Perspectives on Human Differences

Selected Readings on Diversity in America

Perspectives on Human Differences

Selected Readings on Diversity in America

Kent L. Koppelman
Emeritus, University of Wisconsin - La Crosse

Boston   Columbus   Indianapolis   New York   San Francisco
Upper Saddle River   Amsterdam   Cape Town   Dubai   London   Madrid
Milan   Munich   Paris   Montreal   Toronto   Delhi   Mexico City   Sao Paulo
Sydney   Hong Kong   Seoul   Singapore   Taipei   Tokyo

Acquisitions Editor: Kelly Villella Canton
Editorial Assistant: Annalea Manalili
Vice President, Director of Marketing: Quinn Perkson
Senior Marketing Manager: Darcy Betts Prybella
Production Editor: Janet Domingo
Editorial Production Service: Kathy Smith/Publishers' Design and Production Services, Inc.
Composition Buyer: Linda Cox
Manufacturing Buyer: Megan Cochran
Electronic Composition: Publishers' Design and Production Services, Inc.
Interior Design: Publishers' Design and Production Services, Inc.
Cover Designer: Linda Knowles
Cover Administrator: Elena Sidorova

For related titles and support materials, visit our online catalog at www.pearsonhighered.com.

Cataloging-in-Publication is on file at the Library of Congress

Printed in the United States of America

10 9 8 7 6 5 4 3 2 1   RRD-VA   13 12 11 10 09

www.pearsonhighered.com

www.pearsonhighered.com

ISBN-10: 0-13-714503-9
ISBN-13: 978-0-13-714503-4

To Jan

My wife deserves the credit or blame for first suggesting that I create an anthology on diversity issues, and I have a deep sense of gratitude for her support through every step of this long process. She is, of course, the love of my life, but I am one of the lucky ones who can say that my wife is also my best friend. As the old song says, "Who could ask for anything more?"

About the Author

Kent Koppelman attended the University of Nebraska-Lincoln, earning a BA and an MA in English. He taught in high schools for six years, then accepted a teaching assistantship at Iowa State University and earned his doctorate in Education. He accepted a position at the University of Wisconsin-La Crosse, and spent the next 28 years teaching courses in educational foundations, diversity, and multicultural education. He was the recipient of a state award for outstanding teacher educator in 1988, but the following year, his 19-year-old son died in an auto accident. He described his grief experience in *The Fall of a Sparrow: Of Death and Dreams and Healing* (1994).

Dr. Koppelman's book of essays on diversity issues, *Values in the Key of Life: Creating Harmony in the Human Community*, was published in 2000, and in 2005, Allyn & Bacon published his textbook *Understanding Human Differences: Multicultural Education for a Diverse America*. Since retiring in 2007, Dr. Koppelman has written another book on grief issues, *Wrestling with the Angel: Literary Writings and Reflections on Death, Dying and Bereavement* (2009). In 2010, Allyn & Bacon published the third edition of *Understanding Human Differences*. Dr. Koppelman is currently working on a book that addresses conflicting perceptions and beliefs about diversity and pluralism in the United States. He and his wife Jan still live in La Crosse, and their daughter Tess is a television reporter in Kansas City.

Contents

SECTION TWELVE

Pluralistic Responses to the Diversity of American Society   326

Introduction

Residents of the United States today are living in the most diverse society on the planet, perhaps the most diverse in the history of human societies. This diversity was present even in colonial times and at the birth of our nation, as were the difficulties and challenges that diversity often presents. When colonists arrived from various European nations, there were already culturally diverse groups of Native Americans living here. The immigrants who came were Scots, English, Irish, Dutch, French, German, Spanish, and many other nationalities—and all were seeking economic success in the promised land of America. As Jennings has noted, this immigration felt more like an invasion to the indigenous people.[1] In addition, these immigrants brought Africans by force to work as slaves; thus the seeds of oppression and deprivation were planted by those bearing dreams of freedom and prosperity for themselves.

When the new nation was born, the dreamers announced their vision in the words of the documents written for posterity. They proclaimed the principles to which they affixed their signatures: that "all men are created equal, that they are endowed by their creator with unalienable rights, that among these are Life, Liberty and the pursuit of Happiness." They did not mean the Indians or the Africans or even the women among them, except insofar as she gained happiness from her husband's pursuit of it. But there it was, for all to see: the principles by which these new Americans would live, and for which they would die. It was so in the beginning, and it is so today.

The primary change since the beginning has been the people who are referenced by those words. Initially they included mainly white, property-owning males. Power and privilege were disproportionately placed in their hands, and even they weren't fully trusted to use their power wisely. They were allowed to vote for their representative in the House, but not for the man representing them in the Senate. They were permitted to vote for the electors who would choose the President and Vice President of the United States. This new "representative democracy" was a cautious form of self-government, but people living in the United States have always known that the power to vote meant the ability to participate in the governing of this nation, and the slow but steady extension of suffrage in our history represents a record of achievement. As diverse groups gained the right for members to participate in choosing their leaders, it was an acknowledgment of the diversity that existed in the United States.

The first group to be enfranchised was adult (at least 21 years old) white males who did not own property. Throughout the early 1800s, Congress was lobbied extensively to eliminate property restrictions and tax requirements that denied the franchise to adult white males. By 1850, these restrictions had largely been eliminated, paving the way for more changes in voting eligibility to enfranchise other groups of people:

1870 – The 15th Amendment to the U.S. Constitution granted suffrage to black males (not females), but before long, they would be deprived of the right to vote and it would take nearly a hundred years to regain it.

1913 – The 17th Amendment to the U.S. Constitution allowed eligible voters to directly elect their senators.

1920 – The 19th Amendment to the U.S. Constitution granted suffrage to adult women.

1924 – The Indian Citizenship Act provided citizenship and voting rights to adult American Indians.

1971 – The 26th Amendment to the U.S. Constitution extended voting rights to individuals who are 18 years old, in response to concerns that if members of this group could be drafted to die in foreign wars, then they should be allowed to vote for the leaders empowered to send them there.

Gaining the power to vote did not open all the doors of power and privilege, and diverse groups have continued to demonstrate, protest, and lobby to make their voice heard and to ensure that their concerns were addressed.[2] This is why the history of all these groups includes many "firsts" – the first black person to do this, the first woman to do that, the first Latino or Latina to attain a certain goal or status.[3] But as a colleague of mine once said, behind each of these "firsts" is a history of denial and oppression. *The Crisis*, a journal published by the NAACP, continues to identify and celebrate the first African American to gain particular leadership roles or other achievements. And so they should. The struggle by diverse groups to have the opportunity for full participation in our society is ongoing.

Amy Chua asserts that all Americans who care about the continued strength and success of our nation ought to support the efforts of these diverse groups; indeed, her analysis of the historical record found that accepting diversity was advantageous to the most successful societies in history. Based on her study of world empires, Chua (2007)[4] reported that every nation achieving a position of global dominance sufficient to merit the designation of "empire" did so in part because of pluralistic attitudes toward diversity. Beginning with the Persian empire established by Cyrus in 539 BCE and including the Greek and Roman empires, the Mongol empire, and up to the British empire that emerged in the 19th century, Chua provides historical evidence to support the claim that in each of these empires, the society flourished because of the acceptance of diverse people within its boundaries. She also provides historical evidence that the demise of these empires was always related to a growing intolerance of diversity within the society.

Each of these empires achieved global dominance by allowing conquered people the right to maintain their identification with their different racial, ethnic, religious, and linguistic heritages. Further, each empire recruited the best and brightest individuals within the empire, regardless of such differences, to contribute their talents to peaceful or military activities that helped to maintain the empire's status. Chua says that the United States is certainly a hyperpower in today's world, but it does not yet satisfy the definition of "empire" that includes a form of global dominance similar to past empires. Being an empire in the modern world will likely be based more on influence than on conquest as it was in the past, but if Chua's analysis is correct, the United States will never achieve such global influence unless there is greater progress toward establishing and reinforcing pluralistic attitudes that value and support the presence of diversity in our society.

This anthology is designed to promote pluralistic attitudes by providing examples of the voices of diverse people and their perspectives on American society. The book includes essays describing the experiences, opinions, and conclusions of Americans who are black, Asian, Latino, Indian or mixed, Americans who have lived in poverty or who are living with a disability, Americans who are recent immigrants or who came to school speaking a language other than English, Americans who are female or gay or lesbian, Americans from a minority faith or with no faith at all. Some of these voices reflect the experiences of individuals who represent multiple categories, and their voices especially emphasize the complexity of diversity in the United States today. Finally, there are also voices of white male Americans who are allies with one or more of these groups. As an ally, the author has listened to the voices of those from oppressed groups and made a commitment to share their stories and to advocate for their cause.

Structure and Content of the Book

Each section of *Perspectives on Human Differences* begins with an introduction that addresses the topic for that section, discusses the reasons for choosing the selections included, and provides an overview for each reading selection. Quotations and an occasional anecdote are included to remind the reader that diversity issues did not originate in the 21st century, and that people in prior generations offer unique perspectives and insights on issues of diversity. Many of the selected essays simply describe one person's experience, highlighting instances when diversity was not accepted or when people achieved their goals despite societal barriers. Some essays are case studies of a family or of individuals from a particular group and describe issues that affect many or all members of that group. Each narrative has been selected because it provides a unique contribution to the mosaic of diverse experiences in America. The selections as a whole compose a contemporary stained glass window that reflects images and stories illustrating diverse experiences as well as common human joys and sorrows within our multicultural society. And we can learn from both. Finally, each section concludes with a short story or literary reminiscence, providing another way of engaging in individual analysis or group discussions of diversity issues. All of us have read short stories that present provocative views of complex issues that often are ineffectively addressed by research studies or biographical narratives. A good writer of fiction can express truth in a way that provides a better understanding of a unique perspective or highlights a social injustice, or that uses the example of an individual experience to suggest a larger truth. Some of the liveliest discussions my students ever had came from reading a powerful short story that challenged their comfortable views of reality.

Although this anthology is designed for use in any classroom dealing with diversity issues, it is especially intended for teacher education courses that explore these issues in order to help aspiring teachers become more aware of the perspectives of individuals from diverse groups in our society. Such awareness is necessary if these young teachers want to be effective as they work with diverse children in their classrooms. Each section of the book includes selected readings about diversity issues directly related to schools, such as Jack Weatherford's essay in Section One, which discusses how school curricula can distort history simply by omission of information; Mamle Kabu's short story in Section Four, which chronicles life for students of color in a British boarding school; and Reggie Sellars's essay in Section Ten, which describes what it was like to be a gay black man in school both when he was a student and later as a teacher. All of the essays in Section Twelve address some aspect of implementing multicultural education in our nation's schools.

My purpose in selecting the readings for this book was not to find works that would manipulate readers into reaching a predetermined conclusion about diversity; rather, the works were chosen to surprise readers with a new perspective on something that seems familiar or to challenge them with an experience far removed from the world as they know it. In selecting these works, the main point was to find experiences and ideas that would stimulate thought and discussion. Since readers of this book should be as diverse as the society we live in, the sections represent a range not only of experiences but also of writing styles. Some of the professors who reviewed the manuscript identified certain selections as their favorites; other reviewers said they didn't like those same selections. Such different reactions to the same essay are a good indication that the content and writing of the readings selected for this book are varied enough to appeal to the preferences of different individuals. It is unrealistic to expect that every reader will like every selection, but every reader should be able to see the purpose and value of each selection because all of them offer useful observations or insights about diversity.

Acknowledgments

I want to thank all of the contributors to this book for allowing me to bring their work together in what I hope will prove to be a valuable resource for all those involved in teaching about diversity issues. In addition, I want to extend a special thanks to Jan Koppelman for her suggestion to edit an anthology on diversity issues, and for her help on numerous aspects of the lengthy process involved in completing this book. I am most grateful to my editor, Kelly Villella Canton, for her support, and to Kelly's editorial assistant, Annalea Manalili, for her assistance on a multitude of tasks. I also want to thank the reviewers: Christine Canning-Peterson, University of Northern Iowa; Amy L. Freyn, Indiana University Southeast; Emilio Garza, California State University-Bakersfield; Constance J. Goodman, University of Central Florida; Lisa A. Jones, University of Houston-Clear Lake; Kimberly Lockwood,

Troy University; Rosalie M. Romano, Western Washington University; Jerri Shepard, Gonzaga University; Peter Steinfeld, Buena Vista University; Anna V. Wilson, Chapman University; Roberta Wallitt, Ithaca College.

Notes

[1] Frances Jennings, *The invasion of America: Indians, colonialism, and the cant of conquest*. New York: W.W. Norton (1976).

[2] Lawrence H. Fuchs, *The American kaleidoscope: Race, ethnicity, and the civic culture*, Hanover, NH: University Press of New England (1990).

[3] Joan Potter, *African American firsts: Famous, little-known and unsung triumphs of blacks in America*, New York: Kensington Books (2002).

[4] Amy Chua, *Day of empire: How hyperpowers rise to global dominance—and why they fall*. New York: Doubleday, (2007).

Differences, Conflicts, and Resolutions

> **"**A loving person lives in a loving world. A hostile person lives in a hostile world. Everyone you meet is your mirror.**"**
>
> **Ken Keyes, Jr. (1921–1995)**

Keyes's comment reminds us that people are not passive beings who have no influence over their world; an individual's attitudes are a significant factor in shaping the reality in which he or she functions. For that reason, this first section focuses on individual perceptions and relationships with others in a diverse society. With the exception of gender differences, the relationships Americans have with others may not necessarily be diverse if individuals choose to associate only with people of similar backgrounds. Yet, even limited interactions with community institutions and organizations such as schools, businesses, medical clinics, and other services are likely to bring any American into contact with some degree of diversity. This diversity may or may not include racial or ethnic groups, but certainly everyone should encounter differences based on social class, religion, or disability. A person who only has close relationships with people from similar backgrounds and with similar experiences will

inevitably shape an identity that is markedly different from the person who cultivates relationships with others from diverse backgrounds and varied experiences. Furthermore, according to a number of studies,[1] associating with a diverse group of people enhances one's ability to interact effectively with people from groups other than one's own.

Although individual attitudes are fundamental in the development of a sense of identity, so are the perceptions of others. Such perceptions will likely stem from a range of factors starting with appearance, but also including how a person treats people. It's not what a person says, but what a person does in certain situations that will project authenticity and create a sense of trust. When an 88-year-old African American washerwoman gave $150,000 to the University of Southern Mississippi in 1995, this act of generosity was reported in newspaper headlines and on the evening news, but her purpose was not to achieve her fifteen minutes of fame. Oseola

1

McCarty had worked hard and had been frugal all her life before she decided to give up a significant portion of her life savings to help students with financial need. She would never know which students she helped nor how many, but she was content to know that deserving students were being helped.

Whether applauding the diversity of people in the United States or viewing diversity as problematic, many Americans speak of diversity as a contemporary issue. They seem to believe that we didn't have so much diversity in the past, and some even lament the mythical "good old days" when we didn't have the problems we have today. This often includes criticisms of events from the 1960s, which many people regard as a time when diversity issues were the basis of protests and demonstrations that resulted in laws for civil rights and affirmative action—and we haven't been the same since. Yet Section One begins with an essay describing the incredible diversity that has always been unique to America and has always provided Americans with the potential to benefit from that diversity.

This historic misconception was addressed in 1946 by community organizer Saul Alinsky when he described the "People of America" more than a quarter of a century before the American Association of Colleges of Teacher Education (AACTE) published its statement on pluralism called "No One Model American."[2] Consistent with the AACTE statement, Alinsky refutes the idea that a single image can accurately portray "an American" because the reality is that Americans are a heterogeneous group. To illustrate why we must reject simplistic images, Alinsky provides numerous specific examples of diverse housing and food, diverse races and faiths, diverse origins and dialects, diverse occupations and incomes, all the while constantly reminding us that all of the people he is describing are Americans. Alinsky also discusses prejudices based on people belonging to certain groups and concludes by calling on all Americans to accept this incredible American diversity and work with others to make a better and a stronger nation.

We have yet to meet Alinsky's challenge. Why is it so difficult for Americans to appreciate human diversity? In "Fear and Danger," Paul Kivel discusses how individual differences persuade some people to be wary of others. Kivel argues that the fears white people have of people of color have been exacerbated by our society's ongoing racial segregation. He explains why these fears are misplaced, and how they corrupt the ability of white people to have a realistic understanding of racial and ethnic groups. Such isolation and fear contributes to inaccurate assumptions that foster negative perceptions based on group stereotypes. Kivel criticizes politicians and others in leadership roles who manipulate such fears and stereotypes to implement policies and programs that keep different groups from interacting with and learning about each other.

Branch Rickey was the President and General Manager of the Brooklyn Dodgers when he re-

> **❝** If you want to feel proud of yourself, you've got to DO things you can be proud of. Feelings follow actions. **❞**
>
> **Oseola McCarty (1908–1999)**

cruited Jackie Robinson to be the first black player in professional baseball. He believed that simply bringing people together would resolve racial problems, but today we know that proximity is not enough. Although reducing and finally ending racial segregation is the necessary first step to improving race relations, individuals must also make a commitment to expand their knowledge of America's diversity before they can develop realistic perceptions of people who are members of these groups.

Steve Olson suggests that genome research may provide a good starting point by teaching us about our similarities as human beings. Despite the physical differences between human groups such as skin color, average height, eye shapes, and other facial features, the vast majority of genetic characteristics available in the human gene pool are shared by people around the world. As he blends history and science in describing the spread of human beings around the world, Olson also describes the tragedy of human oppression based on perceived and assumed differences. Today, Americans continue to be affected by the reality of human differences; our individual sense of identity will likely be influenced as we learn more about the genetic characteristics we share, as we read accurate historical accounts of diverse groups in our society, and as we continue to follow the evolution of scientific knowledge about human diversity.

Reading accurate historical accounts of diverse groups is the focus of "The Founding Indian Fa-

thers" by Jack Weatherford. Many scholars have written about the omissions and inaccurate information about people of color in the curriculum, but Weatherford's essay focuses on the historic role and contributions of American Indians. Nieto (2004) has argued that providing students only one perspective on history presents them with a distorted version of reality.[3] To illustrate Nieto's point, Weatherford describes some examples from history that most American students are not likely to know concerning the influence of American Indians on such things as the organization of our government as outlined in the U.S. Constitution, our use of the caucus in politics, and our preference for egalitarian attitudes. The omissions in the curriculum of the perspectives and achievements of individuals of color and from other groups may be a significant factor in the lack of interest that some students display in the classroom. It is easy to blame the students, and many have done so, but we should also heed Sidney Harris's words:

> It is an absolute libel on childhood to say that children resist being taught. Children love to be taught and when they resist it is because something has already gone wrong with the child or with the system of teaching.

Arnold Zweig's short story concludes the section by describing the role that personal values play in our beliefs and actions. In the story, a father stumbles into a situation that offers what he initially views as an opportunity to teach his son a moral lesson. He insists on not making the

> **"** Proximity – if we can get enough of it – can solve these problems of racial prejudice and bigotry. **"**
>
> **Branch Rickey (1881–1965)**

decision for his son, but rationally explains the financial benefits that are included in the decision the boy is being asked to make. As the financial rewards increase, the father is the one who learns an unexpected lesson about the power of those who have adequate financial resources and the vulnerability of those who don't.

Notes

[1]See www.diversityweb.org/research_and_trends/ research_evaluation_impact/index.cfm and select *Benefits of Diversity* to get numerous studies on diversity including "The impact of diversity on college students: The latest research" by Debra Humphreys; see also Sidanius, J., Levin, S., van Laar, C, and Sears, D.O. (2008). *The diversity challenge: Social identity and intergroup relations on the college campus.* New York: Russell Sage Foundation. Based on a five-year study of 2000 UCLA students, researchers reported positive outcomes for students who had consistent interactions with diverse members of the campus community.

[2]Download the 1972 statement "No One Model American" at the web site for the American Association of Colleges for Teacher Education – www.aacte .org.

[3]Nieto, S. (2008). *Affirming Diversity: The Sociopolitical Context of Multicultural Education.* Boston, MA: Pearson/ Allyn & Bacon.

The People of America

What does it mean to be an American? For a long time, many people used the dominant group to identify an American: a white person with blonde hair and blue eyes. But Saul Alinsky told us over 60 years ago that there was no single American image, that we were a nation made up of diverse people shaped by race, ethnicity, social class, and more.

The people of America live everywhere from Back Bay Boston to the Bottoms of Kansas City. From swank Lake Forest, Illinois, to slum Harlem, New York. From the gentlemen farmers of Connecticut to the sharecroppers of Arkansas. From the marble swimming pools of magnificent Bel-Air, California, to the muck of the Flats of Cleveland. From sooty Harlan County, Kentucky, to impeccable Bar Harbor, Maine.

The people of America are red, white, black, yellow, and all the shades in between. Their eyes are blue, black, and brown, and all the shades in between. Their hair is straight, curly, kinky, and most of it in between. They are tall and short, slim and fat, athletic and anemic, and most of them in between. They are the different peoples of the world. Their face is the face of the future.

The people of America include followers of all the major religions on the face of the earth. They are Christians, regardless of which one of the two hundred or more different major varieties or sects that compose Christianity. They are Baptists, both Northern and Southern, Episcopalians, Lutherans, Catholics, Mennonite, Methodists, Mormons, Seventh-Day Adventists, Christian Scientists, and a hundred odd more. There are many who believe in Christianity but who do not have any formal membership in any one of these organized religious groups. There are Jews, whether they be Orthodox, Conservative, or Reformed. There are Muslims, Buddhists, and followers of Confucius. There are atheists and agnostics. The steeples and the domes of America's houses of worship are to be found on every hill, in every valley, and in every nook and cranny of America. From these houses of worship come the stiff formal Episcopalian hymns, the wild orgiastic shouts of the (Pentacostalists), the chants of the synagogue, the liturgical music of the Catholic church, the singsong medleys of Confucius and Mohammed, and the cold logic of atheists – all combining into a synthesis of divine faith that is truly the American prayer.

The people of America are the people of the world. They have come from all corners of the earth. They are Slavs, Czechs, Germans, Hispanic, Irish, English, Spanish, French, Russian, Chinese, Japanese, and African Americans.

The people of America live as they can. Many of them are pent up in one-room crumbling shacks and a few live in penthouses. They live in cold-water flats and air-conditioned town houses. A vast segment of our people are confined by color to the dingiest of tenements. In between are many of the

Have-Something, Want-More's in apartments or one-family homes.

The American people have worked hard. Most of them have worked with their hands. They hewed their own log cabins and carved out the railroads, the dams, and the skyscrapers that made America what it is. They have sweated in doing so. They smell like the people of the world. The *Have's* smell toilet water, the *Have-Not's* smell just plain toilet.

They speak an American language all their own, from the "youse guys" of Brooklyn to the "you-alls" of Georgia. There are New England nasal twangs and the slow soft drawl of the Far West. Listen to the people of America talk. Whether you stand on New York's Times Square, Chicago's State and Madison streets, Kansas City's Twelfth and Grand, small South St. Paul's Concord Street, Atlanta's Peachtree Street, San Francisco's Market and Powell, Los Angeles's Hollywood and Vine, or Butte's Park and Main streets. In New York they even talk differently from one part of the city to another, from the soft cultured tones of Park Avenue to the flat screech of The Bronx.

The people of America behave like the people of the world. They scratch their itches; in Chicago they belch in Back of the Yards and they politely burp in the Ambassador East. They are sweaty and they are suave. Their interests range far out over society or they are narrowly confined to their street. They are grubby and grand. They look and dress differently. From the blue denim Levis of the west to the black full-dress suit of the East. From the patched gingham dress of the sharecropper's wife to the latest French importation on Philadelphia's Main Line.

What do Americans eat? They eat mulligan stew alongside the railroad tracks or they eat breast of guinea hen in the dining cars that ride over the tracks. They eat smorgasbord and they eat hot dogs. They eat pig's knuckles and the eat gefilte fish. They eat chicken booya and they eat corned beef and cabbage. They eat hominy and grits and Italian spaghetti. They eat hot cakes and syrup and crepes suzettes. They eat apple pie and they eat strudel. They eat ham and eggs and they eat octopus. They eat steak and they eat Russian borscht. They eat corn on the cob and Wiener-schnitzel. They drink Coca-Cola and Heineken's beer.

They have fried chicken and hot biscuits at their church socials and chicken Kiev at sophisticated night spots. They eat baked beans at the Automat

and French food in the Bull and Bear restaurant at the Waldorf. They are vegetarians, food faddists, and vitamin takers. They eat what their forefathers ate and their forefathers came from everywhere. The diet of America is the diet of the world.

The American people were, in the beginning, Revolutionaries and Tories. The American people ever since have been Revolutionaries and Tories. They have been Revolutionaries and Tories regardless of the labels of the past and present. Regardless of whether they were Federalists, Democrat-Republicans, Whigs, Know-Nothings, Free Soilers, Unionists or Confederates, Populists, Republicans, Democrats, Socialists, Communists, or Progressives. They have been and are conservatives, liberals, and radicals.

The clash of radicals, conservatives, and liberals which makes up America's political history opens the door to the most fundamental question of what is America? How do the people of America feel? It is in this feeling that the real story of America is written. There were and are a number of Americans – few, to be sure – filled with deep feeling for people. They know that people are the stuff that makes up the dream of democracy. . . . Psychiatrists, psychologists, sociologists, and other learned students call this feeling "identification" and have elaborate and complicated explanations about what it means. For our purposes it boils down to the simple question: How do you feel about people?

Do you like people? Most people claim that they like people with, of course, a "few exceptions." When the exceptions are added together it becomes clear that they include a vast majority of the people. It becomes equally clear that most people like just a few people, their kind of people, and either do not actively care for or actively dislike most of the "other" people.

You are white, native-born, and Protestant. Do you like people? You like your family, your friends, some of your business associates (not too many of them), and some of your neighbors. Do you like Catholics, Irish, Italians, Jews, Poles, Mexicans, Blacks, Puerto Ricans, and Chinese? Do you regard them with the warm feeling of fellow human beings or with a cold contempt symbolized in Papists, Micks, Wops, Kikes, Hunkies, Greasers, Niggers, Spics, and Chinks? If you are one of those people who think of people in these derogatory terms, then you don't like people.

You may object to this and say that you do not fall into this classification. You don't call people by such names. You are broad-minded and respect other peoples if they *know their place* – and that place is not close to your own affections. You feel that you are really very tolerant. The chances are that you are an excellent representative of the great American class of Mr. But. Haven't you met Mr. But? Sure, you have. You met him at Community Fund meetings, at housing conferences, at political rallies, and most likely he has greeted you every morning from the mirror in your bathroom. Mr. But is the man who is broad-minded, sensible, practical, and proud of his Christianity. You have heard him talk many times, just as you have heard yourself talk many times. What does he say? Listen to the great American, Mr. But:

"Nobody can say I'm not a friend of the Mexicans or that I am prejudiced, BUT – "

"Nobody can say I'm anti-Semitic. Why some of my best friends are Jews, BUT – "

"Surely nobody can think of me as a reactionary, BUT – "

"I don't think anyone in this room feels more sympathetic toward (Blacks) than I do. I've always had a number of them working for me, BUT – "

"It's perfectly all right for these people to have equal opportunities for work, and after all we are all Americans, aren't we? BUT – "

"Anybody knows that I would be the first to fight against this injustice, BUT – "

"Labor unions are all right, BUT – "

"Sure, I say that all Americans should have the right to live any place they want to regardless of race, color, or creed, BUT – "

You are very probably a typical Mr. But. You make "tolerant" jokes behind the backs of your fellow Americans, about their clothes, complexions, speech, manners, and names. You regard yourself as tolerant, and in that one adjective you most fittingly describe yourself. You really don't *like* people you *tolerate* them. You are very tolerant, Mr. But. You leave a luncheon meeting at which you sat next to a Black man and talked with him (and you tell your friends about it for months to come). You are so flushed and filled with your own goodness that if the thought could father the deed you would take flight on your new angelic wings.

Thomas Jefferson saw this very clearly in his letter to Henry Lee on August 10, 1824:

Men by their constitution are naturally divided into two parties:

1. Those who fear and distrust the people, and wish to draw all powers from them into the hands of the higher classes.
2. Those who identify themselves with the people, have confidence in them, cherish and consider them as the most honest and safe, although not the most wise depository of the public interests.

In every country these two parties exist, and in every one where they are free to think, speak, and write, they will declare themselves. Call them, therefore, Liberals and Serviles, Jacobins and Ultras, Whigs and Tories, Republicans and Federalists, Aristocrats and Democrats, or by whatever name you please, they are the same parties still and pursue the same object. . . .

During Jefferson's lifetime the words democrat and radical were synonymous. Just as people then were divided between those who feared and disliked people and those who liked them, so is Jefferson's observation as true today as it was in 1824 and as true as it always has been since the beginning of mankind.

There were those few, and there will be more, who really liked people, loved people – all people. They were the human torches setting aflame the hearts of men so that they passionately fought for the rights of their fellow men, all men. They were hated, feared, and branded as *radicals*. They wore the epithet . . . as a badge of honor. They fought for the right of men to govern themselves, for the right of men to walk erect as free men and not grovel before kings, for the Bill of Rights, for the abolition of slavery, for public education, and for everything decent and worthwhile. They loved men and fought for them. Their neighbor's misery was their misery. They acted as they believed. . . .

Believing in people . . . they moved ahead to realize those values of equality, justice, freedom, the preciousness of human life . . . Democracy is not an end but the best means toward achieving these values. These values are not even debatable in a free society; they are accepted; they are the reasons for the democratic society. They cannot be placed on the ballot; no state has the right to vote segregation or any other violation of these values. If the democratic process is used to subvert freedom then the process prostitutes the purpose of an open society and democracy is dead. . . .

Many of their deeds are not and never will be recorded in America's history. They were among the grimy men in the dust bowl, they sweated with the sharecroppers, they were at the side of the Okies facing the California vigilantes, they stood before the fury of lynch mobs, they were on the picket lines gazing unflinchingly at the threatening, flushed, angry faces of the police. They were with Chicago's Catholic Bishop Sheil when, ignoring threats from the highest vested authorities, he took his place at the side of thousands of packinghouse workers who had squared off against the hitherto invulnerable meat trust. . . .

Each victory (brings) a new vision of human happiness, for man's highest end is to create – total fulfillment or total security would dull the creative drive. Ours is really the quest for uncertainty, for that continuing change which is life. *The pursuit of happiness is never ending – the happiness lies in the pursuit.*

PAUL KIVEL

Fear and Danger

A major obstacle to cross-cultural communication is that people tend to fear "others" who are different, especially when the differences are racial. The author explores those fears and explains why we need to acknowledge our own fears in order to get beyond them; if we can accomplish this, then political leaders and others will not be able use our fears to manipulate us.

Many of us in the United States today are afraid. We worry about crime, drugs, our children's future, and our own security. Our fear is a result of many economic, social, political, and personal factors. It is also linked to violence in news media, television, and the movies.

In a society where we are constantly presented with tales of danger and violence and told how vulnerable we are, it is not surprising that most of us are fearful. Racism produces a fear-based society in which no one feels safe. However being afraid is not the same as being in danger.

For example, white people often fear people of color, and most people of color fear white people. White people are not usually in danger from people of color. People of color are in danger of individual acts of discrimination, hate crimes, and police brutality at the hands of white people, as well as of institutional practices that kill people due to lack of health care, lack of police protections, and unequal legal prosecution. White people are rarely killed, harassed, or discriminated against by people of color.

To understand whiteness, we need to look at how fear of people of color is manufactured and used to justify repression and exploitation of communities of color.

- Have you ever been in your car when a person of color drove past? Did you reach over to lock your car door?
- When a man of color walks by do you touch your wallet or purse or hold it tighter?
- Have you ever closed a window, pulled a blind, or locked a door when you saw a person of color in your neighborhood?
- Have you ever had an adult or young person of color in your house and wondered, ever so briefly, if valuables were out?
- Have you seen a person of color with quality clothes, an expensive car, or other valuable items and wondered how they got the money to buy them?

I have done all of these things. I was taught to fear people of color. I was told that they were dangerous and that they would steal, cheat, or otherwise grab whatever I had.

Many of these motions were practically involuntary. My hand was on my wallet before I realized it. Of course I tried to turn the gesture into a casual motion so that what I had done would not be

From *Uprooting racism: How white people can work for racial justice* (Gabriola Island, British Columbia: New Society Publishers, 2002).

apparent. For many years I did not realize I was doing this. Then I listened to people of color, particularly African-American men (the group we have been trained to fear the most), describe how white people were always afraid of them. I began to notice my own and other people's gestures – the tensing, the guardedness, the suspicion, the watchfulness.

White fear is primarily fear of men of color. (We also have fears about women of color, but they are not as visceral or pervasive.) For example, I grew up playing cowboys and Indians, always wanting to be the brave cowboy who protected the innocent homesteaders and settlers from the vicious (male) Indians ready to sweep down and destroy white outposts. I was learning that as a man I would have to protect (white) womanhood and (white) civilization.

Growing up in Los Angeles . . . I heard repeated stories about the masses of Mexican and Central-American people pushing against our borders, pressing to get in, to overwhelm us. I remember a discussion with my parents in which I said I didn't think I ever wanted to have children because there were already so many people in the world. My parents tried to convince me that it was important that I have children because I was smart and educated and we needed more of our kind. I understood "our kind" to be white. Again I was getting the message that we had to defend ourselves, reproduce ourselves, and protect what was ours because we were under attack.

Many of the racial images that we hear today such as "illegal alien," "border patrol," "drug wars," and "the invasion of Japanese capital" are based on images of protection, defense, borders, and danger. Many of us feel besieged. We talk as if we are under attack in many areas of our lives where we used to feel safe. We complain that we can't say what we want with impunity; we can't go where we want. We notice that people of color in the United States and abroad are demanding a more equitable distribution of the world's wealth. To counter these attacks on white power and to divert attention from the benefits we have accrued, we have created a fear of potential retaliatory violence from people of color.

This pattern has a long history. Individual white settlers who took Native American lands feared retaliation. But many white people lived in cities and were not worried about Indian attack. White set-

tlers, in conjunction with the U.S. government, which wanted to "open up" Native American land, had to convince the public that Native Americans were dangerous and needed to be exterminated. A campaign, using books, pictures, and the media, created images of Indians as primitive, cruel savages who wanted to kill white men and rape white women. This campaign made it easier to justify the appropriation of Native American lands and the killing or removal of Native Americans themselves. In the process, generations of us learned to fear Indians. Many children growing up today still do, even though there are only about three million Native Americans in all of the United States and Canada. They are the ones who have suffered the effects of racial violence.

Over the course of 240 years of slavery, white slave owners created the illusion that African Americans were dangerous to justify the harshness of their treatment and to scare other white people into supporting their subjugation. White people feared African Americans even though they were so thoroughly dominated and brutalized as to offer little threat to whites. Slaves were brutalized publicly and routinely. Some fought back, but most were more interested in escaping than in retaliation.

This pattern of white fear and violence continues today. We still see selected news coverage that presents African American men as the embodiment of danger itself. It is difficult for any white American not to have an immediate feeling of fear in the presence of an African American male. This fear, in turn, has justified massive and continuous control of the African American community through the schools, police, legal system, jails, prisons, and the military. This control starts in pre-school or elementary school. It limits educational opportunities, jobs, skills, and access to health care. It is enforced by police brutality and various forms of discrimination. These conditions produce stress, despair, and desperation for African American young men, leading to their killing each other and themselves at high rates, living six years less than white men on the average. White violence leads to fear, which is used to justify further white violence. African American men, not white people, are the victims of this cycle of violence.

Similarly Arabs and Arab Americans are portrayed as fanatical terrorists who will stop at nothing to kill us. After the bombing of the Oklahoma City Federal Building, law enforcement officials and the media immediately began talking about the possibility of Arab terrorists being involved. On the one hand, Arab Americans are victims of discrimination, stereotyping, and hate crimes. On the other hand, the U.S. government bombed Iraq (under Saddam Hussein) and maintained a blockade that prevented food and medical supplies from being shipped to that country, leading to the deaths of thousands of Iraqi children every month. In the recent past, the United States also bombed Libya, the Sudan, and Afghanistan, and American arms have been used by Israelis to subjugate the Palestinians. While the fear between Arabs, Arab Americans, and white Americans may be mutual, white Americans are in little danger. But the fear is used to justify the scapegoating, abuse and violence directed against Arabs and Arab Americans. The misrepresentation and demonization is so extreme that I cannot remember the last time I saw a positive image of an Arab or Arab American in the media.

Many times we use stories to justify the fear that we feel toward people of color. We might introduce them by such phrases as "I was attacked once by . . ." "I don't want to sound prejudiced, but I know someone who had a bad experience with . . ." or "It's unfortunate, but my one negative experience was . . ." We then use these single examples to reinforce a stereotype about a whole category of people and to prove the legitimacy of our fear of them.

- Is there a story that you use to justify your fears of people of color?
- What are stories that you've heard other white people use?

These shared stories can be a way to strengthen white solidarity by implying that we share a common danger. They reinforce our desire to be with white people and to avoid people of color. They also raise the stakes if we challenge racism, because to do so seems to threaten our own security. How can we challenge other whites when we may need them in case of an attack?

Sometimes, when I realize the extent of the stereotypes I have learned and act from, I want to disavow the fear altogether and convince myself that there is nothing to be afraid of. Or, to counter the stereotype, I try to assume that all men of color are safe and all white men are dangerous. Yet I know that I am foolish if I simply reverse the stereotypes. In a society in which many people are dangerous and violence is a threat, we need to evaluate the danger from each person we're with. Any preconceived notions of danger of safety based on skin color are dysfunctional – they can actually increase our danger and make us less able to protect ourselves. For example, even as white women have moved to the suburbs, put locks on their doors and windows, and avoided urban streets at night, they have remained vulnerable to robbery and assault from white male friends, lovers, neighbors, and co-workers.

This example shows how racism turns our attention away from real exploitation and danger as we create myths about family violence and sexual assault. We are taught that men of color and men from other cultures are dangerous. We have stereotypes about rapists being dark strangers in alleys, about Asian men being devious and dishonest, about Latinos being physically and sexually dangerous. Racism has produced myths about every group of nonwhite, non-mainstream men being dangerous to white women and children.

The reality is that approximately 80 percent of sexual violence is committed within the same racial group by heterosexual men who know their victim.[1] If we and our children are beaten up, sexually assaulted, or abused it is most likely to be by heterosexual white men, but we continue to believe that we need to protect ourselves from men who are different. We justify public policies that disproportionately lock up men of color, primarily Latino and African American men, but these changes do not make it appreciably safer for us. Because we are led to believe that we need "our" men to protect us from men "out there," we are slow to recognize the violence of men in our family and dating relationships.

We are often awarded a presumption of innocence if we are white. This works to our benefit when we are stopped by the police, shopping in a store, walking down the street, or renting equipment such as cars, tools, or movies. Other white people assume we are safe until we are proven dangerous.

- Was there ever a time when you heard about violence that a white man committed and said to yourself, "I never would have imagined that so-and-so could have done something like that?
- Have you ever been surprised that an African American or Latino man could commit a particular act of violence?

We expect men of color to be dangerous. When Susan Smith killed her two children, she claimed that an African American man had kidnapped them. When Charles Stuart killed his pregnant wife in Boston, he stabbed himself and claimed an African American man had attacked them. When the federal building in Oklahoma City was bombed, most people immediately suspected Arab men as the culprits. Many of us accepted these statements without question because they fit with our expectations. In each situation the search for the guilty white man was temporarily diverted toward men of color.

We fear people of color in great disproportion to any danger they may hold for us. We trust white men in spite of the danger some of them pose. These fears become expectations that influence whom we trust and how we evaluate danger. Our personal vigilance is often increased when people of color are present and relaxed when only white people are around.

These expectations translate into feeling uneasy whenever there are significant numbers of people of color around us. Statistics show that whites are most comfortable in interracial situations where people of color constitute a small percentage of the population. When the percentage rises to 15 or 20, white people often begin to feel that "they" are dominating or are unfairly represented. When people of color constitute 20 or 25 percent of the population, white people begin to describe people of color as the majority or as having taken over. . . .

As white people, we can start by acknowledging the violence we have done to people of color throughout our history. We must understand how we have demonized them to justify that violence. Our fear of violence to ourselves is related to the violence we have done and continue to do to people of color. Therefore one way to lower our fear is to acknowledge and reduce our own violence. . . .

Jewish people in the United States have been subject to verbal and physical attack, bombings, desecration of cemeteries, intimidation, and murder by white Christians. Jews have not attacked Christians for being Christian. Again we can see that although the fear is mutual, Jewish people are in some danger from Christians whereas Christians are in no danger of being attacked by Jews.

Economically, most banks, major corporations, and other institutions that make the financial decisions about jobs, pensions, and health care are owned by Christians. They make the decisions to close down factories in our cities, steal from the government, move jobs overseas, create unsafe working conditions, bust unions, and dump cancer-producing toxins into our rivers and lakes. Christian fear works, like all racial fear, to divert people from the source of danger – people inside the mainstream who hold political, economic, and social power. Jews are blamed for economic problems for which they are not responsible, and they become the targets of further anti-Semitic violence.

All Jews experience the stereotypes and fear that white Christians and other non-Jews have of them. Jewish people know what it's like to be attacked because others have been trained to fear you. Jews who are white are feared and are taught to fear people of color. Many white Jewish concerns about violence focus on danger from African Americans, even though most anti-Semitic violence is committed by white Christians. Anti-Semitism should be challenged wherever it occurs, but primary energy should always go to defend against those with most power to do harm. . . .

The focus by white Jews on external danger from people of color also helps conceal the significant levels of domestic violence, sexual assault, and child abuse within the Jewish community. When Jewish family violence is denied and minimized, and Jewish family values are held up as better than those of African Americans, then racism is perpetuated. This racism justifies violence against African Americans while obscuring violence against Jewish women and children.

All of us who are white need to recognize just how deeply we have been trained to fear and distrust people of color and how much that fear guides our behavior, because that fear is easily manipulated by politicians, the media, or corporate leaders. Christians need to acknowledge their fear and distrust of Jews for the same reasons. Our fear often leads us to misconstrue our own best political interests because our racial fear overrides our best thinking. . . . As our fears of people of color increase, we are more easily deceived by white leaders who have an aura of trustworthiness simply because they are white.

Notes

[1]*Sexual Violence Facts and Statistics*, brochure from the Illinois Coalition Against Sexual Assault, 1993.

The African Diaspora and the Genetic Unity of Modern Humans

Personal identity is often shaped by a sense of group identity based on differences from others. Yet as scientists continue to engage in genome research, they have reported some surprising findings about our common human heritage and the degree of genetic mixing revealed in our genes. In the following essay, the author reviews this recent research.

The city where I live, Washington, D.C., is one of the most diverse in the world. More Ethiopian expatriates live in Washington than in any other city. The population of Vietnamese, Cambodians and Laotians exceeds 50,000. One of every eight Washington residents was born outside the United States. Within one downtown block, you can order food from the national cuisines of Ghana, India, Thailand, Malaysia, China, Japan, Italy, France, El Salvador, and Brazil.

But by far the largest ethnic group in Washington consists of African Americans. Of the 570,000 people who live in the District of Columbia proper, 60 percent are African American, as are about 25 percent of the metropolitan area's 5.5 million people. Many are the descendants of African Americans who moved to Washington from the southern United States after World War II in search of better jobs and better schools for their children. Some can trace their ancestry back to African Americans, free

or slave, who lived in and around Washington before the Civil War.

The suffix "American" in this essay has a particular connotation. I use the term "Central African" to refer to the largest population group in Africa. Many of the ancestors of today's African Americans were in fact Central Africans. But almost all African Americans also have a large number of European-American ancestors.[1] On average, one-fifth to one-quarter of their DNA comes from Europeans. If any African American other than a recent immigrant were to construct a family tree for the past four hundred years, a substantial fraction of the names on that tree between ten and twenty generations ago would be individuals of European ancestry.

By the same token, many European Americans have relatively recent African American ancestors.[2] In some cases the ancestor was one member of an openly interracial marriage. But in most cases the ancestor was an African American whose skin was so light that he or she was passing as a European American. These "passers" as they are called, have been a powerful force for demographic mixing in the United States.[3] Several of the children of Thomas Jefferson and his African American slave Sally Hemings eventually blended into the majority population.[4] Certain cities in the southern United States had large numbers of passers, whose descendants gradually spread into the rest of the country. Some light-skinned African Americans entered the armed forces, were classified as whites, and joined all-white units. Once discharged, many simply continued to define themselves as white.

Thus the suffix "American" here implies an especially high degree of genetic mixing. Such mixing is common in many parts of the world: South Africa is a good example of how people from different continents can produce highly varied populations. But the United States' reputation as a melting pot is borne out by the DNA of its citizens. Few Americans today can claim that all of their ancestors several generations back were from a particular part of the world.

Given this extensive history of mixing, the strength of racial prejudice in the United States can seem perplexing. Throughout the country's history, Americans have drawn rigid distinctions between black and white, Indian and European, Asian and non-Asian, Latino and Anglo. Furthermore, these distinctions have been rooted in the belief that sharp genetic differences separate groups, differences that shape behavior as well as appearance.

Scientific research has shown that these claims have no merit. Given the history of our species, the behaviors characteristic of a group must be the product of culture – of what people learn – not of genetics. That these behaviors seem so ingrained is not a measure of our biological heritage; it is a measure of history's power to shape the collective consciousness of nations and peoples.

All non-Africans descend from Africans who left the continent within the past 100,000 years. But the flow of people out of Africa must have waxed and waned over time. Once the Middle East was settled by modern humans, the people there would have presented an obstacle to new migrations, because incoming groups would have had to compete with them for resources. The prehistoric peoples of the Middle East and the Nile River delta undoubtedly exchanged mates. But the geography of the Old World – especially the barrier posed by the Sahara Desert and the fact that everyone traveling from Africa to Eurasia has to pass through the narrow isthmus of the Sinai – suggests that in prehistoric times people moved between the continents in rather low numbers.

More people journeyed between Africa and Eurasia following the rise of civilization in the Middle East. Black Africans from south of the Sahara began serving as merchants, sailors, servants, and soldiers throughout the Mediterranean world. The invention of oceangoing ships gave people a new way to move between continents. Many Africans settled in Europe and Asia and married non-Africans, and their descendants gradually were absorbed into the population. Even today, mitochondrial and Y haplotypes characteristic of Africa are found in people throughout Europe and Asia, and some of the haplotypes date to these early African exoduses.

The early movements of people out of Africa were dwarfed by the population movements associated with the international slave trade. Slavery was a common feature of ancient societies; in classical Greece and Rome, slaves constituted as much as 30 percent of the population. But slave masters in the ancient world did not discriminate by geographic origin. In Rome, African slaves worked alongside slaves from Iberia, Gaul, northern Europe, Thrace, Sarmatia, Indian, the Arabian Peninsula, Egypt, and Carthage. In fact, many of the early slaves were destitute Romans who had sold themselves into slavery to pay off debts.

In the Middle Ages, the geographic origins of slaves in the western world began to change. The numbers of slaves from Europe and Asia gradually fell, while the number from Africa grew. By 1700, Africa was the world's primary source of slaves.

Scholars have cited many reasons for Africa's rise as a slave producer.[5] Tropical climates and poor soils in Africa limited agricultural productivity, so the overall economic return from selling a young male into slavery was greater than if that man became a farmer. Africans captured and sold slaves in exchange for manufactured goods, which delayed the continent's economic development and further depressed the value of labor within Africa. The rise of sugar production in the New World created a need for huge numbers of agricultural laborers, and Africans were more resistant to the diseases of tropical sugar plantations than were people from other parts of the world. The slave trade was highly profitable to those who provided, transported, and used slaves, and the continent's political fragmentation made it difficult for African leaders to stop the practice. All of these factors tended to reinforce one another. Once Africa became established as the leading exporter of slaves, the trade gained a momentum that was very difficult to reverse.

The slave trade was responsible for one of the largest human migrations the world has ever seen. Even before Europeans began shipping African slaves to the New World, millions were sent to Europe, the Middle East, and as far away as China. Sizable communities of sub-Saharan Africans arose in cities from Lisbon in the west to Hyderabad in the east, from London in the north to Cairo in the south. Some of these communities have survived to the present, but in most places Africans gradually intermarried with non-Africans and blended into the surrounding populations.

The flow of Africans to the new World eventually exceeded that to the Old. Between the early 1500s, when the first slaves were transported directly from Africa to the Americas, and 1870, when the last verified shipment of African slaves made landfall in Cuba, approximately 12 million enslaved Africans traveled across the Atlantic.[6] Africans quickly became a major portion of the population in the Americas, especially as indigenous populations were decimated by Old World diseases. As late as 1800, several times as many Africans as Europeans lived in the New World.

Perhaps two million Africans died during the hellish "Middle Passage" from Africa to the Americas (so called because it was the middle section of a triangular trade route from Europe to Africa, Africa to the Americas, and the Americas back to Europe). Chained together in tiny fetid spaces under unimaginably horrible conditions, they died of dysentery, smallpox, hunger, thirst, suicide, and suicidal rebellions. A slave who exhibited the first signs of sickness was often thrown overboard to prevent an epidemic. Others willingly jumped overboard to drown and escape their captors.

By far the majority of Africans shipped to the New World disembarked in South America and the Caribbean. The mortality of slaves shipped to these areas was shockingly high. Working a slave to death and buying a new one was cheaper than supporting the development of long-term communities and families. But many slaves did survive, and many eventually gained their freedom. By the time slavery was abolished in Brazil in 1888, nearly half the population of the country had ancestors who had been slaves.

The British colonies of North America received far fewer slaves than did Central and South America. But mortality was lower than in South America and the Caribbean (although still much higher than it was for Europeans), and Africans were always a major fraction of the nonnative populations. At the time of the first official U.S. census in 1790, about 20 percent of the country's 4 million people were African American. (As of the 2000 census, African Americans represented 13 percent of the total population of 280 million.)

The large-scale emigration of Africans, Europeans, and, later in the nineteenth century, Asians to the Americas created a human medley unprecedented in history. In the Old World, skin color, facial features, and other physical characteristics have tended to vary continuously. As a result, people in Europe, Africa, and Asia generally interacted with people who were much like themselves physically. Only in the mixing bowl around the Mediterranean and on long-range trade routes did groups that looked substantially different from each other frequently come into contact.

In the New World, the situation was the reverse. The three major groups of American immigrants came from geographic extremes of their respective continents – western Africa, northwestern Europe, and eastern Asia. These groups were overlaid on a fourth group – Native Americans – that had Asian roots but differed substantially from Chinese and Japanese populations. A mischievous god moving groups of people around the globe would have a difficult time assembling a more disparate collection.

The physical differences among the new occupants of the Americas did little to slow the natural human tendency to interbreed.[7] Today most of the people of South and Central American are of mixed European, American Indian, and African descent. In Brazil, for example, African slaves had more ways of becoming free than in other countries, and settlers from Portugal had a history of absorbing people from elsewhere. As a result, intermarriage has been extensive, and the physical characteristics of Brazilians today extend across a broad range.

Racism is not absent in Brazil, despite claims that all races are blending. People with darker skin have more trouble finding good jobs, good housing, and good schools. But skin color in Brazil varies along a continuum, and social distinctions vary continuously as well.

Things turned out differently in the United States, where slave owners and their political allies had a strong interest in maintaining a sharp distinction between African Americans and European Americans. Children born of slaves and slave owners represented a blurring of the distinction between slave and free, between property and property owner. To deal with this problem, these children almost always were treated as black. Thus arose the "one drop" rule, which held that having a single black ancestor made a person black. Today, a strict application of this rule would make African Americans a substantial fraction of citizens of the United States. But it served the purposes of slave owners eager to add to their holdings.

Laws reinforced this distinction.[8] As early as 1691 a statute in colonial Virginia barred "[male] negroes, mulattos and Indians intermarrying with English or other white women," conveniently overlooking the fact that relations between European-American males and African American females were much more common than those prohibited by the statute. Later laws in other states, including many in the North and the West, banned all interracial marriages, including those between people of Asian and European descent. Not until 1967 did the U.S. Supreme Court declare such bans unconstitutional.

These laws reflected a powerful sense of separateness in the United States. Despite the continuous mixing of Africans and Europeans, many European Americans displayed a strong psychological need to believe that the two groups were fundamentally different. This belief accorded with Europeans' view of their place in the world, which arrayed various non-European people beneath the exemplar of European civilization. It also gave Europeans a way to justify their barbarous treatment of African slaves.

Many scientists lent their support to their cause. Throughout the Enlightenment, scientists studied different human groups in an effort to put them into discrete categories. In 1758, for example, the Swedish botanist Carolus Linnaeus gave the human species its formal name, *Homo sapiens*. He then divided the species into four subcategories: red Americans, yellow Asians, black Africans, and white Europeans. He described *Homo sapiens americanus* as "ill-tempered, . . . obstinate, contented, free." *Homo sapiens asiaticus* were "severe, haughty, desirous." *Homo sapiens afer* were "crafty, slow, foolish." And *Homo sapiens europaeus* were, of course, "active, very smart, inventive."[9]

Over the last few decades, scientific efforts to divide human beings into discrete categories have all but collapsed. The categories were clearly artificial, since all groups blend into each other. And the campaign to define human races came to be seen for what it was, a misguided attempt to use the methods of science to excuse the inexcusable.

The failure to define races scientifically has not ended racism. On the contrary, the pronouncements of racist organizations and individuals are as bigoted as ever. And a pervasive if less blatant racism remains deeply embedded in the broader society, despite all the progress that has been made against prejudice. To take just one example, racist groups have never been particularly large in absolute terms. But their activities receive real media attention because they play on fears that cut deeply into the American psyche.

These fears also have made the United States susceptible to another kind of media phenomenon. Every few decades the country undergoes a spasm of self-doubt occasioned by the publication of a book purporting to reveal innate mental differences among groups. These books make more or less the same arguments. They contend that particular groups in U.S. society have inborn traits that make them inherently less able to succeed. Inequities between groups therefore do not reflect different access to education, good jobs, and decent housing. They reflect genetic differences that are impossible to change.

Even before much was known about the genetics of human groups, these arguments were unconvincing.[10] Take the most notorious example – the differences in IQ scores among African Americans, European Americans, and Asian Americans. The average scores of African Americans and European Americans in the United States typically differ by ten to fifteen points, while Asian Americans tend to score about ten points above European Americans.

Hereditarians repeatedly cite these scores as proof that groups have different genetic capabilities. Yet the available evidence points instead toward the overwhelming influence of environmental factors:

- When IQ tests were developed in the early twentieth century, people from different parts of Europe had different average scores. . . . hereditarians used these differences to distinguish among Nordics (northern Europeans, roughly speaking), Alpines (eastern and central Europeans), and Mediterraneans (southern Europeans). Today the descendants of these immigrants score equally well on IQ tests. Yet the same arguments are now applied, through a sort of bracket creep, to African, European, and Asian Americans.
- If genetics were the cause of IQ differences, then African Americans who have higher proportions of European genes should score higher on IQ tests than those with fewer European ancestors, but no such effect has been found. The critical difference is not whether a person is genetically African American; it is whether a person has been treated (discriminated against) as an African American.
- Throughout the twentieth century, IQ scores have been going up for all groups, according to a variety of tests conducted in many different countries. These rises have occurred much too rapidly to be the product of genetic changes. They must result from better diets, better health care, and better education.
- Many studies show that children who receive good prenatal care and early childhood education on average score higher on IQ tests than children who do not. Since proportionally more African Americans than European Americans live in poverty in the United States, their scores on IQ tests tend to be lower.
- When researchers tracked down the children born to German mothers and U.S. soldiers during the Allied occupation of Germany in World War II, they found no difference in the IQ scores of children with African American versus European American fathers.
- Minorities in many countries score lower on IQ tests than do the majorities, regardless of their ancestry. An example is the Buraku of Japan, a minority that is severely discriminated against in housing, education, and employment. Their children typically score ten to fifteen points below

other Japanese children on IQ tests. Yet when the Buraku immigrate to other countries, the IQ gap between them and other Japanese gradually vanishes.

Figuring out why some groups score lower on IQ tests than others is not difficult. Disadvantaged social groups must shoulder many burdens, some of which are imposed on them, some of which they create for themselves. They may have higher dropout rates, lower incomes, more illegitimate births, higher levels of substance abuse, fewer opportunities in housing and employment, and so on. With such liabilities, it makes little sense to pin group differences on biology. But that has always been the easy way out. If group differences are believed to be inborn, efforts to improve the lives of the disadvantaged are unnecessary because they inevitably will fail.

That the supposed influence of genes on intelligence evaporates under closer scrutiny is not surprising. People are too genetically similar to have developed the kinds of intelligence differences cited by the hereditarians.

By comparing the DNA sequences of people from many locations around the world, geneticists have been able to measure the genetic differences between individuals and between groups. What they have found is that about 85 percent of the total amount of genetic variation in humans occurs *within* groups and only 15 percent between groups. In other words, most genetic variants occur in all human populations. Geneticists have to look hard to find variants concentrated in specific groups. . . .

Still, human groups do have different frequencies of some genetic variants – that's how geneticists can track human history using our genes. These differences provide people committed to a racial worldview with one last argument. If groups can differ in appearance for genetic reasons, they say, why can't they differ as well in temperament, character, or intelligence?[11] For example, maybe cold climates exerted some sort of selective pressure on the brain as well as on skin color. If people had to be smarter to survive in far northern areas, maybe intelligence was somehow concentrated in their descendants.

The argument doesn't work for two reasons. First, no mechanism has been identified that could sort complex attributes within such a genetically homogeneous and interconnected species. The idea that natural selection favored different cognitive traits on different continents seems designed more to justify social prejudice than to establish testable hypotheses. The people most adapted to the rigors of the European climate were the Neanderthals, not modern humans. Population levels declined several times in Africa following the appearance of modern humans, and the declines would have imposed the same sorts of selective pressures on Africans as those that non-Africans presumably faced. Animal species with worldwide distributions aren't more intelligent in cold climates than in warm ones. No evidence at all exists that different human groups have ever been under different selective pressures for cognitive traits.[12]

Even if a potential differentiating mechanism could be identified, the case for group differences fails for a second reason. A fundamental distinction exists between a simple trait such as skin color and a complex cognitive attribute such as intelligence.[13] Skin color is determined by a handful of genes and does not depend on the experiences a child has in the womb and while being raised. The development of the brain involves thousands of genes and is indissolubly linked to experience. In a species as genetically homogeneous as ours, showing that the distinctive behaviors of a group have a biological origin will never be possible, because the complexity of the gene-environment interaction will always dwarf any genetic difference between groups. . . .

The desire to attribute complex behaviors to unknown genetic forces is somewhat puzzling. After all, individuals and groups differ for many obvious reasons. Individuals have unique experiences from the moment of conception. They receive varying levels of nutrition and medical care. They are not treated uniformly by adults, teachers, and peers. They are born into cultures with particular histories and beliefs. Why ascribe group differences to genetic forces when the agents of differentiation are right in front of our faces? . . .

This will be a contentious issue over the next few decades. As more is learned about how genetic variants differ in frequency among groups, people will try to link those differing frequencies to the cultural attributes of groups. The reality will always be much more complicated than these simple correlations would indicate. But these efforts will receive great attention because they accord with popular prejudices.

Notes

[1]Ranajit Chakraborty, Mohammad Kamboh, M. Nwankwo, and Robert E. Ferrell, Caucasian genes in American blacks: New data (pp. 145–155), *American Journal of Human Genetics 50*, 1992.

[2]Brent Staples, The real American love story: Why America is a lot less white than it looks, *Slate*, Oct. 4, 1999.

[3]G. R. Daniel, Passers and Pluralists: Subverting the racial divide, in M. Root (Ed.) *Racially mixed people in America* (Newbury Park, CA: Sage Publications, 1992).

[4]Shannon Lanier and Jane Feldman, *Jefferson's children: The story of an American family* (New York: Random House, 2000).

[5]Patrick Manning, Chapter Two, *Slavery and African life: Occidental, Oriental and African slave trades* (New York: Cambridge University Press, 1990).

[6]Philip Curtin, *The Atlantic slave trade: A census* (Madison: University of Wisconsin Press, 1969).

[7]Monica Sans, Admixture studies in Latin America: From the 20th to the 21st century, (pp. 155-177), *Human Biology 72*, 2000; Joseph Page, *The Brazilians* (Reading, MA: Addison Wesley, 1995).

[8]David Greenberg, White weddings: The incredible staying power of the laws against interracial marriage, *Slate*, June 14, 1999.

[9]Jonathan Marks, Chapter Three, *Human biodiversity: Genes, race, and history* (New York: Aldine de Gruyter, 1995).

[10]B. Devlin, S. Fienberg, D. Resnick, and K. Roeder (Eds.), *Intelligence, genes, and success: Scientists respond to The Bell Curve* (New York: Springer-Verlag, 1997); Stephan Jay Gould, *The mismeasure of man* (New York: W. W. Norton, 1996).

[11]J. Philippe Rushton, *Race, evolution and behavior: A life history perspective* (New Brunswick, N.J.: Transaction Books, 1995).

[12]C. Loring Brace, An anthropological perspective on 'race' and intelligence: The non-clinal nature of human cognitive capabilities (pp. 245–264), *Journal of Anthropological Research 55*, 1999.

[13]Ned Block, How heritability misleads about race (pp. 99–128), *Cognition 56*, 1995; Jonathan Michael Kaplan, *The limits and lies of human genetics research: Dangers for social policy* (New York: Routledge, 2000).

The Founding Indian Fathers

The United States has always benefited from its diversity, but often the contributions of people of color and other groups have not been recognized. The author explains how Native American values prevailed over European traditions to create the democratic values and traditions that we now revere as they guide our political processes.

Every day of the school year, troops of children march across the lawn of the United States Capitol perched atop the District of Columbia's highest elevation. The building dominates the Washington skyline, a model of classical symmetry and precision. Two giant wings of precisely equal proportion reach out from a Roman dome that surveys the city of Washington. If reduced to a ruin, the forest of Greek columns decorating the building would appear to be as much at home in Rome or Naples as in Athens or Corinth. The building revels in its Old World heritage. . . .

The children pass under doorways that bear weighty engravings and quotations from European documents such as the Magna Carta interspersed with quotes from the United States Declaration of Independence or Constitution. The building and its appointments proudly proclaim their part in the great march of European progress and civilization. They portray the blessed dove of democracy hatching in Athens and then taking wing for a torturous flight of two millennia, pausing only momentarily over Republican Rome, the field of Runnymede, and the desk of Voltaire before finally alighting to rest permanently and securely in the virgin land of America.

A child standing squarely in the middle of the Capitol beneath the great dome sees a painted band circling the upper wall representing the history of America. In that work, the Indians appear as just one more dangerous obstacle, like the wild animals, the Appalachian Mountains, the Mississippi River, and the western deserts that blocked the progress of European civilization and technology in the white man's march across America. The most peaceful picture with an Indian theme in the rotunda shows the baptism of Pocahontas, daughter of the Indian leader Powhatan. Surrounded by Europeans and dressed in English clothes, she symbolically renounces the savage life of the Indians for the civilization of the British.

The lesson in this august setting presents itself forcefully on every visitor. The United States government derives from European precedents, and the Americans gave civilization to the Indians. Nothing in the Capitol hints that contemporary Americans owe the slightest debt to the Indians for teaching us about democratic institutions.

Despite these civic myths surrounding the creation of American government, America's settlers from Europe knew little of democracy. The English came from a nation ruled by monarchs who claimed that God conferred their right to rule and even allowed them to wage wars of extinction against the Irish. Colonists also fled to America from France, which was wandering aimlessly through history under the extravagances of a succession of kings named Louis, most of whom pursued debauched and extravagant reigns that oppressed, exploited, and at times even starved their subjects. . . .

The Founding Fathers faced a major problem when it came time to invent the United States. They represented, under the Articles of Confederation, thirteen separate and sovereign states. How could one country be made from all thirteen without each one yielding its own power?

Reportedly, the first person to propose a union of all the colonies and to propose a federal model for it was the Iroquois chief Canassatego, speaking at an Indian-British assembly in Pennsylvania in July 1744. He complained that the Indians found it difficult to deal with so many different colonial administrations, each with its own polity. It would make life easier for everyone involved if the colonists could have a union which allowed them to speak with one voice. He not only proposed that the colonies unify themselves, but told them how they might do it. He suggested that they do as his people had done and form a union like the League of the Iroquois.[1]

Hiawatha and Deganwidah founded the League of the Iroquois sometime between A.D. 1000 and 1450 under a constitution they called the *Kaianerekowa* or Great Law of Peace. When the Europeans arrived in America, the league constituted the most extensive and important political unit north of the Aztec civilizations. From earliest contact the Iroquois intrigued the Europeans, and they were the subject of many amazed reports. Benjamin Franklin, however, seems to have been the first to take their system as a potentially important model by which the settlers might be able to fashion a new government.

Benjamin Franklin first became acquainted with the operation of Indian political organization in his capacity as official printer for the colony of Pennsylvania. His job included publication of the records and speeches of the various Indian assemblies and treaty negotiations, but following his instinctive curiosity, he broadened this into a study of Indian culture and institutions. Because of his expertise and interest in Indian matters, the colonial government of Pennsylvania offered him his first diplomatic as-

signment as their Indian commissioner. He held this post during the 1750s and became intimately familiar with the intricacies of Indian political culture and in particular with the League of the Iroquois. After this taste of Indian diplomacy, Franklin became a lifelong champion of the Indian political structure and advocated its use by the Americans.

Echoing the original proposal of Canassatego, Franklin advocated that the new American government incorporate many of the same features as the government of the Iroquois.[2] Speaking to the Albany Congress in 1754, Franklin called on the delegates of the various English colonies to unite and emulate the Iroquois League, a call that was not heeded until the Constitution was written three decades later.[3] Even though the Founding Fathers finally adopted some of the essential features of the Iroquois League, they never followed it in quite the detail advocated by Franklin.

The Iroquois League united five principal Indian nations – the Mohawk, Onondaga, Seneca, Oneida, and Cayuga. Each of these nations had a council composed of delegates called sachems who were elected by the tribes of that nation. The Seneca Nation elected eight sachems to its council, the Mohawk and Oneida nations each had councils of nine sachems, the Cayuga Nation had a council of ten, and the Onondaga Nation had a council of fourteen. Each of these nations governed its own territory, and its own council met to decide the issues of public policy for each one. But these councils exercised jurisdiction over the internal concerns of that one nation only; in this regard they exercised powers somewhat like the individual governments of the colonies.

In addition to the individual councils of each separate nation, the sachems formed a grand Council of the League in which all fifty sachems of the six nations sat together to discuss issues of common concern. The sachems represented their individual nations, but at the same time they represented the whole League of the Iroquois, thereby making the decisions of the council the law for all five nations. In this council each sachem had equal authority and privileges, with his power dependent on his oratorical power to persuade. The council met in the autumn of at least one year in five in a longhouse in the Onondaga Nation; if needed they could be called into session at other times as well. Their power extended to all matters of common concern among the member nations. In the words of Lewis Henry Morgan, America's first modern anthropologist, the council "declared war and made peace, sent and received embassies, entered into treaties of alliance, regulated the affairs of subjugated nations, received new members into the League, extended its protection over feeble tribes, in a word, took all needful measures to promote their prosperity, and enlarge their dominion."[4]

Through this government the nations of the Iroquois controlled territory from New England to the Mississippi River, and they built a league that endured for centuries. Unlike European governments, the league blended the sovereignty of several nations into one government. This model of several sovereign units united into one government presented precisely the solution to the problem confronting the writers of the United States Constitution. Today we call this a "federal" system in which each state retains power over internal affairs and the national government regulates affairs common to all. Henry Steele Commager later wrote of this crucial time that even "if Americans did not actually invent federalism, they were able to take out an historical patent on it."[5] The Indians invented it even though the United States patented it.

Another student of the Iroquois political organization was Charles Thomson, the perpetual secretary of the Continental Congress. . . . Following Thomas Jefferson's request, Thomson wrote at length on Indian social and political institutions for inclusion in an appendix to Jefferson's *Notes on the State of Virginia*. According to his description of Indian political tradition, each Indian town built a council house for making local decisions and for electing delegates to the tribal council. The tribal council in turn elected delegates to the national council.[6] Even though Thomson wrote this several years before the Constitutional Convention, this description reads like a blueprint for the United States Constitution, especially when we remember that the Constitution allowed the state legislatures (rather than the general populace) to elect senators. . . .

If the conduct of any sachem appeared improper to the populace or if he lost the confidence of his electorate, the women of his clan impeached him and expelled him by official action, whereupon the women then chose a new sachem.[7] This concept of

impeachment ran counter to European tradition, in which the monarch ruled until death, even if he became insane or incapacitated, as in the case of George III. The Americans followed the Iroquois precedent of always providing for ways to remove leaders when necessary, but the Founding Fathers saw no reason to follow the example of the Iroquois in granting women the right to vote or any other major role in the political structure. . . .

Another imitation of the Iroquois came in the simple practice of allowing only one person to speak at a time in political meetings. This contrasts with the British tradition of noisy interruptions of one another as the members of Parliament shout out agreement or disagreement with the speaker. Europeans were accustomed to shouting down any speaker who displeased them; in some cases they might even stone him or inflict worse damage. . . .

From Hollywood films and adventure novels American often conclude that strong chiefs usually commanded the Indian tribes. More often, however, as in the case of the Iroquois, a council ruled, and any person called the "head" of the tribe usually occupied a largely honorary position of respect rather than power. Chiefs mostly played ceremonial and religious roles rather than political or economic ones. Unlike the words "caucus" and "powwow," which are Indian-derived and indicative of Indian political traditions, "chief" is an English word of French origin that British officials tried to force onto Indian tribes in order that they might have someone with whom to trade and sign treaties. . . .

In almost every North American tribe, clan, or nation for which we have detailed political information, the supreme authority rested in a group rather than in an individual. It took many generations of close interaction between colonists and Indians before the principles of group decision-making replaced the European traditions of relying on a single supreme authority. The importance of these Indian councils and groups shows clearly in the English lack of words to explain such a process.

One of the most important political institutions borrowed from the Indian was the caucus. The word comes from the Algonquian languages. The caucus permits informal discussion of an issue without necessitating a yea or nay vote on any particular question. This agreed with the traditional Indian way of talking through an issue or of making a powwow; it made political decisions less divisive and combative. The caucus became a mainstay of American democracy both in the congress and in political and community groups all over the country. The caucus evolved into such an important aspect of American politics that the political parties adopted it to nominate their presidential candidates. In time this evolved into the political convention. . . .

Even after the founding of the United States, Indians continued to play a significant role in the evolution of democracy because of their sustained interactions with Americans on the frontier. The frontiersmen constantly reinvented democracy and channeled it into the eastern establishment of the United States.

Time and again the people of the frontier rebelled against the entrenched and conservative values of an ever more staid coastal elite. . . . Even Alexis de Tocqueville, who denigrated the achievements of the Indians, noticed that the settlers on the frontier "mix the ideas and customs of savage life with the civilization of their fathers."[8] . . .

Most democratic and egalitarian reforms of the past two hundred years in America originated on the frontier and not in the settled cities of the east. The frontier states dropped property and religious requirements for voters. They extended the franchise to women, and in 1916 Montana elected Jeannette Rankin as the first woman in Congress four years before the Nineteenth Amendment to the Constitution gave women the right to vote. The western states started the public election of senators in place of selection by the legislature. They also pioneered the use of primary elections and electoral recalls of unpopular officers. Even today they have more elective offices, such as judges; such offices in the east are usually filled by appointment by the governor or the legislature. This strong bias toward the electoral process and equal votes for all has been reinforced repeatedly by the people who have had the closest and the longest connections with the Indians on the frontier. . . .

Washington D.C. has never recognized the role of the Indians in the writing of the United States Constitution or in the creation of political institutions that seem so uniquely American. But an inadvertent memorial does exist. An older woman from

Israel pointed this out to me one spring day as I cut across the lawn of the United States Capitol. She stopped me, and in a husky voice asked me who was the Indian woman atop the Capitol dome. Suddenly looking at it through her eyes, I too saw the figure as an Indian even though I knew that it was not.

When the United States government embarked on an expansion of the Capitol in the middle of the nineteenth century, the architects proposed to cap the dome with a symbol of freedom. They chose for this a nineteen-foot bronze statue of a Roman woman who would stand on the pinnacle of the Capitol. Sculptor Thomas Crawford crowned the woman with a Phrygian cap, which in Roman history had been the sign of the freed slave. At that time Jefferson Davis, the future president of the Confederate States of America, still served as the secretary of war for the United States, and he objected strongly to what he interpreted as an antisouthern and anti-slavery symbol. He compelled Crawford to cap her with something less antagonistic to southern politicians. Crawford designed a helmet covered with a crown of feathers, but in putting this headdress on the figure, her whole appearance changed. Now instead of looking like a classical Greek or Roman, she looked like an Indian.

She still stands today on the pseudoclassical Capitol overlooking the city of Washington. The Washington Monument rises to the same height, but no other building has been allowed to rise higher than she. Even though no one intended her to be an Indian, she now reigns as the nearest thing to a monument that Washington ever built to honor the Indians who contributed to the building of a federal union based on democracy.

Notes

[1]Bruce E. Johansen, *Forgotten Founders*. (Ipswich, MA: Gambit, 1982), p. 12, 61.

[2]Edmund Wilson, *Apologies to the Iroquois*. (New York: Farrar, Straus and Giroux, 1959), p. 46.

[3]Robert A. Hecht, *Continents in Collision*. (Washington, D.C.: University Press of America, 1980), p. 71.

[4]Lewis Henry Morgan, *League of the Iroquois*. (Rochester: Sage, 1851), pp. 66–67.

[5]Henry Steele Commager, The empire of reason: How Europe imagined and America realized the enlightenment. (Garden City, NY: Anchor Books, 1978), p. 207.

[6]Charles Thomson, Appendix 1. In Thomas Jefferson, *Notes on the State of Virginia*. (Chapel Hill: University of North Carolina Press, 1955), p. 203.

[7]Alexander A. Goldenweiser, Iroquois social organization. In R. C. Owen, J. J. F. Deetz, and A. D. Fisher (Eds.) *The North American Indians*. (New York: Macmillan, 1967), p. 570.

[8]Alexis de Tocqueville, *Democracy in America*. 2 volumes. Henry Reeve Text, edited by Phillips Bradley. (New York: Random House, 1945), Vol. 1, p. 334.

Kong at the Seaside

In this story, an incident occurs that makes a father decide to test his son's values, but in the end it is the father's values that are tested. This results in the father reflecting upon the influence that poverty can have on one's values and one's choices in life.

Kong got his first glimpse of the sea as he ran on the beach, which stretched like a white arc along the edge of the cove. He barked vociferously with extravagant enthusiasm. Again and again, the bluish-white spray came dashing up at him and he was forbidden to hurl himself into it! A tall order for an Airedale terrier with a wiry brown coat and shaggy forelegs. However, Willie, his young god, would not permit it; but at any rate he could race at top speed across the firm sand, which was still damp from the ebbing waters, Willie following with lusty shouts.

Engineer Groll, strolling after, noticed that the dog and his tanned, light-haired, eight-year-old master were attracting considerable attention among the beach-chairs and gaily striped bathing-houses. At the end of the row, where the sky was pale and dipped into the infinite – whereas it was vividly blue overhead and shed relaxation, happiness, and vigor on all these city people and their games in the sand – some controversy seemed to be in progress. Willie was standing there, slim and defiant, holding his dog by the collar. Groll hurried over. People in bathing suits looked pretty much alike, social castes and classes intermingled. Heads showed more character and expression, though the

bodies which supported them were still flabby and colorless, unaccustomed to exposure and pale after a long winter's imprisonment within the darkness of heavy clothing. A stoutish man was sitting in the shade of a striped orange tent stretched over a blue framework; he was bending slightly forward, holding a cigar.

"Is that your dog?" he asked quietly.

A little miss, about ten years old, was with him; she was biting her underlip, and a look of hatred for the boy and the dog flashed between her tear-filled narrow lids.

"No," said Groll with his pleasant voice, which seemed to rumble deep down in his chest, "The dog belongs to the boy, who, to be sure, is mine."

"You know dogs aren't allowed off the leash," the quiet voice continued. "He frightened my daughter a bit, has trampled her canals, and is standing on her spade."

"Pull him back, Willie," laughed Groll. "You're quite right, sir, but the dog broke away and, after all, nothing serious has happened."

Willie pushed Kong aside, picked up the spade and, bowing slightly, held it out to the group. Its third member was a slender, remarkably pretty young woman, sitting in the rear of the tent; Groll decided she was too young to be the mother of the girl and too attractive to be her governess. Well gotten up, he reflected; she looks Irish with those auburn eyebrows.

From *Playthings of Time* (New York: Viking Press/Penguin, 1935).

No one took the spade from the boy, and Willie, with a frown, stuck the toy into the sand in front of the girl.

"I think that squares it, especially on such a beautiful day," Groll smiled and lay down. His legs behind him, his elbows on the sand, and his face resting on his hands, he looked over the hostile three. Willie has behaved nicely and politely; how well he looks with his Kong. The dog, evidently not as ready to make peace, growled softly, his fur bristling at the neck; then he sat down.

"I want to shoot his dog, Father," the girl suddenly remarked in a determined voice; "he frightened me so." Groll noticed a gold bracelet of antique workmanship about her wrist – three strands of pale green-gold braided into the semblance of a snake. These people need a lesson. I shall give it to them.

Groll nodded reassuringly at his boy, who was indignantly drawing his dog closer to him. These grown-ups seemed to know that the girl had the upper hand of them, or, as Groll told himself, had the right to give orders. So he quietly waited for the sequel of this charming conversation; after all, he was still there to reprimand the brat if the gentleman with the fine cigar lacked the courage to do so because the sweet darling was not accustomed to proper discipline.

"No one is going to shoot my dog," threatened Willie, clenching his fists; but, without deigning to look at him, the girl continued.

"Buy him from the people, Father; here is my checkbook." She actually took the thin booklet and a fountain pen with a gold clasp from a zipper-bag inside the tent.

"If you won't buy him for me, I'll throw a soup plate right off the table at dinner; you know I will, Father." She spoke almost in a whisper and was as white as chalk under her tan; her blue eyes, over which the sea had cast a greenish glint, flashed threateningly.

The gentleman said: "Ten pounds for the dog."

"The dog is not mine; you must deal with my boy. He's trained him."

"I don't deal with boys. I offer fifteen pounds, a pretty neat sum for the cur."

Groll realized that this was an opportunity of really getting to know his eldest. "Willie," he began, "this gentleman offers you fifteen pounds for Kong

so he may shoot him. For the money, you could buy the bicycle you have been wanting since last year. I won't be able to give it to you for a long time, we're not rich enough for that."

Willie looked at his father, wondering whether he could be in earnest. But the familiar face showed no sign of jesting. In answer he put an arm about Kong's neck, smiled up at Groll, and said: "I won't sell him to you, Father."

The gentleman in the bathing suit with his still untanned pale skin turned to Groll. Apparently the argument began to interest him. "Persuade him. I offer twenty pounds."

"Twenty pounds," Groll remarked to Willie; "that would buy you the bicycle and the canoe, which you admired so much this morning, Willie. A green canoe with double paddles for the water, and for the land a fine nickel-plated bicycle with a headlight, storage battery, and new tires. There might even be money left over for a watch. You only have to give up this old dog by handing the leash to the gentleman."

Willie said scornfully: "If I went ten steps away, Kong would pull him over and be with me again."

The beautiful and unusual young woman spoke for the first time. "He would hardly be able to do that," she said in a clear, sweet, mocking voice – a charming little person, thought Groll – then she took a small Browning pistol, gleaming with silver filigree work, out of her handbag. "This would prevent him from running very far."

Foolish of her, thought Groll. "You see sir, the dog is a thoroughbred, pedigreed, and splendidly trained."

"We've noticed that."

"Offer fifty pounds, Father, and settle it."

"Fifty pounds," repeated Groll, and his voice shook slightly. That would pay for this trip, and if I handled the money for him, his mother could at last regain her strength. The sanatorium is too expensive; we can't afford it. "Fifty pounds, Willie! The bicycle, the watch, the tent – you remember the brown tent with the cords and tassels – and you would have money left to help me send mother to a sanatorium. Imagine, all that for a dog! Later on, we can go to the animal welfare society, pay three shillings, and get another Kong."

Willie said softly: "There is only one Kong. I will not sell him."

"Offer a hundred pounds, Father. I want to shoot that dog. I shouldn't have to stand such boorishness."

The stoutish gentleman hesitated a moment, then made the offer. "A hundred pounds, sir," he said huskily. "You don't look as though you could afford to reject a small fortune."

"Indeed, sir, I can't," said Groll, and turned to Willie. "My boy," he continued earnestly, " a hundred pounds safely invested will within ten years assure you of a university education. Or, if you prefer, you can buy a car to ride to school in. What eyes the other boys would make! And you could drive mother to market; that's a great deal of money, a hundred pounds for nothing but a dog."

Willie, frightened by the earnestness of the words, puckered up his face as though to cry. After all, he was just a small boy of eight and he was being asked to give up his beloved dog. "But I love Kong, and Kong loves me," he said, fighting down the tears in his voice. "I don't want to give him up."

"A hundred pounds – do persuade him, sir! Otherwise my daughter will make life miserable for me. You have no idea," he sighed – "What a row such a little lady can kick up."

If she were mine, thought Groll, I'd leave marks of a good lesson on each of her dainty cheeks; and after glancing at his boy, who, with furrowed brow, was striving to hold back his tears, he said the thought aloud, quietly, clearly, looking sternly into the eyes of the girl. "And now, I think, the incident is closed."

Then the most astounding thing happened. The little girl began to laugh. Evidently the tall, brown man pleased her, and the idea that anyone could dare to slap her, the little lady, for one of her whims, fascinated her by its very roughness.

"All right, Father," she cried; "he's behaved well. Now we'll put the checkbook back in the bag. Of course, Father, you knew it was all in fun!"

The stoutish gentleman smiled with relief and said that, of course, he had known it and added that

such a fine day was just made to have fun. Fun! Groll didn't believe it. He knew too much about people.

Willie breathed more freely and, pretending to blow his nose, wiped away two furtive tears. He threw himself down in the sand next to Kong, happily pulled the dog on top of himself, and began to wrestle with him; the shaggy brown paws of the terrier and the slim tanned arms of the boy mingled in joyful confusion.

However, Groll, while he somewhat reluctantly accepted a cigar and a light from the strange gentleman and silently looked out into the blue-green sea which lay spread before him like shimmering folds of silk with highlights and shadows – Groll thought: Alas for the poor! If this offer had come to me two years ago when my invention was not yet completed and when we lived in a damp flat dreaming of the little house we now have, then – poor Willie! – this argument might have had a different outcome, this struggle for nothing more than a dog, the love, loyalty, courage, and generosity in the soul of an animal and a boy. Yet, speaking in terms of economics, a little financial security was necessary before one could indulge in the luxury of human decency. Without it – he reflected – no one should be asked to make a decision similar to the one which has just confronted Willie and me; everyone was entitled to that much material safety, especially in an era that was so full of glittering temptations.

The little girl with the spade put her slim bare feet into the sand outside of the tent and called to Willie: "Help me to dig new ones." But her eyes invited the man Groll, for whose approval she was striving.

She pointed to the ruined canals. Then, tossing her head, she indicated Kong, who lay panting and lazy in the warm sunshine, and called merrily: "For all I care, he can trample them again."

The whistle of an incoming steamboat sounded from the pier.

The Construction of Personal Identity in a Diverse Society

> **"**Two deer, two owls will behave differently from each other. I have studied many plants. The leaves of one plant, on the same stem, none is exactly alike . . . If the Great Spirit likes the plants, the animals, even little mice and bugs to do this, how much more will he abhor people being alike, doing the same thing . . . and, worst of all, thinking alike.**"**
>
> **John Lame Deer (1903–1976)**

John Lame Deer encourages people to develop their own individual identity, but a larger question needs to be addressed: What influence does the increasing diversity in the United States have on the development of individual identity in America? Because of ongoing segregation in neighborhoods and schools, many Americans might appear to have minimal exposure to that diversity. On the other hand, it is impossible for any American to be completely isolated from diversity in our nation: Consider the athletes Americans support and admire in professional and collegiate sports; the performers we applaud in music, films, and other forms of entertainment; and the advertisements we encounter in newspapers, magazines, and television. American diversity has always been reflected in our language, and today this is especially true for slang terms. Americans who join the military or enter the corporate world inevitably encounter diversity, and most will participate in some form of diversity training. So the question remains: How do Americans determine their sense of identity in the context of the widespread diversity existing in our society?

> **"**The task that remains is to cope with our interdependence – to see ourselves reflected in every other human being and to respect and honor our differences.**"**
>
> **Melba Patillo Beals (1941–)**

Beverly Daniel Tatum examines the issue of the influence of group membership on individual identity, especially during adolescence. She emphasizes the important point that an individual identity may encompass several categories. Each of us has a gender, a race, a social class, a sexual orientation, and so on. Experiences in each of these categories may provide individuals with power and privilege or prejudice and oppression, and these experiences have an impact on the person that we become. Tatum describes how membership in dominant.or subordinate groups influences one's consciousness of identity and examines the dynamics involved in schools or in the larger society as individuals who belong to dominant and subordinate groups seek for affirmation of their identity.

Many students of color in the United States do not often feel affirmed while they are in school, but instead may feel oppressed by a system demanding that they achieve without acknowledging the challenges they face or their struggle to maintain a sense of individuality. Sören Wuerth illustrates this dilemma in "Edwina Left Behind," where Edwina is a 12th grade Cu'pik Indian attending school in the Eskimo village of Chevak in western Alaska. As one of Edwina's teachers, Wuerth respects her not only for her achievements in the face of adverse circumstances, but also for her unique identity and personality. Despite speaking a linguistically distinct form of English (like the other Cu'Pik students in the village), Edwina maintains an "A" average in her high school course work. But to receive a diploma, students must pass Alaska's High School Graduation Qualifying Exam, a difficult test for Cu'Pik students because of the questions about vocabulary terms and concepts that are culturally irrelevant to their lives. Edwina prepares for the test as well as she can, but she fails and does not receive a diploma. Wuerth rejects the validity of such "one size fits all" tests, and insists that the failure here was not Edwina's. It is hard to disagree. Teachers hope that students like Edwina will adhere to the advice of social activist Marian Wright Edelman:

> Don't let anything keep you from struggling and seeking to be a decent, striving human being. It is where you are headed not where you are from that will determine where you end up.

Barack Obama's essay operates at the intersection of Tatum's theoretical discussion and Edwina's lived experience. In "Origins," he describes his experience as a biracial high school student who was trying to understand who he is and where he belongs. He has black friends and white friends, and too often it seems that he must choose one or the other. If he must reject his white friends because they are white, then must he reject his white mother and the white grandparents who raised him? He chooses to search for an alternative to this literally black and white choice, and his search eventually involves becoming familiar with ideas from James Baldwin, Maya Angelou, and Malcolm X.

"We should know that diversity makes for a rich tapestry and we must understand that all the threads of the tapestry are equal in value no matter what their color."

Maya Angelou (1928–)

Although diversity may influence identity for each American, the influence will be different for each one. Na'im Akbar explores differences in identity development for both black and white Americans through the lens of privilege. Akbar describes and provides examples of white privilege, but he also discusses black privilege in a way that few scholars have addressed. A sense of privilege certainly influences one's sense of identity, and Akbar believes that African Americans who benefit the most from their privilege have a special obligation to other members of their group. He challenges them to honor the sacrifices of all those in the past who made their current accomplishments possible, and to support black people today as they continue to confront barriers that make it more difficult to achieve their goals and dreams.

Finally, Rawi Hage's short story offers the example of a subtle relationship that can develop even in the context of numerous impersonal contacts within an urban society. "The Salad Lady" is the name given to a customer who eats a salad for lunch every Wednesday at the same restaurant. The relationship begins as the formal one of waiter to regular customer until the waiter accidentally spills coffee on her. Following this incident, the apologetic waiter offers to share an umbrella and walk her home because it has begun to rain. In a brief conversation while walking to her apartment, they find out more about each other as individuals and a human connection is established. In her subsequent appearances at the restaurant, she and the waiter call each other by name. When she begins wearing a hat, and later when she no longer appears at the restaurant, the waiter knows the reason why. This poignant story becomes a parable illustrating the idea that our identity is shaped by the relationships we form with those around us, even strangers; it also reminds us that it takes more than simply being around other people to build a bond with them.

> 66It is one thing to throw people from different worlds together in a classroom or an Army boot camp and yet another thing to make them feel a connection that produces a sense of community and mutual commitment. More is needed than proximity.99
>
> Christopher Edley, Jr. (1953–)

The Complexity of Identity – "Who Am I?"

Creating a sense of identity is a complex process encompassing factors such as race, social class, ethnicity, and religion. It involves not only how you see yourself, but also how others see you. A person's identity is also significantly influenced by their being a member of a dominant or subordinate group. The author examines all of this and more in the following essay.

The concept of identity is a complex one, shaped by individual characteristics, family dynamics, historical factors, and social and political contexts. Who am I? The answer depends in large part on who the world around me says I am. Who do my parents say I am? Who do my peers say I am? What message is reflected back to me in the faces and voices of my teachers, my neighbors, store clerks? What do I learn from the media about myself? How am I represented in the cultural images around me? Or am I missing from the picture altogether. As social scientist Charles Cooley pointed out long ago, other people are the mirror in which we see ourselves.[1]

A "looking glass self" is not a flat one-dimensional reflection, but multidimensional. Because the focus of this (essay) is racial identity in the United States, race is highlighted in these pages. Yet, how one's racial identity is experienced will be mediated by other dimensions of oneself: male or female; young or old; wealthy, middle-class, or poor; gay, lesbian, bisexual, transgender, or heterosexual; able-bodied or with disabilities; Christian, Muslim, Jewish, Buddhist, Hindu, or atheist. . . .

Who I am (or say I am) is a product of these and many other factors. Erik Erikson, the psychoanalytic theorist who coined the term *identity crisis*, introduced the notion that the social, cultural, and historical context is the group in which individual identity is embedded. Acknowledging the complexity of identity as a concept, Erikson writes:

> We deal with a process "located" *in the core of the individual* and yet also *in the core of his communal culture.* . . . In psychological terms, identity formation employs a process of simultaneous reflection and observation, a process taking place on all levels of mental functioning, by which the individual judges himself in the light of what he perceives to be the way in which others judge him in comparison to themselves . . . while he judges their way of judging him in light of how he perceives himself in comparison to them . . . This process is, luckily, and necessarily, for the most part unconscious except where inner conditions and outer circumstances combine to aggravate a painful, or elated, "identity-consciousness."[2]

Triggered by the biological changes associated with puberty, the maturation of cognitive abilities, and changing societal expectations, this process of simultaneous reflection and observation, the self-creation of one's identity, is commonly experienced in the United States and other Western societies during the period of adolescence.[3] Though the foundation of identity is laid in the experiences of childhood, younger children lack the physical and cognitive development needed to reflect on the self in this abstract way. The adolescent capacity for self-reflection . . . allows one to ask, "Who am I now?" "Who was I before?" "Who will I become?" The answers to these questions will influence choices about who one's romantic partners will be, what type of work one will do, where one will live, and what belief system one will embrace. Choices made in adolescence ripple throughout the lifespan.

Integrating one's past, present, and future into a cohesive, unified sense of self is a complex task that begins in adolescence and continues for a lifetime. . . . My students' autobiographical narratives point to a similar complexity, but the less developed narratives of late adolescents that I teach highlight the fact that our awareness of the complexity of our own identity develops over time. The salience of particular aspects of our identity varies at different moments in our lives. The process of integrating the component parts of our self-definition is indeed a lifelong journey.

Which parts of our identity capture our attention first? While there are surely idiosyncratic responses to this question, a classroom exercise I regularly use with my psychology students reveals a telling pattern. I ask my students to complete the sentence, "I am _____," using as many descriptors as they can think of in sixty seconds. All kinds of trait descriptions are used – friendly, shy, assertive, intelligent, honest, and so on – but over the years I have noticed something else. Students of color usually mention their racial or ethnic group: for instance, I am Black, Puerto Rican, Korean American. White students who have grown up in strong ethnic enclaves occasionally mention being Irish or Italian. But in general, White students rarely mention being White. When I use this exercise in coeducational settings, I notice a similar pattern in terms of gender, religion, and sexuality. Women usually mention being female while men don't usually mention their maleness. Jewish students often say they are

Jews, while mainline Protestants rarely mention their religious identification. A student who is comfortable revealing it publicly may mention being gay, lesbian, or bisexual. Though I know most of my students are heterosexual, it is very unusual for anyone to include their heterosexuality on their list.

Common across these examples is that in the areas where a person is a member of the dominant or advantaged social group, the category is usually not mentioned. That element of their identity is so taken for granted by them that it goes without comment. It is taken for granted by them because it is taken for granted by the dominant culture. In Eriksonian terms, their inner experience and outer circumstance are in harmony with one another, and the image reflected by others is similar to the image within. In the absence of dissonance, this dimension of identity escapes conscious attention.

The parts of our identity that *do* capture our attention are those that other people notice, and that reflect back to us. The aspect of identity that is the target of others' attention, and subsequently of our own, often is that which sets us apart as exceptional or "other" in their eyes. In my life I have been perceived as both. A precocious child who began to read at age three, I stood out among my peers because of my reading ability. This "gifted" dimension of my identity was regularly commented upon by teachers and classmates alike, and quickly became part of my self-definition. But I was also distinguished by being the only Black student in the class, an "other," a fact I grew increasingly aware of as I got older.

While there may be countless ways one might be defined as exceptional, there are at least seven categories of "otherness" commonly experienced in U.S. society. People are commonly defined as other on the basis of race or ethnicity, gender, religion, sexual orientation, socioeconomic status, age, and physical or mental ability. Each of these categories has a form of oppression associated with it: racism, sexism, religious oppression/anti-Semitism,[4] heterosexism, classism, ageism, and ableism, respectively. In each case, there is a group considered dominant (systematically advantaged by the society because of group membership) and a group considered subordinate or targeted (systematically disadvantaged). When we think about our multiple identities, most of us will find that we are both dominant and targeted at the same time. But it is the targeted identities that hold our attention and the dominant identities that often go unexamined.

In her essay, "Age, Race, Class, and Sex: Women Redefining Difference," Audre Lorde captured the tensions between dominant and targeted identities co-existing in one individual (when she) wrote:

> Somewhere, on the edge of consciousness, there is what I call a *mythical norm*, which each one of us within our hearts knows "that is not me." In america, this norm is usually defined a white, thin, male, young, heterosexual, christian, and financially secure. It is with this mythical norm that the trappings of power reside within society. Those of us who stand outside that power often identify one way in which we are different, and we assume that to be the primary cause of all oppression, forgetting other distortions around difference, some of which we ourselves may be practicing.[5]

Even as I focus on race and racism in my own writing and teaching, it is helpful to remind myself and my students of other distortions around difference that I (and they) may be practicing. It is an especially useful way of generating empathy for our mutual learning process. If I am impatient with a White woman for not recognizing her White privilege, it may be useful for me to remember how much of my life I spent oblivious to the fact of the daily advantages I receive simply because I am heterosexual, or the ways in which I may take my class privilege for granted.

It is also helpful to consider the commonality found in the experience of being dominant or subordinate even when the sources of dominance or subordination are different. Jean Baker Miller, author of *Toward a New Psychology of Women*, has identified some of these areas of commonality.[6]

Dominant groups, by definition, set the parameters within which the subordinates operate. The dominant group holds the power and authority in society relative to the subordinates and determines how that power and authority may be acceptably used. Whether it is reflected in determining who gets the best jobs, whose history will be taught in school, or whose relationships will be validated by society, the dominant group has the greatest influence in determining the structure of the society.

The relationship of the dominants to the subordinates is often one in which the targeted group is labeled as defective or substandard in significant ways. For example, Blacks have historically been characterized as less intelligent than Whites, and women have been viewed as less emotionally stable than men. The dominant group assigns roles to the subordinates that reflect the latter's devalued status, reserving the most highly valued roles in the society for themselves. Subordinates are usually said to be innately incapable of being able to perform the preferred roles. To the extent that the targeted group internalizes the images that the dominant group reflects back to them, they may find it difficult to believe in their own ability.

When a subordinate demonstrates positive qualities believed to be more characteristic of dominants, the individual is defined by dominants as an anomaly. Consider this illustrative example: Following a presentation I gave to some educators, a White man approached me and told me how much he liked my ideas and how articulate I was. "You know," he concluded, "if I had had my eyes closed, I wouldn't have known it was a Black woman speaking." (I replied, "This is what a Black woman sounds like.")

The dominant group is seen as the norm for humanity. Jean Baker Miller also asserts that inequitable social relations are seen as the mode for "normal human relationships." Consequently, it remains perfectly acceptable in many circles to tell jokes that denigrate a particular group, to exclude subordinates from one's neighborhood or work setting, or to oppose initiatives which might change the power balance.

Miller points out that dominant groups generally do not like to be reminded of the existence of inequality. Because rationalizations have been created to justify the social arrangements, it is easy to believe everything is as it should be. Dominants "can avoid awareness because their explanation of the relationship becomes so well integrated in other terms; they can even believe that both they and the subordinate group share the same interests and, to some extent, a common experience."[7]

The truth is that dominants do not really know what the experience of subordinates is. In contrast, the subordinates are very well informed about the dominants. Even when firsthand experience is limited by social segregation, the number and variety of images of the dominant group available through television, magazines, books, and newspapers provide subordinates with plenty of information about the dominants. The dominant worldview has saturated the culture for all to learn. Even the Black or Latino child living in a segregated community can enter White homes of many kinds daily via the media. However, . . . information about subordinates is often limited to stereotypical depictions of the "other." For example, there are many images of heterosexual relations on television, but very few images of gay or lesbian domestic partnerships beyond the caricatures of comedy shows. There are many images of White men and women in all forms of media, but relatively few portrayals of people of color. . . .

In a situation of unequal power, a subordinate group has to focus on survival. It becomes very important for the subordinates to become highly attuned to the dominants as a way of protecting themselves from them. For example, women who have been battered by men often talk about the heightened sensitivity they develop to their partners' moods. Being able to anticipate and avoid the men's rage is important to survival. . . .

Because of the risks inherent in unequal relationships, the subordinates often develop covert ways of resisting or undermining the power of the dominant group. As Miller points out, popular culture is full of folk tales, jokes, and stories about how the subordinate – whether the woman, the peasant, or the sharecropper – outwitted the "boss."[8] In his essay, "I Won't Learn from You," Herbert Kohl identifies one form of resistance, "not-learning," demonstrated by targeted students who are too often seen by their dominant teachers as "others."

> Not-learning tends to take place when someone has to deal with unavoidable challenges to her or his personal and family loyalties, integrity, and identity. In such situations, there are forced choices and no apparent middle ground. To agree to learn from a stranger who does not respect your integrity causes a major loss of self. The only alternative is to not-learn and reject their world.[9]

The use of either strategy, attending very closely to the dominants or not attending at all, is costly to members of the targeted group. Not-learning may mean there are needed skills which are not acquired. Attending closely to the dominant group may leave little time or energy to attend to one's self. Worse yet, the negative messages of the dominant group about the subordinates may be internalized, leading to self-doubt or, in its extreme form, self-hate. There are many examples of subordinates attempting to make themselves over in the image of the dominant group – Jewish people who want to change the Semitic look of their noses, Asians who have cosmetic surgery to alter the shape of their eyes, Blacks who seek to lighten their skin with bleaching creams . . . Whether one succumbs to the devaluing pressures of the dominant culture or successfully resists them, the fact is that dealing with oppressive systems from the underside, regardless of the strategy, is physically and psychologically taxing.

Breaking beyond the structural and psychological limitations imposed on one's group is possible, but not easily achieved. To the extent that members of targeted groups do push societal limits – achieving unexpected success, protesting injustice, being "uppity" – by their actions they call the whole system into question. Miller writes, they "expose the inequality, and throw into question the basis for its existence. And they will make the inherent conflict an open conflict. They will then have to bear the burden and take the risks that go with being defined as 'troublemakers. . . .'"[10]

Many of us are both dominant and subordinate. Clearly racism and racial identity are at the center of discussion in this (essay), but as Audre Lorde said, from her vantage point as a Black lesbian, "There is no hierarchy of oppression." The thread and threat of violence runs through all of the isms. There is a need to acknowledge each other's pain, even as we attend to our own.

For those readers who are in the dominant racial category, it may sometimes be difficult to take in what is being said by and about those who are targeted by racism. When the perspective of the subordinate is shared directly, an image is reflected to members of the dominant group which is disconcerting. To the extent that one can draw on one's own experience of subordination – as a young person, as a person with a disability, as someone who grew up poor, as a woman – it may be easier to make meaning of another targeted group's experience. For those readers who are targeted by racism and are angered by the obliviousness of Whites, it may be useful to attend to your experience of dominance where you may find it – as a heterosexual, as an able-bodied person, as a Christian, as a man – and consider what systems of privilege you may be overlooking. The task of resisting our own oppression does not relieve us of the responsibility of acknowledging our complicity in the oppression of others.

Our ongoing examination of who we are in our full humanity, embracing all of our identities, creates the possibility of building alliances that may ultimately free us all.

Notes

[1]See C. Cooley, *Human nature and the social order.* (New York: Scribner, 1922). George H. Mead expanded on this idea in his book, *Mind, self, and society* (Chicago: University of Chicago Press, 1934).

[2]E. H. Erikson, *Identity, youth, and crisis.* (New York: W. W. Norton, 1968) p. 22.

[3]For a discussion of the Western biases in the concept of self and individual identity, see A. Roland, "identity, self, and individualism in a multicultural perspective," pp. 11–23 in E. P. Salett and D. R. Koslow (Eds.), *Race, ethnicity, and self: Identity in multicultural perspective* (Washington, DC: National MultiCultural Institute, 1994).

[4]*Anti-Semitism* is a term commonly used to describe the oppression of Jewish people. However, other Semitic peoples (Arab Muslims, for example) are also subject to oppressive treatment on the basis of ethnicity as well as religion. For that reason, the terms *Jewish oppression* and *Arab oppression* are sometimes used to specify the particular form of oppression under discussion.

[5]A. Lorde, Age, race, class, and sex: Women redefining difference (pp. 445–451). In P. S. Rothenberg (Ed.), *Race, class, and gender in the United States: An integrated study,* 3rd ed. (New York: St. Martin's Press, 1995), p. 446.

[6]J. B. Miller, Domination and subordination (pp. 3–12). In *Toward a new psychology of women.* (Boston: Beacon Press, 1976)

[7]Ibid., p. 8.

[8]Ibid., p. 10.

[9]H. Kohl, I won't learn from you: Confronting student resistance (pp. 134–135). In *Rethinking our classrooms: Teaching for equity and justice.* (Milwaukee: Rethinking Our Schools, 1994), p. 134).

[10] Miller, "Domination and subordination," p. 12.

Edwina Left Behind

Even when they are fluent English speakers, students from diverse cultural and ethnic backgrounds encounter obstacles in America's schools. The following essay describes a specific example of a student who is trying to succeed despite the obstacles.

The woman from the state education department had come to show us "the data." She stood in an auditorium, in front of Ketchikan school district's some 300 teachers and staff and began a choppy Power Point presentation describing the standards on how students should soon be judged.

The official called herself a "recovering" math and middle school teacher. During her presentation, we were quizzed on the meaning of acronyms and asked multiple-choice questions about No Child Left Behind. Judging from comments and muffled heckling behind me, I was not the only teacher who considered the education department's presentation demeaning.

As I listened, I reflected on Edwina, a student in the 12th-grade language arts class I taught last year in the remote Cu'pik Eskimo village of Chevak. Chevak School is the dominant feature in the rural, western Alaska village. Just over 300 students shuffle from small, modular homes to the K-12 school, leaning into the wind most of the year to get there, crossing swells of snow drifts in the winter.

Edwina was tough. She had a round face, always wore the same sweatshirt and oval glasses, and maneuvered through two communities rife with drugs and alcohol like a running back moving past hapless opponents.

Edwina's family lived in the coastal village of Hooper Bay, but she attended Chevak's school 20 miles inland, hoping her education would be superior to that of the neighboring village. On weekends, she'd leave her grandmother's place and drive a snowmobile 40 miles across frozen tundra, in weather that dipped to 60 below, to visit her home village. Edwina beat up boys who picked on her brothers, swore, and chewed tobacco. She turned to her schoolwork with the same rugged self-assurance.

A senior, Edwina needed to pass the state's High School Graduation Qualifying exam to receive a diploma. Early in the year, I downloaded practice tests the state education department offered on its web site. The sample test was three years old and students were so familiar with it they had many of the answers memorized.

Edwina didn't complain. She took the test seriously, as she did most of her school assignments. She remained after class to finish projects, always smiling, easily falling into laughter. She was a good writer. One of her stories, detailing the time she got lost riding through a blizzard behind her father on his snowmobile, eventually appeared in a journal of high school writing. A disciplined student, Edwina maintained a straight-A average throughout her school career. When a storm gripped the village and

From *Rethinking Schools*, 2007, Vol. 21, #4. Reprinted with permission of Rethinking Schools, www.rethinkingschools.org.

other students decided not to go to school, Edwina would invariably trudge through wind-packed snow to ensure an immaculate attendance record.

As the woman from the state droned on about formulaic assessment, I thought of how, as far as I was concerned, Edwina's entire education – all that she'd learned and all that she had endured to obtain it – would come down to one test. Kids in the village struggle to memorize vocabulary and concepts with which they have no connection. A counselor in my village told me the story of an elementary student who began crying during a test. When the counselor asked her what was wrong, the girl pointed to the word "curb" and said she didn't know what it meant. In her community, on a dusty knoll above thousands of acres of barren tundra, residents travel on dirt paths with four-wheelers and snowmobiles. There are no curbs.

It seems every teacher who has worked in Alaska's rural school system has a story of the cultural ignorance of standard tests. A question that stumped a student in my wife's 2nd-grade class asked for the best choice on how to get to a hospital: boat, ambulance, or airplane. Since the nearest hospital was 300 miles away, the student circled the logical, yet "incorrect," answer: airplane.

In Alaska, only about 40 percent of Native students graduate from high school, compared to almost 70 percent for all other ethnicities combined. There were 13 dropouts in Chevak the year I taught there. Generally, white students pass high-stakes tests at double the rate of their Native counterparts. In the region encompassing Chevak, an area the size of Iowa and dotted with more than 50 villages, only about a quarter of the students pass reading tests.

Edwina had lived her entire life in the remote villages of Hooper Bay and Chevak. It's a desolate region where the wind blows almost constantly across a vast delta of winding rivers, sloughs, and sub-arctic tundra. Edwina had to work hard to support her family. Her anna (grandmother) and atta (grandfather) as well as other family members relied on her to help prepare food, cook, wash laundry, run to the village store, and perform hundreds of other tasks.

She tried to stay awake in class and, when I joked with her once about her sleepiness, she erupted in uncharacteristic anger: "I've been up all night working, babysitting, helping my anna and atta!"

Yet, the state graduation-qualifying exam would not ask about her snowmobiling experience, subsistence hunting on the frozen ocean, collecting driftwood, or preparing a traditional sauna called a "steam."

Worried about her lackluster test results in previous years, Edwina took a supplementary class from another teacher, designed specifically to "teach to the test." In my classroom, I deviated from language arts units geared toward critical thinking, inquiry-based learning, and cultural literacy, and devoted several weeks of classroom instruction to review test strategies, test content, and preparation. We analyzed sample tests, practiced using the process of elimination to discard distracting choices, and even discussed cultural biases in test questions.

But in a village where kids are raised with a linguistically distinct form of English – called village English – and where young people struggle daily with the effects of economic hardship, domestic violence, and cultural disintegration, tests that ask students to compare personal digital assistants are irrelevant. Alaska Natives in rural villages have far greater concerns. With Alaska's Native communities suffering from the highest rates of Fetal Alcohol Syndrome, teen suicide, and child abuse in the nation, staying healthy – and even alive – is the paramount motive.

I tried to take these real concerns into consideration in my classroom by making learning relevant to conditions my students faced in their communities while maintaining high expectations in an academically rigorous curriculum. We read books by Native American authors such as Sherman Alexie, reconstructed traditional narratives into plays, and analyzed comparisons between "home" language and Standard English.

I conducted a grant-writing unit so students could realize an authentic outcome for composition. Edwina wrote an introduction to a grant that was ultimately awarded to her senior class.

Little did I know, however, how severely high-stakes tests would undercut my efforts to motivate my Alaska Native students for reading and writing.

Near the end of the year, the counselor came into my classroom. She stood solemnly by the door, as someone would who is about to deliver the news of a death in the family. She held the test results and waited until students were sitting down.

When the seniors looked at their test scores, some seemed unfazed by the results. Edwina, however, said she felt sick.

Because she didn't pass the test, Edwina didn't get a diploma when she graduated later that spring. None of her female classmates did.

Edwina wrote a letter about her shattered hopes and her view of schools – how she'd "been working hard in school all this time" since kindergarten, how she wanted to earn the diploma her older sis-

ter never received, how she's afraid she'll end up living with her mother the rest of her life. When she read her letter aloud, other students in class fell silent.

I suggested she send her letter to the editor of the Bethel paper, but drawing attention to oneself and one's problems is not customary among the Cu'pik Eskimo. In Ketchikan, the department of education representative closed her presentation saying, "Everyone's goal is to increase student achievement."

Edwina accomplished that goal. The state and the school district failed her.

Origins

In this excerpt from his memoir, the author's mother has just left Hawaii to do field work for her masters degree in anthropology and he has moved into an apartment with Gramps and Toot, his white grandparents, while he finishes high school. He is also in the midst of a struggle to find his identity as the child of an interracial marriage. The excerpt begins with the author recalling how he first became interested in playing basketball.

The University of Hawaii basketball team had slipped into the national rankings on the strength of an all-black starting five that the school had shipped in from the mainland. That same spring, Gramps had taken me to one of their games, and I had watched the players in warm-ups, still boys themselves but to me poised and confident warriors, chuckling to each other about some inside joke, glancing over the heads of fawning fans to wink at the girls on the sidelines, casually flipping layups or tossing high-arcing jumpers until the whistle blew and the centers jumped and the players joined in furious battle.

I decided to become part of that world, and began going down to a playground near my grandparents' apartment after school. From her bedroom window, ten stories up, Toot would watch me on the court until well after dark as I threw the ball with two hands at first, then developed an awkward jump shot, a crossover dribble, absorbed in the same solitary moves hour after hour. By the time I reached high school, I was playing on Punahou's teams, and could take my game to the univer-

sity courts, where a handful of black men, mostly gym rats and has-beens, would teach me an attitude that didn't just have to do with sport. That respect came from what you did and not who your daddy was. That you could talk stuff to rattle an opponent, but that you should shut the hell up if you couldn't back it up. That you didn't let anyone sneak up behind you to see emotions – like hurt or fear – you didn't want them to see.

And something else too, something nobody talked about: a way of being together when the game was tight and the sweat broke and the best players stopped worrying about their points and the worst players got swept up in the moment and the score only mattered because that's how you sustained the trance. . . .

I was living out a caricature of black male adolescence, itself a caricature of swaggering American manhood. Yet at a time when boys aren't supposed to want to follow their fathers' tired footsteps, when the imperatives of harvest or work in the factory aren't supposed to dictate identity, so that how to live is bought off the rack or found in magazines, the principal difference between me and most of the man-boys around me – the surfers, the football players, the would-be rock-and-roll guitarists – resided in the limited number of options at my disposal. Each of us chose a costume, armor against uncertainty. At least on the basketball court I could find a community of sorts, with an inner life all its own. It was there that I would make my closest white friends, on turf where blackness couldn't be a disadvantage. And it was there that I would meet Ray and the other blacks close to my age who had begun to trickle into the islands, teenagers whose confusion and anger would help shape my own.

"That's just how white folks will do you," one of them might say when we were alone. Everybody would chuckle and shake their heads, and my mind would run down a ledger of slights: the first boy, in seventh grade, who called me a coon; his tears of surprise – "Why'dya do that?" – when I gave him a bloody nose. The tennis pro who told me during a tournament that I shouldn't touch the schedule of matches pinned up to the bulletin board because my color might rub off; his thin-lipped, red-faced smile – "Can't you take a joke?" – when I threatened to report him. The older woman in my grandparents' apartment building who became agitated when I got on the elevator behind her and ran out to tell the manager that I was following her; her refusal to apologize when she was told that I lived in the building. Our assistant basketball coach, a young wiry man from New York with a nice jumper, who, after a pick-up game with some talkative black men, had muttered within earshot of me and three of my teammates that we shouldn't have lost to a bunch of niggers; and who, when I told him – with a fury that surprised even me – to shut up, had calmly explained the apparently obvious fact that "there are black people, and there are niggers. Those guys were niggers."

That's just how white folks will do you. It wasn't merely the cruelty involved; I was learning that black people could be mean and then some. It was a particular brand of arrogance, an obtuseness in otherwise sane people that brought forth our bitter laughter. It was as if whites didn't know they were being cruel in the first place. Or at least thought you deserving of their scorn.

White folks. The term itself was uncomfortable in my mouth at first. I felt like a non-native speaker tripping over a difficult phrase. Sometimes I would find myself talking to Ray about white folks this or white folks that, and I would suddenly remember my mother's smile, and the words that I spoke would seem awkward and false. Or I would be helping Gramps dry the dishes after dinner and Toot would come in to say she was going to sleep, and

those same words – *white folks* – would flash in my head as if I had secrets to keep.

Later, when I was alone, I would try to untangle these difficult thoughts. It was obvious that certain whites could be exempted from the general category of our distrust: Ray was always telling me how cool my grandparents were. The term *white* was simply a shorthand for him, I decided, a tag for what my mother would call a bigot. And although I recognized the risks in his terminology – how easy it was to fall into the same sloppy thinking that my basketball coach had displayed ("There are white folks, and then there are ignorant motherfuckers like you," I had finally told the coach before walking off the court that day) – Ray assured me that we would never talk about whites as whites in front of whites without knowing exactly what we were doing. Without knowing that there might be a price to pay.

But was that right? Was there still a price to pay? That was the complicated part, the thing that Ray and I never could seem to agree on. There were times when I would listen to him tell some blond girl he'd just met about life on L.A.'s mean streets, or hear him explain the scars of racism to some eager young teacher, and I could swear that just beneath the sober expression Ray was winking at me, letting me in on the score. Our rage at the white world needed no object, seemed to be telling me, no independent confirmation; it could be switched on and off at our pleasure. Sometimes, after one of his performances, I would question his judgment, if not his sincerity. We weren't living in the Jim Crow South, I would remind him. We weren't consigned to some heatless housing project in Harlem or the Bronx. We were in goddamned Hawaii. We said what we pleased, ate where we pleased; we sat at the front of the proverbial bus. None of our white friends, guys like Jeff or Scott from the basketball team, treated us any differently than they treated each other. They loved us, and we loved them back. Shit, seemed like half of 'em wanted to be black themselves – or at least Doctor J.

Well, that's true, Ray would admit.

Maybe we could afford to give the bad-assed nigger pose a rest. Save it for when we really needed it.

And Ray would shake his head. A pose, huh? Speak for your own self.

And I would know that Ray had flashed his trump card, one that, to his credit, he rarely played.

I was different, after all, potentially suspect; I had no idea who my own self was. Unwilling to risk exposure, I would quickly retreat to safer ground.

Perhaps if we had been living in New York or L.A., I would have been quicker to pick up the rules of the high-stake game we were playing. As it was, I learned to slip back and forth between my black and white worlds, understanding that each possessed its own language and customs and structures of meaning, convinced that with a bit of translation on my part the two worlds would eventually cohere. Still, the feeling that something wasn't quite right stayed with me, a warning that sounded whenever a white girl mentioned in the middle of conversation how much she liked Stevie Wonder; or when a woman in the supermarket asked me if I played basketball; or when the school principal told me I was cool. I did like Stevie Wonder, I did love basketball, and I tried my best to be cool at all times. So why did such comments always set me on edge? There was a trick there somewhere, although what the trick was, who was doing the tricking, and who was being tricked, eluded my conscious grasp.

One day in early spring Ray and I met up after class and began walking in the direction of the stone bench that circled a big banyan tree on Punahou's campus. It was called the Senior Bench, but it served mainly as a gathering place for the high school's popular crowd, the jocks and cheerleaders and partygoing set, with their jesters, attendants, and ladies-in-waiting jostling for position up and down the circular steps. One of the seniors, a stout defensive tackle named Kurt, was there, and he shouted loudly as soon as he saw us.

"Hey, Ray! Mah main man! Wha's happenin'!"

Ray went up and slapped Kurt's outstretched palm. But when Kurt repeated his gesture to me, I waved him off.

"What's his problem?" I overheard Kurt say to Ray as I walked away. A few minutes later, Ray caught up with me and asked me what was wrong.

"Man, those folks are just making fun of us," I said.

"What're you talking about?"

"All that 'Yo baby, give me five' bullshit."

"So who's mister sensitive all of a sudden? Kurt don't mean nothing by it."

"If that's what you think, then hey – "

Ray's face suddenly glistened with anger. "Look," he said, "I'm just getting along, all right? Just like I

see you getting along, talking your game with the teachers when you need them to do you a favor. All that stuff about 'Yes, Miss Snooty Bitch, I just find this novel so engaging, if I can just have one more day for that paper, I'll kiss your white ass.' It's their world, all right? They own it, and we in it. So just get the fuck outta my face."

By the following day, the heat of our argument had dissipated, and Ray suggested that I invite our friends Jeff and Scott to a party Ray was throwing out at his house that weekend. I hesitated for a moment – we had never brought white friends along to a black party – but Ray insisted, and I couldn't find a good reason to object. Neither could Jeff or Scott; they both agreed to come so long as I was willing to drive. And so that Saturday night, after one of our games, the three of us piled into Gramps's old Ford Granada and rattled our way out to Schofield Barracks, maybe thirty miles out of town.

When we arrived the party was well on its way, and we steered ourselves toward the refreshments. The presence of Jeff and Scott seemed to make no waves; Ray introduced them around the room, they made some small talk, they took a couple of the girls out on the dance floor. But I could see right away that the scene had taken my white friends by surprise. They kept smiling a lot. They huddled together in a corner. They nodded self-consciously to the beat of the music and said "Excuse me" every few minutes. After maybe an hour, they asked me if I'd be willing to take them home.

"What's the matter?" Ray shouted over the music when I went to let him know we were leaving. "Things just starting to heat up."

"They're not into it, I guess."

Our eyes met, and for a long stretch we just stood there, the noise and laughter pulsing around us. There were no traces of satisfaction in Ray's eyes, no hints of disappointment, just a steady gaze, as unblinking as a snake's. Finally he put out his hand, and I grabbed hold of it, our eyes still fixed on each other. "Later, then," he said, his hand slipping free from mine, and I watched him walk away through the crowd, asking about the girl he'd been talking to just a few minutes before.

Outside the air had turned cool. The street was absolutely empty, quiet except for the fading tremor of Ray's stereo, the blue lights flickering in the windows of bungalows that ran up and down the tidy lane, the shadows of trees stretching across a base-ball field. In the car, Jeff put an arm on my shoulder, looking at once contrite and relieved. "You know, man," he said, "that really taught me something. I mean, I can see how it must be tough for you and Ray sometimes, at school parties . . . being the only black guys and all."

I snorted. "Yeah. Right." A part of me wanted to punch him right there. We started down the road toward town, and in the silence, my mind began to rework Ray's words that day with Kurt, all the discussions we had had before that, the events of that night. And by the time I had dropped my friends off, I had begun to see a new map of the world, one that was frightening in its simplicity, suffocating in its implications. We were always playing on the white man's court, Ray had told me, by the white man's rules. If the principal, or the coach or a teacher, or Kurt, wanted to spit in your face, he could, because he had power and you didn't. If he decided not to, if he treated you like a man or came to your defense, it was because he knew that the words you spoke, the clothes you wore, the books you read, your ambitions and desires, were already his. Whatever he decided to do, it was his decision to make, not yours, and because of that fundamental power he held over you, because it preceded and would outlast his individual motives and inclinations, any distinction between good and bad whites held negligible meaning. In fact, you couldn't even be sure that everything you had assumed to be an expression of your black, unfettered self – the humor, the song, the behind-the-back pass – had been freely chosen by you. At best, these things were a refuge; at worst, a trap. Following this maddening logic, the only thing you could choose as your own was withdrawal into a smaller and smaller coil of rage, until being black meant only the knowledge of your own powerlessness, of your own defeat. And the final irony: Should you refuse this defeat and lash out at your captors, they would have a name for that, too, a name that could cage you just as good. Paranoid. Militant. Violent. Nigger.

Over the next few months, I looked to corroborate this nightmare vision. I gathered up books from the library – Baldwin, Ellison, Hughes, Wright, DuBois. At night I would close the door to my room, telling my grandparents I had homework to do, and there would sit and wrestle with words, locked in suddenly desperate argument, trying to reconcile the world as I'd found it with the terms of my birth. But there was no escape to be had. In every page of every book, in Bigger Thomas and invisible men, I kept finding the same anguish, the same doubt; a self-contempt that neither irony nor intellect seemed able to deflect. . . .

Only Malcolm X's autobiography seemed to offer something different. His repeated acts of self-creation spoke to me; the blunt poetry of his words, his unadorned insistence on respect, promised a new and uncompromising order, martial in its discipline, forged through sheer force of will. All the other stuff, the talk of blue-eyed devils and apocalypse, was incidental to that program, I decided, religious baggage that Malcolm himself seemed to have safely abandoned toward the end of his life. And yet, even as I imagined myself following Malcolm's call, one line in the book stayed me. He spoke of a wish he'd once had, the wish that the white blood that ran through him, there by an act of violence, might somehow be expunged. I knew that, for Malcolm, that wish would never be incidental. I knew as well that traveling down the road to self-respect my own white blood would never recede into mere abstraction. I was left to wonder what else I would be severing if and when I left my mother and my grandparents at some uncharted border.

And, too; If Malcolm's discovery toward the end of his life, that some whites might live beside him as brothers in Islam, seemed to offer some hope of eventual reconciliation, that hope appeared in a distant future, in a far-off land. In the meantime, I looked to see where the people would come from who were willing to work toward this future and populate this new world.

NA'IM AKBAR

Privilege in Black and White

An essay on white privilege could be included under a variety of topics, but in this essay the author is describing black privilege as well as white privilege, and how both function psychologically to shape individual perspectives, personalities, and behavior.

It is my preference to approach the issue of white privilege by suggesting some things that "White Privilege" is *NOT.* In order to avoid some frequent confusion, it is important to distinguish this phenomenon from several similar conditions. Without some clarity in this distinction we are likely to fall victim to a frequent logical fallacy whereby some analogous manifestations are described and approached as synonymous events. First of all, white privilege is not "masculine prerogatives," chauvinism and the similar expressions that characterize sexism. White Privilege is not class snobbery or aristocratic elitism. Such elitism often takes on forms that are reminiscent of some aspects of white privilege but it is faulty to see them as the same event. Judeo-Christian dogmatic intolerance looks like, acts like and very often produces many of the same outcomes. The privilege assigned to people by the dogma of the Judeo-Christian faith is not the same intolerance that is at the root of white privilege. The presumption of Anglo hegemony – the imposition of the Anglo worldview as the normative *zeitgeist* for all cultures – is similar to and has similar consequences as white privilege but it is not the same as white privilege.

An early version of this essay was presented at the 4th Annual White Privilege Conference on April 11, 2003, at Central College in Pella, Iowa. Used by permission of the author.

White Privilege

White privilege is a set of options, opportunities, and opinions that are gained as a consequence of one's race at the expense of people classified as racially non-white. It is not just an issue of one-upmanship in a situation where there is a hierarchy. It is a very specific set of options that one is able to exercise; opportunities that one has access to, and opinions that one is able to hold (and impose on others) that are systematically gained and maintained simply because you are designated as "white." People are deprived of these privileges not because of their gender, their sexual preference, their religious affiliation, but simply because they happen not to be classified as "white." This biological illusion of skin color is presumed to endow people with special and exclusive access to the options, opportunities and opinions that are characteristic of this phenomenon called "white privilege."

What does white privilege permit white people to do? First of all, and most significantly, it permits white people to define reality as they see fit. They are able to define origins and terminations as the juncture at which they enter or leave. For example: despite its thousands of years of precedent history, America is defined as originating at the moment white people appeared on these shores a little over 1500 years ago. America is suddenly "discovered" with the entrance of the white man. The Aztecs, the Incas and their numerous antecedents had populated this land for thousands of years before

43

Europeans accidentally stumbled out of their mythology that presumed the world was flat and limited to a few square miles out into the sea that was known to them.

The definition of this moment (of white arrival) as the "beginning" of America served a very important purpose for the people who claimed that privilege. They could freely engage in ignoring any reality that preceded their arrival and they could begin to effectively eliminate any contradiction to the imposed redefinition of reality that they dictated. This allowed them to wipe out any native inhabitants because native people were simply a contradictory nuisance, a "savage" hindrance to the expansion of the "Great White Empire." Within their logical construction, these natives really didn't exist because the reality of this place began when white people arrived. The process of erasing these logical barriers and clearing the land of these obstacles to their definition became a completely legitimate endeavor.

This is not only true in terms of the definition of what America is, it is also true in terms of their definition of the world's history; its classical culture; even so-called "civilized" life itself. The logical methods known as science and mathematics are presented as *their* (white) creative genius. Architecture, art, philosophy, religion, or any other arena of human endeavor begins at the white privileged benchmark. An essential aspect of white privilege is the presumption of power to completely ignore any reality prior to white presence and to designate it as "prehistoric" at best, or irrelevant at worst.

Such privilege to define can selectively ignore healing practices of non-whites by relegating them as magic (witchcraft) and superstition until white scientists decipher the codes and define these same herbs and methods as medicinal and scientifically legitimate. Whatever was known before white people started knowing is considered pre-knowledge, "folk knowledge" or simple superstition whereas real knowledge begins when white people begin to know. With such a presumptuous epistemology which comes with the privilege of simply being white, they conclude that civilization begins with them and the only information worthy of knowing is information about or from them. Such definitional dismissal permits them to conclude that the means of communicating with language is their exclusive right and anything else is considered to be

pre-literacy rather than alternative interaction. Again their designation of themselves as the norm pre-supposes that any other aspect of human experience is minor, inferior or simply: insignificant.

For example there is a significant following of white social scientists who have described a rather idiosyncratic relationship that they identified between white people and their parents and then proceeded to force the rest of the world into that mold. Imagine going to New Guinea and looking for an "*Oedipus complex!*" Here again we find the considerable arrogance of people taking the example of their small compartment of human experience and going out around the globe with the expectation that human personality develops and morphs around concepts of penis envy, castration anxiety, and other rather dubious manifestations of incestuous family romance. Even the very narrow definition of family as a nuclear unit that is celebrated as normative only in their narrow arena of human experience is an example of how they forge opinions from privilege.

White privilege is the ability to create a racially based society and make your race so presumptive that you can declare that race does not matter to you or to your children. White privilege permits you to buy a band aid that is "flesh colored" and not have to worry about it contrasting with the color of your flesh. White privilege is being able to let your children engage comfortably in the fantasy of being Superman, Spiderman, Barbie or even God's "only begotten Son" (or His Holy Mother) and not deal with the misfit between the color of the portrayal and the complexion in the mirror.

It is a supreme privilege to have your children conceptualize the God of the Universe as reflective of your racial features. This privilege of Divine Identification is then reinforced by an artistic and cultural aesthetic that reaffirms and reifies your presumptive selective favor in the eyes of the Divine Architect of the Universe. Whether it's the DaVinci portrait of the "Last Supper" or Michelangelo's frescos of the Creator himself in the ceiling of St. Peter's Basilica, your racial authenticity is affirmed and celebrated. Whether it's Old St. Nick or the Companions of God's earthly son, your legitimacy is celebrated in all aspects of your culture – both in mythology and biology. It is not surprising that those who are marinated in such images of their supremacy grow to declare with unquestioned authority those who constitute the "Axis of Evil" and the Angels of Mercy. You can declare yourself as singularly qualified to declare what is right and righteousness.

If you are white, you have the privilege of assuming that William Shakespeare, Aristotle, and Thomas Jefferson are the pillars of human civilization. You don't have to know the genius of W. E. B. DuBois. You can declare Erasmus as the premier example of a "Renaissance man" and ignore the much earlier African multi-genius, Imhotep; you can celebrate the military genius and eminence of Joan of Arc and the beauty of Helen of Troy ("whose face launched a thousand ships") while not knowing the contemporary courage and fortitude of Harriet Tubman who single-handedly launched a freedom train. White privilege permits you to minimize the prophetic leadership of Martin Luther King, Jr. as someone who had a dream and gave a speech. Being white allows you to talk about paranoia as a form of mental disorder and to dismiss the possibility that paranoia may be superior reality testing and intuitive perception of a divergent reality.

White privilege permits you to have a situational conscience where you can change your values or change the rules of the game arbitrarily. You can condemn human injustice, even genocide and call it savagery in one setting and implement it in the name of bringing salvation to the heathen or declare it as an aspect of the "white man's burden" when it achieves your objectives. No one else has the right to preserve and defend their self-determined "way of life" while you grant yourself complete authority to engage in any type of barbaric coercion or torture to preserve your "way of life." This privilege permits you to decide what is an authentic "nation" and which nation has veto power to negate the input of "lesser nations." Revolt under tyranny is your claim to fame and any other nation or people who are non-white and revolt against tyranny or oppression are characterized as savage uprisings or anarchy. The option of white privilege is to declare your situation as viable and legitimate as long as it operates in accordance with your objectives but when it is at odds with those objectives then the privileged white decides: "I will simply change the rules and do as I damn well please."

White privilege permits you to classify crazy white people as exceptional; to assert that people

like David Duke (and other notorious whites who designate themselves as "Grand Dragons" or other overtly racist demagogues) an exception, a peculiarity, an oddity while exaggerating the antics and fanaticism of a non-white person like Idi Amin (former president of Uganda) as a savage cannibal – typical of uncivilized non-white leadership. White privilege claims that these utterly bizarre and often numerous white people who often articulate the ideology that is being taught in many institutions of the white privileged environment must somehow be viewed as being the exception even when they articulate what the masses may be thinking. This is a privilege that goes with being white.

If you are a white person who happens to be a minority because you challenge the status quo of your cultural mainstream, white privilege permits you to claim that real white people are like you, even though you may be an exception with limited credibility in your own environment. Yet white privilege permits you to declare that you are a typical white person when all evidence suggests that you are the atypical white person. If you are a white person who acknowledges white privilege, the majority of white people would see you as being deranged. The fact that America still has failed to issue a legislative and reparative apology for 300 years of African slavery with only a small minority suggesting that it would be appropriate exonerates the overwhelming majority who commiserate with the atrocities of slavery as legitimate, justifiable, and even advantageous to the former captives.

Black Privilege

There are those who question the rather one-sided critique of "white privilege" and legitimately ask: Is there such a thing as "Black privilege?" I would venture to conclude that there is, even though I believe that the character of these two privilege classes is quite different. The primary difference is that Black privilege is a by-product of white privilege and is not a self-generated or a self-serving phenomenon.

First of all, Black privilege is the right to be angry! It is the justifiable right to be mad as hell, righteously indignant and consider that anger a legitimate, natural and normal reaction. Black privilege authorizes the Black person to argue that the unnaturalness of the last 400 years thoroughly legitimizes any level or degree of rage any Black person may choose to have once he understands the circumstances of his confrontation with white privilege. It means that as a Black person, I do not have to answer the question: "Why are you so bitter?" I do not have to explain why I have such passion about these issues because Black privilege authorizes me to discard objectivity. I can be completely subjective when it comes to an analysis of the Black experience and I do not have to justify my subjectivity because this is *MY* experience. This is a privilege I have because I am Black.

Another example of Black privilege is to be able to tell the secrets of white folks to anybody in the world. As a consequence of the effort to dehumanize Black people and to ignore Black presence as irrelevant or nonexistent, white people have exposed many of their secrets to Black people. With their privileged assumption of the absence or limitation of intelligence on the part of Black people, they failed to conceal what they sought to keep hidden from people who they acknowledged as competent and comparably human. With the accrued arrogance that accompanied their privilege, white people assumed that Black people could not hear or comprehend questionable white conduct. The obvious example is the way that wealthy (and particularly privileged) white people will reveal secrets in front of their Black servants with only very superficial camouflage. They would never suspect that their "incompetent" servant would be capable of understanding the true implication of their conduct. The myopic privileged person would speak as one speaks in front of their pets or pre-literate children. This practice generalizes into the broader intellectual culture as well. They expose the most graphic and morally abhorrent details of their character with the assumption that Blacks were incapable of critique or communication to others.

In my graduate studies of (their) human conduct, they revealed that their primal and essential motivation was for pleasure and gratification, particularly of a sexual and aggressive nature. They concluded that their behavior, both pathological and normal, was a result of the frustration of their sexual, aggressive drives and incestuous desires during childhood. Despite my disbelief, their great geniuses such as Sigmund Freud insisted that this was the source of their fundamental motivational

life. My esteemed white professors (I had no Black ones by the design of the privileged white academy) insisted that I accept this formulation of their fundamental make-up, become an expert in the assessment of such ethically questionable conduct, and required that I develop techniques to free them from their frustration so they could approach their Nirvana of free hedonistic expression. They thoroughly examined me on it and gave me a Ph.D. when I demonstrated that I understood their understanding of themselves. I have taken their revelations and now declare to the world: "White people are preoccupied with sex and aggression; they will do whatever gives them pleasure because in their view the objective of human life, the ultimate drive of human conduct – whether it is being described from a Freudian point of view or a Behaviorist point of view – is to gratify their material desires by whatever means necessary.

By their own admission these experts admitted that they weren't talking about Black folks, that their theories did not apply to Black people because they don't bother to include Black people in their investigations or their theories. From their privileged place of observation and analysis, they assume that white conduct is normal (even correctly abnormal) and Black people in their inferior human status are deviants from whatever white people are. From my intimate inside view at the white academic table of privilege I can say to non-white (so-called) Yellow, Brown, Red, and definitely Black people that the peculiar and violent behavior of white people as they dominate, assault and seduce the inhabitants of the earth is what they consider to be their human prerogative.

By their own admission, they accept the preeminence of the individual and the ultimate narcissism of individual rights to the exclusion of the collective good. Their concept of themselves is ultimately an egotistical analysis and based on empirical data as they understand their essence as being limited to what is perceptible by the senses. According to the best minds of the privileged white scientists, there is no moral or informational authority above what is empirically identifiable.

These characteristics are ones that white experts have concluded about the nature of white people, and I am able to critique them because they let me "in the house" and they proceeded to discuss who they were in my presence. They examined me on their theories and conclusions and I passed their tests. When I write a paper deconstructing western psychology, my critique is based on what they have concluded about themselves. My independent observations of my reality as a Black person permit me to suggest fundamentally different assumptions about Black reality that the privileged white experts failed to consider in their jaundiced projection onto the Black experience. With the license of their privilege they dismissed my reality. So they can't critique who I am because they only know about themselves. They only speak their own language. They only experience the world through their eyes so they don't know that there's another way to see things. My educational experience within the curriculum of white privilege equipped me to deconstruct their reality and subsequently to engage in reconstruction of my own reality. This capacity to critique white reality within the authorized mindset of white privilege and then to reveal their secrets is a part of Black privilege.

Black privilege permits us to blame everything that's wrong in Black lives as a consequence of white privilege. I can (with considerable justification) claim that Black people would be essentially flawless had it not been for slavery, racism, and the history of oppression. As a Black person using the evidence and history of white exclusionary policies, I can claim that I am not one of those people responsible for imposing American reality on the world. Even though our sons, uncles, fathers, grandfathers, even our mothers defended militarily, economically and intellectually the often misguided policies of the white government, we are guiltless of its moral flaws. I am not responsible for events such as the deadly slaughter of white enemies such as the genocide of Native American people. It was not my decision to drop the atomic bomb on the Asian people of Nagasaki and Hiroshima. I don't have to take responsibility for the thousands of dead Iraqi, Vietnamese or Cambodian women and children whose lives were needlessly taken or abused because of the folly of certain privileged white men who presumed that they had the right to kill people in order to give those people their definition of freedom.

Even though a significant number of people who look like me are in the ranks and engaged in these "killing fields," even though a Black man and a Black woman in recent years actually became the voice that articulated and offered justification for such murderous policies, they can legitimately be exonerated from responsibility for the consequence of those policies because of the historical exclusionary policies that were wrought by white privilege. Black privilege permits us to claim that they were being obedient servants of those who created such reprehensible policies. Privilege authorizes us to claim that we were simply doing what "*Boss*" told us to do. When the white world is called to account for its conduct, it must answer to a superior moral authority about the reasons for so many dead children in the deserts of Iraq and the explanation for the Tigris and Euphrates rivers running with blood with no apparent justification other than white greed. When this happens, we can claim from our position of Black privilege that our historical exclusion permits us to declare: "We aren't responsible; we didn't make those dubious and deadly decisions because by *their* own admission, white people largely excluded us from the privileged decision-making bodies."

Black privilege also means that when Black people act crazy we can say it's because of the insanity of discrimination. If we act foolish or just plain silly we can say that it's because of racism or that it's because we've been robbed of our culture, and we can make that claim with a great deal of legitimacy.

Black privilege permits us to move conveniently in and out of white reality at will. On any given occasion, I can act like a white person better than most white people and do it with finesse and elegance, and two seconds later I can become *super* Black, declare my history of exclusion and deny ownership of my own behavior. I can wear a multiple personality and act in thoroughly contradictory ways and be comfortable with my contradictions. That's a privilege of being Black. This is a consequence of being present and excluded for so many centuries; of being in the white world and treated without the privileges of being white at the same time; of being human and having our humanity ignored and denied at the same time. As a student of the system of white privilege I have been able to master its ways and reject it at will while claiming its rewards when it serves my needs.

This is actually a very special privilege for some Blacks, those of us who have been permitted "privileged matriculation" or acceptable achievements in mastering the "Great White Way." We get to do exciting and wonderful things because of our ability and competence in dealing with multiple cultures. Many other people can claim expertise as multiculturalists, but in order to survive we have had to master multiple cultures, multiple languages and multiple mores. We know two worlds, because white privilege insisted that we master them well. Sometimes many of us know the other world better than we know our own world because our very survival demanded it. I have a PhD in the psychological functioning of white people, but there isn't one white person in the world who has a legitimately approved PhD in the psychological functioning of Black people. There is no white person who knows what I know because I have mastered who I am and I have learned how white people function as well, and by the unrelenting standards of white privilege I was declared competent and qualified in the "white way." There are other Black people who know what I know, but even the most sincere and intimately engaged white person has no institutionally legitimate way of knowing about being Black in the same way that I (and many others) know about being white. This is another example of inadvertent Black privilege.

Black Collaboration with White Privilege

The closing point that I must make is to express my concern about Black collaboration with white privilege. I believe that white privilege today is being buttressed and legitimized by the collaboration of Black people. Large numbers of Black people who have been given influential positions have internalized the mythology that justified white privilege so that they believe it, permit it, authorize it, legitimize it and lose access to their own ways while learning to survive in the white way of privilege.

Initially white privilege was imposed barbarically: by violence, by intimidation, by terrorist tactics and intentional propaganda. For centuries there were deliberate strategies to block access to the empowering self-knowledge of Black people. We were forced to learn white reality because our reality was degraded or hidden from us. There was an intentional effort to rob us of the tools (especially literacy and investigative capabilities) by which we could gain alternative information. Literacy was not only prohibited among slaves, but severely restricted by well-meaning whites who dared to share these tools with the captives. There are tortured, mutilated and murdered Blacks who were indicted as subversive because they taught themselves and others to read. This was the strictly enforced rule of the privileged of this land for over 300 years. It has only been just over 100 years that it was legal for most Black people to develop the tools of literacy and it has only been during the last half century that Black students were granted legal access to information outside of certain restricted, deprived and controlled environments. For most of our experience in America, Black people have been prohibited from learning. Privilege and opportunity were not given to us as a right of birth, we had to take every privilege we have – whether it was spelling, reading, writing or counting. It was a privilege won with the price of blood and death in order to access information or regain skills for learning.

This is especially important to remember if you have the contemporary privilege in this 21st century to be the only (or one of a few) Black person sitting in a previously enforced all white classrooms; the only one granted admission to developing certain specialized skills; the only one who can buy a home in a certain neighborhood or participate in a certain political venue. If you happen to be one of those "firsts," one of the exceptional or privileged Blacks that have been permitted access to opportunities that were recently won, then it's imperative that you remember that you aren't there simply because of your individual merit. You are where you are because Fannie Lou Hamer and many others now in their graves refused to let the system continue on the basis of white privilege.

It is a cruel betrayal for Black people (and white people) to forget that everything Black people have in America today was gained at considerable cost – including death – of Black and white people who defied the system of white privilege. Fortunately, there have always been white people "crazy" enough to go against the order of their own family, their own country, their own nation. They used their privilege to declare that racism was wrong, and they died for the abolition of slavery; they died in the struggle for civil rights.

So when Black people reach positions of influence, we have a responsibility not only to keep the door open so that others can get in, we need to make sure that those who follow will know what to do when they get there. We have a responsibility to promote the development of a critical mass of people who look like us wherever we are.

Sometimes Black people in such positions are reluctant to help other Black people for fear of being viewed as biased or unfair, but we must take primary responsibility to build that critical mass of Black people. It is often comfortable and safe for privileged "exceptional" Black people to stay in the shadows, to be pleasant and not rock the boat. If the boat had not been rocked we would not be sitting "on deck," and we could easily have found ourselves still perceived as property rather than persons. We must "rock the boat" the way that Harriet Tubman did; rock the boat the way that Frederick Douglass did; rock the boat the way that Adam Clayton Powell did; rock the boat the way that Thurgood Marshall and yes, Martin Luther King, Jr. did. Whenever we find ourselves in an exclusive boat, we must rock it. Black collaboration authorizes white society to define the condition of our presence and discredit the boat rockers as militant, radical, "reversed racists" and in opposition to our own objectives. When we legitimize their definitions by our silence, then we are collaborating with their privilege.

We must remember that we are the experts of our self-conscious experience – a privilege won by those who refused to die. When we assume and assert our right to define ourselves we are denying white privilege the option to define us in such a way to perpetuate their privilege and their illegitimate power.

The Salad Lady

(In memory of Eva Elias)

*Individuals do not construct their individual identity in a vacuum, but
in the context of where they live and the people they know. Sometimes a
brief acquaintance can have an impact on a person's life. In this story,
the author only refers to the salad lady by name one time, but it
affirms a genuine human connection made between two strangers.*

I met Sarah at a restaurant. I was the waiter; she, the quiet customer with the soft voice and long gaze that passed through her puffed cigarette smoke, crossed the glass window and always landed on the same spot on the paved sidewalk. She came every Wednesday and ordered the same Greek salad. Whenever she came in, Stavros, the owner, would call me in his thick Crete accent, "Your lady-salad is here." I would rush with a glass of water and greet her calmly with a soft nod, careful not to shatter her deep meditative mood. I never asked her if she wanted "the usual," though I was tempted every time. To say it, I felt, might acknowledge her existence, expose her routine, make her visible to the world. She was the kind of customer who wanted to be left alone. You know, the kind who erects barriers and turns tables into refuges of contemplation and solitude.

I made sure her coffee cup was always filled and warm; the little glass bottles of olive oil and vinegar, which she poured slowly and always after the first bite of her salad, were also always filled. I would leave her the check, usually after the third coffee and right after her ashtray was filled with crushed cigarettes – a kind of subtle acknowledgment on my part of her routine, and my timing skills. She would walk to Stavros, pay him, walk back, give me the tip, and leave. Stavros, with his thick droopy mustache, would wish her a good day from behind his mechanical cash register that opened with a loud ancient voice. The machine was covered with Orthodox icons and Greek flags; on the wall behind him, a series of postcards from Crete showed a deep blue sea and white clay houses; and at his side were two signed photos of seventies Hollywood celebrities.

Stavros was a pain in the ass.

In the kitchen worked Ahmad, the Egyptian, whose conversation and obsession with cars bored the hell out of me; at the end of the kitchen, there

From *Dinarzad's Children: An Anthology of Contemporary Arab American Fiction* (Fayetteville, AR: University of Arkansas Press, 2004). Reprinted by permission of the author.

was François, the Haitian dishwasher, whose overzealous Jehovah's Witness preaching was a joke among all of us. Outside the kitchen there was Claire, the waitress, who served the left-side tables and the bar. Claire had worked in the restaurant for fifteen years. She never stopped reminding everyone about it. She talked about horoscopes, the weather, and her trip on the morning train to work. We all knew she lived in the Bronx and took the R-train every day. She had a very peculiar relationship with Stavros; and when she talked to him, she always reminded him of what a gorgeous broad she once was, and what a fat and stingy pig he turned out to be. She had met Stavros on a Greek island in the eighties, during a trip that she won on a radio show. There Stavros, young and handsome, seduced her that same night in a Greek bar that had no ceiling to keep the stars from shining on the bouzouki band that played loud and happy music, and no walls to keep the Mediterranean Sea breeze from mingling with the tourists' sunburned thighs. Claire and Stavros spent two weeks together. He showed her the rough beaches outside the city, and they danced and drank every night. He took her to his birth village up in the hills and, in a cold flowing river, bathed her naked in his arms. He made her feel what no northern man was ever able to. And when she left the island, she wept and he kept her address. A few months later he showed up at her door with a suitcase. She took care of him. Then, slick Mediterranean that he was, he took care of himself, and in a few years had made enough money to open a small Greek diner with Claire as his manager. No one knew how Claire became the waitress and Stavros her boss, nor how he managed to hold her for such a long time under his command, nor why he, all these years, tolerated her contempt and verbal abuse.

Her relationship with me was also a paradox. In private she often told me that I was doing the right thing by going to school; she told me to study well and not to waste my life. But in public she would call me "college boy," and once in a while she would say that people never learn at school.

Though she had gone to the Mediterranean once, Claire had no clue about geography nor where I came from. She often confused Lebanon

with Libya; and the few times Qaddafi was on the news she tried to talk about him with me with some dismay and confusion.

When I spoke to Ahmad in Arabic, she would often shout, "English, English here. It is America – English!" Ahmad would laugh and ask her for a kiss and a date, insinuating one sexual favor or another. Claire knew that he did it to embarrass François, the pious dishwasher. François would shake his head and splash water at Ahmad and go back to tossing dishes and humming to God.

One bright Wednesday, the sun poured its light on the city from a bucket filled with rays and warmth. Some of it splashed on Stavros's place and fell on the Wednesday table. The table was warm, the cigarette was lit, and the Greek salad flew from the kitchen to her mouth. And then just when the world of her dreams had started to form and to veil the salad lady from the universe, I walked to her with a coffee cup in my hand, in silence. Somehow, I tripped and spilled the coffee in her lap, slashed through her dreams, and stained her morning and day. Frantically, with my sleeves, I tried to stop the brown liquid from dripping more on her black skirt; Claire and Stavros ran, and we all held white cloths, wiping away my shame and the horror that penetrated her thighs.

Claire, who acted like a chambermaid, helped her. Stavros was apologizing to her like a troubadour who had lost his tongue. I stood dumbfounded with nothing to say. I waited at the counter, and as soon as she walked out from the ladies room, Stavros started pushing me and asked me to apologize to her again. All along she was quiet and silent. When I approached her, she waved her hand to me and mumbled something that I interpreted as a gesture of forgiveness, but Stavros kept on pushing me toward her. I approached her and said I was sorry again.

She went back to her seat and lit a cigarette.

She left earlier than usual that day. And Stavros waved her bill and wondered if she would ever come back again.

The next Wednesday, the clouds poured their water on the gloomy city from a bucket filled with water and mist. Stavros's place looked dim and empty. Claire stood there in silence, smoking at the bar, tapping the dead ashes of her long cigarette into a plastic white tray that said "Greece" on it. Stavros stood like a bronze statue, gazing at the rain outside. And I wondered if the salad lady would come that day. The door opened and with the pouring rain, she showed up, Stavros ran with a towel and gave it to the salad lady. He smiled when her head was hidden under the towel. I ran and poured water in a glass, feeling triumphant and relieved. She sat and I approached her with caution and uneasiness. Her cigarette lit the place with assurance; she gazed outside and her quiet dreams came with the water of the outside rain. She finished, paid and stood at the door, waiting for the rain to stop. Stavros called to me, handed me an umbrella and asked me to walk her to her destination.

Under the black umbrella, the salad lady and I hid from the rain and walked. Her hair was still wet, and our shoulders touched. I looked at her closely for the first time. She had high cheekbones, black eyes, and a hooked nose that stopped short of being narrow at its end. She was in her forties, and her gentle quiet manner gave assurance and comfort to me.

"What is your name?" she asked me.

"Khaled," I said.

"What language is that?" she asked.

"Arabic," I said.

"What does it mean?"

"Eternal."

"Eternal?" she repeated. "Eternal?" she said and smiled.

I shrugged my shoulders.

"I am sorry about dropping the coffee the other day," I said. "We all thought that you would never come back again."

"And I thought the man with the mustache would fire you."

"You come every Wednesday," I said.

"Yes. You noticed."

"Why every Wednesday? And you eat that same thing."

"You notice that too, eh?"

"Well, yes, you have been doing it for a while."

"It is the only routine I have in my life. We all need a ritual, don't we?"

"What do you do?" I asked her.

"Nothing now. I have money and I am waiting to die," she said.

"Are you sick?"

"Yes . . . I am home now. Do you want to come up for some tea? You must be cold now," she said.

"I do not know how Stavros would feel about it."

"The place is empty anyway. Come. I will make you some tea."

We entered and the doorman greeted her. I folded the umbrella and watched the water drip on the marble floor through the elevator all the way to her door.

"You can leave it outside," she said.

I did and entered her place. There was a mirror at the entrance, with a vase that held dried dead flowers.

"Come in, take off your shoes and come in. I will put the water on the stove."

I took off my shoes and entered.

Her house was filled with books. She had a large painting of a wolf under a dead tree and an orange sky. The floor was brown shiny wood. Her desk held piles of paper and newspaper clippings, and a red phone. There were no family photographs anywhere to be seen.

She asked me to sit and she brought tea.

She asked few questions. And I answered. I told her that I was going to school at night and that I shared an apartment with a friend. And that I had come alone to America.

She told me that she would be starting her chemotherapy the next week. And that she would be smoking pot.

I finished my tea and went down the stairs.

The next Wednesday, the sun came and shed a graceful, tasteful light on the city. The taxis that passed seemed more yellow than before. The vendors on the streets sold more liquid than the day before. And the salad lady entered the restaurant and we called each other by name.

The Wednesday after, there was a murder on the train, and the tabloid showed pictures of a dead man. And the salad lady came with a hat on her head, and that day Claire had a big fight with Stavros.

The Wednesday after, somewhere next to a bench, pigeons were fed crumbs by an old lady. And the salad lady came with the same hat on her head, and François told Ahmad that he forgave his sins.

The Wednesday after, the churches in the city were empty. Businesspeople walked, it seemed, a little faster, and talked on their phones louder. And the salad lady came with the same hat on her head, and Stavros was on vacation in Greece.

The Wednesday after that same light came back and shone again; the trees absorbed every little ray and drove it to the ground, mixed it with water and earth and turned it to bigger leaves. And Claire quite her job, the salad lady did not come, and I never saw her again.

Perspectives on the Immigrant Experience and Nativism

> 66 We are all wanderers on this earth. Our hearts are full of wonder, and our souls are deep with dreams. 99

Gypsy Proverb

As the Gypsy proverb notes, human beings have always wandered from place to place looking to find new homes and achieve new dreams. Because of its ongoing history of immigration, the United States has been called a "nation of immigrants," but this term is inaccurate since it neglects millions of indigenous people who had probably made their journey centuries earlier and were well established on the North American continent at the time the first European immigrants arrived. (Estimates of native populations at that time range from a total of over two million to eighteen million.) Yet it is fair to say that immigration has been a driving force not only for our nation's growth and prosperity but also for its ever expanding diversity.

Some immigration has been temporary or cyclic as certain immigrants returned to their native country after achieving some economic success, and there were migrants (primarily from Mexico) who came for seasonal work and went home when the work was done. Yet the majority of immigrants intended to stay permanently, and historically, most of them settled in urban areas. Two major changes in recent immigration trends are that the majority of immigrants are people of color and that they are more likely to be located in small cities and towns where people of color have had little or no presence in the past. Such communities now find themselves changed not just because of the new ethnic diversity but also by linguistic diversity in schools and religious diversity in churches. The presence of these new immigrants has renewed the ongoing, often bitter debate among American citizens about how many immigrants should be permitted to settle here. It is a curious debate whose dynamics John Steinbeck described in *America and Americans,* a book written and published almost 50 years ago:

> To all these (immigrants) we gave disparaging names: Micks, Sheenies, Krauts, Dagos, Wops, Ragheads, Yellowbellies, and so forth. The turn against each group continued until it became sound, solvent, self-defensive, and economically anonymous – whereupon each group joined the

older boys and charged down on the newest ones. . . . Having suffered, one would have thought they might have pity on the newer come, but they did not.[1] (p. 15)

Despite the hostility, there is ample evidence that the United States, historically and currently, has enjoyed enormous benefits from the talents that immigrants have brought to this nation. For example, in the late 1800s Charles Steinmetz immigrated to America and became an exceptional electrical engineer, working mainly for General Electric. After he retired, he got a call from G.E. managers, who begged him to come to a factory where their best experts could not locate the cause of a breakdown among some complicated machinery. Steinmetz walked around the equipment, testing one part and then another. At last, he took some chalk from his pocket and marked an "X" on one of the machines. After the machine was disassembled the experts examined parts from behind the place that Steinmetz had marked and discovered the defect that had eluded them. Later, when Steinmetz asked for $10,000 compensation for his work, G.E. insisted that he submit an itemized bill justifying such a large amount. Steinmetz sent a note that said: "Making one chalk mark = $1.00. Knowing where to place it = $9,999."[2]

Like Steinmetz, many immigrants today come with professional training and degrees, or they receive their education here and go on to distinguish themselves in an array of occupations. On the other end of the spectrum are the laborers who take menial jobs for minimal compensation. All of them contribute to the American economy, to their families, and to their communities. For the many laborers who immigrate here, the issue that ought to receive more attention is not simply their contributions to our society but whether they are exploited and inadequately compensated for what they do. Yet many Americans insist that we are letting too many immigrants into the United States and that these immigrants aren't contributing to the country, thus perpetuating myths and misperceptions of immigrants and strengthening anti-immigrant attitudes.

The selections for this section begin with a well-established pattern of migration–that of Mexicans and Mexican Americans who join the migrant stream primarily into the Midwest to harvest crops such as tomatoes or beets. Elva Treviño Hart was a small child that summer when she first went with her family to Minnesota and Wisconsin, and she provides a detailed portrait of the migrant experience from a child's point of view. Much has been written about this ongoing migration pattern and many statistics have been gathered and reported, but Hart's essay offers a very personal and human perspective describing the experiences of one migrant family.

Immigrants have always had different reasons for coming to the United States. For some it was to seek their dreams; for others it was to escape from a nightmare. After the Vietnam War when

"What the people want is very simple. They want an America as good as its promise."

Barbara Jordan (1936–1996)

the communists took over South Vietnam, thousands of Southeast Asians immigrated to America, not only Vietnamese but also Laotians and the Hmong. These refugees have encountered significant cultural and linguistic challenges, and Sonia Nieto captures some of their difficulty in this excerpt from her "Case Study: Hoang Vinh." After a brief introduction to her subject, Nieto lets Hoang Vinh tell his own story. He describes the enormous amount of information he has to master. Developing English skills and a vocabulary adequate to function in everyday life is difficult enough, but Hoang must achieve enough fluency in the language to be able to attend college because a college education is required to gain access to economic opportunity. In addition, Hoang must understand the nuances of the dominant culture while also learning about the diverse racial and ethnic groups that he interacts with in his urban community. Hoang's story reflects the experience of many refugees, but especially those from Southeast Asia.

Refugees are a unique category of immigrants because the injustice they have faced has caused them to flee from violence, persecution, or simply chaos in their native lands. In the past, refugees were usually placed in large urban areas on the east or west coasts, but in recent years they have been sent to smaller cities and communities across the nation. In "Arrival Stories and Acculturation," Mary Pipher describes the lives of refugees who have settled in Lincoln, Nebraska. Unlike other immigrants, refugees do not tend to be fluent in English when they arrive, so they must immediately enroll in English classes as they look for employment. Pipher describes some misconceptions Americans have of the refugees, but also some misconceptions that refugees have about America. Part of their adjustment to living

in the United States requires the refugees to adapt to a reality that is quite different from what they expected. Despite the difficulties, refugees work hard, learn what they must, and usually embrace the traditional vision of the American Dream, a Dream that that they believe is possible for them to achieve. What they want from America is what every American wants.

The most emotional immigration issue today concerns undocumented workers, typically referred to as "illegal aliens," mostly Latinos and primarily from Mexico. Although Americans seem to tolerate refugees, the condemnation of undocumented or illegal immigrants has caused many Americans to insist that we secure the Mexican border to keep undocumented workers out of the United States. In response, Congress approved funds for a proposal from George W. Bush's administration to erect a fence along a portion of the Mexican border, but as Michael Scherer reports in "Scrimmage on the Border," this issue is far too complicated to be resolved by such simplistic solutions. Scherer describes the efforts of the Border Patrol and the so-called "Minuteman" groups of volunteers patrolling the border. In interviews with these volunteers, Scherer discovers the racism and prejudice that fuels their efforts to prevent undocumented Mexicans (and other Latinos) from coming to the United States. Although he presents the anti-immigrant perspective of Tom Tancredo, the Congressman from Colorado who was a candidate for President in the 2008 Republican primaries, Scherer also interviewed Americans who understand how the United States is benefiting from the cheap labor of undocumented workers. Although the battle of the border is likely to continue, Scherer's essay provides us with the context in which it is being fought.

After exploring the concerns facing refugees, migrants, and undocumented workers, Section Three appropriately concludes with a literary memoir written by a Haitian immigrant. In "Dyaspora," Joanne Hyppolite describes the immigrant experience of leaving her native land to live in another culture. As she was growing up, her Haitian family maintained their language, their favorite foods and music, and even furniture that reminded them of "home." But since she was a child, she had to go to school and try to understand the new culture outside their home. Because of ongoing racial segregation, the neighborhood where the Haitian family lives is populated by African American families. Hyppolite's childhood memories include encounters with prejudicial attitudes that her family had never experienced in Haiti, but these experiences are well understood by African Americans. Although they share a similar skin color, the black families in her neighborhood do not share the same heritage as the Haitian immigrants, so the diaspora child is largely on her own to sort out the complexities of her situation: to understand who she is, where she fits in, and to find a voice that will allow her to tell her story.

Notes

[1]Steinbeck, John, E Pluribus Unum, *America and Americans*, New York, The Viking Press, p. 15.

[2]Anecdote adapted from: Clifton Fadiman, *Party of One: The selected writings of Clifton Fadiman*, (Cleveland: World Publishing, 1955).

Barefoot Heart:
Stories of a Migrant Child

The author grew up in Texas, and in this excerpt, an experienced migrant worker has offered her family a chance to come with him to the Midwest to work on farms there. Although the family experiences economic gains, the author describes the hardships of migrant life, especially for the children. Today, many of the migrants working in the fields travel illegally from Mexico, which makes their lives even more difficult.

When my father (*Apá*) had told us we were going to Minnesota with El Indio to work in the beet fields, all the kids had different responses – all silent and internal – we never said anything. He was taking a bunch of children to Minnesota, but he didn't see it that way. My father knew nothing about children. He treated us all like adults, expecting adult responses from us. We were a team going to work.

Delia was in her first year of high school. It was the first of May. She would have to leave the new boy who smiled at her in a secret way in the hall. Her friend Chayo liked him, too. Would the new boy remember Delia when she came back in September or would Chayo have prevailed?

Delmira looked around her eighth-grade class, full of adolescent juices. She would miss her eighth-grade graduation. She didn't know how she could ever tell them that she was being taken out of school to go in the back of a canvas-covered truck

to work in the fields. She knew their responses would be cruel. She decided to face the problem at the end of the summer. So she told no one – just walked out of school at the end of the day with a fake smile and said, "See you tomorrow!" and didn't return until September.

Luis, in the sixth grade, was not so mortified. So he bragged to his friends that he would be doing a man's job that summer. But in his heart of hearts he was afraid. He had worked in the peanut fields for years, but he suspected the beet fields would be much crueler and Apá a harder taskmaster.

Diamantina, in the fifth grade, was terrified. She worried about everything anyway, and she wanted to do well. Would they make her work all day? Would they make her go to a new school? Would there be gringos there? Or would it be a Mexican school for the migrants? She hoped so. She didn't like the gringos – they made her feel ashamed to wear her hand-me-down clothes. She bit her nails until they bled, and then she bit the inside of her lip. At night, she couldn't go to sleep for the pain at the ends of her fingers.

Rudy, in the fourth grade, didn't care about anything. He didn't care to tell anyone, but he didn't consider it an ugly secret either – he would just do what was needed. He was the one who responded best to my father's need to have all of us be adults, albeit short ones.

The gringo who owned the farm and the mayor-domo came to see Apá the day after we got there to talk about the kids' schooling. All the school-age children at the migrant camp had to attend school until the end of the school year or the gringo would get in trouble.

This was a new development my father hadn't expected. But actually, he was glad. His dream was for all of us to finish high school and to have better lives than he had. So he told my mother to get everyone ready for school.

Amá, already overwhelmed with the new challenges, exploded, "I didn't know they would have to go to school! You told me to pack light! We brought mostly work clothes! The girls only brought a couple of dresses to wear in case there was an occasional day off! How can you expect me to dress five children for a month in a gringo school when we didn't bring anything! I'll have to wash clothes daily after being in the fields all day! ¡Esto es el colmo!"

My father looked distressed as he always did when my mother yelled at him with a legitimate point. He mumbled something about having to make do and went outside to sharpen the hoes.

When he left, my mother started to cry. We watched, helpless. Delia said, "Amá, Delmira and I will wash the clothes when we get home from school – for everyone. It's only for a month. We can do it, Amá. You won't have to wash clothes at all." . . .

The next morning, everyone except me prepared to go to school. . . . Rudy was the first one to see the bus, a yellow speck on the featureless horizon. . . . I stood there watching the bus drive away. My brothers and sisters would do what they had to do; they always did. I felt forlorn and abandoned. We had been together, all of us, for days. When I turned around to go back to my parents, I saw a black Ford pull up next to the migrant camp. Three nuns in black habits got out. . . .

I burst through the door and told my mother we had company. When she came out, the nuns asked her how the children would be cared for while the parents worked in the fields. It was the first time my mother had been on the migrant circuit with six children. She said she didn't know.

They offered to take the littlest ones with them for the summer. It would cost only what we could afford – a dollar a week, they said. It was a charity the church offered for the migrants.

My mother felt she had no choice but to send me there. Leaving me at the edge of the field while they worked was dangerous since the rows of beets were half a mile long and I was only three. My eleven-year-old sister, Diamantina, was too young to work. The child labor laws said you had to be twelve to work in the fields. So Diamantina would go with me and be schooled there. . . .

They took the two of us on Sunday. Apá borrowed a car and everyone went. Amá cried quietly and sighed despairingly all the way. Everyone else was silent. . . . When we got there, Apá gave us each a little money. He said they would come to visit us the next time it rained and the fields were unworkable, if he could borrow a car.

The school was huge, with an asphalt playground and a tall, wrought-iron fence surrounding everything. When it was time, Diamantina and I clutched the bars of the fence and pushed our faces through to say goodbye. We were overwhelmed with abandonment and sadness. And it was still daytime.

When nighttime came, then I really knew what it was to feel abandoned. They took us to a really big room, a gymnasium, with a long row of cots. This was where all the children lay down together. Thanks to God, they gave me a cot next to my sister. I covered myself with the sheet while the tears leaked out. I didn't want to cry. I wanted to be strong, as my father liked for me to be, but the tears wouldn't obey me . . . and they kept wetting the small pillow.

"Diamantina," I said to my sister very quietly, "would you hold my hand? I'm afraid and I feel very sad. I want my mother . . . I don't want to be here."

"Shhh, be quiet. Don't be afraid. Give me your hand. I'll take care of you. Don't be afraid."

The nuns walked up and down the rows of cots. I didn't want them to see me cry. I didn't want them even to see me. I closed my eyes very hard to keep the tears in and to make my heart hard. But the lump in my throat wouldn't go away and I felt more alone and sad.

I squeezed my sister's hand tightly . . . it was my only link to the life that I had known up until that time. She squeezed it back. Then I felt less alone. And the lump in my throat got smaller. The tears dried on my cheeks. . . .

The next morning, the nuns made us bow our heads and pray to thank God for breakfast. I prayed for rain.

During recess a vendor sold popsicles through the bars of the fence. My sister took our money out of her sock and bought us each one. They were yellow and deliciously cool in the summer heat of the asphalt playground. The next day we only got one and shared, to conserve our money.

"Do you think they're coming back to get us?" I asked Diamantina as we took turns with the popsicle.

"Of course they are, silly!" she said. But then her eyes got a sad, faraway look.

I imagined them hoeing the beets and wondered if they were thinking about us as they hoed. Maybe Apá wished he had given us more money in case it didn't rain for a while. Maybe Amá missed my laying my head on her lap after dinner when all the work was done. I missed it too. Her apron was soft from being washed a thousand times. It smelled like tortillas and dinner and soap. She rubbed my head with her fingers.

Maybe Amá felt like crying as she hoed, as I did at the school.

When Amá wrote a letter, I made Diamantina read it over and over. Especially the part that said "Your amá, who loves and appreciates you." She let me sleep with it under my pillow. I put it in my sock during the day. The sweat of the playground made it get wet and the letters blurred, but it didn't matter. I couldn't read, anyway.

One night, a clap of thunder woke me from a dead sleep. My eyes were round by the next flash of lightning.

I looked over and Diamantina was awake too. The thunder had awakened some of the little ones and they were crying. I had never been afraid of weather. I loved the wildness of thunder, lightning, and driving rain. My wild nature reveled in it.

"Do you think they'll be here tomorrow? I asked her."

"It may not be raining where they are. It might only be raining here," she answered.

When it continued to rain all night and into the morning, we started to feel hopeful. The rain stopped around mid-morning. We waited all day

with our hearts in our throats. Every car that drove by took our full attention.

After dinner, neither of us spoke. Words wouldn't help, anyway. Our heads were swimming with disappointment. We were becoming older too fast. A part of our childhood was dying.

In bed, I stared at the high gymnasium ceiling. My eyes would fill and empty as the sad thoughts came in waves. Diamantina was crying too.

The next morning, I was in the playroom, feeling terribly lonely. . . . I looked at the nuns and ran out of the room, down the hall, out of the building, and across the asphalt school yard, the nuns screaming and chasing me.

I was determined and hell-bent to be with my sister since I couldn't be with my family. I struggled with the big church door and ran down the aisle, headlong into Diamantina, who was practicing for her first communion. I wrapped myself around her legs, sobbing now, and screaming. The nuns came up to us out of breath. "She ran out. Not supposed to be here," they gasped. They tried to take my hand, but it just dug deeper into my sister's leg. Embarrassed, she tried to talk sense into me. Senseless, I couldn't listen. I just screamed louder, my little soul feeling as if it were going to fly apart. Pandemonium in front of the altar now, the priest coming out of the sacristy to see.

I couldn't tell them what was going on inside of me. How could I? Maybe if I screamed louder they would know. My wild screams would tell them. Diamantina could see. She saw into my eyes and knew.

And the conflict started for her. All these adults wanting us to make nice. And my screams and imploring eyes saying that I couldn't leave her, begging her to help me. She couldn't do it. She was too small and only eleven and my father had taught her too well to mind.

"What happened?" she asked. I just screamed and shook my head wildly. I couldn't say the words, not here, in front of all these people. . . .

"Shhh, ya. You have to go back with them," she said quietly.

"NOOOO! NOOO!" I begged, but I knew I couldn't fight this crowd. They would do what they wanted to with me.

They peeled me off her, still screaming, but only hopeless screams now, knowing that there was no help for me.

She watched them carry me off, but I forgave her. She couldn't do more; I knew that.

Later, we found out that my father hadn't been able to borrow a car. Naturally, on the first rainy day off, all the migrants wanted to use their cars to go to town – to grocery shop, to buy supplies that they had forgotten to bring with them. . . .

The whole family had wanted to visit us, but he couldn't make it work. His powerless feeling had made my father crazy. So he had talked to the mayordomo about helping him get a used car. It had become obvious to the mayordomo and to the gringo that our family was hard working and reliable. Together, Apá and the mayordomo went to the gringo and he agreed to advance my father the money for a used car if he promised to come back to this farm next year. Half the amount would be due this year and half the next. The money would be taken out of his paycheck at the end of the season.

The next time it rained, they arrived bright and early in a gray and white Chevy. It felt like Christmas. I could love the rain again even though it had disappointed me so badly last time. My brothers and sisters were glad to see us, thrilled to have a holiday, and ecstatic about our car. My father proudly drove us around town.

We stopped at a grocery store and got snacks for a picnic. We ate at a picnic table in the park with the grass glistening all around in the sunlight after the rain. I had never been happier.

When they left us later in the afternoon, it was not so sad. We would miss them. But now we knew they had missed us too. We had a car, whereas before we had nothing. Things were looking up. . . .

After leaving us with the nuns for three months, the whole family came to get us at the end of July. The beet thinning and weeding season was over. Beet topping and harvest season wouldn't start until mid-September. All the migrants packed up and went elsewhere to work for a month and a half. Apá said we would follow El Indio's truck to Wisconsin. . . .

We were heading to the farm where El Indio's family had gone the previous year. He had warned us that Wisconsin was not like Minnesota in that nothing was certain there. If the fields were ready, then there would be work. If there were no fields ready to be picked, then either you went on to the next farm or you went to the lake and fished. Also, in Wisconsin, the season was short and there were no contracts with the migrants, so people went to different farms every year.

The farm we went to that first year had plenty of work, but no place for us to stay right away. The house where we could stay was rented and the occupants wouldn't be out for several days. The farmer really wanted his fields picked, though, so he said we could stay in the barn until the house became vacant.

The barn? Everyone looked at Apá, alarmed. The barn was for pigs and cows.

"Sí, bueno," he said. The barn was fine with him as long as there was work. The accommodations didn't matter; we were there to work and make money. No one could argue. But everyone, even Rudy this time, seemed upset and ashamed. The barn was no longer used to house animals, but it was full of rusty old equipment that we had to move out of the way before we had room to live there for a few days.

The work in Wisconsin was to pick green beans, cucumbers, and occasionally tomatoes. . . . The rows were short, so our car was nearby. I kept watching for nuns, but none came. In Wisconsin, even Diamantina worked, as it didn't require much skill just to get the fruit off the plant. All the kids were used to this kind of work. . . . Being used to it didn't mean they liked it, though. In fact, they hated it more than the beet fields.

In Minnesota, they worked standing up, touching only the hoe. Except for the days after a rain, they could stay fairly clean. Not so in Wisconsin. To pick the green beans and cucumbers, you had to put your hands right into the plant, soaked with dew early in the morning. In half an hour your work gloves and shirt were soaked up to the elbow. After they dried in the sun, the prickles from the plants started to make your skin itch. At first, people couldn't decide whether it was better to work bent over at the waist, and have the lower back hurt, or to squat down, and have the knees hurt. Most people started bent over at the waist, but after the first day or two they would go for knee pain instead. At least knee pain stayed localized. The back pain made you feel bad all over. . . .

That year the crops were plentiful and work was continuous, seven days a week for several weeks. . . . By early September, we could feel a chill in the air and smell the coming of winter. The sycamores were already dropping their leaves.

There came a day, finally, when there were no fields that were ready to be picked. The farmer wanted to wait two more days, and then do the final picking of the season. . . .

Four days later we left for Texas. Many of the migrants, including El Indio's family, went back to Minnesota to work on "el tapeo," the beet topping and harvest. The Minnesota farmer wanted us to come back, but Apa insisted on getting his children back into their regular school. His dream was for all of us to graduate from high school. The kids wouldn't quite make the beginning of the school year, but they wouldn't miss by much. So he decided to forego the money that he could have made by staying another month.

Case Study: Hoang Vinh

Although Hoang Vinh's parents couldn't leave Vietnam, they sent him and his four siblings to the United States in the hope that they would have a better future than they could have in their communist-controlled nation. He was a high school senior at the time of this interview, and in this story he describes many of the difficulties that other immigrants, especially refugees, encounter after arriving in America.

"For Vietnamese people, [culture] is very important. . . . If we want to get something, we have to get it. Vietnamese culture is like that. . . . We work hard, and we get something we want."

Hoang Vinh's[1] hands move in quick gestures as he tries to illustrate what he has to say, almost as if wishing that they would speak for him. Vinh[2] is very conscious of not knowing English well enough to express himself how he would like and he keeps apologizing, "My English is not good." Nevertheless, his English skills are quite advanced for someone who has been in the United States for just a short time.

Vinh is 18 years old. He was born in the Xuan Loc province of Dong Nai, about 80 kilometers from Saigon. At the time he was interviewed, he had been in the United States for three years and lived with his uncle, two sisters, and two brothers in a midsize New England town. They first lived in Virginia, but moved here after a year and a half. Vinh and his family live in a modest house in a residential neighborhood of a pleasant, mostly middle-class college town. The family's Catholicism is evidenced

From Nieto, Sonia. *Affirming Diversity: The Sociopolitical Context of Multicultural Education*, 4e. Published by Allyn and Bacon/Merrill Education, Boston, MA. Copyright 2004 by Pearson Education. Reprinted by permission of the publisher.

by the statues of Jesus and the Virgin Mary in the living room. Everyone in the family has chores and contributes to keeping the house clean and making the meals. In addition, the older members make sure that the younger children keep in touch with their Vietnamese language and culture. They have weekly sessions in which they write to their parents; they allow only Vietnamese to be spoken at home and they cook Vietnamese food, something that even the youngest is learning to do. When they received letters from their parents, they sit down to read them together. Their uncle reinforces their native literacy by telling them many stories. Vinh also plays what he calls "music from my Vietnam," to which they all listen.

Because Vinh's father was in the military before 1975 and worked for the U.S. government, he was considered an American sympathizer and educational opportunities for his family were limited after the war. Vinh and his brothers and sisters were sent to the United States by their parents, who could not leave Vietnam, but wanted their children to have the opportunity for a better education and a more secure future. Vinh and his family came in what has been called the "second wave" of immigration from Indochina,[3] that is, they came after the huge exodus in 1975. Although Vinh and his family came directly from Vietnam, most of the second-wave immigrants came from refugee camps in Thailand,

Malaysia, and elsewhere. This second wave has generally been characterized by greater heterogeneity in social class and ethnicity, less formal education, fewer marketable skills, and poorer health than previous immigrants. During the 1980s, when Vinh and his family came to the United States, the school-age Asian and Pacific Islander population between the ages of 5 and 19 grew by an astounding 90 percent. About half of the 800,000 Asian refugees who arrived between 1975 and 1990 were under 18 years of age.[4] The Asian population has grown dramatically since that time. The 2000 census reported that there are currently 10.2 million Asian and Asian Americans in the United States; of these, 1.1 million are Vietnamese.[5]

Vinh's uncle works in town and supports all the children. He takes his role of surrogate father very seriously and tries to help the children in whatever way he can. He discusses many things with them; Vinh speaks with gratitude of the lengthy conversations they have. Mostly, he wants to make sure that all the children benefit from their education. He constantly motivates them to do better.

Vinh's older brother makes dried flower arrangements in the basement and sells them in town. During the summers, Vinh works to contribute to his family here and in Vietnam, but during the school year he is not allowed to work because he needs to focus on his studies ("I just go to school, and, after school, I go home to study," he explains). He uses the money he makes in the summer to support his family because, he says, "We are very poor." They rarely go to the movies, and they spend little on themselves.

Vinh will be starting his senior year in high school. Because the number of Vietnamese speakers in the schools he has attended has never been high, Vinh has not been in a bilingual program. He does quite well in school, but he also enjoys the opportunity to speak his native language and would no doubt have profited from a bilingual education. He is currently in an ESL class at the high school with a small number of other Vietnamese students and other students whose first language is not English. Some teachers encourage Vinh and his Vietnamese classmates to speak Vietnamese during the ESL class to improve their understanding of the curriculum content, but other teachers discourage the use of their native language. All of Vinh's other classes are

in the "mainstream program" for college-bound students: physics, calculus, French, music, and law. Vinh's favorite subject is history because he says he wants to learn about this country. He is also interested in psychology.

Homework and studying take up many hours of Vinh's time. He places great value on what he calls "becoming educated people." His parents and uncle constantly stress the importance of an education and place great demands on Vinh and his brothers and sisters. He also enjoys playing volleyball and badminton and being with his friends in the gym. Because he loves school, Vinh does not enjoy staying home. He is a good student and wants desperately to go to college, but, even at this late date, he had not received any help or information about different colleges, how to apply, how to get financial aid, and admission requirements. He says he does not want to bother anyone to ask for this information. Added to his reluctance to ask for assistance is the economic barrier he sees to getting a college education. Because he wants to make certain that his brothers and sisters are well cared for, housed, and fed, he may have to work full time after graduating from high school. . . .

On Becoming "Educated People"

In Vietnam, we go to school because we want to become educated people. But in the United States, most people, they say, "Oh, we go to school because we want to get a good job." But my idea, I don't think so. I say, if we go to school, we want a good job also, but we want to become a good person.

[In Vietnam] we go to school, we have to remember every single word. . . . We don't have textbooks, so my teacher write on the blackboard. So we have to copy and go home. . . . So, they say, "You have to remember all the things, like all the words. . . ." But in the United States, they don't need for you to remember all the words. They just need you to understand. . . . But two different school systems. They have different things. I think in my Vietnamese school, they are good. But I also think the United States school system is good. They're not the same. . . . They are good, but good in different ways.

When I go to school [in Vietnam], sometimes I don't know how to do something, so I ask my teachers. She can spend all the time to help me, anything I want. So, they are very nice. . . . My teacher, she was very nice. When I asked her everything, she would answer me, teach me something. That's why I remember. . . . But some of my teachers, they always punished me.

[Grades] are not important to me. Important to me is education. . . . I [am] not concerned about [test scores] very much. I just need enough for me to go to college. . . . Sometimes, I never care about [grades]. I just know I do my exam very good. But I don't need to know I got A or B. I have to learn more and more.

Sometimes, I got C but I learned very much. I learned a lot, and I feel very sorry, "Why I got only C?" But sometimes, if I got B, that's enough, I don't need A.

Some people, they got a good education. They go to school, they got master's, they got doctorate, but they're just helping themselves. So that's not good. . . . If I got a good education, I get a good job, not helping only myself. I like to help other people. . . . I want to help other people who don't have money, who don't have a house. . . . The first thing is money. If people live without money, they cannot do nothing. So even if I want to help other people, I have to get a good job. I have the money, so that way I can help them.

In class, sometimes [students] speak Vietnamese because we don't know the words in English. . . . Our English is not good, so that's why we have to speak Vietnamese.

In school, if we get good and better and better, we have to work in groups, like four people. And we discuss some projects, like that. And different people have different ideas, so after that we choose some best idea. I like work in groups.

Sometimes, the English teacher, they don't understand about us. Because something we not do good, like my English is not good. And she say, "Oh, your English is great!" But that's the way the American culture is. But my culture is not like that. . . . If my English is not good, she has to say, "Your English is not good. So you have to go home and study." And she tell me what to study and how to study to get better. But some Americans, you know, they don't understand about myself. So they just say, "Oh! You're doing a good job! You're doing great! Everything is great!" Teachers talk like that, but my culture is different. . . . They say, "You have

to do better. . . ." So, sometimes when I do something not good, and my teachers say, "Oh, you did great!" I don't like it. . . . I want the truth better.

Some teachers, they never concerned to the students. So, they just do something that they have to do. But they don't really do something to help the people, the students. Some teachers, they just go inside and go to the blackboard. . . . They don't care. So that I don't like.

I have a good teacher, Ms. Brown. She's very sensitive. She understands the students, year to year, year after year. . . . She understands a lot. So when I had her class, we discussed some things very interesting about America. And sometimes she tells us about something very interesting about another culture. But Ms. Mitchell, she just knows how to teach for the children, like 10 years old or younger. So some people don't like her. Like me, I don't like her. I like to discuss something. Not just how to write "A," "you have to write like this." So I don't like that. . . . She wants me to write perfectly. So that is not a good way because we learn another language. Because when we learn another language, we learn to discuss, we learn to understand the word's meaning, not about how to write the word.

I want to go to college, of course. Right now, I don't know what will happen for the future. . . . If I think of my future, I have to learn more about psychology. If I have a family, I want a perfect family, not really perfect, but I want a very good family. So that's why I go to school, I have good education to teach them. So, Vietnamese want their children to grow up and be polite and go to school, just like I am right now. . . . I just want they will be a good person.

I don't care much about money. So, I just want to have a normal job that I can take care of myself and my family. So that's enough. I don't want to climb up compared to other people, because, you know, different people have different ideas about how to live. So I don't think money is important to me. I just need enough money for my life.

Demanding Standards

I'm not really good, but I'm trying.

In Vietnam, I am a good student. But at the United States, my English is not good sometimes. I cannot say very nice things to some Americans, because my English is not perfect.

Sometimes the people, they don't think I'm polite because they don't understand my English exactly. . . . I always say my English is not good, because all the people, they can speak better than me. So, I say, "Why some people, they came here the same year with me, but they can learn better?" So I have to try.

When I lived in Vietnam, so I go to school and I got very good credit [grades], but right now because my English is not good, sometimes I feel very sorry for myself.

[My uncle] never told me, 'Oh, you do good,' or "Oh, you do bad." Because every time I go home, I give him my report card, like from C to A, he don't say nothing. He say, "Next time, you should do better." If I got A, okay, he just say, "Oh, next time, do better than A! . . ." He doesn't need anything from me. But he wants me to be a good person, and helpful. . . . So he wants me to go to school, so someday I have a good job and so I don't need from him anymore.

He encourages me. He talks about why you have to learn and what important things you will do in the future if you learn. . . . I like him to be involved about my school. . . . I like him to be concerned about my credits.

Some people need help, but some people don't. Like me, sometimes I need help. I want to know how to . . . apply for college and what will I do to get into college. So that is my problem.

I have a counselor, but I never talk to him. Because I don't want them to be concerned about myself because they have a lot of people to talk with. So, sometimes, I just go home and I talk with my brother and my uncle.

If I need my counselor every time I got trouble, I'm not going to solve that problem. . . . So, I want to do it by myself. I have to sit down and think, "Why did the trouble start? And how can we solve the problem? . . ." Sometimes, I say, I don't want them to [be] concerned with my problem.

Most American people are very helpful. But because I don't want them to spend time about myself, to help me, so that's why I don't come to them. One other time, I talked with my uncle. He can tell me whatever I want. But my English is not good, so that's why I don't want to talk with American people.

I may need my counselor's help. When I go to college, I have to understand the college system and how to go get into college. . . . The first thing I have to know is the college system, and what's the difference between this school and other schools, and how they compare. . . . I already know how to make applications and how to meet counselors, and how to take a test also.

Sometimes I do better than other people, but I still think it's not good. Because if you learn, you can be more than that. So that's why I keep learning. Because I think, everything you can do, you learn. If you don't learn, you can't do nothing.

Right now, I cannot say [anything good] about myself because if I talk about myself, it's not right. Another person who lives with me, like my brother, he can say something about me better than what I say about myself. . . . Nobody can understand themselves better than other people.

I don't know [if I'm successful] because that belongs to the future. . . . I mean successful for myself [means] that I have a good family; I have a good job; I have respect from other people.

Trying to Understand Other Cultures

Some [Black] people very good. . . . Most Black people in [this town], they talk very nice. . . . Like in my country, some people very good and some people very bad.

I am very different from other people who are the same age. Some people who are the same age, they like to go dancing, they like to smoke, they want to have more fun. But not me. . . . Because right now, all the girls, they like more fun [things] than sit down and think about psychology, think about family. . . . I think it's very difficult to find [a girlfriend] right now. . . . If I find a girlfriend who not agree with any of my ideas, it would not be a good girlfriend. . . . I don't need [her to be] very much like me, but some . . . we would have a little in common. . . . It is not about their color or their language, but their character. I like their character better.

I think it's an important point, because if you understand another language or another culture, it's very good for you. So I keep learning, other cultures, other languages, other customs.

I have Chinese, I have Japanese, I have American, I have Cambodian [friends]. Every kind of people. Because I care about character, not about color.

Strength from Culture and Family

Sometimes I think about [marrying] a Vietnamese girl, because my son or my daughter, in the future, they will speak Vietnamese. So, if I have an American girlfriend, my children cannot speak Vietnamese. Because I saw other families who have an American wife or an American husband, their children cannot speak Vietnamese. It is very hard to learn a language. . . . In the United States, they have TV, they have radio, every kind of thing, we have to do English. So, that why I don't think my children can learn Vietnamese.

When I sleep, I like to think a little bit about my country. And I feel very good. I always think about . . . my family . . . what gifts they get me before, how they were with me when I was young. . . . Those are very good things to remember . . .

I've been here for three years, but the first two years I didn't learn anything. I got sick, mental. I got mental. Because when I came to the United States, I missed my father, my family, and my friends, and my Vietnam.

So, every time I go to sleep, I cannot sleep, I don't want to eat anything. So I become sick.

I am a very sad person. Sometimes, I just want to be alone to think about myself. I feel sorry about what I do wrong with someone. Whatever I do wrong in the past, I just think and I feel sorry for myself.

I never have a good time. I go to the mall, but I don't feel good. . . . I just sit there. I don't know what to do.

Before I got mental, okay, I feel very good about myself, like I am smart, I learn a lot of things. . . . But after I got mental, I don't get any enjoyment. . . . I'm not smart anymore.

After I got mental, I don't enjoy anything. Before that, I enjoy lots. Like I listen to music, I go to school and talk to my friends. . . . But now I don't feel I enjoy anything. Just talk with my friends, that's enough, that's my enjoyment.

My culture is my country. We love my country; we love our people; we love the way the Vietnamese, like they talk very nice and they are very polite to all the people.

For Vietnamese, [culture] is very important. . . . I think my country is a great country. The people is very courageous. They never scared to do anything. . . . If we want to get something, we have to get it. Vietnamese culture is like that. . . . We work hard, and we get something we want.

If I have children, I have to teach them from [when] they grow up to when they get older. So, when they get older, I don't have to teach them, but they listen to me. Because that's education, not only myself, but all Vietnamese, from a long time ago to now. That's the custom. So that's why I like my customs and my culture.

Every culture . . . they have good things and they have bad things. And my culture is the same. But sometimes they're different because they come from different countries. . . . America is so different.

[My teachers] understand some things, just not all Vietnamese culture. Like they just understand some things outside. . . . But they cannot understand something inside our hearts.

[Teachers should] understand the students. Like Ms. Mitchell, she just say, "Oh, you have to do it this way." "You have to do that way." But some people, they came from different countries. They have different ideas, so they might think about school in different ways. So maybe she has to know why they think in that way. . . . Because different cultures, they have different meanings about education. So she has to learn about that culture.

I think they just think that they understand our culture. . . . But it is very hard to tell them, because that's our feelings.

When I came to United States, I heard English so I say, "Oh, very funny sound." Very strange to me. But I think they feel the same like when we speak Vietnamese. So they hear and they say, "What a strange language." Some people like to listen. But some people don't like to listen. So, if I talk with Americans, I never talk Vietnamese.

Some teachers don't understand about the language. So sometimes, my language, they say it sounds funny. And sometimes, all the languages sound funny. Sometimes, [the teacher] doesn't let us speak Vietnamese, or some people speak Cambodian. Sometimes, she already knows some Spanish, so she lets Spanish speak. But because she doesn't know about Vietnamese language, so she doesn't let Vietnamese speak.

[Teachers] have to know about our culture. And they have to help the people learn whatever they want. From the second language, it is very difficult for me and for other people.

I want to learn something good from my culture and something good from American culture. And I want to take both cultures and select something good. . . . If we live in the United States, we have to learn something about new people.

[To keep reading and writing Vietnamese] is very important. . . . So, I like to learn English, but I like to learn my language too. Because different languages, they have different things, special. [My younger sisters] are very good. They don't need my help. They already know. They write to my parents and they keep reading Vietnamese books. . . . Sometimes they forget to pronounce the words, but I help them.

At home, we eat Vietnamese food. . . . The important thing is rice. Everybody eats rice, and vegetables, and meat. They make different kinds of food. . . . The way I grew up, I had to learn, I had to know it. By looking at other people – when my mother cooked, and I just see it, and so I know it.

Right now, I like to listen to my music, and I like to listen to American music. . . . And I like to listen to other music from other countries.

We tell [our parents] about what we do at school and what we do at home and how nice the people around us, and what we will do better in the future to make them happy. Something not good, we don't write.

They miss us and they want ourselves to live together. . . . They teach me how to live without them.

[Note: After discussing the goals and difficulties just described by Hoang Vinh in this interview, the author concludes this case study with the following comments.]

Schools are expected to take the major responsibility for helping children confront these difficult issues, but often they do not. Given the changing U.S. demographics and the large influx of new immigrants, the rivalry and negative relationships among different groups of immigrants and native-born students will likely be felt even more. Interethnic hostility needs to be confronted directly through changes in curriculum and other school policies and practices. Students such as Vinh clearly need this kind of leadership to help them make sense of their new world.

Hoang Vinh is obviously on a long and difficult road to adaptation, not only in cultural and linguistic terms, but also, and probably not coincidentally, in terms of his mental health. Many of his issues are based on the traumas he has endured as an immigrant. Whether or not his school is able to help him solve these problems is certain to have an impact on his future.

Notes

[1] I am grateful to Haydée Font for the interviews and transcripts for this case study. When she did these interviews, Haydée was a graduate student in multicultural education at the University of Massachusetts.

[2] The Vietnamese use family names first, given names second. The given name is used for identification. In this case, Vinh is the given name and Hoang is the family name. According to *A Manual for Indochinese Refugee Education, 1976-1977* (Arlington, VA: National Indochinese Clearinghouse, Center for Applied Linguistics, 1976), whereas in the U.S. society John Jones would be known formally as Mr. Jones and informally as John, in Vietnam, Hoang Vinh would be known both formally and informally as Mr. Vinh or Vinh.

[3] See Ronald Takaki, *Strangers from a different shore: A history of Asian Americans* (New York: Penguin Books, 1989); "The biculturalism of the Vietnamese student." *Digest* (Newsletter of the ERIC Clearinghouse on Urban Education), no.152 (March 2000).

[4] Peter N. Kiang and Vivian Wai-Fun Lee, "Exclusion or Contribution? Education K-12 Policy." In *The state of Asian Pacific America: Policy issues to the year 2020* (Los Angeles: LEAP Asian Pacific American Public Policy Institute and the UCLA Asian American studies Center, 1993): 25-48; Digest, 1990.

[5] U.S. Bureau of the Census, *Profile of selected social characteristics: 2000* (Washington, DC: U.S. Government Printing Office, 2000).

MARY PIPHER

Arrival Stories and Acculturation

Although immigrants to America have to satisfy certain criteria that demonstrate their readiness to be self-sustaining when they arrive, refugees are those immigrants who face persecution in their home countries and are admitted even though they may not have job skills or speak English. The author worked with refugees who were placed in the Midwest and describes the difficulties they encountered.

Arrival Stories

Most of the refugees who arrive in Lincoln (Nebraska) didn't choose to come to our city. They were handed a plane ticket to Lincoln by INS officials when they got off a plane in New York or Los Angeles. They may know nothing about the Midwest and they may have been separated from their closest friends by the assignment process. They may have bodies adapted to tropical climates or skills such as deep-sea fishing that they cannot use in the Midwest. They may be moving into a town where no one speaks their language or even knows where their country is.

Most newcomers arrive broke. In fact, I have never met a rich refugee. All arrive worried about jobs and housing, as well as about their legal status in the United States. Especially if they have been tortured or lost family members, they are not at peak mental efficiency. In many cases, refugees don't speak English and have never lived in a developed country. They have been warned not to trust strangers, yet everyone is a stranger. They have no

way to sort out whether people are kind and helpful or psychopaths. All of us look alike to them. They fear robbers, harassment, getting lost, or being hit by a car.

Here in Lincoln, most refugees are met at the airport by people from their homeland and by someone from church services. An interesting thing happens at the airports. When the newcomers and their hosts meet, they all burst into tears. The moment of arrival has an intensity and poignancy that sweeps everyone away. From the airport, refugees are driven to a furnished apartment stocked with food and used furniture. Their first day in town they get their social security cards and their immunizations. They enroll their kids in school, and, if needed, they receive emergency doctors' appointments. Sometimes refugees get off the plane with life-threatening illnesses and go directly to a hospital.

Each adult is given fifty dollars per week, plus food, rent, and temporary medical insurance. They go through an orientation that explains everything from how to use the city bus and library to marriage laws and taxes. Adults are encouraged to get jobs quickly. The goal of our resettlement agencies is self-sufficiency in four months. In fact, within a few weeks, refugees are often working. In addition to their other financial burdens, all refugees must repay their airfares from the country they fled.

A woman from Kazakhstan arrived in Lincoln with her father. She waited three hours at the airport for her sponsor who was at a party and had forgotten her. Later that night her father had a heart attack from the stress of the journey. From television, she knew she could call 911. Yet even when the translation service finally kicked in, she could give no address. Amazingly, her father lived through this attack.

Zainab arrived at JFK Airport in New York City. Before arriving she and her husband had spent years in a camp in the Saudi Arabian desert. They had two children in the camp and Zainab was again pregnant. She walked off the plane, looked at all the electric lights and the people who were walking fast and talking loudly, and she said to her husband, "Let's go back to the camp. At least there we had friends and family." He said, "I don't own the plane. I don't own anything."

Telling me this later, Zainab laughed. She said, "All he had was money for a Pepsi, so he bought me one. Drinking that cheered me up."

Zainab and her husband had hoped they would be assigned Lincoln, where they knew a few families, but an official sent them to Fargo, North Dakota. They boarded another plane and arrived in Fargo late at night. They were picked up and taken to a hotel room. Too tired to clean up or eat, they fell into deep sleep. In the morning they awoke and looked out the window. They saw green trees, grass, a squirrel, and two dogs. Zainab said, "We had spent years in a place with no plants or animals. My husband asked me if we were in heaven."

They had never seen people in shorts or with dyed green hair. They didn't know how to use a phone. A homeless guy gave them thirty-five cents and dialed for them.

Soon they managed to move to Lincoln. Zainab had troubles with our foods. In Iraq there were not many kinds of vegetables, mostly just tomatoes and cucumbers, but they were fresh and delicious. Zainab said Nebraskans had a huge variety, but nothing tasted flavorful.

Zainab came from an area where men and women did not touch each other except in families. The American handshake was a problem. When a man held out his hand to her, she had to explain that Iraqi women do not shake hands. She learned to hug American women and say, "Hug your husband for me."

When I was in college, I remember reading about a tribe in Central America who thought that Americans never got sick or died. All the Americans they'd seen were healthy anthropologists, tall and well-nourished. They'd never seen Americans die.

Modern refugees often come here equally naïve about us. Some have Nebraska and Alaska confused and expect mountains, ice, and grizzlies. Some think of Nebraska as a western state with cowboys, and they are ill-prepared for our factories, suburbs, and shopping malls. Many newcomers have never seen . . . escalators or elevators. Inventions such as duct tape, clothes hangers, aluminum foil, or microwaves often befuddle new arrivals.

Someone once said, "Every day in a foreign country is like final exam week." It's a good metaphor. Everything is a test, whether of one's knowledge of the language, the culture, or of the layout of the city. Politics, laws, and personal boundaries are different. Relations between parents and children, the genders, and the social classes are structured differently here. The simplest task – buying a bottle of orange juice or finding medicine for a headache – can take hours and require every conceivable skill.

Some refugees believe they will be given a new car and a house when they arrive. Some people ask government workers, "Where is my color TV? My free computer?" Others have seen *Dallas* or *Who Wants to Marry a Millionaire?* and think they will soon get rich.

This belief that it's easy to get rich in America is exploited by con artists. An Azerbaijani man received a Reader's Digest Sweepstakes notice informing him he was a millionaire. He fell to his knees and thanked Allah for his riches. A Vietnamese family called relatives in Ho Chi Minh City to tell them the great news that they had won the Publisher's Clearinghouse sweepstakes. A Siberian couple laughed and danced around their kitchen, already spending their expected pickle card winnings on a new car, a dishwasher, and a swimming pool for the kids. Later, when it became clear they hadn't won, they weren't so happy.

Some newcomers don't know the number of weeks in a year or what the seasons are. Others are well-educated but have gaps. Once when I was talking to a well-educated Croatian woman about our history, I brought up the sixties. I said, "It was a hard time with war and so many assassinations, those of John and Bobby Kennedy and Martin Luther King." She asked in amazement, "You mean Martin Luther King is dead?" When I said yes, she began to cry.

Our casual ways of dealing with the opposite sex are without precedent in some cultures. Our relaxed interactions between men and women can be alarming to some people from the Middle East. Some traditional women are suspicious of American women; it seems to them as if the American women are trying to steal their husbands because they speak to them at work or in stores.

An Iraqi high school student told of arriving in this country on a summer day. As she and her father drove through Lincoln, there were many women on the streets in shorts and tank tops. Her father kept saying to her, "Cover your eyes; cover your eyes." Neither of them had ever seen women in public without a head covering.

There are two common refugee beliefs about America – one is that it is sin city; the other is that it is paradise. I met a Cuban mother whose sixteen-year-old daughter got pregnant in Nebraska. She blamed herself for bringing the girl to our sinful town, weeping as she told me the story. And she showed me a picture of the daughter, all dressed in white. A Mexican father told me that his oldest son was now in a gang. He talked about American movies and the violent television, music, and video games. He said, "My son wears a black T-shirt he bought at a concert. It has dripping red letters that read, 'More Fucking Blood.'" He looked at me quizzically. "America is the best country in the world, the richest and the freest. Why do you make things like this for children?"

On the other hand, some refugees idealize our country. They talk endlessly of the mountains of food in buffets, the endless supply of clean water, the shining cars, and the electricity. Flying into a city such as New York or Seattle, many refugees experience their first vision of America and are overwhelmed by the shining stars of light on the ground, more light than they had ever seen. One refugee from Romania captured both ideas when he said, "America is the beauty and the beast."

When I ask refugees what America means to them, many say, "Freedom." This may mean many things. To the Kurdish sisters (Nasreen and Zeenat) it is the freedom to wear stylish American clothes and walk about freely. It's the freedom to go swimming and shopping and make a living. To many of the poor and disenfranchised, it is the radical message that everyone has rights, even though at first many refugees do not know what their rights are.

America means a system of laws, a house, a job, and a school for every child. In America people can strive for happiness, not even a concept in some parts of the world. They are free to become whoever they want to become. Refugees learn they can speak their minds, write, and travel. They shed the constraints of more traditional cultures. As one Bulgarian woman put it to me, "In America, the wives do not have to get up and make the husbands' breakfasts."

People from all over the world want to come here. They want a chance at the American dream. They come because they want to survive and be safe and anywhere is better than where they were. However, the process of adjusting is incredibly traumatic. The Kurdish sisters were in culture shock for about six months. After a year, they are still deeply in debt, lonely, haunted by the past, and struggling to master our language and our culture. They are overwhelmed every time their bills arrive. Nasreen and Zeenat still dream nightly of their homeland.

It is difficult to describe or even imagine the challenges of getting started in a new country. Imagine yourself dropped in downtown Rio de Janeiro or Khartoum with no money, no friends, and no understanding of how that culture works. Imagine you have six months to learn the language and everything you need to know to support your family. Of course, that isn't a fair comparison because you know . . . what a bank is, and how to drive a car. And you have most likely not been tortured or seen family members killed within the last few months.

Picture yourself dropped in the Sudanese grasslands with no tools or knowledge about how to survive and no ways to communicate with the locals or ask for advice. Imagine yourself wondering where the clean water is, where and what food is, and what you should do about the bites on your feet, and your sunburn. . . . Unless a kind and generous Sudanese takes you in and helps you adjust, you would be a goner.

Acculturation

In their first stage after arrival newcomers briefly experience relief and euphoria. They are here and they are safe.

In the second stage reality sets in. Refugees have lost their routines, their institutions, their language, their families and friends, their homes, their work and incomes. They have lost their traditions, their clothes, pictures, heirlooms, and pets. They are without props in a new and alien environment.

They experience cultural bereavement. The old country may have been a terrible place, but it was home. It was the repository of all their stories, memories, and meanings. Many times newcomers' bodies are in America, but their hearts remain in their homeland.

Ideally, the third stage is the beginning of recovery. Newcomers begin to grasp how America works. In the fourth stage, also ideally, newcomers are bicultural and bilingual. They can choose to participate in many aspects of the culture.

In general, there are four reactions refugees' families have to the new culture – fight it because it is threatening; avoid it because it's overwhelming; assimilate as fast as possible by making all American choices; or tolerate discomfort and confusion while slowly making intentional choices about what to accept and reject. Alejandro Portes and Rubén Rumbaut published the results of long-term studies on newcomer adaptation in a book called *Legacies*.[1] They found that this last reaction, which they called "selective acculturation," was best for refugees.

They described two other less-adaptive ways of adjusting. Dissonant acculturation is when the kids in the family outstrip the parents. This can undercut parental authority and put the kids at risk. Consonant acculturation is when members of the family all move together toward being American. At one time this rapid acceptance of American ways was considered ideal, but now it appears that this makes families too vulnerable to the downside of America.

In *Legacies*, Portes and Rumbaut report that most immigrants move into the middle-class mainstream in one or two generations. That is the good news. The bad news is that if they don't make it quickly into the middle class, they won't make it at all. With the passage of time, drive diminishes, and by the third generation, assimilation stops. If two generations fail to make it into the middle class, the following generations are likely to be stuck at the bottom.

Failure to succeed will drive refugee families away from mainstream culture into what Portes calls "reactive ethnicity." Newcomers will revert to enclaves and see failure as inevitable, thus, in many cases, dooming their children to fail.

Portes's research obviously has implications for social policy. We need to help refugees and immigrants early with job training, education, language, and business loans. It's hard to study physics when one is sick and hungry, or to attend GED classes when one has worked all night at a factory. If we miss our chance to help them, we miss our chance to create well-adjusted, well-educated citizens.

. . . I want to tell another archetypal success story. The family arrived here badly traumatized after wandering across many countries looking for a home. But they were a strong family with many attributes of resilience. In Nebraska, their community helped them survive and their hard work enabled them to build a life for themselves. Thirty-seven million people watched the last episode of the (original) TV show Survivor. This family's story and the stories of most refugees are much more compelling than any contrived reality-television program could ever show.

I interviewed Kareem and Mirzana at their high school. Mirzana was small and blond. Kareem was heartbreakingly handsome, with thick eyebrows and black hair. But he was shy and let his older sister do most of the talking.

The family had lived in a village in northern Bosnia. Their father was an engineer, and their mother worked in a store. They were a hardworking middle-class family. Mirzana said she and Kareem had an easy life, consisting mainly of school and play. Their grandparents lived nearby. Kareem said, "We had everything we wanted. We were never lonely."

Nearby there was a war in Croatia, but their parents didn't think the war would come to Bosnia. One day the Serbs came and put their father and all the men in their village into a concentration camp. The siblings and their mother fled to Croatia.

Mirzana told me about her father's camp. She said, "Many men were in a small, empty room. They had nothing to eat, no papers, and no money."

Their father developed a lung infection. Still, he was lucky – he was only there for a month and not too badly beaten. He suffered most hearing the pain of others when the soldiers took them out and beat them. He listened to men scream for hours.

Their father saw many bad things, most of which he didn't tell them. He did tell of a drunken soldier who came into their cell and shouted, "Run to the corner. The last one there will be shot." One man didn't run and was killed by this soldier. Mirzana shook her head sadly as she said, "This man was deaf."

Eventually their father was released. Before he could escape the country, he was ordered to fight the Serbs. He didn't even have a weapon and, as Mirzana put it, "He was there to be shot." After a while, he managed to run away and find his family in Croatia. When he came to their door, none of them recognized him. In the two months he had been away, he'd aged ten years.

The family lived in Croatia for two years. Eventually a friend helped them get into Germany. They spoke no German and lived in one small room, which Kareem didn't like. He said no one could ever be alone and there were fights about space and sharing.

Mirzana and Kareem learned German, but their family couldn't become German citizens and they had no hope of improving their situation. In 1998 the Germans kicked them out and they came to the United States.

They were optimistic on the plane here, but when they arrived in Lincoln they were taken to a small dirty apartment. They were exhausted from the thirty-hour flight, but they couldn't sleep. Their mother was in shock. She cried, "I want to go back." The father said, "You forget, we have no choices. We have no country to return to."

They had no car and they didn't know anyone. No one in the family spoke English. But after five days they moved into their own apartment and they discovered next door a family that the father had known as a child. The two families cried with joy to be reunited. Now the family knows all of the Bosnian community. Bosnians in Lincoln share meals and throw parties. The men help each other find jobs and the women help each other learn English and shop for bargains.

When I met them, Kareem and Mirzana had been here only three months, but already they were speaking pretty good English, their fourth language. They laughed as they talked about early experiences in Nebraska. A neighbor gave them bananas, but they thought they tasted like soap and threw them away. They missed European bakeries. In America everything supposed to be sweet was salty and vice versa. Here herring was sweet and butter was salty.

Kareem and Mirzana like it here. Mirzana is making A's and, after school, she is a stocker at a supermarket. Mirzana laughed as she explained. "The staff teaches me a new word each day." Kareem is too young to work, so he cleans the house, does laundry, and studies after school. Both Kareem and Mirzana want to go to college and get good jobs. They want to care for their parents.

Their parents are ambitious, too. They have difficult factory jobs because their English is still poor. They work from two until ten. But in the morning they study English. Mirzana said, "In a year or two they will have better jobs."

This family is lucky. They have each other and a supportive community. Everyone has many of the attributes of resilience. The family carries with them a great deal of human capital. The external environment has been pretty harsh, but most likely, they will eventually transcend it.

Sometimes Mirzana wishes that her life these last few years were just a dream and she would wake up in Bosnia in their old house. Her grandmother would be calling her to come work in the garden. There would be no war. Kareem disagrees. He is filled with newcomer zest. He said, "I could smell freedom in America."

Notes

[1] Alejandro Portes and Rubén Rumbaut, *Legacies* (Berkeley: University of California Press, 2001).

MICHAEL SCHERER

Scrimmage on the Border

The author addresses the hotly debated issue of "illegal immigration." Unlike many politicians pandering to get votes, his essay demonstrates why there are no simple solutions to this complex problem.

At its southern border, where the United States of America ends in a tangle of barbed wire and manzanita bushes, the red dirt desert fills each night with thousands of men and women trudging north from Mexico. This is the new Ellis Island, the port of entry for more than a million people every year. They come because immigration helps drive our prosperity, and because, as George W. Bush says, there are jobs that U.S. citizens won't do, and because the president of Mexico, Vicente Fox, has made their migration – and gainful employment in El Norte – a linchpin of his nation's economy. They come because American companies have an unquenchable desire for more strawberry pickers and meatpackers and dishwashers, and because few will check to see if their Social Security cards are real. They come alone or as families, cradling babies in their arms, braving freezing nights and sweltering days, border bandits and mesquite trees with thorns like knives. They pay guides thousands of dollars for the privilege of walking 5 or 10 or 20 miles to hide by the side of a desolate road, hoping their ride to Phoenix or Las Vegas or Los Angeles shows up. Every year, hundreds die along the way. Those who do make it are greeted as criminals. In the broken logic of the nation's current immigration policy, they are enticed and needed, but illegal.

On the first Sunday in April, five migrant men huddled in the shade under a cement culvert that passed beneath Arizona's Route 92 in the border town of Hereford. Though it was the middle of the day, with temperatures approaching 80 degrees, they were dressed like New England schoolkids in heavy jackets and wool caps, clothing that had kept them warm as they hiked through the Huachuca Mountains and down into the San Pedro River valley. . . . They were heading north, and might have made it to Phoenix, to a new job and another life, but for a group of citizen soldiers, a ragtag bunch of men and women armed with walkie-talkies, binoculars, and not a few pistols, who were lying in wait. These self-described patriots had chosen this Sunday to do what their president and Congress would not . . . to stop what they called the "illegal invasion of America."

"We found them and called Border Patrol," said Marc Johannes, a 40-year-old auto mechanic from Tucson, who had been manning a post along the road. The five migrants solemnly lowered their heads as they climbed into the back of the patrol truck, saying not a word. "I'm fed up," Johannes said. "This whole country is being over-run." Johannes stands well over 6 feet tall . . . wore desert camouflage pants, and in his bag he had a Russian-made, first-generation infrared scope, the better to see immigrants at night. He didn't want to be mistaken for a racist. "I consider myself a scientist," he continued. "And I know that all people on the planet are the same. If I were living in a Third

World cesspool, I would probably look for another job too. But the entire Third World is moving north on a global scale." One of Johannes' friends' vehicles had been stolen and recovered in Mexico. A neighbor had recently moved away so his daughter would not have to attend a largely Latino school. "I've been denied jobs because I don't speak Spanish," he said. "I'm more affected by this than anybody else."

A few days earlier, Johannes had traveled to Tombstone, Arizona, for the first day of what was billed as "The Minuteman Project," a month-long protest against illegal immigration. The idea, to recruit American citizens for border patrols, was not new. In recent years, a half-dozen groups, including fully armed paramilitary militias and local ranchers, have walked the desert searching for migrants, defying federal officials who warn against civilian bravado. But those groups have largely worked in the shadows. The Minuteman Project was designed as a national coming-out party, less an effort to capture Mexicans crossing the border than to capture airtime on the cable news channels.

"We are done writing letters and sending emails and showing up at town hall meetings," said one of the project's organizers, Chris Simcox, before a bank of television cameras at Tombstone's Masonic Hall. He stood next to Rep. Tom Tancredo (R-Colo.), the House's leading opponent of illegal immigration. . . . Tancredo wore black cowboy boots and a pin that read "Undocumented Border Patrol Agent." In his shirt pocket he kept a fresh cigar. "For the first time in seven years," he told the press, "I can actually tell our friends and supporters that we are on the offensive."

Tombstone is a tourist town, a place of reenactment, simulation. Acting troupes stage Old West gunfights every hour or two, and the stores sell period costumes and posters of Doc Holliday. It is, in many ways, the perfect backdrop for a televised passion play. Minutemen with handlebar mustaches and minutewomen in hip holsters and Wrangler shirts posed before satellite relay trucks. They'd arrived by the hundreds from every corner of the country, with a common sense of outrage and similar sets of talking points – working people and retired people, many of whose parents or grandparents had come from Europe. They'd spent their lifetimes framing houses or driving trucks or digging

wells or trimming trees. Now they felt their country was changing around them. The government was allowing a trampling of the law, a dilution of American culture, and a burgeoning of the welfare state. It was turning a blind eye to a gateway for terrorists. America was being lost. And nobody was stopping it, not the U.S. Border Patrol, not Congress, not the president.

Weeks earlier, appearing at a press conference with Mexico's President Fox, President Bush had said, "I'm against vigilantes in the United States of America." He was dismissing not just the citizen soldiers in the desert but a growing movement within his own Republican Party, for the backlash against immigration in America involves more than the fringe right. Even as the Minutemen gathered, pollsters for NBC News and the *Wall Street Journal* found that 48 percent of Americans believed that immigration "detracts from our character and weakens the United States." In a nation of immigrants, only 41 percent said immigration betters the republic. . . . California Governor Arnold Schwarzenegger declared in an April speech that the United States needs to "close the borders." Though the governor apologized for the remarks, a week later he praised the Minutemen on a Southern California radio show.

Outside the Minutemen's Tombstone headquarters, Don Wooley, a retired pawnbroker with a chiseled jaw and bright eyes, was making his stand. Wooley was proud to have fought in Vietnam because "I don't think it's ever dishonorable to go kill communists." He'd driven down from Lawton, Oklahoma, in December to make sure the Minuteman organizers were not racists or hucksters. Now he was back to do his part. "If you and your kids are going to speak English and live the lifestyle you live today, somebody is going to have to pay the price," he told me. He didn't live near many Spanish-speaking people, but he had heard of the problems. "There are government offices where all the clerks don't speak English," he said. "I wouldn't speak Spanish on a bet. I speak English." He certainly spoke with determination. "Nothing happens in Washington unless there is a crowd with pitchforks and torches."

Representative Tancredo's press secretary, Carlos Espinosa, has one of the toughest jobs in Washington. "Damage control," he called it – constantly parrying and rebutting charges that his boss is a bigot. But if media exposure is the measure of a press secretary's success, Espinosa ranked among the best. In early April, Tancredo was booking at least 30 radio, newspaper, and television interviews a week. "We were sitting in the office yesterday," Tancredo told me, once we settled at a corner table in a deserted cafeteria. ". . . Think about where we were just a few short years ago. And how amazing it is to now be on the cusp of a major shift in public policy."'

When Tancredo arrived in Congress in 1999, no one seemed to care about Mexican migration. The Immigration Reform Caucus he founded attracted only 16 members, all Republicans, and just about the only Americans who ever heard him speak were late-night C-SPAN viewers. "I really didn't know what else to do," he said. "Then 9/11 happened and everything changed. We got 60 members overnight."

Tancredo turned illegal immigration into a national-security issue. He spread word that Islamic prayer rugs and a diary written in Arabic had been found in the border scrubland. "Can anybody explain to me why we shouldn't be paranoid?" he asked a reporter for Fox News. He began appearing regularly on conservative talk radio, and with Lou Dobbs on CNN. He complained about open borders to the *Washington Times* editorial board, and said that "the blood of the people killed" by a second terrorist attack would be on the hands of President Bush and Congress. That prompted a phone call from Bush adviser Karl Rove, one so rife with vulgarity and vitriol that Tancredo, who was driving to work at the time, had to pull his car to the side of the road. Rove called him a "traitor to the president" and told him never to "darken the doorstep of this White House." Unbowed, Tancredo went on to raise money last year to defeat several House Republicans he considered soft on immigration, earning the ire of House Majority Leader Tom DeLay. "I will never be a chairman of any committee around here," Tancredo said, cracking a smile. "I will never be in the 'in' crowd."

But Tancredo did not come to Washington to climb the rungs of power. He came to draw the battle lines in a clash of cultures. "You have to understand there is a bigger issue here. . . . Who are we? Do we have an understanding of what it means to be an American, even if we are Hispanic or Italian

or Jewish or black or white or Hungarian by ancestry? Is there something we can all hang on to? Are there things that will bind us together as Americans?" He continued into a monologue about the identity crisis in America, the "cult of multiculturalism," schoolkids ashamed to love their country, and textbooks that say Christopher Columbus "destroyed paradise." Tancredo believes that many immigrants today, unlike his grandparents, who came over from Italy, no longer feel the need to assimilate. "You have, at least, divided loyalties," he said. . . .

Tancredo led a coterie of insurgent Republicans in a revolt against the White House. They delayed passage of the intelligence reform bill because it failed to include a provision called Real ID, which would make it far more difficult for illegal immigrants to get state driver's licenses. In February, nearly two-thirds of the House, including 42 Democrats, voted for the Real ID measure, which was later endorsed by the Senate and signed by the president. This is only the beginning of what Tancredo hopes will be a series of legislative victories this year. He plans to derail a bipartisan effort, supported by the president, that would allow illegal immigrants to find legal employment in the U.S. He's reintroducing a bill that would suspend legal work visas, increase fines for employers who hire illegal immigrants, and deploy the military to protect the borders. He is also helping groups in seven states push new initiatives or laws that would deny government services to illegal immigrants. Last fall Arizona voters approved Proposition 200, a ballot initiative nicknamed "Protect Arizona Now," which requires government workers to report undocumented residents who seek out government aid. The law garnered 56 percent of the vote, including, according to one exit poll, more than 40 percent of the state's Latino voters. . . .

The minutemen set up their operational headquarters in the run-down dormitories of the Miracle Valley Bible College, a faded compound near Hereford built in the late 1950s by the Reverend Asa Alonzo Allen, a faith healer famous for exorcising demons before tent crowds of 20,000 until he died of alcoholism at the age of 59. At the front gate, an armed guard screened cars. Inside was a communications center, equipped with ham radios and topographic maps of well-known immigration trails. For security, all registered Minutemen wore orange badges. The men slept four to a room. A surplus of American flags festooned the front lawn.

Minuteman founder Jim Gilchrist, a retired accountant, seemed thrilled by the layout and its trappings. He'd served as a Marine outside of Khe Sanh during Vietnam, and took easily to the role of commanding general, always talking up the enemy and warning of possible ambushes. He leaked rumors to the conservative press, claiming that a Latin American gang called Mara Salvatrucha, or MS-13, was planning to attack his volunteers. During a desert patrol one day, he received a tip from an informant he would not identify suggesting an imminent armed assault from across the wire. "Do whatever you want with that," he told a skeptical *Los Angeles Times* reporter between drags of a cigarette. "I didn't personally gather this info. . . ." He wore a crumpled straw cowboy hat, and what appeared to be a brand-new military equipment belt, to which he affixed his cellular phone and water bottles. When volunteers came to him with concerns that their walkie-talkies were being intentionally jammed by human smugglers across the border, he announced, with some elation, "This has been like a real war."

Like many Minuteman volunteers, Gilchrist hails from Southern California, a land adrift in a demographic sea change. Between 2000 and 2020, the number of Latino residents there is set to increase by nearly two-thirds, and the number of Asian residents will increase by 40 percent. Once-lily-white suburbs in Orange County, where Gilchrist lives, will soon count whites as a minority. He says he doesn't mind the diversity of races, but he cannot tolerate the diversity of cultures. "I saw the country change literally overnight into a foreign country," he told me over a hamburger at the Trading Post Diner on Route 92. "The Fourth of July was not being celebrated, but Cinco de Mayo was. All the billboards would be in foreign languages. It's not just Spanish. It's Korean. I saw the nation being segregated."

Gilchrist's co-organizer, Chris Simcox, worked as an elementary school teacher in Los Angeles until 2001, when he moved to Tombstone and founded an armed border patrol called Civil Homeland Defense. "Where are all these gangs coming from, who don't speak English?" he remembered thinking after he took a job teaching in South Central in the late 1990s. "We have people that came to this country saying, Your laws mean nothing, your citizenship means nothing." Around the same time, former Southern California resident Glenn Spencer, a former radio talk show host, founded American Border Patrol at the base of the Huachuca Mountains, where he launched regular patrols, some of which he broadcast in infrared video on the Internet. Another Los Angeles native, Casey Nethercott, recently bought a ranch that abuts the border and founded the Arizona Guard, a militia that he says is prepared to fight the Mexican army if the U.S. government is not. They came to Arizona because it has all the action. . . .

Many locals take the torrent in stride. They sleep with their screen doors locked and their front doors open, and if someone comes knocking late at night, searching for food, water, or a telephone, they try to help out. "I got to the point where I was buying extra bread and peanut butter for those people," said Eric Nelson. Crime against locals is extremely rare, though in January 2004, three illegal immigrants attacked Hereford resident Sandy Graham as she warmed up her Chevy Suburban to drive her 14-year-old daughter to school. The men, who had been hiding in the mesquite, stabbed Sandy with a pen, kicked her daughter, and sped away in the car. They were promptly caught and arrested, but at least one resident, Cindy Kolb, began strapping a .38 to her ankle before driving her seven-year-old to the bus stop.

Local newspaper columnist Jim Dwyer calls the anti-immigrant activists "crusading carpetbaggers," and the governments of Douglas, Tombstone, and Cochise County have passed resolutions condemning civilian patrols. Undaunted, Simcox worked without sleep for much of the first week of the Minuteman Project, cautioning his volunteers to act responsibly on the border, to phone Border Patrol, and to not engage the migrants. He wore a bulletproof vest and kept an armed guard at his side. Because he was on probation for carrying a pistol into a nearby national park, he can no longer pack his own weapon. "My family is very concerned with me taking on a multimillion-dollar crime syndicate," Simcox said after finishing breakfast one morning. . . . "It's the government of Mexico in bed with the government of the United States that has created a subculture of human smuggling and drug smuggling and gangsters, and it's a mess. This border is worth a billion dollars of business at least."

Since he began his work, he said, his group has alerted Border Patrol to nearly 5,000 illegal migrants in the desert, and rescued 158 people in need of food or water. Later that day, he had an interview scheduled on *The O'Reilly Factor,* which would be broadcast from a relay truck parked on the border.

Locals like Herb Linn would just as soon Simcox stay in Los Angeles. At Johnny Ringo's, a biker bar named after the gunfighter who shot a man in 1879 for refusing a shot of whiskey, Linn stopped pouring drinks when I mentioned Simcox. "He's a self-serving son of a bitch who wants his 15 minutes of fame," said the barkeep, a former city councilor. "If the Minutemen succeed in sealing the border, are they going to spend as much time picking the crops? I don't want to pay five bucks for a can of string beans."

James "Butch" Peri, owner of one of the largest onion farms in Nevada, knows all about the costs and benefits of migrant labor. He pays legal immigrants around $8 an hour to shovel onions into 90-pound burlap bags, a job for which he says there are no U.S.-born applicants. At a meeting of Tancredo's Immigration Reform Caucus on Capitol Hill, Peri stood before congressional staffers making the case that U.S. agriculture depends on Mexico. Americans, he said, have become spoiled. "It belittles them to pull weeds in a lawn. Kids don't wash cars anymore. They don't mow lawns."....

Immigration as an issue, it turns out, can be great for radio ratings, creating all the impassioned binaries that keep listeners from turning the dial. It pits the working man against the lawbreaker, the common voter against the elite politician, the radio host against the mainstream media. "Our language is being destroyed by George Bush and Bill Clinton to pay off their buddies who put them in power," ranted nationally syndicated Michael Savage over a southern Arizona station broadcast one day during the Minuteman protest. "Our culture is being destroyed to the point where there is no culture. We have no common culture. They want us to become a culture of the international. That's why I tell you that civil upheaval in this country might also not be more than a few years off, sparked by this flood of illegal aliens that both the Democrats and Republicans are foisting upon this nation."

John Stone thought he saw something move in the brambles.... He held binoculars up to his face.

"No, it's just a bush. I've been looking at this landscape so long that every bush looks like a person and every person looks like a bush." The Minutemen had spaced themselves out over two miles on a stretch of dust called Border Road.... Their task was mercilessly boring. They sat on chairs or in their trucks, gazing over a wide desert plain that passed five or six miles into Mexico to a distant highway where the migrants would, on a normal day, be dropped off for the long walk to the United States. No one was coming now. The Mexican government, wary of gun-toting vigilantes, had mounted its own patrols. Every few hours, on the other side of the short barbed-wire fence, you could see another group of migrants get rousted from the bush, loaded into the back of a Mexican government truck, and driven back into the country's interior.

In the absence of action, the Minutemen bided their time with the steady stream of international media who showed up to interview them. Behind them, up on a hill, sat a group of volunteers from the ACLU and the American Friends Service Committee, mostly students from Stanford Law School and Prescott College.... They wore T-shirts that read "observadores legales." They videotaped the Minutemen, and the Minutemen videotaped them. Mexican television stations came to shoot pictures of the spectacle, only to find elderly men and women sitting in lawn chairs aiming their own camcorders. It wasn't exactly the sort of border standoff most participants had expected....

A few miles down the road, Casey Nethercott, the militant leader of the Arizona Guard, kept watch over his border property, a place he calls "Warrior Ranch." It holds about 100 acres of dirt and tumbleweed, a few buildings, and a windmill with no blades. He keeps a 120-pound rottweiler trained to tackle grown men, and two black sport utility vehicles reinforced with steel plates to stop bullets when his militia patrols the desert.

"Migration from Mexico is the catalyst that is starting the demise of America," he told me, sitting in his cramped office, which was decorated with diagrams of military attack formations. "It's being flooded with illegals, people that are substandard humans. They don't educate themselves. They don't care about themselves. And if you think that's racist, I'm sorry, you're wrong. If a black man with a white wife and two adopted Mexican and

Chinese children moved in next door to me, first thing I'd do is take over a bottle of wine and say welcome to the damned neighborhood. And if he was in the Army I would hit him up to join the organization. But these are illegals. They are illegal."

Nethercott . . . had just been released after serving six months in prison, the result of a dispute with the local Border Patrol. Federal officers had tried to pull him over, but he drove onto his ranch and shut the gate . . . and a standoff ensued until local sheriffs arrived. A few weeks later, the FBI tried to serve Nethercott and his fellow militia member, Kalen Riddle, a warrant for threatening federal officers. The FBI said Riddle refused an order to stop moving in a Safeway parking lot, and an agent shot and injured him. Nethercott was acquitted of all charges, but he still faces a 2003 aggravated assault charge in Texas (that he) pistol-whipped an illegal Salvadoran migrant he found sneaking into the country during a patrol in 2003, a charge Nethercott denies. . . .

Back at the Bible College in Miracle Valley, Gilchrist arrived at the communications center to prepare for another radio interview. . . . Outside on the front lawn, Mike Bird, a 22-year-old volunteer from Georgia, was pacing around, awaiting instructions for his night patrol up along Route 92. Bird . . . planned to spend the full month in Arizona. "You'll never hear it from any of these guys," he confided between drags of a Dunhill, "but I have too big a gun." A .44 Magnum, the sort of cannot made famous by Dirty Harry, stretched down his right thigh. Bird was unemployed, but he hoped to get a job back home sampling air quality at the local coal plant. . . .

Word had filtered down from Gilchrist about the success that the Minutemen were having, about the waiting migrants backed up like cars in a traffic jam on the other side of the border. Mike was ready. "Tonight is the night," he told me, imagining them in the wilderness. "Think about it. They are hungry. They have been waiting two days. They are going to rush the line."

Dyaspora

This first-person narrative describes the life of immigrants from Haiti living in Boston. It also captures the feelings shared by many immigrant children and youth as they try to maintain their native culture, but struggle to be accepted by their peers, even those peers who are from the same racial group.

When you are in Haiti they call you *Dyaspora*. This word, which connotes both connection and disconnection, accurately describes your condition as a Haitian American. Disconnected from the physical landscape of the homeland, you don't grow up with a mango tree in your yard, you don't suck *kenèps* in the summer, or sit in the dark listening to stories of *Konpè* Bouki and Malis. The bleat of *vaksins* or the beating of a *Yanvalou* on *Rada* drums are neither in the background or the foreground of your life. Your French is non-existent. Haiti is not where you live.

Your house in Boston is your island. As the only Haitian family on the hillside street you grow up on, it represents Haiti to you. It was where your *granmè* refused to learn English, where goods like ripe mangoes, plantains, *djondjon*, and hard white blobs of mints come to you in boxes through the mail. At your communion and birthday parties, all of Boston Haiti seems together in your house to eat *griyo* and sip *kremas*. It takes forever for you to kiss every cheek, some of them heavy with face powder, some of them damp with perspiration, some of them with scratchy face hair, and some of them giving you a perfume head-rush as you swoop in. You are grateful for every smooth, dry cheek you encounter. In your house, the dreaded *matinèt* which your parents imported from Haiti just to keep you, your brother, and your sister in line sits threateningly on top of the wardrobe. It is where your mother's *andeyò Kreyòl* accent and your father's *lavil* French accent make sometimes beautiful, sometimes terrible music together.

On Sundays in your house, "Dominika-anik-anik" floats from the speakers of the record player early in the morning and you are made to put on one of your frilly dresses, your matching lace-edged socks, and black shoes. Your mother ties long ribbons into a bow at the root of each braid. She warns you, your brother and your sister to "respect; your heads" as you drive to St. Angela's, never missing a Sunday service in fourteen years. In your island house, everyone has two names. The name they were given and the nickname they have been granted so that your mother is Gisou, your father is Popo, your brother is Claudy, your sister is Tinou, you are Jojo, and your grandmother is Manchoun. Every day your mother serves rice and beans and you methodically pick out all the beans because you don't like *pwa*. You think they are ugly and why does all the rice have to have beans anyway? Even with the white rice or the *mayi moulen*, your mother makes *sòs pwa* – bean sauce. You develop the idea that Haitians are obsessed with beans. In your

From E. Danticat (Ed.) *The butterfly's way: Voices from the Haitian dyaspora in the United States*, (New York: Soho Press, 2001). Reprinted by permission of the author.

house there is a mortar and a pestle as well as five pictures of Jesus, your parents drink Café Bustelo every morning, your father wears *gwayabèl* shirts and smokes cigarettes, and you are beaten when you don't get good grades at school. You learn about the infidelities of husbands from conversations your aunts have. You are dragged to Haitian plays, Haitian *bals*, and Haitian concerts where in spite of yourself *konpa* rhythms make you sway. You know the names of Haitian presidents and military leaders because political discussions inevitably erupt whenever there are more than three Haitian men together in the same place.

Every time you are sick, your mother rubs you down with a foul-smelling liquid that she keeps in an old Barbancourt rum bottle under her bed. You splash yourself with Bien-être after every bath. Your parents speak to you in *Kreyòl*, you respond in English, and somehow this works and feels natural. But when your mother speaks English, things seem to go wrong. She makes no distinction between he and she, and you become the pronoun police. Every day you get a visit from some *matant* or *monnonk* or *kouzen* who is also a *marenn* or *parenn* of someone in the house. In your house, your grandmother has a porcelain *kivèt* she keeps under her bed to relieve herself at night. You pore over photograph albums where there are pictures of you going to school in Haiti, in the yard in Haiti, under the white Christmas tree in Haiti, and you marvel because you do not remember anything that you see. You do not remember Haiti because you left there too young but it does not matter because it is as if Haiti has lassoed your house with an invisible rope.

Outside of your house, you are forced to sink or swim in American waters. For you this means an Irish-Catholic school and a Black-American neighborhood. The school is a choice made by your parents who strongly believe in a private Catholic education anyway, not paying any mind to the busing crisis that is raging in the city. The choice of neighborhood is a condition of the reality of living here in this city with its racially segregated neighborhoods. Before you lived here, white people owned this hillside street. After you and others who looked like you came, they gradually disappeared to other places, leaving you this place and calling it bad because you and others like you live there now. As any *dyaspora* child knows, Haitian parents are

not familiar with these waters. They say things to you like, "In Haiti we never treated white people badly." They don't know about racism. They don't know about the latest styles and fashions and give your brother hell every time he sneaks out to a friend's house and gets his hair cut into a shag, a high-top, a fade. They don't know that the ribbons in your hair, the gold loops in your ears, and the lace that edges your socks alert other children to your difference. So you wait until you get to school before taking them all off and out and you put them back on at the end of your street where the bus drops you off. Outside your house, things are black and white. You are black and white. Especially in your school where neither you nor any of the few other Haitian girls in your class are invited to the birthday parties of the white kids in your class. You cleave to these other Haitian girls out of something that begins as solidarity but becomes a lifetime of friendship. You make green hats in art class every St. Patrick's Day and watch Irish step-dancing shows year after year after year. You discover books and reading and this is what you do when you take the bus home, just you and your white schoolmates. You lose your accent. You study about the Indians in social studies but you do not study about Black Americans except in music class where you are forced to sing Negro spirituals as a concession to your presence. They don't know anything about Toussaint Louverture or Jean-Jacques Dessalines.

In your neighborhood when you tell people you are from Haiti, they ask politely, "Where's that?" You explain and because you seem okay to them, Haiti is okay to them. They shout, "Hi, Grunny!" whenever they see your grandmother on the stoop and sometimes you translate a sentence or two between them. In their houses, you eat sweet potato pie and nod because you have that too, it's made a little different and you call it *pen patat* but it's the same taste after all. From the girls on the street you learn to jump double-dutch, you learn to dance the puppet and the white boy. You see a woman preacher for the first time in your life at their church. You wonder where down South is because that is where most of the boys and girls on your block go for vacations. You learn about boys and sex through these girls because these two subjects are not allowed in your island/house. You keep your street friends separate from your school friends and this is how it works and you are used to it. You get so you can jump between worlds with the same ease that you slide on your nightgown in the evening.

Then when you get to high school, things change. People in your high school and your neighborhood look at you and say, "You are Haitian?" and from the surprise in their voice you realize that they know where Haiti is now. They think they know what Haiti is now. Haiti is the boat people on the news every night. Haiti is where people have tuberculosis. Haiti is where people eat cats. You do not represent Haiti at all to them anymore. You are an aberration because you look like them and you talk like them. They do not see you. They do not see the worlds that have made you. You want to say to them that you are Haiti, too. Your house is Haiti, too, and what does that do to their perceptions? You have the choice of passing but you don't. You claim your *dyaspora* status hoping it will force them to expand their image of what Haiti is but it doesn't. Your sister who is younger and very sensitive begins to deny that she is Haitian. She is American, she says. American.

You turn to books to lose yourself. You read stories about people from other places. You read stories about people from here. You read stories about people from other places who now live here. You decide you will become a writer. Through your writing they will see you, *dyaspora* child, the connections and disconnections that have made the mosaic that you are. They will see where you are from and the worlds that have made you. They will see you.

Challenges for Linguistically and Culturally Diverse People

" True (education), unlike assimilation, is a two-way street. It involves cultural sharing, a genuine respect and interest in difference, not cultural submergence by one party to please another. "

Clarence Page (1947–)

Unfortunately, American schools have been more likely to provide examples that contradict journalist Clarence Page's insight rather than illustrate it. One of the most dramatic examples is the historic experience of American Indian children who have attended schools that emphasize competition and individual achievement. Culturally, children from most American Indian communities would only want to excel if their achievement would enhance the regard given to their peers or their community. If an individual student's achievements in school could be viewed as creating a derogatory perception of his or her peers or community, the student might feel an obligation to conceal his or her talent.

In the early 1960s, anthropologists who were fluent in the Lakota language were engaged in research observing Indian children and white teachers in schools on the Pine Ridge Reservation. The researchers saw numerous instances where teachers called on a student who did not know an answer, and then called upon a more academically gifted student to get the right answer so they could proceed with the lesson. And often, before the student could answer, his or her peers would make comments in Lakota such as: *Go ahead, show the teacher how smart you are. Make the rest of us look bad.* The teachers did not understand Lakota, so they did not understand why the bright student would suddenly appear confused and unable to respond. Frustrated teachers just assumed that the other students were having a bad influence on the bright students.[1]

Most native cultures emphasize a concern for collaboration and for the collective good. Yet even when these cultural beliefs could have been used to help Indian students succeed in schools, teachers did not respond appropriately. As part of his doctoral research, Harry Wolcott taught in a one-room Indian school. Wolcott lived in the community for a year and became well acquainted with the children and the adults, but he felt uncertain about how much his pupils were learning because no matter what sort of an assignment he gave them, the children would always work with others. Nothing he could say or do would persuade them to do their homework individually.[2] Times have changed, and such stories from the past have motivated multicultural educators today to advocate for creating culturally responsive classrooms, especially with the evolving yet continuous cultural and linguistic diversity of students in America's schools.

In the first essay, Dennis Baron provides the history of linguistic diversity in the United States. Immigrants came speaking German, Italian, Polish, Spanish, Dutch, and other languages. Most of them lost their language in two or three generations, but the efforts of German immigrants to maintain their native tongue led to the first English-Only legislation. Today Spanish-speaking immigrants are trying to preserve their first language, and once again there is opposition from Americans who insist that English is the only acceptable language. Baron describes the historic and current activities of English-Only proponents in schools and society, and concludes that the history of this movement has more to do with nativist animosity toward immigrants than with a sincere desire for immigrants to achieve linguistic competence in English.

How best to attain competence in English is the focus of Earl Shorris's essay, but "Late Entry, Early Exit" also describes some dilemmas stemming from inadequate responses in U.S. schools to the needs of bilingual children. For too many children, entry into programs that could help them be successful in school and in their careers comes too late (if ever), which leads to an early exit – a reference to the high Latino drop out rate. Shorris discusses programs such as submersion, immersion, teaching English as a second language, and bilingual education, and he provides examples of outcomes from some specific school programs. Although Shorris does not advocate for any particular approach, he does affirm the value of people being both bilingual and bicultural, and argues that U.S. schools have a special responsibility to promote diversity. Shorris would applaud this comment by the American educator Rosa Guerrero about the diversity of the American people:

> We are all Americans who, because of our cultural heritage, contribute something unique to the fabric of American life. We are like the notes in a chord of music – if all the notes were the same, there would be no harmony, no real beauty, because harmony is based on differences, not similarities.

In "Maintaining Bilingualism and Cultural Awareness," Irene Villanueva reinforces Shorris's perspective by describing the actions of seven Latino families who want their children to be both bilingual and bicultural. She incorporates interviews with the parents (in a bilingual format) from her research that explain why these parents place so much importance on their children maintaining fluency in Spanish, from simply being able to communicate with grandparents (and other family members) to the positive influence it can have on their children's sense of identity. Villanueva's research with these families reveals the difficulties of finding good bilingual programs in U.S. schools, forcing one family to stay temporarily in Mexico so the children could attend Mexican schools to strengthen their Spanish-speaking skills before returning to the United States. All of these parents believe that their children do not have to reject their native language and culture in order to become fluent speakers of English.

Shirley Brice Heath discusses language fluency in the context of race and class in her essay on "Oral Traditions." Based on many years of ethnographic research in the Piedmont Plateau region of South Carolina, Heath and her research team recorded how black and white children from two segregated low-income communities in the rural South developed different types of language skills and different communication styles. In comparing their language development with that of the black and white children of middle class professionals, Heath and her researchers provide some disturbing but compelling insights on the impact that differences in learning how to communicate have on the children's performance and academic success in school. Even though the differences in language development can create problems for children, there are many teachers who have been able to work effectively with linguistically diverse students.

Aurora Cedillo is a gifted teacher who describes some of the reasons for her success in the interview entitled "Working with Latino and Latina Students." As a bilingual educator, Cedillo knows the value of having fluency in two languages. Knowing certain cultural characteristics shared by many Latinos has enabled her to work effectively with Latino/a students. She discusses the need for teachers of Latino/a students to address the history of Latino countries, the rea-

sons for Latino immigration to the United States, and the contributions Latinos/as have made to American society. Cedillo reinforces Shorris's concern about Latinos leaving school by noting that children of Latino immigrants as well as first and second generation Latino youth are the two main groups responsible for producing one of the highest dropout rates among all ethnic groups. Because cultural differences can result in educators misinterpreting Latino students' behaviors, Cedillo describes some specific instructional strategies to use and explains why they have been successful for her.

Sometimes viewing diversity experiences in other cultures may help us to understand diversity issues in our own country. The final selection is an excerpt from the short story "Human Mathematics" by Ghanian author Mamle Kabu, about a British boarding school where cultural and linguistic diversity were not accommodated. The narrator is Claudia, a Ghanian student who has attended this boarding school for several years and has assimilated to British culture. With the arrival of a new Ghanian student named Folake, Claudia is reminded of her own struggle to be accepted when she first came to the school, especially the difficulties she encountered during her first year, which primarily stemmed from linguistic differences. In talking with Folake, Claudia finds herself switching in and out of her Ghanian accent, which reminds her of what she has given up in order to be accepted by others. When a cultural misunderstanding leads to physical confrontation between Folake and a British girl, Claudia is forced to make a choice between being neutral or supporting Folake. It is a choice without enough options, but the lack of options in the past has been a problem not only in Great Britain but also in the United States. As Andrew Young has said, accepting and promoting diversity must be one of the options being offered to children and adults living in a diverse society:

> We can embrace our diversity, find strength in it, and prosper together, or we can focus on our differences and try to restrict access to resources by members of ethnic and racial groups different from ours and limit prosperity for all.

Notes

[1]Murray L. Wax & Rosalie H. Wax, Great Tradition, little tradition, and formal education. In *Anthropological Perspectives on Education*, M.L. Wax, S. Diamond, & F.O. Gearing, (Eds.). (New York: Basic Books, 1971)

[2]Harry, F. Wolcott, Handle with care: Necessary precautions in the anthropology of schools. In *Anthropological Perspectives on Education*, M.L. Wax, S. Diamond, & F.O. Gearing, (Eds.). (New York: Basic Books, 1971)

DENNIS BARON

English in a Multicultural America

The author explains the linguistic history of the United States and its implications for the current linguistic concerns of people in the English-Only Movement or those demanding a Constitutional Amendment making English the official language of the United States.

The protection of the Constitution extends to all, – to those who speak other languages as well as to those born with English on the tongue. Perhaps it would be highly advantageous if all had ready understanding of our ordinary speech, but this cannot be coerced by methods which conflict with the Constitution, – a desirable end cannot be promoted by prohibited means.

> Associate Supreme Court Justice
> James Clark McReynolds
> Meyer v. Nebraska, 1923

In the United States today there is a growing fear that the English language may be on its way out as the American lingua franca, that English is losing ground to Spanish, Chinese, Vietnamese, Korean, and the other languages used by newcomers to our shores.

However, while the United States has always been a multilingual as well as a multicultural nation, English has always been its unofficial official language. Today, a greater percentage of Americans speak English than ever before, and the descendants of nonanglophones or bilingual speakers still tend to learn English – and become monolingual English speakers – as quickly as their German, Jewish, Irish, or Italian predecessors did in the past.

Assimilated immigrants, those who after several generations no longer consider themselves "hyphenated Americans," look upon more recent waves of newcomers with suspicion. Similarly, each generation tends to see the language crisis as new in its time. But reactions to language and ethnicity are cyclical, and the new immigrants from Asia and Latin America have had essentially the same experience as their European predecessors, with similar results.

As early as the 18th century, British colonists in Pennsylvania, remarking that as many as one-third of the area's residents spoke German, attacked Germans in terms strikingly familiar to those heard nowadays against newer immigrants. Benjamin Franklin considered the Pennsylvania Germans to be a "swarthy" racial group distinct from the English majority in the colony. In 1751 he complained,

> Why should (Germans) be suffered to swarm into our Settlements, and by herding together establish their Language and manners to the exclusion of ours? Why should Pennsylvania, founded by the English, become a Colony of Aliens, who will shortly be so numerous as to Germanize us instead of our Anglifying them, and will never adopt our Language or Customs, any more than they can acquire our Complexion?

From *Social Policy Magazine,* 1991, spring.

The Germans were accused by other 18th-century Anglos of laziness, illiteracy, clannishness, a reluctance to assimilate, excessive fertility, and Catholicism (although a significant number of them were Protestant). In some instances they were even blamed for the severe Pennsylvania winters.

Resistance to German, long the major minority language in the country, continued throughout the 19th century, although it was long since clear that, despite community efforts to preserve their language, young Germans were adopting English and abandoning German at a rate that should have impressed the rest of the English-speaking population.

After the US entered World War I, most states quickly banned German – and, in some extreme cases, all foreign languages – from school curricula in a wave of jingoistic patriotism. In 1918, for example, Iowa Governor William Harding forbade the use of foreign languages in schools, on trains, in public places, and over the telephone (a more public instrument then than it is now), even going so far as to recommend that those who insisted on conducting religious services in a language other than English do so not in churches or synagogues but in the privacy of their own homes.

Similarly, in 1919 the state of Nebraska passed a broad English-only law prohibiting the use of foreign languages at public meetings and proscribing the teaching of foreign languages to any student below the ninth grade. Robert T. Meyer, a teacher in the Lutheran-run Zion Parochial School, was fined twenty-five dollars because, as the complaint read, "between the hour of 1 and 1:30 on May 25, 1920," he taught German to ten-year-old Raymond Papart, who had not yet passed the eighth grade.

Upholding Meyer's conviction, the Nebraska Supreme Court found that most parents "have never deemed it of importance to teach their children foreign languages." It agreed as well that the teaching of a foreign language was harmful to the health of the young child, whose "daily capacity for learning is comparatively small." Such an argument was consistent with the educational theory of the day, which held as late as the 1950s that bilingualism led to confusion and academic failure, and was harmful to the psychological well-being of the child. Indeed, one psychologist claimed in 1926 that the use of a foreign language in the home was a leading cause of mental retardation. . . .

The US Supreme Court reversed Meyer's conviction in a landmark decision in 1923. But the decision in *Meyer v. Nebraska* was to some extent an empty victory for language teachers: while their calling could no longer be restricted, the ranks of German classes had been devastated by the instant linguistic assimilation that World War I forced on German Americans. In 1915 close to 25 percent of the student population studied German in American high schools. Seven years later only 0.6 percent – fewer than 14,000 high school students – were taking German.

Like German in the Midwest, Spanish was the object of vilification in the American Southwest. This negative attitude toward Spanish delayed statehood for New Mexico for over 60 years. In 1902, in one of New Mexico's many tries for statehood, a congressional subcommittee held hearings in the territory, led by Indiana Senator Albert Jeremiah Beveridge, a "progressive" Republican who believed in "America first! Not only America first, but America only." Witness after witness before the Beveridge subcommittee was forced to admit that in New Mexico, ballots and political speeches were either bilingual or entirely in Spanish; that census takers conducted their surveys in Spanish; that justices of the peace kept records in Spanish; that the courts required translators so that judges and lawyers could understand the many Hispanic witnesses; that juries deliberated in Spanish as much as in English; and that children, who might or might not learn English in schools, as required by law, "relapsed" into Spanish on the playground, at home, and after graduation.

One committee witness suggested that the minority language situation in New Mexico resembled that in Senator Beveridge's home state of Indiana: "Spanish is taught as a side issue, as German would be in any State in the Union. . . . This younger generation understands English as well as I do." And a sympathetic senator reminded his audience, "These people who speak the Spanish language are not foreigners; they are natives, are they not?"

As Franklin did the Germans in Pennsylvania, Senator Beveridge categorized the "Mexicans" of the American Southwest as non-natives, "Unlike us in race, language, and social customs," and concluded that statehood must be contingent on assimilation. He recommended that admission to the

Union be delayed until a time "when the mass of the people, or even a majority of them, shall, in the usages and employment of their daily life, have become identical in language and customs with the great body of the American people; when the immigration of English-speaking people who have been citizens of other States does its modifying work with the 'Mexican' element." Although New Mexico finally achieved its goal of statehood, and managed to write protection of Spanish into its constitution, schools throughout the Southwest forbade the use of Spanish among students. Well into the present century, children were routinely ridiculed and punished for using Spanish both in class and on the playground.

As the New Mexican experience suggests, the insistence on English has never been benign. The notion of a national language sometimes wears the guise of inclusion: we must all speak English to participate meaningfully in the democratic process. Sometimes it argues unity: we must speak one language to understand one another and share both culture and country. Those who insist on English often equate bilingualism with lack of patriotism. Their intention to legislate official English often masks racism and certainly fails to appreciate cultural difference: it is a thinly-veiled measure to disenfranchise anyone not like "us" (with notions of "us," the real Americans, changing over the years from those of English ancestry to northwestern European to "white" monolingual English speakers).

American culture assumes monolingual competence in English. The ability to speak another language is more generally regarded as a liability than a refinement, a curse of ethnicity and a bar to advancement rather than an economic or educational advantage.

In another response to non-English speaking American citizens, during the nineteenth century, states began instituting English literacy requirements for voting to replace older property requirements. These literacy laws generally pretended to democratize the voting process, though their hidden goal was often to prevent specific groups from voting. The first such statutes in Connecticut and Massachusetts were aimed at the Irish population of those states. Southern literacy tests instituted after the Civil War were anti-Black. California's test (1892) was aimed at Hispanics and Asians. Alaska's

in 1926 sought to disenfranchise its Native Americans. Wyoming's (1897) was anti-Finn and Washington state's (1889) was anti-Chinese.

The literacy law proposed for New York State in 1915, whose surface aim was to ensure a well-informed electorate, targeted a number of the state's minorities. It was seen both as a calculated attempt to prevent New York's one million Yiddish speakers from voting and as a means of stopping the state's German Americans from furthering their nefarious war aims. When it was finally enacted in 1921, supporters of the literacy test saw it as a tool to enforce Americanization, while opponents charged the test would keep large numbers of the state's newly enfranchised immigrant women from voting. Later, the law, which was not repealed until the Voting Rights Act of 1965, effectively disenfranchised New York's Puerto Rican community.

Although many Americans simply assume English is the official language of the United States, it is not. Nowhere in the US Constitution is English privileged over other languages, and while a few subsequent federal laws require the use of English for special, limited purposes – air traffic control, product labels, service on federal juries – no law establishes English as the language of the land.

In the xenophobic period following World War I, several moves were made to establish English at the federal level, but none succeeded. On the other hand, many states at that time adopted some form of English-only legislation. This included regulations designating English as the language of state legislatures, courts, and schools, making English a requirement for entrance into such professions as attorney, barber, physician, private detective, or undertaker, and in some states even preventing nonanglophones from obtaining hunting and fishing licenses.

More recently, official language questions have been the subject of state and local debate once again. An English Language Amendment to the US Constitution (the ELA) has been before the Congress every year since 1981. In 1987, the year in which more than 74 percent of California's voters indicated their support for English as the state's official language, thirty-seven states discussed the official English issue. The next year, official language laws were passed in Colorado, Florida, and Arizona. New Mexico and Michigan have taken a stand in favor of English Plus, recommending that everyone have a knowledge of English plus another language. . . .

Official American policy has swung wildly between toleration of languages other than English and their complete eradication. But neither legal protection nor community-based efforts has been able to prevent the decline of minority languages or to slow the adoption of English, particularly among the young. Conversely, neither legislation making English the official language of a state nor the efforts of the schools has done much to enforce the use of English: Americans exhibit a high degree of linguistic anxiety but continue to resist interference with their language use on the part of legislators or teachers.

A number of states have adopted official English. Illinois, for example, in the rush of post-war isolationism and anti-British sentiment, made *American* its official language in 1923; this was quietly changed to English in 1969. Official English in Illinois has been purely symbolic; it is a statute with no teeth and no discernible range or effect. In contrast, Arizona's law . . . required all government officials and employees – from the governor down to the municipal dog catcher – to use English and only English during the performance of government business.

Arizona's law was challenged by Maria-Kelley Yniguez, a state insurance claims administrator fluent in Spanish and English, who had often used Spanish with clients. Yniguez feared that, since she was sworn to uphold the state constitution, speaking Spanish to clients of her agency who knew no other language might put her in legal jeopardy. [In 1990] Arizona's law was ruled unconstitutional by the US District Court for the District of Arizona.

Judge Paul G. Rosenblatt, of the US District Court for the District of Arizona, found that the English-only article 28 of the Arizona constitution violated the First Amendment of the US Constitution protecting free speech. The ruling voiding the Arizona law will not affect the status of other state official English laws. However, it is clear that other courts may take the Arizona decision into consideration.

Perhaps the most sensitive area of minority-language use in the US has been in the schools. Minority-language schools have existed in North America since the 18th century. In the 19th century bilingual education was common in the Midwest – St. Louis and a number of Ohio cities had active English-German public schools – as well as in parochial schools in other areas with large nonanglophone populations. More commonly, though, the schools ignored non-English speaking children altogether, making no curricular or pedagogical concessions to their presence in class. Indeed, newly instituted classroom speech requirements in the early part of this century ensured that anglophone students with foreign accents would be sent to pathologists for corrective action. And professional licensing requirements that included speech certification tests were used to keep Chinese in California and Jews in New York out of the teaching corps.

The great American school myth has us believe that the schools Americanized generations of immigrants, giving them English and, in consequence, the ability to succeed. In fact, in allowing nonanglophone children to sink or swim, the schools ensured that most of them would fail: dropout rates for non-English speakers were extraordinarily high and English was more commonly acquired on the street and playgrounds or on the job than in the classroom.

We tend to think past generations of immigrants succeeded at assimilation while the present generation has (for reasons liberals are willing to explain away) failed. In fact, today's Hispanics are acquiring English and assimilating in much the same way and at the same pace as Germans or Jews or Italians of earlier generations did.

California presented an extreme model for excluding children with no English: it segregated Chinese students into separate "oriental" English-only schools until well into the 20th century. The ending of segregation did little to improve the linguistic fortunes of California's Chinese-speakers, who continued to be ignored by the schools. They were eventually forced to appeal to the Supreme Court to force state authorities to provide for their educational needs. The decision that resulted in the landmark case of *Lau v. Nichols* (1974) did not, however, guarantee minority-language rights, nor did it require bilingual education, as many opponents of bilingual education commonly argue. Instead the Supreme Court ordered schools to provide education for all students whether or not they spoke English, a task our schools are still struggling to carry out.

Confusion over language in the schools seems a major factor behind official language concerns. Bilingual education is a prime target of English-only lobbying groups, who fear it is a device for minority language maintenance rather than for an orderly transition to English. Troubling to teachers as well is the fact that bilingual programs are often poorly defined, underfunded, and inadequately staffed, while parents and students frequently regard bilingual as a euphemism for remedial. In its defense, we can say that second language education did not come into its own in this country until after World War II. Bilingual education, along with other programs designed to teach English as a second language, are really the first attempts by American schools in more than two centuries to deal directly with the problem of non-English speaking children. They represent the first attempts to revise language education in an effort to keep children in school; to keep them from repeating the depressing and wasteful pattern of failure experienced by earlier generations of immigrants and nonanglophone natives; to get them to respect rather than revile both English (frequently perceived as the language of oppression) and their native tongue (all too often rejected as the language of poverty and failure).

Despite resistance to bilingual education and problems with its implementation, the theory behind it remains sound. Children who learn reading, arithmetic, and other subjects in their native language while they are being taught English will not be as likely to fall behind their anglophone peers, and will have little difficulty transferring their subject-matter knowledge to English as their English proficiency increases. On the other hand, when nonanglophone children or those with very limited English are immersed in English-only classrooms and left to sink or swim, as they were for generations, they will continue to fail at unacceptable rates.

Those Americans who fear that unless English is made the official language of the United States by means of federal and state constitutional amendments they are about to be swamped by new waves of non-English speakers should realize that even without restrictive legislation, minority languages in the US have always been marginal. Research shows that Hispanics, who now constitute the nation's largest minority-language group, are adopting English in the second and third generation in the same way that speakers of German, Italian, Yiddish, Russian, Polish, Chinese or Japanese have done in the past. However, as the experience of Hispanics in southern California suggests, simply acquiring English is not bringing the educational and economic successes promised by the melting-pot myth. Linguistic assimilation may simply not be enough to overcome more deep-seated prejudices against Hispanics.

Nonetheless, there are many minority-language speakers in the US, and with continued immigration they will continue to make their presence felt. . . . Even if the courts do not strike down English-only laws, it would be difficult to legislate minority languages out of existence because we simply have no mechanisms in this country to carry out language policy of any kind (schools, which are under local and state control, have been remarkably erratic in the area of language education). On the other hand, even in the absence of restrictive language legislation, American society enforces its own irresistible pressure to keep the United States an English-speaking nation. The Census also reports that 97 percent of Americans identify themselves as speaking English well or very well. English may not be official, but it is definitely here to stay.

. . . English-only legislation, past and present, no matter how idealistic or patriotic its claims, is supported by a long history of nativism, racism, and religious bigotry. While an English Language Amendment to the US Constitution might ultimately prove no more symbolic than the selection of an official bird or flower or fossil, it is possible that the ELA could become a tool for linguistic repression. Those who point to Canada or Belgium or India or the Soviet Union as instances where multilingualism produces civil strife would do well to remember that such strife invariably occurs when minority-language rights are suppressed. In any case, such examples have little in common with the situation in the United States.

The main danger of an ELA, as I see it, would be to alienate minority-language speakers, sabotaging their chances for education and distancing them further from the American mainstream, at the same time hindering rather than facilitating the linguistic assimilation that has occurred so efficiently up to now in the absence of legal prodding.

Late Entry, Early Exit

The author supports the idea of enabling people to be bilingual and bicultural, but he is not certain that bilingual education has proven to be the best way to achieve that goal. He discusses some issues related to how we determine bilingual competence, and concludes with an example of a school that succeeded in achieving this goal.

"When I went to the first grade," Awilda Orta said, "I had a vision that the room was split. There were no lights on my side of the room. I sat in darkness. Many years later, I went back to visit the nuns, and I saw the room again. On the side where I sat, there were floor-to-ceiling windows; the room was bathed in light. I realize then that I felt myself in darkness, because I spoke no English."

Sylvia Sasson (Shorris), who entered school speaking some English, was the only child with a Spanish surname in her class. "I remember the sound of the other children's names," she said. "I was so different. The lunches my grandmother fixed for me were an embarrassment. I never got peanut butter and jelly like the other kids. For a while, I wanted to be anything but Spanish; at one time I thought of telling people I was Estonian." . . . Every morning, before going to school, she was sick.

Submersion, the method of learning a language endured by Sylvia, has generally been the American experience. At various times during the history of immigration, the submersion method has been replaced by a less traumatic variant known as the immersion method. In both methods classroom in-struction is entirely in English, but in the immersion method all of the children come to class speaking only a foreign language.

Immersion uses the coercive value of the peer group; submersion depends on shame. In the submersion method children learn to devalue their culture as well as their language. Sylvia wanted only to be named O'Brien or Goldberg or Perini, like the other children in her class. Awilda Orta prayed to be in the light. Richard Rodriguez, whose autobiography, *Hunger of Memory*, can be read as the experience of submersion writ large, wished to shed the "private" language of his home and family for a "public" language and the life that accompanied it. . . .

How to learn a new language and adopt a new culture would seem to be a thoroughly understood process in a country often described as a nation of immigrants. It is not. On the contrary, as observers from Tocqueville to the present have noted, a state lacking in some of the qualities of a nation over-compensates for its youth and diversity by requiring the highest degree of conformity from all of its citizens. During its relatively brief history the United States has shown varying degrees of acceptance of foreign-language speakers. Until the last decade of the nineteenth century most states permitted private "nationality" schools, which carried out what are now know as maintenance programs in languages other than English. Ten years later, most states had outlawed such schools. During World

War I, nationalistic and patriotic feeling led to legal xenophobia: A town in Ohio fined people twenty-five dollars for speaking German in public. Not until 1923 did the Supreme Court strike down laws prohibiting private schools from teaching in languages other than English. Even so, children were forbidden to speak Spanish in the classroom or the schoolyard in the Southwest for most of the twentieth century.

The Bilingual Education Act was passed in 1968 and strengthened and clarified by amendments in 1974 and 1978. Its survival was assured by the *Lau v. Nichols* decision of the Supreme Court in 1974, which held that under the provisions of the Civil Rights Act of 1964 children who could not understand the language in which they were being taught were not offered equal education. Yet by the end of 1980, the law that made Spanish, as well as English, an official language of Dade County, Florida, was voted out, and in the realm of commerce, the federal courts had upheld a ruling that an employer could prohibit the use of a foreign language in the workplace. As the Latino population increased and bilingual instruction became more widespread, the Reagan administration cut funding for bilingual programs and English-only laws were passed in sixteen states, including Florida and California.

For most of its history the United States has feared bilingualism and biculturalism as impediments to the forging of a nation. Assimilation or destruction have generally been the choices offered to those who differed from the majority. The brutality inherent in democracy made it so. And the Constitution, which has served well in mitigating the dangers of raw democracy in most areas, has few explicit views on culture. On such matters as an official language, for example, the intentions of the framers must be discerned from their omissions. With interpretation left to the Congress and the courts, the effect of the Constitution on pluralism has been less consistent and less salutary than one might have hoped for. Only during brief peaks of liberal toleration have the pluralistic implications of the Constitution been allowed to moderate the nation's politics.

As a rule, the educational arguments for and against bilingualism have been less important than the general willingness in the nation to tolerate the eccentricity of a second language and a nonstan-dard culture. Economics have almost always been the determining factor. The Depression years, when as many as a million people of Mexican descent were deported, had a devastating effect on biculturalism in the United States. Spanish-language theaters, newspapers, and publishing houses closed. Hard times produced xenophobia and exacerbated racism; Latinos, being both racially and culturally different, were easy targets. The desire then among Latinos for racial, cultural, and linguistic assimilation was overwhelming. Everyone wanted to be re-born in the melting pot; in a troubled democracy, it was the only safe response to xenophobia. . . .

In retrospect, the melting pot theory was coercive, illiberal in the extreme, but probably a necessary part of creating a nation in the unique circumstances of the United States. Whether a stable political and economic union could have been made of a population Balkanized by language and culture is an academic question; one theory serves as well as the next. . . .

No educational method so perfectly mirrors the experience of the melting pot as submersion; it is the street of strangers brought into the school. After two weeks in the barrio, an eleven-year-old girl from Ecuador described New York as *frío y corrumpido*, and she made it clear that the cold and corruption did not end when she entered the schoolroom. Merely to survive physically the submerged student must learn to communicate; otherwise, she may never find the lunchroom or the bathroom. But elemental communication is one thing, education by submersion another; the student can get through the educational system without learning and can even succeed by manipulating the definition of success.

The choice of how to respond to the new environment must be made quickly. In the first days and months of school the submerged student is faced with making or accepting a series of definitions and then making decisions about them. The pressure is terrible, for it is mostly negative, a demand to rebel against the newly imposed culture, yet the children know that they cannot do well in the world either by maintaining their old culture or by adopting the culture of rebellion. The conflict leaves some of them paralyzed, mute in the classroom, raging in the schoolyard. I have heard many teachers describe these children as "the dead."

Although submersion seems a murderous system, examples of survival and success run into the millions. The economic and intellectual prowess of the United States, it could be argued, is a direct result of the effectiveness of the submersion method of education. Of the three children described at the beginning, all of whom had difficult submersion experiences, none failed. Sylvia Sasson, who fared badly in the early grades, won the English prize by the time she graduated from a prestigious high school and became a published writer in English. Awilda Orta, who sat in the emotional dark, became a brilliant teacher and educational administrator. Richard Rodriguez went on to earn a Ph.D. in Renaissance literature and to write an autobiography so preciously English it used single quote marks in the British style.

One factor common to all three is their facility for language. They are astonishingly verbal people and almost equally at home speaking or writing. Sasson and Orta are bilingual; only Rodriguez does not speak Spanish. Perhaps their natural ability enabled them to overcome the trauma of abruptly converting to a new language. Perhaps it was the schools they attended that brought them through. Orta and Rodriguez both went to Catholic schools; Sasson attended a girls' high school noted for its rigorous academic program. Perhaps they are merely anomalies.

On the other hand, if the sampling were done at a prison in New York or Texas or California, the conclusions would be very different. Most pintos (prisoners) did not have successful school careers. . . . The curious thing about ex-pintos is that they are not comfortable either in English or standard Spanish; they speak Caló, which has a vocabulary of between a thousand and fifteen hundred words and is used in conjunction with standard and non-standard English and Spanish. . . .

In the end, submersion performs a kind of social triage. Enough succeed to keep the method from being thrown out, but most fail, enabling the majority, who control the educational system, to maintain their social and economic advantages. Submersion functions like a sieve, which can be made coarse or fine by adding or subtracting such things as ESL classes, counseling programs, and orientation classes.

Submersion, which is a spur to the few, is too cruel for the many. The Chinese, French, Germans, Jews, Poles, Russians, and Scandinavians of earlier times knew enough to save their children with schools and newspapers in their own languages, ethnic clubs, religious clubs, anything they could do to mitigate the Darwinian cruelty of the submersion system. Since the passage of the Bilingual Education Act, public schools in the United States have been attempting to help children with limited English proficiency (LEP) learn to listen, speak, read, and write in a new language in the most efficient way. But so far, bilingual education has not, of itself, solved the educational problems of Latino children. If submersion caused them to fail, bilingual education has not caused them to succeed.

Meanwhile, more Latino children enter kindergarten and fewer finish high school. And the country, which once embraced men and women who could work with their hands and arms, wants people who can use their minds; (the) immigration law passed in 1990 makes provision for people with skills to enter the country on a priority basis. The immigrants of the early part of the twentieth century, who could grunt or nod while they attached themselves to machines, levers, tools, whatever needed the strength of an arm and a human reflex to operate it, lived to enjoy union wages without adopting much of the new language or culture. It is not so easy now. The Latino population is burgeoning at a difficult time. Too many Latinos have no English when a little English is not enough.

So far, no one has produced the one study that proves now and forever whether bilingual education works. The studies are inconclusive, in part, because they do not adequately define the goal of bilingual education. . . .

The minimum definition of bilingualism is to be able to listen to someone speaking another language and understand what the speaker is saying. Such a definition, however, might mean that understanding kitchen Spanish makes one bilingual. Maybe speaking is a better skill to use as a minimum, but speaking about what? lunch? love? logarithms? literature? The quality and complexity of the conversation will have to be considered. Or should one be required to read and write two languages in order to be considered bilingual? And if so, how well? As well as Conrad? And didn't Conrad speak with a heavy Polish accent?

The most demanding definition insists that one be accepted as a native in speaking, listening, reading, and writing two languages. The *Oxford English Dictionary,* in the supplement published in 1987, states that bilingualism is the "ability to speak two languages; the habitual use of two languages colloquially." Assuming that either of the two definitions in the *OED* is acceptable and that the failure even to hint at standards of literacy betrays carelessness and not despair, is bilingualism the goal of bilingual education? Or is the goal to convert children to monolingual English speakers?

Before addressing the social and political goals of bilingual education, the question of how people learn two languages and how they think after they have learned a second language needs to be considered. If educating people to have the ability to speak two languages is relatively easy and not harmful to their thinking in either language, that goal would appear to be a good one.

But what if speaking, listening, reading and writing two languages fluently leads people to think more slowly, to have just a little bit less facility than they might have had with only one language? Research can be found to prove the "jack of all trades, master of none" theory of language acquisition. And there is an enormous amount of research proving that bilingual education lowers performance (test scores) in English.

Unfortunately, every statement about bilingualism and bilingual education requires an "on the other hand." For every paper proving the "jack of all trades" theory, there is another defending the notion that whoever doesn't know two languages doesn't know one. When the two sides meet, . . . most of the argument focuses on statistics, and the best anyone seems to be able to say about the statistics is that they "suggest" something or other. Nobody is quite sure what. As Jim Cummins wrote in *Bilingualism in Education,* "It is clear, then that there is little consensus as to the exact meaning of the term bilingualism, and that it has been used to refer to a wide variety of phenomena. Research associated with bilingualism reflects this semantic confusion. It is essential, therefore, in reconciling contradictory results associated with bilingualism . . ."

Meanwhile, the question of the goal of bilingual education remains unresolved. All Latino parents want their children to learn English, and all proponents of bilingual education agree that in the end the children must be able to speak, listen, read, and write in English. The survival of English is not at issue, only the death of Spanish. With the question unresolved, the monolingual Spanish-speaking student entering school in the United States participates in a linguistic lottery: Depending on which public school, even which class, the child attends, he or she may encounter a method ranging from instruction entirely in Spanish to one in which the teachers and students do not use any language but English.

The tragic aspect of this lottery is that the number of losers far exceeds the number of winners; for Latinos, especially those who enter school speaking no English, the educational system is not a good bet. Optimists put the dropout rate for all Latino children in the U.S. at 35.8 percent. Realists think the national rate is over 40 percent. . . .

There is no standard by which the education of Latino children in the United States can be considered adequate, fair, or morally acceptable. If one of the goals of the Bilingual Education Act was to educate Spanish-speaking children as well as English-speaking white or black children, the act has failed. If the goal was to improve the education of Latino and other language-minority children, there is still not much evidence to support its success. . . .

The issue of who is an educated adult has been discussed widely in the United States, but when it comes to children, a few standardized tests are thought to be enough. Rarely, if ever, is the moral character of the child considered part of his education. Rarely does anyone ask what happens to the values of one culture when that culture is denigrated by the teaching of a new one. A superbly educated Latino professional man said to me about his parents, "They speak broken English," but it did not occur to him to add that they speak beautiful Spanish. In America, the old culture dies easily; the tragedy . . . is that it is replaced with drugs, violence and rock and roll.

The late nineteenth- and early twentieth-century schools set up by the Germans, Italians, Jews, Norwegians, Poles, and Swedes and the more recent schools run by the Chinese and Japanese have endeavored to help their students retain the old culture as much or more than the language. The founders of those schools, many of whom were tied to the religious center of the community, feared the new or different or modern morality, which they understood as no morality at all. In many instances the conservation of values undoubtedly led to serious emotional conflict. The literature of the early part of the twentieth century is filled with such cases. Writers from Dreiser to Fitzgerald to Roth told stories of the clash of cultures.

Now the clash is different, no longer between opposing sets of values but between values and the violent vacuum. The substitute for culture presented to newcomers was invented at the conjunction of entertainment and advertising; it may still be called culture, but neither Rambo nor Madonna has the character required to get a troubled child through the night. If submersion, which sets out to destroy every vestige of the old language and culture, is to be supplanted, bilingual education will have to offer something beyond words, or it will be no more than a mask to hide the old method.

The nature of the beginning, Spanish or English, bilingualism or submersion, early exit (transition) or late exit (maintenance), will determine how children understand school. If it is a place of failure and ridicule rather than comfort and hope, the child may choose to play dead. . . .

. . . When the home language is different from the school language and the home language tends to be denigrated by others . . . , it would appear appropriate to begin initial instruction in the child's first language, switching at a later stage to instruction in the school language.
. . . Where the home language is a majority language valued by the community . . . then the most efficient means of promoting an additive form of bilingualism is to provide initial instruction in the second language.

Jim Cummins, *Bilingualism in Education*

The Bilingual Education Act, even with a tuck taken here and there to make it fit the politics of the interested, does not deal with the problem of the death of the Spanish language. This death hides behind the myth of the Promethean immigrant who bears his language in a basket, another treasure hidden among his few belongings. It is only a myth, no more than that, yet it has sustained the faith of those who love the sound and soul of Spanish. In reality, many Latinos now speak Spanish only to their parents or grandparents, if at all. Most newcomers live in the worst of the social and economic world, where the only middle-class Latinos they have contact with are shopkeepers or the grim officials who try to keep order among the crowds at the bottom of the social scale. To depend on continuing waves or newcomers, many of whom speak ungrammatically, using the tiniest vocabulary, is to ensure the death of the language. Third or fourth generation Latinos who live in suburbs of Minneapolis or Atlanta have no more reason to know Spanish than Polish-Americans need to know Polish or German-Americans to know German.

Spanish probably would go the way of French, German, and Italian in the United States, unless one thinks of it rather than English as the lingua franca of the hemisphere. And that is where the practical, political, and economic difference lies. Miami was the first city to make a business decision to maintain Spanish. So much of the city, its banking and export sectors, is concerned with Latin America that Spanish has become the preferred language of business. Everyone speaks English, of course, but it lacks the comfort of Spanish; it is not at home in Panama or Peru.

Latino businessmen in Texas, New York, California, and Illinois make the same argument. And if the hemisphere is declared a free trade zone . . . the practical value of Spanish will increase tenfold or a hundredfold or more.

In the battle between maintenance and transition, late and early exit from bilingual programs, the emotional issues of nationalism and the arguments for cultural enrichment may eventually give way to the business proposition expressed at Coral Way Elementary: People who know two languages have a better chance of getting ahead in life. If that is so, however, why should Anglos be denied the opportunity to succeed? Shouldn't bilingual education at the maintenance level be available to everyone who wants it? Wouldn't that begin to overcome some of the deficiencies in U.S. culture? Wouldn't that make the United States a more formidable competitor in the world?

Children in Latino neighborhoods could all learn Spanish as well as English. Where the Chinese language is strong, they could learn both Chinese and English, and so on. In larger cities, with several ethnic populations, children or their parents might be permitted to choose between many languages. Cummins explains exactly where to begin for both

Anglo and Latino children. His method is not radical, but practical, the homely logic of a man hoping to avoid the wars of chauvinism.

Coral Way Elementary School in Miami put Cummins's notions into practice. In bilingual schools the Anglos learn Spanish as a second language, attending special immersion classes from the earliest grades, just as their Latino counterparts attend immersion ESL classes. Before long, all the children are fluent in both English and Spanish. To continue the process after the elementary grades, high school students may take courses in Spanish after school for extra credit. If they do well in both their English and Spanish studies, those who take the extra courses are awarded a second diploma from a high school in Spain.

It is not a sentimental system; Dade County doesn't operate that way. Nor is it racist or ethnocentric. The method grew out of a sense of the equality of languages, cultures, and economic capabilities. It worked. Whether it will continue to work will be the test. When the federal government first provided money for a bilingual program at Coral Way Elementary in Little Havana in 1963, the students were the children of middle- and upper middle-class Cuban exiles. They arrived with great facility in Spanish, most of which was easily transferable to English. Many of the Cubans have moved away now. The newest immigrants are poor people who fled the war in Nicaragua or the death squads in Guatemala and El Salvador. . . .

The Spanish-speaking teachers and the administrators at Coral Way Elementary are still Cuban, and their methods have not changed. They still believe that the maintenance of two languages is the proper form of bilingual education. It is still the culture of the school that accommodates the child, rather than attempting to force the child to learn in an alien environment. Only the students are different. Some of them come to school not knowing how to hold a pencil, never having touched a book, speaking only rudimentary Spanish, emotionally wounded by the experiences of war or drug addiction. This new cohort stands in terrible contrast to its predecessor, as if in one famous bilingual public school a test of the relative importance of school and home had been devised and the lives of the children had been committed to it.

Unfortunately, many of the children who do not learn Spanish well do not become proficient in English either. The failure of schools to teach English to Latino children by any method – submersion, immersion, transition, or maintenance – is so common in the United States that almost every successful Latino in business or the professions attributes part of his or her success to the ability to read, write, and speak English, a set of skills that second-generation European-Americans took for granted. Their view of the basis for success emphasizes the true horror of the education of Latinos in the United States: The system destroys one language, but does not replace it with another, creating a great class of mutes, victims who cannot even speak of their pain.

Maintaining Bilingualism and Cultural Awareness

When Carlos Cortez went to school as a child, he was told to speak only in English, so he lost the ability to speak Spanish. Later he enrolled in college, where he was told that he should learn another language because it was good to be bilingual. He wondered why his teachers did not recognize this in elementary school. This author describes the efforts of several families who understand that it is valuable to be both bilingual and bicultural, and relates how they are helping their children achieve both goals.

Much research has been conducted on language attrition, the diminution of bilingualism across time, and the fact that within three generations of migrating to the United States the native language is eliminated.[1] A conflicting view of this reality is often cited by English Only advocates who are concerned about cultural assimilation.

US English, an offshoot of the Federation for American Immigration Reform, promotes tighter restrictions on immigration, organized around the supposed need to establish English as the official language in the United States. Their efforts are based on the misconception that recent immigrants are indifferent toward learning English and that the use of English is threatened by the sheer numbers of speakers of other languages. In fact, nothing could be farther from the truth. Spanish speaking immigrants, for instance, are known to convert to English after residing for a number of years in the United States, with each successive generation shifting more and more in that direction.[2] In this monolingual context, institutionalized efforts toward maintaining a dual language facility among youth are often actually nothing more than programs which help to make the transition to English.[3]

For this study, I focused on a small group of highly educated Chicano parents and their attempts to secure bilingualism for their children. . . . Six of the seven Chicano families in Southern California that participated in this study indicated that Spanish was the native language of the children. . . .

These parents made a conscious effort to create a bilingual environment during their children's early childhood years. For example, if the mother worked outside the home, the parents provided either a Spanish-speaking nanny, grandmother, or another member of the extended family to care for the children during the day. Thus, thirteen of the seventeen children were native Spanish speakers and all of them had contact with grandparents and extended family. These children also had exposure to English through formal preschool experience as well as informal experiences and interaction with bilingual members of the extended family, friends, in the neighborhood, television and so on. . . .

In the Sánchez family, mother and father acknowledged that at family functions, the children's interactions were limited to Spanish with grandparents and other adults, and English with their peers.

Q: ¿Con quién hablan inglés?
[With whom do they speak English?]

T: Con los amigos de la escuela.
[With their friends from school.]

F: En la escuela, con nosotros, con sus primos.
[In school, with us, with their cousins.]

T: Sí con sus primos, puro inglés.
[Yes, with their cousins, only in English.]

F: Mis sobrinos no hablan español.
[My nieces and nephews do not speak Spanish.]

As the children began to acquire a second language, it became apparent that the forces outside of the home were strong. Even for three-year-old Analisa, who had no formal preschool experience of English instruction, both parents had become aware of her preference for English and were consciously striving to maintain Spanish as a means of communication in the home.

Q: Y la niña, ¿siempre habla español o inglés?
[And the child, does she always speak Spanish or English?]

J: Ahora, el inglés es el idioma preferido de ella. Sí puede hablar español. Sí entiende todo, pero . . .
[Now, English is her preferred language. She can speak Spanish. She understands everything, but . . .] . . .

As the children got older the tendency to speak English was stronger. Yet the Sánchez children, Maya and Jojo, spoke only Spanish to the baby, but the parents had to remind the children to respond in Spanish when they spoke to them.

Q: Los ninos hablan español o inglés?
[Do the children speak Spanish or English?]

F: Entre ellos mismos, inglés.
[Between themselves, English.]

A: Y con Uds?
[And with your parents?]

F: Si los acordamos que tiene que ser español, hablan español, si no, haablan . . .
Pero al niño, al bebe le hablan español, los dos.
[If we remind them that it has to be Spanish, they speak Spanish, if not, they speak . . .
But to the baby, to the baby they speak in Spanish, both of them.]

Thus, while Spanish was spoken in the home and appeared to be the native language of the children, it was used through the children's infancy and early childhood years by all members of the family.

According to six of the seven sets of parents, the intrusion of English began at the preschool age. As the children began their formal schooling, the emphasis on English presented a dilemma for these parents who were struggling to provide a bilingual atmosphere and maintain Spanish in the home. . . .

Two parents spoke of their children's inclination to speak more English and less Spanish. Bertha and Francisca said their children were native Spanish speakers until they began school. By the time they reached ages eight and ten, English had become their dominant language. This shift was attributed to the fact that Spanish has predominantly informal and oral functions while English has formal and academic functions. . . .

Early in this study, two families (Reyes/Fuentes and Sánchez) with preschool age children stated that they were seeking bilingual preschools, while the Carrera family decided to move to a more "bilingual" neighborhood in order for their children to hear Spanish in their environment. These families researched the availability of bilingual preschool programs and found that the emphasis was on teaching English as a second language rather than development of the native language in a bilingual environment.

H: Esas, estamos buscando uno. Per todavía no hallamos un lugar que podemos decir que va ir allí. Sí queremos un programa que enseña inglés y español.

[Those, we're looking for one. But we still haven't found a place that we can say that she's going to. We do want a program that teaches English and Spanish.]

J: No hay programa bilingüe aquí, programas bilingües aquí. Sí hay, pues no, no son. Como Head Start, esos no son bilingües. Son para que ellos aprenden inglés.

[There isn't a bilingual program here. There are, but no, they're not. Like Head Start, they're not bilingual. They're for them to learn English.]

Although her parents continued to search for a bilingual program until Analisa was four years old, they didn't consider those available to be true bilingualism, rather they were to transition to English.

While the Reyes/Fuentes family contemplated the possibility of living in a Spanish-speaking country in order for Analisa to develop her bilingualism and become biliterate, and the Sanchez family considered enrolling the children in a Mexican school in order to develop literacy skills in Spanish, the Carrera family had in fact lived in Mexico for two years. As Carla was beginning kindergarten, Jorge was entering second grade, and Tino was approaching junior high school, the family decided to enroll the children in Mexican schools to read in Spanish before returning to the United States and continuing their education. . . .

When they returned to the United States at midyear, Carla was placed in an "English-only" first-grade class because there was no bilingual program in the neighborhood school. In second and third grades, however, she was placed in a bilingual program and transitioned to English in fourth grade. Jorge, who had been in bilingual kindergarten and first grade in the United States, continued his Spanish instruction in Mexico for grades two and three, and was placed in an "English only" fourth grade on his return. Although Tino had also been enrolled in the Mexican schools, he had never been in a bilingual program in the United States and continued his high school education in the regular English program. Thus, both Carla and Jorge were transferred to all English classes by fourth grade. This placement corresponded to the transitional type of bilingual programs in the United States which em-

phasized transition to English rather than the development of true bilingualism.

The importance of bilingualism and biliteracy is a dilemma for parents who seek to maintain and develop the native language of their children with little support from society and educational institutions. Thus, the learning and development of Spanish as well as English, and becoming biliterate, are considered important goals of these families. . . .

None of the parents stated that they believe that their children must reject their native language and culture in order to succeed. On the contrary, they emphasized the belief that their children need to become bilingual, biliterate, and bicultural in order to succeed in the United States. All of the parents declared their rationale for maintaining bilingualism as instrumental and utilitarian, in that it was necessary in order to converse with the grandparents and other monolingual Spanish-speaking relatives. As Javier put it:

J: … por la razón de que vivimos en una area predominantemente bilingüe y a parte de eso también por la cuestión de que muchos de nuestros familiares todavía hablan español primeramente.

[. . . because we live in a predominantly bilingual area and besides that also because many of our relatives are still native Spanish speakers.]

Although they use Spanish in the home and in their work, these parents found that it is difficult to maintain bilingualism in their children. Those who sought bilingual preschools for their children were unsuccessful. In fact, the parents discovered that rather than working to develop and strengthen the children's native language, most of the preschools, like the elementary schools, emphasize ESL instruction and treat the bilingual child as requiring remedial education. Thus, these parents found it necessary to prepare their children for preschool by either keeping their children at home in a predominantly Spanish environment until about age four, while gradually increasing the use of English at home and providing a familiar bilingual environment until the child could accommodate to an all-English setting. Those parents who sent their first child to preschool or Head Start were discouraged by the emphasis on English.

In retrospect, the parents consider problems the children had in school a result of not having fully developed their linguistic and academic foundation in the native language. Other parents provided what they felt was a strong foundation in Spanish, preparing their children with "readiness" concepts and an awareness that instruction would be conducted in English. In addition, five of the seven families had researched the preschool and elementary schools before enrolling their children, so that while they may not have been able to fulfill a bilingual need, they also sought schools which would provide a positive, creative, affective, and nurturing learning environment. . . .

While the schools emphasize transition to English, these parents have sought other means of encouraging and developing their children's bilingualism. In addition to encouraging academic success in English, the parents have also provided interaction in Spanish at home, as well as with grandparents and other Spanish-speaking adults. These parents and their associates also serve as models of educated and bilingual professionals. They work in occupations in which knowledge of Spanish is regarded as an asset, for example, the legal profession, education, and in community or social service agencies. Thus, the children are in contact with positive role models who acknowledge their bilingualism and culture as resources and qualities of which they are proud.

In addition to the home environment and extended family, the parents also provided extracurricular activities for the children which promote and encourage the use of Spanish for cultural activities – music, dance, arts, and sports. These organized activities provide opportunities for the children to participate and interact in Spanish with other bilingual children and families.

All parents and children are involved in the teaching and learning of culture. These children, because of their interaction with their parents, extended families, friends, and classmates, were also becoming bicultural. Their parents consciously selected various cultural experiences, some of which were more mainstream, others more Chicano or Mexican, and all of which the parents believe are important for the child, for example, . . . activities

such as soccer, San Diego/Tijuana children's choir and folkloric dance. . . .

In addition to these organized activities, . . . the families also participated in social functions and cultural traditions such as weddings, baptisms, birthday parties, and family gatherings which provided much of their children's social and cultural experiences. . . . The children were also involved in numerous cultural and social activities in the Chicano community such as Hispanic Future Leaders workshops and summer programs for teens; community cultural celebrations of Mexican holidays; music appreciation and familiarity of Mexican music; as well as daily preparation of traditional foods.

Recognizing the realities of schooling in the United States, the children have become English-dominant in order to succeed in school. Yet they have also been able to maintain and use Spanish. . . . Like their parents who consider themselves bicultural, the children are developing a cultural awareness and identity as Mexican or Chicano in contrast to some members of their extended families who not only lose Spanish language skills, but also desire to assimilate into the mainstream society. . . .

For example, fifteen-year old Florencia related a story about an incident with a high school counselor in which she and a cousin were counseled to take an "easy class" rather than a college preparatory course. Florencia decided for herself which course she needed in order to satisfy college admission requirements and proceeded to counsel her cousin. However, the counselor directed her to leave the office and her cousin was made to stay alone with the advisor. Florencia interpreted the "guidance" of the counselor as discriminatory based on their surnames rather than academic achievement or potential.

Another example of the children's awareness of cultural identity was that of Jose Antonio. When he was twelve years old, a number of children at his school were interviewed to participate in the filming of an educational program on early California history. Jose correctly determined that the interviewer was looking for someone to play the part of the child/narrator. Thus, he offered information about his family, his knowledge of Spanish and English, and demonstrated pride in his Mexican heritage. He was selected as the narrator of the program.

Most of these children had experienced discrimination and prejudice, and they were able to identify social injustice as institutional and not only affecting themselves as individuals but all others with whom they identified. For example, in seventh grade, Jorge wrote an autobiography in which he discussed his personal struggle to maintain a high academic standing as it conflicted with peer pressure and his personal need for group membership. . . .

The parents in this study are clearly extraordinary in their goals of maintaining bilingualism and cultural identity. In a society where one language, English, has more prestige than another, and where "success" is judged in terms of attaining proficiency in that language as a means of assimilating to the mainstream culture, these parents have taken extreme steps in their efforts to maintain their language and culture. . . . When one considers the fact that, in general, the native language is eliminated within three generations of migrating to the United States, these second-and third-generation parents are working against all odds to provide a bilingual environment for their children. . . .

In spite of these efforts to make Spanish the native language of the children, and creating an environment in which the children would be encouraged to become bilingual, all of these children were sensitive to the outside forces which emphasize the dominance of English in the society. Thus, once they became enrolled in school . . . they quickly became English-dominant. Although most of the children have not developed Spanish academically, that is, literacy in Spanish, they have maintained oral proficiency in Spanish. . . .

The children's early exposure to Mexican and Chicano practices and activities provided positive experiences in the Chicano community and enabled the children to identify themselves as members of the community. Thus, as the children grew,

they began to voice their cultural awareness and identify with the community in a positive way. The children had a positive attitude about their cultural identity. Their cultural pride and self-esteem was evident by the way in which they identified others as lacking "the culture," the way in which they volunteered to demonstrate their knowledge of their heritage to strangers, and their awareness of social issues, such as discrimination and inequality, which affect the community as a whole as well as themselves as students. . . .

Because these children have been able to maintain Spanish, develop a cultural awareness and identity, while at the same time developing an awareness of larger social issues, they have also set goals for themselves. Their parents, as the first generation to attend college, did not consider themselves prepared for college. However, these children have been prepared by their parents to expect to attend college, to carry on the legacy of a committed and concerned Chicano with a goal to create social change. . . . Their goals and efforts toward maintaining bilingualism illustrate a consciousness of identity, one that is successful in two languages and two cultural environments.

Notes

[1]Irene Villanueva, The voices of Chicano families: Life stories, maintaining bilingualism, and cultural awareness. In M. Seller and L. Weis (Eds.) *Beyond black and white: New faces and voices in U.S. schools.* (Albany, NY: State University of New York Press, 1997), pp. 61–79.

[2]C. Veltman, *The future of the Spanish language in the United States* (Washington D.C.: Hispanic Policy Development Project, 1988); R. Sánchez, *Chicano discourse: Socio-historic perspectives.* (Rowley, MA: Newbury House, 1983).

[3]K. Hakuta, *Mirror of language: The debate on bilingualism.* (New York: Basic Books, Inc., 1982).

Oral Traditions

Although people may share the same language, learning to communicate is not always the same process with the same outcome. A team of ethnographic researchers studied two rural communities in the Piedmont area of the Carolinas. "Roadville" was populated by low-income white families; "Trackton" had low-income black families. Both relied on a local mill for employment. In the following excerpts, the author describes differences between how children in these communities learned to communicate, and the implications of this learning when the children entered elementary school.

Roadville: A piece of truth

Roadville residents worry about many things. Yet no Roadville home is a somber place where folks spend all their time worrying about money, their children's futures, and their fate at the hands of the mill. They create numerous occasions for celebration, most often with family members and church friends. On these occasions, they regale each other with "stories." To an outsider, these stories seem as though they should be embarrassing, even insulting to people present. It is difficult for the outsider to learn when to laugh, for Roadville people seem to laugh at the story's central character, usually the story-teller or someone else who is present.

A "story" in Roadville is: "something you tell on yourself, or on your buddy, you know, it's all in good fun, and a li'l something to laugh about." Though this definition was given by a male, women define their stories in similar ways, stressing they are "good fun," and "don't mean no harm." Stories recount an actual event either witnessed by others

or previously told in the presence of others and declared by them "a good story." Roadville residents recognize the purpose of the stories is to make people laugh by making fun of either the story-teller or a close friend in sharing an event and the particular actions of individuals within that event. However, stories "told on" someone other than the story-teller are never told unless the central character or someone who is clearly designated his representative is present. The Dee children sometimes tell stories on their father who died shortly after the family moved to Roadville, but they do so only in Mrs. Dee's presence with numerous positive adjectives describing their father's gruff nature. Rob Macken, on occasion, is the dominant character in stories which make fun of his ever-present willingness to point out where other folks are wrong. But Rob is always present on these occasions and he is clearly included in the telling ("Ain't that right, Rob?" "Now you know that's the truth, hain't it?"), as story-tellers cautiously move through their talk about him, gauging how far to go by his response to the story.

Outside close family groups, stories are told only in sex-segregated groups. Women invite stories of other women, men regale each other with tales of their escapades on hunting and fishing trips, or their run-ins (quarrels) with their wives and children. Topics for women's stories are exploits in cooking, shopping, adventures at the beauty shop, bingo games, the local amusement park, their gardens, and sometimes events in their children's lives. Topics for men are big-fishing expeditions, escapades of their hunting dogs, times they have made fools of themselves, and exploits in particular areas of their expertise (gardening and raising a 90-lb pumpkin, a 30-lb cabbage, etc.). If a story is told to an initial audience and declared a good story on that occasion, this audience (or others who hear about the story) can then invite the story-teller to retell the story to yet other audiences. Thus, an invitation to tell a story is usually necessary. Stories are often requested with a question: "Has Betty burned any biscuits lately?" "Brought any possums home lately?" Marked behavior – transgressions from the behavioral norm generally expected of a "good hunter," "good cook," "good handyman," or a "good Christian" – is the usual focus of the story. The foolishness in the tale is a piece of truth about everyone present and all join in a mutual laugh at not only the story's central character, but at themselves as well. One story triggers another, as person after person reaffirms a familiarity with the kind of experience just recounted. Such stories test publicly the strength of relationships and openly declare bonds of kinship and friendship, with no "hard feelings." Only rarely, and then generally under the influence of alcohol or the strain of a test in the relationship from another source (job competition, an unpaid load), does a story-telling become the occasion for an open expression of hostility.

Common experience in events similar to those of the story becomes an expression of social unity, a commitment to maintenance of the norms of the church and of the roles within the mill community's life. In telling a story, an individual shows that he belongs to the group: he knows about either himself or the subject of the story, and he understands the norms which were broken by the story's central character. Oldtimers, especially those who came to Roadville in the 1930s, frequently assert their long familiarity with certain norms as they tell stories on the young folks and on those members of their own family who moved away. There is always an unspoken understanding that some experiences common to the oldtimers can never be known by the young folks, yet they have benefited from the lessons and values these experiences enabled their parents to pass on to them.

In any social gathering, either the story-teller who himself announces he has a story or the individual who invites another to tell a story is, for the moment, in control of the entire group. He manages the flow of talk, the staging of the story, and dictates the topic to which all will adhere in at least those portions of their discourse which immediately follow the story-telling. . . .

Perhaps the most obligatory convention . . . is that which requires a Roadville story to have a moral or summary message which highlights the weakness admitted in the talk. "Stories" in these settings are similar to testimonials given at revival meetings and prayer sessions. On these occasions, individuals are invited to give a testimonial or to "tell your story." These narratives are characterized by a factual detailing of temporal and spatial descriptions and recounting on conversations by direct quotation ("Then the Lord said to me:"). Such testimonials frequently have to do with "bringing a young man to his senses" and having received answers to specific prayers. The detailing of the actual event is often finished off with Scriptural quotation, making it clear that the story bears out the promise of "the Word.". . .

In Trackton: Talkin' junk

Trackton folks see truth and the facts in stories in ways which differ greatly from those of Roadville. Good story-tellers in Trackton may base their stories on an actual event, but they creatively fictionalize the details surrounding the real event, and the outcome of the story may not even resemble what indeed happened. The best stories are "junk," and anyone who can "talk junk" is a good story-teller. Talkin' junk includes laying on highly exaggerated compliments and making wildly exaggerated comparisons as well as telling narratives. Straightforward factual accounts are relatively rare in Trackton and are usually told only on serious occasions: to give a specific piece of information to someone who has requested it, to provide an account of the troubles of a highly respected individual, or to exchange information about daily rounds of activities when neither party wishes to intensify the interaction or draw it out. Trackton's "stories," on the other hand, are intended to intensify social interactions and to give all parties an opportunity to share in not only the unity of the common experience on which the story may be based, but also in the humor of the wide-ranging language play and imagination which embellish the narrative.

From a very early age, Trackton children learn to appreciate the value of a good story for capturing an audience's attention or winning favors. Boys, especially on those occasions when they are teased or challenged in the plaza, hear their antics become the basis of exaggerated tales told by adults and older children to those not present at the time of the challenge. Children hear themselves made into characters in stories told again and again. They hear adults use stories from the Bible or from their youth to scold or warn against misbehavior. The mayor captures the boys' conflict in the story of King Solomon which features a chain of events and resolutions of a conflict similar to that in which they are currently engaged. Children's misdeeds provoke the punchline or summing up of a story which they are not told, but are left to imagine: "Dat póliceman'll come 'n git you, like he did Frog." The story behind this summary is never told, but is held out as something to be recreated anew in the imagination of every child who hears this threat.

Trackton children can create and tell stories about themselves, but they must be clever if they are to hold the audience's attention and to maintain any extended conversational space in an ongoing discourse with a story, but if they do not succeed in relating the first few lines of their story to the ongoing topic or otherwise exciting the listeners' interests, they are ignored. An adult's accusation, on the other hand, gives children an open stage for creating a story, but this one must also be "good," i.e. highly exaggerated, skillful in language play, and full of satisfactory comparisons to redirect the adult's attention from the infraction provoking the accusation.

Adults and older siblings do not make up sustained chronological narratives specially for young children, and adults do not read to young children. The flow of time in Trackton, which admits few scheduled blocks of time for routine activities, does not lend itself to a bedtime schedule of reading a story. The homes provide barely enough space for the necessary activities of family living, and there is no separate room, book corner, or even outdoor seat where a child and parent can read together out of the constant flow of human interactions. The stage of the plaza almost always offers live action and is tough competition for book-reading. Stories exchanged among adults do not carry moral summaries or admonitions about behavior; instead they focus on detailing of events and personalities, and they stress conflict and resolution or attempts at resolution. Thus adults see no reason to direct these stories to children for teaching purposes.

When stories are told among adults, young children are not excluded from the audience, even if the content refers to adult affairs, sexual exploits, crooked politicians, drunk ministers, or wayward choirleaders. If children respond to such stories with laughter or verbal comments, they are simply warned to "keep it to yo'self." Some adult stories are told only in sex-segregated situations. Men recount to their buddies stories they would not want their wives or the womenfolk to know about; women share with each other stories of quarrels with their menfolk or other women. Many men know about formulaic toasts (long, epic-like accounts of either individual exploits or struggles of black people) from visitors from up-North or men returned from the armed services, but these are clearly external to the Trackton man's repertoire, and they do not come up in their social gatherings. Instead, Trackton men and their friends focus on recent adventures of particular personalities known to all present. All of these are highly self-assertive or extol the strength and cleverness of specific individuals.

Women choose similar topics for their stories: events which have happened to them, things they have seen, or events they have heard about. Considerable license is taken with these stories, however, and each individual is expected to tell the story, not as she has heard it, but with her own particular style. Women tell stories of their exploits at the employment office, adventures at work in the mill, or episodes in the lives of friends, husbands, or mutual acquaintances. Laced through with evaluative comments ("Didja ever hear of such a thing?" "You know how he ak [act] when he drunk." "You been like dat."), the stories invite participation from listeners. In fact, such participation is necessary re-inforcement for the story-teller. . . .

The traditions of story-telling

Roadville members reaffirm their commitment to community and church values by giving factual accounts of their own weaknesses and the lessons learned in overcoming these. Trackton members announce boldly their individual strength in having been creative, persistent, and undaunted in the face of conflict. In Roadville, the sources of stories are personal experience and a familiarity with Biblical parables, church-related stories of Christian life, and testimonials given in church and home lesson-circles. Their stories are tales of transgressions which make the point of reiterating the expected norms of behavior of man, woman, hunter, fisher-man, worker, and Christian. The stories of Road-ville are true to the facts of an event; they qualify exaggeration and hedge if they might seem to be veering from an accurate reporting of events.

The content of Trackton's stories, on the other hand, ranges widely, and there is "truth" only in the universals of human strength and persistence praised and illustrated in the tale. Fact is often hard to find, though it is usually the seed of the story. Playsongs, ritual insults, cheers, and stories are assertions of the strong over the weak, of the power of the person featured in the story. Anyone other than the story-teller/main character may be subjected to mockery, ridicule, and challenges to show he is not weak, poor, or ugly.

In both communities, stories entertain; they provide fun, laughter, and frames for other speech events which provide a lesson or a witty display of verbal skill. In Roadville, a proverb, witty saying or Scriptural quotation inserted into a story adds to both the entertainment value of the story and to its unifying role. Group knowledge of a proverb or saying, or approval of Scriptural quotation reinforces the communal experience which forms the basis of Roadville's stories.

In Trackton, various types of language play, imitations of other community members or TV personalities, dramatic gestures and shifts of voice quality, and rhetorical questions and expressions of emo-tional evaluations add humor and draw out the interaction of the story-teller and audience. Though both communities use their stories to entertain, Roadville adults see their stories as didactic: the purpose of a story is to make a point – a point about the conventions of behavior. Audience and story-teller are drawn together in a common bond through acceptance of the merits of the story's point for all. In Trackton, stories often have no point; they may go on as long as the audience enjoys the story-teller's entertainment. Thus a story-teller may intend on his first entry into a stream of discourse to tell only one story, but he may find the audience reception such that he can move from the first story into another, and yet another. Trackton audiences are unified by the story only in that they recognize the entertainment value of the story, and they approve stories which extol the virtues of an individual. Stories do not teach lessons about proper behavior; they tell of individuals who excel by outwitting the rules of conventional behavior.

Children's stories and their story-telling opportunities are radically different in the two communities. Roadville parents provide their children with books; they read to them and ask questions about the books' contents. They choose books which emphasize nursery rhymes, alphabet learning, animals, and simplified Bible stories, and they require their children to repeat from these books, and to answer formulaic questions about their contents. Roadville adults similarly ask questions about oral stories which have a point relevant to some marked behavior of a child. They use proverbs and summary statements to remind their children of stories and to call on them for comparisons of the stories' contents to their own situations. Roadville parents coach children in their telling of stories, forcing them to tell a story of an incident as it has been pre-composed in the head of the adult.

Trackton children tell story-poems from the age of two, and they embellish these with gestures, *inclusios*, questions asked of their audience, and repetitions with variations. They only gradually learn to work their way into any ongoing discourse with their stories, and when they do, they are not asked questions about their stories, nor are they asked to repeat them. They must, however, be highly creative and entertaining to win a way into an ongoing conversation. They practice the skills which they must learn in order to do so through ritualized insults, playsongs, and of course, continued attempts at telling stories to their peers.

In Roadville, children come to know a story as either a retold account from a book, or a factual account of a real event in which some type of marked behavior occurred, and there is a lesson to be learned. There are Bible stories, testimonials, sermons, and accounts of hunting, fishing, cooking, working, or other daily events. Any fictionalized account of a real event is viewed as a lie; reality is better than fiction. Roadville's church and community life admit no story other than that which meets the definition internal to the group.

The one kind of story Trackton prides itself on is the "true story," one in which the basis of the plot is a real event, but the details and even the outcome are exaggerated to such an extent that the story is ultimately anything but true to the facts. Boys excel in telling these stories and use them to establish and maintain status relations once they reach school age, and particularly during the preadolescent years. To Trackton people, the "true story" is the only narrative they term a "story," and the purpose of such stories is to entertain and to establish the story-teller's intimate knowledge of truths about life larger than the factual details of real events. . . .

The story in school

When Trackton and Roadville children go to school, they meet very different notions of truth, style, and language appropriate to a "story" from those they have known at home. They must learn a different taxonomy and new definitions of stories. They must come to recognize when a story is expected to be true, when to stick to the facts, and when to use their imaginations. In the primary grades, the term "story" is used to refer to several types of written and oral discourse. When the first-grade teacher says in introducing a social studies unit on community helpers, "Now we all know some story about the job of the policeman," she conjures up for the children different images of policemen and stories about them, but the concept of story which holds in this school context is one which refers to factual narratives of events in which policemen are habit-

ually engaged. Following their home model, Roadville children might conceive of such a story as "telling on" a policeman or recounting his failure to follow certain rules. Trackton children would expect stories of a policeman to exaggerate the facts and to entertain with witticisms and verbal play. During rest time after lunch, the primary teacher may read to the student the "story" of "Curious George," a monkey who talks, gets involved in a wide range of antics, and always comes out the victor. Roadville children have had little experience with such wild fantasy stories, and Trackton children have not heard stories about such animals read to them from books. Neither group has had the experience of helping negotiate with an adult the meaning of the story: "Isn't he crazy?" "Do you think they'll catch him?" "What would have happened if . . .?"

For Roadville children, their community's ways of learning and talking about what one knows both parallel and contradict the school's approach to stories. In the classroom, occasions for story-telling between adults and children are established by adult request, just as they are in Roadville at home. Teachers sometimes politely listen to very young children's spontaneous stories (for example, those volunteered during a reading lesson), but these are not valued as highly as those specifically requested by adults as digressions. When teachers ask children to "make up" a story or to put themselves "in the shoes of a character" in a story from their reading book, they prefer fanciful, creative, and imaginative accounts. In Roadville, such stories told by children would bring punishment or a charge of lying. The summary of one story can be related to the summary of another, and the moral of one story can be linked with another, but extension of the facts of a story by hyperbole without qualification, and the transfer of characters, times, and places would be unacceptable features of stories in Roadville.

For Trackton children entering school, the problems presented by the school's conventions and expectations for story-telling are somewhat different. Questions which ask for a strict recounting of facts based on a lesson and formulated in the teacher's mind which simply recounts facts accurately has no parallel in their community. Their fictive stories in response to assignments which ask them to make up a story often fail to set the scene or introduce characters, and often the point of their stories is not clear to either teachers or other students. Inside the classroom, their language play, incorporation of commercial characters, and many of their themes are unacceptable. The close personal network which gives Trackton stories their context and their meaning at home has no counterpart in the school. For each community, the story whose features are marked here are only those produced and recognized as "a story" by community residents – modified nonfictive for Trackton and nonfictive for Roadville. "Story" in the school being the type most often used in language arts contexts (reading and writing lessons) and the nonfictive (being) that most frequently used in social studies and science lessons. . . .

The significance of these different patterns of language socialization for success in school soon becomes clear. After initial years of success, Roadville children fall behind, and by junior high, most are simply waiting out school's end or their sixteenth birthday, the legal age for leaving school. They want to get on with family life and count on getting a high school diploma when and if they need it in the future. Trackton students fall quickly into a pattern of failure, yet all about them they hear that they can never get ahead without a high school diploma. Some begin their families and their work in the mills while they are in school. But their mood is that of those who have accepted responsibilities in life outside the classroom, and that mood is easily interpreted negatively by school authorities who still measure students' abilities by their scores on standardized tests. Trackton students often drift through the school, hoping to escape with the valued piece of paper which they know will add much to their parents' and grandparents' pride, although little to their paychecks. . . .

An ethnographer of communication has no more talent for accurately predicting the future

than any other social scientist. However, our examination here of the maintenance of patterns of language use and their mutually reinforcing cultural patterns leaves us with ample possibilities for speculation. Through the numerous geographic and economic moves of (the 20th) century, both Roadville's and Trackton's forefathers maintained habits which were forged in the social, regional, and economic milieus of preceding centuries. In the 1920s, the schools of the Piedmont began to articulate their mission as preachers of culture to the mill people, the poor whites, and the mountain folks who had come to the mill villages. Through the decades, the schools maintained this goal while mill people kept their faith in the power of the schools to help them get ahead. When blacks came to school with whites in the late 1960s, most people saw no need for a change of mission or methods. . . .

Will the road ahead be altered for the students from Trackton and Roadville who have, through the efforts of some of their teachers, learned to add to their ways of using language learned at home? Will their school-acquired habits of talking about ways of knowing, reporting on uses of language, and reading and writing for a variety of functions and audiences be transmitted to their chances of the next generation? Internalization and extension of these habits depend on opportunities for practice as well as on a consciousness that these ways may have some relevance to future vocational goals. Maintenance of these habits depends on both sustained motivation for entrance into some vocation in which they are seen as relevant, and exposure as adults to multiple situations in which the habits can be repeatedly practiced. . . . In short, the orientation toward uses of language must include not only the interactions of the present, but also the needs of the future.

Working with Latino and Latina Students

"Hispanic" is a term created by the U.S. Census Bureau to identify people who are Spanish-speakers; Latinos/as is an alternative term preferred by many. Chicano is a term chosen by Mexican-Americans who strongly identify with their indigenous cultural heritage. The author has worked successfully with many Latino/a students, and she shares some of the reasons for and the strategies behind that success.

As the 21st century begins, it is apparent that Latinos have influenced U.S. society in a variety of areas such as music, entertainment, and even the English language. Mexican cuisine can be found almost everywhere from fine restaurants to fast food; salsa recently surpassed ketchup as the most popular American condiment. Latinos have also made significant contributions to the American economy. Although anti-immigrant critics claim that Mexican immigrants in particular contribute primarily to the Mexican economy by sending much of their money to families and relatives in Mexico, yet Ramos (2002) cites a National Academy of Science study reporting that both legal and illegal Mexican immigrants spend more than $10 billion each year in the United States.[1] From 2001 to 2003, Latinos' disposable income increased by about 30% to total $652 billion (Grow, 2004).[2] As this population continues to increase, so will their influence and their purchasing power – estimated to exceed $1 trillion by 2010.

Aurora Cedillo was born in south Texas, but when she was 12 years old she came with her family to harvest crops in Idaho and Montana. Her family decided to stay in Oregon where she graduated from North Salem high school. She attended college with assistance from a federally funded career ladder teacher-preparation program. Upon graduating, Salem-Keizer schools hired her as their the first bilingual-bicultural teacher. Twenty years later she earned a Masters degree in Bilingual Education Administration from the University of Oregon. She has currently completed her doctoral studies at Oregon State University and will be awarded her doctoral degree upon completion of her dissertation.

Aurora describes herself as "a holistic bilingual and multicultural educator, consultant, interpreter, and conference presenter," but she is more than that. Although her parents had eighteen children, she is the oldest female of her ten surviving siblings. She is also a single mother and grandmother.

Originally appeared in *Cultural competence: A primer for educators* by Jerry V. Diller and Jean Moule (Belmont, CA: Wadsworth, 2005). Reprinted by permission of author.

She has always enjoyed telling family and cultural stories, and has written about her beliefs and experiences. She believes that "the words I speak today were at one time spoken by my grandmothers in the past. Therefore, I am the words my grandmothers and my mother spoke." The following is an interview conducted by Jerry V. Diller and Jean Moule (2005) with Aurora Cedillo.[3]

Could you talk about your own ethnic background and how it has impacted your work?

I'm caught between ethnicities. As I've grown older, I realize I have a multiple identity. I describe myself as Chicana, of Mexican-American heritage (but) as I look deeper, I realize that Mexican means mixed race. My mom is French. My dad is more indigenous, though his last name was Cedillo, a very Spanish name. Therefore, I am French and Spanish and indigenous. My father's father, my grandfather, lived with my mom at the beginning of her marriage, so she learned a lot from him about his indigenous culture. Many of his ideas, belief, and practices were taught to us. Therefore, I would describe my ethnic background as Mexican American, Chicana, and all of my responses in this interview derive from my *lived* experience. . . .

As a bilingual of diverse language, culture, and color, my work involves balancing the cultural, linguistic, and socioeconomic scale for students, staff, and parents. Opening means of communication, increasing awareness and acceptance between the groups is a continuous daily task. I confirm the efforts of the groups and value their input, but progress is slow in coming. Success comes one grain of sand at a time; teachers are overwhelmed with students that don't understand the language and culture of the school, parents that seem to not care about the education of their children, and administrators that can't support the teachers' efforts. Institutional historical practices of silencing and promoting invisibility are alive and vital constantly in every element of the educational experience for teachers, students, and parents of color. . . .

What characteristics do Latinos/Latinas share as a group?

. . . A characteristic Latinos share is a belief in destiny. The belief is that we are not in complete control of everything that happens in our lives. "Si Dios Quiere" (God willing) is a typical yet simple statement of such belief. A higher being, God, has a purpose and a plan destined for each of us. . . . To Latinos destiny is being. No plan, no objective, no road map, no timeline. I never planned to be in this interview. I never planned to attend Oregon State University as a student participating in a doctoral program. I never planned to be a teacher, to travel nationally and internationally to share my teaching experience. Terms like *goal setting* and *objectives* and *plans* are words I learned in the mainstream world. I learned to use them; however, I can tell you that the plans I have made have very rarely been achieved. Our beliefs on destiny are based in our indigenous experience of European conquest, of genocide, of never having choice in our lives. I can't choose my place of employment. I can't choose where to live my life; I can't choose my doctor. I can't even tell you I will see you tomorrow, because even that depends on someone else.

Another fundamental belief that guides Latinos is the belief that we are born into a family and that the family becomes the most important element in life in this world and beyond. The family is the centerpiece, the glue that bonds one to nature. Family is plural and multifaceted. It is elastic and fluid-like. To Latinos, family is much more than the biological members one is born into. Family is broad and deep. It is inclusive of several generations, social relationships, and local community members. Family includes mother, father, sister, and brother. It includes sister cousins, political sisters, and growth sisters; also . . . aunts, uncles, grandparents, and great-grandparents. It includes children, grandchildren, and great-grandchildren. . . .

The community family includes members of a rural community meeting in faraway places and uniting to assist one another in surviving in the new place. Individuals share housing, food, medicine, and money. They provide guidance in survival in the community, employment, and resources. Once able to sustain themselves, they leave and set up another place to assist the newcomers. Everyone from your birth farm, community, or state is a brother and sister. The term paisano relates to the brotherhood.

So, we are community centered in the family, defined by destiny, and our connections extend socially, religiously, and politically. We are one. This belief, if misunderstood, creates problems on the job and in relations in mainstream culture. Something as simple as a statement in an invitation to an event can be misunderstood. For example, the statement "no children please" to some Latinos may mean that he/she wasn't really welcomed because if one is invited, all are invited.

Another characteristic of Latino culture is collaboration and cooperation. "One" does not know "it" all. However, everyone knows something. So collectively, as a family or as a community, we Latinos are able to solve the immediate concerns. All members are responsible for something. Some are good at speaking and negotiating; others are good at thinking; others are good at math; others are more spiritually inclined; others are better caregivers. Everyone in the family is an expert in something. Depending on the task . . . different leaders arise. When we came to Oregon, my father did not speak, read, or write English. He could not read a map, a road sign, or was unable to ask for directions. My sixteen-year-old brother took the map, read it, and another brother asked directions. The rest of us participated by cleaning and feeding the crew in the cabin. . . .

What historical experiences should educators be aware of in relationship to the Latino/a community and Latino/a students?

Historical events that include the histories of the students in the classroom are very important. Teachers must be inclusive of the countries represented in the classroom. For Latino students, a teacher must look to include members of communities represented in her class. For Mexican Americans, . . . a teacher must include Cesar Chavez. . . . It's amazing how quickly Heroes of Color fade

away in the daily tasks of teaching. Once I asked third-grade students to tell me about Cesar Chavez. Eager and enthused students discussed a boxer also named Cesar Chavez. In less than ten years, Cesar Chavez had been lost to a new generation of teachers and students!

Teachers must celebrate the sixteenth of September, Mexico's day of independence, as well as many other Central American countries that celebrate their independence day in September. As teachers, we must know what event happened on the fifth of May and why we celebrate that day. For Mexican Americans and Chicanos, Cinco de Mayo is especially important. The battle in Puebla, Mexico, on the fifth of May is a day to remember – that regardless of poverty, training, or language, positive change can happen if we fight a battle as a united people.

Teachers must be inclusive when discussing historical events. Many of our teachers were not exposed to the history of Latino countries and are not informed. I would suggest that teachers invite community members, parents, or minority staff within the school to come and share with the students. . . . Also important is the discussion of the contributions made by members of these communities in the development of this powerful nation. . . .

Are there any subpopulations in the Latino/a community you feel deserve additional attention in the classroom?

The two groups that I think deserve additional attention are the newly arrived to our communities from indigenous backgrounds and the locally born and grown Latino children. Our indigenous Indian populations intermixed racially with Latino/as as they come from Mexico, Central America, and Guatemala. We know very little about their background, how they learn, where their historical places are, or their lifestyles in their countries of origin. We are unfamiliar with their social practices and do not speak their language if it is not Spanish. Frankly we are at a loss. Right now in our schools, we are looking for representatives from these indigenous communities who will come and share with us information on how we can reach their students and families. They tend to be even harder to reach than Chicano students, fall through the cracks, drop out, and underachieve at even higher levels.

A second group, particularly at high risk, are the first- and second-generation Latinos, both immigrant and U.S.-born. These students grow up in two worlds. They learn two languages at one time. They live between worlds and have not developed a strong foundation in either one. The minute they are born, they're listening to English as well as to the Spanish of their parents. So they must learn two languages. Educators in charge of instructing these students have little knowledge about bilingualism. In desperation, Spanish-language experts from Mexico and other Central Americans are hired to work with these students. These teachers know Spanish but do not know how to work with bilingual students. Just because you speak two languages does not make you a teacher of bilingual students.

Inappropriate or no assessment of these students' academic skills leads to inappropriate placements and instruction. Many of these students attend high-risk schools where the least experienced teachers tend to teach. Since they require a bilingual placement, they are taught by teachers who are just learning Spanish as their second language. They have not yet developed the depth or the breadth of the language in order to provide students with rich embedded language required in academics.

Students from these two Latino subgroups tend to be the ones who drop out of school the most. They are also the fastest growing population in penal institutions. They also tend to be disconnected from the cultural practices and linguistic foundation that strengthen the first generation.

Research shows that if you teach children in the language they understand, they will be successful. But there are political pressures coming from the educational establishment that allow non-English students three years in special programs and then push them out. Research, however, says that it takes five to seven years for a child to develop the academic proficiency of an English speaker. But new educators want to keep their jobs and want to make sure they are doing what the system tells them to do. Older educators who have seen the research and know from firsthand experience are more likely to challenge the political pressures and push for teaching (students) in their native language. But basically, educators are caught between these forces, and what are you going to do?

Another great controversy is the misalignment in bilingual education. So-called programs are planted on hard soil. Allocated funding is misused; programs are left to the discretion of unqualified staff; and resources are either lacking or inappropriate.

Higher education institutions provide very little in bilingual education courses. Bilingual teachers have to figure it out on their own. Due to the lack of bilingual staff, multicultural education, language acquisition, and foreign language are somehow supposed to prepare bilingual educators. Bilingual education is very political. It involves learning the rights and the Constitution. It involves moving student, parents, and staff to question the system. This is very scary, and few teachers feel strong enough to battle.

All of these misalignments take a toll on teachers who are on the front lines. She is the one who sees the failure, the student dropout rate . . . (yet) she is blamed for the lack of support given to non-English speakers at such a crucial time in their development. . . .'

Could you talk a little more about the controversy among bilingual educators, their approaches and what needs to be done for bilingual students?

Controversy among bilingual educators centers on pressures from the mainstream society dictating that English is the only language to be taught.

How do different cultural styles, values, and worldviews affect education of Latino/Latina students?

The biggest thing I see . . . is that the teacher tends to come from an "I" perspective and is in charge of teaching students who are from a culture with a "we" perspective. Not being aware of this cultural difference can result in confusion and arrogance on the part of the teacher who desires to control everything. The "I" perspective is an egocentric attitude that predominates in Anglo culture. I need to plan, I need to do, or I need to fix. For the mainstream culture, the idea is that you fail because (you) failed to plan. This "I" perspective creates misunderstanding toward people that have a "we" perspective. In order for "I" to do something, "we" needs to happen. In order for "I" to attend, "we" need to have a car, pay the insurance, get a license, learn to read English, and learn to drive. "I" is dependent on how many resources "we" can gather.

. . . The element of time heavily impacts the class. In situations where the relationship is more important than the event, measuring time can be problematic. For mainstream culture the clock runs the show. In Latino culture, the relationship runs the show. So it is more important to save the relationship than is to save time. In Latino culture, the concept of time is different; *luego, despues, al rato, al ratito, ya* all have a different time value. If a teacher does not know that, it could cause disruptions in transitioning times.

Another issue is the concept of collective ownership. In Spanish the word *la, el* is used instead of *my* or *mine*. In English we say "my car," "my house," or "my pencil." . . . In Spanish we say *el carro, la casa, el lapiz*. Even your personal parts don't belong to you. So it's *los manos,* the hands, . . . Not wash *your* hands; wash the hands, wash the face, clean the ears. But in Anglo culture, it's I washed *my* hands, I washed *my* face.

So this little boy or girl comes to school. He or she needs a pencil, so they pick one up off a desk. Not my pencil or her pencil, but the pencil. Another child yells out, "He stole my pencil. She took my pencil!" The Latino child says, "I did not take your pencil." "You have the pencil right there!" The teacher intercedes: "Is that her pencil? Give her back her pencil!" "But why?" Now he goes home and he takes a dinner plate. He had that plate yesterday, now his sister has it today. "That's my plate!" he says, and his mother disciplines him, feeling the need to remind him about sharing. "This is not your plate; it belongs to the family; it belongs to whoever gets it first." . . .

There is also the high respect given to food in Latino culture. It is a community where everything is shared, especially food. Nothing is thrown away, and you share your food rather than throw it away. You don't play with it. At home one gets scolded or spanked for wasting or throwing away food. In the classroom, when food like rice or salt or macaroni or beans are used in learning activities, that is playing with it; the child is put in a difficult bind. He doesn't participate. He refuses to play with it. He may be graded down. But if the teacher is aware of these cultural things, they can use rocks or popsicle sticks, anything but food.

What are some of the factors important in assessing the learning style of Latino/Latina students and what classroom factors could be manipulated to match these styles?

Learning styles are basically the different ways humankind learns. We learn by seeing. We learn by doing. We learn by acting out. We learn by observing others and modeling their behavior. We teach children by modeling the things we expect from them. It's a continual process in the classroom. You reach out to the kids, you model, you show, you do, you explain. You have other people explain. Look at Jose; he did it really well. Could you tell us how you did that, could you show us? I do much of my teaching in the context of small cooperative learning groups. You give them tasks to practice, problems to solve, explain your expectations step by step. Put things on the wall that reinforce the lessons, always giving them references to what they need to do. Reviews for when they are absent from the classroom. All of these little efforts or bricks of support provide scaffolding for learning and succeeding. Especially where language is an issue . . .

In working in small groups, it is important to find a student leader who understands the lesson and is able to tell what he learned. I always tell my bilingual teachers, when you set up your cooperative groups, you want to find someone to lead who is fluent in English as well as someone who is fluent in Spanish (and) a balance of gender, girls and boys. In classes for bilingual children, everyone must be a teacher to each other. English speakers are going to learn Spanish; the Spanish speaker is going to learn English. The bilingual children are going to learn everyday.

Also look to language ability when you're forming groups. With different levels of ability, you're not the only teacher. You cannot teach such a classroom alone. You need your environment to help you. You need your students and their peers to help you. You need the materials to support you, and above all you need the cultural awareness of where those kids are coming from and their home experience. Finally, learn by doing. Create the experience for and with students. Learning involves all the senses. Use them. If you do all of these things and make all of these connections, kids will be more successful.

I have spoken of many strategies throughout the interview. Of all the ones I've spoken about, communicating is the most important. . . . (If) you leave parents out of the learning loop (or) the aunts or the grandmothers, you are only using half of your resources. You need to bring the families into the learning environment. . . . They know their children the most. They know if their children are morning people or afternoon people, their abilities and capabilities, their individual histories. We have a lot of kids who bring trauma with them

to the classroom: abandonment, abuse, neglect, just being poor, not having the right foods, medical care, attention. We can't expect them to read and write when their teeth are falling out or they have an ear infection that has never been corrected. . . .

Our schools witness families who have experienced death, drownings, and fires. We tend to be quicker to help them if they are English speaking. The school gets together, brings boxes of food and clothes, making sure that the family gets the support its needs. When Latino kids get hurt or their families have problems, there is a tendency to expect other agencies to take care of things. Somebody else will take care of it. We need the kind of system that will respond equally to all students who are hurting. And in a language and style they can understand.

Notes

[1]Jorge Ramos, *The Other Face of America*. (New York: Rayo, 2002)

[2]Brian Grow, Is America Ready? *Business Week*, 2004, Issue 3874, pp. 58–70.

[3]Jerry V. Diller and Jean Moule, *Cultural competence: A primer for educators*. (Belmont, CA: Wadsworth, 2005, interview excerpts from pp. 194–206).

Human Mathematics

Folake is a new arrival at Ridgefield, a boarding school in England. Although the narrator is also from West Africa, she has been at the school for two years and has adapted to her surroundings. This excerpt from the short story begins after Folake has been at the school for a year and has begun the process of adaptation; it ends following a conflict that stems from cultural and linguistic differences.

Folake and I were often compared with each other because we had several things in common beyond our West African blood.

There were other Nigerian girls in the school, but none were both in Folake's year and in her boarding house, as I was. There were also a few girls from other West African countries and a handful from Eastern and Southern Africa. In addition, there was a strong representation from Asia. In fact, although not officially international, Ridgefield had a strong foreign contingent. There were different degrees of foreignness, however. There were the fresh arrivals from abroad, and then there were the ones who looked foreign but had spent much, most, or all of their lives in England.

The one other Ghanaian girl in the school, Stella Amissah-Smith, fell into this latter category. She had been in the school since the earliest level and had spent all of her life in England. I had been quite excited to meet her at first, but somehow we had never formed a real friendship. My social circle was a veritable league of nations, while hers comprised almost exclusively British girls. The two circles simply did not intersect. Once we both understood that, we maintained a neutral distance from each other.

In these divergent social constellations there was another important difference between us, which, incidentally, also distinguished Folake from me. Strictly speaking and certainly in biological terms, I was only half African. My other half was German, European, Caucasian – white. This distinction, which in purely racial terms might have bracketed Folake and Stella together and placed me outside their subset, did not, in reality, constitute any common ground for the two of them. In fact, the distance between them was even greater than that between Stella and me. On a line with three equidistant points, I would have been the midpoint with the two of them at either extreme. Midpoint was the natural position for me.

The subtle complexities of this situation demonstrated the inefficiency of color as a lowest common denominator for human mathematics. Fortunately for me, I had realized early in life that the ability of color labels to seem hopelessly superficial at best and ridiculously inaccurate at worst, was, like the tip of the proverbial iceberg, the very indication that a dense, hulking mass lurked beneath.

Strangely enough, growing up in Ghana as a visibly brown child, I had been labeled "white." Yet I had metamorphosed into a "black" the first time I traveled to a white country. However, like the chameleon, another creature of distinct in-betweens, I had already learned that it was I who had to make the adjustment, not my surroundings.

In my years at Ridgefield Girls' the ease with which I moved between the colors of my spectrum was as involuntary as the changes in my accent. When I spoke to Folake, her Nigerian accent teased out and propped up my languishing Ghanaian one. When I spoke to the teachers and the British girls, their clipped tones braced and nurtured my burgeoning British accent.

Some of my classmates had teased me about my Ghanaian English in my first year at the school. What seemed to stand out most was intonation. This had caused some embarrassment in my first week when Sarah, a girl who sat next to me in class, had been unable to understand my request to borrow an eraser. The problem was that I pronounced the word with a heavy stress on the first rather than the second syllable. Sarah had obviously never been asked for an "ee-raser" before and wasn't sure what to make of my request. After a few efforts to make myself understood, I realized we were drawing attention to ourselves and tried to put her off, but it was too late.

"What's the matter over there?" asked the teacher.

"Oh, nothing," we chorused. I was anxious for the fuss to die down, and Sarah was sensitive to that. But the teacher genuinely wanted to help because I was the new girl.

"Did you need something, Claudia?" she persisted gently.

"Well, I was just trying to borrow an ee-raser," I mumbled, hot with shame and cold with dread.

"Oh, you mean an eraser," she said straight away. Apparently it was not the first time she had heard it pronounced that way. Her correction had been completely involuntary and was not mocking or patronizing. I was grateful for that but still had to endure the snickers of my classmates.

Although embarrassing for me, the incident had been a genuine misunderstanding on Sarah's part. She was not one of the girls who made fun of my accent. In fact, she later became one of my closest British friends. In my first year at Ridgefield, which I had entered at the third form level, we had sat next to each other in our classroom preceding assembly every morning.

In the fourth form we were in the same dormitory together with four other girls. We were not close in the way best friends were, but we liked each other and had an easy familiarity that came from being thrown together in several settings within the school environment. She sometimes teased me good naturedly by calling me "Ee-raser." My interactions with her, as with the other white girls, generally featured the more Caucasian me.

My Caucasian identity, thus far in my life, had consisted of looking different, being "white" in a black home country, knowing European foods, having an ear for my mother's favorite classical composers. It was being dropped at parties long before they began and collected long before they ended because we were operating by European time in Africa. It was calling my grandparents, even the Ghanaian ones, "Oma" and "Opa."

Thus it was that I was more easily accepted, warmed up to by the white girls, safer territory for them than the pure African girls from Africa. The same situation pertained in reverse. In Folake's first year at Ridgefield I could sense that she was grateful to me for stopping at her downstairs dormitory on the way to breakfast. She had an amicable but still slightly stiff relationship with her dormitory mates and was more at ease with me. She probably sensed that she could be more herself in the few minutes of our walk than for the rest of the day. This was despite the presence of my best friend, Mira. Perhaps Mira's being Indian and strongly accented made Folake comfortable too.

In the fifth form we outgrew large dormitories and earned the privilege of double rooms. Although we were not given a choice of roommates, there was some effort to pair well-known sets of friends and I was happy to discover that I was placed with Mira. Next door were Stella Amissah-Smith and her best friend, Jenny James. Those who were not part of an obvious friendship were randomly paired. And that was how Folake and Sarah became roommates.

There seemed no immediate problem with this pairing. The two had known each other for a year and had often been in my company at the same time in the common areas. However, we had not advanced very far into the term when undercurrents of tension began to hum. Although I had initially been pleased that I could see two friends at the same time, I quickly discovered that I did not feel comfortable when they were both present.

For the first time I became conscious of the switches in my accent. What was normally an automatic, involuntarily transition became a linguistic quandary. As often happens when switching rapidly between languages, elements from one linguistic set soon started to jump into the other like nerve impulses firing out of control. The result was not the smooth, natural blend of the two that I effortlessly used with Mira. It was a jarring, clumsy combination that made me feel awkward like a tuneful songbird that had unexpectedly produced a squawk. Under these tensions conversations dwindled to pleasantries and flat jokes until I found myself looking for an exit.

I started to question myself – my very being and my genuineness. I did not like feeling awkward and fake, and did not understand why I should feel that way in their room when I never did otherwise. Was it false and deceitful to be black with a black friend and white with a white one? And to be yet a third, perhaps "brown," person with friends who were neither black nor white? Did it make me two- or even three-faced? If it did, could I help it?

For a while I avoided Sarah and Folake, trying to make the echoes go away. Deep down, I knew they were with me to stay, but at least I could quiet them by staying in as neutral territory as possible. In a school like Ridgefield, however, this was not easy and my concerns returned with renewed vigor on the day of the row.

I was always grateful to have missed the main action of that fight. In theory, it had little to do with me anyway. Yinka and Alison were not even in my year. They were younger, and at that stage of our lives and in our highly structured school environment, a year's age difference was worth as much as a decade's in later life. However, both girls were in my house. It was natural for quarrels to break out once in a while in that populous, hormone-charged atmosphere. They usually affected only the two girls involved and perhaps their closest friends. But this one was different. This one became a fight between black and white.

One of the girls had been talking on the phone while the other was listening to a radio program.

One had complained that the other was being too noisy, but neither was prepared to compromise. In the end, both radio and telephone were forgotten while they screamed at each other in the corridor. It was never firmly established which of them had first brought color into it, but the myriad versions of "you white girls don't respect anybody" and "go back to your country if you don't like the way we are" that later flew around the school clearly indicated the direction the quarrel had taken.

What disturbed me most was the divisive aftermath of the conflict. There was a tacit need for everyone to take a stance. I feigned a senior's indifference to the immature carryings-on of the juniors, but Mira was not fooled. At lunchtime Stella and Jenny joined our table. I longed to hear Stella's opinion on the topic but did not want to ask her. So I almost dropped my fork when I heard Mira say in a bantering tone: "Hey, so you two are flouting the new rule of segregation, are you?"

"Nothing to do with me," said Stella with a dismissive shrug.

"Pathetic," said Jenny as she passed the ketchup. "I wish they'd grow up."

Stella squirted the ketchup all over her chips and dug into them with gusto. I could see that the topic had already vacated her mind, and I envied her detachment. I was quiet on the way back to classes, and when Mira said, "You don't have to take sides you know, Claudia," I pretended to be brooding over my upcoming mathematics lesson.

But Folake would not allow me to forget the incident. She knew Yinka and her family from Nigeria and was outraged on their behalf.

"Do you know what that small girl said to her?" she fumed when she came to our room that evening. "She told her that she couldn't even speak English properly and then she and her white friends imitated her accent and laughed. Ah! How I wish I could take a lot of them to Nigeria, just for one day. They would smell pepper!"'

My African blood boiled up. "Couldn't speak English properly?" I shouted, "Can she speak Yoruba? Why didn't they ask her how many languages she can speak? Someone who can speak only one language, insulting a person who can speak three or four! Chia! They feel so superior, but they don't know that in Africa even the children speak two or three languages."

With every sentence my voice grew louder, faster, and more Ghanaian. Mira shot me a look of mingled awe and amusement. As the conversation heated up she kept up with us by waggling her head from side to side in that uniquely Indian way, that blend of a nod and a shake which looks like no but means yes.

Folake invited us back to her room to share some Nigerian food her aunt had brought on the weekend. Mira was tactful enough to know that Folake really wanted to be alone with me, to bathe in the surging African tide. And indeed, it seemed like an appropriate moment to do such a thing, almost like drinking a toast to the renaissance of our African unity, our enlistment in the war against the insolence of spoiled white girls.

I watched Folake mix the gari and water with that deft grace with which Africans handle food. I was already being transported back to Ghana, even before I caught the pungent, mouthwatering aroma of the salt fish stew. She had warmed it on the little stove in the upstairs kitchen and beamed with pride as she brought it in.

"It's my favorite," she said, spooning it over the moist mounds of gari in the two plates. With eager anticipation I watched the steaming orange rivulets of palm oil trickle over the white sides of the gari like lava from a volcano. We settled on her bed, plate in our laps, relishing the saltines and the added pleasure that eating with one's fingers always seems to impart to a meal. The unique flavor of the palm oil, the coarsely chopped slivers of onion so characteristic of a West African stew, and the fiery tang of the chili pepper were like old friends found again.

"Ah! Ah! Ah! Tell your auntie I said her stew is tooooooo sweet!" I sniffed, sinuses streaming and eyes watering from the pepper. Folake smiled at my African turn of phrase, understanding the compliment. She asked if my mother ever prepared food like that." Not anymore," I said. "She made the effort when we were in Ghana. But as for the salt fish . . ." I laughed and she nodded knowingly.

"Yes, the smell! As for that one, the oyibos can't stand it."

"Hmm, you know already! How she hated it! She didn't want that fish in the house at all! I used to ask her how she could complain about it when she loved eating those moldy, stinking cheeses. Kai! I could never bring that stuff close to my mouth."

Folake heartily agreed and as we marveled over this gastronomic puzzle, the door opened and Sarah walked in.

Astonishment registered on her face as she saw me seated cross-legged on Folake's bed, plate balanced in my lap, oily orange fingers halfway to my mouth. I could tell at once that the greatest shock had been to discover that the loud African voice chatting and laughing with Folake did not belong to one of her Nigerian friends, but to me.

"Hi, Sarah!" I said too quickly and too brightly.

"Hello, Claudia," she said in a voice which could easily have continued, "pleased to meet you." The shock had been so great that she could not hide her discomfort. She had entered her own room to find herself in alien territory.

"You're invited," I said, unable to think of anything else to say.

"Invited?" she echoed, shaking her head in irritated confusion. "Invited to what?" I pointed at the food.

"No thanks," she said. She was polite enough not to put into words what her eyes said, which was, "How can you eat something that smells like that?" Instead she said, "I was just coming to get my glasses." She grabbed them from her night table and, without further ado, fled the smell of salt fish and the two aliens sitting in the African den that had once been her room. There was an uncomfortable silence that Folake broke with, "My friend, as for dis one she no fit chop am!"

"No, you're right of course. She doesn't know how to eat it," I replied, using a Ghanaian expression that had always infuriated my mother. "What do you mean you don't know how to eat it?" she would say. "Just put it in your mouth, chew it, and swallow it!" But Africans knew what it meant. Sarah could no more have eaten that food than performed a Yoruba dance on the spot.

I giggled at the expression because the memory of my mother's indignation always made it amusing to me. Folake giggled at her own use of broken English. Some tension was released, and I started to feel sorry for Sarah and a little disloyal.

"I hope we didn't offend her," I said.

"Ah-ah! Why should she be offended?" asked Folake. "We didn't do anything wrong. This is also my room."

"Yes, of course, I know," I said hastily. "But I think we made her uncomfortable. She's such a nice girl," I added lamely.

"Well, you may find her nice but you don't have to live with her."

"I just don't know why two people as nice as you and her can't get on," I said with some exasperation, finally giving voice and life to that delicate topic.

"Claudia, please! That girl looks down on me because I'm a Nigerian. She doesn't like my music because it's too 'noisy,' she doesn't like the smell of my food – you saw her just now, didn't you, turning up her nose at it. She doesn't like my African friends coming to the room. She thinks she's better than me just because she's oyibo. And she always wants the window open when it's freezing cold. I can't even feel comfortable in my own room because of her. Ah-ah!"

"Folake, Sarah is not like that. Honestly. She's not one of those girls who looks down on people just because they're black. I've known her longer than you, you know. I mean, she's always been perfectly nice to me."

"Yes, but you aren't really black are you? I mean, you can also be an oyibo when you want to. She doesn't see you as a black. That's why she's so nice to you. As far as she's concerned, you're one of them."

I was not happy with the turn the conversation was taking. I felt somehow offended without being sure exactly which part of what she had said had upset me. I was not even sure if the offensive part had been explicitly stated or implied. Or whether it just hung there between the lines, with or without the intent of the speaker. I also felt that familiar sense of unease that always pervaded me when the issue of taking sides, of being "one of them or one of us" was so bluntly articulated. What I was sure about was that I was no longer comfortable in that room.

I finished my food a little too quickly and told Folake I was sleepy. She had already sensed that the mood was spoiled and did not make it any more awkward for me. That was one of the reasons I liked her: she was sensitive and intuitive. I knew she would not have said what she had if I had not brought up a delicate topic. I had only myself to blame.

After that incident I renewed my resolve to stay in neutral territory. However, as if the cosmos itself had determined to make me face up to my own duality, things came to a head a mere fortnight later. It is amazing how an event of barely a minute's duration can generate hours, even days of discussion, then years of reflection. Yet a minute was probably all it took from the moment Sarah placed the wastepaper bin on Folake's bed until we burst into their room to find a handprint emblazoned on her cheek. Five fingers, long and graceful, stamped beautifully in scarlet on a background white with shock. I had always envied Folake's elegant fingers.

They were locked in a thrashing embrace, clawing, tearing, swaying dangerously. As Mira and I pried them apart, Stella and Jenny came running down the corridor from their room.

"What the – oh my God!" gasped Jenny.

"She hit me, she hit me!" Sarah screamed, as if it weren't evident. Folake stood there with a face like thunder, looking as if she would like to slap her again. I looked from one to the other, lost for words. Mira pulled Sarah away, sat her down on her own bed, and put her arms around her. Sarah collapsed into sobs, ruining the perfect contrast as the red of outrage and humiliation spread all over her face and neck.

The doorway was crowded now as more girls arrived to see what all the noise was about. In her fury Folake addressed us all as one.

"That bitch put the dustbin on my bed!"

Where Sarah's feelings seemed to be composed of equal parts anger, fear, and humiliation, Folake's consisted of pure, unadulterated rage.

"How dare you?" she spat in Sarah's direction, making the word "dare" sound like an explosion. As all eyes turned to Sarah, she wailed: "I didn't even realize what I was doing, I was just trying to sweep the floor."

"Oh please!" snorted Folake. "You knew exactly what you were doing, you wanted to insult me. To tell me I am no better than rubbish." The more impassioned she became, the more Nigerian she sounded.

Realizing the futility of talking to her, Sarah addressed herself to the rest of us. "I always lift up the bin when I'm sweeping – sometimes I put it on the table, sometimes on my own bed, it doesn't really matter. I just wasn't thinking when I put it on her bed. I wasn't trying to insult her. I don't know why she has to be so touchy." And she started crying again.

At that moment the housemistress arrived at the scene. She took in Sarah's weeping distress and Folake's icy fury in a glance. Aware that she might not obtain a clear picture of events from either of them, she allowed Jenny and Stella to acquaint her with the basic facts before ordering all of us back to our rooms. Before we left I went up to each of them briefly.

"Sorry, Sweetheart," I said patting Sarah's shoulder awkwardly. "You'll be fine. Can I get you anything in town?" It was harder to look at Folake, her unrepentant rage more daunting to face than tearful misery. So I just said, "Let's talk about it later, OK?"

Out of the corner of my eye I saw Stella watching me with an amused expression and as we walked down the corridor, she said with a smirk, "Poor old Claudia, always trying to be everyone's friend." The sting of that well-timed remark lasted for years, but over time, my resentment mellowed into something bordering on pity for her.

After speaking to the two girls, the housemistress telephoned their homes and asked for them to be collected from school. They returned on Monday, Sarah with her mother and Folake with her aunt who served as her guardian in England. After a long meeting in the headmistress's office it was decided that Folake, as the primary aggressor, should be suspended for the rest of the term. This would also neatly postpone the need to solve the accommodation problem for the two of them until the next term. Since Christmas holidays were little more than a week away, it was not such a long sentence,

however it did mean that it was Folake's last day of school until the new year.

Sarah was punished with a detention for engaging in a fight. She was furious as she felt she had only been defending herself, but as she later recounted, the headmistress said she should have walked away and reported the situation immediately. Both girls were reminded in the crispest terms that fighting was unseemly, unladylike, and utterly forbidden at Ridgefield.

I had little chance to discuss events with Folake before she left that day or indeed to do much beyond saying good-bye and wishing her a Merry Christmas. Although I spent some time with her while she packed her things, we could not talk properly in front of her aunt. Only when her aunt carried the bags downstairs did she hug me.

Perhaps she read in my eyes that I felt let down, that I wanted to ask her why she had done it – why had she lived up to their stereotypes? – for she said in a rush: "Claudia, I'm not usually a violent person, you know that. But she really offended me and it was the last straw. I can't put up with that sort of thing anymore. I have my dignity too. I know she's your friend too, and I'm sorry you're . . . caught in the middle, but it's OK, you don't have to take sides."

Folake was put in a different boarding house the following term. Several of her Nigerian friends were there so she fit in easily and became even more a part of their set than she had been before. These changes, combined with our increased workload as we prepared for our examinations, facilitated a natural loosening of our relationship. Mira and I chatted with her whenever we sat together in the dining hall, but things were never quite the same as they had been before the fight. . . .

Perspectives on Religious Diversity and Intolerance

> ❝The faith in which I was brought up assured me that I was better than other people; I was saved and they were damned. Our hymns were loaded with arrogance – self-congratulations on how cozy we were with the Almighty and what a high opinion He had of us and what hell everybody else would catch come judgment day. ❞
>
> **Robert Heinlein (1907–1988)**

Science fiction writer Heinlein expresses the sense of supremacy that often consumes people of various faiths, but he is specifically addressing his Christian faith. It was the sort of arrogance he describes that was not only reflected in the Nazi attitudes toward the Jews but also in the attitudes of some Americans who applauded the Nazis. Because of the repugnance most Americans have felt about Nazis after they became aware of the Holocaust, many young people today are surprised to learn that not all Americans reviled Hitler and the Nazis prior to World War II. When Jewish writer Laura Zamekin married Thayer Hobson, she was not trying to conceal her Jewish identity, but simply followed convention and took his last name. By the mid-1930s, Americans were hearing rumors about anti-Semitic activity in Germany. At a New York dinner party, some people were deploring the Germans' brutality toward the Jews, but Hobson overheard others defending the Nazis. One person argued that the Jews had "asked for it" because of such things as claiming to be "the chosen people." One party-goer politely disagreed by saying, "Some of my best friends are Jews." At this point Laura Hobson entered the conversation: "Some of mine are, too, including my mother and father." After a brief silence, the discussion proceeded to another topic.[1] Laura Hobson wrote about such experiences in her novel, *Gentleman's Agreement*. It was made into a movie in 1948, and received the Academy Award for Best Picture. It was later said that this award demonstrated that Americans were starting to confront their religious prejudices.

> **❝Man is the Religious Animal . . . He is the only animal that loves his neighbor as himself, and cuts his throat if his theology isn't straight. He has made a graveyard of the globe in trying his honest best to smooth his brother's path to happiness and heaven.❞**
>
> **Mark Twain (1835–1910)**

Religious prejudice has not merely existed between Christians and Jews. Twain's comment addresses religious differences between people worldwide, creating conflicts throughout Europe and Great Britain for centuries and causing widespread violence and bloodshed. This history inspired leaders of the fledgling experiment in democracy in the new nation they called the United States of America to make sure that religion and state were kept apart. In the first essay, "The Framers and the Faithful," Steven Waldman provides a history lesson about the principle of separation of church and state as he describes the diversity that existed in the United States, including Catholics, mainstream Protestant sects, and evangelical Christians. He explains why most evangelical Christians were motivated to oppose the practice of having an established church supported by taxpayer money, and why they were among the staunchest supporters of Jefferson's "wall of separation." As a minority faith, evangelical Christians understood the importance of not mandating established churches in the separate states or in the nation as a whole.

Being perceived as a religious minority has always been a reality for American Muslims, but especially following the terrorist attacks on September 11, 2001. In "The Morning After the Morning After," Michelle Fine presents her interviews with Muslim teenagers about their experiences in the years since that tragedy occurred. They described incidents that involved being confronted with stereotypes, including observing police writing down the license plate numbers of their family's vehicle, challenging a teacher's comments related to the war in Iraq, and females being criticized by their non-Muslim peers for wearing their "hijab" (headscarf). Despite the many examples they reported of people's ignorance about Islam, these Muslim youth have persisted in explaining and clarifying the precepts of Islam to others and in strengthening their identities as both Muslims and Americans.

Like Muslims, atheists in the United States historically have been viewed with suspicion and even have been persecuted. Yet, in reviewing research on such "godless people," Andrew Newberg and Mark Robert Waldman reported favorable findings concerning their mental and physical health. In their essay, "Atheism and the Pursuit of Happiness," the authors argue that religion, or the lack of religion, was not the most critical factor in whether individuals achieved a positive outlook on life. One study found that people with a strong religious faith tended to be less tolerant of those who were different, and

> **❝All beliefs on which you bet your life are fundamentally religious beliefs, and atheism can be as much a religion as theism.❞**
>
> **Horace M. Kallen (1882–1974)**

another study found that an acceptance of atheism was one of the indicators of a "healthy" society. The authors stress the need to be critical when examining research, but also emphasize that it is important to be just as critical when encountering stereotypes and prejudices about atheists or people from a different religious faith. As some scholars (like Horace Kallen) have said, we should understand religion as a word denoting the deepest beliefs a human being has about what it means to live ethically in this life, and what happens after we die.

Diana Eck extends the discussion of prejudice and stereotyping of religious minorities in the United States by describing how negative attitudes from some Americans toward such groups have become more intense as religious diversity in America has increased. Although Eck provides several examples of prejudice leading to negative behaviors against non-Christians, she concludes with her belief that most Americans want to be "good neighbors," even if the person living next to them is from a different faith. Finally, the last essay in this section addresses the intersection of differences based on religion, sexual orientation, and ethnicity to explain how past and present oppression can serve as the motivation for being committed to overall issues of social justice.

As a gay man, Warren Blumenfeld has encountered anti-gay attitudes, and as a Jew, he has been personally affected by anti-Semitism – some members of his family were Holocaust victims. "A Letter to My Great-Grandfather" is a personal statement written to one of those victims, deploring the prejudice that results in people being attacked, beaten, and even killed for belonging to a minority group. After reviewing historic examples of anti-Semitic and anti-gay attitudes, he describes contemporary examples of violence in response to differences of race, ethnicity, or sexual orientation. In memory of his Great-Grandfather, he is committed to doing what he can to reduce prejudice and bigotry, and to be a voice for all oppressed people to honor those specific individuals whose voices were silenced by the Nazi genocide.

Despite the difficulties people have experienced due to religious differences, Diana Eck and Warren Blumenfeld both remain optimistic about people accepting our religious diversity and overcoming prejudice based on differences. Almost a century ago, Leo Tolstoy provided a parable to reinforce their optimism in his tale about "The Three Hermits." Tolstoy implies that there is no Christian God or Muslim God or Hindu God or any other divine being exclusively attached to one group. How people live from day to day will say more about their goodness and their closeness to God than a lifetime of prayers and professions of faith. People from many other cultures have expressed this view, but perhaps none as eloquently as this comment from an American Indian leader:

Notes

[1]Anecdote taken from: Laura Hobson's autobiography, *Laura Z: A life*. (New York: Arbor House, 1983).

> 66 The Great Spirit who has made us all has given us different complexions and different customs. Why may we not conclude that he has given us different religions, according to our understanding? 99
>
> **Red Jacket (Seneca) (1757–1830)**

The Framers and the Faithful

Even though Christianity has historically been the dominant faith in the United States, its followers have rarely spoken with one voice on various social issues. The author explains how the position of many evangelical Christians regarding the issue of the separation of church and state has changed since the founding of our nation.

Thomas Jefferson stood, dressed in a black suit, in a doorway of the White House on January 1, 1802, watching a bizarre spectacle. Two horses were pulling a dray carrying a 1,235-pound cheese – just for him. Measuring four feet in diameter and 17 inches in height, this cheese was the work of 900 cows.

More impressive than the size of the cheese was its eloquence. Painted on the red crust was the inscription: "Rebellion to tyrants is obedience to God." The cheese was a gift from religious leaders in western Massachusetts.

It may seem surprising that religious leaders would be praising Jefferson, given that his critics had just months earlier been attacking him as an infidel and an atheist. In the 1800 election, John Adams had argued that the Francophile Jefferson would destroy America's Christian heritage just as the French revolutionaries had undermined their own religious legacy. Adams supporters quoted Jefferson's line that he didn't care whether someone believed in one god or 20, and they argued that the choice in the election was: "God – And a religious president . . . [or] Jefferson – and no God."

From the *Washington Monthly*, April, 2006, 38(4). Reprinted with permission from the *Washington Monthly*. Copyright by Washington Monthly Publishing, LLC, 1319 F Street NW, Washington, DC 20004, (202) 393–5155. Web site: www.washingtonmonthly.com.

But in a modern context, the most remarkable thing about the cheese is that it came from evangelical Christians. It was the brainchild of the Rev. John Leland – a Baptist and, therefore, a theological forefather of the Rev. Jerry Falwell and Franklin Graham. Even though Jefferson was labeled anti-religion by some, he had become a hero to evangelicals – not in spite of his views on separation of church and state, but because of them. By this point, Jefferson had written his draft of the Virginia statute of religious freedom, and he and James Madison were known as the strictest proponents of keeping government and religion far apart. Because Baptists and other evangelicals had been persecuted and harassed by the majority faiths – the Anglicans in the South and the Puritan-influenced Congregationalists in the North – these religious minorities had concluded that their freedom would only be guaranteed when the majority faiths could not use the power of the state to promote their theology and institutions.

Each side of our modern culture wars has attempted to appropriate the Founding Fathers for their own purposes. With everything from prayer in school to gay rights to courtroom displays of the Ten Commandments at stake, conservative and liberal activists are trying to capture the middle ground and win over public opinion. Portraying their views as compatible with – even demanded by – the Founding Fathers makes any view seem more sensible, mainstream, and in the American tradition. And in truth, you can find a Jefferson or Adams quote to buttress just about any argument. But there are a few facts that might actually be stipulated by both sides in the culture wars. First, the original Constitution didn't say all that much about religion. God is not mentioned, and the only reference to religion is a ban on providing religious tests for holding office. (Ask why, . . . Conservatives say the Founders left it out because they wanted the states to regulate religion; liberals say it was because the framers were secularists who wanted strict separation between religion and government.)

Second, there was a widespread view among religious people of all flavors that the Constitution would be much stronger if it had a Bill of Rights that more explicitly guaranteed religious freedom. The 18th-century evangelicals were among the strongest advocates of this view and of the Bill of Rights, which declared that: "Congress shall make no law regarding the establishment of religion." Throughout the states, evangelicals pushed hard for ratification of the Bill of Rights in the state legislatures. Indeed, part of what made Jefferson cheeseworthy in the eyes of a Baptist leader like Leland was his advocacy of a Bill of Rights.

Modern Christian conservatives concede that point and hail the First Amendment, but they argue that it by no means follows that either the Founders or the evangelicals wanted a strict separation of church and state. They point out – accurately – that neither the Constitution nor the Bill of Rights includes the phrase "separation of church and state." And they argue that what the First Amendment intended to do was exactly what it says – and no more: prevent the "establishment" of an official state church, like the ones that had been prevalent in the colonies up until the time of the revolution. In the book *The Myth of Separation*, religious conservative David Barton argues that the Founders simply did not support separation of church and state. Indeed, he maintains, this was a Christian nation founded by Christian men who very much wanted the government to support religion. The contemporary intellectual battle over the role of religion in the public square will be determined in part on who can own the history.

It is ironic that evangelicals – so focused on the "true" history – have neglected their own. Indeed, the one group that would almost certainly oppose the views of 21st-century evangelicals would be the 18th-century evangelicals. John Leland was no anomaly. In state after state, when Americans met to debate the relationship between God and government, it was the early evangelicals who pushed the more radical view that church and state should be kept far apart. . . . It was the 18th century evangelicals who provided the political shock troops for Jefferson and Madison in their efforts to keep government from strong involvement with religion. Modern evangelicals are certainly free to take a different course, but they should realize that in doing so they have dramatically departed from the tradition of their spiritual forefathers.

To understand why, we need to go back to the period known as the Great Awakening, a spiritual movement of the 1730s and 1740s that challenged the style and theology of the existing churches. The dramatic wave of revivalism started in New Jersey and western Massachusetts, where ministers such as Jonathan Edwards preached about the importance of personal born-again experiences. These isolated revivals became a mass movement with the arrival in the fall of 1739 of an English preacher named George Whitefield. A friend of John and Charles Wesley, the founders of Methodism, Whitefield had developed a following after writing about his conversion experiences and travels from depravity to salvation. . . . His voice was powerful, almost hypnotic. He attacked the Church of England for its lethargy and lack of emphasis on the simple message that only God's mercy keeps us from damnation. Churches banned him from their pews, so he went into the fields, where he drew worshippers by the thousands.

Whitefield was what we would now call an evangelical. . . . Like modern evangelists, Whitefield used the latest media innovations to spread the gospel far and wide. In his case, that meant tapping into a burgeoning network of newspapers that had sprung up in the colonies – one of the most important being the *Pennsylvania Gazette*, a small publication purchased by Benjamin Franklin in 1729. For six months before Whitefield's arrival, the *Gazette* had printed dispatches about his preaching in England – the 20,000 who showed up at Kensington Common, or the time he delivered a sermon on a tombstone, or how he used tree limbs as pews. Once Whitefield arrived, Franklin offered saturation coverage of his every move, the huge crowds in Charleston and Wilmington, and the money he was raising for an orphanage in Georgia.

Franklin strongly disagreed with Whitefield's central message. A strict Calvinist, Whitefield believed that good behavior could not get us into heaven; Franklin, self-described Deist, did. But there was much about Whitefield, and the evangelicals, that Franklin liked. Whitefield relentlessly attacked the established clergy not only for its stodginess, but also for its lackadaisical attitudes toward moral evils. He denounced mistreatment of slaves, endorsed education for blacks, and established several charities. Because he was preaching in open fields, he drew people from a variety of denominations, classes, and even races.

When local clergy stopped giving Whitefield a place to speak, Franklin helped build a new hall for him – and for clergy of any other religion. Franklin boasted that it was "expressly for the use of any preacher of any religious persuasion who might desire to say something to the people at Philadelphia; the design in building not being to accommodate any particular sect, but the inhabitants in general; so that even if the Mufti of Constantinople were to send a missionary to preach Mohammedanism to us, he would find a pulpit at his service." For Franklin, evangelicals represented the democratic spirit railing against authority and insular institutions.

In part for this reason, the Great Awakening transformed the colonial approach to the separation of church and state. Throughout the colonies, churches divided into "Old Lights" and "New Lights," with the latter group tending to oppose the established churches more vigorously. As the years proceeded, the Church of England and the official churches became closely linked in the public mind with royal tyranny in general. For the New Lights, opposition to the official church became opposition to English rule, and vice versa.

This idea, seeded by the Great Awakening, was revolutionary in itself. Most of Europe had for centuries operated under the theory that the state took its authority from God. It had both the responsibility and right to intervene in religious matters. Conversely, the religious institutions tended to rely on the state to help enforce their doctrine. More important, most of the colonies had imported the idea that an official "established" church was an absolute necessity for promoting religion. In the South, it was the Anglican church, while in the North, the Puritan-influenced Congregationalist church was dominant. In both cases, there was a broad accep-

tance among the colonial elites of the idea that established churches were traditional and sensible. By equating political and religious persecution, the evangelicals helped lay the foundation for a radical political shift in the colonies.

One of the fastest growing of the evangelical groups was the Baptists, the current heart of the "religious right." As the Baptist influence grew, so did the Anglican backlash against it. In May of 1771, an Anglican minister and a sheriff interrupted one Baptist preacher's hymn singing, put a horsewhip in his mouth and dragged him away from the meeting to be whipped in a nearby field. In Virginia, four Baptist preachers were imprisoned for their emotional sermons. . . .

As a result of this persecution, the evangelicals were strong supporters of revolution, believing that their fight for religious freedom would rise or fall with the war against political tyranny. After the revolution, they pressed their opposition to the official church establishments and their support for separation of church and state.

Historians on both sides of the modern culture wars have attempted to study the writing and passage of the First Amendment looking for clues about the Founders' intent. But to understand the role of broader public opinion, there's much more to be learned from the individual state fights over religious freedom. Right before the Declaration of Independence and for two decades after, state legislatures grappled with church-state issues with much greater specificity than the federal constitutional convention had. These battles were fought not only with a few elites in a committee room but also among a broad range of local landowners, merchants, and churchgoers. One of the most significant of these battles took place in Virginia.

After the revolution, there was a sense throughout the state that religion was in decline: Churches were struggling, and immorality was on the rise. Leaders of the dominant Anglican Church – which had turned into today's Episcopal Church – began pressing for state support of religion.

In 1784, Patrick Henry, the most popular leader in the state, campaigned for a law that would tax Virginians to support the promotion of Christianity. . . . He was taking the liberal view that religion in general should be aided. Under his proposal, voters could designate the denomination, or even the specific church, that their tax dollars would fund. Baptists could give money to the Baptist Church, and Presbyterians to their own church. Henry's bill even went so far as to provide that those who didn't want to support religion could have the option of targeting their tax dollars toward education in general.

The measure, "A Bill for establishing a Provision for the Teachers of the Christian Religion," gained wide support. It was viewed as a gentle and flexible approach to encouraging religions while remaining consistent with the spirit of the revolution. Richard Henry Lee . . . (and) even George Washington supported the approach.

One major Virginia leader stood in opposition to Henry and this popular proposal: James Madison. Though not as well known as Henry, Madison had just played the central role in the constitutional convention and had growing influence within the legislature. He fervently believed that even though the assessment did not create a religious establishment, it posed a severe threat to religious freedom.

On November 11, 1784, the tall, charismatic Patrick Henry and the frail, brainy James Madison faced off in the legislature. Henry argued that nations that had neglected religion had suffered and declined. Madison tried to counter by pointing out lands where religion had flourished without government support. Madison lost. By a vote of 47 to 32, the legislature voted for a resolution declaring that the people of the Commonwealth "ought to pay a moderate tax or contribution annually for the support of the Christian religion."

During a legislative hiatus that followed, Madison tried to turn public opinion by writing one of the most important documents in the history of American religious freedom, the "Memorial and Remonstrance." He asserted that even though the assessment would support Christianity in general . . . it was still akin to an "establishment."

"Who does not see that the same authority which can establish Christianity, in exclusion of all other Religions, may establish with the same ease any particular sect of Christians, in exclusion of all other Sects?" he asked. The bill, he said, was "an offense against God," and previous efforts throughout history to provide financial support for religion had backfired. "During almost fifteen centuries has the legal establishment of Christianity been on trial. What have been its fruits? More or less in all places, pride and indolence in the Clergy, ignorance and

servility in the laity, in both, superstition, bigotry and persecution."

Madison's paper was circulated widely throughout the state. He went from town to town arguing on its behalf. . . . What soon became clear is that Madison did have allies in his radical view that even the gentle assessment constituted a threat to religious freedom: the evangelical Christians.

"This scheme should it take place is the best calculated to destroy Religion," declared one petition from evangelical Presbyterians in Rockbridge. . . . The Baptist General Association in Orange, Virginia, rejected the idea that government aid was necessary to help religion as "founded neither in Scripture, on Reason, on Sound Policy; but is repugnant to each of them."

When the legislators returned to Richmond to vote on the measure, the tide had shifted. . . . It's worth noting that the focus of the evangelical argument against state aid to religion was not merely fear of persecution. After all, the assessment law had made it clear that Baptists could funnel their taxes to Baptist churches. Rather, the evangelicals believed that Christians were to render unto Caesar what was his – that the religious and political spheres were meant, by Jesus, to be separate. . . . They further argued that the approach ignored an important lesson of Christian history – that the greatest flowering of Christianity occurs without government support. . . .

With the evangelicals providing the political ground troops, the legislature then went even further, approving Thomas Jefferson's statute on religious freedom. The statute prohibited not only formal establishments, but also the use of government funds to aid any particular religion on the grounds that no man's taxes should be used to support religious beliefs with which he does not agree. "To compel a man to furnish contributions of money for the propagation of opinions which he disbelieves, is sinful and tyrannical."

A similar dynamic developed during the ratification of the Bill of Rights. The evangelicals provided the political muscle for the efforts of Madison and Jefferson, not merely because they wanted to block official churches but because they wanted to keep spiritual and secular worlds apart. . . .

Some religious conservatives today point to a slew of comments and actions from the Founding Fathers indicating their support for an intermingling of religion and state. These are not hard to find – in part for a reason rarely acknowledged by either side in the culture wars: The founders did not agree with one another on how to interpret the First Amendment.

John Adams, Patrick Henry, and others believed the First Amendment really was meant to block the formal establishment of an official church, but allowed much mixing of church and state. For instance, Adams endorsed national days of fasting and prayer and appointments of congressional chaplains. Jefferson and Madison were on the other end of the spectrum, demanding the clearest separation of church and state. . . . As president, Jefferson reversed the practice initiated by Washington and Adams and refused to have a national day of prayer. Madison agreed. He also cited the appointment of chaplains as being a direct violation of the "pure principle of religious freedom." . . . The Founding Fathers were divided on separation of church and state – but most of the evangelicals weren't. They overwhelmingly sided with Jefferson and Madison. . . .

Today's Christian conservatives often note that Jefferson's famous line declaring that the first amendment had created "a wall separating church and state" was not in the Constitution but in a private letter. But in that letter, Jefferson was responding to one sent to him by a group of Baptists in Danbury, Connecticut. We usually read Jefferson's side of that exchange. It's worth re-reading what the Danbury Baptists had to say because it reminds us that for the 18th-century evangelicals, the separation of church and state was not only required by the practicalities of their minority status, but was also demanded by God. "Religion is at all times and places a matter between God and individuals," the Baptists wrote, warning that government "dare not assume the prerogatives of Jehova and make Laws to govern the Kingdom of Christ." Government had no business meddling in the affairs of the soul, where there is only one Ruler.

The evangelical wariness of the political world persisted for many of the next 200 years. The creation of the Moral Majority changed that. Angry about court rulings allowing abortion and banning prayer in school, Jerry Falwell and others argued that Christians should dive aggressively into the public realm in order to promote Christian values. The election of Ronald Reagan, the emergence of the Christian Coalition, and the enormously important role that religious conservatives played in the election of George W. Bush all seemed to validate that strategy. At this moment in history, the evangelical movement in politics is so strong – and their advocacy of greater government support for religion so persistent – it's difficult to remember that this view is relatively recent . . . (but) the spirit of John Leland can be discerned in some modern evangelicals.

The popular commentator Cal Thomas and the author Ed Dobson, both former officials of the Moral Majority, wrote a courageous book called *Blinded by the Might,* arguing that proximity to power had prompted religious conservatives to abandon their principles and distracted them from their religions mission. . . . And the Baptist legacy reappeared after George W. Bush's election when a number of religious conservatives surprised pundits by suggesting that churches should not accept money from the faith-based initiative. . . .

A small group of influential evangelical historians have tried to rebut the notion that the country was founded as a Christian Republic. Mark Noll, George Marsden, and Nathan Hatch, the preeminent evangelical historians, wrote a book called *The Search for Christian America* in which they gently, but firmly, attempted to correct a number of misconceptions that modern religious conservatives have about their own past. "The tragedy is that we come to believe that we are attuned to the wisdom of the ages," they noted, "when in fact the sound we really hear is but an echo of our own voice."

So far these individuals – the ones we might call the Original Intent Evangelicals – have been overshadowed by higher-profile Christian conservative leaders like James Dobson, Pat Robertson, and Charles Colson. These leaders insist that the Founders meant only to block the establishment of an official state religion, not to stop all government support of specific religions. Therefore, they argue, the Constitution should be read to allow vouchers for schools that teach religion, prominent displays of the Ten Commandments in government offices, even open proselytizing by military chaplains. In some cases, they go even further. In 2005, the GOP-controlled Virginia House of Delegates passed a measure that would amend the state constitution – and override language that Jefferson himself had written – to allow prayer and proselytizing on all public property (a Senate panel ultimately killed the measure). And a plank in the 2004 Texas Republican platform declares that: "the United States of America is a Christian nation" and disparages "the myth of the separation of church and state."

Contemporary religious conservatives can certainly find quotes from Founding Fathers to support their claims that government should aggressively support religion. They'll have a harder time finding quotes from 18th-century evangelicals. (They) are free to chart a different course from earlier Christians, but they should do so with the knowledge that some very pious evangelical leaders believed this was a dangerous path.

The Morning After the Morning After

In the United States, people should feel free to worship as they please without fear of persecution, but our history reveals frequent failures to live up to that principle. As this essay makes clear, since the terrorist attack on 9/11, many non-Christians, especially Muslims, have felt victimized by stereotypes and suspicion from the majority.

August 12, 2005

A 15-year-old student named Basil who attends a racially and ethnically integrated, middle-class public high school says, "When I walk down the street, I know they're thinking I may be a terrorist."

Over the last year, I joined colleague Selcuk Sirin of New York University in conversations with Muslim-American youth in the New York metropolitan region, in a small effort to bear witness to the collateral damage at home, in the bodies and souls of U.S. Muslim-American youth, a small but deeply affected part of a great mass of people [who are] compelled to find their voice. These young people, aged 12 to 18, were unsuspecting teenage citizens of the United States of America – until 9/12/01.

Between then and now, our nation has invaded Afghanistan and Iraq, exchanging Osama bin Laden for Saddam Hussein. We have constructed, detained, and abused at Guantanamo; passed the Patriot Act; and orchestrated mass detentions of Muslim Americans, including some young people under 18. We have elected George Bush to a second term, witnessed the atrocities of Abu Ghraib. Esti-

From *Forever After: New York City Teachers on 9/11*. Edited by Teachers College Press with Maureen Grolnick (New York: Teachers College Press), Copyright © 2006 by Teachers College, Columbia University. All rights reserved.

mates range from 25,000 to 1 million Iraqis who have been killed, as we near the 2,000 mark for the number of American soldiers killed.

"How do you know they're thinking you might be a terrorist?"

"I know," Basil replies, his voice dropping. "I just feel constantly violated . . . even if they say nothing."

As the Muslim-American youth talk to us, they tell us – one of us Turkish and raised Muslim, the other a Jew from the Northeast United States – that on September 12, 2001, they were evicted from the moral community of psychological citizenship in the United States. From that point forward, maybe before, these young people and their families have experienced a relentless undertow of challenges to their psychological well-being, social relations, and public life; placed at once under intense surveillance and rendered fundamentally invisible as human, critical, engaged citizens. Marian, age 18, told us:

I remember that day [9/11/01] my father drove home a number of children from school, a religious school. As he dropped them at the elementary school where they would meet their parents, the police were there, taking names, phone numbers, and licenses. That was frightening enough, but as we drove off we found ourselves in a big traffic jam, and some woman screamed out of her car, "Why don't you just go home?" I knew then that everything was going to be different.

These young people describe daily walks to school, being on the streets, at the mall, in the library, on the bus, escorted by the specter of *terrorist* (for boys) and *oppressed/uneducated* (for girls). Living in the new "world," they were now outsiders within their own communities and schools. We heard stories of airport delays, dates broken because "my parents wouldn't understand," tongues bitten in history class for fear of being sent to the principal for a dissenting opinion. Abid, a sophomore at a public high school, told us, "My history teacher got mad when I challenged him about the war . . . I think his son is fighting there." Ahab, at age 11 the youngest and smallest in our discussion group, joined our conversation with a whisper, "I don't like it either when people think me, or my father, is going to throw a bomb."

When we asked whom they turn to, in the face of these difficult adolescent interactions, they explained: "I don't really tell my parents. They have enough to contend with." Salma elaborated with a story about her father and his job. Originally from Macedonia, Salma's father works in the food industry at a major hotel. Importing a long and deep history of hiding his Muslim identity, at the hotel he remains silent about his ethnic and religious commitments. Asked by the hotel chef to "taste" a new chicken dish dipped in wine, he politely refused and later told his family that he told the chef he was "allergic" to chicken." Salma laughed, "Dad, this is America. You can say you are Muslim, and you don't drink wine." And then turning to the focus group, she continued, "My parents hide everything, but we're free here." Protecting parents from knowledge of persistent discrimination and "parenting parents" about U.S. ways of life appear to be two of the related labors of adolescent hyphenated selves.

We asked these teens to draw identity maps, to reveal how their "American" selves and their "Muslim" selves overlap/interact/negotiate life in the United States post-9/11. As the identity maps reveal, Muslim-American youth craft *hyphenated cultural selves* in a sea of contested global relations and representations. *How* young people negotiate at the hyphen varies widely, and often by gender, class, and type of schooling (public, religious, home schooling). But they all have to negotiate.

Consider the words and images on the map created by Omar, age 14, who humanizes what we

heard from so many of the young men we interviewed: the factors of being Muslim and being American have seared him in half, filling him with "tears for racism," a frowning face, a severed soul. Living with the haunting ghosts of "terrorist" looming around him, he, like so many young men, feels swallowed by a representation he can't actively resist, lest he embody the hegemonic trope – young Muslim filled with rage. To resist, he tries to contain the anger, to protect himself and his family.

The identity map for Selina, age 15, has a distinct yet equally powerful visual narrative of fluid selves – American and Muslim – at the hyphen, voicing what so many of the young women told us. Actively refusing to separate the currents of Islam and America that move through the river of her body, she nevertheless recognizes the distinct pools of water from which they gather a fluid sense of identity, rightfully claiming both currents at the same time, decorated with smiles and (in color) a beautiful blending of shade.

Not at all naive to the flood of stereotypes held about Muslim women as uneducated, oppressed, or dupes of religion, the female students look for ways to educate those who stereotype and "don't know any better."

Many of the young people mentioned times in school when everyone "turns to me, like about the war. Like I am supposed to educate them." We asked if they mind being singled out as an authority. Most said no, they didn't mind, although they were a bit discomforted by the attention. Amira offered an elaborate retort:

> I guess it's better that I educate them than they stay ignorant. I want to tell them there is more to know than just today, them alone, the mall, boys, music. I want to tell them to learn about what's going on in the world. But they don't watch the news or read the paper. I listen to CNN, Fox News, Al-Jazeera, and French news every night. So maybe it's best that I do answer their questions. There is a big world out there, and I personally believe I am just one small dot in this world. There is something much bigger than any of us. I wish the American students understood that.

Both boys and girls are equally frustrated by the absurdity of questions tossed their way (Are you a terrorist? Why do you dress like that?), but the girls are nevertheless eager for others to "just ask me a question – don't assume I'm gonna throw bombs . . . or I'm an uneducated woman!" They want the opportunity to share themselves, to teach, and to change minds.

We thought that Muslim girls who are veiled and therefore more visible would have a more difficult path than [relatively invisible] Muslim boys, but we were wrong. Amira helped us understand what seemed initially like an anomaly: "I finally figured out what to tell people about the *hijab*. I wear it like a bicyclist wears a bike helmet. It protects me from danger, and it gives me the freedom to wander where I dare not without it. Then they leave me alone!!"

Filled with confidence and wonder, the young women voiced concern that "people are afraid to talk to me because I wear a hijab." They nevertheless seek contact with a larger world. When asked, "If you were on MTV, what would you tell other teenagers about being Muslim-American?" they were eager to tell their peers:

"Yes, we shower!"

"No, we don't swim in a *hijab!*"

"It's not that my parents won't let me go to the dance, I don't want to go!"

"We use cell phones, and can tuck them in. Look – I'm hands free!"

In contrast, in our discussions with the young men, hyphenated cultural selves were splintered with the weight of the world; split open with the searing knife of global conflict. As Omar (the 14-year-old) articulates in his identity map, so many of the young men view the United States as an oppressive force on their souls ("get rich," war, country sucks). Some wax eloquent with a mystifying romance ("wanna go home") to return to their "homelands of peace." This is despite the fact that an overwhelming majority of the participants were born in the United States and have very limited, if any, real-life experiences outside of this country.

Adamant about the splits between the United States and "Muslim countries," Adnan wrote in his map, under "U.S.A.": "Land of opportunity, rich, war, get drafted and die." On the other side of his map, the heading reads "Muslims in Other Countries" and under that is written: "People are accused but are not hurt or no action is taken against them. Muslims love each other and take care of each other. Land of peace." Torn between the land where they live and are persecuted and a strong imaginary picture about peace abroad, taunted often at school and on the street, these young men try to prove the stereotype wrong and struggle to contain the anger, the rage, and not fight back.

While so many of the young men – as teens – come to see themselves as homeless or displaced, most of the young women – like those shown in this article – present themselves as transnational citizens or citizens of the world. And still, all yearn for a conversation, in school and out, with educators and peers about the global conflicts they carry in their souls.

Like the Arab and Muslim students with whom we spoke, many students today may find themselves part of the "collateral damage," exiled from mainstream culture. As teachers, we are charged with the responsibility of helping all students find a voice, and guiding them toward a deeper understanding of the multilayered circumstances that define a complicated, and often difficult, world.

If we do not teach about conditions of oppression and terror (state- and corporate-sponsored, interpersonal, domestic, and suicide bombs), even in times of relative prosperity and peace, we relinquish the space of public education to the globalization of terror, greed, fear, obedience, and silencing. By so doing, we surrender democracy, hollow the souls of educators and youth, and threaten our collective futures.

Today's students will become tomorrow's voters, policy makers, and world leaders. With such important responsibilities to look forward to, they deserve an education that interrogates what they know, and what they need to know.

Atheism and the Pursuit of Happiness

The authors are a medical doctor and a therapist, respectively. Dr. Newberg also teaches at the University of Pennsylvania, where his expertise in Radiology, Psychiatry, and Religious Studies has spurred his research into how the brain constructs reality and forms beliefs. This essay describes how atheists function in society compared to religious people.

Many studies have attempted to correlate religion with health, but none has clearly shown that atheism is an unhealthy belief system. By itself, a belief system cannot predict whether an individual will be happy or healthy. For example, a religious person who struggles with the tenets of his or her religion is likely to experience anxiety and stress, whereas a nonreligious person who derives great pleasure from secular beliefs will probably experience a high degree of satisfaction with life. Happiness is generated from multiple factors that involve social and family life, physical and emotional health, satisfaction with work, intellectual stimulation, and even altruistic pursuits. Religious beliefs are but one part of this complex interaction.

In a study conducted at the University of Illinois, 222 undergraduates were screened for happiness using several assessment filters. The researchers reported the following:

> We compared the upper 10% of consistently very happy people with average and very unhappy people. The very happy people were highly social, and had stronger romantic and other social relationships than less happy groups. They were more extraverted, more agreeable, and less neurotic, and scored lower on several psychopathology scales of the Minnesota Multiphasic Personality Inventory. Compared with the less happy groups, the happiest respondents did not exercise significantly more, participate in religious activities significantly more, or experience more objectively defined good events.[1]

Thus, happiness is not necessarily related to one's religious or spiritual beliefs. The most important element, according to these researchers, was maintaining a network of good social relationships. What, then, is one to make of the hundreds of studies supporting the notion that religious involvement enhances one's emotional and physical health? There are four important issues to consider in reviewing studies on religion and spirituality.

First, we have to recognize that the beneficial impact of religion, though statistically significant in many studies, is often small. More important, many factors not relating to spirituality per se are also involved. For example, religions offer social interaction; meaning in life; rules against unhealthy behaviors such as excessive drinking, smoking, or promiscuity; and a variety of psychological coping mechanisms. However, a person can also have access to these healthful elements through nonreligious groups. When religion does provide these healthy elements, it can be very beneficial; but the question is whether there is something intrinsic to religiousness itself that makes it healthier than other belief systems. In this sense, no one has yet designed the "perfect" study to account for all the variables that are involved in religious activities and personal health.

Second, most studies involve self-reports, which tend to be optimistically biased. In other words, nearly everyone tends to believe that the activities he or she chooses to engage in are beneficial, even when they are shown to be otherwise. People will also tend to ignore behaviors known to be unhealthy. Alcoholics, for example, will underrreport their drinking,[2] and nearly half of all adolescents will deny that they have every had a sexually transmitted disease, even though their medical records state otherwise.[3]

Third, the wording of many studies biases the outcome. This is not done deliberately; it's just one of the problems researchers face when trying to define their terms. The best a research study can do is point to a possible answer rather than an absolute truth.

Fourth, researchers often include experiences such as optimism, pleasure, peacefulness, forgiveness, and kindness as indicators of spiritual, mystical, and transcendent states. In fact, these attitudes promote health in both religious and nonreligious individuals.

When you take all these influences into account, it is difficult to argue convincingly that, on an individual basis, nonreligious people are less happy and less healthy than those who believe in God. In fact, according to the research by Phil Zuckerman, a professor of sociology at Pitzer College, "In sum, countries marked by high rates of organic atheism are among the most societally healthy on earth, while societies characterized by non-existent rates of organic atheism are among the most destitute. Nations marked by high degrees of organic atheism tend to have among the lowest homicide rates, infant mortality rates, poverty rates, and illiteracy rates, and among the highest levels of wealth, life expectancy, educational attainment, and gender equality in the world."[4] Citing the findings from contemporary research, Zuckerman concludes that a healthy society tends to promote widespread atheism whereas societal insecurity causes widespread belief in God.

Perhaps the most important thing to keep in mind is that all statistical surveys have built-in limitations. As the largest independent social research institute in Britain points out, pollsters incorrectly assume that respondents understand their questions in the ways the pollsters intended, and they also assume that all respondents answer in similar ways.[5] With this in mind, let's take a look at some of the more respectable surveys and the problems they raise.

In a study conducted by the Barna Group, atheists had a lower divorce rate than religious groups,[6] but in a study with over 10,000 participants, ARIS reported that atheists also had the lowest marital rate.[7] If you believe in the sanctity of marriage, poor statistical logic might lead you to the conclusion that you should give up your religious beliefs the day after your wedding in order to stay married.

In another reputable study, atheists reported higher levels of stress and less satisfaction in life than evangelicals.[8] Does this mean that strong religious beliefs are healthy for you? On one hand, this might be the case, but on the other hand, a recent study by the Mayo Clinic reported that compared with atheists and agnostics, highly religious people had more obsessional symptoms, showed more intolerance for uncertainty, needed to control thoughts, and had an inflated sense of responsibility.[9]

In a study that statistically analyzed the beliefs of people in sixty-six countries, religious people tended to trust others more, including the government, and were less willing to break the law. However, they also tended to be more racist, showed less concern for the rights of working women, and expressed greater intolerance towards other religious groups.[10] Buddhists, by the way, showed the greatest tolerance toward others. Atheists were more tolerant of others who held different beliefs, but were less trusting of the government and more willing to break the law.

The problem is this: opposing groups will selectively use data to support their point of view. Proponents of religion might say that atheists are thieves; and atheists might counter by pointing to the racism that religious groups generate. Both sides, however, would have adapted the findings to their own beliefs. When you look at data from a broader perspective, it seems clear that each individual is free to decide what is right or wrong, and that everyone, no matter what his or her religious orientation may be, has certain weaknesses and strengths. Human beings are full of faults. If religion helps some improve, great; and if being an atheist means fighting religious injustices, then this outlook also makes a contribution to our society. It all depends on your innermost beliefs and how you choose to manifest them in the world. . . .

In conclusion, the evidence suggests that we should be very careful about making causal connections in the accumulating data concerning spiritual and religious believers. There are compassionate, creative atheists; and there are murderers who act in God's name. This suggests that it is important to judge people not only on their beliefs but also on the behaviors that arise from those beliefs. Spiritual beliefs – all beliefs, for that matter – reflect the way we choose to understand reality, and this is a unique experience for every individual. Truth, beauty, compassion, morality – all such ideals can be embraced by religious and nonreligous people alike.

Different beliefs can open the mind to possibilities previously undreamed of, and this open-mindedness can be best achieved by maintaining a compassionate dialogue between all sides of the spiritual debate, especially between scientific and religious views. I believe that this is what Einstein was suggesting when he said that: "science without religion is lame, religion without science is blind." Whether we are gazing through a telescope, or contemplating our soul, we all can marvel at the beauty and mysteriousness of the universe. It is in the nature of our brain to search for its deepest truths, and although we may never grasp truth in its entirety, it is our right, and our biological heritage, to try.

Notes

[1] E. Diener and M. E. Seligman, Very happy people. *Psychological Science 13*(1), 2002, pp. 81–84.

[2] J. R. Nevitt and J. Lundak, Accuracy of self-report of alcohol offenders in a rural midwestern county, *Psychological Reports 96*(2), 2005, pp. 511–514.

[3] L. R. Clark, C. Brasseux, D. Richmond, et al. Are adolescents accurate in self-report of frequencies of sexually transmitted diseases and pregnancies? *Journal of Adolescent Health, 21*(2), 1997, pp. 91–96.

[4] P. Zuckerman, Atheism: Contemporary rates and patterns, in M. Martin (Ed.) *Cambridge Companion to Atheism* (Oxford: Cambridge University Press, 2006).

[5] D. Collins, Pretesting survey instruments: An overview of cognitive methods. *Quality of Life Research 12*(3), 2003, pp. 229–238.

[6] Barna Group, *Christians are more likely to experience divorce than are non-Christians,* Dec. 21, 1999. See www.barna.org.

[7] American Religious Identification Study (ARIS), 2001. For further information, see www.gc.cuny.edu/faculty/research_briefs/aris/aris_index.htm

[8] Barna Group, *People's faith flavor influences how they see themselves,* Aug. 26, 2002. See www.barna.org.

[9] J. S. Abramowitz, B. J. Deacon, C. M. Woods, and D. F. Tolin, Association between Protestant religiosity and obsessive-compulsive symptoms and cognitions. *Depression and Anxiety 20*(2), 2004, pp. 70–76.

[10] L. Guiso, P. Sapienza, , and L. Zingales, People's opium? Religion and economic attitudes. *Journal of Monetary Economics 50,* 2003, pp. 225–282.

Afraid of Ourselves

While a professor at Harvard, the author was the director of a research team known as the "Pluralism Project," which documented current religious diversity in the United States. This excerpt is from her book, A New Religious America, *which describes that diversity.*

"We the people of the United States of America" are now religiously diverse as never before, and some Americans do not like it. For the Fourth of July edition of the *Los Angeles Times* a few years ago, I wrote an op-ed piece on the many places we might find the American flag flying on the holiday – on the grand staircase of the Hsi Lai Buddhist Temple in Hacienda Heights, for example, or next to the blackboard in the fourth-grade classroom of an Islamic school in Orange County. A few weeks later I received a letter from a gentleman in Tampa, Florida, expressing astonishment at my article, which had been syndicated in a Florida newspaper. He was clearly upset by the piece and proffered his own conclusion: "If this is indeed the case, as you have alleged, then I wonder how all these people got here. Now is the time to close the doors. I suggest they go back where they came from." It is clear to me that the religious controversies of the American public square are just beginning.

I have often suspected that many Americans, like the man from Tampa, do not really know how much more complex our "sweet land of liberty" has become. When I read his letter, I thought of the days I had spent in another part of Florida, in the Miami area, visiting with Trinidadi immigrants at a Caribbean Hindu temple set in behind a shopping mall in Oakland Park, then finding my way to an Islamic center in a suburban area of Pompano Beach, finally heading to a Thai Buddhist temple that translates its name as "Temple of the Good Lord" in the flats south of Miami. I had to go looking for these places, as did all of our Pluralism Project researchers. The new religious America did not simply present itself in a coherent group photo. Rather, we made it a point to search out its various expressions. So I often wondered as I drove America's highways from temple to mosque to gurdwara just how many people had any idea that this is all here and what they would think if they did. The man from Tampa gave it a voice. He did not know about all these new neighbors, and when he found out he did not like it. Alas, he is also not alone. The climate of suspicion created by a new spate of American xenophobia has given rise to a thousand stories of insult and insinuation, assault and hatred.

New religious communities keep their stories of trouble within the oral histories of their own communities or in the pages of their local newspapers. The Muslim community of Flint, Michigan, remembers the night everyone ended up with flat tires. They had all come out of the mosque at the close of the Eid-al Fitr celebrations at the end of the month of Ramadan, only to discover, too late, that the parking lot had been strewn with hand-welded triangular spikes. The Hindu community in Kansas City

remembers the day a side of beef was hung belliger-
ently on the door of its temple, a clear statement by
someone that vegetarian Hindus had no place in a
city famous for its red meat. The Hindus of Pitts-
burgh remember the day that the Hindu temple in
Monroeville was desecrated and the word *Leave*
written across the altar. . . .

The perpetrators of such harassment surely sense
that change is in the air, and they are apprehensive.
New people have moved into their neighborhoods
about whom they know little except they are "different." When President Clinton spoke on the new
hate crimes legislation in April of 1999, he said,
"Our diversity is a godsend for us, and the world of
the twenty-first century. But it is also the potential
for the old, haunting demons that are hard to root
out of the human spirit." The haunting demons
surely include the fear of the foreign and the deni-
gration of the different, whether we speak of race,
ethnicity, or religion. The U.S. Department of Justice has started keeping records on hate crimes and
has reported a steady rise through the past decade,
with hate crimes motivated by race topping the list,
followed by those motivated by religion.[1]

. . . America is well on the way to becoming a
"minority-majority" country, with the numbers of
foreign born higher than at any time in the past
century. How we move from being a nation that
puts up with what are infelicitously called "aliens"
to being a nation that welcomes newcomers of
every religion – how we move from being strangers
to neighbors – is one of the great challenges of
America's new century of religious life. Nothing is
more central to most religious traditions than hos-
pitality toward the neighbor, even toward the
stranger. But we also know too well that our suspicions of neighbors, nurtured in an environment
where walls are many and bridges few, can create
the climate in which neighbors become enemies
overnight, as we have seen so tragically in multiethnic nations around the world. . . .

The newsman Walter Lippman spoke of stereotypes as the "pictures in our heads," the sketchy and
distorted images created by one group to describe,
label, and caricature another. These pictures,
shaped by media, reading, and hearsay, inevitably
yield images that don't match the human being.
They are stereotypes, some romantic and others
denigrating. Harold Isaacs's book on American images of Asia first published in the 1950s was entitled

Scratches on Our Minds. Some of the "scratchings" are
not even full-blown images for, as Issacs concludes,
"Vagueness about Asia has been until now the natural condition even of the educated American."[2]

Prejudice is prejudging people and groups on the
basis of these images, often half-formed caricatures.
As the quip goes, prejudice is "being down on
something you're not up on." People "known"
through stereotypes do not have the opportunity to
tell us who they are. We do not let them get close
enough to speak for themselves. We define them in
their absence, on the basis of the images already
present in our minds. Lata, a Boston Hindu friend,
put it this way: "People have a prejudged opinion
about you. Just seeing you, they already know who
you are, even though they never want to take the
time to really know who you are." . . .

Religious prejudice takes many forms, and
among the most destructive is simply erasing a
group's legitimacy as a religion. Anglo-Saxon newcomers to the continent did not see Native Americans as people with a "different" religious tradition
but rather as "pagans" with no religion at all. Native
people are sensitive to this negative image even
today. Anne Marshall, a Muscogee Creek Indian
and an executive in the United Methodist Church,
says, "Our Native traditions are not pagan, they are
sacramental. They have allowed our people to survive for five hundred years, no matter what was
done to us. But people don't even classify our religion as a religion, along with Hinduism and Islam."
Fellow citizens who identify religiously as Pagans
also face an uphill climb toward recognition. Most
people have no idea about the spiritual ecology of
American Paganism, a path that emphasizes humans' intimate dependence upon the Earth and its
ecosystems. They know little of Pagan ethics and
the principle of the Threefold Return, reminding
Pagans that every word and action directed outward, whether for good or ill, whether generous or
miserly, will return to them threefold. Instead, people tend to identify Paganism with broad negative
strokes, classifying it with Satanism and their worst
stereotypes of witchcraft. Other religious communities have also felt the sting of being left out of majority consciousness, like the young Sikh college
student who told us, "The thing that really bothered
me about stereotyping and discrimination was just
the fact that we're not really even recognized as a
religion. You're Sikh? How do you spell that? You

know, like, I've never heard of this before. I honestly feel I'm not accepted as fully having a religion here." . . .

The new immigrants of the late twentieth century faced denigrating stereotypes planted in the soil of ignorance and fed by a stream of negative media images. Terms like *Sikh militant* or *Islamic fundamentalist* express a shorthand version of complex political struggles abroad, and they shape in profound ways the mental images people hold of all Sikhs and Muslims. Muslims feel especially vulnerable to the stereotypes that so readily pair the word *Muslim* with *fundamentalist, terrorist,* or *holy war.*

Mary Lahaj, my third-generation Muslim-American friend, told us "Muslims are stereotyped as terrorists, fanatics. These kinds of labels (really) dehumanize the Muslim. This means that you literally don't look at the Muslim as another human being." . . .

Couple a deep negativity toward religious difference with a deep ignorance of other religious traditions, and we have a recipe for prejudice. For example, in 1990 a small item in the *New York Times* caught my eye under the headline "Yoga and the Devil: Issue for Georgia Town."[3] The dateline was Toccoa, Georgia, and apparently officials barred a town-sponsored yoga class "because the relaxation of yoga exercises would open practitioners to the influence of the devil. 'The people who are signed up for the class are just walking into it like cattle to a slaughter,' said a leader of a local group comprised of Baptists, Lutherans, and other Christians." Defenders of the class insisted that the class was only for stretching and relaxing, not for promoting religion. Clearly what to many Americans has been a spiritual practice is perceived as a threat in what must be a fairly homogeneous town. The small town of Winter, Wisconsin, was the scene of another such incident. A high school student found the computers of the school district blocked, preventing her from access to information on Wicca, and a member of the school board accused her of being a "devil worshiper" for seeking such information. The district had installed a computer filter system to restrict Internet access to subjects deemed controversial. The student complained, "I tried to look up Buddhism and it was blocked. Then I tried to look up Wicca and it was blocked. Then I looked up Christian churches and you could find anything you want."[4] The case attracted nationwide atten-

tion, and eventually the school district changed the system before the case reached the courts. But at the civic level, it is yet another example of the potent mixture of fear and ignorance that sparks so many incidents of outright discrimination.

In New Jersey . . . the dot, or *bindi*, on the forehead worn by many Hindu women stood for the strangeness of the whole Indian immigrant community in the eyes of a racist group calling themselves the Dot Busters. The attacks had nothing to do with Hinduism as a religion but were directed at all South Asian immigrants. In 1987 in Jersey City, a climate of constant low-level harassment turned to violence. A thirty-year-old Indian immigrant, Navroze Mody, was beaten to death by a gang changing "Hindu, Hindu!" They conflated race, religion, and culture in one naked cry of hatred. . . .

A few weeks later, a young resident in medicine, Dr. Sharan, was assaulted by three young men with baseball bats as he walked home late one night in Jersey City. He was beaten severely and left unconscious with a fractured skull. Sharan was in a coma for a week and suffered severe neurological damage. He recalled that one of the young people yelled, "There's a dothead! Let's get him!" as they set out after him with their bats.

These incidents were a severe blow to the Indian immigrant community and jarred the community into taking political action seriously. A group called Indian Youth Against Racism (IYAR) was formed with a base at Columbia University. The group helped in getting a bill passed in the New Jersey legislature in 1990 that raised the mandatory penalties for "bias crimes." It documented instances of violence against Indians in New Jersey, and it helped implement a series of educational programs on South Asian cultures for students and faculty at a Jersey City high school. But the attacks have not ceased. In 1991 there were fifty-eight cases of hate crimes against Indians in New Jersey. In 1992 an Indian physician was hit on the head and sprayed with Mace, and an Indian businessman was struck on the head with a bat. In 1998 an Indo-Caribbean man was beaten on the street of Queens. The Asian American Legal Defense and Education Fund has started tracking incidents and organizing community awareness.[5]

. . . A new immigrant religious community may first encounter its neighbors not over a cup of tea but in a city council or zoning board hearing. Every religious tradition in America has faced zoning boards, but new and struggling religious communities often feel more acutely the sting of this civic scrutiny. (While) questions of zoning and traffic, and even the need for more recreational space, are real concerns, they also are ways of articulating, in concrete terms, some of the amorphous fears that residents may have about new neighbors. . . . I have often told my students and researchers that if you want to know how things are going in the new religious America, go to the zoning boards and city councils. There you will hear how people express their anxieties about the change that is afoot.

"I'm not a prejudiced person. I just don't want this to suddenly start changing the neighborhood."[6] These words of a New Jersey woman could well be the epigram of a chapter on America's zoning controversies. She was reflecting on the conversion of an old Jewish summer camp (near) her home into a Jain religious retreat center. The truth is, many people simply do not like change, and change is in the American air. . . .

The story of Dwarakadish Temple in Sayreville, New Jersey, sums up the building issues new immigrant communities have faced. We visited this temple before in our exploration of Hindu devotion in America, for it is a lively community of Krishna devotees called the Pushti Marga, the Path of Grace. The Hindus of northern New Jersey thought the old YMCA building in Sayreville would be the perfect site for a new temple to Lord Krishna, and they first negotiated to buy the building in May 1992. A year later, however, more than two hundred people packed the planning board meeting – only twenty-five of them New Jersey Hindus who supported the temple. After detailed discussions of how much traffic the temple would generate, the Hindus' plan was rejected by the board, citing issues of traffic and parking. But many at the hearing felt the deeper issue was sheer animosity toward the Hindus. "They only challenged us on traffic, but they were not in favor of having a temple here," concluded one temple member.

The fears of the Hindu community were confirmed when the YMCA building, still standing empty, was sprayed with graffiti. The newspaper *India Abroad* reported, "The mayor of Sayreville, New Jersey, John B. McCormack, says he is 'not taking lightly' anti-Hindu slogans that were painted on the walls of a proposed Hindu temple site. Writ-ten on several walls of the building were such expressions as 'Get out Hindoos' and 'KKK.'"[7]

The Hindu temple filed suit in U.S. District Court against the Sayreville Planning Board for "bias and discrimination against Asian Indians and practitioners of the Hindu faith." The Hindus insisted their religious freedom was being denied in the decision of the board to reject their proposal for a temple. As an article in the *New Jersey Law Journal* put it, "The plaintiffs also note that the board cited traffic concerns in denying the permit even though the state's Municipal Land Use Law prohibits use of off-site traffic considerations as a basis for making planning decisions. In addition, the suit alleges that the use of the YMCA as a temple conforms to the borough's zoning regulations and that even the board's chairman recognized that there was no legal basis for denying the trust permission to operate its temple.[8]

The case eventually was settled by mediation between the Hindu community and the planning board. The temple agreed to add more on-site parking, to prohibit on-street parking on its three major holy days, and to make other parking arrangements for those days. A representative of the planning board said, in retrospect, "The main consideration had to do with traffic. There is already a lot of traffic on the street, Washington Road. But the temple was a small part of the traffic problem and should not be asked to bear the burden of correcting an already existing problem."

Finally, the temple opened in 1994. Priests came from India for the occasion. More than three thousand people flocked to the temple opening. The newly renovated building had been painted a pale pink and decorated with thousands of flower garlands for the occasion. Every day since the temple opened, the devoted service of Lord Krishna has brought immigrant Hindu Americans to the temple on Washington Road. . . .

This is one of the hopeful signals of America's new multireligious experiment. Time and again, stories that begin with incidents of hatred or conflict evolve in time into stories of new neighbors who have, in the course of their conflict, learned much more about one another. Distant images have become people with faces, voices, and problems. Strangers, in time, become neighbors. And neighbors, even those who differ from us, become allies in creating our common society.

Notes

[1]William J. Clinton, *Remarks in the Roosevelt Room, The White House,* April 6, 1999. For hate crimes statistics, see the U.S. Department of Justice FBI Web site: www.fbi.gov/ucr/hatecm/htm#bias.

[2]Harold Isaacs, 1958, *Scratches on our minds: American images of China and India* (Armonk, NY: M. E. Sharpe, Inc. 1980), p. 37.

[3]"Yoga and the Devil: Issue for Georgia Town," *New York Times,* Sept. 7, 1990.

[4]Doug Grow, "Wisconsin Teen Victorious in Her Free-Speech Fight," *Minneapolis Star Tribune,* March 31, 1999.

[5]See also the India Abroad Center for Political Awareness.

[6]*Newark Star Ledger,* August 12, 1996.

[7]*India Abroad,* May 28, 1993.

[8]*New Jersey Law Journal,* December 20, 1993.

A Letter to My Great-Grandfather

The author discusses his legacy from his Jewish family, even though many of them were killed during the Holocaust, and his struggle to be honest with his family about being a gay man. Being aware of the prejudice and violence that persists against those perceived as "other," he argues that the best way to honor the legacy from his family is to follow Gandhi's advice: "Be the change you want to see in the world."

Dear Great-Grandfather Wolf,

Though I have never written to you, I have carried your image and felt your comforting presence ever since that first day when your son (my maternal grandfather, Simon) told me about you and his mother—my great-grandmother, Basha. One day, when I was very young, I sat upon Simon's knee. Looking down urgently, but with deep affection, he said to me, "Varn," (he always pronounced my name Varn), "you are named after my father, Wolf Mahler, who was killed by the Nazis along with my mother and most of my 13 brothers and sisters." When I asked why they were killed, he responded simply, "Because they were Jews." Those seemingly simple words have reverberated in my mind, haunting me ever since.

As you know, according to Ashkenazi Jewish tradition, a newborn infant is given a name in honor of a deceased relative. The name is formed by taking the initial letter of the name of the ancestor being honored. I had the good fortune to be named after you. As it has turned out over the years, you not only gave me my name, but you also gave me a sense of history and a sense of my identity.

Originally appeared in Angela Brown (Ed.) *Mentsh: On Being Jewish and Queer.* (Los Angeles: Alyson Books, 2004). Reprinted by permission of the author.

Simon left Krosno in 1912 bound for New York, leaving you and nine of his siblings. (Already in this country were one brother and three sisters.) As he left, a series of pogroms targeting Jews had spread throughout the area. He often explained to me that he could only travel by night with darkness as his shield to avoid being attacked and beaten by anti-Semites. He arrived in the United States on New Years' Eve in a city filled with gleaming lights and frenetic activity, and with his own heart filled with hope for a new life.

In 1929, Simon returned to Krosno with my grandmother, Eva, to a joyous homecoming —for this was the first time he had seen you since he left Poland. He took with him an early home movie camera to record you on film. While in Poland he promised that once back in the United States, he would try to earn enough money to send for his remaining family members who wished to leave, but history was to thwart his plans. During that happy reunion, he had no way of knowing that this was to be the last time he would ever see you and the others he left behind alive. Just 10 years later, the Nazis invaded Poland.

Simon heard the news sitting in the kitchen of his home in Brooklyn. He was so infuriated, so frightened, so incensed that he took the large radio from the table, lifted it above his head, and violently hurled it against a wall. He knew what this invasion meant. He knew it signaled the end of the Jewish population in Eastern Europe as he had known it. He knew it meant certain death for people he had grown up with, people he had loved, people who had loved him.

Simon's fears soon became real. He eventually learned from a brother who had escaped into the woods with his wife and young son that you, Basha, and a number of his siblings were tossed alive into a massive bon fire in the streets of Krosno by Nazi troops. Hundreds of Jews were burned alive that day, and those who were not were eventually loaded onto cattle cars and transported to Auschwitz concentration camp.

Simon never fully recovered from those days in 1939. Though he kept the faces and voices from that distant land within him throughout his life, the Nazis also invaded my grandfather's heart, killing a part of him forever. My mother told me that Simon became increasingly introspective, less spontaneous, less optimistic of what the future would hold.

In this country, my own father suffered the effects of anti-Jewish prejudice. One of only a handful of Jews in his school in Los Angeles in the 1920s and '30s, many afternoons he returned home injured from a fight. To get a decent job, his father, Edmond, was forced to anglicize the family name, changing it from "Blumenfeld" to "Fields."

My parents did what they could to protect my sister and myself from the effects of anti-Jewish prejudice, but still I grew up with a constant and gnawing feeling that I somehow did not belong. The time was the early 1950s, the so-called "McCarthy Era" – a time of fear, a time when difference of any sort was held suspect. In addition to being different because of their religion, many Americans believed that Jews were communists. On the floor of the U.S. Senate, a brash young Senator from Wisconsin, Joseph McCarthy, sternly warned that "Communists corrupt the minds and homosexuals corrupt the bodies of good upstanding Americans," and he proceeded to have them officially banned from government service. In terms of gay and lesbian people, during this era there were frequent police raids on gay and lesbian bars, which were usually Mafia owned; the U.S. Postal Service raided gay organizations and even published the names of their mailing lists in local newspapers, and people lost their jobs. Gays and lesbians were often involuntarily committed to mental institutions and many underwent Electro-shock therapy; some were even lobotomized.

My parents feared that I might be gay (or, to use the terminology of the day, "homosexual"). Not knowing what else to do, they sent me to a child psychologist from the time that I was four years old until I was twelve. And as it turned out, their perceptions were indeed correct.

While Simon was alive, my mother asked me not to discuss my sexual orientation with him – for he often expressed to me that it was now my responsibility to eventually marry and raise children so I could help perpetuate the Jewish people, a people who had been decimated in Europe. My mother worried that information concerning my sexual orientation would upset Simon, and that he probably wouldn't understand. Yet something within me felt that he knew anyway and that he most certainly did understand. I know it grieved him that I never married and that I did not give him any great-grandchildren; I saw how it pleased him to be around the children of my cousins. It hurt me not to be able to be fully open with him. I think now that if I had, it could have ultimately brought us closer.

Great-grandfather Wolf, you would have been proud of Simon. He was a loving and caring father, grandfather, and great-grandfather. He gave me so much: my enjoyment for taking long walks and sitting in quiet solitude, pride in my Jewish heritage, and most of all, my ability to love.

My journey of "coming out" as gay over successive years was often difficult and painful, but looking back, I conclude that it was certainly rewarding, for it has been the prime motivator for my work as a writer and social justice educator. I am committed to this work to ensure a better future for the young people growing up today, but to be completely honest, I have another major motivation. I still don't feel safe in the world, and therefore I have a deep personal stake in the work I am doing. Often, when I leave my little university enclave, I tend to feel like an outsider in my own country. Maybe that feeling will never completely leave me; I don't really know. I can take solace, at least, that the fear has diminished somewhat over the years.

A few years ago, great-grandfather, I felt your presence, your touch strongly as I co-facilitated a workshop in Eastern Massachusetts for 31 German teachers of English who were taking a summer course on U.S. culture at a local college. During the workshop, I heard you telling me that I was doing something exceptionally important. In my own small way, I was having an impact on these teachers who soon would be traveling back home to Germany, teachers who themselves would have an impact on German youth. I was proud to be an integral link in that chain. I knew I could not undo the terrible things that happened to you, but somehow I was doing my part to ensure that it never happened again.

Of course, I too have my own biases and prejudices, which I acknowledge and am taking responsibility to heal. I tend automatically to stiffen whenever I hear the German language being spoken. Growing up with Simon, I leaned to be wary of even buying German products. I recall a conversation, or should I say an argument, many years ago between him and my sister, Susan, in which Simon voiced his immediate and vehement protest when Susan brought up the notion of purchasing a Volkswagen. Until that day, I hadn't realized how deep were his wounds.

In my own case, on a number of occasions my wounds surfaced. For example, while attending an opera in Boston with a friend, I lost my ability to concentrate on the production as the German couple seated behind me spoke in their native tongue. And a few years earlier while traveling through Germany en route from Holland to Copenhagen on a train, my anxiety seemed almost paralyzing until we finally reached Denmark, clear of the German border.

During the workshop with the German teachers, my apprehension collided with the reality that these teachers were warm, good people whom I could begin to trust. I was overwhelmed with conflicting feelings and felt as though I were blanking out. While my co-facilitator led the group through an exercise, I walked out into the hallway of the building and up a short flight of stairs. As I looked out the window onto a courtyard, I saw a young mother and her toddler son walking slowly below me. Scenes from the film that Simon and Eva took when they visited you back in 1929 flashed through my mind. In those black and white images were pictured the inquisitive young children in their long night shirts, smiling proud women some with small infants in their arms, relatives of all ages self-consciously walking quickly toward the camera, for some inexplicable reason moving their arms around in tightly closed circles.

Great-grandfather, you know that I am gay. Even though you lived at a time and place in which homosexuality was little discussed, your presence offers me support and comfort, for you saw first-hand how parallel forms of oppression run side-by-side and at points intersect. Though you may not have actually witnessed those "accused" of same-sex attractions tortured and put to death, you no doubt heard about how they were treated. Hitler, in his ultimate fashion, showed the world the direct links in the various forms of oppression.

I recently looked up the word "holocaust" in the dictionary. Among the listings was the definition: "genocidal slaughter." As I read this, the same nagging questions came to me as they did that first day Simon told me about your death—questions concerning the very nature of human aggression, our ability for compassion, and, especially for those generations following World War II, our capacity to prevent similar tragedies in the future.

I write to you today, great-grandfather, with both bad and good news. The bad news is that I fear we are repeating many of the mistakes of the past. With the rise of nationalistic movements throughout Eastern Europe, long suppressed feelings of anti-Semitism and other forms of racism and ethnic hatred are once again resurfacing. "Ethnic cleansing" has become the sanitized term for hatred, forced expulsions, and murder. Hate-motivated vandalism and violence are on the increase in the United States too. For example, the series of incidents in 1999: fire bombings at three synagogues in and around Sacramento, California; the shooting spree in Indiana and Illinois singling out Jews and Koreans; the spraying of bullets into a Los Angeles Jewish Community Center wounding a number of Jewish adults and children, and eventually, the killing of an Asian postal worker. We have witnessed the brutal attacks on Rodney King in Los Angeles, the barbarous slaying of James Byrd, Jr. in Jasper, Texas, and the fierce rape and murder of a seven-year-old girl in a Las Vegas casino bathroom.

In addition, the numbers of lesbian, gay, bisexual, and transgender people who are the targets of violence are escalating. Almost every week we hear of brutal and senseless attacks, so-called "gay bashings." In our schools and on our streets, groups of males wielding baseball bats and guns target anyone who acts or looks "different." For example, two men in Alabama bludgeoned to death Billy Jack

Gaither, a thirty-nine-year-old gay man, with an ax handle and tossed his limp body onto a pyre of burning tires. Brandon Teena, a female-to-male transgender person, was gang raped in Nebraska. Teena reported the incident to local police officials who basically discounted his story. Soon thereafter, the perpetrators entered Teena's home and murdered him along with two of his friends.

There is a tradition in the western states of the United States of ranchers killing a coyote and tying it to a fence to scare off other coyotes, and to keep them from coming out of their hiding places. On October 6, 1998, two young men lured a twenty-one-year-old gay college student at the University of Wyoming in Laramie into their pickup truck. They drove Matthew Shepard to a remote spot on the Wyoming prairie, pistol whipped him, and shattered his skull. As if he were a lifeless coyote, they tied him to a wooden fence where he was bound for over eighteen hours in near freezing temperature. The message from his attackers seemed quite clear: to all lesbian, gay, bisexual, and transgender people, stay locked away in your suffocating closets of denial and fear and don't ever come out into the light of day.

Great-grandfather, I like to think that you were there with me in the winter of 1991 when I had the opportunity to travel with my friend Derek to Amsterdam on vacation. This city is truly magical, especially in winter when its intricate series of canals freeze over offering a veritable ice highway to a country of skaters. Of all the amazing sites I visited, none attracted my interest more than the Homo-monument and the Anne Frank House.

The monument consists of three separate triangles of pink granite, which together form one larger triangle. Over one of the triangles hangs the following inscription: "HOMOMONUMENT commemorates all women and men oppressed and persecuted because of their homosexuality, supports the International lesbian and gay movement in their struggle against contempt, discrimination, and oppression, demonstrates that we are not alone, calls for permanent vigilance." The theme of the monument is "Past, Present, and Future," and the three pink triangles relate to the three aspects of this theme.

Following my visit to the monument, I walked the short distance to the Anne Frank House. On my first visit to the House in 1972, I was too overcome with grief to remain for more than a few minutes. This time, as I mounted the narrow steps leading to

her hiding place, I envisioned her faint image and could almost see her writing her secret thoughts in the diary that would one day become a chronicle, a testimony to all the world.

It is no coincidence that these two historic sites (one to commemorate the Jews of Holland, the other to a sexual minority) rest a mere few hundred meters apart. Though clearly not identical, there are connections between the pain and suffering endured by Anne, her family, and countless other European Jews, and the pain and suffering of gay and lesbian people forced into the camps under the pink and black triangle cloth.

In 2000, I again visited Europe, and this is the good news I alluded to earlier. In November when I was visiting my mother and sister at their home in Nevada, I checked my email and found a personal invitation to give a presentation at an international colloquium to be held in Berlin, Germany the following February. The topic of the colloquium was *Die Verfolgung Homosexueller im Dritten Reich* (The Persecution of Homosexuals under the Nazis) and the colloquium organizers were aware of my work on this topic. They wanted me to give one of my slide presentations titled "The German Homosexual Emancipation Movement from 1860 to 1933" to lay an historical foundation for the colloquium. I immediately accepted their kind invitation, expressing how enormously honored I was and how much I looked forward to joining what I believed would be a truly remarkable program.

Over the next few weeks before traveling to Berlin, however, the reality set in, filling me with a constant and overwhelming anxiety from which I could not escape. I lay in my bed late into the night unable to sleep, thoughts of you and Basha, Simon and Eva flashing into my consciousness. Difficult and seemingly unanswerable questions filled my mind: "Will my going to Germany be tantamount to betraying my kin?" or "Would they approve of this trip?" And "What about my personal safety? How secure is Germany for Jews today?" Also, self doubt concerning my abilities engulfed me: "What right do *you* have?," I questioned myself. "You are an American, you don't speak German, and you are traveling to Germany to present German history to Germans? What sense does that make?" My heart raced many nights and I often wept before I went to sleep. On a few occasions, I nearly got out of bed to email the colloquium organizers to say that I would not be able to attend. Throughout the days leading up to the colloquium, my apprehension was intense; I withdrew from friends, becoming increasingly melancholy, isolated, depressed. My friend Leah reached out to me saying, "You bring with you a clear and resounding voice, one that your relatives were denied. You can speak in their memory and speak in a way that they never could." Her words resonated in my mind at Boston's Logan airport as I boarded the Lufthansa plane that was to transport me to Berlin. It was a profoundly emotional journey, tears flowing unencumbered throughout that long flight.

I arrived on a cloudy and drizzly morning. On the cab ride to my hotel, except for a small segment of the Berlin Wall that stood as a reminder of the city's not-so-distant past, the landscape appeared strangely familiar, for this could have been any of a number of European or even U.S. cities: urban factories, small shops, rush-hour traffic, pedestrians toting raised umbrellas walking to work, and children on their way to school. Once in my hotel room, I turned on the TV and viewed a children's program in which a young girl and boy demonstrated the proper way to assemble a tropical aquarium. This seeming ordinariness was somehow reassuring to me.

I ventured downtown walking through a number of neighborhoods and riding the subway. People appeared relaxed and friendly.

By the day of the colloquium, I had begun to feel that I had made the right decision in coming here. The first panel was composed of preeminent researchers in the persecution of homosexuals under the Third Reich, followed by curators of Holocaust Museums and concentration camps. Next, two gay men, both survivors of the death camps, gave moving testimonials. I then shared the platform with a college student whom I had met in Florida one year prior and whom I invited to join me in the presentation.

As the lights lowered, I pressed the "advance" button on the remote-control switch to display the first slide. Toward the end of my presentation, I concluded on a personal note choking back tears: "This has been a difficult presentation for me," I acknowledged, "for I come to you today speaking not only as a gay man, but also as a Jew. I feel honored to have been invited to come to Berlin to be able to speak on behalf of my family members whose voice was extinguished." I dedicated my talk to your memory, and to Basha, Simon, and Eva. I continued:

> And to their memory, I raise a central tenet of Jewish tradition, which is *Tikkun Olam:* meaning the transformation, healing, and repairing of the world so that it becomes a more just, peaceful, nurturing, and perfect place. As we look back over the unconscionable horrors of the Nazi era, I have a hope—a hope that we can all join together as allies to counter the hatred so we can make real the true potential of *"Never Again."* I end then by asking us all to join and go out into our lives, and work for *Tikkun Olam.* Let us transform the world.

Throughout the colloquium and my time in Berlin, I felt your presence, great-grandfather, and the power of *Tikkun Olam*, for I continued my own healing journey as someone from the third generation, someone who has been touched very deeply by the German Holocaust.

As you know, I am by no means a very religious person, though I strive to become more spiritual and connected to you. Before the end of my days, I know I must travel back to Krosno if I want to be able to say that I have truly accomplished all I needed to accomplish in this world. Simon's son, my uncle Jack, has informed me that your small village no longer exists. Although the Nazis destroyed Krosno, I want to walk upon the soil that you once walked upon, to witness the hallowed ground on which you prayed, and to feel the Polish sun nurturing me as it had once nurtured and illuminated you—that same sun which they eclipsed from you all too soon.

I don't know if there really is a purpose to life, or if we are placed here for a reason. If it is true that we all have a unique mission or calling in this world, I believe mine is to continue doing the work I am doing, with you as my guide. You are that still and quiet voice within me, that voice that keeps me on course and prevents me from sinking under the waters of doubt and fear. The mistakes I have made along my path most assuredly occurred when I refused to heed your counsel.

Being both Jewish and gay, I truly believe I am "twice blessed." I ask that you now, great-grandfather, stay with me and continue to be my teacher, my light, my guide. With you by my side, I can never be alone.

With love forever and ever, Warren

The Three Hermits

An Old Legend Current in the Volga District

*No matter what religion a person follows, the challenge of all faiths is to live with a sense
of love and compassion for each other and the world. The author believes that the real
proof of faith is seen not in the differing rituals of religions, but in the way we live each
day, and he offers a parable based on an ancient legend to illustrate this point.*

> **And in praying use not vain repetitions,
> as the Gentiles do: for they think that they
> shall be heard for their much speaking.
> Be not therefore like them: for your
> Father knoweth what things ye have
> need of, before ye ask Him.**
>
> **Matthew VI: 7,8.**

A Bishop was sailing from Archangel to the
Solovétsk Monastery, and on the same vessel
were a number of pilgrims on their way to
visit the shrines at that place. The voyage was a
smooth one. The wind favorable and the weather
fair. The pilgrims lay on deck, eating, or sat in
groups talking to one another. The Bishop, too,
came on deck, and as he was pacing up and down
he noticed a group of men standing near the prow
and listening to a fisherman who was pointing to

the sea and telling them something. The Bishop
stopped, and looked in the direction in which the
man was pointing. He could see nothing, however,
but the sea glistening in the sunshine. He drew
nearer to listen, but when the man saw him, he
took off his cap and was silent. The rest of the people also took off their caps and bowed.

"Do not let me disturb you, friends," said the
Bishop. "I came to hear what this good man was
saying."

"The fisherman was telling us about the hermits," replied one, a tradesman, rather bolder than
the rest. "What hermits?" asked the Bishop, going
to the side of the vessel and seating himself on a
box. "Tell me about them. I should like to hear.
What were you pointing at?"

"Why, that little island you can just see over
there," answered the man, pointing to a spot ahead
and a little to the right. "That is the island where the
hermits live for the salvation of their souls."

"Where is the island?" asked the Bishop. "I see
nothing."

"There, in the distance, if you will please look
along my hand. Do you see that little cloud? Below
it, and a bit to the left, there is just a faint streak.
That is the island."

From *Twenty Three Tales* (translated and edited by Louise
and Maude Aylmer), (Oxford: Oxford University Press,
1947). By permission of Oxford University Press.

The Bishop looked carefully, but his unaccustomed eyes could make out nothing but the water shimmering in the sun.

"I cannot see it," he said. "But who are the hermits that live there?"

"They are holy men," answered the fisherman. "I had long heard tell of them, but never chanced to see them myself till the year before last."

And the fisherman related how once, when he was out fishing, he had been stranded at night upon that island, not knowing where he was. In the morning, as he wandered about the island, he came across an earth hut, and met an old man standing near it. Presently two others came out, and after having fed him and dried his things, they helped him mend his boat.

"And what are they like?" asked the Bishop.

"One is a small man and his back is bent. He wears a priest's cassock and is very old; he must be more than a hundred, I should say. He is so old that the white of his beard is taking a greenish tinge, but he is always smiling, and his face is as bright as an angel's from heaven. The second is taller, but he also is very old. He wears a tattered peasant coat. His beard is broad, and of a yellowish grey color. He is a strong man. Before I had time to help him, he turned my boat over as if it were only a pail. He too is kindly and cheerful. The third is tall, and has a beard as white as snow and reaching to his knees. He is stern, with overhanging eyebrows; and he wears nothing but a piece of matting tied around his waist."

"And did they speak to you?" asked the Bishop.

"For the most part they did everything in silence, and spoke but little even to one another. One of them would just give a glance, and the others would understand him. I asked the tallest whether they had lived there long. He frowned, and muttered something as if he were angry; but the oldest one took his hand and smiled, and then the tall one was quiet. The oldest one only said: 'Have mercy upon us,' and smiled."

While the fisherman was talking, the ship had drawn nearer to the island.

"There, now you can see it plainly, if your Lordship will please to look," said the tradesman, pointing with his hand.

The Bishop looked, and now he really saw a dark streak – which was the island. Having looked at it a while, he left the prow of the vessel, and going to the stern, asked the helmsman:

"What island is that?"

"That one," replied the man, "has no name. There are many such in this sea."

"Is it true that there are hermits who live there for the salvation of their souls?"

"So it is said, your Lordship, but I don't know if it's true. Fishermen say they have seen them; but of course they may only be spinning yarns."

"I should like to land on the island and see these men," said the Bishop. "How could I manage it?"

"The ship cannot get close to the island," replied the helmsman, "but you might be rowed there in a boat. You had better speak to the captain."

The captain was sent for and came.

"I should like to see these hermits," said the Bishop. "Could I not be rowed ashore?"

The captain tried to dissuade him.

"Of course it could be done," said he, "but we should lose much time. And if I might venture to say so to your Lordship, the old men are not worth your pains. I have heard say that they are foolish old fellows, who understand nothing and never speak a word, any more than the fish in the sea."

"I wish to see them," said the Bishop, " and I will pay you for your trouble and loss of time. Please let me have a boat."

There was no help for it; so the order was given. The sailors trimmed the sails, the steersman put up the helm, and the ship's course was set for the island. A chair was placed at the prow for the Bishop, and he sat there, looking ahead. The passengers all collected at the prow, and gazed at the island. Those who had the sharpest eyes could presently make out the rocks on it, and then a mud hut was seen. At last one man saw the hermits themselves. The captain brought a telescope and, after looking through it, handed it to the Bishop.

"It's right enough. There are three men standing on the shore. There, a little to the right of that big rock."

The Bishop took the telescope, got it into position, and he saw the three men: a tall one, a shorter one, and one very small and bent, standing on the shore and holding each other by the hand.

The captain turned to the Bishop.

"The vessel can get no nearer in than this, your Lordship. If you wish to go ashore, we must ask you to go in the boat, while we anchor here."

The cable was quickly let out; the anchor cast, and the sails furled. There was a jerk, and the vessel shook. Then, a boat having been lowered, the oarsmen jumped in, and the Bishop descended the ladder and took his seat. The men pulled at their oars and the boat moved rapidly towards the island. When they came within a stone's throw, they saw three old men: a tall one with only a piece of matting tied round his waist: a shorter one in a tattered peasant coat, and a very old one bent with age and wearing an old cassock – all three standing hand in hand.

The oarsmen pulled in to the shore, and held on with the boathook while the Bishop got out.

The old men bowed to him, and he gave them his blessing, at which they bowed still lower. Then the Bishop began to speak to them.

"I have heard," he said, "that you, godly men, live here saving your own souls and praying to our Lord Christ for your fellow men. I, an unworthy servant of Christ, am called, by God's mercy, to keep and teach His flock. I wished to see you, servants of God, and to do what I can to teach you, also."

The old men looked at each other smiling, but remained silent.

"Tell me," said the Bishop, "what you are doing to save your souls, and how you serve God on this island."

The second hermit sighed, and looked at the oldest, the very ancient one. The latter smiled, and said:

"We do not know how to serve God. We only serve and support ourselves, servant of God."

"But how do you pray to God?" asked the Bishop.

"We pray in this way," replied the hermit. "Three are ye, three are we, have mercy upon us."

And when the old man said this, all three raised their eyes to heaven, and repeated:

"Three are ye, three are we, have mercy upon us!"

The Bishop smiled.

"You have evidently heard something about the Holy Trinity," said he. "But you do not pray aright.

You have won my affection, godly men. I see you wish to please the Lord, but you do not know how to serve Him. That is not the way to pray; but listen to me, and I will teach you. I will teach you, not a way of my own, but the way in which God in the Holy Scriptures has commanded all men to pray to Him."

And the Bishop began explaining to the hermits how God had revealed Himself to men; telling them of God the Father, and God the Son, and God the Holy Ghost.

"God the Son came down on earth," said he, "to save men, and this is how He taught us all to pray. Listen, and repeat after me: 'Our Father.'"

And the first old man repeated after him, "Our Father," and the second said "Our Father," and the third said, "Our Father."

"Which art in heaven," continued the Bishop.

The first hermit repeated, "Which art in heaven," but the second blundered over the words, and the tall hermit could not say them properly. His hair had grown over his mouth so that he could not speak plainly. The very old hermit, having no teeth, also mumbled indistinctly.

The Bishop repeated the words again, and the old men repeated them after him. The Bishop sat down on a stone, and the old men stood before him, watching his mouth and repeating the words as he uttered them. And all day long the Bishop labored, saying a word twenty, thirty, a hundred times over, and the old men repeated it after him. They blundered, and he corrected them, and made them begin again.

The Bishop did not leave off till he had taught them the whole of the Lord's Prayer so that they could not only repeat it after him, but could say it by themselves. The middle one was the first to know it, and to repeat the whole of it alone. The Bishop made him say it again and again, and at last the others could say it too.

It was getting dark and the moon was appearing over the water, before the Bishop rose to return to the vessel. When he took leave of the old men they all bowed down to the ground before him. He raised them, and kissed each of them, telling them to pray as he had taught them. Then he got into the boat and returned to the ship.

And as he sat in the boat and was rowed to the ship he could hear the three voices of the hermits loudly repeating the Lord's Prayer. As the boat drew near the vessel their voices could no longer be heard, but they could still be seen in the moonlight, standing as he had left them on the shore, the shortest in the middle, the tallest on the right, the middle one on the left. As soon as the Bishop had reached the vessel and got on board, the anchor was weighed and the sails unfurled. The wind filled them and the ship sailed away, and the Bishop took a seat in the stern and watched the island they had left. For a time he could still see the hermits, but presently they disappeared from sight, though the island was still visible. At last it too vanished, and only the sea was to be seen, rippling in the moonlight.

The pilgrims lay down to sleep, and all was quiet on deck. The Bishop did not wish to sleep, but sat alone at the stern, gazing at the sea where the island was no longer visible, and thinking of the good old men. He thought how pleased they had been to learn the Lord's Prayer; and he thanked God for having sent him to teach and help such godly men.

So the Bishop sat, thinking, and gazing at the sea where the island had disappeared. And the moonlight flickered before his eyes, sparkling, now here, now there, upon the waves. Suddenly he saw something white and shining, on the bright path which the moon cast across the sea. Was it a seagull, or the little gleaming sail of some small boat? The Bishop fixed his eyes on it, wondering.

"It must be a boat sailing after us," thought he, "but it is overtaking us very rapidly. It was far, far away a minute ago, but now it is much nearer. It cannot be a boat, for I can see no sail; but whatever it may be, it is following us and catching up to us."

And he could not make out what it was. Not a boat, nor a bird, nor a fish! It was too large for a man, and besides a man could not be out there in the midst of the sea. The Bishop rose, and said to the helmsman:

"Look there, what is that, my friend? What is it?" the Bishop repeated, though he could now see plainly what it was – the three hermits running upon the water, all gleaming white, their grey beards shining, and approaching the ship as quickly as though it were not moving.

The steersman looked, and let go the helm in terror.

"Oh, Lord! The hermits are running after us on the water as though it were dry land!"

The passengers, hearing him, jumped up and crowded to the stern. They saw the hermits coming along hand in hand, and the two outer ones beckoning the ship to stop. All three were gliding along upon the water without moving their feet. Before the ship could be stopped, the hermits had reached it, and raising their heads, all three as with one voice, began to say:

"We have forgotten your teaching, servant of God. As long as we kept repeating it we remembered, but when we stopped saying it for a time, a word dropped out, and now it has all gone to pieces. We can remember nothing of it. Teach us again."

The Bishop crossed himself, and leaning over the ship's side, said:

"Your own prayer will reach the Lord, men of God. It is not for me to teach you. Pray for us sinners."

And the Bishop bowed low before the old men; and they turned and went back across the sea. And a light shone until daybreak on the spot where they were lost to sight.

Perspectives on Race and Confronting Racism

"Do you know what it is like to feel you are of no value to society? To know people come to help you because they believe you have nothing to offer? You hold out your hand and beckon me to come . . . I shall not come as an object of your pity; I shall come in dignity or I shall not come at all."

Chief Dan George (1899–1981)

Chief Dan George is describing the pain of racism and the courage of those who refused to be defeated by it. It is important that all Americans never forget the overt racism of the past, and that we continue to honor the abilities and achievements of those people of color who persisted and broke through barriers to realize their goals. They inspired communities of color; whether it was the scholarly brilliance of W. E. B. DuBois or the boxing skills of Jack Johnson and later Joe Louis, their accomplishments contradicted the lie of white supremacy. Some of the most significant refutations of racial stereotyping occurred in competitive sports. Today we still celebrate Jackie Robinson breaking the color line in professional baseball and it is still inspirational to watch the old black and white films of Jesse Owens using his athletic ability at the 1936 Olympics in Berlin to demolish the Nazi propaganda of Aryan supremacy. And twenty-four

years before that, a Sac and Fox Indian named Jim Thorpe proved that he was the greatest athlete of his time (and some say for all time) by winning gold medals in the pentathlon and decathlon at the 1912 Olympics in Stockholm.

Jim Thorpe was a hero to many American Indians even before his achievements in the Olympics. There is story that many Indians tell and a few others have heard that goes back to his days as a track athlete at the Carlisle School for Indians. The story not only celebrates Thorpe's incredible talents, but it is a parable for why racism contradicts the fundamental values of American society. In 1909 the coach at Lafayette College, Harold Anson Bruce, sent an invitation to Carlisle's coach, "Pop" Warner, to compete in a dual track meet between the two schools. Bruce was so anxious to see this almost legendary track team that he guaranteed a significant sum of money to the school if Carlisle would accept the invitation. They did and the track meet quickly sold out. Bruce was excited as he went to Central Station to meet the train bringing the Carlisle team, but he was surprised to find only a few young men gathered around their coach. Bruce approached the group and asked Pop Warner about the rest of his athletes. Warner said they were all there. There were only six Indian athletes standing beside the coach.

Bruce shook his head and said, "Pop, I've got a team of forty-six; it's an eleven event program. You won't stand a chance." Warner told him not to worry about it, and it was clear that he wasn't worried. When the track meet began, Jim Thorpe won first place in the 120-yard high hurdles and the 220-yard low hurdles. He also won first place in the high jump, broad jump, pole vault, and shot put. He was third in the 100-yard dash. Two of Thorpe's classmates won first and second place in the half-mile, the mile, and the two-mile. Another Indian athlete won the quarter-mile, and another was fifth place in the high hurdles. Carlisle won the dual meet, 71-41.[1] Imagine if that story had never happened, or if other talented people of color – not just athletes but poets, novelists, lawyers, doctors, artists, social activists, scholars and more – were not allowed to use their abilities to benefit our society. America was founded on the idea of the right of each individual to pursue happiness. When our society interferes with that pursuit for any of us, then all of us are diminished and our society edges closer to the drab and dreary world of dystopias. The author of *Black Like Me* stated this point unequivocally:

> Racism always involves an injustice committed by one person or group against another person or group . . . It is fatal in the end because it always works to damage *both* groups.

John Howard Griffin (1920–1980)

Although race has never been established by legitimate scientific criteria, it has proven to be a remarkably durable concept. Many human beings worldwide still perceive physical differences in racial terms that may also include hierarchical assumptions about superior and inferior racial groups. Recent genome research may be approaching a more scientific description of race, but as Wade (2006) points out, these racial categories have nothing to do with a person's appearance.[2] The genetic markers involved are related to ancestry and geography ("continent of origin") rather than physical attributes. Time will tell how far down that road we will go. The bigger issue for now is the need to understand how people form negative attitudes about race and what forms of overt and covert discrimination are based on perceptions of race. All of the selections for this section will address the varied examples of contemporary racism.

In the essay "Brave Warrior," Karen Coody Cooper focuses on racism in language used to refer to Native Americans that could be considered overt or covert, depending on the perceptions of the individual reader. Hopefully most Americans agree that the term "redskin" is racist. Referring to the history of the term, Cooper demonstrates why this word is inappropriate for use in any context, and certainly not as the nickname for a professional football team. She also discusses the implications of other terms such as "brave," "warrior," "pioneer," and "squaw." She concludes with an admonition that words are important, and that the choice of words may say more about people's negative attitudes than the actual content of the statements they make.

The excerpt from Nathan McCall's autobiography describes the covert racism that he encounters after he has finished serving his time in prison and tries to create a new life as a free man. Although McCall would eventually become a successful journalist, the experience he recalls in "Starting Over" is his testimony that it wasn't easy. McCall describes obstacles that he encountered immediately after his release from prison and the frustrations he felt trying to overcome stereotypes associated with being not only a black man but an "ex-con" as well. His story illustrates the poignant comment that tennis star Arthur Ashe made a few years before his tragic and untimely death:

> A pall of sadness hangs over my life and the lives of almost all African Americans because of what we as a people have experienced historically in America, and we as individuals experience each and every day.

While McCall was trying to overcome the negative stereotypes associated with being a black man and a former convict, Benji Chang and Wayne Au describe another kind of stereotype in "Unmasking the Myth of the Model Minority." Many white people regard the "model minority" image of Asian Americans as a realistic and positive image and not a stereotype. The authors explain where the model minority stereotype originated and they assert that although this stereotype is often viewed as positive, it actually has been damaging for Asian Americans. In addressing this myth, the authors also describe the diversity that exists among Asian Americans, and conclude with specific suggestions of effective ways for teachers to interact with Asian American students in their classrooms.

In "The New Racial Reality," Ellis Cose discusses the potential impact increasing numbers of biracial people in the United States will have on our traditional notions of race. While biracial

people have experienced overt and covert racism, they have also been confronted with unique issues. For example, biracial individuals continue to feel pressured to choose one race to identify with, as if others need you to choose before they know how to treat you. As Ellis notes, contemporary biracial people are more likely to reject the "us and them" mentality and to insist on claiming and identifying with whatever racial groups are included in their family heritage. We have already seen an example of this attitude in the excerpt from Barack Obama's book in Section Two. Cose shares the stories of several biracial individuals and the strategies they have used in dealing with other people who still want to pigeonhole them into a single racial category. Many of them are actively working to build bridges between racial groups as a way to combat racism.

In "Like Crabs in a Barrel: Why Inter-Ethnic Anti-Racism Matters Now," George Lipsitz also addresses strategies for combating racism, and he insists that no matter what racial category or categories someone identifies with, all people of color (and he would include biracial people) must become allies of other people of color who are confronting racism and trying to bring about social change. He discusses the "divide and conquer" tactic that has been used effectively against people of color in the past, and he provides examples of how this strategy is still being employed. He proposes that people of color need to form alliances with other groups and individuals across racial lines because only by working together can they hope to defeat racism. Lipsitz argues that those fighting against racism must cultivate a pluralistic awareness of others and not be limited to one perspective. He emphasizes that racism involves power, and that power can only

> ❝It does not help the cause of racial equality for white people to content themselves with being non-racist. Few people outside the Klan or skinhead movements own up to all-out racism these days. White people must take the extra step. They must become anti-racist.❞

Clarence Page (1947–)

be defeated by maintaining solidarity with all those who oppose it.

To conclude this section, Danny Romero's short story "Crime" is about the exercise of power on an individual level. Romero describes a scene from the life of a Latino named Libertad. As he is walking home from work, two policemen stop him and force him to get down on his knees for no apparent reason. They question him and they demand to see some identification — without providing any explanation for their actions. And then this Kafkaesque scene ends; even though Libertad has not done anything wrong and did not commit a crime, there is no doubt that a "crime" of injustice has been committed by the forces employed to enforce justice. The story

illustrates experiences that people of color have had with local police forces that are quite different from those of most white people. White people can choose to remain oblivious to these injustices or perhaps merely agree that an injustice has occurred, or they can feel the same sense of outrage that people of color feel, and work with others engaged in anti-racist activities to create a society that does not tolerate racial injustices.

Notes

[1] R. W. Wheeler, *Jim Thorpe, world's greatest athlete.* (Norman, OK: University of Oklahoma Press, 1978).

[2] Nicholas Wade, *Before the dawn: Recovering the lost history of our ancestors.* (New York: The Penguin Press, 2006).

Brave Warrior

The author reminds us that words matter, especially when the words are referring to an entire group of people. As an education professional working for the Smithsonian, the author was involved in the creation of the verbal and visual displays at the American Indian Museum in Washington D.C.

> **Sticks and stones may break my bones, but words can never hurt me.**

How many of us, as children, chanted that line to our tormentors as we ran away holding back tears? The ditty is not true. Words are extremely important and they can be very hurtful. Words can cause, or prevent, wars. Communication is often touted as one of the main difficulties in the workplace. Many arguments occur because we misunderstand the words used by someone. But, more often than not, arguments begin because words were formed specifically to hurt, abuse, antagonize, marginalize, or incite. This brief exploration will look at some of the words applied to American Indians and examine how the interpretation of the words affects our understanding of American Indians as fellow humans.

When preparing educational materials, it is important to prepare student readers regarding the meaning, history, and context of the quotes they will encounter. In past centuries and decades, majority newspapers and other publications were not sensitive to other cultures. The words they used to refer to "Others" were often pejorative, demeaning, belittling, and unfriendly.

Redskin is one such word.

L. Frank Baum, beloved author of *The Wizard of Oz*, wrote in 1890, while editor of the *Aberdeen Saturday Pioneer*, "the Redskin is extinguished, and what few are left are a pack of whining curs who lick the hand that smites them . . . the best safety of the frontier settlements will be secured by the total annihilation of the few remaining Indians."[1]

Major John Vance Lauderdale, the attending physician for the U.S. Army at the Wounded Knee Massacre of December 29, 1890, noted, "every redskin must be killed from off the face of the plains."[2] The term *redskin* was often linked with statements advocating genocide of America's indigenous populations. Surprisingly, this odious work continues in seemingly acceptable usage today due to the nation's capital serving as home of a football team called the Washington Redskins. Any efforts to get the name changed meets with rebuttals claiming that the name "honors" American Indians.

A popular early biography of Abraham Lincoln includes, "A savage was in the act of lifting his little

From *Multicultural Perspectives*, 2003, 5(1). Reprinted by permission of the Taylor and Francis Group who may be contacted at www.informaworld.com.

brother from the ground, whereupon Mordecai, aiming his gun through the hold in the loft, fired, and killed the "redskin."[3] What do the terms *savage* and *redskin* accomplish in this sentence? They determine that American Indians are something different from the hero's people, and further, the intent of these negative words is to say that American Indians are less human than the hero's people. According to *Merriam Webster's Collegiate Dictionary*, the word savage is related to the beautiful word *sylvan*. Both words derive from the same root which refers to forests and explains why some colonists wrote "salvage" when mentioning native people. Savage came to mean uncivilized and brutish, although earlier it might have meant simply people who lived in the woods.

Even words seemingly less pejorative than *savage* and *redskin* can be harmful. It might be hard for educators to understand that *brave* and *Indian warrior* should also be avoided, or used carefully, in modern educational materials.

When writers use the terms *braves* or *warriors*, they are generally referring to the hale and hearty male members of the community. Logically, the young, strong male was ideal to call on for defense and to train as a militia member. The same could be said of any White frontier settlement's young men. Those communities had their braves and warriors as well. But, by calling American Indian defenders braves or warriors, and not calling White fighters braves or warriors, authors portraying American Indians as the Other, something different, and something not of the same caliber. Our mind's eye, fed by television, cinema, and literature, can easily see braves and warriors as savage beings. We hardly see them as fathers, brothers, sons, husbands. The use of the term *braves* and *warriors* serves to separate them, rather than equate them, with what should be viewed as counterparts in nearby White communities.

American Indian men did not constantly roam the forests or prairies in search of battle. They had families to feed, tools to make, politics to discuss and enact, children to instruct, horses to train (depending on the area and the time period), trips to undertake to quarries and bartering centers, and manual labor to offer to their wives and mothers and for community projects. In other words, they were as busy as their White male counterparts. An Indian man's permanent life status was not as a brave or warrior.

The *New Book of Knowledge*, a children's encyclopedia, provided the following information on "Indian wars:"

> In the dark woods around Jamestown, Virginia, wild war whoops shrilled on a March morning in 1622. Swooping down on the farms and tobacco plantations along the James River, Indian warriors slaughtered 422 men, women, and children . . . their final conquest by the white settlers was certain. They were a primitive people struggling against a powerful civilization.[4]

The author creates an emotional scene with the balance tipped against American Indians. The woods are dark, the sounds are shrill, the "warriors" (something other than defending home guards) swoop like predatory fowl. The author judges Indians to be deserving of losing their homes because they were "primitive." Power, in this author's judgment, is not only might but equates to being right. Nothing in the section on Indian wars explains what American Indians were fighting for, and there is no description of any of the numerous massacres enacted upon peaceful American Indian communities. For descriptions of such massacres, see Helen Hunt Jackson's highly regarded expose, *A Century of Dishonor.*

Other difficulties with words occur in the usage of terms like *frontier, settler,* and *explorer.* We rarely seem to see American Indians as frontier dwellers, as settlers, and as explorers. But as a group, they experienced all of these roles. In fact, America's explorers were generally led by Indian guides as in the case of Sacajawea leading Lewis and Clark, and Delaware guide Black Beaver leading a variety of western explorers.[5]

American Indians were not unsettled, except during limited periods of displacement. They either had seasonal settlements or permanent settlements. Nothing rankles an American Indian reader more than to read about some historic White man who was the "first settler" in the area, or to read about the "first baby" born west of some landmark. The implication is that the land was empty of people, or worse, that Indians were not people.

Textbooks have steadily improved, but students will undoubtedly stumble on older books when researching American Indian topics. It perhaps is not necessary to engage in classroom discussions about whether students will encounter the same exclusionary language their grandparents encountered, but it is important to ensure that classroom materials are appropriate and to ascertain that today's students are not regurgitating yesterday's language attitudes in their current work.

As for the term *frontierspeople*, American Indians were living on that mysterious front line of the frontiers as much as non-Indians were. In fact, much of the frontier became a three-layered cultural mix of untreatied Indians to the west of the line, displaced Eastern Indians pushed to the line, and White "frontier" settlers ever pressuring them to keep moving out of the way. Eastern Indians like the Delaware were constantly on the edge of the ever-moving frontier.[6] Yet the terms *frontiersman* and *frontierspeople* are generally used to not only differentiate American Indians from White sylvan dwellers, but to exclude them from the human realm. It seems the use of words that could include American Indians, but instead, that actually were written with the purpose to exclude them, are designed to say that American Indians were not of the same human caliber as those who are included in the terms popularly reserved for Caucasian people.

Just as *Civil War Soldier* conjures up a White image even though there were American Indian[7] and African American Civil War soldiers, so too do *settler, farmer, pioneer, frontiersman,* and *trader* exclude American Indians from the human occupations in which they fully participated because we have not been conditioned to see those terms inclusively. Today, words like *artist, writer, doctor, professor, scientist,* or *entrepreneur* seemingly exclude American Indians in the same way that *pioneer, explorer,* and *settler* did in the past.

Words that separate American Indians from mainstream American terms serve to strengthen the idea that mainstream American words do not pertain to American Indians. For a writer to use the term *squaw* as a substitute for the term *American Indian woman* implies that American Indian women are some other category entirely. If the sentence is in English, why would the author select a native word unless the author intended to create a foreign or Other sensation in the reader? Squaw was not actually a stand-alone word, but instead is an Algonquian suffix or syllable appearing in various forms depending on the particular language or dialect, and may appear as *–quau, -queu, -kwa, -ska,* and other variations.[8] For many decades the newly coined frontier term *squaw* was often used in a derogatory manner to refer to American Indian women. The American Indian author Mourning Dove demonstrates the abusive nature of the word *squaw* as long ago as 1927 in her novel *Cogewa the Half-blood* by having a character say, "Why is this squaw permitted to ride? This is a ladies race!"[9] The author clearly felt the word separated, and denigrated American Indian women as they related to White women in people's minds. Her heroine is a victim of such stereotypes throughout the novel.

Intermixing native-language words with English often confuses place, time, and people in strange juxtapositions. Too often it occurs as a mish-mash, rather like someone writing about a European woman in France and calling her *frau*.

Users of educational materials should also watch how the word *papoose* is used. The word derives from the Algonquian language. Again, unless the word is being used to teach something about native language, references to American Indian children should be about babies and infants, not papooses. If *papoose* is used to refer to American Indian children, it can set the reader on the path to considering that American Indian children are different in terms of value, that they may be harder to teach, slower to learn, uglier, smellier, more brutish than other babies. Such value judgments occur subliminally because other value words like *stinking savage, dirty pagan, screeching heathen, skulking varmint,* and *lousy redskin* occurred in historic accounts about American Indians and in popular novels and movies, and continued on television, contributing to the continuing development of poor images regarding American Indians.[10]

Ask any poet about the value of just the right word and you will be told that words are everything. Teachers and authors must evaluate materials prior to placing them before students, or before encouraging students to look at older resources. Is the material inflammatory? Does it provide a balanced point of view? Make sure students encounter the right words, or that you, or they, can put right the words they do encounter.

Notes

[1] L. Frank Baum, Editor, *Aberdeen Saturday Pioneer,* (Dec. 20, 1890), Aberdeen, SD.

[2] J. Green, *After wounded knee.* (Lansing: Michigan State University Press, 1996).

[3] W. M. Thayer, *A pioneer boy and how he became president: A story of his life,* (Boston: Walker & Wise, 1863).

[4] F. Downey, Indian wars, *The new book of knowledge,* (Danbury, CT: Grolier, 1985), p. 212.

[5] L. Hauptman, *Between two fires,* (New York: Free Press Paperbacks, 1995), p. 24.

[6] Helen Hunt Jackson, *A Century of dishonor,* (New York: Harper, 1881).

[7] A. H. Abel, *The American Indian in the Civil War, 1862-1865,* (Cleveland, OH: H. Clark Company, 1919).

[8] C. Masthay, Ed., *Schmidt's Mahican dictionary,* (Philadelphia: American Philosophical Society, 1991).

[9] Mourning Dove, *Cogewea the half-blood,* (Boston: Four Seas Co., 1927)

[10] L. A. Fiedler, The Indian in literature in English. Volume 4, History of Indian White Relations. In W.E. Washburn (Vol. Ed.) and W.C. Sturterant (Gen. Ed.), *Handbook of North American Indians* (Washington, DC: Smithsonian Institution, 1988), pp. 573-581.

Starting Over

The author came from a middle class African American home, but experiences with prejudice and discrimination led him into drug use and then he was convicted for his involvement in an armed robbery. While in prison he participated in a program to develop skills as a printer, and when he returns home to Virginia he hopes to find a job in the printing trade. This excerpt begins with his release from prison on parole.

My parole officer was a cockeyed young white guy with a big watermelon head and thin, stringy hair that he combed from one side of his head all the way across the top to cover his bald spot. Right away, I resented him. I resented the whole notion of being on parole. I felt I'd paid my debt to society . . . and that the slate should be squeaky clean.

During our first meeting, my P.O. lectured me about what I could and couldn't do. It was humiliating and made me feel like a child: I had to report to him once a month. I couldn't own a firearm. I couldn't vote. I couldn't travel outside the immediate area without his written permission. Finally, putting on his best stern-faced look, he added, "And you're not to associate with other ex-felons."

I wanted to slap my knee and laugh in that white man's face. I wanted to say, . . . *you may as well ship me to the desert to live, 'cause half the niggahs in Portsmouth are ex-felons*. But I didn't say it. I kept quiet and nodded my head, signaling that I understood.

Right away, my P.O. pressured me to find a job. He said I'd have to report to him weekly until I got employed. That was incentive enough to get hustling. The problem was, he also told me I was required by law to tell the truth on job applications. If they asked, I had to tell I was a convicted felon.

I hit the streets hard, starting with applications to area print shops. Armed with my Offset Printing and Lithography certificate, I went in feeling confident that I could talk knowledgeably about any phase of the printing process, and I did. At one point, a print shop in Norfolk was set to bring me on. They had openings. The interview went extremely well. The fleshy-faced shop supervisor was smiling at me big-time. "You'll like it here. You'll do just fine."

Then, as I sat there, he scanned my application. His big blue eyes stopped near the bottom – the section where they ask, *Have you ever been convicted of a felony?* I had put "Yes" in that section.

The supervisor looked at me, turned the application my way, pointed at that section, and said, "What's this about?"

"Well, uh, I was convicted of armed robbery and served three years. I'm out on parole." I heard the words as if they'd been spoken by someone else. The supervisor played it off, like it was no big deal. Then he went into that "We'll call you" mode and walked me to the door.

I knew it was over. I knew I'd never hear from him again, and I didn't.

Several times, I missed out on plum printing jobs like that one, jobs that I really wanted, all, it seemed, because I came clean about my record. It didn't make me feel good about telling the truth, especially to white folks. Most blacks understand that a brother with a rap sheet is commonplace, like being circumcised. But white folks take that shit to heart. They don't understand, and they don't forgive.

Job-hunting is expensive. The little money I'd saved from working in a prison was gone in no time. I had to rely on my parents for bus fare. My pride wouldn't let me ask them for much. I walked wherever I could, but most places I went were not within walking distance. The frustration of going from door to door to businesses in Norfolk and Portsmouth brought to mind a line about job-hunting in a rendition of "Inner City Blues" by Gil Scott-Heron:

> Walk a big hole in a brand-new pair of shoes
> and you've had your first look
> at the inner city blues . . .

Every time I filled out an application and ran across that section about felony convictions, it made me feel sick inside. I felt like getting up and walking out on the spot. What was the use? I knew what they were going to do. No white folks would hire me. It was bad enough that I was black. A black man with a felony record didn't stand a chance, no matter how many trade certificates or degrees he had.

The thing that irritated me the most was that everywhere I went it seemed white folks were always asking if they could "help" me. Every time I walked into a store or into a building, white people rushed up to me before I could get in the door good and asked, "May I help you?" They'd look at me like I was a germ, like they thought I was there to steal something or stick up the place. "May I help you?" They always said it loud enough to make other people stop and stare. I knew the deal. That was their way of alerting everybody else. That was their way of announcing, "Beware! There's a *black* man in here!"

It still pisses me off now when white folks rush up to me and ask, "May I help you?" Hell, they were doing everything in their power to hold me *back*. When they asked if they could help me back then, I wanted to cuss them out. I wanted to say, *Yeah, motherfucka, you can help me! Help me get a JOB!*

Seeing how frustrated I was getting, my parents suggested that I get away for a while, so I went to Washington, D.C., to job-hunt. There, I lived with the family of one of my father's old Navy buddies. I wandered around downtown D.C. applying for jobs at print shops and other places. It felt refreshing being in a city where nobody knew me. In D.C., I didn't have a street image to contend with. I had a clean slate. But that comfort didn't last long. After a few weeks, I ran out of money and had to return home and start the job search there again.

Over time, the frustration worsened. My P.O. kept bugging me, and I stayed broke all the time. There was nothing to give Liz for child support. Every now and then, she'd make some sarcastic remark about me not doing anything for my son. For a while, I stopped going around to see (them) because I was so ashamed that I had no money.

With no money, no car, no apartment, I began to feel like less of a man, like I was a grown child depending on my parents. My self-esteem started slipping. Every day I got more uptight and madder at the world.

One day, while driving my stepfather's car, I pulled into the drive-in window of the Burger King on Victory Boulevard. I ordered. "Gimme a fish sandwich, fries, and a shake."

The server, a white man who appeared to be in his mid-twenties, hurriedly took the order, handed me the food, and shut the window. I needed more change. I waited as the server spoke on the intercom, apparently taking orders from other customers driving in behind me. Noticing I was still there waiting, he frowned and opened the window to see what I wanted. I could tell he was annoyed.

I asked, "Could you give me change for a ten, please?"

Without saying a word, the clerk clucked his tongue in disgust, snatched the ten-dollar bill from my hand, and slammed the window shut. After changing the bill from the cash register, he opened the window and all but threw the money back at me. Quarters dropped from my hand and landed in my lap. The clerk rolled his eyes, slammed the window shut again, and waited for me to leave.

That old fire – the fire I used to feel all the time before I went to prison – resurfaced, and blood rushed *hot* to my head. Before I knew it, I'd sped the car away from the drive-in window and wheeled into a nearby parking space. I jumped out of the car, bolted through the front door of the Burger King, and leaped onto the front counter. All the nerves in my body had readied for battle. Just as I was about to swing my legs across the counter, a black store manager stepped forward and held his hand aloft, almost pleadingly. "Be cool, brother. Be cool."

Those few words, spoken in a soft sincere tone that suggested that he understood, were enough to make me stop long enough to reconsider my actions. I got off the counter and stood there, breathing heavily. Customers and other Burger King employees stopped and stared. The white server, his eyes wide, stood back behind the manager. I glared into his eyes and felt hatred seething in my soul. I wanted him bad. I wanted him bad enough to risk thirty days in jail. By then, I was feeling that if I could get across that counter and reach that white boy, I would try to knock his teeth through the back of his head. I'd punch him in his face and slam his head against the ice cream machine so hard he'd have nightmares about me the rest of his life.

Looking at the manager, I pointed at the white boy and said, "You better teach that *punk* how to treat people!" Then I turned and stormed out of the store.

I'd read somewhere that 85% of inmates return to prison within five years of being released. Just about all the guys I knew who'd gotten out were returning so fast it seemed they had been home on furlough rather than parole. Bonaparte stuck up a restaurant and was wounded during a shoot-out with the law. Another dude went back on an armed-robbery beef shortly after he got out. I'd heard Pearly Blue died in prison of hepatitis. Jim, who was living about ninety miles away in Richmond, was the only person who seemed to be doing all right for himself. . . .

I knew I had to work hard to reach the five-year mark. And yet as the harshness of the outside world started taking a toll, fears began dancing around in my head. Doubts seeped in. All the spiritual and philosophical principles I had studied in prison seemed to go out the window when contending with the reality of that white man's world.

Oddly, there were times when I actually missed the solitude and security of prison. For three years I hardly had to deal with racism. It hadn't mattered whether or not white people gave me a job. I was guaranteed work in prison, and I had a place to eat and sleep, three hots and a cot. I wondered if Bone and some of the others who'd gone back had subconsciously found ways to get busted because things got too heavy for them out in the world. I wondered if I might mess around and do the same. I'd read about the power of the subconscious, and I believed it was true. I figured that if I went back to the joint for anything, it would be for going off on some white person for insulting me. But there was always the possibility of getting busted on a humble, being in the wrong place at the wrong time. I was determined not to let anything like that happen, but every now and then I wondered about it and got uptight and started thinking that it just might happen if I didn't get a better grip.

One night, while driving my stepfather's car, I stopped at a convenience store. It was located on a small, deserted street. It was late and there was only one attendant in the store. While I browsed, he went to a back room to get something. When I went to the counter, I noted: *There's no one else here. No customers. No cameras.* When the clerk returned, I made my purchase and went back to the car. I climbed in and sat there a moment, thinking. I looked up and down the street, and there was no one in sight. I thought, *I can take this place by myself. I can stick my hand in my coat like I've got a gun, and take this place.*

I'd been doing that a lot lately. I'd enter stores, case them, and assess my chances of being able to pull off another job. *Just one job, no more. All I need is some funds to tide me over until I can find work. Just this one time.*

Every person who ever did time can tell you what he did wrong to get caught. Every one feels that all he has to do is rectify that one mental error and he's on his way. I knew what had gone wrong in the McDonald's stickup. We hadn't planned carefully. I *knew* I could do it right this time.

I sat there for a long while, struggling inside my head. It was a real rumble between right and wrong. It was a struggle that on the surface didn't make sense, an internal battle that should not have been taking place in light of all that I had suffered and learned from prison. And yet, there I was, thinking about making another hit.

Sitting there in the car, I thought my plan through like a chess match. I envisioned the job step by step and mapped out my getaway route. Then I thought about something else. I remembered that I had something that most cats coming out of the joint did not: I had supportive parents. I thought about my mother and stepfather, who had suffered through three years of hell with me, from start to finish. I thought about how hard they'd pulled for me since I'd gotten out. They gave me money. I had a place to lay my head. They let me use their car. They cared about me. *They cared about me.* I couldn't let them down.

I thought about something else, too. The lessons about perseverance I learned in the joint. I'd learned about the strength of the mind and seen that mental toughness, more than brawn, determines who survives and who buckles. When I left prison, I knew I was armed with a different kind of weapon than I had relied on before going in. I had knowledge.

I started the car and drove away.

Note: The author gets an opportunity to go to college and earn a journalism degree, but he continues to have difficulty getting a job because of his criminal record. He is finally hired after submitting an application form where he does not to admit to having committed a felony.

Unmasking the Myth of the Model Minority

Can a "positive stereotype" be beneficial? The authors show how the "model minority" perception of Asian Americans distorts the diversity within this group and creates problems for individual Asian Americans. Their recommendations for how teachers should address this myth in schools also suggest some things we all need to learn.

Have you ever sat next to an Asian student in class and wondered how she managed to consistently get straight A's while you struggled to maintain a B-minus average?

From: *Top of the Class*

In January 1966, William Petersen penned an article for *The New York Times Magazine* entitled, "Success Story: Japanese American Style."[1] In it, he praised the Japanese-American community for its apparent ability to successfully assimilate into mainstream American culture, and literally dubbed Japanese Americans a "model minority" – the first popular usage of the term.

By the 1980s, *Newsweek, The New Republic, Fortune, Parade, U.S. News and World Report,* and *Time* all had run articles on the subject of Asian American success in schools and society, and the Myth of the Model Minority was born. The Myth of the Model Minority asserts that, due to their adherence to traditional Asian cultural values, Asian-American students are supposed to be devoted, obedient to authority, respectful of teachers, smart, good at math and science, diligent, hard workers, cooperative, well-behaved, docile, college-bound, quiet, and opportunistic.

Top of the Class: How Asian Parents Raise High Achievers – and How You Can Too (quoted above) is a perfect modern example.[2] Published in 2005, the authors claim to offer readers 17 "secrets" that Asian parents supposedly use to develop high school graduates who earn A-pluses and head to Ivy League colleges. It's a marketing concept built purely on the popular belief in the Myth of the Model Minority.

However, in both of our experiences as public school teachers and education activists, we've seen our share of Asian American students do poorly in school, get actively involved in gangs, drop out, or exhibit any number of other indicators of school failure not usually associated with "model minorities."

A critical unmasking of this racist myth is needed because it both negatively affects the classroom lives of Asian American students and contributes to the justification of race and class inequality in schools and society.

Reprinted with permission from *Rethinking Schools*, Winter 2007-2008, Vol. 22, #2, www.rethinkingschools.org.

Masking Diversity

On the most basic level, the Myth of the Model Minority masks the diversity that exists within the Asian-American community. The racial category of "Asian" is itself emblematic of the problem. Asia contains nearly four billion people in over 50 countries, including those as diverse as Turkey, Japan, India, the Philippines, and Indonesia.

The racial category of "Asian" is also historically problematic. Similar to those categories used to name peoples from Africa and the Americas, the definition of Asia as a continent (and race) and division of Asians into various nations was developed to serve the needs of European and U.S. colonialism and imperialism.

The category of Asian gets even fuzzier in the context of the United States since there are over 50 ways to officially qualify as an Asian American according to government standards. Pacific Islanders and "mixed race" Asians are also regularly squished together under the banner of Asian or Asian Pacific Islander (which, out of respect for the sovereignty of Pacific peoples, we refuse to do here).

The Myth of the Model Minority, however, masks another form of diversity – that of economic class division. As Jamie Lew explains in her 2007 book, *Asian Americans in Class*,[3] there are increasing numbers of working-class Korean-American students in New York City performing more poorly in schools than their middle-class counterparts.

Similarly, Vivian Louie found class-based differences in her study of Chinese-American students.[4] Her research indicated that middle-class Chinese-American mothers tended to have more time, resources, and educational experience to help their children through school and into college than mothers from working-class Chinese-American families, who had longer work hours, lower-paying jobs, and lower levels of education.

These class differences are sometimes rooted in specific immigrant histories and are connected to the 1965 Immigration Act. The Act not only opened up the United States to larger numbers of Asian immigrants, but, among a handful of other criteria, it granted preference to educated professionals and those committing to invest at least $40,000 in a business once they arrived.

As a consequence, some Asian immigrants, even those within the same ethnic community, enter the United States with high levels of education and/or with economic capital attained in their countries of origin. Others enter the United States with little or no education or money at all. These educational and financial heritages make an important difference in how well children gain access to educational resources in the United States.

In other words, whether we are talking about African-American, white, Latina/o, indigenous, or "model minority" Asian-American students, the first rule of educational inequality still applies: Class matters.

To add to the complexity of Asian-American diversity, many of the class differences amongst Asian Americans also correlate with ethnic differences. According to the 2000 census, 53.3 percent of Cambodians, 59.6 percent of Hmong, 49.6 percent of Laotians, and 38.1 percent of Vietnamese over 25 years of age have less than a high school education. In contrast, 13.3 percent of Asian Indians, 12.7 percent of Filipinos, 9.9 percent of Japanese, and 13.7 percent of Koreans over 25 years of age have less than a high school education.

These educational disparities are particularly striking considering that, for instance, 37.8 percent of Hmong, almost 30 percent of Cambodians and 18.5 percent of Laotians have incomes below the poverty line (compared to 12.4 percent of the total U.S. population). Indeed, the 2000 census reveals relatively consistent high education rates and income amongst South Asian, Korean, and Chinese Americans, and relatively low education rates and low income amongst Cambodian, Lao, and Hmong Americans. Hence, the Myth of the Model Minority serves to obscure the struggles of poor or "undereducated" families working to gain a decent education for their children.

One of the most cited statistics proving the Myth of the Model Minority is that Asian Americans even out earn whites in income. What is obscured in this "fact" is that it is only true when we compare Asian American *household* income to white *household* income, and the reality is that Asian Americans make less per person compared to whites. Statistically, the average household size for Asian Americans is 3.3 people while for whites it is 2.5 people.

Consequently, Asian-American households are more likely than white households to have more than one income earner, and almost twice as likely to have three income earners. When we take these issues into account, Asian-American individuals earn $2,000 on average less than white individuals.

The statistics on Asian-American income are further skewed upward when we look at the economies of the states where the majority live. The three states with the highest proportion of Asian Americans, Hawai'i, California, and New York, all have median income levels in the top third of states. This means that regardless of statistically higher household incomes, the high cost of living in states with large Asian-American populations guarantees that Asian Americans, on average, are more likely to have less disposable income and lower living standards than whites.

While the above statistics may be remarkable in the face of the Myth of the Model Minority, they also point to another serious problem: The myth is regularly used as a social and political wedge against blacks, Latina/os, and other racial groups in the United States.

The racist logic of the model minority wedge is simple. If, according to the myth, Asian Americans are academically and socially successful due to particular cultural or racial strengths, then lower test scores, lower GPAs, and lower graduation rates of other groups like African Americans and Latina/os can be attributed to their cultural or racial weaknesses. Or, as a high school guidance counselor in Stacey J. Lee's book, *Unraveling the Model Minority Stereotype,* puts it, "Asians like . . . M.I.T., Princeton. They tend to go to good schools . . . I wish our blacks would take advantage of things instead of sticking to sports and entertainment."[5]

The Myth of the Model Minority also causes Asian-American students to struggle with the racist expectations the myth imposes upon them. An Asian-American high school student in Lee's book explains, "When you get bad grades, people look at you really strangely because you are sort of distorting the way they see an Asian."

Unfortunately, some East and South Asian Americans uphold the myth because it allows them to justify their own relative educational and social success in terms of individual or cultural drive, while simultaneously allowing them to distance themselves from what they see as African American, Latina/o, indigenous, and Southeast-Asian educational failure.

As Jamie Lew observes, the Myth of the Model Minority ". . . attributes academic success and failure to individual merit and cultural orientation, while underestimating important structural and institutional resources that all children need in order to achieve academically." In doing so, the Myth of the Model Minority upholds notions of racial and cultural inferiority of other lower achieving groups, as it masks the existence of racism and class exploration in this country.

One of the difficulties of unmasking the Myth of the Model Minority is that the diversity of the Asian American experience poses substantial challenges, particularly in relation to how race, culture, and ethnicity are typically considered by educators. For instance, Asian-American students challenge the categories commonly associated with the black-brown-white spectrum of race. Many Asian-American students follow educational pathways usually attributed to white, middle-class, suburban students, while many others follow pathways usually attributed to black and Latina/o, working-class, urban students.

Other Asian-American groups challenge typical racial categories in their own identities. Pilipinos,[6] for instance, don't quite fit into the typical categories of South, East, or Southeast Asian, nor do they quite fit the category of Pacific Islander. Further, some argue that Pilipinos have a lineage that is more closely related to Latina/os because they were in fact colonized by Spain. Consequently, because of their particular circumstances, many Pilipinos more strongly identify with being brown than anything else. As another example, many high-achieving, middle-class South Asians consider themselves "brown," especially after the discrimination endured after 9/11.

Asian-American students also challenge typical notions of immigration and language by blurring the typical dichotomies of native language vs. English and immigrant vs. American-born. Some Southeast Asian refugees, like those from Laos, may develop fluency in multiple languages and attend universities, even as their parents are low-income and do not speak English. On the other hand, there are groups of Pilipinos who grow up highly Americanized, who have been taught English their whole lives, but who have some of the highest dropout and suicide rates.

Asian-American students also challenge popularly accepted multicultural teaching strategies because they are often a numerical minority in classrooms, and multicultural teaching strategies designed to meet the needs of classroom majorities can leave out the culturally specific needs of Asian-American students. These can include the language acquisition needs of students who come from character-based languages (e.g. Chinese, Japanese), social and ideological differences of students from majority Muslim nations (e.g. Pakistan, Indonesia), and psychological issues that emerge from student families traumatized by U.S. intervention/war policies (e.g. Korea, Vietnam, Thailand).

From the Fukienese-Chinese student in an urban Philadelphia classroom with mostly Black or Latino/a students, to the Hmong student who sits with two or three peers in a mostly white school in rural Wisconsin, to the Pilipino student in a San Diego suburb with predominantly Pilipino classmates and some white peers, Asian-American youth do not fit neatly into the typical boxes of our educational systems.

Unmasking the Myth In Our Classrooms

Despite the diversity and complexity inherent in working with Asian-American populations, there are many things that educators can do to challenge the Myth of the Model Minority. Similar to other communities of color, effective steps include recruiting more educators from Asian-American backgrounds, promoting multilingual communications in instruction and parent involvement, and developing relationships between parents, community groups, and schools.

Within the classroom, teachers can make use of several strategies to counter the Myth of the Model Minority. The following list offers a starting point . . .

Don't automatically assume that your Asian-American students are "good" students (or "bad" for that matter) and get to know them.

Personally get to know students and their family's practices, which widely vary from home to home, despite their "membership" in specific ethnic or linguistic groups. Start by researching the specific histories and cultures of the students in your classroom to better understand the historical and political contexts of their communities. Also, bring the lives of all of your students, Asian Americans included, into your classroom. Have them consider, reflect, and write about how their home lives and experiences intersect with their school lives and experiences.

Develop strategies to personally engage with students and their communities, whether through lunchtime interactions or visits to their homes, community centers, and cultural or political events. While we recognize the limited resources of all teachers, learning about your Asian-American students and their communities takes the same energy and commitment as learning to work with any specific group of students.

Rethink how you interpret and act upon the silence of Asian-American students in your classroom.

Asian-American student silence can mean many things, from resistance to teachers, to disengagement from work, to a lack of understanding of concepts, to thoughtful engagement and consideration, to insecurity speaking English, to insecurity in their grasp of classroom content. Rather than assume that Asian-American student silence means any one thing, assess the meaning of silence by personally checking in with the student individually.

Teach about unsung Asian-American heroes.

Teachers might include the stories of real-life woman warriors Yuri Kochiyama and Grace Lee Boggs.

Kochiyama has been involved in a range of efforts, from working closely with Malcolm X in Harlem, to Puerto Rican sovereignty, to freeing political prisoners like Mumia Au Jamal. Boggs' efforts have included work with famed Humanist Raya Dunayevskaya, organized labor, and the Detroit Freedom Summer schools.

Or perhaps teach about Ehren Watada, the first commissioned officer to publicly refuse to go to war in Iraq because he believe the war is illegal and would make him a part to war crimes. Learning about heroes like these can help students broaden the range of what it means to be Asian American.

Highlight ways in which Asian Americans challenge racism and stereotypes. Schools should challenge racist caricatures of Asians and Asian Americans, including viewing them as penny-pinching convenience store owners, religious terrorists, kung fu fighting mobsters, academic super-nerds, and exotic, submissive women.

One way to do this is to introduce students to stereotype-defying examples such as Kochiyama, Boggs, and Watada. There are also many youth and multi-generational organizations of Asian Americans fighting for social justice in the U.S. These include Khmer Girls in Action (KGA, Long Beach) and the Committee Against Anti-Asian Violence/Organizing Asian Communities (CAAAV, New York).

These organizations are extremely important examples of how youth can be proactive in challenging some of the issues that affect our communities, and their work challenges the stereotype of Asian Americans as silent and obedient.

Illustrate historical, political, and cultural intersections between Asian Americans and other groups.

There are historical and current examples of shared experiences between Asian Americans and other communities. For instance, teachers could highlight the key role of Asian Americans in collective struggles for social justice in the United States. Possible examples include: Philip Veracruz and other Pilipino farm workers who were the backbone and

catalyst for the labor campaigns of Cesar Chavez and the United Farm Workers in the late 1960s and early 1970s; Chinese students and families who challenged the racism of public schools in the *Lau v. Nichols* case of the 1970s that provided the legal basis for guaranteeing the rights of English language learners and bilingual education; Asian-American college students who in 1967-69 organized with Black, Latina/o, and Native Americans at San Francisco State University in a multiethnic struggle to establish the first ethnic studies program in the nation, united under the banner of "Third World Liberation."

Weave the historical struggles, culture, and art of Asian-American communities into your classroom.

As part of a curriculum that is grounded in the lives of all of our students, teachers can highlight Asian-American history, culture, and art in their classroom practices to help Asian-American students develop not only positive self-identity, but also empathy between Asian Americans and other racial, cultural, or ethnic groups. Teachers might use novels by Carlos Bulosan, John Okada, Nora Okja Keller, Lê Thi Diem Thúy, Jessica Hagedorn, Jhumpa Lahiri, or Shawn Wong; poetry by Lawson Inada, Li-Young Li, Marilyn Chin, Nick Carbón, or Sesshu Foster; spoken word by Reggie Cabico, Ishle Park, Beau Sia, or I Was Born With Two Tongues; hip-hop music by Blues Scholars, Skim, Native Guns, Himalayan Project, or Kuttin Kandi; and history texts by Ron Takaki, Sucheng Chan, Peter Kwong, or Gary Okihiro.

When it comes to dealing with Asian Americans in education, it is all too common for people to ask, "What's wrong with the Myth of the Model Minority? Isn't it a positive stereotype?" What many miss is that there are no "positive' stereotypes, because by believing in a "positive" stereotype, as, admittedly, even many Asian Americans do, we ultimately give credence to an entire way of thinking about race and culture, one that upholds the stereotypical racial and cultural inferiority of African Americans and Latina/os and maintains white supremacy.

The Myth of the Model Minority not only does a disservice to Asian-American diversity and identity, it serves to justify an entire system of race and class inequality. It is perhaps for this reason, above all else, that the Myth of the Model Minority needs to be unmasked in our classrooms and used to challenge the legacies of racism and other forms of inequality that exist in our schools and society today.

Notes

[1] Petersen, William, Success Story: Japanese American Style, *The New York Times Magazine,* (1966, January).

[2] Abboud, Soo Kim, and Kim, Jane Y., *Top of the class: How Asian parents raise high achievers – and how you can too,* (New York: Penguin Group, 2005).

[3] Lew, Jamie, *Asian Americans in Class: Charting the achievement gap among Korean American youth,* (New York: Teachers College Press, 2006).

[4] Louie, Vivian, Parents' aspirations and investment: the role of social class in the educational experiences of 1.5 and second-generation Chinese Americans, *Harvard Educational Review,* 2001, *71,* 438–474.

[5] Lee, Stacey J. *Unraveling the model minority stereotype: Listening to Asian American youth,* (New York: Teachers College Press, 1996).

[6] Pilipino is a term used by some activists in the Pilipino-American community as a means of challenging the way that Spanish and U.S. colonization of the islands also colonized the language by renaming them the Philippines after King Phillip, and introducing the anglicized "f" sound which did not exist in the indigenous languages there.

The New Racial Reality

The author discusses the impact of biracial people on our traditional notions of race and identity, and considers whether it would be a good idea to have a category where one could designate "multiracial" in the U.S. Census and other data-gathering activities.

America's racial composition is quite different (today). It is less "monoracial," less black and white, more intermarried, and a hell of a lot more confusing.

At the time of the 1970 census, America had few shades of gray. Whites (at 87.5 percent) and blacks (at 11.1 percent) accounted for more than 98 percent of the total U.S. population. Other racial minorities added up to just over 1 percent. Hispanics, who could be of any race, stood at 4.5 percent. Twenty years later, the nation was spinning from a demographic whirlwind. Newcomers were pouring in from Mexico, the Philippines, Korea, Cuba, India, mainland China, and other non-European countries, while Europeans – no longer favored by U.S. immigration laws – had dwindled to a trickle. America, in short, was no longer nearly so black and white. . . .

After reanalyzing U.S. Bureau of the Census's survey data for 1985 and 1990, scholars Douglas Besharov and Timothy Sullivan concluded that black and white marriages were growing faster than had previously been thought.[1] . . . To multiracialists, America's approximately three million multiracial

Excerpts from pages 4-8, 10-12, 19-26 from *Color Blind* by Ellis Cose. Copyright © 1996 by Ellis Cose. Reprinted by permission of HarperCollins Publishers

children are a forceful argument for the recognition of a new race and a new racial reality. . . .

Lise Funderburg, author of *Black, White, Other*, which profiles several children of black-white interracial unions, extracted the following comment from one of the persons she interviewed: "A lot of Blacks get upset if they ask you exactly what you are and you come back and say, 'Biracial.' One response is, 'What? Are you too good to identify with Blacks?' I say, 'It's not that I'm too good at all, but I'm composed of two different races and I choose to value each of those.' It's not as though I'm going to write off my mother's race for the convenience of pleasing somebody else's view of what I should or should not be doing."[2] . . .

Clearly, the multiracialists have flagged a nettlesome problem. Forcing multiracial children into prefabricated "monoracial" boxes is illogical. It is preposterous – not to mention cruel – to ask any child of mixed race to choose one race (and symbolically one parent) arbitrarily over the other. As Gish Jen, a Chinese American married to a man of Irish descent, acknowledged, there is pain in seeing her child stripped of what he considers to be an essential part of his identity. Yet many Americans insist on seeing multiracial children through monochromatic eyes. Some spiteful schoolmates gave her son a taste of what his future might hold when they taunted him for being "Chinese" – even as he futilely insisted that he was not. Though Jen and her husband originally had hoped their son would "grow up embracing his whole complex ethnic heritage," they have had to accept a harsher reality and recognize that their son "is considered a kind of Asian person."[3]

It's unclear whether the federal government's official adoption of a multiracial category would lead to broader public acceptance of multiracialism and eventually make things easier for children such as Jen's son. It is even less clear what effect a multiracial box would have on statistical analyses of America's racial stock. "Multiracial," after all, is not a particularly precise description. It simply means that a person theoretically fits "other." Consequently, a multiracial designation conceivably could end up being less accurate (in the sense of grouping people together who are deemed to be phenotypically similar) than the groupings we have now, depending on how it is defined and who decides who belongs to it. . . .

Indeed, many critics would argue – some for scientific and others for sociopolitical reasons – that the creation of more racial pigeonholes is precisely what America doesn't need. The bigger problem in short, may not be that the current groupings are insufficient, but that they foster a belief that there is something logical, necessary, scientific, or wise about dividing people into groups called races.

Certainly, when it comes to racial "science," not much has changed since 1942, the year anthropologist Ashley Montagu published the first edition of Man's *Most Dangerous Myth: The Fallacy of Race.* "In earlier days we believed in magic, possession, and exorcism, in good and evil supernatural powers, and until recently we believed in witchcraft. Today many of us believe in 'race.' 'Race' is the witchcraft of our time. The means by which we exorcise demons. It is the contemporary myth. Man's most dangerous myth," wrote Montagu.[4]

Montagu acknowledged that racial groups were real. He rejected the notion, however, that the categories amounted to anything important. Racial groups were merely people with geographic origins in common who, to certain European taxonomists, looked somewhat alike. "No one ever asks whether there are mental and temperamental differences between white, black, or brown horses – such a question would seem rather silly,"[5] he pointed out,

suggesting that the question was no less silly when applied to humans. Having rejected the idea that race represents different evolutionary paths taken en route to becoming Homo Sapiens or is linked to fundamentally different capabilities or traits or indicates the existence of any "hard and fast genetic boundaries," Montagu concluded that it is little more than an excuse for prejudice.

Americans are no closer than we were half a century ago to coming up with a sound scientific rationale for the myriad ways we regard race. Certainly, as Montagu admitted, different races exist – if only because we have decided that they do. We can theoretically create races at will. If Americans agreed, for instance, that people with red hair constitute a separate race, these people would be one. And if we proceeded to treat all people with red hair differently from everyone else, they would soon take on all the attributes we associate with "real" races. If, for instance, they were allowed only to do menial labor, refused an education, compelled to intermarry, forced to live in predominantly redhead communities, and told that their only real gifts were drinking and song, they would eventually develop a culture that embodied the new redhead stereotype. But all we would have proved is that human beings have the power to define (and thereby create) races – not that the classification has any value or makes any sense.

Race, in and of itself, is a harmless concept. It is the attributes and meaning we ascribe to race that make it potentially pernicious. And, unfortunately, race began as a value-loaded conceit. As paleontologist Stephen Jay Gould noted, eighteenth-century German naturalist Johann Friedrich Blumenbach created the modern system of racial classification as a "hierarchy of worth, oddly based upon perceived beauty, and fanning out in two directions from a Caucasian ideal."[6] Blumenbach's racial pyramid had Africans and Asians on the bottom, Malays and American Indians in the middle, and whites at the top. That history and the uses to which race was subsequently put go a long way toward explaining why the movement to create a new multirace makes some people uncomfortable. . . .

It is certainly true that people of unclear race or ethnicity often have particular concerns. Adrian Piper, an artist and philosopher who is light enough to "pass" for white but considers herself black, at one point took to handing out cards that read:

> Dear Friend,
> I am black. I am sure you did not realize this when you made/laughed at/agreed with that racist remark. In the past, I have attempted to alert white people to my racial identity in advance. Unfortunately, this invariably causes them to react to me as pushy, manipulative, or socially inappropriate. Therefore, my policy is to assume that white people do not make these remarks, even when they believe there are no black people present, and to distribute this card when they do. I regret any discomfort my presence is causing you; just as I am sure you regret the discomfort your racism is causing me.
>
> Sincerely yours,
> Adrian Margaret Smith Piper

She stopped giving out the cards, Piper told a *Washington Post* reporter, "after a man I met at a party said he was trying to think of a racial slur so he could get one of my cards."[7]

In recent years, a host of writers have attempted to illuminate the special situation of being racially ambiguous.... In *Notes of a Black White Woman*, Judy Scales-Trent, a law professor at the State University of new York at Buffalo and a "black" woman who is often assumed to be white, discussed the problem of "coming out": "When do I tell someone that I am black? And how will they respond? And if I don't tell people (the apartment rental agent, the cab driver), aren't I 'passing'?"[8] ...

Shirlee Taylor Haizlip's *The Sweeter the Juice* is, among other things, the saga of her search for relations who had cut off all contact with her family and passed into the white world. With the help of a detective agency, she found a long-lost aunt. The woman was then eighty-eight years old and living in Anaheim, California. Initially, when the detective called, she claimed no relationship to the family who was looking for her, but eventually she owned up. Haizlip, in detailing her first encounter with her newly found aunt, wrote that she ended up asking herself, "Was it my responsibility to remind Grace who she was, to dredge up a past she had buried? Despite all the years of longing and conjecture, de-

spite the fact that race was the central issue, I could not bring myself to broach it."[9]

In the end, Haizlip managed to get the "white sister" and the "black sister" (Haizlip's mother) together for a visit. "Watching the sisters sit side by side in the restaurant booth, I sensed a budding comfort," she noted. "But I also thought it was just as well that after this visit they would be three thousand miles apart. Race still separated them. I understood now in ways I had not that Grace was indeed white. She could not give up being white, nor could she tear down the alabaster walls she had built around her life. She would be content to see us as often as we might like to visit, as long as no one in her circle knew who or what we were. In other words, she would be satisfied to continue the pattern of the past."[10] . . .

Haizlip believes that people are growing weary of racial polarization. "I think we have come to the end of our rope, and we want to say, 'God, what is the answer? We've tried everything, and *what* is the answer?'" The question, she suspects, may ultimately lead people to accept the notion that one racial label for everyone is the only course that makes sense. Once we recognize that everyone is mixed, that we all share genes from a common pool, perhaps "we can look at each other as extended family and distant cousins." If we begin to do that, Haizlip said, "we're going to be more tolerant of each other. We don't love everybody in our family, but we are more tolerant of them."[11]

America, of course, has not quite gotten to that point; it insists not only on racial labels, but on treating people differently on the basis of perceived differences, (and) not all shades of black are always seen as equal. In *The Color Complex*, authors Kathy Russell, Midge Wilson, and Ronald Hall pointed out, "For light-skinned blacks, it simply remains easier to get ahead. Take a close look at Black urban professionals, or 'buppies,' with their corporate salaries, middle class values, and predominantly light-brown to medium-brown skin color. They benefit not only from their social contacts with other light-skinned blacks but also from looks that, in a predominantly White society, are more mainstream."[12]

Professors James Johnson and Walter Farrell attempted to quantify the color advantage. In their report of their study of two thousand male job seek-ers in the Los Angeles area in the *Chronicle of Higher Education*, they stated that color seemed to play a role in determining who worked and who did not; being African American and dark reduced the odds of working considerably: "In our sample, only 8.6 percent of white males were unemployed, com-pared with 23.1 percent of black males in general and 27 percent of dark-skinned black males," and among light-skinned black men, it was 20 percent. Even among those who were relatively well edu-cated, Johnson and Farrell indicated, skin tone seemed to make a difference: "We found that only 10.3 percent of light-skinned African-American men with 13 or more years of schooling were un-employed, compared with 19.4 percent of their dark-skinned counterparts with similar education. Indeed, the unemployment rate for the light-skinned black males was only a little higher than the 9.5 percent rate for white males with compara-ble schooling."[13] Johnson and Farrell's point was not that light skin ensures success or that dark skin guarantees failure, but that complexion is far from a neutral trait, that skin tone had a great deal to do with how warmly one is received by the world.

That a lighter complexion may be related to suc-cess is not news to many blacks, who have long ac-knowledged – if not always openly – that color sometimes matters nearly as much as does race. As Teresa Wiltz, a light-skinned black journalist, ob-served in the *Chicago Tribune:* "From the beginning black wealth and skin color have been inextricably linked. The lighter you were – and most likely, that meant you were the descendant of a wealthy white slaveowner – the more likely you were to be middle class."[14] Precisely because that linkage has always been there, some blacks are suspicious of those with lighter complexions. . . .

Much of the uneasiness engendered by the mul-tiracialists is rooted in such frustration, in unpleas-ant and ugly racial memories, in racial insecurities, in anxieties about race and rank, and in the knowl-edge that race has never been neutral in America but has inevitably forced people to take sides. The debate, in short, is really not so much about a mul-tiracial box as it is about what race means – and what it will come to mean as the society approaches the millennium. Juliet Fairly, a New York-based

journalist whose white mother was born in France and whose father is African American, recalled the difficulty growing up with a split identity and des-perately wanting to fit in. She went through a phase when she wanted to be totally "black" and even sported an Afro pick in her straightish dark hair. Eventually, she decided that she could not ignore the part of herself that is also her mother, and she has come around to support a multiracial category – but only "if it has no consequences." . . .

Tomorrow's multiracial people could just as eas-ily become the next decade's something else. A name, in the end, is just a name. The problem is that we want those names to mean so much – even if the only result is a perpetuation of an ever-more-refined kind of racial madness.

On the one hand, it makes perfect sense for chil-dren of parents of identifiably different races to in-sist that all their heritages are "honored" in what they are called. Yet, the assumption runs aground of an inescapable reality: that the very function of groups within racial classification is to erase iden-tity, to render us less individuals (whatever our con-stituent parts) than undifferentiated members of groups within a previously heterogeneous mass. By what logic, for instance, can one take countless African tribes – and the offspring of individuals comprised of any combination of those tribes – and make them all into one race called black? The rea-soning is certainly no less specious than that which allows us to ignore the fact that a "black" American may also be Irish and Greek.

In the past, Americans (which is not to exclude much of the rest of the world) have made much more of racial labels than we should. We have seen race as a convenient way of sorting out who is en-titled to which rewards, who is capable of what ac-complishments, and who is fit to associate with whom. In light of that history, asking whether we should have a new racial category is a trivial ques-tion. The infinitely more important question is whether it is possible to divorce any system of racial classification from the practice of racial discrimina-tion, whether a nation splintered along racial lines – a nation that feels compelled to rank people on the basis of race (aesthetically; professionally; so-cially; and, most insistently, intellectually) – is capa-ble of changing that propensity any time soon.

Notes

[1]Douglas J. Besharov and Timothy S. Sullivan, One flesh, *The New Democrat*, July-August, pp. 19–21.

[2]Lise Funderburg, *Black, White, Other*. (New York: William Morrow, 1994).

[3]Gish Jen, An Ethnic Trump. *New York Times Magazine*, July 7, 1996, p. 50.

[4]Ashley Montagu, *Man's Most Dangerous Myth: the Fallacy of Race*. (New York: Oxford University Press, 1974).

[5]Ibid.

[6]Stephen Jay Gould, The Geometer of Race. *Discover*, November, 1994, pp. 65–69.

[7]Adrian Piper, Passing for White, Passing for Black (pp. 6-32). *Transition: An International Review*. 1992, Vol. 58.

[8]Judy Scales-Trent, *Notes of a Black White Woman*. (University Park: Pennsylvania State University Press, 1995).

[9]Shirlee Taylor Haizlip, *The Sweeter the Juice*. (New York: Simon and Schuster, 1994).

[10]Ibid.

[11]Ibid.

[12]Kathy Russell, Midge Wilson, and Ronald Hall Sacks, *The Color Complex*. (San Diego: Harcourt Brace Jovanovich, 1992).

[13]James Johnson and Walter Farrell, Walter, Race Still Matters. *Chronicle of Higher Education*, July, 1995, p. A48.

[14]Carrie R. Leana, Why downsizing won't work, *Chicago Tribune Magazine*, April 14, 1996, pp. 15–18.

Like Crabs in a Barrel: Why Inter-Ethnic Anti-Racism Matters Now

Individuals of color may have negative attitudes toward other people from other oppressed groups, causing them to ignore discrimination against a group that doesn't affect them directly. The author explains why it is in the self-interest of anyone who has experienced oppression to challenge discrimination against any oppressed group.

In places near the ocean where merchants sell live crabs, they display their wares in open barrels. When the crabs try to escape by climbing up the sides of the barrel, they always fail. As soon as one starts to climb, it gets pulled back down by the others, who are also trying to escape.

When we try to overcome racism, sexism, homophobia, or class oppression, we often find ourselves in the position of crabs in a barrel. We work as hard as we can, but all our efforts fail to free us. Instead of pulling ourselves up, we only pull someone else down.

It's not hard to figure out why this happens. People with power want us to be divided and to fight each other so we will not unite and fight them. If any of us make gains, they want us to make them at each other's expense instead of demanding a fundamental redistribution of resources and power.

The "divide and conquer" strategy has been used more and more in recent years. Malcolm X used to say that racism was like a Cadillac because they came out with a new model every year. There is always racism, but it is not always the same racism. Unlike past segregation and white supremacy which produced a relatively uniform system of exclusion, today's racism employs practices that produce differentiation rather than uniformity, that give excluded groups decisively different relationships to the same oppression.

For example, the opponents of affirmative action make appeals to Asian Americans, arguing that its dismantling will secure "advantages" for Asians that now go to blacks and Latinos. Anti-immigrant groups try to enlist African Americans in efforts to deprive Asian American and Latino immigrants of social services, health care, and education on the grounds that immigrants are responsible for the declines in economic status and political power experienced by blacks in recent years. Racist legislators intent upon dismantling the political gains won by African Americans over the past three decades invite Latinos to support budget cuts, redistricting, term limits and other measures designed to undercut the seniority, control over resources, and political influence of black legislators.

From *ColorLines*, Winter, 1999. Reprinted by permission of the author.

At the same time, enemies of rights for women and gays and lesbians seek alliances with men of color. They encourage men from aggrieved racial groups to make gains within their own groups rather than outside them, to gain power at the expense of women and gays and lesbians in their own communities rather than at the expense of wealthy white men with power.

These new divisions can also produce unexpected affiliations and alliances. Attacks on bilingual education and immigrants' rights harm both Latinos and Asian Americans. Irrational and alarmist policies about AIDS stigmatize both homosexuals and Haitians. Puerto Ricans on the mainland are both Spanish speakers from a colonized homeland, like Mexicans, and U.S. citizens, like blacks. Filipinos are non-citizen immigrants from Asia, but they share with Mexicans the experience of being immigrants from a Catholic nation colonized by Spain whose patron saint is the Virgin of Guadelupe.

Yet the same forces that create unexpected affinities and alliances can also generate new forms of division and differentiation. All racialized groups face problems because of environmental racism, but Native Americans suffer particularly from lead poisoning, Asian American and Pacific Islanders from underweight births and childhood malnutrition. Unemployment has hit African Americans harder than Asian Americans or Latinos, but women immigrants from Asia, Mexico, and Central America are over-represented in hazardous low-wage jobs.

Under these conditions, inter-ethnic anti-racism is emerging as a tactical necessity. This strategy does not erase purely national or racial identities, nor does it permanently transcend them. There is always room for more than one tactical stance in struggles for social justice, and ethnic nationalism and autonomous single-group struggles will always be legitimate and meaningful under some circumstances. But the current historical moment is generating new forms of struggle, forms eloquently described by scholar activist Lisa Lowe as "alternative forms of practice that integrate yet move beyond those of cultural nationalism."[1]

Alliances across racial lines offer some obvious advantages. They produce strength in numbers; we are more powerful with allies than we would be alone. If we are there for other people's struggles, there is a greater likelihood that they will be there for us in the future if we need them. By standing up for someone else, we establish ourselves as people with empathy for the suffering of others; it shows that we will not turn our backs on people simply because they seem powerless.

Angela Davis points to the work of workers' centers like Asian Immigrant Women Advocates that address the whole lives of workers – not just their class, racial, or gender identities. These centers combine literacy classes with legal advice about domestic violence and divorce while they address issues about wages, hours, and working conditions.

Because there is no way to improve the lives of Asian American immigrant workers without attending to the concerns of Latinas who often work at their side, and because entrepreneurs from their own ethnic group are often part of the problem, these efforts inevitably lead to inter-ethnic alliances. They lead to cross-class alliances because there is no way to deal with domestic violence as a class-specific or race-specific problem. They also lead to the formation of temporary affinities and alliances across gender, class, and racial lines through tactics like consumer boycotts of goods created under unsafe or unfair working conditions.

Consider also some of the less obvious advantages of inter-ethnic anti-racism. Coordinated actions against racism enable aggrieved groups to focus on the fact of oppression itself rather than merely on the identities of the oppressed. Inter-ethnic anti-racism can shift the focus away from defensive concerns about "minority" disadvantages and toward an analysis of white "majority" advantages, thus helping to define the target.

This might show that racialized groups are not merely disadvantaged, but also taken advantage of. It might make visible the new forms of racialization created day after day in the present, not just those attributable to histories of slavery, conquest, genocide, immigrant exploitation, and class oppression.

In the final analysis, the most important reason for inter-ethnic anti-racism is that it provides the most effective way for us to see exactly how power works in the world. We will always misread and misunderstand our circumstances if we see things from only one perspective.

Solidarities based on single identity are limited; solidarities based on multiple identities are unlimited. All social movements need some form of organic solidarity. But people who must see themselves as exactly the same in order to wage a common struggle will be poorly prepared for struggles for social justice against a power structure that constantly creates new forms of differentiation among the oppressed.

Yet precisely because no unified identity encompasses anyone's social world, inter-ethnic anti-racist activism offers the opportunity to make struggles for social justice as mobile, fluid, and flexible as the new forms of oppression. They enable us to create places like the ones envisioned by Patrick Chamoiseau's narrator in *Texaco*, an epic novel about anti-racist struggle in Martinique: "those places in which no one could foresee our ability to unravel their History into our thousand stories."[2]

Notes

[1] Lisa Lowe, Work, immigration, gender: New subjects of cultural politics, *The politics of culture in the shadow of capital*. (Durham, NC: Duke University Press, 1997), p. 369.

[2] Patrick Chamoiseau, *Texaco: A novel*. (New York: Vintage International, 1997), p. 54.

Crime

After the terrorist attack on 9/11, the Dean of Washington National Cathedral, Reverend Nathan Baxter, cautioned Americans: "As we act, let us not become the evil we deplore." This short story can be read as a parable illustrating this concern as it describes a brief encounter between the police and a Latino man on an urban street.

On his way home from work Libertad waited at a stoplight. Out of the corner of his eye he saw Mr. Charlie drive up behind dark sunglasses. Two screws sat in the car. They waited to turn in the direction Libertad was taking down the boulevard. This was the only way to the subway. He thought he saw one of the screws lean out of the car window to get a better look at him, but Libertad did not turn in their direction to see for certain. He felt their eyes on him as he crossed in front of them. He kept on his way, as nonchalant as possible, trying to recount the contents of his shoulder bag and wrestling with the urge to run.

The siren sounded for an instant. A voice over the loudspeaker said, "Hold it right there. Punk."

Libertad halted.

The voice said, "Turn around."

Libertad turned and saw the lights atop the car spinning, flashing, red and blue. *What's this crap?* thought Libertad. A spotlight turned on him, blinding, "Get on your knees," said the voice over the loudspeaker. "Keep your hands where I can see them."

Libertad did. He tried to shield his eyes with his hands out in front of him.

From I. Stavans, Ed. *New World: Young Latino Writers* (New York: Delta Books, 1997). Copyright © 1996 by Danny Romero. Reprinted by permission of author.

"Where you moving to so fast?" said a second voice from the brightness.

"You weren't trying to get away from me, punk?" said the first screw over the loudspeaker.

"Let's see some ID," said the second screw.

"You speak English, punk?"

Libertad was silent for a moment, trying to shield his eyes from the spotlight shining in his face. "Hey, man," he said, "what's the problem?" He reached for his wallet.

A revolver was cocked, a certain click-click, turning the cylinder, a fresh cartridge now before the barrel. Libertad froze.

"Wha'cha doing, punk?" said the first screw. The loudspeaker crackled.

"I'm getting my goddamn ID," said Libertad, not moving. "It's in my wallet."

"Dumb-ass motherfucker, you move again an' I'll send you back across the border. Dead. Punk." Again the loudspeaker crackled.

Sweat trickled down the middle of Libertad's back. He had never been across the border in his life. When he was younger, all his friends went to visit family or for smuggling. They brought back fireworks and switchblades. It used to be $100 for a pound of grass, $150 for a kilo. They bragged about the pussy and the one dirty theater where for $2 a person could watch cheap sex acts. He remembered summer nights when he was a teenager, when he and his friends walked through the streets, tossing quarter sticks of dynamite, M-1000s they were called. Not much later Frank and his brother Clown were shot and killed outside a liquor store by the screws responding to reports of sporadic gunfire. The media reported the screws had acted in good faith. Libertad wished he had an M-1000 with him now.

"I have to get my ID," he said.

"Go ahead," said the second screw. Again there was the sound of a revolver being cocked, a certain click-click, turning the cylinder, a fresh cartridge now before the barrel. "Slowly."

Libertad reluctantly brought down his right hand, still holding the left one up, and reached back. He closed his eyes; it was more comfortable. The backs of his eyelids stung. He tilted his head downward.

"Uh, you think you could turn off that light, please?"

"'Please' even," mocked the first screw. "We're videotaping this punk," he went on. "You're on *Candid Camera*. Ha-ha-ha. We're doing a little training film." The second screw laughed nervously. The first screw said to the second screw, "You know, I hate these punks that complain."

"You know it," said the second screw.

The spotlight burned on Libertad. He brought his wallet out. He opened it and removed the first card out of the plastic window insert. He held it out in front of him.

"Hey, you do that real good," said the first screw. "What else you do real good? Ha-ha-ha. Punk."

It sounded to Libertad as if the screw still stood near the car. His ID was torn out of his hand from the left side. The spotlight blinked once, twice, then flashed back on again. The first screw laughed loudly.

"Check this out," said the second screw. His words trailed back over to the car.

Libertad could not hear their words. He imagined they were looking at his picture. In it he was four years younger. He had gone to renew his ID on the day after his birthday. At a party a few days earlier he had met this woman and spent the next seven days with her drinking, screwing, and swallowing Valium, 50 mg at a time. The Valium kept him so hard that week, he joked to his friends, that the wrinkles on his face had been stretched taut, and there was the reason he looked so much younger in the photo. And there was the reason he looked to be in a stupor.

Laughter came from the squad car.

On the boulevard the traffic was heavy as usual, traveling east and west. One hot rod, from the sound of it, roared down the street, the occupants screaming out, "Hhheeeyyy, sssuuucckkkeeerrr . . ." as they passed.

Libertad had his hands up all the while. His knees ached on the uneven concrete surface of the broken sidewalk. He thought for a second that the sun was out but realized it was the heat from the light. Libertad wondered if this was how his brother had ended up. Was this what happened that night three years ago when he left work and was never seen again? Did they stop him and have him kneeling in the street?

Three or four times this month Libertad remembered scenes such as this as he traveled on the boulevard. He had always considered himself lucky not to be that person in the street, but as he knelt there now, he guessed it had been only a matter of time before he was rounded up also.

He heard one screw, keys jingling, walk over to him. "When did you get out of prison?" asked the second screw, now standing nearby.

"Why are you stopping me?" asked Libertad.

"Shut up, punk," shouted the first screw from over near the car.

The second screw said, "You fit the description of the suspect."

"What suspect? asked Libertad.

"You don't worry 'bout that unless you're him," said the second screw. "When did you get out of prison?"

"I've never been there," answered Libertad. He wondered if he was carrying anything suspicious in his shoulder bag. It still lay near him, he thought.

"What have you been arrested for? Punk," shouted the first screw.

"Drunk in public," said Libertad. He heard the first screw reading off the ID information into the two-way radio. Libertad hoped his name came up clean. A person never knew what might happen. People had identical names and outstanding warrants for arrest. Mr. Charlie did not keep good records. They could take you in on fines already paid, time already served.

The first screw said, "L-i-b-e-r-t – "

"Any major crimes?" asked the second screw.

"—libber-todd, I guess . . . I don't care what the—"

"No, I haven't," said Libertad.

"—yeah, you know, the street in the ghetto part of town—"

"How many times you been arrested?" asked the second screw.

"I don't know," said Libertad. "Too many times, I guess."

"—this says he's thirty, but he looks older . . . Pancho Villa mustache motherfucker . . . looks like someone hit him in the forehead with a bottle or something . . . Frankenstein . . . dope fiend . . . and you should see him . . . we'll check it out."

The second crew walked back over to the car. The two screws spoke too low for Libertad to hear them. The keys jingling walked up and stood near Libertad. "How long you been using?" the second screw asked.

"Hey, I don't do that," said Libertad.

"You know the routine," said the second screw. "Put your sleeves up."

Libertad brought his hands down and pushed his sleeves up.

"Any tattoos?" asked the second screw.

"No," said Libertad. He held his arms out in front of him so the screw could check for needle marks. "I don't do that," repeated Libertad. There were cars honking on the boulevard.

"Wha'cha have in the bag?" asked the second screw. "You got a bomb in there?"

"Just books and paper," said Libertad.

"You wanna open it up," said the second screw.

Libertad felt on the ground in front of him for his bag. He heard another car drive up and stop. Two doors opened and closed. Libertad opened the bag slowly and held it out. Another car drove up and stopped. One door opened and closed.

"What about that little pocket right there?" asked the second screw. "You wanna open it up too."

"Pens. Cigarettes," said Libertad. He opened it and held it out. On his left side he could feel pedestrians moving past him. He wondered if it might be someone from his work. "That's all," he said. He heard two car doors open and close. One car drove off.

"You got a gun or a knife on you?" asked the second screw. He stood closer to Libertad on his right side.

"No, I don't," said Libertad.

"Stand up," said the second screw. "Spread your legs and lace your fingers together on top of your head." The screw kicked his legs farther apart. He stood behind Libertad and began to pat him down. Two pairs of footsteps walked over to them.

"What are you doing around here?" asked a new voice.

"I work over on the next street," said Libertad. The second screw was feeling his coat pocket. "That's a book," said Libertad.

"Take it out," said the second screw.

"Why don't you go back to where you came from? Punk," said the first screw.

Libertad took the book out of his pocket and held it out. "I was born in this country," he said. The second screw took the book out of his hand, then felt the pocket to make certain it was empty.

"Why did you start walking away so fast when you saw us back there? Punk," said the first screw.

"I just got off from work," said Libertad. "I'm walking to the corner to catch the subway."

"You read that shit," said the second screw. He dropped the book to the ground.

Libertad stood in the middle of a circle of the three men, eyes closed, hands on head, fingers laced. "I just want to catch the subway," he said.

The first screw said, "We don't want to see you around here no more. Punk." He walked right up to him and stood rock hard against Libertad. "Get out of here. Punk," he said. They all three walked away.

Libertad opened his eyes by accident. They hurt. "Can I have my ID?" he asked, eyes closed again.

"This your current address?" asked the second screw.

"One-nine-four-zero East Seventy-third Street," said Libertad. "I work just over on the next street."

"Telephone number?" asked the second screw.

"Five-five-five-four-three-six-nine," said Libertad. "At work it's Q-Z-five-three-three-eight-one."

He felt his ID brush off his face as it was thrown at him. He could hear the three men climbing into the car, doors opened, then closed. He noticed for the first time their engine was still running. They gunned it; there was laughter. The spotlight went off. Libertad blinked his eyes open, trying to focus his vision. The car drove off. Libertad still blinked, on his knees, groping for his belongings.

Perspectives on Classism and Its Consequences

> "Unless we start to fight and defeat the enemies of poverty and racism in our own country and make our talk of equality and opportunity ring true, we are exposed as hypocrites in the eyes of the world when we talk about making other people free."
>
> **Shirley Chisholm (1924–2005)**

Throughout her political career Shirley Chisholm articulated the problems of people burdened by poverty and racism. She recognized that discrimination based on race often overlaps with social class discrimination, especially when schools continued to be as segregated as Jonathan Kozol (2005) documented in *The Shame of the Nation.*[1] John Powell (2008) summed up the situation by saying "We can tell much about someone's life opportunity by his or her zip code."[2] Chisholm challenged her colleagues in the House of Representatives to vote their values and not succumb to expediency and to the power of lobbyists for the rich and powerful. The necessity of fundraising for one's campaign has put increased pressure on politicians to attend to the priorities of those making significant campaign contributions and, to a lesser degree, to the needs of the large middle class who constitute the majority of voters. The needs of the poor have often been ignored or discussed as an afterthought, and only if there were enough resources available after addressing the priorities of corporate and middle class America.

During the Great Depression, politicians were forced to pay attention to the needs of the poor more than ever before because so many Americans suddenly found themselves living in poverty. The sympathy for their plight was reflected in legislation for Social Security and Aid to Dependent Children, but it was also at times reflected in individual actions of political leaders. Flamboyant New York City Mayor Fiorello La Guardia often presided at police court so he would be aware of the social problems in his city. On a day that was bitterly cold, an old man was brought before the Mayor who was presiding at the court and wearing his famous sombrero. The old man was charged with stealing a loaf of

179

bread. Asked if he was guilty, the man admitted his crime, but he also said that he had to steal because there were no jobs, he had no money, and his family was starving.

La Guardia responded, "I've got to punish you. The law makes no exceptions. I can do nothing but sentence you to a fine of ten dollars." La Guardia reached into his pocket and pulled out some dollar bills from which he took a $10 bill, "Here's the ten dollars to pay your fine." La Guardia took off his sombrero and held it upside down. "And now I remit the fine." He dropped the ten-dollar bill into it. "Furthermore, I'm going to fine everyone in this courtroom fifty cents for living in a town where a man has to steal bread in order to eat. Bailiff, collect the fines and give them to the defendant." The bewildered old man left the courtroom with a total of $47.50.[3]

This man now had the resources to buy food for himself and his family for a little while, but as kind as such assistance may be, charity can never be the solution to the problems of people living in poverty, especially for those who don't get enough food. For Loretta Schwartz-Nobel, engaging in research on poverty for decades has meant traveling around the United States and visiting homes of low-income families. She has also interviewed people who provide services such as health care to poor people. In "A Story Without an End," she examines the extent of malnutrition and hunger in the United States and describes what happens to malnourished children physically and cognitively. She discusses predictable negative consequences for a society that allows children's development to be sabotaged by inadequate nutrition. Unlike third world countries, the United States has the resources to feed its hungry children, but Schwartz-Nobel questions whether

Americans have the moral commitment to do so. This was the moral challenge Martin Luther King, Jr., issued over forty years ago, and the challenge has yet to be met:

> There is nothing new about poverty. What is new, however, is that we now have the resources to get rid of it.

Although poverty includes issues of unemployment, hunger, homelessness, and even destitution, it also includes issues affecting people with jobs and homes who are barely getting by. In the excerpt from his book on the working poor, David K. Shipler attempts to correct some distortions of poverty by describing the lives of low-income people and citing statistics to illustrate the economic difficulties for Americans living below or near the poverty line. "At the Edge of Poverty" presents a portrait of "the forgotten America" as Shipler describes how the working poor struggle to make ends meet while Americans who are financially comfortable blame the poor for being poor, as if poverty resulted only from personal deficiencies rather than being a consequence of circumstances beyond an individual's control.

Viewing personal deficiencies as the cause of an individual's poverty is a common and historic rationalization in the United States, but even when poor people have extraordinary abilities, they still struggle to escape from poverty. In his book *And Still We Rise*, Miles Corwin offers a unique perspective on poverty by focusing on the lives of low-income high school students in Los Angeles who are enrolled in a talented and gifted program. In the chapter "My Safe Haven," Corwin describes the life of Olivia, a brilliant student who works as a lap dancer in the evenings to earn the money necessary to have her own apartment and avoid living in a foster home.

> 66 For every talent that poverty has stimulated, it has
> blighted a hundred. 99

John Gardner (1912–2002)

Despite her intelligence and her desire, Olivia may not be able to afford to go to college even though she is committed to overcoming all obstacles and to continuing to make progress toward that goal. Americans still have a great attraction to the "rags to riches" story, regardless of the many scholars and social activists who have tried to explain the difficulties involved in escaping poverty.

What about those low-income people who are not "gifted and talented" like the students Corwin writes about? What about all those families and children of average abilities who are growing up in segregated urban neighborhoods with inadequate schools and services? Alex Kotlowitz describes the lives of such people in his book, *There Are No Children Here*. In this excerpt, it is the Christmas season and the Rivers family leaves their home at the Henry Horner Projects in Chicago to take a bus downtown so the children can enjoy the Christmas decorations and window displays. When they return home, they hear the news that their older brother might be sent to prison for ten years, and the delight of Christmas fades in the gloom of another defeat in this struggle to survive amid the crime and chaos of the inner city. Once again the issue is not that we don't have the resources to assist such families, but that we choose other priorities. This is not a conservative or a liberal issue; it is a moral issue that was articulated in the 1950s by Republican President Dwight David Eisenhower:

> Every gun that is made, every warship launched, every rocket fired signifies . . . a theft from those

who hunger and aren't fed, those who are cold and are not clothed.

Ursula Le Guin addresses this issue in an unusual way by describing what would seem to be an ideal world in her short story "The Ones Who Walk Away from Omelas." But the beautiful fantasy doesn't seem so ideal once we learn that this utopian society is based on the misery and suffering of one small child. In the utopia Le Guin creates, the child is a compelling metaphor for a society whose prosperity is built on exploiting the weak, the poor, the disadvantaged. By the end of the story the author describes the moral choice that exists for every citizen of this utopia. Any human being who wants his or her society to be one that is moral and just has to decide what the responsibilities are for individuals and for governments to respond to the needs and the sufferings of those who are most vulnerable in that society. Civil rights activist Andrew Young echoes Shirley Chisholm in stating the challenge for those who live in America:

> One must question the values of a society that tolerates the kind of poverty that exists in the United States.

Notes

[1]Jonathan Kozol, *The shame of the nation: The restoration of apartheid schooling in America*. New York: Crown Publishers (2005).

[2]John A. Powell, Race, Place, and Opportunity, *The American Prospect, 19*(10) (2008, October).

[3]Benett Cerf, *Try and Stop Me*. (New York: Simon & Schuster, 1944).

A Story Without an End

The author has written about poverty for many years, exploring rural, urban, and suburban communities consisting of diverse racial, religious, and ethnic groups. She has not merely relied on statistical reports; she has visited the homes of the poor and talked to them. In this essay, she tells us what she learned from her research.

In writing (about poverty), I have often traveled alone in uncharted territory. I have zigzagged through dirty streets, lonely towns and unfamiliar cities. I have climbed the steps of tenements, heard the glass of broken windows cracking under my feet and held the hands of hungry children on flea-infested beds. I have knocked on countless unfamiliar doors, seeking the eyes of strangers in the opening cracks, hoping they would see beyond the uncertainty in my eyes and read the friendship.

I am by nature a timid person with a poor sense of direction and a fear of the unfamiliar. Sometimes, when I got lost and the tiny screen on the red cell phone that linked me to my home and family read "no service," I wondered why I had come and why I felt so compelled to take on this massive self-imposed task. . . .

I knew that I had taken on this work partly because I felt more richness in the empty homes of poor strangers than I did at lavish cocktail parties where I stood making small talk on the heels of too-tight shoes, feeling the weight of my small evening bag like a heavy backpack after weeks on the open road.

But I also knew that it was because, in these homes, I would always find children whose eyes still sparkled with hope, innocent children, peeking around the safety of their mothers' skirts to stare at me before venturing out, eager children whose hands and hearts still opened in the anticipation that life would be full, silent children fluent only in the language of dreams. I knew that I was there because I found, in the eyes and hands and hearts of these children, the core of all that was profound and meaningful in my life. . . .

In the decades that followed, the questions that haunted me were asked again and again by politicians, scholars, hunger task forces and groups of physicians. But to this day, none of them have found and implemented an answer that solved the problem. There has always been a dream in America, a dream that anyone willing to work hard enough could succeed. Americans love the story of the poor boy who grew up in a log cabin and became the president of the United States. But the reality is that, most of the time, family legacy plays a larger role in our lives than the work ethic.

George Bush Senior knew that the presidency was a real possibility for his sons the same way the poor know that hunger is a real possibility for theirs. Just as the children of doctors and lawyers build their hopes on their parents' successes, so the children of the poor often have their paths marked out for them by their parents' poverty and by the hunger and malnutrition they experience as a result.

Dr. Debbie Frank, a Boston pediatrician who has been running the Failure to Thrive program at the Grow Clinic at Boston Medical Center since November 1984, says that all of the children she sees in her practice are poor and malnourished. They get sent to her because the primary-care physicians find them "too scary" to deal with.

In her seventeen years at the clinic, the biggest shift she has observed is in the increasing number of hungry and malnourished children from working families. That is because access to food stamps and other benefits always depends on the last month's income, and families with uncertain income who run out of food can't wait until the next month. They need the help immediately because without it they will soon become so desperate that they will eat anything they can find, beg or steal.

Since malnutrition impairs the immune system, especially the ability to fight off viruses and gastrointestinal impairment, the malnourished kids she sees get sick a lot more often than well-nourished ones. Like all sick children, they frequently throw up, lose their appetite and lose weight. The difference is that when these kids get over their illness, there's nothing extra in the house to feed them and help them gain back the weight they've lost. So each time the cycle repeats, the child loses more weight. Since malnourished children acquire illnesses faster, with each weight loss they become more susceptible and less able to quickly recover from the next episode.

As Dr. Frank puts it, "Child hunger is a health issue, a very serious one. My kids don't have AIDS but they function as if they did. The difference is that their immune systems were fine until they became malnourished. Now, they just continue to decline and decline. That downward spiral is what I worry about most in the short term, but in the long term, I worry about their cognitive mental development. The first thing malnourished children do is cut down on discretionary activity like talking, reading and interacting. They sleep more, they play less and they connect less.

"By the time most kids get to me, they have become so listless and tired that they have slept through many opportunities for learning. Even before their growth has been noticeably compromised, the high cognitive cost of hunger has been felt. Since learning is cumulative, just think how much learning is lost over many years of hunger."

Some of the effects of malnutrition are silent and almost invisible to the average person. Like yo-yo dieters, poor children who have experienced hunger frequently gorge when they have access to food. They also tend to fill up on fried foods and soda because they are cheap, and the fat and the bubbles make them feel full. But the kids Debbie Frank sees don't even get enough french fries or soda.

"The impoverished Asian population gets a lot of thin soup," she explained. "The African-American population often eats oatmeal and the Spanish population subsists mostly on rice and beans." Dr. Frank keeps a food pantry right there at the clinic. "I have to," she said. "What's the point of telling them what their child needs to eat and watching them burst into tears because they don't have the money or the food stamps to get it. Malnourished kids don't just need to eat, they need to eat one and a half times the food the average kid consumes in order to make up for the nutritional deprivation they've already experienced.

"When I got involved here in the mid-1980s, I thought it was a short-term thing, but the hunger I've seen in America is like a famine that sometimes recedes but never goes away. That's because it's not an act of God, it's an act of legislature. It increases whenever our public programs decrease. We see a lot of kids here who are hungry now because of the 1996 Welfare to Work changes. We see others that are victims of the Family Cap policy. That's the program that will not increase payments to a family when another child is born. As a result, when families grow in size, each kid gets even less to eat. We don't punish the parents; we punish the kids. Since '96 our federal policies have really become punitive policies because on top of the federal cuts, we've had such high housing costs and such high fuel costs that the need for emergency food has been driven up even further.

"Politicians and legislators seem to be in very serious denial about the fact that they are voting on policies and choosing programs that starve children.

"Even if a family got all the food benefits from WIC, welfare and food stamps combined, they'd still only be getting two-thirds of what a growing child needs to be healthy, and that's if they weren't already undernourished. It's like me giving a kid half a dose of penicillin and expecting him to get well.

"It's not that these programs aren't useful," Dr. Frank added. "It's that there isn't enough food provided by them. Just like with medicine, you have to give the right dose. Politicians and legislators have to be realistic. They have to understand that, even if they say the cuts are for the able-bodied family members, the children will also eat less because the food in these families is shared. Poor families aren't going to let Uncle Harry starve because he can't find work and his food stamps have been cut off. Little as they have, the poor are often kinder and more generous to each other than the larger population is to them.

"One pregnant mother I saw here recently looked hungry so I said, 'Have you eaten today?' She said, 'Not yet, but don't worry, my son Johnnie will bring some of his free lunch home to me in his pockets.' The spirit of sharing is wonderful, but because these families lack an adequate supply of food to share, the whole family often ends up chronically malnourished." . . .

In economic terms, we have always known that in a land of plenty, hunger and malnutrition make no sense. . . . As the Children's Defense Fund puts it, "All segments of society share in paying the costs of children's poverty just as they would all share in the gains if child poverty were eliminated. In fact, the American labor force is projected to lose as much as $130 billion in future productive capacity (an amount twice the size of the U.S. annual trade deficit with Japan) for every year that 14.5 million American children continue to live in poverty."

"I don't see it as very different here than it is in third world countries," Larry Brown said the first time we met. "The impact is still morbidity and mortality. The latest research on cognitive function shows us that there is really no mild undernutrition.

"What we found in our field studies was often similar to what I saw in third world countries. What we do in this country is not really very different from taking people who are desperate into a refugee camp and then threatening them under the guise of helping them. I've been in those refugee camps and I've seen the faces of people who are lost and terrified. I've also been in our welfare

offices and our food stamp offices. At the slight risk of a little hyperbole, I saw the same kind of faces, the same kind of people and the same kind of fear. I saw them being treated in the same kind of mean-spirited, threatening, intimidating way.

"I've seen hunger in the third world and I've seen hunger in America and I've seen very similar outcomes. In America there are not as many lives being crippled and perhaps not as deeply but it is clearly a continuum and not a dichotomy. Where is the line to be drawn between a child in a third world country who has chronic hunger and a child in America who doesn't get enough to eat? Both kids' minds are being sapped. Both kids are never going to live up to their potential. Both have their health compromised and have to have altered senses about the adult worlds and about what love and care mean.". . .

Brown's eyes narrowed. "I work with about two hundred food banks now, and as far as I'm concerned they are at the right hand of God. They have their finger in the dike. I see all of them as saints but I see the need for their charity as the failure of a nation.

"The problems are so easy for the federal government to solve that if the president and Congress really wanted to they could do so in six months. It's a failure of will and a failure of political leadership that they haven't done so.". . .

What is needed is a change in vision, a change that acts on the American belief that every child in this country has the right to food, a change that converts that belief into a workable plan.

One such plan was actually handed to us back in 1990. At that time, growing anguish about hungry children had caused the Center on Hunger and Poverty to convene a group of concerned experts at Tufts University in Medford, Massachusetts. Over several months, the group drafted a document that became known as the Medford Declaration. The committee was made up of the members of several national hunger organizations, including the World Hunger Year and the Food Research and Action Center. The document they created was reviewed by corporate chairpersons, foundation presidents and community leaders. It was revised six times based on their comments.

The committee believed that we had the knowledge, the programs and the resources to end hunger in "a matter of months."

The program itself required two steps. The first step was to see that food was made available to the hungry on an adequate and consistent basis by expanding existing public food programs so that, when they were combined with the "heroic efforts" of voluntary food providers, the food needs of hungry and starving Americans could finally be met in an adequate way.

They suggested that until federal programs were expanded to that level, we could meet the emergency food needs of our families by moving surplus food into the communities in much the same way that we ship goods to feed our military personnel overseas or respond to starvation in third world countries.

The second, more long-term step, was to attack the causes of hunger by increasing the earning power, independence and self-reliance of poverty-stricken American families.

The middle class is used to receiving help in ways that the poor have largely been denied. They have received loans, mortgages, retirement accounts and tax breaks that have helped them build equity capital and other assets.

With the poor, the government has done just the opposite. They have insisted that the poor have nothing left at all, no house, no car of any value, no savings and no income that is large enough to lift them out of poverty before they can receive even short-term help with food.

The Medford Declaration sought to change that. It got substantial press coverage when it was released but did not have the long-term impact that its founders had hoped for. They saturated Congress and the press with thousands of copies of the two-sided red, white and blue declaration but found that it was very hard for a single document to drive public opinion and create far-reaching permanent change. While there have been other plans to end hunger since then, most have followed the same basic principles.

The concepts behind the Medford Declaration are as usable and as sound today as they were in 1990. If we had the will, it could still become a standard by which this nation expresses its values, its goals and its commitment to end hunger and starvation among American children and their parents.

But our legislators not only failed to respond to the Medford Declaration of 1990, they introduced the massive cuts of 1996. As a result, over 100 million more children have needlessly gone hungry. . . .

Ending poverty and hunger means more than just ending welfare and asking charity to do the impossible by picking up the shortfall caused by massive food stamp cuts. It means training people to do meaningful work at fair wages and it means caring enough to make sure that their families don't starve during the process. It means providing food stamps and food aid to the children and adults who need them without intimidation or humiliation. It means adequate pay to all working people, including immigrants and military families. It means a minimum wage that can actually support and feed families.

On the iron gates of the Nazi concentration camps, there was a sign that read, *Arbeit macht frei* (Work will make you free). But work only makes people free when they are not imprisoned by the circumstances of their lives and when they are justly compensated for it. Setting people free from poverty and starvation is not only economically wise and morally just, it is at the very heart of America's value system. It is also within our grasp.

During the mid to late 1960s when the Johnson administration declared its war on poverty, the number of poor children in the country actually decreased by 45 percent from 17.6 million to 9.7 million. During the next two decades, however, the number of children in poverty increased again by over 37 percent.[1]

That is because, once again, at the start of the 1980s, the Reagan administration decided to reduce the role of the government's food aid and poverty measures. Some domestic programs were eliminated entirely while funding for others was reduced.

"In the quiet of American conscience," George W. Bush said during his inauguration speech twenty years later, "we know that deep persistent poverty is unworthy of our nation's promise and whatever our views of its cause, we can agree, children at risk are not at fault."

The word "hunger" was never mentioned. The reference to America's vulnerable children was as close as George W. Bush came to publicly acknowledging that hunger still ran rampant, starving the souls and the bodies of 12.1 million of America's children in the year that he took office. Perhaps that is because he genuinely did not know or perhaps it is because acknowledging America's starving children would require responding to them swiftly, urgently and as a top priority. . . .

In the winter that followed the terrorist attacks (of September 11), 800,000 more Americans lost their jobs, and hunger in America increased dramatically. . . .

In New York City alone, one and a half million people now counted on food pantries. Sixty percent of them were seeking emergency food for the first time. But many who lined up hungry at sunrise received only a numbered ticket that allowed them to return at dusk for something to eat.

The director of one New York church reported that before September 11, when three hundred people arrived for food on a single day, he thought it was a lot. Now he expected to see more than a thousand each day.[2]

The story was the same all over the country.

At the same time that the newly unemployed continued to create an unprecedented level of need, cutbacks, hiring freezes, and fierce new competition made it harder than ever for people to find jobs. A surge of evictions spread across America. Suddenly, in New York, Philadelphia, Boston, Cleveland, Milwaukee, and other cities, social workers and tenant advocates reported frantic calls from men and women desperately searching for ways to shelter their children while getting out of leases they could no longer afford. By February 2002, evictions had surged to an all-time high, so had pleas for emergency food. . . .

President Bush's primary response to the burgeoning crisis that followed September 11 was to call for another $48 billion for the Pentagon and refuse to revisit the issue of tax cuts that primarily benefited the rich.

As Matthew Miller of the *Philadelphia Inquirer* perceptively pointed out, no one could really demand a tax increase or challenge a wartime President by saying he wanted too much for defense in a time of real national danger. But those priorities effectively ruled out funding the unmet social needs of Americans for perhaps another generation.

It should be acknowledged that soon after the war in Afghanistan began, President Bush took to the airways and, in an admirable and compassionate gesture, he spoke openly of hunger and homelessness. His speech was effective. The need was dire, and his power to lead was obvious. Within two weeks, more than 1.5 million children had each sent a dollar to help feed the hungry children . . . *of Afghanistan.*

Notes

[1] *Two Americas, Alternative futures for child poverty in the U.S.,* Center on Hunger and Poverty, p. 9; (Also, *The consequences of hunger and food insecurity for children — evidence from recent scientific studies,* June, 2002).

[2] Alan Fever, Hungry, Cold and Stuck on Line, *New York Times,* Dec. 27, 2001, p. D1.

At the Edge of Poverty

The author is a respected journalist who carefully researched the conditions affecting the working poor whose lives he described in his book, The Working Poor: Invisible in America. This excerpt comes from the Introduction to that book.

The man who washes cars does not own one. The clerk who files cancelled checks at the bank has $2.02 in her own account. The woman who copyedits medical textbooks has not been to a dentist in a decade.

This is the forgotten America. At the bottom of its working world, millions live in the shadow of prosperity, in the twilight between poverty and well-being. Whether you're rich, poor, or middle class, you encounter them every day. They serve you Big Macs and help you find merchandise at Wal-Mart. They harvest your food, clean your offices, and sew your clothes. In a California factory, they package lights for your kids' bikes. In a New Hampshire plant, they assemble books of wallpaper samples to help you redecorate.

They are shaped by their invisible hardships. Some are climbing out of welfare, drug addiction, or homelessness. Others have been trapped for life in a perilous zone of low-wage work. Some of their children are malnourished. Some have been sexually abused. Some live in crumbling housing that contributes to their children's asthma, which means days absent from school. Some of their youngsters do not even have the eyeglasses they need to see the chalkboard clearly.

. . . While the United States has enjoyed unprecedented affluence, low-wage employees have been testing the American doctrine that hard work cures poverty. Some have found that work works. Others have learned that it doesn't. Moving in and out of jobs that demand much and pay little, many people tread just above the official poverty line, dangerously close to the edge of destitution. An inconvenience to an affluent family – minor car trouble, a brief illness, disrupted child-care – is a crisis to them, for it can threaten their ability to stay employed. They spend everything and save nothing. They are always behind on their bills. They have minuscule bank accounts or none at all, and so pay more fees and higher interest rates than more secure Americans. Even when the economy is robust, many wander through a borderland of struggle, never getting far from where they started. When the economy weakens, they slip back toward the precipice.

Millions have been pushed into a region of adversity by federal welfare reform's time limits and work mandates. Enacted in 1996 during an economic boom, the reform is credited by many welfare recipients for inducing them to travel beyond the stifling world of dependence into the active, challenging, hopeful culture of the workplace. They have gained self-confidence, some say, and have acquired new respect from their children. Those with luck or talent step onto career ladders toward better and better positions at higher and higher pay. Many more, however, are stuck at such low wages that their living standards are unchanged. They still cannot save, cannot get decent health care, cannot move to better neighborhoods, and cannot send their children to schools that offer a promise for a successful future. These are the forgotten Americans, who are noticed and counted as they leave welfare, but who disappear from the nation's radar as they struggle in their working lives.

Breaking away and moving a comfortable distance from poverty seems to require a perfect lineup of favorable conditions. A set of skills, a good starting wage, and a job with the likelihood of promotion are prerequisites. But so are clarity of purpose, courageous self-esteem, a lack of substantial debt, the freedom from illness or addiction, a functional family, a network of upstanding friends, and the right help from private or governmental agencies. Any gap in that array is an entry point for trouble, because being poor means being unprotected. You might as well try playing quarterback with no helmet, no padding, no training, and no experience, behind a line of hundred-pound weaklings. With no cushion of money, no training in the ways of the wider world, and too little defense against the threats and temptations of decaying communities, a poor man or woman gets sacked again and again – buffeted and bruised and defeated. When an exception breaks this cycle of failure, it is called the fulfillment of the American Dream.

As a culture, the United States is not quite sure about the causes of poverty, and is therefore uncertain about the solutions. The American Myth still supposes that any individual from the humblest origins can climb to well-being. We wish that to be true, and we delight in examples that make it seem so, whether fictional or real. The name of Horatio Alger, the nineteenth-century writer we no longer read, is embedded in our language as a synonym for the rise from rags to riches that his characters achieve through virtuous hard work. The classic immigrant story still stirs the American heart, despite the country's longstanding aversion to the arrival of "the wretched refuse" at "the golden door," in the words etched on the Statue of Liberty. Even while resenting the influx of immigrants, we revel in the nobility of tireless labor and scrupulous thrift that can transform a destitute refugee into a successful entrepreneur. George W. Bush gave voice to the myth when he was asked whether he meant to send a message with the inclusion of two blacks, a Hispanic, and two women in the first senior appointments to his incoming administration. "You bet," the president-elect replied: "that people who work hard and make the right decisions in life can achieve anything they want in America."[1]

The myth has its value. It sets a demanding standard, both for the nation and for every resident. The nation has to strive to make itself the fabled land of opportunity; the resident must strive to use that opportunity. The ideal has inspired a Civil Rights Movement, a War on Poverty, and a continuing search for ways to ease the distress that persists in the midst of plenty.

But the American Myth also provides a means of laying blame. In the Puritan legacy, hard work is not merely practical but also moral; its absence suggests an ethical lapse. A harsh logic dictates a hard judgment: If a person's diligent work leads to prosperity, if work is a moral virtue, and if anyone in the society can attain prosperity through work, then the failure to do so is a fall from righteousness. The marketplace is the fair and final judge; a low wage is somehow the worker's fault, for it simply reflects the low value of his labor. In the American atmosphere, poverty has always carried a whiff of sinfulness. Thus, when Judy Woodruff of CNN moderated a debate among Republican presidential candidates in March 2000, she asked Alan Keyes why he thought morality was worsening when certain indicators of morality were improving: Crime was down, out-of-wedlock births were down, and welfare was down, she noted. Evidently, welfare was an index of immorality.

There is an opposite extreme, the American Anti-Myth which holds the society largely responsible for the individual's poverty. The hierarchy of racial discrimination and economic power creates a syndrome of impoverished communities with bad schools and closed options. The children of the poor are funneled into delinquency, drugs, or jobs with meager pay and little future. The individual is a victim of great forces beyond his control, including profit-hungry corporations that exploit his labor.

In 1962, Michael Harrington's eloquent articulation of the Anti-Myth in his book *The Other America* heightened awareness; to a nation blinded by affluence at the time, the portrait of a vast "invisible land" of the poor came as a staggering revelation.[2] It helped generate Lyndon B. Johnson's War on

Poverty. But Johnson's war never truly mobilized the country, nor was it every fought to victory.

More than forty years later, after all our economic achievements, the gap between rich and poor has only widened with a median net worth of $1,430,100 among the top 10 percent and just $1,700 for the bottom 25 percent.[3] Life expectancy in the United States is lower, and infant mortality higher, than in Japan, Hong Kong, Israel, Canada, and all the major nations of Western Europe.[4] Yet after all that has been written, discussed, and left unresolved, it is harder to surprise and shock and outrage. So it is harder to generate action.

In reality, people do not fit easily into myths or anti-myths, of course. Working individuals are neither helpless nor omnipotent, but stand on various points along the spectrum between the polar opposites of personal and societal responsibility. Each person's life is the mixed product of bad choices and bad fortune, of roads not taken and road cut off by the accident of birth or circumstance. It is difficult to find someone whose poverty is not somehow related to his or her unwise behavior – to drop out of school, to have a baby out of wedlock, to do drugs, to be chronically late to work. And it is difficult to find behavior that is now somehow related to the inherited conditions of being poorly parented, poorly educated, poorly housed in neighborhoods from which no distant horizon of possibility can be seen.

How to define the individual's role in her own poverty is a question that has shaped the debate about welfare and other social policies, but it can rarely be answered with certainty, even in a specific case. The poor have less control than the affluent over their private decisions, less insulation from the cold machinery of government, less agility to navigate around the pitfalls of a frenetic world driven by technology and competition. Their personal mistakes have larger consequences, and their personal achievements yield smaller returns. The interaction between the personal and the public is so intricate that for assistance such as job training to make a difference, for example, it has to be tailored to each individual's needs, which include not only such "hard skills" as using a computer or running a lathe, but also "soft skills" such as interacting with peers, following orders willingly, and managing the deep anger that may have developed during years of adversity. Job trainers are discovering that people who

have repeatedly failed – in school, in love, in work – cannot succeed until they learn that they are capable of success. To get out of poverty, they have to acquire dexterity with their emotions as well as their hands.

An exit from poverty is not like showing your passport and crossing a frontier. There is a broad strip of contested territory between destitution and comfort, and the passage is not the same distance for everyone. "Comfortable is when I can pay my rent with one paycheck – I don't have to save for two weeks to pay one month's rent," said Tyrone Pixley, a slender man of fifty in Washington, D.C. He was especially undemanding, having emerged from a tough life as a day laborer and a heroin user. "I don't want to have to scuffle," he said simply. "I want to be able to live comfortable, even if it's in a ten-by-ten room. And in the course of a month I can pay all my bills out of my pay. I don't have to have anything saved." For me to be comfortable, I don't have to have a savings account.

In such a rich country, most people have more appetite than Tyrone Pixley. Surrounded by constant advertising from television sets that are almost always turned on, many Americans acquire wants that turn into needs. "You're living in the projects, your mom's on welfare, . . . (yet) you be wantin' things all your life, and you can't have," explained Frank Dickerson, a janitor who dealt drugs in Washington to get things he didn't have. You got kids want to have the nice tennis shoes, the jackets; they can't get that with a mom . . . on welfare. How they gonna get it? They may be getting older, growing up; they want to have nice stuff, so the only way to get that is turn to drugs. That's right. You go out there, you deal, and you get the things that you need. Car, apartments, clothes." Frank Dickerson spent three years in prison, but he and his wife also bought a house in the Maryland suburbs with the money he made from drugs.

Poverty, then, does not lend itself to easy definition. It may be absolute – an inability to buy basic necessities. It may be relative – an inability to buy the lifestyle that prevails in a certain time and place. It can be measured by a universal yardstick or by an index of disparity. Even dictionaries cannot agree. "Want or scarcity of means of subsistence," one says categorically. "Lack of the means of providing material needs or comforts," says another. "The state of one who lacks a usual or socially acceptable amount of money or material possessions," says a third.

By global or historical standards, much of what Americans consider poverty is luxury. A rural Russian is not considered poor if he cannot afford a car and his home has no central heating; a rural American is. A Vietnamese farmer is not seen as poor because he plows with water buffalo, irrigates by hand, and lives in a thatched house; a North Carolina farmworker is, because he picks cucumbers by hand, gets paid a dollar a box, and lives in a run-down trailer. Most impoverished people in the world would be dazzled by the apartments, telephones, television sets, running water, clothing, and other amenities that surround the poor in America. But that does not mean that the poor are not poor, or that those on the edge of poverty are not truly on the edge of a cliff. . . .

Indeed, being poor in a rich country may be more difficult to endure than being poor in a poor country, for the skills of surviving in poverty have largely been lost in America. Visit a slum in Hanoi and you will find children inventing games with bottles and sticks and the rusty rims of bicycle wheels. Go to a slum in Los Angeles and you will find children dependent on plastic toys and video games. . . .

In the United States, the federal government defines poverty very simply: an annual income, for a family with one adult and three children, of less than $21,100 in the year 2007. That works out to $10.14 an hour or $4.29 above the federal minimum wage, assuming that someone can get a full forty hours of work a week for all fifty-two weeks of the year, or 2,080 working hours annually.[5] With incomes rising through the economic expansion of the 1990s, the incidence of official poverty declined, beginning the new decade at 11.3 percent of the population, down from 15.1 percent in 1993. Then it rose slightly in the ensuing recession, to 12.3 percent in 2006.

But the figures are misleading. The federal poverty line cuts far below the amount needed for a decent living, because the Census Bureau still uses the basic formula designed in 1964 by the Social Security Administration, with four modest revisions in subsequent years. That sets the poverty level at approximately three times the cost of a "thrifty food basket." The calculation was derived from spending patterns in 1955, when the average family used

about one-third of its income for food. It is no longer valid today, when the average family spends only about one-tenth of its budget for food, but the government continues to multiply the cost of a "thrifty food basket" by three, adjusting for inflation only and overlooking nearly half a century of dramatically changing lifestyles.[6]

The result burnishes reality by underestimating the numbers whose lives can reasonably be considered impoverished. More accurate formulas, being tested by the Census Bureau and the National Academic of Sciences, would rely on actual costs of food, clothing, shelter, utilities, and the like. Under those calculations, income would include benefits not currently counted, such as food stamps, subsidized housing, fuel assistance, and school lunches; living costs would include expenditures now ignored, such as child-care, doctor's bills, health insurance premiums, and Social Security payroll taxes. . . . Such a change would presumably make more families eligible for benefits that are linked to the poverty level; some programs, including children's health insurance, already cover households with incomes up to 150 or 200 percent of the poverty threshold, depending on the state.

Even if revised methods of figuring poverty were adopted, however, they would provide only a still photograph of a family's momentary situation. In that snapshot, the ebb and flow of the moving picture is lost. By measuring only income and expenses during a current year and not assets and debts, the formulas ignore the past, and the past is frequently an overwhelming burden on the present. Plenty of people have moved into jobs that put them above the threshold of poverty, only to discover that their student loans, their car payment, and the exorbitant interest charged on old credit card balances consume so much of their cash that they live no better than before.

When the poor or the nearly poor are asked to define poverty, however, they talk not only about what's in the wallet but what's in the mind or the heart. "Hopelessness," said a fifteen-year-old girl in New Hampshire.

"Not hopelessness – helplessness," said a man in Los Angeles. "Why should I get up? Nobody's gonna ever hire me because look at the way I'm dressed, and look at the fact that I never finished high school, look at the fact that I'm black, I'm brown, I'm yellow, or I grew up in the trailer."

"The state of mind," said a man in Washington, D.C. "I believe that spirituality is way more important than physical."

"I am so rich," said a woman whose new job running Xerox machines was lifting her out of poverty, "because – not only material things – because I know who I am, I know where I'm going now."

Another woman, who fell into poverty after growing up middle class, celebrated her "cultural capital," which meant her love of books, music, ideas, and her close relationships with her children. "In some senses, we are not at all poor; we have a great richness," she said. "We don't feel very poor. We feel poor when we can't go to the doctor or fix the car."

For practically every family, then, the ingredients of poverty are part financial and part psychological, part personal and part societal, part past and part present. Every problem magnifies the impact of the others, and all are so tightly interlocked that one reversal can produce a chain reaction with results far distant from the original cause. A rundown apartment can exacerbate a child's asthma, which leads to a call for an ambulance, which generates a medical bill that cannot be paid, which ruins a credit record, which hikes the interest rate on an auto loan, which forces the purchase of an unreliable used car, which jeopardizes a mother's punctuality at work, which limits her promotions and earning capacity, which confines her to poor housing. . . . If she or any other impoverished working parent added up all of her individual problems, the whole would be equal to more than the sum of its parts. . . .

If problems are interlocking, then so must solutions be. A job alone is not enough. Medical insurance alone is not enough. Good housing alone is not enough. Reliable transportation, careful family budgeting, effective parenting, effective schooling are not enough when each is achieved in isolation from the rest. There is no single variable that can be altered to help working people move away from the edge of poverty. Only where the full array of factors is attacked can America fulfill its promise.

Notes

[1]Bush was quoted in Richard A. Oppel, Jr., *New York Times,* Dec. 18, 2000, p. A19.

[2]Michael Harrington, *The Other America.* (Baltimore: Penguin, 1963).

[3]"2004 Survey of Consumer Finances," Board of Governors of the Federal Reserve System, Feb 28, 2006.

[4]*World in Figures* (London: The Economist Newspaper, 2003), pp. 76, 79.

[5]The Census Bureau "counts money income before taxes and does not include capital gains and noncash benefits (such as public housing, Medicaid, and food stamps)." The poverty threshold is adjusted annually on the basis of the consumer price index. See http://www.census.gov/hhes/poverty/povdef.html.

[6]For more on the poverty index, Gordon M. Fisher, "The Development of the Orshansky Poverty Thresholds and Their Subsequent History as the Official U.S. Poverty Measure," http://www.census.gov/hhes/poverty/povmeas/papers/orshansky.html.

My Safe Haven

Olivia is a talented and gifted student who has had to live in foster homes because her mother abused her. The author describes her life during her senior year in high school as she approaches graduation, hoping to go on to college and escape her poverty.

While Braxton searches for an inexpensive child care center for Toya, he is heartened by the fact that, at least, his other problem student – Olivia – has returned to school. As long as she remains on the lam from the county, however, Braxton knows her future is uncertain. He knows that county authorities can get a court order to apprehend her and contact police. Officers can then track her down, pull her out of school, and toss her in the county's shelter for abused and neglected children.

During Olivia's first few weeks at school, Braxton continually encourages her to return to foster care. She just has to make it until June, he tells her, and then she will walk the stage at graduation, head for Babson College in Massachusetts, where she plans to apply for a scholarship, and finally free herself from county supervision. A few years ago Olivia read a magazine article that rated Babson as the best business college in the nation, and since then she has dreamed of enrolling there. The school offers a major in entrepreneurial studies, which Olivia feels would be perfect for her. She eventually wants to own her own business and make a lot of money, as quickly as possible, because she never wants to be poor again, never wants to rely on another governmental agency for her survival.

Olivia has written a brief autobiographic essay in preparation for her Babson application:

"Die, you little bitch!" the woman roared as she caught the young girl by her hair. Struggling to escape, the girl was dragged to the bathroom. The Girl's tear-drenched face screamed for the woman to stop, as she was thrown into the shower, her head bouncing off the tiled wall. Her skin burned as the hot water soaked through her clothes.

The woman lifted an extension cord. Crack, crack, crack, it resounded, until the girl's yells drowned out its sound . . .

I was that little girl, and the woman, my mother. I wanted to die rather than endure it. Dealing with a situation I did not create, and could not change, became more than I could bear. Society teaches one to honor thy father and mother, for it is morally correct. But what is one to do when they aren't morally correct and being beaten becomes an everyday event?

So one windy March afternoon I ran until my breath escaped me. Later that night, I called a runaway shelter, which began my trek through many group and foster homes.

My life hasn't been an easy one. Group homes are full of teenage pregnancy, high school dropouts, thieves and drugs. The staff only work there. And since caring isn't included in their salary, they don't.

Through it all, school has been my only safe haven. It is my main focus, even though I have allowed the surrounding negativity to sidetrack me at times. I can truly appreciate what an education means, for it is the only factor that separates me from the hoodlums. It is imperative in order for me to attain the success that I deeply desire in my future.

Braxton tells Olivia that to ensure her future, to earn a scholarship to Babson, she must keep her grades up this year and stay focused on school until June.

To Olivia, graduation day seems so far in the future that it is an abstraction rather than an inevitability. During the second week of school, she loses her job at the women's clothing store because her sputtering, 1977 Volkswagen bug continues to stall on her and she is late to work several days in a row. She hears about a job as a graveyard-shift dispatcher at an aerospace company. Olivia figures she will be able to do her homework and catch a few hours of sleep during the quiet early morning hours. When her shift ends, she will have enough time to make it to class in the morning. She tries to schedule an interview for the job as soon as possible because she is down to her last few dollars and is desperate for money. She scans the ads in the newspaper for temporary night work where she can earn some quick cash to tide her over.

Olivia is embarrassed to tell Braxton, or her classmates, but she eventually takes a job as a taxi dancer. She wears a black, low-cut, spaghetti strap dress, and dances, talks, and plays pool with customers for six dollars an hour and tips. The club is located in a desolate, industrial section of downtown Los Angeles, on the top floor of a grimy brick building, above an electrical supply company and down the street from a printing plant and a cigar factory.

The black awning outside the club advertises: HOSTESS DANCING in large block letters. There is a five dollar cover charge, and a sign by the door: PROSTITUTION & LEWD CONDUCT ARE UNLAWFUL AND IMPERMISSIBLE ACTIVITIES. Inside the dim, smoky club, downtown factory workers and laborers, and a few businessmen in sports coats and ties, ogle the women, who sit on a padded bench at the edge of the bar. The women, dressed in short skirts, halter tops, and skimpy, low-cut dresses, look bored as they smoke cigarettes, chat, and wait for customers to approach them. In her heavy makeup and thick eyeliner, Olivia looks as if she is in her twenties. Only an occasional girlish gesture or nervous giggle betrays her as a seventeen-year-old high school senior with a fake ID.

In the club's dark recesses, in the padded corner booths, some of the women engage in what is euphemistically called "lap dancing," and afterward obtain "tips" from the men. The empty Trojan wrappers scattered about the floor of the men's bathroom indicate that more goes on in this club than dancing.

Olivia carefully avoids the dark corners of the club. When a man wants to dance or talk with her, he has to line up at a booth by the bar, punch a time card, and pay twenty-one dollars an hour for the privilege. Dancing with the men is distasteful to Olivia, and she tries to persuade them to buy her a Snapple and just sit and talk at a well-lit table near the dance floor. She usually takes home from fifty to seventy dollars a night in tips, but some nights she does not return home until 2:00 a.m. She wakes up at 6:30 the next morning, stumbles into class, bleary-eyed and yawning, and fights to stay awake. Other students are penalized for being tardy or for missing class. But most of the teachers cut Olivia some slack. Even though she often is late now for her 8:00 a.m. classes, is occasionally absent, and sometimes turns in her homework late, her teachers know her circumstances are anomalous.

In her AP U.S. Government class, the teacher, Scott Allen, asks students to sign a contract with him, agreeing to obey the class rules regarding homework assignments, attendance, and exams. Allen also asks the students to have a parent sign it. On the day the contract is due, Olivia approaches Allen after class. From a distance, she could pass for a teacher, and Allen, who is thirty-five years old, could pass for a student. He has light brown, shoulder-length hair and wears faded jeans, sneakers, and a T-shirt. Olivia is dressed up again today, in a chocolate brown skirt, matching blazer, stockings, and brown lizard high heels. After school, she is interviewing for the job as the graveyard-shift dispatcher.

"I can't turn the contract in," Olivia tells Allen.

"Why not?" he asks, not looking up from his roll book.

"I don't have any parents to sign it," she says matter-of-factly.

He studies her, now, with genuine concern.

"Are you eighteen?"

"No."

"Well . . ." Allen says, struggling to think of a solution that does not embarrass her. "Just sign it yourself. Don't worry about the rest of it."

She nods and saunters out the classroom, earrings jangling, her high heels clicking on the linoleum, echoing in the hallway.

Olivia's schedule is so hectic now, with school and taxi dancing, that she has little time for homework, so she tries to do most of it during her AP computer science class. While the other students write down the problems and furiously fill pages of paper with their attempts to solve them, Olivia computes the problems in her head. In a moment, she can conceptualize computer or mathematical problems and quickly reach solutions. Her teacher boasts that Olivia is one of the most gifted computer science students she ever taught at Crenshaw and expects her to pass the AP exam this spring with a five – the highest score.

As the other students labor and surreptitiously ask Olivia for help, she quickly whips through her class assignments. She has no computer at home, so despite admonitions from her teacher, she frequently uses her spare class time to write papers and finish homework for other courses.

After a few weeks of taxi dancing four and five nights a week, trying to keep up with her AP courses, and sleeping only a few hours a night, Olivia finally concedes defeat. She cannot sustain this pace until October, much less until June. She does not want to return to a group home, but she has heard about a pilot program for older foster children that provides apartments, stipends, and loose supervision. Olivia decides this could be the solution to her problems.

She decides to cut her computer science class on a September afternoon and visit Ron Johnson, whose firm has a county contract to run the housing program. Johnson knows Olivia because she was a long-time student in a martial arts class he taught for foster children. And she trusts him, partly because he, too, grew up poor and had a tumultuous childhood; because he, too, was once a bright

student with a troubled home life. A former gang member from a Brooklyn housing project, Johnson straightened out his life and graduated from Columbia University.

Olivia pulls out of the high school parking lot and speeds around a corner, grinding her gears, her Volkswagen rattling down the street. On this still, smoggy afternoon, the gauzy haze that encircles Los Angeles seems to compress the horizons and shrink the city. The air is so thick with pollutants, the veiled sun and vaporous shadows create a spectral twilight in the middle of the day.

"If Ron can get me an apartment, all my problems will be solved," Olivia tells me. At a stop sign she puts her hands together, as though praying, and says, "I hope, I hope he can. I'd rather be AWOL than have to deal with another crowded, dirty foster home with another foster mother who doesn't give a damn about anything but her paycheck."

She races down Crenshaw Boulevard and screeches to a halt in front of Johnson's office, housed on the ground floor of a sooty brick building, facing a body shop and down the street from a pawn shop, a hat store, and a strip of boarded-up businesses. She sits on a chair next to his desk. He brings a Coke and she explains her predicament to him, how she is tired of living in foster homes, how his program would be perfect for her.

He shrugs and says, "I understand what you're saying. But as long as you're AWOL, I can't do anything for you. You've got to get back into the system. You've got to let your social worker place you in a home. Once you're placed I can see about getting you an apartment."

"Why can't I get an apartment right now? I'm turning myself in to you."

"You know that's not the way it works."

The office's front door is open, but there is not much of a breeze, just the rumble of traffic. Olivia cools her forehead with the Coke can. "I can't live like that again," she says. "I can't go back to one of those places."

"Your last placement seemed like a good situation. Why'd you go AWOL?"

"I haven't had a mom since I was twelve. All of a sudden someone wanted to be my mom. It didn't work."

"Part of being an adult is making it work," he says. "It was an impulse decision. You can't make life decisions based on impulses."

"I never respected my mom," Olivia says. "She never deserved respect. And I never respected my foster mothers. They never cared about me." Olivia stares off into the distance. "So I don't care about them."

"Any problem you've got, you just replay your battle with your mother," he says. "You're angry. You resent authority. You've got to give people some respect."

"I give people respect who deserve respect," she says angrily. "I respect my teachers. I respect Mr. Braxton. I respect you."

"Physically, you're okay," he says. "But you've got a lot of emotional problems. Hey, you come from a situation that would make anyone angry and hurt. But you've got to be in the system before I can help you."

She frowns and twirls an earring. "If I go back, how long will I have to be there before you can get me in an apartment?"

"One to two months," he says. "That's all I need."

"I can't handle another two months in one of those homes," she says plaintively.

"Olivia!" he shouts. "We're talking a few months." He pats her shoulder and says softly, "We're talking about what's best for you, what's best for your future."

She slinks down in her chair and her eyes begin to tear.

"You're jammed up right now," he says. "But you know you've got to go back. It's you only way out." He pauses, grips her by the shoulders, and asks, "Will you go back?"

"I guess so," she says mechanically.

"Okay," he says, clapping his hands once. "We got that straightened out. You still working?"

"Yeah. I got a kind of temporary job now. And I've applied for this night job as a dispatcher. I'm waiting to hear whether I got the job. It's perfect for me –"

He interrupts her. "When you get back into a foster home, I hope you stop working."

"I can't."

"Why not?"

"I can't live poor," she says, sounding desperate. "I gotta buy clothes. I gotta pay for gas."

"None of that stuff really matters," he says. "Look, you can't play basketball. You're not a musician. But you're bright. School's your ticket out of

here. It was my ticket out, too. School should be your priority now, not clothes and your car."

The teenagers he advises often stare at him sullenly, their eyes opaque with boredom. But Olivia is listening to him now, nodding in assent.

"So first thing you do is call your social worker. Get back into the system. Whatever foster home they send you to – go. Don't get nasty with anyone. Don't give anyone a hard time. Don't go AWOL again."

"Okay," she says. "But I don't want to be there indefinitely."

"You won't be," he says. "Just don't blow it now. All you have to do is hang on nine more months. Then all this is behind you and you're on your way to college. It's almost over. Can you hang on nine more months?"

She takes a sip of Coke and says weakly, "I'll try."

The next day at school, Olivia explains her predicament to Braxton. While he leaves to attend a meeting, he lets her use his office. She closes the door, calls her social worker and county social services and sets in motion the move to yet another foster home – her thirteenth residence in the past five years. Although resigned to her fate, she remains in a surprisingly upbeat mood. Despite constant obstacles, she does not stay despondent for long. She usually brims with energy and ideas, laughs easily and is generally so high-spirited people are surprised when they discover her background.

On a Friday morning, Olivia misses (her English) class because her social worker has found a new home for her. Olivia stuffs all her belongings into a few green plastic garbage bags and drives to her new residence: a four-bedroom foster home, where five other girls and the foster mother live. From a distance, the foster home, which is only a few miles from Crenshaw, looks like a standard beige, Southern California ranch-style house. But a closer inspection reveals the fortress-like security measures. Stucco walls and a rusty, six-foot-high metal fence with spiked tips encircle the house. Each window is latticed with thick bars, and at the front of the house there is a heavy, steel-mesh security door. The house faces a major thoroughfare – with no stop signs or traffic lights nearby – and a constant stream of cars race by at breakneck speed.

Olivia's social worker orders her to sell her Volkswagen because she has no driver's license and no insurance. Instead, Olivia parks the car at the top of a hill near the house. Every morning she tells the foster mother she is walking to the bus stop, and instead, climbs the hill and drives off to school – if the car starts.

The Volkswagen is not much to look at, just a battered, rusting, nineteen-year-old Bug with torn upholstery, a mangled bumper, and only one headlight. But to Olivia, it is a prized possession. She lovingly washes the car each week. She buys magazines that feature custom Volkswagens and studies them in bed at night. She spends afternoons at auto part shops, shopping for gold hubcaps and chrome shift knobs that will give her car a little flash. Her friends cannot understand why she is so attached to such a wreck, why she continues to drive it and risk arrest. But for a girl who has never owned anything that could not fit in a plastic garbage bag, who never received a gift that she cared about – from someone whom she cared about – who never bought anything for herself, except clothes, this car signifies more to her than just transportation.

A few days after she moves into the foster home, Olivia's car breaks down again. I drive her and her best friend Julia to the foster home because Olivia has to pick up a book. She rings the bell. No one answers. Suddenly a girl inside the house shouts, "I'm calling the police!" Another girl yells, "I'll kill you, bitch!"

The foster mother lets Olivia in the house. Several girls argue at the top of their lungs. One girl in the hallway screams at another girl for stealing her clothes. In the kitchen, a girl sprawls on the floor, eyes shut, hands over her ears, sobbing. Another girl in the living room, whose father is dying of AIDS, accuses her roommate of betraying a confidence by telling everyone. She grabs Olivia by the shoulders.

"My dad has HIV and TB," she says, tears streaming down her face. "It's true. I'm not ashamed. But why does she have to tell everyone?" she says, pointing to a girl across the room. "Why does she have to put my business on the street?" She shakes Olivia and begins sobbing.

Olivia leads her over to the sofa and tries to calm her. The sofa is gold crushed velvet covered in plastic. The coffee table is made of wood burl, with a matching wood burl clock on the wall. On the opposite wall looms a large black velvet Jesus, who graces the bedlam below with a beatific look.

Wide-eyed, Julia glances around nervously. "These foster homes," Olivia tells her, "are always like this. There's always a lot of yelling and dissension and fights over stealing. There's always a lot of craziness. Night and day." She opens the door to her bedroom and sees her roommate curled up on a bed, eating caramel corn and watching cartoons. The dim, musty room is a mess: the floor is strewn with shoes, hair brushes, and empty cereal boxes. The orange carpet is ripped and stained. A broken mirror leans against a wall. A small desk is covered with Olivia's makeup, shampoo, detergent, and a few school books. A floor lamp with no bulb teeters in the corner. Olivia's roommate has cut pictures of rap stars from magazines and taped them to the walls. A cascade of socks, T-shirts, and blouses topples from the roommate's chipped dresser. Green plastic garbage bags, filled with Olivia's clothes, surround her bed.

Olivia sees that the clothes in one of her bags, which she had neatly folded, are in a jumble. "Did you go through my things?" she asks her roommate in an even tone.

"I didn't touch yo' motherfucking shit!" screams her roommate, a tall, skinny, gap-toothed girl with wild hair. "You fucking bitch!" She leaps off the bed and charges Olivia, fists clenched, eyes flashing.

Olivia holds up a palm and says calmly, "Slow down. I'm not violent. I don't like to fight. I just want to know."

The roommate stops suddenly, startled by Olivia's sangfroid. "I ain't gone through nobody's stuff. But some motherfucker done gone through mine and stole my toothpaste and my sponge."

"Don't get so defensive," Olivia says. "Calm down. It was a simple question."

The roommate returns to her cartoons. Olivia finds the book and heads out the door.

There Are No Children Here

LaJoe and Paul had eight children, including triplets, before Paul got into drugs and lost his job, and the family had to go on welfare. LaJoe's son Terence is in jail waiting to be sentenced, and 13-year-old Lafeyette and his younger brother, Pharoah, are trying to survive the drugs, crime, and violence of Chicago's Henry Horner projects.

As it did every winter, the temperature in the apartment approached a dry, crackling 85 degrees. Stripping down to their underwear was of no relief to Lafeyette and Pharoah; it was like being inside an oven. Their only remedy was to open a window, even in the dead of winter, but then they had to put up with a frigid draft. Pharoah had developed a blistering cough; his throat was parched and sore. The scorching heat tired the boys and put everyone on edge. LaJoe wanted to find some excuse to get them out of the apartment. Weekends were the worst. Besides the Boys Club, the kids had nowhere to go, so they would sit around all day. As Christmas approached, LaJoe wanted to do something special, for herself and the children. She had already promised them they would be getting bunk beds for the holidays, but that was beginning to seem unlikely. After buying the children their Christmas presents, she didn't have the money for the beds. They'd have to wait until spring.

LaJoe decided to take the younger ones to see the Christmas windows downtown, something she had done with her mother as a child. The triplets

had never before been in the Loop; Pharoah, only a couple of times. LaJoe didn't think to ask Lafeyette. She figured he'd feel too grown for such a tour.

So on a Thursday after school, two weeks before Christmas and a few days after she'd won $38 playing cards, LaJoe gathered the children. In addition to Pharoah, and the triplets, she invited three of her grandchildren, Tyisha, Baldheaded, and Snuggles, and a friend of the triplets whom everyone called Esther B.

She walked the young battalion to Madison Street, where they hopped the bus and where all the kids, including ten-year-old Pharoah, got on for free. As LaJoe and the eight youngsters filed on, the driver joked, "Next time you get on the bus, you pay nine dollars." LaJoe, already tired, managed a half smile. The trip, she hoped, would lift her spirits.

"Why's that window so clean?"

"Where them lights come from?"

"Ooooh, look at them tall buildings."

"Them's glass."

"No, they aint."

"Is too."

"If a hurricane hit them buildings, everybody gonna die. The glass will get them."

"Ain't no hurricane gonna hit it."

"Stop lying."

And so the banter went as the bus was swallowed by the city's downtown; the skyscrapers

197

seemed to rise forever into the darkening sky. The children tried to look straight up, to spot the buildings' tops, but, with their necks craning back as far as they would go and their faces pressed against the bus windows, their warm breath clouded the glass. Frantically, they rubbed off the mist as they caught a few more glimpses of the high-rises that dared to tower over their own.

LaJoe began to share their excitement. "When we're through," she promised the distracted crew, "I'll buy you some popcorn like you never tasted before." She remembered the popcorn her mother treated her to when as a young girl she had visited her at her job in the downtown county building. LaJoe was beginning to feel a part of an ordinary family, a family without problems.

"Here you go, ma'am," the bus driver told LaJoe as he pulled up to State Street, home of the downtown's major department stores and their elaborate Christmas windows. The children pushed and tumbled off the bus.

"Ain't no one going anywhere," LaJoe shouted. All except Pharaoh, who felt he was big enough to go it on his own, clamored to hold LaJoe's hands. "I can't hold you all. Pharoah! Pharoah!" she called. But Pharoah was mesmerized by the afternoon rush. Men in suits and ties walked past him, their eyes focused straight ahead, their faces fixed with determination. And the women. They looked so pretty in their long wool coats, brightly colored scarves draped around their rosy faces. He twirled 180 degrees as his gaze followed one passerby after another.

"Pharoah!" LaJoe shouted again. "PHAROAH!" He drew upright at the sound of his name, which for the past minute had fluttered by him like the rush-hour shoppers. "Pharoah, take Tammie's and Tiffany's hands." He gripped the bare hands of the two five-year-olds. Tyisha grabbed Timothy and Snuggles. LaJoe picked up Baldheaded in one arm and held Esther B. with the other. Like paper chains, the eight of them floated down State Street, in and around the hurried businessmen and women, toward the crowds surrounding the windows.

The children screamed in delight at the sight of the two-foot-high mechanical children in the windows, some singing carols, two celebrating Christmas in a spaceship. "Are they real little kids?" Timothy asked.

"No," LaJoe told him. "Them's dolls and they make them move by battery."

"I wish I could go in there and live with them," Timothy said.

The kids argued. Was it real or fake snow? How about all the Santas ringing bells on the street corners? How could there be so many? "Them Santa Clauses just want money to buy people gifts," Pharoah explained to the younger ones. Pharoah himself had begun to doubt Santa's existence. "I don't think there's a Santa Claus," he whispered to his mother. "I don't think he could make it in every state in one day. He couldn't go to Detroit in one whole day."

Pharoah guided LaJoe and the others from window to window, block to block. He'd fly ahead of the pack, with Tammie and Tiffany as his wings. "Mama, come see this! Mama, come see this!" he'd scream. At one window, Pharoah read for the little ones: "Singing carols on the steps of the Art Institute has a way of making even Scrooge look cute . . . There's Tiny Tim and Bob Cratchit from Dicken's past. But who's teasing the dogs?"

"Perfect," said a young couple who had stopped to listen. Pharoah smiled proudly.

LaJoe led the children to McDonald's, where they ate and talked feverishly. "Where we going next?" they asked. "Mama, where?"

"One more stop. The big Christmas Tree," she told them.

They hiked one more block, where they oohed and aahed at the huge city tree, which was actually tens of smaller trees neatly sculptured to look like one. "Is that God's tree?" Tiffany asked. "It's almost in the sky."

"No, that's everybody's tree. But God probably be around here somewhere," LaJoe told them, as their small bodies moved in rhythm to the Christmas carols emanating mysteriously from the tree's center. Finally, LaJoe brought them to Garrett's, a downtown popcorn emporium, where, despite Pharoah's protestations that she keep the rest of the money for herself, she bought them two huge bags, one of cheese-flavored and the other of caramel popcorn. She popped a kernel of each in each of their mouths as they giggled and chewed and asked for more. It was, they told LaJoe, the best popcorn they'd ever had.

On the bus ride home, Tiffany and Tammie walked up and down the aisle and in clear and precise tones, meant to imitate adults', said to each other and the other children: "Oh, we had a lovely day. Didn't you have a lovely day?" Before long, all eight had joined in the game. "Oh, we had a lovely time, Mama," one would say to the giggles of the others. LaJoe sat back in the seat, her head against the cold window. She was physically exhausted, but, in an odd sort of way, had more energy than she had had in a long time. It felt good to see the children giddy with excitement. They seemed so unencumbered. She promised herself she'd take the children on more trips. It gave them – and her – such satisfaction. "Oh, what a lovely day," she repeated to herself, imitating her daughters. She laughed softly.

Pharaoh, too, sat in the bus exhausted. It had been an extraordinary day for him. He got to help his mother take care of the kids and to read to them from one of the windows. But more than that, he liked just spending time with his mother. He wished she'd take him on more trips. "I'd like to go again, Mama," he told LaJoe.

"Me too." LaJoe smiled and patted Pharaoh's head.

LaJoe's only regret was that she hadn't asked Lafeyette. She didn't think he would have wanted to go; he would have thought himself too old for such a tour. But when they got home, Lafeyette was seated on the couch.

"Why didn't you take me, too?" he demanded.

"I didn't think you'd want to see a Santa Claus and a Christmas tree and the windows with all those dolls in it," she said.

"I wanted to go."

Next time, LaJoe promised herself. She had to remind herself that Lafeyette, despite his adult worries, was still a thirteen-year-old boy.

Lafeyette got angry when he heard the news. There was no way their brother could go to prison for ten years. No way. He wasn't *that* bad. When LaJoe had told Lafeyette, all he could muster was "I hope Terence get less time than ten years." He then disappeared into the bathroom, where he remained for nearly half an hour. Like his father, he felt his stomach tie up into knots when he got anxious. He had terrible bouts of diarrhea.

When Pharaoh heard that his brother might be sent away for ten years, his face dropped. "I be thinking," he told his mother, "why they be locking people up and taking them away from their par-

ents?" LaJoe tried to explain why it happened; it was a form of punishment for Terence's doing something wrong.

"If he get the ten years, then he'll be home when he's twenty eight. I'll be twenty," Pharaoh said, calculating the years with his fingers.

"Y'all just will have to catch up a little," LaJoe told him. "That'll be all right." LaJoe was concerned about Pharaoh because his teacher had called her one afternoon after school and said that Pharaoh had been daydreaming a lot in his class. Was there something wrong? The teacher had asked LaJoe. She suspected Pharaoh was troubled about Terence. Neither Pharaoh nor Lafeyette liked to let his mother in on his worries, because he thought it would just burden her more. As a result, a lot went unspoken.

"Terence is gonna be a man about what they give him," LaJoe assured Pharaoh. "And you have to be a man for him also, no matter what they do. You have to be Pharaoh and you can't worry about Terence if it make you to the point you have to daydream, thinking on him. Your brother's gonna be all right, so don't worry about him."

"Mama," Pharaoh interrupted, "I'm just too young to understand how life really is."

The prosecution had offered Terence ten years if he would agree to plead guilty. That may have seemed an outrageous offer, particularly since he adamantly proclaimed his innocence. But Terence had been arrested again. Another armed robbery. Only this time, the police had substantial incriminating evidence.

Over the summer, Terence, while out on bond, had been determined to stay out of trouble. He spent some afternoons and evenings shining shoes at the airport, but mostly he lounged in the bedroom he shared with Weasel. Friends would visit him there. He didn't leave the apartment much. He felt good about his public defender, Audrey Natcone. She cared and she believed him. Nonetheless, Terence didn't share her optimism about his getting off. Hadn't he once spent five months in detention for a crime he hadn't done? No one came to his rescue then, he thought. Luck saved him. Had the girl he'd allegedly shot not come forward and changed her testimony, he might have been sent to prison. Because of the severity of the alleged crime, aggravated battery with a gun, he would have been tried as an adult. The judge could have sent him away for ten years. He just didn't trust the system. *They* didn't listen. *They* didn't understand. So if *they* thought he was a bad guy, if they wanted him to be a bad guy, then he'd be a bad guy. If *they* wanted to put him away for something he didn't do, then he'd give them something to put him away with. It was a tangled and tragic form of reasoning, but then it was a tangled and tragic life that had got him into trouble. It was his own confused method of seeking justice. And so he told a friend over the summer, perhaps somewhat presciently, "Man, they ain't gonna convict me with something I ain't do like that. I'm gonna give them something to convict me for."

On September 5, Terence and an acquaintance help up Mazury Tavern, a working-class bar on the city's north side. The stories vary. Terence says he went for a car ride with a few friends, only to learn that they'd planned a robbery. They paid Terence a few hundred dollars to stand as the lookout.

The police reported it differently. Two men, Terence and his friend, entered Mazury Tavern, where the friend held the bartender at bay with a pistol while Terence jimmied open a video game and the cash register and withdrew an estimated $1000 in cash. The police said they found indisputable evidence: Terence's fingerprints. Moreover, the police said Terence gave them an oral confession, though he refused to sign it. In the statement, he said he agreed to accompany his acquaintance to a north side tavern and that for his role in the robbery he received two bags of heroin.

Whatever the true version, Terence knew the prosecution had a good case. The police had reason to prosecute him. Now if he served time, at least it would be for something he'd done, not for some "bogus case." After they arrested him, he didn't confess to Audrey. But she could tell. She just knew.

His arrest upset Audrey, but it didn't come as a surprise. Many of her clients committed crimes while they were out on bond. She had hoped it would be different with Terence. She also felt they had had a strong case. She believed Terence hadn't committed the first armed robbery. The police still hadn't produced the line-up photos, which made her think something was amiss. But now it didn't matter. The prosecutors could try to second case first – and Terence didn't seem to have a chance.

The prosecution, though, was already overburdened with cases. It didn't want to go to trial. The three prosecutors in the courtroom where Terence's case was to be heard handled about 450 cases at a time, up from 250 cases the year before. They suspected part of the reason for the increase was political. Their boss was running for mayor, so the more cases they prosecuted, particularly those related to drugs, the more convinced the electorate would be that he was a strong law-and-order man. In fact, of the twenty-five thousand drug defendants in the county the previous year, over half had had their cases dismissed or their charges dropped, according to one study. As a result, the prosecutors – or state's attorneys, as they are called in Chicago – pleabargained nearly 90 percent of their cases. They just didn't have the time to go to trial.

They had told Audrey they would offer Terence ten years in exchange for a guilty plea. She thought that was too much for him, especially since she believed he didn't commit the first robbery. It was also his first offense as an adult. She wanted to get him six. . . . She believed she could negotiate a shorter term with the prosecution.

(Note: Terence eventually accepted an offer of an eight-year sentence.)

The Ones Who Walk Away from Omelas

This short story begins as an amusing exercise in creating a utopian land, but by the end of the story it becomes clear that the author has a much more serious purpose: exploring the moral and political implications related to how oppressors in any society benefit from the exploitation and suffering of the oppressed.

(Variations on a theme by William James)

With a clamor of bells that set the swallows soaring, the Festival of Summer came to the city of Omelas, bright-towered by the sea. The rigging of the boats in harbor sparkled with flags. In the streets between houses with red roofs and painted walls, between old moss-grown gardens and under avenues of trees, past great parks and public buildings, processions moved. Some were decorous: old people in long stiff robes of mauve and grey, grave master workmen, quiet, merry women carrying their babies, and chatting as they walked. In other streets the music beat faster, a shimmering of gong and tambourine, and the people went dancing, the procession was a dance. Children dodged in and out, their high calls rising like the swallow' crossing flights over the music and the singing. All the processions wound towards the north side of the city, where on the great water-meadow called the Green Fields boys and girls, naked in the bright air, with mud-stained feet and ankles and long, lithe arms, exercised their restive horses before the race. The horses wore no gear at all but a halter without bit. Their manes were braided with streamers of silver, gold, and green. They flared their nostrils and pranced and boasted to one another; they were vastly excited, the horse being the only animal who has adopted our ceremonies as his own. Far off to the north and west the mountains stood up half encircling Omelas on her bay. The air of morning was so clear that the snow still crowning the Eighteen Peaks burned with white-gold fire across the miles of sunlit air, under the dark blue of the sky. There was just enough wind to make the banners that marked the race-course snap and flutter now and then. In the silence of the broad green meadows one could hear the music winding through the city streets, farther and nearer and ever approaching, a cheerful faint sweetness of the air that from time to time trembled and gathered together and broke out into the great joyous clanging of the bells.

Joyous! How is one to tell about joy? How describe the citizens of Omelas?

They were not simple folk, you see, though they were happy. But we do not say the words of cheer much any more. All smiles have become archaic. Given a description such as this one tends to make certain assumptions. Given a description such as this one tends to look next for the King, mounted on a splendid stallion and surrounded by his noble knights, or perhaps in a golden litter borne by great-muscled slaves. But there was no king. They did not use swords, or keep slaves. They were not barbarians. I do not know the rules and laws of their society, but I suspect that they were singularly few. As they did without monarchy and slavery, so they also got on without the stock exchange, the advertisement, the secret police, and the bomb. Yet I repeat that these were not simple folk, not dulcet shepherds, noble savages, bland utopians. They were not less complex than us. The trouble is that we have a bad habit, encouraged by pedants and sophisticates, of considering happiness as something rather stupid. Only pain is intellectual, only evil interesting. This is the treason of the artist: a refusal to admit the banality of evil and the terrible boredom of pain. If you can't lick 'em, join 'em. If it hurts, repeat it. But to praise despair is to condemn delight, to embrace violence is to lose hold of everything else. We have almost lost hold; we can no longer describe a happy man, nor make any celebration of joy. How can I tell you about the people of Omelas? They were not naïve and happy children – though their children were, in fact, happy. They were mature, intelligent, passionate adults whose lives were not wretched. O miracle! but I wish I could describe it better. I wish could convince you. Omelas sounds in my words like a city in a fairy tale, long ago and far away, once upon a time. Perhaps it would be best if you imagined it as your own fancy bids, assuming it will rise to the occasion for certainly I cannot suit you all. For instance, how about technology? I think that there would be no cars or helicopters in and above the streets; this follows from the fact that the people of Omelas are happy people. Happiness is based on a just discrimination of what is necessary, what is neither necessary nor destructive, and what is destructive. In the middle category, however – that of the unnecessary but undestructive, that of comfort, luxury, exuberance, etc. – they could perfectly well have central heating, subway trains, washing machines, and all kinds of marvelous devices not yet invented here, floating light-sources, fuelless power, a cure for the com-

mon cold. Or they could have none of that: it doesn't matter. As you like it. I incline to think that people from towns up and down the coast have been coming in to Omelas during the last days before the Festival on very fast little trains and double-decked trams, and that the train station of Omelas is actually the handsomest building in town, though plainer than the magnificent Farmers' Market. But even granted trains, I fear that Omelas so far strikes some of you as goody-goody. Smiles, bells, parades, horses, bleh. If so, please add an orgy. If an orgy would help, don't hesitate. Let us not, however, have temples from which issue beautiful nude priests and priestesses already half in ecstasy and ready to copulate with any man or woman, lover or stranger, who desires union with the deep godhead of the blood, although that was my first idea. But really it would be better not to have any temples in Omelas – at least not manned temples. Religion, yes, clergy no. Surely the beautiful nudes can just wander about, offering themselves like divine soufflés to the hunger of the needy and the raptures of the flesh. Let them join in the processions. Let tambourines be struck above the copulations, and the glory of desire be proclaimed upon the gongs, and (a not unimportant point) let the offspring of these delightful rituals be beloved and looked after by all. One thing I know there is none of in Omelas is guilt. But what else should there be? I thought at first there were no drugs, but that is puritanical. For those who like it, the faint insistent sweetness of *drooz* may perfume the ways of the city, *drooz* which first brings a great lightness and brilliance to the mind and limbs, and then after some hours a dreamy languor, and wonderful visions at last of the very arcane and inmost secrets of the Universe, as well as exciting the pleasure of sex beyond all belief, and it is not habit-forming. For more modest tastes I think there ought to be beer. What else, what else belongs in the joyous city? The sense of victory, surely, the celebration of courage. But as we did without clergy, let us do without soldiers. The joy built upon successful slaughter is not the right kind of joy; it will not do; it is fearful and it is trivial. A boundless and generous contentment, a magnanimous triumph felt not against some outer enemy but in communion with the finest and fairest in the souls of all men everywhere and the splendor of the world's summer: this is what swells the hearts of the people of Omelas, and the victory they celebrate is that of life. I really don't think many of them need to take *drooz*.

Most of the processions have reached the Green Fields by now. A marvelous smell of cooking goes forth from the red and blue tents of the provisioners. The faces of small children are amiably sticky; in the benign grey beard of a man a couple of crumbs of rich pastry are entangled. The youths and girls have mounted their horses and are beginning to group around the starting line of the course. An old woman, small, fat, and laughing, is passing out flowers from a basket, and tall young men wear her flowers in their shining hair. A child of nine or ten sits at the edge of the crowd, alone, playing on a wooden flute. People pause to listen, and they smile, but they do not speak to him, for he never ceases playing and never sees them, his dark eyes wholly rapt in the sweet, thin magic of the tune.

He finishes, and slowly lowers his hands holding the wooden flute.

As if that little private silence were the signal, all at once a trumpet sounds from the pavilion near the starting line: imperious, melancholy, piercing. The horses rear on their slender legs, and some of them neigh in answer. Sober-faced, the young riders stroke the horses' necks and soothe them, whispering, "Quiet, quiet, there my beauty, my hope . . ." They begin to form in rank along the starting line. The crowds along the racecourse are like a field of grass and flowers in the wind. The Festival of Summer has begun.

Do you believe? Do you accept the festival, the city, the joy? No? Then let me describe one more thing.

In a basement under one of the beautiful public buildings of Omelas, or perhaps in the cellar of one of its spacious private homes, there is a room. It has one locked door, and no window. A little light seeps in dustily between cracks in the boards, secondhand from a cobwebbed window somewhere across the cellar. In one corner of the little room a couple of mops, with stiff, clotted, foul-smelling heads, stand near a rusty bucket. The floor is dirt, a little damp to the touch, as cellar dirt usually is. The room is about three paces long and two wide: a mere broom closet or disused tool room. In the room a child is sitting. It could be a boy or a girl. It looks about six, but actually is nearly ten. It is feeble-minded. Perhaps it

was born defective, or perhaps it has become imbecile through fear, malnutrition, and neglect. It picks its nose and occasionally fumbles vaguely with its toes or genitals, as it sits hunched in the corner farthest from the bucket and the two mops. It is afraid of the mops. It finds them horrible. It shuts its eyes, but it knows the mops are still standing there; and the door is locked; and nobody will come. The door is always locked; and nobody ever comes, except that sometimes – the child has no understanding of time or interval – sometimes the door rattles terribly and opens, and a person, or several people, are there. One of them may come in and kick the child to make it stand up. The others never come close, but peer in at it with frightened, disgusted eyes. The food bowl and the water jug are hastily filled, the door is locked, the eyes disappear. The people at the door never say anything, but the child, who has not always lived in the tool room, and can remember sunlight and its mother's voice, sometimes speaks. "I will be good," it says. "Please let me out. I will be good!" They never answer. The child used to scream for help at night, and cry a good deal, but now it only makes a kind of whining, "eh-haa, eh-haa," and it speaks less and less often. It is so thin there are no calves to its legs; its belly protrudes; it lives on a half-bowl of corn meal and grease a day. It is naked. Its buttocks and thighs are a mass of festered sores, as it sits in its own excrement continually.

They all know it is there, all the people of Omelas. Some of them have come to see it; others are content merely to know it is there. They all know that it has to be there. Some of them understand why, and some do not, but they all understand that their happiness, the beauty of their city, the tenderness of their friendships, the health of their children, the wisdom of their scholars, the skill of their makers, even the abundance of their harvest and the kindly weathers of their skies, depends wholly on this child's abominable misery.

This is usually explained to children when they are between eight and twelve, whenever they seem capable of understanding; and most of those who come to see the child are young people, though often enough an adult comes, or comes back, to see the child. No matter how well the matter has been explained to them, these young spectators are always shocked and sickened at the sight. They feel disgust, which they had thought themselves superior to. They feel anger, outrage, impotence, despite all the explanations. They would like to do something for the child. But there is nothing they can do. If the child were brought up into the sunlight out of that vile place, if it were cleaned and fed and comforted, that would be a good thing, indeed; but if it were done, in that day and hour all the prosperity and beauty and delight of Omelas would wither and be destroyed. Those are the terms. To exchange all the goodness and grace of every life in Omelas for that single, small improvement: to throw away the happiness of thousands for the chance of the happiness of one: that would be to let guilt within the walls indeed.

The terms are strict and absolute; there may not even be a kind word spoken to the child.

Often the young people go home in tears, or in a tearless rage, when they have seen the child and faced this terrible paradox. They may brood over it for weeks or years. But as time goes on they begin to realize that even if the child could be released, it would not get much good of its freedom: a little vague pleasure of warmth and food, no doubt, but little more. It is too degraded and imbecile to know any real joy. It has been afraid too long even to be free of fear. Its habits are too uncouth for it to respond to humane treatment. Indeed, after so long it would probably be wretched without walls about it to protect it, and darkness for its eyes, and its own excrement to sit in. Their tears at the bitter injustice dry when they begin to perceive the terrible justice of reality, and to accept it. Yet it is their tears and anger, the trying of their generosity and the acceptance of their helplessness, which are perhaps the true source of the splendor of their lives. Theirs is no vapid, irresponsible happiness. They know that they, like the child, are not free. They know compassion. It is the existence of the child, and their knowledge of its existence, that makes possible the nobility of their architecture, and poignancy of their music, the profundity of their science. It is because of the child that they are so gentle with children. They know that if the wretched one were not there sniveling in the dark, the other one, the flute-player, could make no joyful music as the young riders line up in their beauty for the race in the sunlight of the first morning of summer.

Now do you believe in them? Are they not more credible? But there is one more thing to tell, and this is quite incredible.

At times one of the adolescent girls or boys who go to see the child does not go home to weep or rage, does not, in fact, go home at all. Sometimes also a man or woman much older falls silent for a day or two, and then leaves home. These people go out into the street, and walk down the street alone. They keep walking, and walk straight out of the city of Omelas, through the beautiful gates. They keep walking across the farmlands of Omelas. Each one goes alone, youth or girl, man or woman. Night falls; the traveler must pass down village streets, between the houses with yellow-lit windows, and on out into the darkness of the fields. Each alone, they go west or north, towards the mountains. They go on. They leave Omelas, they walk ahead into the darkness, and they do not come back. The place they go towards is a place even less imaginable to most of us than the city of happiness. I cannot describe it at all. It is possible that it does not exist. But they seem to know where they are going, the ones who walk away from Omelas.

People with Disabilities – Facing Barriers, Finding Allies

> **"** Disability (is) a natural phenomenon which occurs in every generation, and always will . . . people with a disability are a distinct minority group, subject at times to discrimination and segregation . . . but also capable of taking our rightful place in society. **"**
>
> **Laura Hershey (1962–)**

Disability rights activist Laura Hershey is talking about the injury of oppression that people with disabilities have encountered while also being subjected to the insult of a society that denied the existence of this oppression. In the 1960s when people of color and women were confronting the dominant society with their legitimate accusations about racism and sexism, oppression against people with disabilities didn't even have a name. In 1973, Congress acknowledged problems in the education of children with disabilities and tried to address these issues in Section 504 of the Rehabilitation Act. Congress strengthened this effort in 1975, and continued to amend the law several times, reauthorizing the legislation in 1997 as the Individuals with Disabilities Education Act (IDEA). Despite these efforts to improve the education of students with special needs, schools still make mistakes and many still fail to provide what students need.

The term "ableism" was finally coined in the 1980s as activists within the disability community began to insist on their status as a legitimate "minority group" because they faced problems of prejudice and discrimination not just in schools but in society, similar to what other minority

> **"** When I was young, I was put in a school for retarded kids for two years before they realized I actually had a hearing loss. And they called ME slow! **"**
>
> **Kathy Buckley (1962–)**

groups have experienced. As ableism became a more widely accepted term and research documented the barriers and social injustices encountered by people with disabilities, political leaders responded sympathetically and Congress passed the Americans with Disabilities Act (ADA) in 1990 – a civil rights law that provided legal avenues for people with disabilities to pursue when they believed that they had been discriminated against. Despite this legislative progress, individuals with disabilities are still confronted with negative stereotypes, issues of access, and other social injustices on a daily basis.

Similar to gay people who are in the closet to avoid having to deal with people's homophobia, some individuals who have disabilities that are not obvious try to avoid prejudice and discrimination by not revealing their disability to non-disabled people. This strategy is illustrated in "Covering My Tracks," in which Chloe Atkins describes her efforts to conceal her disability so she can avoid the kinds of problems encountered by people with an observable disability. The sexual orientation comparison is not an abstract issue for Atkins, who is also a lesbian living in Canada and legally married to her partner. In concealing her disability, Atkins's assumption is that if others do not know she is disabled then they will treat her as they would treat anyone else, and that's all that she wants.

The need for people like Atkins to conceal their disability in order to appear "normal" is the subject of anthropologist Jamake Highwater's essay "Transgression as Deformity." Highwater describes cultural attitudes toward deviance and argues that the emphasis on normality in Western cultures results in the perception of abnormal human characteristics as a deformity for the affected individual. Highwater offers cross-cultural examples to illustrate how non-Western cultures have been tolerant of deviance from societal norms, whereas Western societies tend to transform deviations from the norm into deviance, stigmatizing people who exhibit such "imperfections." Highwater's analysis supports the contention of many people with disabilities that their main problem is not the limitations imposed by their disability, but the obstacles they encounter in society that limit them.

Paul Longmore struggled against these societal limitations. As a person with a severe disability, Longmore felt not only stigmatized but punished for his "transgression," as he describes in "Why I Burned My Book." Despite encountering people who discouraged him, Longmore persisted in pursuing his ambitious goals of earning a doctorate in history and teaching in college. In this essay, he explains the barriers he had to overcome, including those stemming from government programs that were intended to help people with a disability. The injustice and frustration that finally culminated in Longmore burning the book he wrote for his dissertation is a case study about attitudes toward and the treatment of people with a disability in our society.

> **❝**I seldom think about my limitations, and they never make me sad. Perhaps there is just a touch of yearning at times; but it is vague, like a breeze among flowers.**❞**
>
> **Helen Keller (1880–1968)**

Longmore generously gives credit to people who were his advocates, and in "The Challenge of Being an Advocate," Craig R. Fiedler explains what is required for anyone, but especially professional educators, to advocate for people with a disability. He provides a clear definition of advocacy and describes the actions of several educators engaged in advocacy efforts. After providing a brief history of advocacy, Fiedler then identifies and describes characteristics that are essential to be an effective advocate. At the conclusion of his essay, Fiedler focuses on schools and the barriers that students with a disability may encounter where they could benefit from the presence of an advocate.

Mara Sapon-Shevin fulfills Fiedler's challenge by being an educator and an advocate for students with disabilities. In "Places Where We All Belong," she identifies the many differences students bring to the classroom in addition to having a disability. She then describes the philosophy of *Inclusion* and how it can create a shared community in the classroom that strengthens learning for all students. She debunks myths about inclusion as well as myths that have been used to resist implementing an inclusive classroom, such as the advantages of ability grouping and problems involved in acknowledging and teaching about human differences. She concludes with specific examples of inclusion that demonstrate

the positive outcomes it can achieve, and in doing so makes possible the creation of the kind of school that educator Robert Barth described:

> I would prefer my children to be in a school in which differences are looked for, attended to, and celebrated as good news, as opportunities for learning.

It is rare for a novelist to use a character with disabilities as the narrator and/or main character of the book, but in Mark Haddon's novel, *The Curious Incident of the Dog in the Night-Time*, the story is being told by a highly functioning autistic teenager. The boy discovers that his neighbor's dog has been killed, and because he is standing over the dog when the police come, they arrest him and take him to jail. As he waits for his father to come to the police station, the boy's mind wanders over a multitude of topics and it becomes obvious that labeling him "autistic" is a simplistic form of shorthand for a much more complex emotional and intellectual phenomenon. By the end of this excerpt, readers will have a better understanding of this unusual narrator, enough to know that he is likely to persist in his efforts and may yet discover who killed the dog. In the process, the reader has become acquainted with a narrator who deviates from the norm but is not deviant, a boy who is special not because of his needs but because of his personality — a person who is part of our diverse human family.

66 We are all one big family, and any one of us can get hurt at any moment. . . . We should never walk by somebody in a wheelchair and be afraid . . . or think of them as a stranger. 99

Christopher Reeve (1952–2004)

Covering My Tracks

People with a disability that cannot be visually observed often feel that they have to hide their disability in order to get a job and to get along with non-disabled people. In one college class I met a man who told me he had multiple sclerosis, but that he had not told people at work nor anyone else except for one friend who also had multiple sclerosis.

As the plane tilted backward to place its rear wheels on the runway, I could feel a familiar pain beginning to sear down deep inside me. . . . Inside the terminal, I scanned various departure screens for my next flight, ten hours away. My plan was to have lunch with my brother and sister-in-law in town and then make my way back to the airport to finish the last leg of my trip to New York. I searched for exit signs. As I walked, sunlight cascaded about me through glass and steel ramps. An escalator finally ejected me into the baggage claim area and soon I was out onto a curb near car rental desks and cab stands.

A slightly overweight, middle-aged man approached. He wore a short-sleeve, white shirt with pocket crest and shoulder epaulets along with a pair of nylon, black trousers. Well-creased, black running shoes completed his uniform. "A Taxi, sir?" He queried.

"Actually, it's ma'am," I corrected him.

He reddened, "Of course, of course. I'm sorry. It was the way the light was hitting you." He gestured plaintively towards me. "Of course I now see you're a woman."

"That's all right; it happens all the time," I assured him. And it did happen, far more frequently than I liked. . . . "I need a cab downtown."

"Okay, where you going?"

"The lakefront, near Shuter Street."

"So, you're staying in one of them grand hotels down there? They're pretty nice."

"No, just lunch." . . .

"Well, there are some good restaurants too."

"How much is the fare?"

"It's by zones. That'll be four zones; so twenty-eight dollars."

A gray minivan pulled up. It had a raised roof and an accessibility sticker in the rear window. I stepped backward: "I don't need something this large."

"Don't worry. It's very comfortable," he assured me, "and very roomy!"

"But shouldn't you save it for someone in a wheelchair?"

"Well, we used to do that, but the government funding changed, so we don't get so many travelers in wheelchairs anymore." He wiped a rivulet of perspiration from his cheek with an exaggerated shrug of his shoulder and motioned impatiently with his hands. "You don't have a thing against wheelchairs do you?"

"No, no, no . . ." I suddenly felt self-conscious again, "I'll take it."

From M. L. Vance (Ed.) *Disabled faculty and staff in a disabling society: Multiple identities in higher education.* (Huntersville, NC: Association on Higher Education and Disability, 2007).

Within seconds I leaned into the van's rear bench as the driver's foot on the accelerator drove my torso into the seat back. . . . Traffic buzzed by us. I contemplated the repetitive landscape of warehouses and suburban malls. . . . The pain within me was growing. Rivers of fire seemed to beach up from the depths of my head and pour themselves into the tributaries of my face and neck. And an irrepressible dread began to overtake my thoughts. I did not want this; I did not need it. Not right now.

A familiar wellspring of self-pity rose up in me. Why did I have to suffer like this? Why me of all people? I had intelligence and talent but they were always reined in by the limits of my body. . . . I groped beneath the seat belt cinched across my hips, probing my trousers' pocket for my pillbox. Flipping it open, I fingered three pills onto my open palm. I had no water with me. I'd drained my last bottle as I walked through the terminal. Puckering my cheeks and rolling my tongue, I tried to conjure up a pool of saliva in my mouth. Over and over I sucked on an imaginary lozenge in an effort to create enough fluid to swallow the medication. Nothing. I despaired. If I didn't take it now, the pain and symptoms could overwhelm me. I threw the tablets into my mouth and tilted my head back. "Come on, come on," I urged, "swallow them." Swishing spittle between my teeth and into the rear of my mouth, I tried to gulp. Two went down. The third lay decaying on the surface of my tongue, spreading an acrid taste throughout my mouth. . . . I turned my gaze and attention back to the roadway.

Two years ago on a similar business trip, I had ended up in the ER of a small Midwestern city, eventually becoming so ill that I landed in ICU for weeks and then the hospital itself for months. Far from home, my morale sunk and my family festered in emotional collapse and near financial ruin. Only now was my eldest son regaining his footing. In the spring he would finally graduate from high school. The hiatus deeply wounded the relationship between my daughter and me. We suffered silences between us that previously we would not have tolerated. On sleepless nights I would hold imaginary conversations with her during which she actually talked, but in reality, during the day, she remained pleasant but guarded. I couldn't fathom her thoughts. Since that terrible year, I had wanted to

rage at her, anything to get closer to her but she held me at bay with lots of smiles, superficial chatter and good behavior.

The cabbie broke through my thoughts, "So, you got any kids?"

"Two, how about you?"

"Three, but they're all grown now. My daughter, she gave me a little grandson a couple of years ago. He's the sweetest little guy. . . ." He eyed me in the rearview mirror. "How old are yours?"

"Oh they're teenagers."

"Teenagers! I remember the hormones, the driving lessons, the curfews. I wouldn't do that again. And my daughter was the worst. You'd think the sons would be bad but it was the girl who caused the problems!" I guffawed good-naturedly. "You work?" I nodded. "What do you do?"

"I'm a professor."

"A professor . . . you must be smart. My son did a master's degree in anthropology." He glanced at me again. "I don't know what to do with that. But now he works in an advertising agency, you know, he helps make up the ads for TV. He does well, so I can't complain. But imagine, anthropology. I don't even try to understand what it is he studied. He married this summer, so now we're waiting for another grandchild to come. . . ." He watched in the mirror for my reaction. "So what does your husband do?" And then, he faltered, "If you're married, you might be single or divorced . . . Or even have just a boyfriend." His cheeks reddened with exertion.

I hated this question. I didn't have a husband. I had a wife. I'm Canadian, and in Canada it is legal for same-sex spouses to marry, but even in my own country I found this question awkward. I may have been a legally married gay person, but being gay wasn't necessarily socially acceptable. I swallowed the pronoun, "Works in health care."

"He's a doctor?"

"No, an administrator."

He nodded. I deliberately turned my head to look out the window. I was a lousy liar. Any more conversation would inevitably result in my slipping up and using a she, her, or hers in a clause. The strain of dissembling made the pain spreading in my head worse.

The restaurant reverberated with the chink of china, flatware and glass. Men and women in dark suits clustered around tables flanked by cherry-veneered walls. Skylights and mirrors illuminated the dining room at odd angles so that it seemed that sunlight spattered every surface, blinding me. Behind my sunglasses, I scanned the diners looking for my sister-in-law's distinctive panama hat. Finally, I spied her and my brother in the back corner. My legs stumbled heavily as I treaded between pillars, chairs and table legs. There was little doubt the paralysis was beginning to settle in.

I suffer from a rare form of muscular dystrophy. It is controlled by an array of drugs but its particular form of weakness can still attack me when I am tired or run down. As the physical crisis endures, the paralysis works its way from the centre of my body outward. I lose my ability to chew and swallow and breathe and then eventually can't move my fingertips. The symptoms can vary in type, duration and degree, but they inevitably invade my daily life. Still, I do my best to conceal my frailties. I wear dark glasses to meetings to obscure any evidence of paresis in my face. On days I can't walk well, I avoid or cancel meetings. My co-workers know that I have a disabled parking space near the elevator, but few places are safe to disclose what ails me. Experience has taught me that providing accurate knowledge of my disability only disadvantages me in the workplace and elsewhere. And so, within the faculty, I endure a muted resentment about the privileged space that my car occupies in the university parking lot. Colleagues with greater seniority have to walk much further than I do to our building's entrance.

My sister-in-law, Wendy, looked up at me and smiled. . . . My brother, Simon, watched me carefully as I sat down. I hung onto the table and the edge of the seat with more determination than I might have had I been feeling well. My brother raised an eyebrow and asked, "You all right?"

"A bit tired . . . We'll see."

"Let's get you something to drink."

"Coffee. I'd love a coffee." I'd discovered that caffeine sometimes boosted me out of trouble. Simon asked a busboy to bring me an espresso.

"We started without you because I have to get back to the office and we didn't know what the traffic would be like from the airport." He leaned over the table and kissed me. "Wendy can drive you back, by the way."

His wife beamed at me. "We can chat on the drive . . . gossip about him!" She looked at Simon and laughed. . . . When the steaming demitasse arrived, I ordered my meal. As I waited for my food, I noticed that when I sipped my coffee, my swallowing was beginning to dis-coordinate. I could no longer really sense where the liquid was in my mouth and throat. I choked a couple of times, unintentionally aspirating the warm fluid into my windpipe.

Simon and Wendy looked at one another and then at me. They said nothing, but their faces squinted unspoken concern. My own worry reasserted itself. How the hell was I going to get to New York? And if I did make it, would I ever leave? Or would my body entomb me in paralysis again? The best idea would be to simply go home with Wendy, inject some of my medication and try to sleep for a day or two. This usually forestalled a major crisis. But I had to be in Manhattan: I was scheduled to speak at a meeting of a specialized branch of a research foundation.

I listened as Simon and Wendy discussed their three children, all of them still in grammar school. I picked at my food, carefully placing small morsels in my mouth and chewing them slowly. My whole being felt as though it was shutting down and even the prospect of digesting incremental portions seemed too strenuous.

"You're not feeling well are you?" Wendy stared earnestly at me.

"No."

"Do you have to go on tonight? Can't you fly out tomorrow?"

I shook my head. "I speak early tomorrow morning, nine a.m."

"I don't know. You don't look right. I think we should call Sarah."

"What will Sarah be able to do? She's at home."

"Well maybe your own spouse can convince you to stay put. You don't look like you should travel."

My brother was already dialing his mobile phone. "Here," he waved it at me, "talk to her. By the looks of you, I think you should stay here."

Within seconds I could hear Sarah's gravelly voice, "Hello Simon?"

"No it's me. I'm using his phone." . . .

"So you made it for lunch. How are they? . . ."

"Yes, and they're fine." I lowered my voice, "We're calling for another reason. I'm getting weaker and the pain is getting bad."

Silence ensued. I could hear Sarah breathing into the receiver. . . . "Shit, I knew I should have gone with you."

"Well that's moot now. Anyway, work wouldn't pay for you to come with me and we couldn't afford it on our own."

"So what do you want to do?"

"Well if the world was perfect, I would stop here and not go on; try to catch some rest for the next couple of days. You know the routine."

"Well that's what you should do."

"But what about the meeting?"

"You'll have to miss it."

"But this is one of those things I really can't miss. It would be bad for my career not to be there."

"Can't you get someone else to present your piece?"

"Maybe . . . I have it all written out. But what would I say? What would be my excuse?"

"Just tell them you have the flu and can't make it."

"I hate using illness as an excuse. It sets a bad precedent."

"But this is different. Everybody gets the flu from time to time. Just tell them you have a fever. You don't even have to tell them that you're not in New York."

"Well, I'll think about it."

"You shouldn't think about it, you should *do* it."

"We'll see."

"Let me know what you decide. . . . I love you."

"I love you too. Bye."

Wendy reached across the table and placed her hand on mine. "So? What did she say?"

"That I should stay."

"So we're all in agreement."

While I was almost persuaded, I fretted about how I could contribute to the discussion without attending the session. "But I need to put in an appearance at this meeting."

"Why not email your talk to the Chair?" Simon suggested.

"That's not a bad idea." I tugged at the zipper of my knapsack underneath the table, feeling for the edge of my laptop. . . . Within moments, I typed a quick note. I lied that I was in New York and that I had come down with a case of stomach flu and I doubted that I could make the early morning meeting. Would he please read my notes to the gathering if I didn't make it? As I wrote, nervous perspiration glistened across my face. I hated lying. I continued, I'll catch up with you at the annual association meeting in six weeks. Even as I closed by thanking him, my fingers jumbled the keyboard, miss-hitting letters and punctuation. My coordination was flagging.

Done. I shut the screen. I tried to sound confident but I worried whether my story would suffice. I pondered what I would tell them at work. I decided to say that I had gone to New York but had come down with food poisoning. My anxieties fanned the fiery pain in my face and limbs. I needed to lie down, and soon. I looked around the restaurant – my vision seemed okay. "I think we should go," I mumbled.

Forty minutes later I lay on my brother's spare bed, with the curtains drawn and a fan rotating in the corner. My medicine bags lay opened on the bedside table revealing pill bottles and an array of syringes and vials. Once naked, I had impelled myself to draw and inject two intramuscular medications in my thighs. I hated doing this, especially when my movements were uncomfortable and clumsy. Usually Sarah did this for me, but I had little choice. . . . I needed to let both my mind and body rest, and to let the drugs have their effect. I settled into the darkness.

The next day I rose only to go to the bathroom. Wendy and Simon checked on me a couple of times by pushing the bedroom door ajar to make sure I was still breathing. I managed to inject more medicine but couldn't swallow any pills. By seven the pain had largely receded. The weakness persisted, but I knew from experience that it would begin to abate. Even as I found my body strain to simultaneously sit up *and* breathe, I suspected that I had averted a debilitating crisis and long hospital stay. Even as Wendy and Simon's voice beckoned to me, I gave into my frailty and sank back down onto the mattress.

I propped myself on pillows so that I could see a small television perched on a bookshelf across the room. I held the remote in my left hand. . . . I needed something mildly engaging but not too intense or threatening. . . . I scanned station after station, finally settling on a PBS piece about Antarctica. I drifted in and out of sleep, waking finally to the bizarre image of penguins swimming in a city pool to the shrieks and delight of children. I switched off the television and rolled over, intending to stand, but the leaden weight of my limbs held me back. I reached for a bottle of water on the bedside table. I carefully held it to my lips and sipped. My swallowing seemed okay. I wondered if I should try to catch up on my steroids and other drugs. Some of the pills could wait, but others pressed more urgently . . . my body needed them. I risked complications without them.

My medications lay within reach on the bedside table. I unzipped one of the satchels and began to fumble through the various plastic containers, seeking out the critical drugs and overlooking others. I corralled a handful of pills and threw them onto my tongue. I sluiced water carefully into my mouth, cautious to neither over fill nor under fill since my throat muscles' coordination was only beginning to return. I looked at my watch – quarter past twelve. I lay on the bed waiting for everything to take effect. Generally it took about forty minutes. I flicked the television back on. . . .

A little after midnight I heard my sister-in-law running water in the kitchen. She and Sarah shared a habit of brewing endless pots of tea. . . . I could hear the hollow drumming of the water hitting the bottom and sides of the kettle as Wendy filled it from the tap. I swung my legs out over the side of the bed; yes, they were stronger. I could sense I was more robust. After a few more seconds of testing my strength by sitting upright with my feet on the floor, I decided I could probably make it to the

kitchen. . . . Out in the hall, my hands reached for furniture and walls. The lit frame of the kitchen doorway drew me onward. . . .

"Oh, it's you. I'm glad to see you're up." Wendy's gaze lingered on me a moment longer. "Are you okay? Do you want an arm?"

"No, no, I'm fine. Well not fine, but much better . . . much, much better. I could do with some tea."

"It's being made."

I eased myself into a wooden armchair at the linoleum table. Wendy stacked dishes into the shelves from an open dishwasher. "So, what's your plan?"

"It's Saturday right?" Wendy nodded. "Well, the research symposium ends today so I've missed all that. I'll have to catch up with someone who was there . . . Do you want to give me the phone?" I nodded at the handset lying on the counter. "I should re-book my flights so I can be back home tomorrow for the work week." . . .

It took almost an hour and fifteen hundred dollars to negotiate a new ticket. I flew home on a small jet without in-flight food or movies. . . . Sarah and my daughter met me at the airport. They stood at the bottom of the exit ramp with my empty wheelchair between them in case I needed it.

On Tuesday morning, a colleague stopped me in front of the faculty elevators. "How was New York?"

"Great," I responded.

He patted me on my shoulder as he turned to walk down an adjacent corridor. "Hey, we should have lunch next week and you can tell me all about it."

Transgression as Deformity

What does it mean to be deviant from the norm? How have other societies regarded such people? The author provides an analysis with cross-cultural examples of how societies have regarded those who were different, disabled, deformed. He argues that when we confuse human variation with deviation, we contribute to the perpetuation of injustice.

Like all the mythic attitudes of the West, our attitudes about normality don't change quickly. The entrenched Western paradigm of "divine law" leaves little room for the impulsiveness of nature. In our illusions of a "steady-state" biology, the seasons may change and creatures may be born and grow old and die, but human nature, having been perfected by God, remains immutable and eternal. It is tacitly assumed that God doesn't make mistakes, doesn't create freaks, unless his intentions are ominous, meaning that his errors are forms of punishment. Behind every disease, anomaly, and deviation is the persistent question: "What did I do to deserve this?" Even for those who revel in their spiritual liberation, there inevitably remains the suspicion that illness and adversity are some inscrutable form of divine justice.

Even the word "freak" is a shortened form of the original Latin *lusus naturae* (freak of nature), suggesting that nature can somehow be unnatural. We rarely grasp the scope of nature's variety because we are obsessed with a model of nature that cannot easily understand anything that doesn't have a clear-cut polarization: It is normal or it is abnormal. Our comprehension of time and identity does not permit us to recognize that everything is constantly

changing – passing silently through the immense space that exists between what exists and what is coming into existence, between what is "normal" and what is "abnormal." By the standard of *lusus naturae*, every mutation essential to evolution and every hybrid plant or beast is a freak, because it cannot and will not *fit* into the narrow context that we take to be god's ultimate "reality."

Despite the importance of nature's whims in the earth's creative process, most of us are so intimidated by the prospect of radical change and so uncertain of exactly what constitutes a "freak" that we plead for reassurances from our peers that we ourselves are exempt from that terrifying category of freakishness. The reassurance we seek, however, is not an affirmation of our *own* normalcy, but a satisfaction that comes from designating the abnormality of *others*.

"We are the freaks!" is what we believe all the oddities of the world constantly assure us, as they look across at us from their dreadful isolation, "Look at us. Can't you see? *We* are the freaks! But not you! Not *you!*" The age-old fascination with humpbacks, dwarfs, transvestites, hermaphrodites, bearded ladies, and giants seems to be rooted in the realization of the curious possibilities of nature, which happily do not overtake the lives of ordinary people. "We are the freaks! Not you!" But this fascination is not built simply on disgust and aversion. In many societies, deformity is regarded as the mysterious connections between the physical and the

From Transgression as deformity (pp. 71–97), in *The mythology of transgression*. (New York: Oxford University Press, 1997).

spiritual. In modern Western society, freaks may be regarded as aberrations, but in many other times and places freaks were and still are regarded with fear and reverence.

So exactly what is a freak? It is the exceptional rather than the ordinary. It is something that is unusual or irregular. In this sense, left-handedness is freakish. A freak can also be an unusually formed organism, a dwarf, a giant, or Siamese twins. An albino African is a freak. Yet in each of these instances, freakishness has no implicit negative cultural significance until a negative value is attributed to specific kinds of irregularity. Freaks occur in nature, but society determines their value, that can as readily be revulsion as wonderment. In our particular society we are instructed to respond to most irregularity with revulsion. Children must be taught not to stare at disabled people. In contrast, the albinos of Central Africa are held in great regard, as exceptional rather than deformed persons.

The basis of freakishness that interests me is the one that arises from a peculiar culture question that repeats itself again and again as we look across the chasm separating people who are different: "Who are we? Are we *us* or are we *them?*" The current wisdom insists that this apprehension about conformity is built on our inherent need to be accepted into our kinship group, but there is also a good deal of evidence suggesting that acceptance is only part of our cultural motive. There are countless societies in which acceptance is not based on our notions of behavioral and physical conformity. To the contrary, in a great many communities, oddities were and still are revered.

People with crossed eyes were greatly admired by the ancient Maya. . . . One of the most revered and pervasive figures of Mesoamerican culture is the so-called Hunched Back Flute Player, who is associated with rain-making and whose image is widely found in Mexico and throughout the southwest United States. In the seventeenth century, the leaders of the tribes of the Congo were admired for their overwhelming obesity. Among the Moche of pre-Columbian Peru, a favored subject of thousands of effigy potteries is a huge range of physical deformities as well as every conceivable sex act involving every possible combination of male and female participants. . . .

But, in the West, diversity is often equated with deformity. We earnestly want assurance from our peers that we are *not different,* that we *don't stand out* except in certain very acceptable ways, such as having wealth or fame, possessing social stature and community prestige, and being conventionally attractive. We don't want to be too tall or too short, too buxom or too flat-chested, too endowed or excessively underendowed, too unnoticeable or too conspicuous. That's why we follow the lead of trendy magazines, dressing and grooming ourselves in terms of the prevailing notion of attractiveness. *Above all, we don't want to be freaks.* We don't want to have extraordinary or exotic looks. We are reluctant to create an entirely new and individual kind of beauty because such beauty might be seen as an aspect of freakishness, until, that is, a person of prominence introduces it into pop repertory. Even our ideas about what is sexy are based on consensus. And what we want more than anything else is to be a lauded imitation of that consensus. At the very most, we want the safety of being sublimely average. But under no circumstances do we want to be freaks.

The ideals of our own social identity entirely prescribe our expectations of and our responses to other people. When we sense an imperfect imitation of the consensus in a stranger, we feel uneasy, and then, as the degree of difference widens, we feel repulsed, which is a response expressed as readily with brutality as with derision. This discriminatory process is how we have been meticulously trained to respond to oddities and freaks as well as strangers from other lands. Since our social attitudes are based on the manipulation of an innate proclivity to be sociable and live in communities, we mistake our imprinted behavior for an inborn reflex; and we take it for granted that our hostile reaction to someone or something "unnatural" is simply a "natural" expression of our God-given knowledge of what is and what is not natural.

The problem with the word "natural" is very much like the problem with the word "unnatural." Such terms presume an infallibility that closes all disagreements and debate. The words alone, without qualification or explanation, represent an unimpeachable judgment. . . .

During the last years of the nineteenth century, anthropologist Matilda Coxe Stevenson conducted a great deal of fieldwork among the Zuni Indians of the American Southwest. Her chief source of information, and her close friend, was an Indian named

We'wha, a Zuni *Ihama* – or male transvestite, whose biological gender was unknown to Stevenson until We'wha's death. That We'wha was a biological male was also unknown by President Cleveland and other politicians whom the Indian visited during a six-month stay in Washington, D.C.

We'wha was greatly admired by members of her tribe. At an early age she lost her parents and was adopted by a sister of her father. She belonged to the Badger clan. Owing to her intelligence, We'wha was often asked by her clan to memorize and recite the long prayers used at Zuni rituals. She was both a religious and a tribal leader. Only when she died did Stevenson know with certainty that We'wha was a male. For her funeral, We'wha was dressed in women's clothing, with the addition of men's trousers. The ambiguity of gender in the Zuni worldview is emphasized by the fact that We'wha was buried on the men's side of the cemetery. This was the only biological demarcation of social gender that countered the gender she had chosen during her lifetime. Her behavior had determined her gender in life; her anatomy only was the determinate of her gender in death. From the Zuni point of view, We'wha's spirit was that of a woman; only her body was that of a man.

Stevenson eventually asked one of We'wha's close friends: "Why didn't someone ever tell me about We'wha?"

It was a question that would have made a good deal of sense to any Anglo whose notion about gender is anatomical and whose notion of reality is a matter of physical facts. The serene answer given to Stevenson came from a very different point of view. "Tell you about what?" responded the Indian with an expression of perplexity.

For the Zuni, We'wha was not stigmatized because he/she was an *Ihamana*. To the contrary, her tribe always referred to her as a female, and the people viewed her as a divine freak. To be different in the way that We'wha was different was understood as a blessing, as the designation by the Great Mystery of a being of extraordinary spirituality and power, to be revered, admire, but also to be feared.

Unexpected things, freakish events are always happening. Meteors plummet to earth. Two-headed calves are born. The caterpillar mysteriously changes into a butterfly. In fact, wherever we look we see evidence of change and mutation despite the fact that we are taught that we are sheltered under a fixed and finite sky.

Our observations of change, in conflict with our belief that the cosmos is in stasis, create a peculiar kind of metaphysical schizophrenia in the West. Because we ignore the process of natural modification, we often mistake variation for deviation. In fact, the perfectly acceptable word "deviation" has assumed a sinister connotation when applied to sexuality. And because we identify deviation with distortion, we suspect that despite the perfection of the world, somehow there are still some things that are imperfect. This knowledge of deviation and transgression impels us to define and defend our standards of normalcy. Those standards are unmistakably aimed at condoning those who are part of the mainstream while condemning those who are marginal. . . .

Despite all the evidence to the contrary, in our minds the world remains a motionless island at the center of the cosmos, and our particular ethnic and religious and gender group remains at the center of all the populations of the world, because we persist in using ourselves to connote as well as to denote human normalcy. It is in this sense – in a prolonged and mindless bias regarding normalcy – that deformity has been institutionalized as a moral and spiritual transgression in the West.

Why I Burned My Book

Government assistance to people with a disability should be designed to help them be as independent as possible, but for many people with disabilities this assistance can be more of a hindrance than a help. The author of the following essay provides an example of the problems that he encountered trying to pursue his educational and career goals.

I want to tell you why I burned my book. A deed as shocking as burning a book demands an explanation. It seems particularly mystifying and, therefore, all the more disturbing when the perpetrator has avowedly devoted his life to books. In order to account for that act, I will have to tell you a good deal about myself. I must say that I feel uncomfortable having to disclose so much about my personal life. I would prefer to keep it private. I would rather write biography than autobiography. But it seems to me that some of us are going to have to talk frankly about what it is really like for us as disabled people if we ever hope to break down the barriers of prejudice and discrimination that "cripple" our lives.

I – and most disabled Americans – have been exhorted that if we work hard and "overcome" our disabilities, we can achieve our dreams. We have heard that pledge repeatedly from counselors and educators and by "experts," and from our government too. We have seen it incarnated by disabled heroes on television, those plucky "overcomers" who supposedly inspire us with their refusal to let

their disabilities limit them. We are instructed that if we too adopt an indomitable spirit and a cheerful attitude, we can transcend our disabilities and fulfill our dreams.

It is a lie. The truth is that the major obstacles we must overcome are pervasive social prejudice, systematic segregation, and institutionalized discrimination. Government social-service policies, in particular, have forced millions of us to the margins of society. Those policies have made the American Dream inaccessible to many disabled citizens.

In saying these things, I risk getting myself labeled as a maladjusted disabled person, a succumber to self-pity, a whining bitter cripple who blames nondisabled people for his own failure to cope with his condition. That charge – or the fear that we might provoke it – has intimidated many of us into silence. As I said, some of us are going to have to risk telling the truth.

The truth is I am a model "rehabilitant." I am, from one perspective, a disabled overachiever, a "supercrip." That shouldn't surprise anyone. I had polio. The rehabilitation system drilled people who had polio in overcoming and then held us up as legendary exemplars of healthy adjustment to disability. American culture has lionized us for our alleged refusal to accept limitations.

So what did I do? I earned my B.A., M.A., and my Ph.D. in American history, intending to become a college teacher. And when I published my first book, one reviewer remarked that it drew on "a truly astounding amount of research." Of course it did. Would a postpolio supercrip do anything less? How characteristically disabled of me to undertake so grandiose a project.

Still, I don't want to reduce my work to "overcoming." At the core of my efforts, I pursued a rather simple personal dream: I wanted to write about American history and to teach it to college students.

A succession of dedicated teachers helped me move toward those goals by demonstrating their belief in my talents. . . . The endorsement of my scholarship and teaching by these mentors, their confidence that I could have a professional future, were especially important because their support buoyed me up against waves of bias from other quarters. Even while they urged me on, other teachers sapped some of my energy with wounding words of prejudice and occasional overt acts of discrimination.

One undergraduate professor told me that because of my disability no college would ever hire me as a teacher. I guess he thought he was helping me face the hard facts. . . . A couple of years later as I was completing my master's degree, the chair of the history department told me he thought I would do well in doctoral studies, because, he said, "You're not bitter like most cripples." Bur he also informed me matter-of-factly that because of my disability no college would ever hire me as a teacher.

I went ahead and applied to several Ph.D. programs in history anyway. One school rejected me because of my disability. Fortunately, the Claremont Graduate School accepted me. At the end of my first year there, I applied for a fellowship, but the departmental committee turned me down. I asked for a meeting with them. I wanted them to tell me to my face why they had refused my fellowship application. They explained that because of my disability no college would ever hire me as a teacher. In other words, they didn't want to squander the department's money on me. They suggested I consider archival work. I pointed out that archival work is more physical than teaching. Besides, I said, I want to teach, and I'm going to teach whether you help me or not. They said they felt sure I would succeed, because "we really admire your courage." . . .

If individual acts of discrimination on the part of some of my teachers hurt or hindered me, over the long run the discrimination institutionalized in government policies and programs was far more debilitating. At the time of my acceptance to graduate school, I applied to the California Department of Rehabilitation for financial aid. A rehabilitation counselor in the Pasadena office told me that DR did not fund doctoral study. But, he said, they could train me to become a computer programmer. I told him no, thanks. Now, there's nothing wrong with computer programming. It's honorable work. It's just not what I wanted to do. I wanted to teach in college.

For several years I hunted for money to pay for my graduate education. I applied for student fellowships. I got none. I asked about financial aid from disability-related charities like the Easter Seal society. They said they didn't provide that kind of help. I even managed, after a considerable campaign, to become a contestant on the TV game show *Tic Tac Dough*. I lost.

Finally one day, not knowing where else to turn for advice or assistance, I happened to call the Rehabilitation Counseling Department at Cal State University, Los Angeles. A secretary put me through to one of the professors. I explained my situation. He told me I had been – how shall I put it? – *misinformed* by the counselor at the state Department of Rehabilitation. Nothing in the law or public policy or DR's own regulations, explained the professor, prevented it from financially supporting my Ph.D. studies in history. DR could help me in whatever way I needed. I just had to persist with them tenaciously, he said, I had to refuse to take no for an answer.

Armed with this information and advice, I went back to the Department of Rehabilitation. This time the people in the Pasadena office agreed to enroll me as a client. DR would begin funding my graduate education. But – here was the catch – it would pay no more than the cost of tuition at one of California's public universities. At the Claremont Graduate School, a private institution, tuition stood at three times the rate of tuition at the state's public institutions such as UCLA. In practical terms, DR's cap on tuition payments meant that I could now take two courses a year, instead of just one. . . .

If the struggle to find ways to pay for my graduate studies slowed my progress, an even greater financial dilemma threatened to stop me altogether. My disability incurs enormous expenses. I have no use of my arms, limited use of my right hand, and, because of a severe spinal curvature I use a ventilator a great deal of the time. As a result, I employ aides in my home to do the housekeeping and to assist me with tasks like showering, shaving, dressing, and eating. At the time I burned my book, the wages paid to my personal assistants, plus the rental of my ventilators, exceeded $20,000 a year. (By the turn of the century, those costs topped $45,000 a year). Disability-related living and work expenses have posed the fundamental problem of my adult life. The plain fact is that I am unlikely ever to earn enough in an academic career to cover such costs.

My situation is not unusual. Enormous numbers of Americans with major disabilities grapple with high disability-related expenses. They too could work, at least part-time, but could never earn enough to pay for the services and devices they need.

Necessity has forced many of us to maintain eligibility for federal Supplemental Security Income (SSI) or Social Security Disability Insurance (SSDI) or both. Both programs provide monthly cash benefits. But that is not what makes them vital to us. Indeed, virtually any of us could earn the $350 to $700 monthly allotments we typically receive.

Far more important, SSI and SSDI eligibility make us eligible for more essential assistance. For instance, throughout my adult life I have paid my personal assistants through California's In-Home Support Services program. Medi-Cal (the California version of Medicaid) has paid for my ventilators. Without this financial aid, I would have had to spend my adult life in some sort of nursing home – at far greater cost to taxpayers, I might add. In most states, people with disabilities like mine have found themselves in a far more horrendous situation: they get little or no aid for independent living. They are shackled to their families or imprisoned in nursing homes. They are denied access to life and to work. Independent living has enabled me to work productively.

The catch is that for most of my adult life, in order to maintain eligibility for this government aid, I had to refrain from work. Using a combination of medical and economic criteria, federal disability policy defined – and still defines – "disability" as the total inability to engage in "substantial gainful activity." . . .

If the policy definition of disability as complete incapacitation for productive work ever made sense, it certainly made none by the late twentieth century. Advances in technology made it possible for even significantly disabled people to work. I completed my doctoral dissertation using a Dictaphone and a word processor. . . .

The mechanisms used to restrict disabled people's access to the labor market and society came in the late twentieth-century to be called, in one of the system's modern euphemisms, "work disincentives." Those so-called disincentives are, in fact, penalties, punishments designed to keep disabled people out of work, out of society, and out of life. Likewise, if we try to marry or raise a family, the government penalizes many of us through – here's yet another euphemism – "marriage disincentives." Throughout the recent decades, politicians have talked incessantly about "family values." Yet the policies they perpetuate have relentlessly undermined the families of disabled Americans. Marriage and work penalties hit disabled women even harder than disabled men. Marriage sometimes mitigates women's poverty, but the disability policy disincentives exacerbate the impoverishment and isolation of women with disabilities by helping to keep their employment and poverty rates high and their marriage rates low. . . .

Meanwhile, invention and maintenance of the disabled caste advanced the ideological and economic interests of an array of professional groups in the modern welfare state. "Disability" became a multibillion dollar industry. Many states still keep adults with physical or developmental disabilities imprisoned in nursing homes and other public and private facilities that exploit them for profit. Even those of us at large in society pull in high profits for vendors of a great many services and products. A few years ago, I designed a device for my use in the bathroom. Knowing it would prove handy for people with similar disabilities, I sought ways to make it available. It would cost only a few dollars to manufacture, but a vendor eagerly told me we could sell it for at least fifty dollars a unit. The government would pay for it, he said. Hence comes the overpricing of everything from hearing aids to wheelchairs. This greedy arrangement between the private and public sectors, between vendors and the government, keeps many people with disabilities in a permanent state of clientage. We have to stay clients in order to get the devices and services we require. . . .

I have spent much of my life seeking ways to elude social sigma and outwit discrimination. I have wanted to escape the roles of dependent cripple or inspirational overcomer. . . . Yet for my entire adult life, many government policies have been designed to prevent me, not just from pursuing my profession, but from attaining the socially respected place in society that goes with honest work. Millions of other Americans with disabilities find their attempts at productivity and pride blocked by these same segregationist work penalties and the social prejudice those policies express. . . .

Finally in 1986, Congress . . . ordered permanent elimination of most work disincentives from SSI. The new rules in Section 1619 would permit recipients to earn up to a threshold amount equivalent to the cash value of all the assistance they received plus the amount of their "impairment-related work expenses."

For twenty years, I had wondered and worried how I would ever fulfill my dream of teaching and writing American history. I had finally finished my Ph.D. . . . but still could not take even a part-time teaching position without jeopardizing the financial aid that paid for my ventilators and in-home assistance. With Section 1619, the work penalties were at long last gone. Or so I thought . . . (then) I learned that although Section 1619 would permit me to earn a living as a college teacher, the reformed rule would not allow research fellowships or publishing royalties. The Social Security Administration would continue to regard such income as "unearned," like royalties from oil well stocks.

The Huntington Library, a world-renowned research institution in San Marino, California, fifteen minutes from where I lived, had just offered me a fellowship to continue my work on George Washington's role in post-revolutionary America. I would have to turn that fellowship down. More problematic, in October the University of California Press would publish my book, *The Invention of George Washington*. I needed that first book to make myself attractive in the college-teaching job market. UC Press expected the book to sell pretty well. That was the problem. Even if it yielded only modest royalties, that money would not fit the Section 1619 de-

finition of "earned" income. So I could lose some or all of the assistance I depended on to work and live, and literally, to breathe. . . .

[*The author communicated with Dorcas Hardy, the commissioner of the Social Security Administration (SSA), to find some way to resolve the problem of people with a disability being denied fellowships and book royalties, but Hardy's advice turned out to be "not just unworkable. It sidestepped the central issue."*]

Finally, Commissioner Hardy notified me that SSA would regard any income I obtained from research fellowships and book royalties as "unearned" and that this would adversely affect my eligibility for SSI.

When I read the commissioner's peremptory warning that SSA would punish me if I received any royalties from my book, something in me reached a breaking point. Years of finding myself trapped and thwarted by this system, years of feeling demeaned and degraded by it, came to a head. I said to myself, "I've had enough." I decided in that moment that when my book came out in October I would burn it in protest. . . .

On October 18, some forty people gathered in front of the federal building on Los Angeles Street in downtown L.A. There were adults with disabilities who were trying to work, or wanted to and could work, but were thwarted by work penalties. There were college students with disabilities who wondered if they would be prevented from following the careers they dreamed of pursuing when they graduated. There were parents of disabled children who wanted those youngsters to have a useful and fulfilling future. There were teachers and counselors who labored to help people with disabilities get an education or job training. They were paid with government funds to do this, but government policies baffled their efforts. We all came together to demand an end to work and marriage penalties.

(A friend) and his aide transported (a) barbecue in his wheelchair-lift-equipped van. We set up on the sidewalk in front of the main entrance to the federal building. Parker Center, the headquarters of the Los Angeles Police Department, stands right across the street. Several LAPD cops, along with security personnel from the federal building, warily stood watch during the protest and book burning.

I had hired a Deaf commercial-art student from Pasadena City College to make brightly colored placards bearing slogans television viewers would be able to read easily. One placard declared: "We Want to Work! Why Won't the Government Let Us?" Another demand I borrowed from the League of the Physically Handicapped: "Jobs. Not Tin Cups."

A row of placard holders stood to one side, as another group of demonstrators paraded in an elongated circle. Two of them led the protesters in disability rights chants. Wheelchair riders carried placards on their laps.

After awhile I stepped up to the wooden lectern I had borrowed and read a statement explaining the reason for our demonstration. Then I moved over to (the) barbecue. A friend handed me a lighted match. I turned and ignited the newspaper wads under the grill. A copy of my book stood on top of the grill. The front cover of the book jacket had a striking design: a photographic reproduction of Antoine Houdon's famous white marble bust of Washington against a red and blue background with the words "The Invention of George Washington" and "Paul K. Longmore" above and below. The image was bold, noble, majestic. At first the flames licked the bottom of the book. Then they engulfed my name and George Washington's head and the book's title.

I somberly watched the fire consume my book. I had planned the protest. I had rehearsed how to burn the book. I had even thought about what sort of expression I should have on my face. But I could never have prepared for the emotional effect on me of the act itself. I was burning my own book, a book I had spent ten years of my life laboring over, a book that had earned my Ph.D. in history, a book I felt proud of and, in fact, loved. It was a moment of agony.

Everyone in the crowd looked on quietly, soberly. Several wept. As with my own reaction, their emotional response surprised me. I asked my friend Carol Gill, a disabled psychologist who participated in the protest, why she thought so many people had reacted so strongly. She said she believed that those friends and colleagues were partly expressing their love for me. At the same time, she said, the entire protest and especially the burning of the book gave tangible form to the pain they felt about their own lives. They too felt thwarted by a government that stymies their efforts to work and make a life. They too felt dehumanized by a society that devalues them. . . .

The core of what I said in my statement just before I burned my book unfortunately remains true today:

"We, like other Americans, should have the right to work productively. Work and marriage penalties . . . , far more than our disabilities, thwart our efforts and our lives. We demand an end to these discriminatory government policies.

"We are here today, not just for ourselves, but on behalf of millions of Americans with disabilities. My book represents, not just my work, but the work that we all want to do and could do. The burning of a copy of my book symbolizes what the government does to us and our talents and our efforts. It repeatedly turns our dreams to ashes. We find that outrageous, and we will no longer quietly endure that outrage.

"We, like all Americans, have talents to use, work to do, our contributions to make to our communities and country. We want the chance to work and marry without jeopardizing our lives. We want access to opportunity. We want access to work. We want access to the American Dream."

The Challenge of Being an Advocate

The author describes why people with disabilities need non-disabled advocates. This is an especially important challenge to those who aspire to teach, but it is not limited to them. Any person who is committed to social justice can get involved with community organizations working with and on behalf of people with disabilities.

Advocacy has been variously defined in the professional literature. After reviewing the many definitions, the following essential characteristics of advocacy emerge:

(1) advocates must give primary allegiance to those they serve and not to the employing agency, (2) advocacy actions typically seek a change in the status quo; (3) advocates speak up for individuals or in concert with another person; and (4) the intent of advocacy is to correct an identified problem or to improve services for children with disabilities. With these characteristics in mind, consider the following four cases:

Mary Kinney was the only speech and language clinician employed by a small, rural school district. In the past five years, the school district had grown dramatically, primarily because of two large industries moving into the area, creating jobs and bringing new families into the community.

Unfortunately, the school budget had not kept pace with the influx of new students. At the beginning of the school year, the director of pupil services informed Mary and other professional staff serving students with disabilities that no additional staff would be employed to address increasing caseloads. In effect, everyone was told to do the best job they

could with limited resources. Mary was serving a full caseload of children eligible for speech and language services. Two months into the school year, she received 12 new referrals of children in potential need of her educational services. Mary suspected that the majority of those newly referred children would qualify for speech and language services; however, she was unable to meet their needs adequately given her full caseload. She decided to meet with the parents of the recently referred children. At this meeting, Mary explained the situation and informed the parents of their educational rights. She encouraged the parents to contact the school administration to demand appropriate services.

The students in Steve Kern's special education program at Central High School were difficult to teach. The school had labeled these students as emotionally/behaviorally disordered and almost all of them had poor school attendance and were involved with the juvenile justice system. For two years Steve complained to school administrators about inadequate vocational/career services, nonexistent participation of community agencies in transition planning, and the use of excessively punitive disciplinary measures such as repeated school suspensions. Steve maintained that the school district lacked sufficient commitment to his students' educational needs and had taken an "out of sight, out of mind" approach. The state protection and advocacy agency was forming a task force to address the

From The challenge of being an advocate in *Making A Difference: Advocacy competencies for special education professionals*, 2nd Ed. (Austin, TX: Pro-Ed, 2007).

transitional needs of secondary students with emo-
tional/behavioral disorders. Through Steve's membership in the state's Council for Exceptional
Children, he was appointed to serve on this task
force. Steve's participation on the task force was
critical in formulating the policy recommendations
they submitted to the state's Department of Education. These recommendations served as an impetus
for the development of new administrative regulations that expanded vocational training for special
needs students, provided closer monitoring of transitional programming, and called for statewide in-
service training on positive behavior management
techniques and procedures.

As principal of Wilson Elementary School, Karen
Snyder was concerned about the appropriate inclusion of students with disabilities into general education classrooms. Karen was convinced that most of
the school's students who were learning disabled
and mildly mentally retarded could be successful,
with support, in general education. The problem
was that many teachers were not implementing the
accommodations listed on the individualized education plans (IEP) of students included in general
education classes. At the monthly staff meeting,
Karen reviewed IEP legal requirements and emphasized each teacher's obligation to adhere to all accommodations listed in an IEP. Karen also
personally reviewed all IEPs and made regular
classroom visits to ensure that teachers complied
with IEP provisions.

Miguel Hernandez worked in a culturally diverse
urban school district. At Martin Luther King Jr.
Middle School, where he served as a counselor, the
school population was 40 percent Hispanic, 40
percent African American, and 20 percent Caucasian. Many of the students at this school lived in
poverty. Miguel met twice a week with seventh-
grader Suzie Ortiz. Susie was in the learning disabilities program, but Susie's mother was dissatisfied
with the program because she felt Susie had not
made any academic progress in two years. Her
mother was also frustrated because whenever she
raised a concern, staff members either dismissed her
or said they would make changes and then didn't.
Although Susie's mother was angry at the school,
she felt incapable of changing the situation. As a
single parent with five children, she was working at
three different jobs to pay the bills. Miguel had a
good relationship with Susie, and both Susie and

her mother trusted him. Aware of Susie's home
situation, Miguel put Mrs. Ortiz in touch with a
food pantry and the local respite care program, a
free financial budgeting service. Miguel also informed Mrs. Ortiz of her options for changing
Susie's IEP, and introduced her to a representative
of a parent advocacy center. The center provided an
advocate who assisted Mrs. Ortiz in preparing for an
upcoming IEP meeting.

What do these four scenarios have in common?
In each, a professional educator is engaged in some
form of advocacy on behalf of students with disabilities and their families. These scenarios also illustrate that special education advocacy work is not
"one size fits all." It is as multifaceted as the needs
and circumstances of children with disabilities and
their families, but the potential impact of advocacy
in special education was captured by one teacher's
comment, "We have the power to make a difference."[1]

As was stated in the first characteristic for advocacy, an advocate's primary loyalty or allegiance
must be to children with disabilities and their families. By being an advocate, educators face potential
conflicts of interest by being employees of a school
district that they may be challenging. Their primary
commitment, however, ethically rests with the children and their families. Because professionals who
challenge their school districts may face disciplinary
sanctions for their perceived "insubordination,"
they must carefully consider possible consequences
of their advocacy actions.

The second characteristic of advocacy was that
an advocate seeks a change in the status quo, meaning that such work is action and change oriented.
Advocacy for change requires dedication, time, energy, and a clear vision of desired outcomes. The
third characteristic talked about empowering parents
as the natural advocates of their children. For various
reasons, not all parents are able to function as effective advocates. When this is the case, educators and
others have an opportunity to fill the advocacy void
by speaking up for children with disabilities. The
fourth characteristic of advocacy emphasizes the
problem-solving nature of this endeavor – identifying
issues and then determining how to address them.
Advocates seek positive change through improved
educational systems and services for children with
disabilities and their families.

The roots of professional advocacy can be traced to the "child-saving" era of the later nineteenth and early twentieth centuries.[2] During this era, professional child advocacy efforts led to the creation of many agencies to address the increasing needs of children and families. . . . Professionals have functioned both as *external advocates,* working for change from outside an organization, and *internal advocates,* committed to changing organizations from within.

Both kinds of advocates were necessary because individuals with disabilities have historically experienced discrimination; that's why they have minority status in this country. They share the conditions of discrimination, segregation, and subordination with certain ethnic, racial, social class, and gender groups.[3] From this perspective, advocacy is needed to foster basic civil rights. Herr stated that, "as a banished and insular minority, such persons were isolated and stigmatized in ways that matched and sometimes exceeded the most vicious regimes of racial segregation."[4] The segregation, isolation, and discrimination experienced by individuals with disabilities take many forms, including separate housing, separate schooling, separate medical care, and separate employment.

The at-risk status of many individuals with disabilities was noted by Fiedler and Antonak:

> The ebb and flow of society's attitudes and treatment of persons with mental retardation resulted in bleak periods where they were thought of as a menace, a threat to society, and where Social Darwinism was the driving force behind perceptions of society's responsibilities. During these bleak times, the societal response to people with mental retardation emphasized solutions such as institutional incarceration, immigration restriction, eugenic control, and sterilization.[5]

These kinds of discriminatory and pernicious practices were justified because individuals with disabilities were considered deviant, as being significantly different from others in aspects that were negatively valued.

In terms of public schooling, children with disabilities were not deemed worthy of any education until the late nineteenth century.[6] This period of total educational neglect was followed by a period of institutionalized, segregated education. Public school programs for children with disabilities were sporadic until the 1960s. When educational services were provided, children with disabilities were placed in segregated, self-contained special education classrooms. This placement model was indicative of a philosophy that children with disabilities must be separated from non-disabled students in the interest of school efficiency.[7]

Clearly, U.S. society and the public educational system have made great strides in the way individuals with disabilities are viewed and treated. New rights and opportunities have evolved over the past 40 years. Most of these societal and educational advancements in both thinking and acting toward individuals with disabilities are directly attributable to advocacy efforts. . . .

Even though the federal special education law – the Individuals with Disabilities Education Act (IDEA) – has been in existence since 1975, there are still legitimate concerns about compliance with legal mandates and best educational practice. For many children, advocacy is the "squeaky wheel that gets the grease," in the form of appropriate, individualized educational services, but children without an effective advocate are more likely to encounter inappropriate educational experiences. . . .

It is widely maintained that many children with disabilities are routinely denied their rights and deprived of appropriate special educational services because those services are not truly individualized.[8] . . . A study of secondary students with emotional/behavioral disorders (EBD) illustrates this criticism. As part of the data collection, the researcher reviewed all of the current IEPs for all 10 students enrolled in a high school EBD program. He was shocked to discover that every single IEP was identical. All of the goals and objectives and the services provided were the same, word for word. The only difference was the demographic information for each student. What was "special" about special education? In this case – nothing.

Many IEP meetings primarily operate as mechanisms for the identification of problems within students and for procedural compliance with the law.[9] That is, many IEP meetings provide limited focus on individualized instruction; instead, these meetings merely legitimize the teacher's identification of the student as the problem. This practice reflects the internal deficit model of disability that blames the student and his or her family for school failure. Instead of the individual needs of children driving the educational programming decisions, as is the legal requirement, too many programming decisions are based primarily on administrative convenience. . . .

Advocates for children with disabilities must first recognize that schools are bureaucracies, and thus are conservative by nature. Schools tend to be inflexible and resistant to change. A common feature of bureaucratic institutions is that they tend to respond more to their own needs rather than to the needs of those they serve.[10] For that reason, schools often base decisions on administrative convenience and not on the individual needs of children with disabilities. For example, a small, rural school district in the Midwest had historically sent their students with severe disabilities to a regional program 20 miles away in another district. The district decided to bring their six students with severe disabilities back to their home district the next year. This decision was based on the legal requirement that children with disabilities be educated as close to their home as possible.

The only problem with the decision to bring the six students back to their home district was where to place them. The district had one elementary building and one secondary building. Both schools were antiquated and overcrowded so there was no space for an additional classroom in either of the two buildings. The district leased a former muffler shop downtown and converted it into a special education classroom. The closest school building was over a mile away. The muffler shop was converted over the summer and the six students started their new school year in this downtown facility.

One parent objected to this arrangement and filed for a due process hearing. The district's rationale for their placement decision was simply that they had no space in any school building; therefore, this was a suitable arrangement in an effort to accommodate students coming back into their home district. It was more convenient to renovate a non-school facility than to disrupt the school environment by rearranging existing classroom space to accommodate these six students. The school district lost this case. . . .

Another feature of schools as bureaucracies is the pressure toward conformity. Schools as institutional work environments demand compliance and conformity from their employees. Teachers have been conditioned to conform rather than to be autonomous and involved as initiators of change. This teacher conditioning was identified by Glickman:

"Administrators prize conformity, privacy, dependency, quietness, and routine in their teachers and consider unconventionality, public attention, creativity, assertiveness, spontaneity, and collective action among teachers to be threatening . . . teachers are rewarded for conforming and penalized for being intellectually critical."[11] Given this work environment, the risks of serving as an advocate are obvious. A destructive consequence of this pressure to conform is that many teachers and administrators who start their careers with idealism and a strong sense of purpose become disillusioned. . . .

In recent years, there has been increased emphasis on the postgraduation success of special education students. . . . Most special education outcomes research has employed Halpern's conceptual model where the desired outcome of special education programming is successful community adjustment that consists of three components: employment, residential adjustment, and establishment of desirable social and interpersonal networks.[12] The vast majority of outcomes studies paint a pessimistic picture. . . . Simply stated, many studies reveal that special education graduates are (1) not employed, (2) not living on their own, (3) not integrated into their communities, and (4) not very satisfied with their lives. . . .

One obvious conclusion to be drawn from all of the evidence is that special education students need to have advocates. The historical discrimination against children's special education rights, the unresponsive and inflexible school bureaucracies, the inability of some families to function as advocates for their children, and the bleak postgraduation adjustment outcomes for special education graduates underscore the critical need for educators and others to engage in advocacy efforts. Rights and services for children with disabilities have improved tremendously in the past 25 years, but improved services and continued progress are necessary. Advocacy is essential in monitoring current practices and seeking improvements.

Notes

[1]D. Taylor, D. Coughlin, and J. Marasco, J. (Eds.), *Teaching and advocacy.* (York, ME: Stenhouse Publishers, 1997), p. 178.

[2]F. Murry, Effective advocacy for students with emotional/behavioral disorders: How high the cost?

pp. 414–429, *Education and Treatment of Children*, 2005, *28*(4).

[3]E. Brantlinger, Home-school partnerships that benefit children with special needs, pp. 249–259, *The Elementary School Journal*, 1991, *91*(3).

[4]S. S. Herr, Advocacy and the future of communitization (pp. 3–15). In J. A. Mulick and B. L. Mallory (Eds.) *Transitions in mental retardation: Vol.1: Advocacy, technology and science*. (Norwood, NJ: Ablex, 1984), p. 3.

[5]C. R. Fiedler and R. F. Antonak, Advocacy, (pp. 23–32). In J. L. Matson & J. A. Mulick (Eds.), *Handbook of mental retardation*. (New York: Pergamon Press, 1991), p. 23.

[6]S. Stainback, W. Stainback, and M. Forest, *Educating students in the mainstream of regular education*. (Baltimore: Brookes, 1989).

[7]T. M. Skrtic, *An organizational analysis of special education reform*. Paper presented at the annual meeting of the American Educational Research Association, Washington, DC, 1987.

[8]B. Audette and B. Algozzine, Re-inventing government? Let's re-invent special education, pp. 214–219, *Journal of Learning Disabilities*, 1997, *30*(4); M. L. Hines, *Don't get mad: Get powerful! A manual for building advocacy skills*. (Lansing: Michigan Protection and Advocacy Service, 1987). (ERIC Document Reproduction Service No. ED 354 683.); J. M. Kauffman, How we might achieve the radical reform of special education, pp. 6–16, *Exceptional Education*, 1993, *60*(1).

[9]C. Christensen and S. Dorn, Competing notions of social justice and contradictions in special education reform, pp. 181–199, *Journal of Special Education*, 1997, *31*(2).

[10]D. Taylor, D. Coughlin, and J. Marasco, J. (Eds.), *Teaching and advocacy*.

[11]C. D. Glickman, *Supervision of instruction: A developmental approach*. (2nd ed.) (Boston: Allyn and Bacon, 1990), p. 38.

[12]A.S. Halpern, Transition: A look at the foundations, pp. 479-486, *Exceptional Children*, 1985, Vol. 51.

Places Where We All Belong

How to teach children to accept people with disabilities is part of a larger question – how do we prepare children to accept the human differences that are so pervasive in our society? The author believes it can start in schools by practicing "full inclusion." She explains the concept and describes how teachers can create inclusive classrooms.

Children differ in many ways. Regardless of what grade is being taught . . . the reality is that all classrooms are actually heterogeneous. Within a class, you may have students who live in different family situations, some living with two parents, some with one parent, some with grandparents, some in foster care or shelters. Children may have two mothers, two fathers, many siblings, stepbrothers and sisters, or no siblings at all.

A class may contain children from different racial or ethnic groups, children of different religions, and children of different socioeconomic levels. You may have students with different dietary requirements, children who speak different languages, and children whose parents are struggling with drug or alcohol abuse.

Without a doubt, students will differ in appearance, size, interests, skills, abilities, and challenges. A class may have students who are athletic and coordinated and students who are not, students who read easily and those who struggle, students who make friends quickly and those who wrestle with forming relationships.

Although all classrooms are already heterogeneous, many schools are moving toward ever more purposive heterogeneity, attempting to limit the negative effects of tracking and recognizing the value of teaching children to interact comfortably with a wide range of people. This philosophy, sometimes referred to as *full inclusion,* represents a commitment to creating schools and classrooms in which all children, regardless of individual educational needs or disabilities are educated together.

What makes a classroom inclusive? Many people use the word *inclusive* to refer to the ways in which special education services are provided. From that perspective, an inclusive classroom can be described as one in which all children, regardless of performance level, are educated with their chronological peers in a "typical" classroom. That is, children are educated in "third grade" even though they do not read "at the third-grade level," and individualized or specialized services that may be required are provided within the context of the general education classroom.

Inclusion, however, can be defined much more broadly, so that it refers to welcoming and accommodating many kinds of student differences, not just those typically labeled as "disabilities." Addressing student differences related to race, class, gender, ethnicity, language, family background, and religion could all be part of creating an "inclusive classroom." A broader definition of inclusion refers to a classroom in which all children are part of a shared community and the following characteristics are present:

- Open discussion of the ways in which people are different and the kinds of support and help they need and want
- A commitment to meeting children's individual needs within a context of shared community and connection
- Explicit attention to the ways in which students' differences can become the basis for discrimination and oppression and teaching students to be allies to one another . . .

There are many challenges to implementing inclusion. Long-held notions of how people learn, how teachers can best teach, and how differences should be responded to can keep us from reinventing schools as cooperative, inclusive communities. Many of the existing structures of school (gifted programs, special education, remedial education services) also make inclusive classrooms difficult to operationalize, and there are myths about inclusion, grouping, and teaching that can get in the way of creating more difference-friendly classrooms.

Myths about Ability Grouping

• *There is such a thing as ability.* Many educational systems are based on a notion of fixed ability levels that define the best a student can do. When we talk about children "not working up to their ability" or sometimes, ironically, "overachieving" (doing better than we predicted they would), we are evoking an image of fixed immutable potential. This belief system leads to classes for students who are "gifted" and classes for students who have "special needs" where we adjust our curricula and expectations accordingly.

In actuality, all people vary along a wide number of dimensions, and ability is not a particularly useful construct. How well any child does is a function of many factors, including the nature of the curriculum, the child's self-concept, and the flexibility and support of those who surround the child. In other words, if conditions were right, we could all do better. Hunt notes, "It is highly unlikely that any society has developed a system of child rearing and education that maximizes the potential of the individuals which compose it. Probably no individual has ever lived whose full potential for happy intellectual interest and growth has been achieved."[1]

We are, then, *a world of underachievers,* and it makes sense for teachers to find ways to help all children achieve more and to create classrooms that nurture and support diversity.

• *Students learn better in homogeneous groups.* Some teachers believe that by "narrowing the range" of abilities in the classroom, children will learn better because tasks will be more appropriate. Actually, despite the fact that many teachers continue to group students by ability, overwhelming research results suggest that homogenous grouping does not consistently help anyone learn more or better.[2] In fact, organizing children into high-, average-, and low-ability groupings actually *creates* differences in what children learn by exposing them to different kinds of materials and vastly different expectations. Although some children in high-ability groups may benefit academically from such arrangements, the children who lose the most are those placed in average- and low-ability groups. Such grouping practices tend to compound racial, ethnic, and economic differences in schools, as poor children and children of color are least likely to be placed in enriched, gifted, or high-ability tracks and are more likely to end up in special education and low-ability groups.

Ability grouping also takes a serious toll on children's self-concept and their opportunities to form meaningful relationships across groups. Children in the lowest groups or in special education classrooms are often painfully aware of the limited expectations adults have for them and are often subjected to teasing, ridicule, and humiliation by their classmates. Similarly, children who are in the top groups or removed to gifted classes are often labeled as "brains" or "nerds" and are sometimes equally excluded or isolated. Grouping children according to some putative ability level creates artificial distance among them as well as amplifying and solidifying whatever actual differences exist.

• *Teaching is easier in homogeneous groups.* Many of us were educated in highly tracked schools and classrooms, and have gone on to organize our own instruction that way. Having three reading groups or grouping by ability for math may seem natural and familiar, but it has been increasingly challenged through the development of multilevel, multi-modality instructional models, the use of cooperative learning, and the increasing recognition of the many intelligences students bring to their learning. Although organizing instruction in heterogeneous groups definitely involves a different kind of planning and preparation, many teachers report increased enthusiasm in their students, as well as greater learning and deeper involvement when curricula and instruction are organized around diverse learners working together.

Myths about Inclusion

• *Inclusion means dumping all students back into the regular classroom.* Unfortunately, in some schools, children previously educated in special education settings have been summarily returned to general education classrooms with little or no teacher preparation or support. This is not inclusion, but is, in fact, "dumping," and it should be resisted. Inclusion requires ongoing preparation and support for teachers and the reorganization of support services for both students and teachers so that resources are available in the regular education classroom.

• *It takes a special person to work with special children – those who have disabilities and those who are gifted.* Idealizing the special education teacher or the teacher of the gifted as someone with unique personality characteristics and a set of instructional tricks foreign to general education teachers has served to deskill general education teachers, removing the motivation and necessity of developing a wider repertoire of skills. Increasingly, the research shows that all children need "good teaching" and that the characteristics of that teaching (learner-centered, responsive, engaging) cut across all categories of students. Inclusion is beyond the reach of the already overburdened general education teacher. There is no question that many general education teachers are overburdened and undersupported. Adding students with disabilities or other special needs without committing the necessary resources and support is unethical as well as ineffective. We must make huge improvements in the kinds and quality of support we provide to teachers, particularly planning and collaboration time with other teachers, modified curricula and resources, administrative support, and ongoing emotional support.

• *Curriculum of general education classrooms will get watered down and distorted.* There is a fear that inclusion will force teachers to "dumb down" the curriculum, thus limiting the options for "typical students" and especially for gifted students. The reality is that curriculum in inclusive classrooms must be structured as multilevel, participatory, and flexible. We must abandon the assumption that all children in the same grade will be working at the same level, completing the same project in the same way, and being evaluated according to the same criteria. We need new models of instruction and assessment.

• *Inclusion favors children with disabilities at the expense of other children's education.* There is currently no evidence that the education of other students suffers in any way from the inclusion process. The film, *Educating Peter,* details the classroom experience of Peter, a boy with Down syndrome during his third-grade year. . . .

Martha Stallings, Peter's third-grade teacher, reports that the students in her class all had a wonderful year, learned their math and their history and their geography, and did a great deal of writing and reading. They also learned to be decent human beings and to understand and support a classmate with major behavioral and learning challenges.[3] That seems like an incredibly successful year to me. . . .

Myths about Teaching about Differences

• *If we do not mention differences, students will not notice them.* Ask any teacher if his or her students know which child comes from a poor family, which child is overweight, and which child reads really "hard" books. Children are extremely aware of their classmates and their differences. Not noticing differences simply tells students that differences are things we should not talk about with the teacher or in class; such discussions become the focus of playground whispering and bathroom secrets.

• *Mentioning differences calls negative attention to them and makes things worse.* We probably all remember a teacher who attempted to address children's social interactions and made things worse ("Now I don't like the way you're treating Jessica. I want you all to be nice to her" or some other well-meaning but ineffective and embarrassing attempt to address friendship and exclusion issues). But there are effective ways to deal with students' social interactions and their differences – ways that are respectful and sensitive and that allow students to develop repertoires of perspective taking and problem solving.

• *People are naturally more comfortable with people "just like them."* Growing up in a highly segregated society in which differences in race, religion, social class, and ability were rarely addressed, it is not surprising that people tend to gravitate to others who look like them. But this is neither inevitable nor desirable. Thoughtful teachers can implement strategies designed to help students learn to be comfortable interacting and socializing with others they perceive as "different" – girls and boys, able-bodied students and those with disabilities, children of different racial or ethnic groups, and so on. Before they can do this, teachers must see the value and importance of this intermingling and connection and not accept as inevitable the ways in which children often separate themselves.

• *Children are cruel and cannot accept differences.* We have all seen (and experienced) horrible examples of teasing and cruelty between children. But many of us have also seen the opposite – a child gently supporting the head of a classmate who has cerebral palsy, a junior-high girl stepping in to defend her overweight friend who is being harassed, and children figuring out ways to include their classmates in projects and field trips. Children learn their responses to differences from the adults with whom they interact – parents and teachers – and they model their behavior closely on the behavior of those adults. Children can be systematically taught and supported in learning repertoires of kindness, support, and caring within classrooms that value those behaviors. . . .

The goal of having an inclusive classroom is not to homogenize differences, pretending that they are not there or do not have an impact on students or their lives. The goal is to acknowledge those differences and create a classroom community that works with those differences (and sometimes around those differences) so that every student can feel a sense of connection and belonging. By setting inclusion as a goal for all our classrooms, we can acknowledge the heterogeneity we already have (and receive support and help for responding to challenges) and we can set a vision of full membership and participation in the forefront of our thinking and planning. . . .

The goal must not be "not noticing" differences. The goal should be to notice, understand, respond, and connect. . . . (We) can make a distinction between noting that Nicole's hair is bright red and making fun of Nicole for being a "carrot top." There is a difference between noting that Nancy's shoes are shaped differently to accommodate her feet and looking away quickly in embarrassment when she mentions buying new shoes. Telling someone that you "don't notice" how they are different is not truly a compliment if it means that you are failing to see all aspects of who that person is.

Within inclusive classrooms, differences are acknowledged and accommodated, and teachers talk honestly and openly about differences and still retain a strong sense of community. . . . Consider the following two possibilities for Marsha, who has diabetes: In Classroom A, the teacher makes special arrangements to buy some sugar-free cookies for the class party, and quietly dispenses those to Marsha so that other students will not know. In Classroom B, the students know that Marsha has diabetes, and they understand why and when she takes insulin. When they are discussing the class party, the students themselves volunteer, "Let's make sure we get snacks that everyone can eat" and they list Marsha's needs as well as the needs of Sarah, who is a vegetarian, Robin, who is allergic to wheat, and Amman, who does not eat pork or pork products such as lard. The goal is not to hide Marsha's unique needs, but to think about Marsha as both an individual and as a member of a cohesive, classroom community.

Similarly, think of how teachers respond to children's noticing differences in academic requirements for different children. In one classroom, children who ask, "How come Matthew gets to do his math on the computer?" or "Why does Sharissa only have five spelling words?" are told to mind their own business. In an inclusive classroom in which the teacher has helped students to know one another well, other students *know* that Matthew works on the computer because his processing difficulties make that strategy much more successful for him than pen and paper. Sometimes they partner up with him and work on the computer together. They also know that people learn spelling in many different ways and that five spelling words for Sharissa is just the right level of challenge. And, since their spelling words are drawn from their own writing and not from a standardized list, it makes sense to them that different people have different lists.

One sometimes hears it said that the "successful" inclusive classroom is one in which "you can't tell the kids with disabilities apart from the regular kids." While the underlying sense of equity and fair treatment reflected in that statement is admirable, the goal itself is often unattainable and probably undesirable. Some of the children included in typical classrooms have differences that are quite noticeable, and no amount of community building or successful accommodation will mask their unique characteristics. Setting a goal of "invisibility" for children with disabilities does not help us think well about how children's differences are responded to or how they are incorporated into the daily life and activities of a classroom. Encouraging Rowena to hide her hearing aids behind her hair so that no one sees them will not help other students learn how to communicate with a classmate with a hearing loss. It also communicates to Rowena that wearing hearing aids is somehow bad or shameful. The goal of an inclusive classroom is that all students feel they belong and are able to contribute to the class. . . .

Making inclusion work also means attending to the beliefs and experiences of parents, whose own school histories may not have included extensive relationships with students they perceived as "different." When it came time for Stacy, a "typically developing child" to go to school, her parents wrestled with not only whether Stacy should be in an inclusive classroom but whether she should go full time to the gifted program as the school district offered:

> . . . we eventually decided that we didn't want her to participate [in the gifted program] because we didn't want her in an isolated classroom away from her friends where she would feel different from everybody else. . . . my husband and I decided . . . to keep her in a regular second grade class. And guess who her seat partner was? It was Madison! We were blown away because . . . her seat partner couldn't read or write. So we decided to get with the program and figure out what all this [inclusion] was all about.[4]

Later that year, after Stacy and Madison, a child with Down Syndrome, had become good friends, Stacy's mother reflected:

> For Stacy it was a turning point. . . . Their friendship was a connection immediately and wasn't something that we could explain to Stacy about Madison, but she found out for herself. In spite of us, the kids wanted this relationship to happen, and it did.[5]

Parents, like students, can learn, through inclusion, that children are children and that individual accommodations need not be overwhelming or frightening. For Stacy's mother, as for Stacy, learning to be comfortable with differences was a growing process:

> After six months into their second grade year together, Stacy must have asked a dozen times if Madison could come over and play. I had so many excuses why Madison couldn't come . . . Finally, after Stacy's persistence, I asked Madison's mother. I was quite embarrassed, but I just blurted out, "You know, Stacy really wants Madison to come over and play, but what does she eat? What do I do if she chokes? What if she wants to go home? Does she know how to use the toilet? . . . You know, our generation is just so ignorant about these things. I was terrified the first time Madison came over to play. Well it took all of about ten minutes to put my worries to rest. Madison was really just another kid. Nothing secret, nothing surprising.[6]

This is what building community is all about. Creating an inclusive classroom means attending to many aspects of the classroom. . . . I sometimes hear teachers and administrators say:

"If we include a student like Daniel, we'll have to modify the curriculum."

"If we include students like Tara, we'll have to change our teaching methods – lecture just doesn't work for those kids."

"If we want to include Natasha, we'll really have to deal with a lot of social issues – the kids in my class can be so cruel."

All of the statements are true! Attempting to integrate students with significant educational and behavioral challenges or other characteristics that could lead to rejection and exclusion shows us what kinds of changes are needed in our schools. When we see how certain children struggle within our system, it points out to us all the ways in which our schools and classrooms are unimaginative, underresourced, unresponsive, and simply inadequate. Remember, the kinds of changes we make for Daniel, Tara, and Natasha are almost always changes that benefit many other children as well. (For any teacher), thinking about your curriculum, your pedagogy, and your social climate in terms of inclusion can help you meet the needs of *all* children better.

Notes

[1] J. M. Hunt, *Intelligence and experience.* (New York: Ronald Press, 1961), p. 346.

[2] Massachusetts Advocacy Center, *Locked in/locked out: Tracking and placement practices in Boston public schools.* (Boston: Author, 1990); J. Oakes, *Keeping Track.* (New Haven, CT: Yale University Press, 1985).

[3] M. A. Stallings, When Peter came to Mrs. Stalling's class. *NEA Today,* May, 1993, p. 22; M. A. Stallings, *Educating Peter.* A presentation at the Association for Persons with Severe Handicaps Conference, Alliance for Action, Dec., 1994, Atlanta, GA.

[4] D. Staub, *Delicate threads: Friendships between children with and without special needs in inclusive settings.* (Bethesda, MD: Woodbine House, 1998).

[5] Ibid.

[6] Ibid.

The Curious Incident of the Dog in the Night-Time

The narrator in this excerpt from a novel is a 15-year-old highly functioning autistic boy who lives in England. The boy's neighbor is Mrs. Shears, and he discovers her dog lying on her front lawn, having been killed with a garden fork. He liked the dog so he hugs it. Mrs. Shears calls the police and they question the boy. When one of them grabs his arm he panics and hits the man. The police arrest him for assaulting a police officer.

23. When I got to the police station they made me take the laces out of my shoes and empty my pockets at the front desk in case I had anything in them that I could use to kill myself or escape or attack a policeman with. The sergeant behind the desk had very hairy hands and he had bitten his nails so much that they had bled.

This is what I had in my pockets

1. A Swiss Army knife with 13 attachments including a wire stripper and a saw and a toothpick and tweezers.
2. A piece of string
3. A piece of a wooden puzzle . . .
4. 3 pellets of rat food for Toby, my rat
5. £ 1.47 (this was made up of a £ 1 coin, a 20p coin, two 10p coins, a 5p coin and a 2p coin)
6. A red paper clip
7. A key for the front door

I was also wearing my watch and they wanted me to leave this at the desk as well but I said that I needed to keep my watch on because I needed to know exactly what time it was. And when they tried to take it off me I screamed, so they let me keep it on.

They asked me if I had any family. I said I did. They asked me who my family was. I said it was Father, but Mother was dead. And I said it was also Uncle Terry, but he was in Sunderland and he was Father's brother, and it was my grandparents, too, but three of them were dead and Grandma Burton was in a home because she had senile dementia and thought that I was someone on television.

Then they asked me for Father's phone number.

I told them that he had two numbers, one for at home and one which was a mobile phone, and I said both of them.

It was nice in the police cell. It was almost a perfect cube, 2 meters long by 2 meters wide by 2 meters high. It contained approximately 8 cubic meters of air. It had a small window with bars and, on the opposite side, a metal door with a long, thin hatch near the floor for sliding trays of food into the cell and a sliding hatch higher up so that policeman could look in and check that prisoners hadn't escaped or committed suicide. There was also a padded bench.

I wondered how I would escape if I was in a story. It would be difficult because the only things I had were my clothes and my shoes, which had no laces in them.

I decided that my best plan would be to wait for a really sunny day and then use my glasses to focus the sunlight on a piece of my clothing and start a fire. I would then make my escape when they saw the smoke and took me out of the cell. And if they didn't notice I would be able to wee on the clothes and put them out.

I wondered whether Mrs. Shears had told the police that I had killed Wellington and whether, when the police found out that she had lied, she would go to prison. Because telling lies about people is called *slander.*

29. I find people confusing.

This is for two main reasons.

The first main reason is that people do a lot of talking without using any words. Siobhan says that if you raise one eyebrow it can mean lots of different things. It can mean "I want to do sex with you" and it can also mean "I think that what you just said was very stupid."

Siobhan also says that if you close your mouth and breathe out loudly through your nose, it can mean that you are relaxed, or that you are bored, or that you are angry, and it all depends on how much air comes out of your nose and how fast and what shape your mouth is when you do it and how you are sitting and what you said just before and hundreds of other things which are too complicated to work out in a few seconds.

The second main reason is that people often talk using metaphors. These are examples of metaphors.

I laughed my socks off.
He was the apple of her eye.
They had a skeleton in the cupboard.
We had a real pig of a day.
The dog was stone dead.

The word *metaphor* means carrying something from one place to another; and it comes from the Greek words μετα (which means *from one place to another*) and φερειν (which means *to carry*), and it is when you describe something by using a word for

something that it isn't. This means that the word *metaphor* is a metaphor.

I think it should be called a lie because a pig is not like a day and people do not have skeletons in their cupboards. And when I try and make a picture of the phrase in my head it just confuses me because imagining an apple in someone's eye doesn't have anything to do with liking someone a lot and it makes you forget what the person was talking about.

My name is a metaphor. It means carrying Christ and it comes from the Greek words χριστζ (which means Jesus Christ) and φερειν and it was the name given to St. Christopher because he carried Jesus Christ across a river.

This makes you wonder what he was called before he carried Christ across the river. But he wasn't called anything because this is an apocryphal story, which means that it is a lie, too.

Mother used to say that it meant Christopher was a nice name because it was a story about being kind and helpful, but I do not want my name to mean a story about being kind and helpful. I want my name to mean me.

31. It was 1:12 a.m. when Father arrived at the police station. I did not see him until 1:28 a.m. but I knew he was there because I could hear him.

He was shouting, "I want to see my son," and "Why the hell is he locked up?" and "Of course I'm bloody angry."

Then I heard a policeman telling him to calm down. Then I heard nothing for a long while. At 1:28 a.m. a policeman opened the door of the cell and told me that there was someone to see me.

I stepped outside. Father was standing in the corridor. He held up his right hand and spread his fingers out in a fan. I held up my left hand and spread my fingers out in a fan and we made our fingers and thumbs touch each other. We do this because sometimes Father wants to give me a hug, but I do not like hugging people, so we do this instead, and it means that he loves me.

Then the policeman told us to follow him down the corridor to another room. In the room was a table and three chairs. He told us to sit down on the far side of the table and he sat down on the other side. There was a tape recorder on the table and I asked whether I was going to be interviewed and he was going to record the interview.

He said, "I don't think there will be any need for that."

He was an inspector. I could tell because he wasn't wearing a uniform. He also had a very hairy nose. It looked as if there were two very small mice hiding in his nostrils. (This is not a metaphor; it is a simile, which means that it really did look like there were two very small mice hiding in his nostrils, and if you make a picture in your head of a man with two very small mice hiding in his nostrils, you will know what the police inspector looked like. And a simile is not a lie, unless it is a bad simile.)

He said, "I have spoken to your father and he says that you didn't mean to hit the policeman."

I didn't say anything because this wasn't a question.

He said, "Did you mean to hit the policeman?"

I said, "Yes."

He squeezed his face and said, "But you didn't mean to hurt the policeman?"

I thought about this and said, "No. I didn't mean to hurt the policeman. I just wanted him to stop touching me."

Then he said, "You know that it is wrong to hit a policeman, don't you?"

I said, "I do."

He was quiet for a few seconds, then he asked, "Did you kill the dog, Christopher?"

I said, "I didn't kill the dog."

He said, "Do you know that it is wrong to lie to a policeman and that you can get into a very great deal of trouble if you do?"

I said, "Yes."

He said, "So, do you know who killed the dog?"

I said, "No."

He said, "Are you telling the truth?"

I said, "Yes. I always tell the truth."

And he said, "Right. I am going to give you a caution."

I asked, "Is that going to be on a piece of paper like a certificate I can keep?"

He replied, "No, a caution means that we are going to keep a record of what you did, that you hit a policeman but that it was an accident and that you didn't mean to hurt the policeman."

I said, "But it wasn't an accident."

And Father said, "Christopher, please."

The policeman closed his mouth and breathed out loudly through his nose and said, "If you get into any more trouble we will take out this record and see that you have been given a caution and we will take things much more seriously. Do you understand what I'm saying?"

I said that I understood.

Then he said that we could go and he stood up and opened the door and we walked out into the corridor and back to the front desk, where I picked up my Swiss Army knife and my piece of string and the piece of the wooden puzzle and the 3 pellets for rat food for Toby and my £ 1.47 and the paper clip and my front door key, which were all in a little plastic bag, and we went out to Father's car, which was parked outside, and we drove home.

37. I do not tell lies. Mother used to say that this was because I was a good person. But it is not because I am a good person. It is because I can't tell lies.

Mother was a small person who smelled nice. And she sometimes wore a fleece with a zip down the front which was pink and it had a tiny label which said **Berghaus** on the left bosom.

A lie is when you say something happened which didn't happen. But there is only ever one thing which happened at a particular time and a particular place. And there are an infinite number of things which didn't happen at that time and that place. And if I think about something which didn't happen I start thinking about all the other things which didn't happen.

For example, this morning for breakfast I had Ready Brek and some hot raspberry milk shake. But if I say that I actually had Shreddies and a mug of tea (But I wouldn't have Shreddies and tea because they are both brown.) I start thinking about Coco Pops and lemonade and porridge and Dr Pepper and how I wasn't eating my breakfast in Egypt and there wasn't a rhinoceros in the room and Father wasn't wearing a diving suit and so on and even writing this makes me feel shaky and scared, like I do when I'm standing on the top of a very tall building and there are thousands of houses and cars and people below me and my head is so full of all these things that I'm afraid that I'm going to forget to stand up straight and hang on to the rail and I'm going to fall over and be killed.

This is another reason why I don't like proper novels, because they are lies about things which didn't happen and they make me feel shaky and scared.

And this is why everything I have written here is true.

41. There were clouds in the sky on the way home, so I couldn't see the Milky Way.

I said, "I'm sorry," because Father had had to come to the police station, which was a bad thing.

He said, "It's OK."

I said, "I didn't kill the dog."

And he said, "I know."

Then he said, "Christopher, you have to stay out of trouble, OK?"

I said, "I didn't know I was going to get into trouble. I like Wellington and I went to say hello to him, but I didn't know that someone had killed him."

Father said, "Just try and keep your nose out of other people's business."

I thought for a little and I said, "I am going to find out who killed Wellington."

And Father said, "Were you listening to what I was saying, Christopher?"

I said, "Yes, I was listening to what you were saying, but when someone gets murdered you have to find out who did it so that they can be punished."

And he said, "It's a bloody dog, Christopher, a bloody dog."

I replied, "I think dogs are important, too."

He said, "Leave it."

And I said, "I wonder if the police will find out who killed him and punish the person."

Then Father banged the steering wheel with his fist and the car weaved a little bit across the dotted line in the middle of the road and he shouted, "I said leave it, for God's sake."

I could tell that he was angry because he was shouting, and I didn't want to make him angry so I didn't say anything else until we got home.

When we came in through the front door I went into the kitchen and got a carrot for Toby and I went upstairs and I shut the door of my room and I let Toby out and gave him the carrot. Then I turned my computer on and played 76 games of Minesweeper and did the Expert Version in 102 seconds, which was only 3 seconds off my best time, which was 99 seconds.

At 2:07 a.m. I decided that I wanted a drink of orange squash before I brushed my teeth and got into bed, so I went downstairs to the kitchen. Father was sitting on the sofa watching snooker on the television and drinking scotch. There were tears coming out of his eyes.

I asked, "Are you sad about Wellington?"

He looked at me for a long time and sucked air in through his nose. Then he said, "Yes, Christopher, you could say that. You could very well say that."

I decided to leave him alone because when I am sad I want to be left alone. So I didn't say anything else. I just went into the kitchen and made my orange squash and took it back upstairs to my room.

Perspectives on Sex Role Stereotypes and Sexism

66 What is enough? Enough is when somebody says, 'Get me the best people you can find' and nobody notices when half of them turn out to be women. 99

Louise Renne (1937–)

The struggle for equal treatment of women has had a long and sometimes surprising history. Based on available evidence, it would appear that from the beginning, human societies had specific roles for men and women, but after examining burial sites and artifacts, Thompson (1981) speculated that during the period before recorded history women held major leadership roles in these simple agrarian societies. Thompson also argued that it wasn't until communities began engaging in violent, physical conflicts that warrior-kings emerged as leaders and what we now regard as traditional sex roles were established.[1] For years many people in Western societies have insisted that traditional gender roles simply reflected innate differences between men and women; yet historical and anthropological research has consistently documented diverse gender functions and activities in different cultures for both men and women (Harris, 1990; Tavris and Wade, 1984).[2] Such cultural differences make it difficult to argue that there is a specific set of gender differences that are universal across centuries and cultures.

Historically Western societies have presumed that woman's place was in the home, but there were always women who found ways to escape the confines of such sex role expectations. In the Middle Ages, women joined convents to be afforded the opportunity to read and think and write without the distractions of a husband and children. Lerner (1993) analyzed the writings of such women and found that many of the ideas they expressed represented the origins of contemporary feminist thought.[3] Women are still contending with echoes of the old sexism – the belief that men's superiority to women is part of nature's (or God's) plan; that women and men have specific roles that are logical and necessary (and some who speculate that we will eventually discover that they are genetically determined); that women who rebel against the roles they are supposed to play will have difficulty finding a

> ❝The Glass Ceiling hinders not only individuals but society as a whole. It effectively cuts our pool of potential corporate leaders by half. It deprives our economy of new leaders, new sources of creativity – the "would be" pioneers of the business world. ❞
>
> **Lynn Martin (1939–)**

man who will marry them. These tired old assertions continue to be used to intimidate women into staying in their "place." Women who reject this intimidation may be subjected to painful consequences in a variety of forms, including the violence of date rape and domestic abuse.

Yet most women continue to do what they need or want to do. Today over half of the workforce in the United States is female and so are about half of the managers. On college and university campuses across the country, women outnumber men. The numbers of women in Congress and in other nontraditional roles have tended to increase steadily. Despite this progress, working women are still exploited through pay inequities and demeaned by sexual harassment at work. Although resistance to change remains strong, women have a history of overcoming this resistance; knowing how women were oppressed in the past provides the context for understanding the resistance that women encounter today. Feminists have studied this history to identify ways in which women have confronted injustice and to discern whether these lessons can be applied when confronting sexist problems today — such as violence against women, demeaning images, and the glass ceiling. Whether conservative or liberal, all women are affected by these issues.

The essays in this section examine the resistance to change and/or the nature of contemporary sexism in a variety of areas. Because

feminists have made extraordinary gains, especially over the past half century, Susan Faludi argues that this success has created a backlash against feminism. As a journalist, she is especially critical of how the media has reported on gender issues and presented research about women's reality. Her analysis of media reports on several studies reveals that journalists have often not been objective but instead have displayed an obvious bias against women. Her analysis provides excellent examples of important questions to ask when confronted by research that seems more designed to satisfy an agenda than to discover the truth.

Whereas Faludi provides a detailed description of the misuse of statistics and research, Stephen Jay Gould uses scientific studies to refute the "natural" argument for male supremacy. Some men insist that the male animal is consistently larger than the female and therefore the female requires a male to protect her. Gould debunks the myth of larger males and dependent females by describing a different pattern in nature and providing examples that contradict this assumption. Gould argues that the lessons of gender from nature, as is generally true of nature's lessons, will always be too complex to be manipulated into the pigeonholes mandated by some human ideology.

Many feminists have argued that sex roles restrict men as well as women, and Norah Vincent addresses this issue in her book, *Self-Made*

> **❝People call me feminist whenever I express sentiments that differentiate me from a doormat or a prostitute.❞**
>
> **Rebecca West (1892–1983)**

Man. Vincent disguised herself as a man for two years so she could experience what it was like to live in "a man's world." In this excerpt, Vincent joins a bowling league and provides some insightful portraits of the working class men she meets. She doesn't ignore their flaws, but she describes some of the difficulties they encounter and the resilience they have developed to cope with them. In the end, Vincent views these men sympathetically, recognizing that they are also struggling to find their way in a world that often seems hostile to them. She concludes that although being male and female creates different experiences for each gender, all of us could learn some important lessons from these differences.

Women have their own set of difficulties to contend with, but as Gloria Steinem suggests, perhaps not as many while they are young, especially if they are in college. In her essay "Why Young Women Are More Conservative," Steinem answers that question by arguing that young women have not yet been exposed to the blatant gender oppression that often motivates older women to become active in feminist causes. As women get partners and jobs and children, the demands and inequities of the gender roles become more obvious. As Steinem has said before, she never encountered a man asking for advice on how to juggle marriage and a career. Young women are more likely to resist being identified with feminist goals and have a more conservative perspective because they are not yet at a point in their lives where they can appreciate the value of feminist perspectives and may even misinterpret

the biting wit of a feminist like Rebecca West as the ranting of an angry woman.

In the next essay, bell hooks builds on Steinem's analysis by arguing that women of all ages may also be reluctant to identify with feminism because they aren't sure what feminism is and what feminists want. What is the goal of feminist activism? The title of hooks's essay asserts what she believes should be forcefully presented as the primary goal – "Feminism: A Movement to End Sexist Oppression." In this excerpt from her book on feminist theory, hooks describes some misperceptions of feminists and how these misperceptions contribute to the reluctance of many women to identify themselves as feminists. Although she discusses the ways that race and class have been divisive factors in the pursuit of feminist goals, hooks also emphasizes the necessity for all women to join the feminist effort to achieve the primary goal of ending sexist oppression. Once women understand feminism, they will also understand why some feminists insist that there are no good alternatives to becoming a feminist.

Finally, many feminists have explored the issue of how gender affects childhood. As children grow up, what are the consequences of changing from "a child" to "a girl"? In her short story "The Monkey Garden," Sandra Cisneros uses the perspective of a young girl to tell the story. The monkey garden is simply a deserted yard that has become a playground for children in the neighborhood. When the last family moved away, no one else moved in, but in the

❝I became a feminist as an alternative to becoming a masochist.❞

Sally Kempton (1943–)

yard flowers continued to grow and the apple tree continued to produce fruit and plant life expanded and obscured the signs of human habitation except for abandoned cars that mysteriously began to appear. The monkey garden was a child's world; no adults intruded on their games. But then a girl named Sally introduces a new kind of game that doesn't belong in a child's world. By the end of the story, the young girl feels a painful sense of loss, and when she leaves the monkey garden, she knows she will never return.

Notes

[1]William Irwin Thompson, *The time falling bodies take to light: Mythology, sexuality and the origins of culture,* New York: St. Martin's Press (1981).

[2]Marvin Harris, *Our kind: Who we are, where we came from and where we are going,* New York: Harper Perennial (1990); Carol Tavris & Carol Wade, *The longest war: Sex differences in perspective,* 2nd ed. San Diego, CA: Harcourt Brace Jovanovich (1984).

[3]Gerda Lerner, *The creation of feminist consciousness: From the Middle Ages to eighteen-seventy,* New York: Oxford University Press (1993).

SUSAN FALUDI

The Myths of the Backlash

The author describes how research was misused by the media to disseminate false information about women, providing a useful case study about the need to be skeptical of reported research results and a guide to learning how to ask the right questions about the findings.

To be a woman in America at the close of the 20th century – what good fortune. That's what we keep hearing anyway. The barricades have fallen, politicians assure us. Women have "made it," Madison Avenue cheers. Women's fight for equality has "largely been won," *Time* magazine announces. . . .

Behind this celebration of the American woman's victory, behind the news, cheerfully and endlessly repeated, that the struggle for women's rights is won, another message flashes. You may be free and equal now, it says to women, but you have never been more miserable. . . .

The prevailing wisdom of the past decade has supported one, and only one, answer to this riddle: it must be all that equality that's causing all that pain. Women are unhappy precisely *because* they are free. Women are enslaved by their own liberation. They have grabbed at the gold ring of independence, only to miss the ring that really matters. . . . But what has made women unhappy in the last decade is not their "equality" – which they don't yet have – but the rising pressure to halt, and even reverse, women's quest for that equality. . . .

Some social observers may well ask whether the current pressures on women actually constitute a backlash – or just a continuation of American society's long-standing resistance to women's rights. Certainly hostility to female independence has always been with us. But if fear and loathing of feminism is a sort of perpetual viral condition in our culture, it is not always in an acute stage; its symptoms subside and resurface periodically. And it is these episodes of resurgence . . . that can accurately be termed "backlashes" to women's advancement. . . .

The backlash line claims the women's movement cares nothing for children's rights – while its own representatives in the capital and state legislatures have blocked one bill after another to improve child care, slashed billions of dollars in federal aid for children, and relaxed state licensing standards for day care centers. The backlash line accuses the women's movement of creating a generation of unhappy single and childless women – but its purveyors in the media are the ones guilty of making single and childless women feel like circus freaks. How is it possible that so much distorted . . . information can become so universally accepted? . . . (The) way the media handled two particular statistical studies may help in part to answer that question.

In 1987, the media had the opportunity to critique the work of two social scientists. One of them had exposed hostility to women's independence; the other had endorsed it. . . . Shere Hite had just published the last installment of her national survey on sexuality and relationships, *Women and Love:*

A Cultural Revolution in Progress, a 922-page compendium of the views of 4,500 women.[1] The report's main finding: Most women are distressed and despairing over the continued resistance from the men in their lives to treat them as equals. Four-fifths of them said they still had to fight for rights and respect at home, and only 20 percent felt they had achieved equal status in their men's eyes. Their quest for more independence, they reported, had triggered mounting rancor from their mates. . . . This was not, however, the aspect of the book that the press chose to highlight. The media were too busy attacking Hite personally. . . .

When the media did actually criticize Hite's statistical methods, their accusations were often wrong or hypocritical. Hite's findings were "biased" because she distributed her questionnaires through women's rights groups, some articles complained. But Hite sent her surveys through a wide range of women's groups, including church societies, social clubs, and senior citizens' centers. The press charged that she used a small and unrepresentative sample. Yet, as we shall see, the results of many psychological and social science studies that journalists uncritically report are based on much smaller and nonrandom samples. And Hite specifically states in the book that the numbers are *not* meant to be representative; her goal, she writes, is simply to give as many women as possible a public forum to voice their intimate, and generally silenced, thoughts. The book is actually more a collection of quotations than numbers. . . .

If anything, the media seemed to be bearing out the women's complaint by turning a deaf ear to their words. Maybe it was easier to flip through Hite's numerical tables at the back of the book than to digest the hundreds of pages of rich and disturbing personal stories. Or perhaps some journalists just couldn't stand to hear what these women had to say; the overheated denunciations of Hite's book suggest an emotion closer to fear than fury – as do the illustrations accompanying *Time*'s story, which included a woman standing on the chest of a collapsed man, a woman dropping a shark in a man's bathwater, and a woman wagging a viperish tongue in a frightened male face.

At the same time the press was pillorying Hite for suggesting that male resistance might be partly responsible for women's grief, it was applauding an-other social scientist whose theory – that women's equality was to blame for contemporary women's anguish – was more consonant with backlash thinking. Psychologist Dr. Srully Blotnick, a *Forbes* magazine columnist and much quoted media "expert" on women's career travails, had directed what he called "the largest long-term study of working women ever done in the United States." His conclusion: success at work "poisons" both the professional and personal lives of women." In his 1985 book, *Otherwise Engaged: The Private Lives of Successful Women,* Blotnick asserted that his twenty-five year study of 3,466 women proved that achieving career women are likely to end up without love, and their spinsterly misery would eventually undermine their careers as well. "In fact," he wrote, "we found that the anxiety, which steadily grows, is the single greatest underlying cause of firing for women in the age range of thirty-five to fifty-five." He took some swipes at the women's movement, too, which he called a "smoke screen behind which most of those who were afraid of being labeled egomaniacally grasping and ambitious hid."[2]

The media received his findings warmly – he was a fixture everywhere . . . national magazines like *Forbes* and *Savvy* paid him hundreds of thousands of dollars to produce still more studies about these anxiety-ridden careerists. None doubted his methodology – even though there were some fairly obvious grounds for skepticism.

For starters, Blotnick claimed to have begun his data collection in 1958, a year in which he would have been only seventeen years old. On a shoestring budget, he had somehow personally collected a voluminous data base ("three tons of files, plus twenty-six gigabytes on disk memory," he boasted in *Otherwise Engaged*) – more data than the largest federal longitudinal studies with multimillion-dollar funding. And the "Dr." in his title was similarly bogus; it turned out to be the product of a mail-order degree from an unaccredited correspondence school. When tipped off, the editors at *Forbes* discreetly dropped the "Dr." from Blotnick's by-line – but not his column.

In the mid-80's, Dan Collins, a reporter at *U.S. News & World Report,* was assigned a story on that currently all-popular media subject: the misery of the unwed. His editor suggested he call the ever quotable Blotnick, who had just appeared in a similar story on the woes of singles in the *Washington Post*. After his interview, Collins recalls, he began to wonder why Blotnick had seemed so nervous when he asked for his academic credentials. The reporter looked further into Blotnick's background and found what he thought was a better story: the career of this national authority was built on sand. Not only was Blotnick not a licensed psychologist, almost nothing on his resume checked out; even the professor that he cited as his current mentor had been dead for fifteen years.

But Collins's editors at *U.S. News* had no interest in that story . . . and the article was never published. Finally, a year later, after Collins had moved to the *New York Daily News* in 1987, he persuaded his new employer to print the piece.[3] Collins's account prompted the state to launch a criminal fraud investigation against Blotnick, and *Forbes* discontinued Blotnick's column the very next day. But news of Blotnick's improprieties and implausibilities made few waves in the press; it inspired only a brief new item in *Time*, nothing in *Newsweek*. And Blotnick's publisher, Viking Penguin, went ahead with plans to print a paperback edition of his latest book anyway. . . . Viking's executive editor explained at the time, "Blotnick has some very good insights into the behavior of people in business that I continue to believe have an empirical basis."[4]

The press's treatment of Hite's and Blotnick's findings suggest that the statistics the popular culture chooses to promote most heavily are the very statistics we should view with the most caution. They may well be in wide circulation not because they are true but because they support widely held media preconceptions. . . .

Valentine's Day 1986 was coming up, and at the Stamford *Advocate*, it was reporter Lisa Marie Petersen's turn to produce that year's story on Cupid's slings and arrows. Her "angle," as she recalls later, would be "Romance: Is It In or Out?" She went down to the Stamford Town Center mall and interviewed a few men shopping for flowers and chocolates. Then she put in a call to the Yale sociology department, "just to get some kind of foundation," she says. "You know, something to put in the third paragraph."[5]

She got Neil Bennett on the phone – a thirty-one-year-old unmarried sociologist who had recently completed, with two colleagues, an unpublished study on women's marriage patterns. Bennett warned her the study wasn't really finished, but when she pressed him, he told her what he had found: college-educated women who put schooling and careers before their wedding date were going to have a harder time getting married. "The marriage market unfortunately may be falling out from under them," he told her.

Bennett brought out the numbers: never married college-educated women at thirty had a 20 percent chance of being wed; by thirty-five their odds were down to 6 percent; by forty, to 1.3 percent. And black women had even lower odds. "My jaw just dropped," recalls Petersen, who was twenty-seven and single at the time. Petersen never thought to question the figures. "We usually just take anything from good schools. If it's a study from Yale, we just put it in the paper."[6]

The *Advocate* ran the news on the front page.[7] The Associated Press immediately picked up the story and carried it across the nation and eventually around the world. In no time, Bennett was fielding calls from Australia.

In the United States, the marriage news was absorbed by every outlet of mass culture. The statistics received front-page treatment in virtually every major newspaper and top billing on network news programs and talk shows. . . . Even a transit advertising service . . . plastered the study's findings on display racks in city buses around the nation, so single straphangers on their way to work could gaze upon a poster of a bereft lass in a bridal veil, posed next to a scorecard listing her miserable nuptial odds.

Bennett and his colleagues, Harvard economist David Bloom and Yale graduate student Patricia Craig, predicted a "marriage crunch" for baby-boom college-educated women for primarily one reason: women marry men an average of between two and three years older. So, they reasoned, women born in the first half of the baby boom between 1946 and 1957, when the birthrate was increasing each year, would have to scrounge for men in the less populated older age brackets. And those education-minded women who decided to get their diplomas before their marriage license would wind up worst off, the researchers postulated – on the theory that the early bird gets the worm.

At the very time the study was released, however, the assumption that women marry older men was rapidly becoming outmoded; federal statistics now showed first-time brides marrying grooms an average of only 1.8 years older. But it was impossible to revise the Harvard-Yale figures in light of these changes, or even to examine them – since the study wasn't published. This evidently did not bother the press, which chose to ignore a published study on the same subject – released only a few months earlier – that came to the opposite conclusion. That study, an October 1985 report by researchers at the University of Illinois, concluded that the marriage crunch in the United States was minimal. Their data, the researchers wrote, "did not support theories which see the marriage squeeze as playing a major role in recent changes in marriage behavior."[8] . . .

In March, 1986, Bennett and his co-researchers released an informal "discussion paper" that revealed they had used a "parametric model" to compute women's marital odds – an unorthodox and untried method for predicting behavior. Princeton professors Ansley Coale and Donald McNeil had originally constructed the parametric model to analyze marital patterns of elderly women who had already completed their marriage cycle. Bennett and Bloom, who had been graduate students under Coale, thought they could use the same method to predict marriage patterns. Coale, asked about it later, was doubtful. "In principle, the model may be applicable to women who haven't completed their marital history," he says, "but it is risky to apply it."[9]

To make matters worse, Bennett, Bloom, and Craig took their sample of women from the 1982 Current Population Survey, an off year in census data collection that taps a much smaller number of households than the decennial census study. The researchers broke that sample down into ever smaller subgroups – by age, race, and education – until they were making generalizations based on small unrepresentative samples of women.

As news of the "man shortage" study raced through the media, Jeanne Moorman, a demographer in the U.S. Census Bureau's marriage and family statistics branch, kept getting calls from reporters seeking comment. She decided to take a closer look at the researchers' paper. A college-educated woman with a doctoral degree in marital demography, Moorman was herself an example of how individuals defy demographic pigeonholes: she had married at thirty-two, to a man nearly four years younger.

Moorman sat down at her computer and conducted her own marriage study, using conventional standard-life tables instead of the parametric model, and drawing on the 1980 Population Census, which includes 13.4 million households, instead of the 1982 survey that Bennett used, which includes only 60,000 households. The results: At thirty, never-married college women have a 58 to 66 percent chance at marriage – three times the Harvard-Yale study's predictions. At thirty-five, the odds were 32 to 41 percent, seven times higher than the Harvard-Yale figure. At forty, the odds were 17 to 23 percent, *twenty-three* times higher. And she found that a college-educated single woman at thirty would be *more* likely to marry than her counterpart with a high-school diploma.

In June 1986, Moorman wrote to Bennett with her findings. She pointed out that more recent data ran counter to his predictions about college-educated women. While the marriage rate has been declining in the general populations, the rate has actually risen for women with four or more years of college who marry between ages twenty-five and forty-five. "This seems to indicate delaying rather than forgoing marriage," she noted.

Moorman's letter was polite, almost deferential. . . . Two months passed. Then, in August, writer Ben Wattenberg mentioned Moorman's study in his syndicated newspaper column and noted that it would be presented at the Population Association of America Conference, an important professional gathering for demographers.[10] . . . Suddenly, a letter arrived in Moorman's mailbox. "I understand from Ben Wattenberg that you will be presenting these results at the PAA in the spring," Bennett wrote; would she send him a copy "as soon as it's available?" When she didn't send it off at once, he called and, Moorman recalls, "He was very demanding. It was, 'You have to do this, you have to do that.'"[11] This was to become a pattern in her dealings with Bennett. . . .

Moorman . . . put the finishing touches on her marriage report with the more optimistic findings and released it to the press.[12] The media relegated it to the inside pages when they reported it at all. At the same time, in an op-ed piece printed in the *New York Times*, the *Boston Globe*, and *Advertising Age*, Bennett and Bloom roundly attacked Moorman for issuing her study, which only "further muddled the discussion," they complained. . . .

Bennett and Bloom's essay . . . criticized Moorman for using the standard-life tables, which they labeled a "questionable technique."[13] So Moorman decided to repeat her study using the Harvard-Yale men's own parametric model. She took the data down the hall to Robert Fay, a statistician whose specialty is mathematical models. Fay looked over Bennett and Bloom's computations and immediately spotted a major error. They had forgotten to factor in the different patterns in college- and high school-educated women's marital histories. (High school-educated women tend to marry in a tight cluster right after graduation . . . College-educated women tend to spread out the age of marriage over a longer and later period of time . . .) Fay made the adjustments and ran the data again, using Bennett and Bloom's mathematical model. The results this time were nearly identical to Moorman's.

So Robert Fay wrote a letter to Bennett. He pointed out the error and its significance. . . . Bennett wrote back the next day. "Things have gotten grossly out of hand," he said. "I think it's high time that we get together and regain at least some control of the situation." He blamed the press for their differences and pointedly noted that "David [Bloom] and I decided to stop entirely our dealings with all media,"[14] a hint perhaps that the Census researchers should do the same. But Bennett needn't have worried about his major error making headlines: Moorman had, in fact, already mentioned it to several reporters, but none were interested. . . .

In all the reportorial enterprise expended on the Harvard-Yale study, the press managed to overlook a basic point: there was no man shortage. As a simple check of the latest Census population charts would have revealed, there were about 1.9 million more bachelors than unwed women between the ages of twenty-five and thirty-four and about a half million more between the ages of thirty-five and fifty-four. In fact, the proportion of never-married men was larger than at any time since the Census Bureau began keeping records in 1890. If anyone faced a shortage of potential spouses, it was *men* in the prime marrying years: between the ages of twenty-four and thirty-four, there were 119 single men for every 100 single women. . . .

If the widespread promotion of the Harvard-Yale marriage study had one effect, it was to transfer much of this bachelor anxiety into single women's minds. In the *Wall Street Journal*, a thirty-six-year-old single woman remarked that being unmarried "didn't bother me at all" until *after* the marriage study's promotion; only then did she begin feeling depressed.[15] A thirty-five-year-old woman told *USA Today*, "I hadn't even thought about getting married until I started reading those horror stories" about women who may never wed.[16] In a *Los Angeles Times* story, therapists reported that after the study's promotion, single female patients became "obsessed" with marriage, ready to marry men they didn't even love, just to beat the "odds."[17] . . . The Annual Study of Women's Attitudes conducted by Mark Clements Research for many women's magazines, found that the proportion of all single women who feared they would never marry had nearly doubled in that one year after the Harvard-Yale study came out, from 14 to 27 percent, and soared to 39 percent for women twenty-five and older, the group targeted in the study.

The year after the marriage report, news surfaced that women's age at first marriage had dropped slightly and, reversing a twenty-year trend, the number of family households had grown faster between 1986 and 1987 than the number of non-family households. . . . These small changes were immediately hailed as a sign of the comeback of traditional marriage. "A new traditionalism, centered on family life, is in the offing," Jib Fowles, University of Houston professor of human sciences, cheered in a 1988 opinion piece in the *New York Times*. Fowles predicted "a resurgence of the conventional family . . . (father working, mother at home with the children)." This would be good for American industry he reminded business magnates who might be reading the article. "Romance and courtship will be back in favor, so sales of cut flowers are sure to rise," he pointed out. And "a return to homemaking will mean a rise in supermarket sales."[18]

This would also be good news for men, a point that Fowles skirted in print but made plain enough in a later interview: "There's not even going to have to be a veneer of that ideology of subscribing to feminist thoughts," he says. "Men are just going to feel more comfortable with the changed conditions. Every sign that I can see is that men feel uncomfortable with the present setup." He admits to being one of them: "A lot of it has to do with my assumption of what it is to be a male."[19]

But will his wife embrace the "new traditional-ism" with equal relish? Having recently given birth to their second child, she returned immediately to her post as secondary education coordinator for a large Texas school district. "She's such a committed person to her job," Fowles says, sighing. "I don't think she'd give up her career."

Notes

[1] Shere Hite, *Women and love: A cultural revolution in progress.* (New York: Knopf, 1987), pp. 12, 39, 41–42, 39, 79, 96, 99, and 774–778.

[2] Srully Blotnick, *Otherwise engaged: The private lives of successful career women.* (New York: Penguin Books, 1985), pp. viii, xii, 265, 278, 316, and 323–324.

[3] Dan Collins, Is he handing readers a line? *New York Daily News,* July 19, 1987, p. 4.

[4] See "Secret of a Success," *Time,* Aug. 3, 1987, p. 61.

[5] Personal interview with Lisa Marie Petersen, Nov. 1989.

[6] Ibid.

[7] Lisa Marie Petersen, They're falling in love, again, say marriage counselors. Stamford (Conn.) *Advocate,* Feb. 14, 1986, p. A1.

[8] R. Schoen and J. Baj, Impact of the marriage squeeze in five western countries (pp. 8–19). *Sociology and Social Research,* 1985, 70(1).

[9] Personal interview with Ansley Coale, June, 1986.

[10] Ben Wattenberg, New data on women, marriage. *Newspaper Enterprise Association,* Aug. 27, 1986.

[11] Personal interviews with Jeanne Moorman, June, 1986, May, 1988, September, 1989.

[12] Jeanne E. Moorman, *The history and the future of the relationship between education and marriage.* (Washington, D.C.: U.S. Bureau of the Census, Dec. 1, 1986).

[13] Neil G. Bennett and David E. Bloom, Why fewer women marry. *Advertising Age,* March 2, 1987, p. 18.

[14] Letter from Neil Bennett to Jeanne Moorman, March 3, 1987.

[15] J. S. Lublin, Staying single: Rise in never marrieds affects social customs and buying patterns. *The Wall Street Journal,* May 28, 1986, p.1.

[16] K. S. Peterson, Stop asking why I'm not married. *USA Today,* July 9, 1986, p. D4.

[17] Elizabeth Mehren, Frustrated by the odds, single women over 30 seek answers in therapy, *Los Angeles Times,* Nov. 30, 1986, Part VI, p. 1.

[18] Jib Fowles, Coming soon, more men than women, *New York Times,* June 5, 1988, p. 3.

[19] Personal interview with Jib Fowles, June, 1988.

Gender in Nature

A common argument to justify the belief that men are superior to women is to say that in the natural world males are the larger of the two and they use their superior strength to protect the female who is therefore willing to be subordinate to the male. The author shows that this sort of thinking does not represent an accurate understanding of nature.

Alfred, Lord Tennyson, never known for egalitarian perspectives, had this to say about the relative merit of the sexes:

> Woman is the lesser man, and all
> thy passions, matched with mine,
> Are as moonlight unto sunlight, and
> as water unto wine.

The couplet may not represent Tennyson's considered view, since the protagonist of "Locksley Hall" had lost his love to another and speaks these words during a grand poetic fit of sour grapes. Still, the literal reading – that women are smaller than men – would be accepted by most of us as a general fact of nature, not as a sexist trap. And most of us would therefore be wrong.

Human males are, of course, generally larger than human females, and most familiar mammals follow the same patterns. Yet females are larger than males in a majority of animal species – and probably a large majority at that. For starters, most animal species are insects and female insects usually exceed their males in size. Why are males generally smaller?

One amusing suggestion was proposed in all seriousness just 100 years ago (as I discovered in the "50 and 100 Years Ago" column in *Scientific American* for January, 1982). A certain M. G. Delaunay argued that human races might be ranked by the relative social position of females. Inferior races suffered under female supremacy, males dominated in superior races, while equality of sexes marked races of middle rank. As collateral support for his peculiar theses, Delaunay argued that females are larger than males in "lower" animals and smaller in "higher" creatures. Thus, the greater number of species with larger females posed no threat to a general notion of male superiority. After all, many serve and few rule.

Delaunay's argument is almost too precious to disturb with refutation, but it's probably worth mentioning that the paradigm case of a "higher" group with larger males – the mammals – is shakier than most people think. Males are large in a majority of mammalian species, of course, but Katherine Ralls found a surprising number of species with larger females, spread widely throughout the range of mammalian diversity. Twelve of 20 orders and 20 of 122 families contain species with larger females. In some important groups, larger females are the rule: rabbits and hares, a family of bats, three families of baleen whales, a major group of seals, and two tribes of antelopes. Ralls further reminds us that since blue whales are the largest animals that have ever lived, and since females surpass males in baleen whales, the largest individual animal of all time is undoubtedly a female. The biggest reliably measured whale was 93.5 feet long and a female.[1]

The sporadic distribution of larger females within the taxonomic range of mammals illustrates the most important general conclusion we can reach about the relative size of sexes: the observed pattern does not suggest any general or overarching trend associating predominance of either sex with anatomical complexity, geological age, or supposed evolutionary state. Rather, the relative size of sexes seems to reflect an evolved strategy for each particular circumstance – an affirmation of Darwin's vision that evolution is primarily the story of adaptation to local environments. In this perspective, we must anticipate the usual pattern of larger females. Females, as producers of eggs, are usually more active than males in brooding their young. (Such male tenders as sea horses and various mouth-brooding fishes must receive eggs directly from a female or actively pick up eggs after a female discharges them.) Even in species that furnish no parental care, eggs must be provided with nutriment, while sperm is little more than naked DNA with a delivery system. Larger eggs require more room and a bigger body to produce them.

If females provide the essential nutriment for embryonic or larval growth, we might ask why males exist at all. Why bother with sex if one parent can supply the essential provisioning? The answer to this old dilemma seems to lie in the nature of Darwin's world. If natural selection propels evolution by preserving favored variants from a spectrum randomly distributed about an average value, then an absence of variation derails the process – for natural selection makes nothing directly and can only choose among alternatives presented. If all offspring were the xeroxed copies of a single parent, they would present no genetic variation (except for rare new mutations) and selection could not operate effectively. Sex generates an enormous array of variation by mixing the genetic material of two creatures in each offspring. If only for this reason, we shall have males to kick around for some time. . . .

The struggle for genetic representation in the next generation can be pursued in a variety of ways. One common strategy mimics the motto of rigged elections: vote early and vote often (but substitute "fornicate" for "vote"). Males who follow this tactic have no evolutionary rationale for large

size and complexity beyond what they need to locate a female as quickly as possible and to stick around. In such cases, we might expect to find males in their minimal state – a small device dedicated to the delivery of sperm. Nature, ever obliging, has provided us with some examples of what, but for the grace of natural selection, might have been my fate.

Consider a species so thinly spread out over such a broad area that males will rarely meet at the site of a female. Suppose also that females, as adults, move very little if at all: they may be attached to the substrate (barnacles, for example); they may live parasitically, within another creature; or they may feed by waiting and luring rather than by pursuit. And suppose finally that the surrounding medium can easily move small creatures about – as in the sea, with its currents and high density. Since males must find a stationary female, and since the medium in which they live can provide (or substantially aid) their transport, why be large? Why not find a female fast when still quite small and young and then hang on as a simple source of sperm? Why work and feed, and grow large and complex? Why not exploit the feeding female? All her offspring will still be 50 percent you.

Indeed, this strategy is quite common, although little appreciated by sentient mammals of different status, among marine invertebrates that either live at great depth (where food is scarce and populations very thinly spread), or place themselves in widely dispersed spots that are hard to locate (as in many parasites). Here we often encounter that ultimate in the expression of nature's more common tendency – females larger than males. The males become dwarfs, often less than one-tenth the length of females, and evolve a body suited primarily for finding females – a sperm delivery system of sorts.

A species of *Enteroxenos*, for example, a molluscan parasite that lives inside the gut of sea cucumbers (echinoderms related to sea urchins and starfishes), was originally described as a hermaphrodite, with both male and female organs. But J. Lutzen of the University of Copenhagen discovered that the male "organ" is actually the degenerated product of a separate dwarf male organism that found the parasitic female and attached permanently to her. The female *Enteroxenos* fastens herself to the sea cucumber's esophagus by a small ciliated tube. The dwarf male finds the tube, enters the female's body, attaches to it in a particular place, and then loses virtually all its organs except, of course, for the testes. After a male enters, the female breaks its tubular connection with the sea cucumber's esophagus, thereby obliterating the pathway of entrance for any future males. . . .

As long as such an uncomfortable phenomenon resides with unfamiliar and "lowly" invertebrates, male supremacists who seek pseudosupport from nature may not be greatly disturbed. But I am delighted to tell a similar story about one group of eminently suited vertebrates – deep-sea anglerfishes of the Ceratioidei (a large group with 11 families and nearly 100 species).

Ceratioid anglerfishes have all the prerequisites for evolving dwarf males as sperm delivery systems. They live at depth in the open ocean, mostly from 3,000 to 10,000 feet below the surface, where food is scarce and populations sparse. Females have detached the first dorsal fin ray and moved it forward over their capacious mouth. They dangle a lure at the tip of this spine and literally fish with it. They jiggle and wave the lure while floating, otherwise immobile, in the midst of the sea. The related shallower-water and bottom-dwelling anglerfishes often evolve elaborate mimetic structures for their lures – bits of tissue that resemble worms or even a decoy fish. Ceratioids live well below the depth that light can penetrate sea water. Their world is one of total ambient darkness, and they must therefore provide the light of attraction themselves. Their lures glow with a luminescence supplied by light glands – a death trap for prey and, perhaps, a beacon for dwarf males.

In 1922, B. Saemundsson, an Icelandic fisheries biologist, dredged a female *Ceratias holbolli*, 26.16 inches in length. To his surprise, he found two small anglerfish, only 2.03 and 2.10 inches long, attached to the female's skin. He assumed, naturally, that they were juveniles, but he was puzzled by their degenerate form: "At first sight," he wrote, "I thought these young ones were pieces of skin torn off and loose." Another oddity puzzled him even more: these small fish were so firmly attached that their lips had grown together about a wad of female tissue projecting well into their mouths and down their throats. Saemundsson could find no other language for his description but an obviously inappropriate mammalian analogy: "The lips are grown

together and are attached to a soft papilla or 'teat' protruding so far as I can see, from the belly of the mother."

Three years later, the great British ichthyologist C. Tate Regan, then keeper of fishes and later boss of the British Museum (Natural History), solved Saemundsson's dilemma. The "young ones" were not juveniles, but permanently attached, sexually mature dwarf males. As Regan studied the details of attachment between male and female, he discovered the astounding fact that has ever since been celebrated as one of the greatest oddities in natural history: "At the junction of the male and the female fish there is a complete blending . . . their vascular systems are continuous."[2] In other words, the male has ceased to function as an independent organism. It no longer feeds, for its mouth is fused with the female's outer skin. The vascular systems of male and female have united, and the tiny male is entirely dependent upon the female's blood for nutrition. . . .

The extent of male submergence has been exaggerated in most popular accounts. Although attached males surrender their vascular independence and lose or reduce a set of organs no longer needed (eyes, for example), they remain more than a simple penis. Their own hearts must still pump the blood now supplied by females, and they continue to breathe with their gills and remove wastes with their kidneys. . . . Nevertheless, however autonomous, the males have evolved no mechanism for excluding other males from subsequent attachment. Several males are often embedded into a single female. . . .

As I sit here wiggling my toes and flexing my fingers in glorious independence (and with a full one-inch advantage over my wife), I am tempted (but must resist) to apply the standards of my own cherished independence and to pity the poor fused male. It may not be much of a life in our terms, but it keeps several species of anglerfishes going in a strange and difficult environment. And who can judge anyway? In some ultimate Freudian sense, what male could resist the fantasy of life as a penis with a heart, deeply and permanently embedded within a caring and providing female? These anglerfishes represent, in any case, only the extreme expression of nature's more common pattern – smaller males pursuing an evolutionary role as sources of sperm. Do they not, therefore, teach us a generality by their very exaggeration of it? We human males are the oddballs.

I therefore take my leave of fused anglerfishes with a certain sense of awe. Have they not discovered and irrevocably established for themselves what, according to Shakespeare, "every wise man's son doth know – journeys end in lovers meeting?"

Notes

[1]Katherine Ralls, Mammals in which females are larger than males, *Quarterly Review of Biology* 51(1976), pp. 245–276.

[2]C. Tate Regan, Dwarfed males parasitic on the females in oceanic anglerfishes (Pediculati: Ceratioidea). *Proceedings of the Royal Society* Series B 97 (1925), pp. 386–400.

Self-Made Man

The author is a lesbian writer who disguised herself as a man called "Ned" and went out into society in this disguise for a two-year period. In this excerpt, she has decided to join a bowling league so that she can quickly become acquainted with a number of men in an all-male setting where the men will be comfortable expressing themselves.

I'd chosen well in choosing a bowling alley. It was just like every other bowling alley I'd ever seen; it felt familiar. The decor was lovingly down at heel and generic to the last detail, like something out of a mail-order kit, complete with the cheap plywood paneling . . . There were the usual shabby cartoons of multicolored balls and pins flying through the air, and the posted scores of top bowlers. The lanes, too, were just as I remembered them, long and glistening with that mechanized maw scraping at the end.

And then, of course, there were the smells; cigarette smoke, varnish, machine oil, leaky toilets, old candy wrappers and accumulated public muck all commingling to produce that signature bowling alley scent that envelops you the moment you enter and clings to you long after. . . .

As I scoped the room . . . I could see then that this was going to be laughable. (Men) were all throwing curve balls that they'd been perfecting for twenty years. I couldn't even remember how to hold a bowling ball, much less wing it with any precision . . .

I was surrounded by men who had cement dust in their hair and sawdust under their fingernails.

They had nicotine-sallowed faces that looked like ritual masks, and their hands were as tough and scarred as falcon gloves. These were men who, as one of them told me later, had been shoveling shit their whole lives. . . .

The league manager led me toward the table where my new teammates were sitting. As we approached, they all turned to face me.

Jim, my team captain, introduced himself first. He was about five feet six, a good four inches shorter than I am, with a lightweight build, solid shoulders, but skinny legs and oddly small feet – certainly smaller than mine. This made me feel better. He actually came across as diminutive. He wore his baseball cap high on his head, and a football jersey that draped over his jeans almost to his knees. He had a mustache and a neat goatee. Both were slightly redder than his light brown head of hair. He was thirty-three, but in bearing, he seemed younger. He wasn't a threat to anyone and he knew it, as did everyone who met him. But he wasn't a weak link either. He was the scrappy guy in the pickup basketball game.

As he extended his arm to shake my hand, I extended mine, too, in a sweeping motion. Our palms met with a soft *pop,* and I squeezed assertively the way I'd seen men do at parties when they gathered in someone's living room to watch a football game. From the outside, this ritual had always seemed overdone to me. Why all the macho ceremony? But from the inside it was completely different. There was something so warm and bonded in this handshake. Receiving it was a rush, an instant inclusion in a camaraderie that felt very old and practiced.

It was more affectionate than any handshake I'd ever received from a strange woman. To me, woman-to-woman introductions often seem fake and cold, full of limp gentility. I've seen a lot of women hug one another this way, too, sometimes even women who've known each other for a long time and think of themselves as being good friends. They're like two backward magnets pushed together by convention. Their arms and cheeks meet, and maybe the tops of their shoulders, but only briefly, the briefest time politeness will allow. It's done out of habit and for appearances, a hollow, even resentful, gesture bred into us and rarely felt.

This solidarity of sex was something that feminism tried to teach us, and something, it now seemed to me, that men figured out and perfected a long time ago. On some level men didn't need to learn or remind themselves that brotherhood was powerful. It was just something they seemed to know. . . .

Next I met Allen. His greeting echoed Jim's. It had a pronounced positive force behind it, a presumption of goodwill that seemed to mark me as a buddy from the start, no questions asked, unless or until I proved otherwise.

"Hey man," he said, "Glad to see you."

He was about Jim's height and similarly built. He had the same goatee and mustache, too. He was older, though, and looked it. At forty-four, he was a study in substance abuse and exposure to the elements. His face was permanently flushed and pocked with open pores; a cigarette-, alcohol- and occupation-induced complexion that his weather-bleached blond hair and eyebrows emphasized by contrast.

Bob I met last. We didn't shake hands, just nodded from across the table. He was short, too, but not lean. He was forty-two and he had a serious middle-aged belly filling out his T-shirt, the unbeltable kind that made you wonder what held up his pants. He had sizable arms, but no legs or ass, the typical beer-hewn silhouette. He had a ragged salt-and-pepper mustache, and wore large glasses with no-nonsense metal frames and slightly tinted aviator lenses.

He wasn't the friendly type. . . .

Being Ned, I had to get used to a different mode (of communication). The discord between my girlish ways and the male cues I had to learn on the fly was often considerable in my mind. For example, our evenings together always started out slowly with a few grunted hellos that among women would have been interpreted as rude. This made my female antennae twitch a little. Were they pissed off at me about something?

But among those guys no interpretation was necessary. Everything was out and aboveboard, never more, never less than what was on anyone's mind. If they were pissed at you, you'd know it. These gruff greetings were indicative of nothing so much as fatigue and appropriate male distance. They were glad enough to see me, but not glad enough to miss me if I didn't show.

Besides, they were coming from long, wearying workdays, usually filled with hard physical labor and the slow, soul-deadening deprecation that comes of being told what to do all day by someone you'd like to strangle. . . . None of them got much satisfaction from their jobs, nor did they expect any. Work was just something they did for their families and for the few spare moments it afforded them in front of the football game on Sundays, or at the bowling alley on Mondays. Jim lived in a trailer park and Allen had lived in one for much of his life, though now it was unclear where he was living. Bob never said where he lived. As always, Jim cracked jokes about his class. With his usual flip wit, he called trailer parks "galvanized ghettos," and Allen chimed in about living in a shithole full of "wiggers," or "white niggers," themselves being foremost among them.

In my presence, none of them ever used the word "nigger" in any other context, and never spoke disrespectfully of black people. In fact, contrary to popular belief, white trash males being the one minority it is still socially acceptable to vilify, none of these guys was truly racist as far as I could tell, or certainly no more than anyone else.

As usual, Jim told a funny story about this. He said that he'd been coming out of a bar late one night, and a black guy had approached him asking for money. He's emerged from a wooded area behind the bar that was well known as one of (the) crack dens in the area. The guy said to Jim, "Hey man. Don't be afraid of me because I'm black, okay. I just wondered if you had some money to spare."

"I'm not afraid of you because you're black," Jim shot back. "I'm afraid of you because you came out of those woods."

They took people at face value. If you did your job or held up your end, and treated them with the passing respect they accorded you, you were all right. If you came out of the woods, you were shady no matter what your color. . . . They were rock bottom utilitarians. Either a guy was good and did what he was hired to do, or he wasn't, and that alone was the basis on which you judged his worth.

The only time I heard the term "reverse discrimination" mentioned, Jim was telling a story, as he did from time to time, about his stint in the army. He'd been promoted to the position of gunner, apparently, and had occupied the post proficiently for some time, when a new superior officer, a black man, was installed in his unit. Jim found himself demoted to KP and a whole host of other shit jobs soon thereafter.

"The guy had taken everyone out of their posts and put all his black friends in them instead," Jim said. "It was blatant discrimination. So I went to the sergeant in charge, who was a black guy and very fair, and told him all about it. He consulted the evidence and told me I was right, and put me back in my position."

Everyone nodded around the table and that was that.

Exposing my own prejudices, I had expected these guys to be filled with virulent hatred for anyone who wasn't like them, taking their turn to kick the next guy down. But the only consistent dislike I ever saw in them was for comparatively wealthy clients for whom they'd done construction, plumbing or carpentry work and the like. But even here they mostly laughed at the indignities inflicted on them . . .

Bob told a funny story about a buddy of his getting a wicked case of the shits on a job and being summarily denied the use of the "old lady's toilet." There was nothing for it, so as Bob described it, the guy took a newspaper and a bucket into the back of their van and camped out. After a while the old lady, wanting to know why they took an unauthorized work stoppage, burst into the van, only to happen upon a very unsavory scene that sent her shrieking from the premises, denouncing the men as barbarians.

There were the occasional gay or sexist jokes, but (these) were never mean-spirited. . . . They each had the usual stories about being propositioned by a gay man, or happening on a gay bar unawares, but they told them with the same disarming bemusement and self-abasement as they told the stories about the habitually mysterious ways of rich people. Gay people and their affairs didn't much interest them, and if gays were the butt of a joke now and then, so was everyone else, including, and most often, themselves. . . .

Nothing was beyond humor, especially for Jim . . . "I remember when I was in the army," he'd say, "and I was drunk off my ass as usual. And there was this huge guy playin' pool in the bar I was in. And I don't know why, but I just flicked a beer coaster at him, and it hit him right in the back of the head. And he turned around really slowly and he looked down at me and he said in this really tired way, 'Do we really need to do this tonight?' And I said, 'Nah, you're right. We don't. Sorry.' So he turned around, and fuck me if I didn't throw another one and hit him again, right in the back of the head. I don't know why I did it. And I knew when I did it that he was gonna kick my ass, so I turned round and tried to run, and I slipped in a puddle of beer and fell on my face, and he just picked me right up and bashed the shit out of me. And the funniest thing about it was that the whole time he was punching me, he kept apologizing to me for having to do it."

This was a source of hilarity to everyone, the stupid crap you felt compelled to do as a guy finding your spot in the scheme of things, and the obligatory beatings you had to give or take. But only Jim really had enough perspective to admit the folly of his masculinity, and to fully appreciate the absurdity of brutish necessity in the male-on-male world. A guy whom you'd just provoked twice, and who'd warned you not to trespass had no choice but to beat you if you crossed the line. That was just how it was among men, and Jim mocked it lovingly.

Bob was more guarded. He didn't readily admit his mistakes or the missteps he'd made in the past. Instead, he held the world at arm's length, projecting a kind of terse authority from his barrel chest, just nodding or frowning at something you'd say. . . . But when it came to something that Bob felt more confident about, he'd engage you. Not that Bob's engagements were ever long or involved, but they packed a rhetorical punch. I asked him once if his workplace was unionized, and his answer surprised me. . . .

"No," he said, "My shop isn't union."

"Why not?" I asked.

"Unions are for the lazy man."

"Why's that?"

"Because they're all about seniority," he said, pausing for effect. "I'll give you an example," he went on. "One place I worked was union, and it was run on the seniority system. The guys who'd been there the longest had the most clout, which meant that when there were layoffs, they'd always have better standing. There was one guy like that there who'd been there forever . . . He used to just hang out and read the newspaper. Never did a lick of work. Meanwhile, I worked my ass off all day long. But when it came time to let people go, I was let go and he wasn't. Now that's not fair, is it?"

"No," I agreed, "It isn't."

I tried to engage him further on the question, but as I came to understand, you'd always know when a conversation with Bob was over. . . .

The bowling part of the evening was clearly secondary to the beer and the downtime with the boys at the table, smoking and talking shit. They cared about their game and the team's standing – more than they let on – but as Jim jokingly put it to me as a way of making me feel better for being the worst bowler any of them had ever seen, the league was really just an excuse to get away from their wives for the evening. . . . Still, they warmed to me more and more as my bowling improved. . . .

They took me under their wings. Another older bowler had also done this. Taking me aside between rounds, he tried to teach me a few things to improve my game. This was male mentor stuff all the way. He treated me like a son, guiding me with firm encouragement and solid advice, an older man lending a younger man his expertise.

This was commonplace. During the course of the bowling season, which lasted nine months, a lot of men from the other teams tried to give me tips on my game. My teammates were constantly doing this, increasingly so as the season wore on. There was a tension in the air that grew up around me as I failed to excel, a tension that I felt keenly, but that seemed unrecognizable to the guys themselves. I

had good frames, sometimes even good whole games, but I still had a lot of bad ones, too, and that frustrated us all. . . .

As men they felt compelled to fix my ineptitude rather than be secretly happy about it and try to abet it under the table, which is what a lot of female athletes of my acquaintance would have done. I remember this from playing sports with and against women all my life. No fellow female athlete ever tried to help me with my game or give me tips. It was every woman for herself. It wasn't enough that you were successful. You wanted to see your sister fail. . . .

One summer when I was a maladjusted teenager, I went to a tennis camp in New Jersey that catered largely to rich princesses and their male counterparts. Most of them couldn't really play tennis on more than a country-club level. Their parents had sent them there to get rid of them. They just stood around most of the time posing for one another, showing off their tans. But I'd had a lot of private coaching in tennis by that time, and my strokes were fairly impressive for my age. I took the tennis pretty seriously.

As for posing, I looked like I'd been raised by wolverines.

The instructors used to videotape each of us playing, so that they could go over the tapes with us and evaluate our techniques. One day, my particular class of about twenty girls was standing around the television watching the tape, and the instructor was deconstructing my serve. He'd had a lot of negative things to say about most of the other girls' serves, but when it came to mine he raved unconditionally, playing my portion of the tape over and over again in slow motion.

At this, one of the prettiest girls in the group, no doubt exasperated by the repetition, said loudly enough for everyone to hear: "Well, I'd rather look the way I do and serve the way I do than serve the way she does and look the way she does."

Now that's female competitiveness at its finest.

But with these guys and with other male athletes I've known it was an entirely different conflict. Their coaching reminded me of my father's whose approach to fatherhood had always been about giving helpful, concrete advice. It was how he showed his affection. It was all bound up in a desire to see us do well. . . .

I guess that's what I respected about those guys the most. I was a stranger, and a nerd, but they cut me all the slack in the world, and they did it for no other reason that I could discern than that I was a good-seeming guy who deserved a chance, something life and circumstance had denied most of them.

I would never have predicted it, but part of me came to really enjoy those nights with the guys. Their company was like an anchor at the beginning of the week, something I could look forward to, an oasis where nothing would really be expected of me. Almost every interaction would be entirely predictable, and the ones that weren't were all the more precious for being rare. . . .

So much of what happens emotionally between men isn't spoken aloud, and so the outsider, especially the female outsider who is used to emotional life being overt and spoken, tends to assume that what isn't said isn't there. But it is there, and when you're inside it, it's as if you're suddenly hearing sounds that only dogs can hear.

I remember one night when I plugged into that subtext for the first time. A few lanes over, one of the guys was having a particularly hot game. I'd been oblivious to what was happening, mourning my own playing too much to watch anyone else. It was Jim's turn, and I noticed that he wasn't bowling . . . (and) all the other bowlers had sat down as well. . . . Then I realized that there was one guy stepping up to the lane. It was the guy who was having the great game. I looked up at the board and saw that he'd had strikes in every frame, and now he was on the tenth and final frame in which you get three throws if you strike or spare in the first two. He'd have to throw three strikes in a row on this one to earn a perfect score. . . .

It was a beautiful moment, totally still and reverent, a bunch of guys instinctively paying their respects to the superior athleticism of another guy.

That guy stepped up to the line and threw his three strikes, one after the other, each one met by mounting applause, then silence and stillness again, then on the final strike, an eruption, and every single guy in that room, including me, surrounded that player and moved in to shake his hand or pat him on the back. It was almost mystical, that telepathic intimacy and the communal joy that succeeded it. . . . The moment said everything all at once about how tacitly attuned men are to each other, and how much of this women miss when they look from the outside in.

Why Young Women Are More Conservative

The author's analysis of the pressures on young women was first published over 20 years ago; therefore, it provides a basis for assessing what has changed and what has not changed since it was written. Those believing much change has occurred on a particular issue should be able to provide evidence and examples to support their view.

If you had asked me a decade or more ago, I certainly would have said the campus was the first place to look for the feminist or any other revolution. I also would have assumed that student-age women, like student-age men, were much more likely to be activist and open to change than their parents. After all, campus revolts have a long and well-publicized tradition, from the students of medieval France, whose "heresy" was suggesting that the university be separate from the church, through the anti-colonial student riots of British India; from students who led the cultural revolution of the People's Republic of China, to campus demonstrations against the Shah of Iran. Even in this country, with far less tradition of student activism, the populist movement to end the war in Vietnam was symbolized by campus protests and mistrust of anyone over thirty.

It has taken me many years of traveling as a feminist speaker and organizer to understand that I was wrong about women, at least about women acting on their own behalf. In activism, as in so many other things, I had been educated to assume that men's cultural pattern was the natural or the only one. If student years were the peak time of rebellion and openness to change for men, then the same must be true for women. In fact, a decade of listening to every kind of women's group – from brown-bag lunchtime lectures organized by office workers to all-night rap sessions at campus women's centers; from housewives' self-help groups to campus rallies – has convinced me that the reverse is more often true. Women may be the one group that grows more radical with age. Though some students are big exceptions to this rule, women in general don't begin to challenge the politics of our own lives until later.

Looking back, I realize that this pattern has been true for my life, too. My college years were full of uncertainties and the personal conservatism that comes from trying to win approval and fit into the proper grown-up and womanly role, whether that means finding a well-to-do man to be supported by or a male to support. Nonetheless, I went right on assuming that brave exploring youth and cowardly conservative old age were the norms for everybody, and that I must be just an isolated and guilty accident. Though every generalization based on female culture has many exceptions, and should never be used as a crutch or excuse, I think we might be less hard on ourselves and each other as students, feel better about our potential for change as we grow older – and educate reporters who announce feminism's demise because its red-hot center is not on campus – if we figured out that for most of us as women, the traditional college period is an unrealistic and cautious time. Consider a few of the reasons.

As students, women are probably treated with more equality than we ever will be again. For one thing, we're consumers. The school is only too glad to get the tuitions we pay, or that our families or government grants pay on our behalf. With population rates declining because of women's increased power over childbearing, that money is even more vital to a school's existence. Yet more than most consumers, we're too transient to have much power as a group. If our families are paying our tuition, we may have even less power.

As young women, whether students or not, we're still in the stage most valued by male-dominant cultures: we have our full potential as workers, wives, sex partners, and childbearers.

That means we haven't yet experienced the life events that are most radicalizing for women: entering the paid-labor force and discovering how women are treated there; marrying and finding out that it is not yet an equal partnership; having children and discovering who is responsible for them and who is not; and aging, still a greater penalty for women than for men.

Furthermore, new ambitions nourished by the rebirth of feminism may make young women feel and behave a little like a classic immigrant group. We are determined to prove ourselves, to achieve academic excellence, and to prepare for interesting and successful careers. More noses are kept to more grindstones in an effort to demonstrate newfound abilities, and perhaps to allay suspicions that women still have to have more and better credentials than men. This doesn't leave much time for activism. Indeed, we may not yet know that it is necessary.

In addition, the very progress into previously all-male careers that may be revolutionary for women is seen as conservative and conformist by outside critics. Assuming male radicalism to be the measure of change, they interpret any concern with careers

as evidence of "campus conservatism." In fact, "dropping out " may be a departure for men, but "dropping in" is a new thing for women. Progress lies in the direction we have not been.

Like most groups of the newly arrived or awakened, our faith in education and paper degrees also has yet to be shaken. For instance, the percentage of women enrolled in colleges and universities has been increasing at the same time that the percentage of men has been decreasing. Among students entering college in 1978, women *outnumbered* men for the first time. This hope of excelling at the existing game is probably reinforced by the greater cultural pressure on females to be "good girls" and observe somebody else's rules.

Though we may know intellectually that we need to have new games with new rules, we probably haven't quite absorbed such facts as the high unemployment rate among female Ph.D.s; the lower average salary among women college graduates of all races than among counterpart males who graduated from high school or less; the middle-management ceiling against which even those eagerly hired new business-school graduates seem to bump their heads after five or ten years; and the barrier-breaking women in nontraditional fields who become the first fired when recession hits. Sadly enough, we may have to personally experience some of these reality checks before we accept the idea that lawsuits, activism, and group pressure will have to accompany our individual excellence and crisp new degrees.

Then there is the female guilt trip, student edition. If we're not sailing along as planned, it must be *our* fault. If our mothers didn't "do anything" with their educations, it must have been *their* fault. If we can't study as hard as we think we must (because women still have to be better prepared than men), and have a substantial personal and sexual life at the same time (because women are supposed to care more about relationships than men do), then we feel inadequate, as if each of us were individually at fault for a problem that is actually culture-wide.

I've yet to be on a campus where most women weren't worrying about some aspect of combining marriage, children, and a career. I've yet to find one where many men were worrying about the same thing. Yet women will go right on suffering from the double-role problem and terminal guilt until men are encouraged, pressured, or otherwise forced, individually and collectively, to integrate themselves into the "women's work" of raising children and homemaking. Until then, and until there are changed job patterns to allow equal parenthood, children will go right on growing up with the belief that only women can be loving and nurturing, and only men can be intellectual or active outside the home. Each half of the world will go on limiting the full range of its human talent.

Finally, there is the intimate political training that hits women in the teens and early twenties: the countless ways we are still brainwashed into assuming that women are dependent on men for our basic identities, both in our work and our personal lives, much more than vice versa. After all, if we're going to enter a marriage system that's still legally designed for a person and a half, submit to an economy in which women still average (far less than) men, and work mainly as support staff and assistants, or *co*-directors and *vice*-presidents at best, then we have to be convinced that we are not whole people on our own.

In order to make sure that we will see ourselves as half-people, and thus be addicted to getting our identity from serving others, society tries hard to convert us as young women into "man junkies"; that is, into people who are addicted to regular shots of male-approval and presence, both professionally and personally. We need a man standing next to us, actually and figuratively, whether it's at work, on a Saturday night, or throughout life. (If only men realized how little it matters *which* man is standing there, they would understand that this addiction depersonalizes them, too.) Given the danger to a male-dominant system if young women stop internalizing this political message of derived identity, it's no wonder that those who try to kick the addiction – and, worse yet, to help other women do the same – are likely to be regarded as odd or dangerous by everyone from parent to peers.

With all that pressure combined with little experience, it's no wonder that younger women are often less able to support each other. Even young women who espouse feminist goals as individuals may refrain from identifying themselves as "feminist": it's okay to want equal pay for yourself (just one small reform) but it's not okay to want equal

pay for women as a group (an economic revolution). Some retreat into individualized career obsession as a way of avoiding this dangerous discovery of shared experience with women as a group. Others retreat into the safe middle ground of "I'm not a feminist but, . . ." Still others become politically active, but only on issues that are taken seriously by their male counterparts.

The same lesson about the personal conservatism of younger women is taught by the history of feminism. If I hadn't been conned into believing the masculine stereotype of youth as the "natural" time for freedom and rebellion, a time of "sowing wild oats" that actually is made possible by the assurance of power and security later on, I could have figured out the female pattern of activism looking at women's movements of the past.

In this country, for instance, the nineteenth century wave of feminism was started by older women who had been through the radicalizing experience of getting married and becoming the legal chattel of their husbands (or the equally radicalizing experience of *not* getting married and being treated as spinsters). Most of them had also worked in the anti-slavery movement and learned from the political parallels between race and sex. In other countries, that wave was also led by women who were past the point of maximum pressure toward marriageability and conservatism.

Looking at the first decade of this second wave, it's clear that the early feminist activist and consciousness-raising groups of the 1960s were organized by women who had experienced the civil rights movement, or homemakers who had discovered that raising kids and cooking didn't occupy all their talents. While most campuses of the late sixties were still circulating the names of illegal abortionists privately (after all, abortion could damage our marriage value), slightly older women were holding press conferences and speak-outs about the reality of abortions (including their own, even though that often meant confessing to an illegal act) and demanding reform or repeal of anti-choice laws.

Though rape had been a quiet epidemic on campus for generations, younger women victims were still understandably fearful of speaking up and campuses encouraged silence in order to retain their reputation for safety with tuition-paying parents. It took many off-campus speak-outs, demonstrations against laws of evidence and police procedures, and testimonies in state legislatures before most student groups began to make demands on campus and local cops for greater rape protection. In fact, "date rape" – the common campus phenomenon of a young woman being raped by someone she knows, perhaps even by several students in a fraternity house – is now being exposed. Marital rape, a more difficult legal issue, was taken up several years ago. As for battered women and the attendant exposé of husbands and lovers as more statistically dangerous than unknown muggers in the street, that issue still seems to be thought of as a largely noncampus concern, yet at many of the colleges and universities where I've spoken, there has been at least one case within current student memory of a young woman beaten or murdered by a jealous lover.

This cultural pattern of youthful conservatism makes the growing number of older women going back to school very important. They are life examples and pragmatic activists who radicalize women young enough to be their daughters. Now that the median female undergraduate age in this country is twenty-seven because so many older women have returned, the campus is becoming a major place for cross-generational connections.

None of this should denigrate the courageous efforts of young women, especially women on campus, and the many changes they've pioneered. On the contrary, they should be seen as even more remarkable for surviving the conservative pressures, recognizing societal problems they haven't yet fully experienced, and organizing successfully in the midst of a transient student population. Every women's history course, rape hot line, or campus newspaper that is finally covering *all* the news; every feminist professor whose job has been created or tenure saved by student pressure, or male administrator whose consciousness has been permanently changed; every counselor who's stopped guiding women one way and men another; every lawsuit that's been fueled by student energies against unequal athletic funds or graduate school requirements: all those accomplishments are even more impressive when seen against the backdrop of the female pattern of activism.

Finally, it would help to remember that a feminist revolution rarely resembles a masculine-style one – just as a young woman's most radical act toward her mother (that is, connecting as women in order to help each other get some power) doesn't look much like a young man's most radical act toward his father (that is, breaking the father-son connection in order to separate identities or take over existing power).

It's those father-son conflicts at a generational, national level that have often provided the conventional definition of revolution; yet they've gone on for centuries without basically changing the role of the female half of the world. They have also failed to reduce the level of violence in society, since both father and sons have included some degree of aggressiveness and superiority to women in their definition of masculinity, thus preserving the anthropological model of dominance.

Furthermore, what current leaders and theoreticians define as revolutions usually are little more than taking over the army and the radio stations. Women have much more in mind than that. We have to uproot the sexual caste system that is the most pervasive power structure in society, and that means transforming the patriarchal values of those who run the institutions, whether they are politically the "right" or the "left," the fathers or the sons. This cultural part of the change goes very deep, and is often seen as too intimate, and perhaps too threatening, to be considered as either serious or possible. Only conflicts among men are "serious." Only a takeover of existing institutions is "possible."

That's why the definition of "political," on campus as elsewhere, tends to be limited to who's running for president, who's demonstrating against corporate investments in South Africa, or which is the "moral" side of some conventional revolution, preferably one that is thousands of miles away.

As important as such activities are, they are also the most comfortable ones when we're young. They provide a sense of virtue without much disruption in the power structure of our daily lives. Even when the most consistent energies on campus are actually concentrated around feminist issues, they may be treated as apolitical and invisible. Asked "What's happening on campus?" a student may reply, "The anti-nuke movement," even though that resulted in one demonstration of two hours, while student anti-rape squads have been patrolling the campus every night for two years and women's studies have begun to transform the very textbooks we read.

No wonder reporters and sociologists looking for revolution on campus often miss the depth of feminist change and activity that is really there. Women students themselves may dismiss it as not political and not serious. Certainly, it rarely comes in the masculine sixties style of bombing buildings or burning draft cards. In fact, it goes much deeper than protesting a temporary symptom – say, the draft – and challenges the right of one group to dominate another, which is the disease itself.

Young women have a big task of resisting pressures and challenging definitions. Their increasing success is a miracle of foresight and courage that should make us all proud. But they should know that they, too, may grow more radical with age.

One day, an army of gray-haired women may quietly take over the earth.

Feminism: A Movement to End Sexist Oppression

Studies have shown that many women who agree with various feminist goals and values refuse to use the term "feminist" to describe themselves. Since part of the problem is confusion about what feminism is, the author offers some clarification of that term and suggests that regardless of whether you call yourself a feminist, you can still be an advocate for feminism.

A central problem within feminist discourse has been our inability to either arrive at a consensus of opinion about what feminism is or accept definitions that could serve as points of unification. Without agreed upon definitions, we lack a sound foundation on which to construct theory or engage in overall meaningful praxis. Expressing her frustrations with the absence of clear definitions, Carmen Vasquez comments:

> We can't even agree on what a "Feminist" is, never mind what she would believe in and how she defines the principles that constitute honor among us. In key with the American capitalist obsession for individualism and anything goes so long as it gets you what you want. Feminism in America has come to mean to mean anything you like, honey. There are as many definitions of Feminism as there are feminists, some of my sisters say, with a chuckle. I don't think it's funny.[1]

It is not funny. It indicates a growing disinterest in feminism as a radical political movement. It is a despairing gesture expressive of the belief that solidarity between women is not possible. It is sign that the political naïveté which has traditionally characterized woman's lot in male-dominated culture abounds.

Most people in the United States think of feminism as a movement that aims to make women the social equals of men. This broad definition, popularized by the media and mainstream segments of the movement, raises problematic questions. Since men are not equals in white supremacist, capitalist, patriarchal class structure, which men do women want to be equal to? Do women share a common vision of what equality means? Implicit in this simplistic definition is a dismissal of race and class as factors that, in conjunction with sexism, determine the extent to which an individual will be discriminated against, exploited, or oppressed. Bourgeois white women interested in women's rights issues have been satisfied with simple definitions for obvious reasons. Rhetorically placing themselves in the same social category as oppressed women, they were not anxious to call attention to race and class privilege.

Women in lower class and poor groups, particularly those who are non-white, would not have defined feminism as women gaining social equality with men since they are continually reminded in

From *Feminist theory: From margin to center* (Boston: South End Press, 1984).

their everyday lives that all women do not share a common social status. Concurrently, they know that many males in their social groups are exploited and oppressed. Knowing that men in their groups do not have social, political, and economic power, they would not deem it "liberating" to share their social status. While they are aware that sexism enables men in their respective groups to have privileges denied them, they are more likely to see exaggerated expressions of male chauvinism among their peers as stemming from the male's sense of himself as powerless and ineffectual in relation to ruling male groups, rather than an expression of an overall privileged social status. From the very onset of the women's movement, these women were suspicious of feminism precisely because they recognized the limitations inherent in its definition. They recognized the possibility that feminism defined as social equality with men might easily become a movement that would primarily affect the social standing of white women in middle and upper class groups while affecting only in a very marginal way the social status of working class and poor women. . . .

In a San Francisco newspaper article, "Sisters Under the Skin," columnist Bob Greene commented on the aversion many women apparently have to the term feminism. Greene finds it curious that many women "who obviously believe in everything that proud feminists believe in dismiss the term 'feminist' as something unpleasant; something with which they do not wish to be associated." Even though such women often acknowledge that they have benefited from feminist-generated reform measures which have improved the social status of specific groups of women, they do not wish to be seen as participants in feminist movement:

> There is no getting around it. After all this time, the term "feminist" makes many bright, ambitious, intelligent women embarrassed and uncomfortable. They simply don't want to be associated with it.
>
> It's as if it has an unpleasant connotation that they want no connection with. Chances are if you were to present them with every mainstream feminist belief, they would go along with the beliefs to the letter – and even if they consider themselves feminists, they hasten to say no.[2]

Many women are reluctant to advocate feminism because they are uncertain about the meaning of the term. Other women from exploited and oppressed ethnic groups dismiss the term because they do not wish to be perceived as supporting a racist movement; feminism is often equated with white women's rights. Large numbers of women see feminism as synonymous with lesbianism; their homophobia leads them to reject association with any group identified as pro-lesbian. Some women fear the word "feminism" because they shun identification with any political movement, especially one perceived as radical. Of course there are women who do not wish to be associated with the women's rights movement in any form so they reject and oppose feminist movement. Most women are more familiar with negative perspectives on "women's lib" than the positive significations of feminism. It is this term's positive political significance and power that we must now struggle to recover and maintain.

Currently feminism seems to be a term without any clear significance. The "anything goes" approach to the definition of the word has rendered it practically meaningless. What is meant by "anything goes" is usually that any woman who wants social equality with men regardless of her political perspective (she can be a conservative right-winger or a communist) can label herself feminist. Most attempts at defining feminism reflect the class nature of the movement. Definitions are usually liberal in origin and focus on the individual woman's right to freedom and self-determination. In Barbara Berg's *The Remembered Gate: Origins of American Feminism,* she defines feminism as a "broad movement embracing numerous phases of woman's emancipation." However, her emphasis is on women gaining greater individual freedom. Expanding on the above definition, Berg adds:

> What is meant by "anything goes" is usually what any woman who wants social equality oppressive restrictions; freedom to express her thoughts fully and to convert them freely into action. Feminism demands the acceptance of women's right to individual conscience and judgment. It postulates that woman's essential worth stems from her common humanity and does not depend on the other relationships of her life.[3]

This definition of feminism is almost apolitical in tone; yet it is the type of definition many liberal women find appealing. It evokes a very romantic notion of personal freedom which is more acceptable than a definition that emphasizes radical political action.

Many feminist radicals now know that neither a feminism that focuses on woman as an autonomous human being worthy of personal freedom nor one that focuses on the attainment of equality of opportunity with men can rid society of sexism and male domination. Feminism is a struggle to end sexist oppression. Therefore, it is necessarily a struggle to eradicate the ideology of domination that permeates Western culture on various levels as well as a commitment to reorganizing society so that the self-development of people can take precedence over imperialism, economic expansion, and material desires. Defined in this way, it is unlikely that women would join feminist movement simply because we are biologically the same. A commitment to feminism so defined would demand that each individual participant acquire a critical political consciousness based on ideas and beliefs.

All too often the slogan "the personal is political" (which was first used to stress that woman's everyday reality is informed and shaped by politics and is necessarily political) became a means of encouraging women to think that the experience of discrimination, exploitation, or oppression automatically corresponded with an understanding of the ideological and institutional apparatus shaping one's social status. As a consequence, many women who had not fully examined their situation never developed a sophisticated understanding of their political reality and its relationship to that of women as a collective group. They were encouraged to focus on giving voice to personal experience. Like revolutionaries working to change the lot of colonized people globally, it is necessary for feminist activists to stress that the ability to see and describe one's own reality is a significant step in the long process of self-recovery; but it is only a beginning. When women internalized the idea that describing their own woe was synonymous with developing a critical political consciousness, the progress of feminist movement was stalled. Starting from such incomplete perspectives, it is not surprising that theories and strategies were developed that were collectively

inadequate and misguided. To correct this inadequacy in past analysis, we must now encourage women to develop a keen, comprehensive understanding of women's political reality. Broader perspectives can only emerge as we examine both the personal that is political, the politics of society as a whole, and global revolutionary politics.

Feminism defined in political terms that stress collective as well as individual experience challenges women to enter a new domain – to leave behind the apolitical stance sexism decrees is our lot and develop political consciousness. . . . By repudiating the popular notion that the focus of feminist movement should be social equality of the sexes and emphasizing eradicating the cultural basis of group oppression, our own analysis would require an exploration of all aspects of women's political reality. This would mean that race and class oppression would be recognized as feminist issues with as much relevance as sexism.

When feminism is defined in such a way that it calls attention to the diversity of women's social and political reality, it centralizes the experiences of all women, especially the women whose social conditions have been least written about, studied, or changed by political movements. When we cease to focus on the simplistic stance "men are the enemy," we are compelled to examine systems of domination and our role in their maintenance and perpetuation. . . .

Feminism is the struggle to end sexist oppression. Its aim is not to benefit solely any specific group of women, any particular race or class of women. It does not privilege women over men. It has the power to transform in a meaningful way all our lives. Most importantly, feminism is neither a lifestyle nor a ready-made identity or role one can step into. Diverting energy from feminist movement that aims to change society, many women concentrate on the development of a counter-culture, a woman-centered world wherein participants have little contact with men. Such attempts do not indicate a respect or concern for the vast majority of women who are unable to integrate their cultural expressions with the visions offered by alternative woman-centered communities. . . .

To emphasize that engagement with feminist struggle as political commitment we could avoid using the phrase "I am a feminist" (a linguistic structure designed to refer to some personal aspect of identity and self-definition) and could state "I advocate feminism." Because there has been undue emphasis placed on feminism as an identity or lifestyle, people usually resort to stereotyped perspectives on feminism. Deflecting attention away from stereotypes is necessary if we are to revise our strategy and direction. I have found that saying "I am a feminist" usually means I am plugged into preconceived notions of identity, role, or behavior. When I say "I advocate feminism" the response is usually "what is feminism?" A phrase like "I advocate" does not imply the kind of absolutism that is suggested by "I am." It does not engage us in the either/or dualistic thinking that is the central ideological component of all systems of domination in Western society. It implies that a choice has been made, that commitment to feminism is an act of will. It does not suggest that by committing oneself to feminism, the possibility of supporting other political movements is negated.

As a black woman interested in feminist movement, I am often asked whether being black is more important than being a woman; whether feminist struggle to end sexist oppression is more important than the struggle to end racism and vice-versa. All such questions are rooted in competitive either/or thinking, the belief that the self is formed in opposition to an *other*. Therefore one is a feminist because you are not something else. Most people are socialized to think in terms of opposition rather than compatibility. Rather than see anti-racist work as totally compatible with working to end sexist oppression, they are often seen as two movements competing for first place. When asked "Are you a feminist?" it appears that an affirmative answer is translated to mean that one is concerned with no political issues other than feminism. When one is black, an affirmative response is likely to be heard as a devaluation of struggle to end racism. Given the fear of being misunderstood, it has been difficult for black women and women in exploited and oppressed ethnic groups to give expression to their interest in feminist concerns. They have been wary of saying "I am a feminist." The shift in expression

from "I am a feminist" to "I advocate feminism" could serve as a useful strategy for eliminating the focus on identity and lifestyle. It could serve as a way for women who are concerned about feminism as well as other political movements to express their support while avoiding the linguistic structures that give primacy to one particular group. It would also encourage greater exploration in feminist theory. . . .

Feminism as a movement to end sexist oppression directs our attention to systems of domination and the inter-relatedness of sex, race, and class oppression. Therefore, it compels us to centralize the experiences and the social predicaments of women who bear the brunt of sexist oppression as a way to understand the collective social status of women in the United States. Defining feminism as a movement to end sexist oppression is crucial for the development of theory because it is a starting point indicating the direction of exploration and analysis.

The foundation of future feminist struggle must be solidly based on a recognition of the need to eradicate the underlying cultural basis and causes of sexism and other forms of group oppression. Without challenging and changing these philosophical structures, no feminist reforms will have a long-range impact. Consequently, it is now necessary for advocates of feminism to collectively acknowledge that our struggle cannot be defined as a movement to gain social equality with men; that terms like "liberal feminist" and "bourgeois feminist" represent contradictions that must be resolved so that feminism will not be continually co-opted to serve the opportunistic ends of special interest groups.

Notes

[1]Carmen Vasquez, Towards a Revolutionary Ethics, *Coming Up,* January, 1983, p. 11.

[2]Bob Greene, Sisters Under the Skin. *San Francisco Examiner,* May 15, 1983, p. 3.

[3]Barbara Berg, *The Remembered Gate: Origins of American Feminism.* (New York: Oxford University Press, 1979).

The Monkey Garden

Are there any consequences when a child becomes aware that he is a boy or she is a girl? The children in this short story enjoy playing in a garden until an incident occurs that forces the narrator to leave the garden, and her childhood, forever.

The monkey doesn't live there anymore. The monkey moved – to Kentucky – and took his people with him. And I was glad because I couldn't listen anymore to his wild screaming at night, the twangy yakkety-yak of the people who owned him. The green metal cage, the porcelain tabletop, the family that spoke like guitars. Monkey, family, table. All gone.

And it was then we took over the garden we had been afraid to go into when the monkey screamed and showed its yellow teeth.

There were sunflowers big as flowers on Mars, and thick cockscombs bleeding the deep red fringe of theater curtains. There were dizzy bees and bow-tied fruit flies turning somersaults and humming in the air. Sweet sweet peach trees. Thorn roses and thistle and pears. Weeds like so many squinty-eyed stars, and brush that made your ankles itch and itch until you washed with soap and water. There were big green apples hard as knees. And everywhere the sleepy smell of rotting wood, damp earth and dusty hollyhocks thick and perfumy like the blue-blond hair of the dead.

Yellow spiders ran when we turned rocks over, and pale worms blind and afraid of light rolled over in their sleep. Poke a stick in the sandy soil and a few blue-skinned beetles would appear, an avenue of ants, so many crusty ladybugs. This was a garden, a wonderful thing to look at in the spring. But bit by bit, after the monkey left, the garden began to take over itself. Flowers stopped obeying the little bricks that kept them from growing beyond their paths. Weeds mixed in. Dead cars appeared overnight like mushrooms. First one and then another and then a pale blue pickup with the front windshield missing. Before you knew it, the monkey garden became filled with sleepy cars.

Things had a way of disappearing in the garden, as if the garden itself ate them, or, as if with its old-man memory, it put them away and forgot them. Nenny found a dollar and a dead mouse between two rocks in the stone wall where the morning glories climbed, and once when we were playing hide and seek, Eddie Vargas laid his head beneath a hibiscus tree and fell asleep there like Rip Van Winkle until somebody remembered he was in the game and went back to look for him.

This, I suppose, was the reason why we went there. Far away from where our mothers could find us. We and a few old dogs who lived inside the empty cars. We made a clubhouse once on the back of that old blue pickup. And besides, we liked to jump from the roof of one car to another and pretend they were giant mushrooms.

Somebody started the lie that the monkey garden had been there before anything. We liked to think the garden could hide things for a thousand years. There beneath the roots of soggy flowers were the bones of murdered pirates and dinosaurs, the eye of a unicorn turned to coal.

This is where I wanted to die and where I tried one day, but not even the monkey garden would have me. It was the last day I would go there.

Who was it that said I was getting too old to play the games? Who was it I didn't listen to? I only remember that when the others ran, I wanted to run too, up and down and through the monkey garden, fast as the boys, not like Sally, who screamed if she got her stockings muddy.

I said, Sally, come on, but she wouldn't. She stayed by the curb talking to Tito and his friends. Play with the kids if you want, she said, I'm staying here. She could be stuck up like that if she wanted to, so I just left.

It was her own fault too. When I got back, Sally was pretending to be mad . . . something about the boys having stolen her keys. Please give them back to me, she said, punching the nearest one with a soft fist. They were laughing. She was too. It was a joke I didn't get.

I wanted to go back with the other kids who were still jumping on cars, still chasing each other through the garden, but Sally had her own game.

One of the boys invented the rules. One of Tito's friends said you can't get the keys back unless you kiss us, and Sally pretended to be mad at first but she said yes. It was that simple.

I don't know why, but something inside me wanted to throw a stick. Something wanted to say no when I watched Sally going into the garden with Tito's buddies all grinning. It was just a kiss, that's all. A kiss for each one. So what, she said.

Only how come I felt angry inside. Like something wasn't right. Sally went behind that old blue pickup to kiss the boys and get her keys back, and I ran up three flights of stairs to where Tito lived. His mother was ironing shirts. She was sprinkling water on them from an empty pop bottle and smoking a cigarette.

Your son and his friends stole Sally's keys and now they won't give them back unless she kisses them and right now they're making her kiss them, I said all out of breath from the three flights of stairs.

Those kids, she said, not looking up from her ironing.

That's all?

What do you want me to do, she said, call the cops? And kept on ironing.

I looked at her a long time, but couldn't think of anything to say, and ran back down the three flights to the garden, where Sally needed to be saved. I took three big sticks and a brick and figured this was enough.

But when I got there Sally said go home. Those boys said, leave us alone. I felt stupid with my brick. They all looked at me as if I was the one that was crazy and made me feel ashamed.

And then I don't know why but I had to run away. I had to hide myself at the other end of the garden, in the jungle part, under a tree that wouldn't mind if I lay down and cried a long time. I closed my eyes like tight stars so that I wouldn't, but I did. My face felt hot. Everything inside hiccupped.

I read somewhere that in India there are priests who can will their heart to stop beating. I wanted to will my blood to stop, my heart to quit its pumping. I wanted to be dead, to turn into the rain, my eyes melt into the ground like two black snails. I wished and wished. I closed my eyes and willed it, but when I got up my dress was green and I had a headache.

I looked at my feet in their white socks and ugly round shoes. They seemed far away. They didn't seem to be my feet anymore. And the garden that had been such a good place to play didn't seem mine either.

Perspectives on Sexual Orientation and Heterosexism

> ❝If some of us don't take on the oppressive labels and publicly prove them wrong, we'll stay trapped by stereotypes for the rest of our lives.❞
>
> **Dave Kopay (1942–)**

As a professional football player, Dave Kopay did not fit the labels or stereotypes traditionally used in reference to gay men, so it was especially important when he came out of the closet after he retired. Gay men and lesbians are athletes, teachers, doctors, lawyers, mechanics, plumbers, soldiers, retirees, and much more. Further, Harris (1990) reported on historical and anthropological research that has identified the presence of gay men and lesbians from the earliest times of recorded history up to the present.[1] Jamake Highwater (1997) noted that societies around the world have had varied cultural attitudes toward individuals who defined themselves as outside cultural norms with regard to their sexual orientation.[2] Regardless of cultural attitudes in societies today, Zeldin's review of the historical data concluded that homosexuals have not always been rejected and persecuted, but that two thirds of societies around the world at one time or another have accepted members who engaged in homosexual activity (1994).[3]

In the United States, however, gay men and lesbians have still not been accepted, and they continue to be associated with stereotypical identities assigned to them by a homophobic society. Today, individuals who happen to be gay or lesbian are defining themselves according to their own perceptions and definitions. Further, individuals who identify themselves as bisexual, transsexual, or transgender challenge others to develop a more complex understanding of the role of gender in shaping identity. Many have adopted the term "Queer" to refer to anyone who does not fit the traditional heterosexual norms, and they are challenging the appropriateness of traditional concepts such as normality and abnormality with regard to human emotions and sexual behaviors.

Although the struggle for civil rights for racial groups and women is not over, it has only begun for Lesbian, Gay, Bisexual, and Transgender (LGBT) people. For many years and in many countries, military leaders have engaged in the

> "Normal is just a cycle on a washing machine."
>
> Emmylou Harris (1947–)

hypocrisy of allowing closeted gay men the right to fight and possibly die for their country, but denied that right if they were openly gay. Although many nations today recruit openly gay men into the military, in the United States the hypocrisy was translated into a policy known as "Don't Ask, Don't Tell." In 2008, California voters denied the legal right of gay and lesbian couples to get married, joining many other states that had passed similar laws. Although the California vote has energized the gay community in California and in other states, it is too early to tell if their efforts will change the minds of enough Americans to gain the civil rights they demand as American citizens.

Opposing discrimination is a major part of the story that Eric Marcus tells in his interview with "The Mixed Couple." The lesbian couple he interviews is referred to as "mixed" because they are interracial – one partner is an African American and the other is a Latina. Early in the interview the women talk about their families and experiences growing up, and their difficulties in being able to identify and acknowledge their sexual orientation. They reminisce about how they met and fell in love. By the time they encounter blatant discrimination at a restaurant, they are quite

comfortable in their identities as lesbians, and that is a major factor in their decision to confront the owner of the restaurant and expose this discrimination to the public.

Like the two women, Reggie Sellars also had to sort out conflicting feelings as a consequence of being an African American and a gay man. As an athlete he could easily hide his sexual orientation because stereotypes of gay men do not include being a football player. Yet, as he entered college, Sellars not only wanted to come out for the football team, he wanted to come out of the closet. He was successful at doing both, and as an openly gay man he applied and was eventually hired for a teaching job. As a teacher he tried to be a role model and an advocate for his gay students, but he continued to encounter people who were uncomfortable with his sexual orientation, even among colleagues of color. Telling his father about being gay was a difficult decision because his father was a minister who believed that homosexuality is a sin. At the end of the essay, Sellars gambles on the sincerity of his father's love and comes out to him.

"The Perversion of Homophobia" begins with another parent/child confrontation in which the parent's religious faith is significant, but this one

> "I believe all Americans who believe in freedom, tolerance and human rights have a responsibility to oppose bigotry and prejudice based on sexual orientation."
>
> Coretta Scott King (1927–2006)

> 66 The only abnormality is the incapacity to love. 99
>
> **Anais Nin (1903–1977)**

involves a mother rejecting her lesbian daughter. It is one of many incidents from the lives of gay men and lesbians that the author uses to create the context for discussing the term "perversion," a term that has historically been used to describe homosexuality. Koppelman argues that the hostile behavior of heterosexuals toward gay men and lesbians more readily illustrates the concept of perversion than does the loving relationship of same-sex partners. Because so many people use their religious faith to justify anti-gay feelings, the essay addresses the religious rationale for denouncing homosexuality and then responds with arguments that refute this rationale – arguments supported by evidence from research in both the sciences and the social sciences. The evidence is even stronger today, but the findings available before the 1980s were compelling enough to cause one leading thinker to conclude:

> I can't understand any discussion of gays and lesbians as if they were something immoral or unsatisfactory. They're doing just what nature wants them to do.

R. Buckminster Fuller (1895–1983)

Although homophobia is primarily a problem for gay men and lesbians, in the essay "Appearances," Carmen Vazquez explains how simply appearing to be gay can result in violence against heterosexual people. From the married couple assaulted on the street to the young man on a dance floor attacked with an ice pick, these heterosexuals have had the opportunity to experience the fury of homophobic wrath. Vazquez introduces the concept of "gender betrayal" to explain why such anti-gay violence occurs, and she challenges both gay and straight people to address anti-gay attitudes by confronting those who express slurs or anti-gay jokes in the media, at school, or at work.

As we have seen in the previous essays, homophobia has serious consequences for gays and lesbians. Yet homophobia is so irrational that Dan Greenburg uses satire as the most effective way to expose its absurdities. In his one-act play entitled "Convention," two businessmen are forced to share a hotel room because so many people have come to the city to attend a convention that there aren't enough rooms. As the two men get acquainted, the issue of homosexuality comes up. For the rest of the play, one character constantly tests the other to see if he has any behaviors that might identify him as a gay man. After being tested with a long list of stereotypical examples of gay behavior, the man being tested finally suggests that the two men engage a prostitute. Thinking that engaging in sexual activity will prove he is not gay, the man being tested discovers that no behavior is safe from the suspicious mind of a homophobe.

Notes

[1]Marvin Harris, *Our kind: Who we are, where we came from and where we are going,* New York: Harper Perennial (1990).

[2]Jamake Highwater, *The mythology of transgression: Homosexuality as metaphor.* (New York: Oxford University Press, 1997).

[3]Theodore Zeldin, *An intimate history of humanity.* (New York: HarperCollins, 1994).

> ❝To hate and to fear is to be psychologically ill . . . it is, in fact, the consuming illness of our time.❞
>
> **Harry Emerson Overstreet (1875–1970)**

The Mixed Couple: Deborah L. Johnson and Dr. Zandra Z. Rolón

This selection provides an intimate account of life at the intersections of gender, race, and sexual orientation. In his introduction, the author stated that when he interviewed them, the women "were living in northern California, where Deborah is a consultant for gay organizations across the country, and Zandra is a chiropractor in private practice."

Zandra: Deborah calls my family a Mexican commune. Three quarters of the population in Brownsville, Texas, are relatives of mine. My mother and father got divorced when I was still a child. I'm the oldest, so I was my mother's right arm with everything. We're very, very good friends and always have been. We've always respected each other as women first. A lot of my feminism I know I've learned from her. I think she was a feminist before she even knew she was.

I got a grip on the fact that I was a little different when I was about ten, maybe twelve. I remember discovering a box underneath my mom's bed that had all these adult novels. Every time she left the house, I'd run to this box and read the books. The descriptions of the women were the parts I liked the most.

I always had crushes on girls at school. In high school I even had a lover. We didn't call ourselves *lovers,* but we messed around all the time. She had her boyfriend; I had my boyfriend – that was just what we did at slumber parties.

I tried to do what was expected of me and got married. I got caught up in the romance of being in a relationship. I liked everything that came with

falling in love. I just happened to fall in love with somebody who happened to be a man. Besides, it wasn't kosher for me to be in tune – nor did I know that I could be in tune – with the fact that I was lesbian. It wasn't until later, when I was going through my divorce in my early twenties, that I realized I had a choice.

After my divorce I left Houston and eventually wound up in L.A., where I worked with battered women and children in a shelter. Then one day about eight months after I started working there, the women I worked with took me to a lesbian club. I saw wall-to-wall women and thought, *This is it! This is it! I'm in heaven!* The light went on: I decided to stop lying and came out.

It was pretty hard for my mom. She went through all the typical things. She cried and she got mad. "What did I do? How did I cause it? Was it because we didn't have a man around the house?" She didn't want me seeing my younger brother and sister. She really tried to alienate me from the family, but I banked on the fact that we had a good relationship. What turned her around was the fact that I waited her out.

Deborah: Our families are very different. I grew up in L.A. in a very upper-middle-class bourgeois black household. We're one of these very well-rooted, extremely well-connected families. I lived a privileged life: A new car when I was sixteen, traveling

From *Making history: The struggle for gay and lesbian equal rights, 1945-1990,* (New York: HarperCollins, 1992).

in Europe, the whole bit. If there was such a thing as grooming the future leadership of America, that was the approach my parents took. They spent a lot of time with their kids.

Growing up was quite traumatic for me because I really thought that I was a little boy trapped inside of a little girl's body. I was supposed to be sweet and docile, but I was a jock. I wanted to grab the world by the balls! It just didn't make any sense to me. And I had sexual feelings very, very early, but boys were not an interest. When the other little girls were starting to get crushes on boys and were talking about weddings, I always knew I wanted to marry a girl – always, always, always.

When I was seven, I remember telling my parents that I was not going to marry a man and all the reasons why. By the time I was ten, I explained to them that I was in love with this little girl. My dad told me that it was just a phase, that I was going to outgrow it. My mother knew better; she had worked for years as a teacher with teenaged girls. My relationship with my parents has been in the toilet ever since then.

I started reading a lot of my father's medical books. He's a pharmacist. I read about wet dreams, and that's what I thought I was having. I didn't know what was going on. I just knew that I was fantasizing about women and girls, and then I'd get this stuff between my legs that looked kind of like what they said semen looked like. So I was scared. I thought that there was something really, really wrong here. I didn't know there was such a thing as lesbianism, women with women, so I just assumed that I would have to be a male if I wanted to be with women. It was very confusing.

It was when I read *The Children's Hour* in seventh grade that I learned about women with women. I was doing a scene with this woman who I had a serious crush on, and she got to the part where she explained how she really felt for her female coworker. It hit me like a ton of bricks. . . .

So it was just about the time where you were starting to hear the *g* word and the *l* word. It was also a time of social turmoil . . . And I'm black, so beyond the gay issue, I was dealing with black pride and the issues of being black. It was a challenging time of looking at who I was and where I fit in.

Right as I was getting a sense of who I was, I started a relationship with a girl in Girl Scouts. I was

about fourteen. We didn't have a real name for our relationship, but it felt right and it felt good. If my parents had had any doubt about my being a lesbian, they knew for sure when they walked in on us in the act.

In the years after that, my parents confiscated my mail and read it. They hired a private investigator. It was very, very serious. You see, this was before the consenting-adult laws were passed in California. The anti-sodomy laws were still on the books. My dad's attitude was, "We're pumping all this money into you, and you're throwing your life down the toilet." He believed that my sexuality would ruin my life because it was bad, evil, and criminal. He really thought I was sick, that there was something hormonally off. My mother was into her whole Satanic stuff, believing that the devil was after my soul. She's a Pentecostal Evangelist. So not only did I have to deal with my mother, I had to listen to the shit from the pulpit that was very condemning of gays.

My way of coping was to be an overachiever and to give my parents something to be proud of. My thinking was, *OK, I'll live one life for you so you'll love me, but then, behind your back I'm going to sneak around and live the life I want to live.* My plan was to infiltrate the system. That way, no one could get rid of me. I was in Girl Scouts all through high school. I was also student body president.

When I got to college – my parents insisted that I go to the University of Southern California [USC], which is where they met – I had my own Girl Scout troop. I was president of my mother's sorority and of the YWCA. It was a lot of women's stuff, but traditional women's stuff. In my other life I had a girlfriend. She lived in another city, so it was difficult for us to see each other a lot. But we kept up with correspondence – at least we did when the letters weren't confiscated.

At school I used to secretly read the Lesbian Tide, a lesbian feminist publication. It came in a brown envelope, and I'd hide it between my mattresses. I used to read it and think, *How could they be so dykey? How could they be playing baseball and have everybody know that they're out?* I was still very much into hiding then. But I eventually had the sense that I was getting a free ride, that there were a lot of people who were putting a lot of shit out on the line, and that I needed to stand up and be counted. I also did it for my life because I thought I was going to die if I didn't.

So . . . I started getting involved in gay activism and went to rap groups at the Gay and Lesbian Community Services Center in Los Angeles. Two years later, by the time I was eighteen, I was leading rap groups. I brought all of the political work that I had been doing in student government and civic things right into the gay movement. I got into the speakers' bureau early on and went to college campuses, church groups, community groups, and radio shows and talked about what it meant to be gay. I did that at my own school, as well. I helped train the campus psychological counselors on issues of homophobia. My therapist at school got me involved in that. She was the head of the counseling service at USC, and my saving grace.

I was one of the youngest people and one of the only blacks at the Gay and Lesbian Community Services Center. You can be sure that being black had an impact on how people dealt with me. I had the advantage of at least being educated on an undergraduate level. This was an advantage because I found there was a lot of academic bias within the gay and lesbian movement. The activists tended to be fairly well educated. If you split infinitives and couldn't write, your opinions were discounted. There are a lot of good grass-roots activists who are very bright people but who don't have college experience. I have watched time and time again for their opinions to be devalued or not to be taken seriously, particularly if they're people of color. I have encountered this attitude constantly. And there was just a lot of racism.

The racism took different forms in the gay community, but perhaps the most blatant kinds I encountered during those years were the exclusionary policies at the gay clubs, at places like Studio One. If you were black, you could only get in on a certain night. We used to call it "Plantation Night." We used to picket all the time. On the nights when blacks weren't welcome, which was most nights, they used the whole ID bullshit.

Zandra: Certain people needed to show two or three picture IDs. How many people carry three picture IDs? They never said it was because you were black. But people of color would get carded heavily.

Deborah: So if I went with a white friend, maybe I wouldn't make it in the door and they would. It made me beyond crazy. My feeling toward the discrimination was . . . *Who do you think you are?* Besides being lesbians, we're both women of color. You can't separate our lesbianism from our racial identities. So we're up against all kinds of stuff in the larger society. But when we came to the gay and lesbian community, we naively expected it to be more sensitive. Ironically, we found that the gay and lesbian community was much further behind than the straight community when it came to basic civil rights.

Zandra: As an oppressed group, how can the lesbian and gay community oppress other people? How can you do that?

Deborah: The clubs were the most blatant. Usually, it was more subtle. Part of the way racism displayed itself was in the lack of cultural sensitivities. If you want a certain kind of people to attend meetings or events, then you have to recruit. You've got to advertise. You have to solicit. You have to make the experience something they would want to be involved in. But what I kept getting over and over again was that people of color didn't matter and that we were somehow ancillary. And when black people showed up at meetings or social gatherings, they would get the cold shoulder. Nobody would ever talk to them. The insensitivities were really bad. And there were racial comments all the time.

Because I felt ostracized and because of my own need to socialize with other women of color, I started a big social-club network for black lesbians when I was twenty-one. We did social events for a number of years and had as many as six hundred women participating. I met Zandy at one of our events. . . .

Zandra: At the time we were with other women. I remember walking in and seeing her at the bar and thinking to myself, *Goddamn! Perfect!* Then I met her and realized, *I am going to get in trouble with this woman. Somehow, somewhere, I will definitely get in trouble with this woman.* It just so happened that Deborah's lover was a really good friend of my lover. So it turned out that we hung out with each other for that whole evening. After that evening, we would party together during the weekends – go to each other's houses for dinner.

Deborah: Zandy and I were working together in the movement, too. Through this social group we started to become more political, and we started rap groups for black lesbians.

Zandra: I was a spokesperson also. Whenever the occasion came up for gay people to speak on gay issues, I would always volunteer, whether that meant on radio talk shows, at colleges, in newspapers – anything and everything.

Well, the energy between the two of us was so strong that we could not be in the same room together. I would get too nervous, and she would be too nervous. The feeling was, "Let's not cross boundaries. We're in relationships." At that time I thought that she was happy in her relationship, and vice versa. Needless to say, we weren't, and two years after we met, we left our relationships to be with each other.

Deborah: We'd been together as a couple for only about six months, when Zandy decided to take me out for a romantic dinner. . . . We were both going to take off work the next day to honor Martin Luther King, Jr.'s birthday . . .

Zandra: Deborah had just gotten her review at work, and we were going out, in part, to celebrate.

Deborah: I was working for Prudential in acquisitions and sales and as a real estate investment manager. I went to work there after I finished my MBA at UCLA. January was my first six-month review, and it was a rave review.

Zandra: A friend of mine, who happens to be straight, told me about this really nice French restaurant, called Papa Choux. She said the restaurant had these six private booths that were very romantic. I thought it would be just perfect. So I made the reservations and requested a booth. This was going to be a surprise for Deborah.

We got to the restaurant, and the waiter who seated us asked, "Are you sure you want a booth?"

We insisted that yes, we did. So he showed us to a booth. It's the kind where you have to move the table out so you can get in. Right in front of the table was a little white sheet curtain that closed. The booths were set in a horseshoe, and in the middle of the horseshoe was a fountain. There was candlelight, and a violinist who came around. It was romantic.

We were taking our jackets off, and the waiter came back and took the table away and said, "You'll have to move. You can't sit here." He kept saying, "It's against the law to sit here." And we said, "What's against the law? What did we do?"

Deborah: He went into all this bullshit about, "It's against the law to serve two men or two women in these booths." That's when we explained to him that we had been activists for a very long time, and that was bullshit. I told him, "If I can get a motel room with this woman, I know I can eat with her."

Zandra: Of course, at that point, everybody was looking out of their little booths to see what was going on. We asked to see the manager.

Deborah: We were not going to move.

Zandra: The manager came over, or at least we thought we were talking to the manager – we found out later that he was the maître d'. He kept giving us the back-of-the-bus type of thing. "Well, you can sit over there and you can have free drinks, but you cannot sit here. You will not be served here." He kept insisting that it was the law.

Deborah: It makes me crazy thinking about it. You have to remember that we were there, in part, because of Martin Luther King's birthday. We were going to take off that next day from work as this real show of solidarity. And if there's anything that King had taught us, it was that we could sit anywhere in the restaurant that we wanted to sit. This was just bizarre. And now I was pissed because this guy was trying to use the law against people he thought didn't know the law. That's what they used to do in the South – deny you your rights by telling you you're breaking the law.

Zandra: The maître d' finally got off it and said, "It is the house policy to serve only couples in these booths, and the manager is very, very adamant about it."

Deborah: We said, "A couple of what?" At one of the press conferences later he said that it was for mixed couples. It's not hard to see that we're a mixed couple. But he kept on and he made it quite plain that the owner was adamant that no two men and no two women were going to be served there. This went on for fifteen minutes. We weren't budging, and we were screaming at each other. He looked at us like, "You can rot. You can freeze your ass over in hell. We will serve you someplace else, but this section is for other kinds of people than you.

Zandra: We left there fuming. We took the names of everyone on staff. I had never, ever blatantly been denied anything because of who I was, ever. I knew about discrimination. My grandfather was discriminated against in the same way that blacks were discriminated against. But never had it happened to me. I had never been told that I couldn't do something or have something or be somewhere because of who I was or because of the color of my skin. How dare you! How dare you! Besides this, they completely blew my romantic date!

Deborah: Zandy had all these expectations about what this evening was going to be. I didn't have any expectations, and to me it was the same old shit. It was like, "OK, here's some more butt we've got to kick." Whereas, for her, that Latin embarrassment came out. Now, I don't know if you know much about Latinos. First off, we're "the family," the two of us. And these people fucked with the family. Latinos have an expectation of respect. When they don't get it, they're hurt and they're pissed. But black people don't have an expectation of respect, so when we get it, we're surprised.

Zandra: We left the restaurant knowing that we had to do something. I didn't know what it was, but we had to do something.

Deborah: . . . We decided that we were going to talk to Gloria Allred, who is a famous civil rights attorney . . . who wins her cases. You name it; she

wins. Gloria is also a media queen – nobody works the media like this woman does. And her law firm is good. They are the best, and they're bad. People tremble when they know Gloria Allred is coming because she wins. And while she's not a lesbian, she has won some of the biggest gay rights cases.

Zandra: She didn't know if we had a case until after she did some research. Then she told us that we did have a case, that there was a city ordinance that prohibited discrimination on the basis of sexual preference.

Deborah: But the ordinance was untested. She told us up front, "It's a very gray area of the law here, but I think we have a chance. And what's more, this case offers the possibility of doing some very important public consciousness-raising concerning issues of discrimination." Having a public case was not our intention. My intention when I went to Gloria was just to get the restaurant to stop discriminating, that's all. Do whatever you've got to do, but we don't want this to go on anymore.

This is the point when I got scared. I was afraid of what kind of impact the publicity would have. Quite frankly, I was afraid for my job. I had just graduated. I worked damn hard to get my MBA. I worked in financial investments in the biggest insurance company in the world. I'm black, and I'm a lesbian. And now I was going to be an out lesbian bringing a public lawsuit? I knew I was putting it all on the line. That made my parents beyond nuts because they felt I was just making it – making good money. "Are you a fool? What's wrong with you?" But I decided to go ahead and do it.

Zandra: I made her do it.

Deborah: No, you didn't make me. But you made it quite plain: "Shit or get off the pot." I made the decision to do it because I was madly in love, and I am still madly in love. To me, that is still the bottom-line issue that people don't understand. As I explained to my mother, "Either this is a country where I can live openly with this woman and love her the way I want to, or it isn't. And if it's not, tell me now – I'll go to Canada; I'll go to Sweden."

As far as my job was concerned, my attitude began to change. I decided that I didn't want to be someplace that didn't really want me. As I told my mother, "If I'm going to get fired because I'm a lesbian, I'm going to get fired because I'm a lesbian whether I sue Papa Choux or not." In other words, if my being a lesbian was going to be an issue, there was going to come a point where I was going to bottom out at that company, and I would rather know now that they don't like lesbians than wait ten years after I've invested sweat and blood someplace where I'm not wanted.

Zandra: What ended up happening was that we announced the lawsuit in front of the restaurant.

Deborah: We had a whole picnic scene. They wouldn't let us eat inside the restaurant, so we were going to eat outside.

Zandra: It was media galore.

When the restaurant found out that we were suing them, instead of saying, "OK, we'll change the policy. Here's a free dinner," they said, "Fuck you!" They put ads in the paper saying, "They can send us to jail. They can hang us by out thumbs. But we're not going to serve two men or two women."

Deborah: They said things like, "This makes a mockery, a charade, out of true romantic dining." Quarter-page ads in the *L.A. Times!*

Zandra: . . . Very quickly our story was front page in the newspapers. Every time you turned on the news, there it was: "Lesbian couple sues restaurant . . ." Then Deborah started chickening out because our story was everywhere.

Deborah: . . . We hadn't been together that long, and when we got together, I was not in the best shape. Emotionally I was just a wreck. And it began to feel like everything I was working for was going down the tubes. When Zandy first came into my life, amazingly my father fully embraced her. I mean, the man never cared about anybody I was with, not even so much as a friend. With Zandy he said, "This is my daughter." He even told her that she was the answer to his prayers for me! God, I was surprised. Then the lawsuit hit in the news, and we got this message on our answering machine. He was furious, "If I hear anymore, ANYTHING, about this GODDAMN restaurant thing, I

am THROUGH with BOTH OF YOU!" The next morning we got a whole page in the *L.A. Times* with our pictures and everything. I was scared. I was scared because my family relationship was going right down the tubes, and at work it was a chill. I was a coward – I was a pure coward.

Zandra: They still talked to her at the office, but nobody would bring up the issue.

Deborah: It was very strained. I would have to leave work to go to court. It was hard to go to court and come back. I always made sure that I clocked out on my vacation time.

My boss and I finally had a discussion about it. He was a young Jewish guy. He liked Zandy and me a lot. He let me know that the attorneys had discussed what to do with me – what to do with this "problem." They had caught the story out there, too, because it was airing everywhere. He said they weren't going to fuck with me. His words were, "If you would sue over a restaurant, imagine what you would do over your job. And they don't want Gloria Allred down there on the steps of our building." He said that I had insulated myself by being so bold.

Then the head honcho came down one day and called the entire office together for an impromptu meeting. He said, "There's a rumor going around here . . . that says if you work here for so many years, you're automatically going to get rewarded and that this is the only way you can get promoted, by staying here long enough. But that's not true. It's performance that counts, and I'm here to congratulate Deborah Johnson." They gave me an early promotion – a year early!

The promotion was encouraging because at the time we were still losing our case in the courts. . . . It was scary because we were losing ground that the gay rights movement had already won. I was afraid we were setting the movement backwards, but I knew in the end that we had to continue the battle because I felt that if I didn't do something, I was never going to be able to sleep. . . .

Zandra: Every time we went to court, every time there was a ruling, there was major press coverage. We were in magazines and every single newspaper.

Deborah: And the restaurant kept taking all these ads out against us. It became this big media zoo.

The appellate court overturned the lower court decisions and said, "You cannot discriminate arbitrarily like that. It's class discrimination. You can't do that." The restaurant petitioned the state supreme court, which declined to hear the case. That meant the appellate court's ruling was going to stand. We had won. The lower court issued the injunction and the motion of summary of judgment. Papa Choux paid all the attorneys' fees. . . . But rather than serve us and comply with the law, Papa Choux just closed the booths. . . . So they had a public wake, with the television cameras from the eleven o'clock news and the whole bit. They gave out free drinks and declared, "True romantic dining died on this day." It's kind of like what they did in Mississippi and Alabama. Instead of letting the black kids swim in the public pools, they just closed the pools. . . .

Deborah: But through our case, we not only put teeth into the local ordinance, which had never been tested before, but on the state level, we became one more instance where the state civil rights act was applied to gays and lesbians. What the appellate court said was that the list that included sex, race, creed, et cetera was meant to be illustrative, not exhaustive, and that we were to be included. So we won under both the local gay rights ordinance and the state civil rights law. We became a precedent-setting case. The case is in the law books now, so for gay rights it's done a lot. They certified it for publication, which is very rare. Now other people can use our suit as precedent anywhere in California. And emotionally, winning was just such a matter of pride.

Zandra: In the end, it turned out to be bigger than what we ever expected. We had no intention of being a test case, and we wound up being heroes to the gay community. The level of respect that came with all of that was incredible. I had never, ever been so out. There was no one I needed to come out to anymore. By bringing this case, we said, "This is who we are. This is our relationship. And we will sue the restaurant – we will sue anybody – if we don't get the respect that we want."

The case also solidified our relationship because the whole thing had been a question of "Are we a family or aren't we?" And it solidified our relationship not only for us, but within the community, with our friends, and with our family.

The relationship was always the number one thing. We were not willing to put our relationship on the line, but we were willing to put everything else on the line for our relationship.

Working My Way Back Home

The author has had to negotiate a number of difficult paths as a gay man: being raised in a Baptist family, being a closeted K-12 student, becoming an openly gay college student and athlete, and finally, an openly gay teacher. In addition, he is also an African American. This essay is from an anthology of writing by gay and lesbian teachers.

Every time I do something like this, it brings up a lot that even I haven't processed. It is pointed out to me again and again and again that I am one of the only black teachers at my school, and the only openly gay teacher. Sometimes the tokenism smacks me right in the face. Writing this for a gay publication, but also knowing my story is "better" because I'm black . . . well, I know it serves its purpose. Mainly, I do it because I hope it will help someone else. But we shall see.

I guess you could say I was born a poor black boy and now I'm a poor black man, but that's only in the financial sense. All of my life I have had loving care from my parents, my friends, and many of my teachers. Being the youngest of six children, I always had plenty of attention from my family. They were always there for me. My family always stayed together, and we're still very close. Another thing that added to the loving atmosphere in my family was that my father is a Baptist minister. Some people ask me if that wasn't an ordeal, growing up in a religion that is so opposed to homosexuality. I say no, because my father then and now doesn't preach a gospel against homosexuality. At the same time, within my own mind was always that internal conversation about what my father might say or do if

he knew his youngest son was gay. I was always afraid that if he found out about me, he would kick me out of the house. So, from early on, I learned to hide that side of myself from my family but especially from my father.

I was born in Winston-Salem, North Carolina, which is the fifth-largest city in North Carolina, but that doesn't make it a very large place. In the city you pretty much know everyone your own age, especially if you are an athlete. I played football since I was six years old. By doing well in football, I was able to garner a lot of support. I realized that if I continued to do well in the sport, people would continue to like "me." Along the same lines, I also did well in my academics. I went to a school where, in my classes, only three students out of thirty-five were black. The vast majority was white. I learned early on that, to be a black person amongst a group of white people, you had to be "nice" – you had to do whatever you could to fit in because, as soon as you did something they didn't deem "appropriate," it was labeled as being a "black" thing.

My saving grace was that, whereas at school I might feel a little restricted to how I could be, whenever I went home I was free to be myself. I lived in an all-black neighborhood so, if I ever had problems at school, I could go home and talk to my parents and friends about the situation. That sustained me throughout my entire educational career. It has also helped that, as an athlete, I was respected by the other students.

From *One Teacher in Ten: Gay and lesbian educators tell their stories* © 1994 by Kevin Jennings (Ed.). Reprinted by permission of Alyson Books.

It was during these years, about fifth grade, that sexuality really made an imprint on my life. It wasn't homosexuality or heterosexuality; it was racial sexuality. Like all students that age, we would have sleepovers. I was always one of the students invited to the sleepovers. But when I went to the parties, which were coed, we would play the "kissing game." One of the rules was explained to me this way: "Hey, Reggie, you know you can't play because you're black, and we can't kiss black people!" I learned that I had my limits to being accepted, even in the *straight* white world.

More and more, sexuality as well as race began to play a bigger role in my life. When I reached junior high school I met another black male student and we became good friends. In seventh and eighth grades we were always together. Since we spent so much time together, we began to call each other "cousins." Eventually it became a sexual relationship. We didn't call it homosexuality; we didn't say we were gay; we just said we really loved one another and cared for one another. Fitting all the norms I was supposed to, I still had my girlfriends, always girlfriends of color, of course, whom I really enjoyed being with as friends. But they always tended to be the best friends of my "cousin" so we could always be together. We would talk about what we would do when we got older. He would talk about his wife and how many kids they would have, and how he would name his first kid after me. My scenario was that I never saw myself with a wife. I knew that I only wanted to be with him for the rest of my life.

About this time, I approached one of my guidance counselors to apply to a boarding school. I loved my school in North Carolina, I loved living with my family, but I also felt that I was missing something. In hindsight, I wanted to leave because I was ready to deal with my sexuality, but I wasn't able to deal with it in such a familiar setting where, if I wasn't accepted, I would be cast out. I applied to and was accepted to Phillips Exeter Academy. At age sixteen, I left for Exeter.

After I was accepted, the football coach contacted me when he learned I was interested in playing for the school. I got there a week before classes started to attend football camp. I was one of two tenth-graders who eventually made the varsity team. Thus, coming into the school year, I already had a reputation. This helped me to be seen as a leader.

Initially at Exeter, one of my dreams was to have a boyfriend. But, due to my being on the football team, I instantly had a reputation and everything that comes along with that reputation of being a football player. Then, sophomore year, a new student named Mark came in and was on the varsity diving team as a freshman. He and I hung out in the same crowd. The word got around that he was gay but didn't have a problem with it. I thought this was pretty intriguing so I resolved to get to know him. He was dealing with it in a more open way than I was ready to deal with it, though. One evening in the dorm he came over and closed my bedroom door. I totally freaked out: "What are people going to think? This guy has a reputation for being gay." I wasn't ready for people to think that about me. I threw open my door and ran out.

In my senior year, another player on the football team had become a little tired of Mark being openly gay. He found Mark and beat him up. Mark then came to me, seeking comfort, and when I saw him, I was outraged. I went out to find the other guy. I'm glad I didn't find him that night because I think I would have hurt him physically. I saw him the next day and told him that if he felt he needed to show how much of a man he was by beating up homosexuals, he should start with me because I was a homosexual. I screamed, "I'm gay! Why don't you try to fight me? You know you can't kick my ass!" He just laughed and said that I was just saying this – "You can't be gay. You're my friend. You're captain of the football team."

Toward the end of my senior year we had sexuality workshops. We did skits where a student would be homosexual, and I always volunteered to play that role. I felt that I could be myself. The health teacher always thanked me for doing this. She thought it was so great that the football captain, the track captain, the heralded student leader, would put himself in such a position. She said that my doing this would help some student who really *was* dealing with his sexuality. I just smiled and laughed to myself, only wishing that she knew that I wasn't role-playing, but was actually being myself.

In college, I decided to come out as a gay person and also go out for the football team. I made the freshman football team and resolved to tell my closest friend on the team I was gay. His response was that he had never really known a gay person before but that, since he now knew me, he realized that all the stereotypes about gay people weren't true. I was shocked, completely taken aback, because I had expected him to tell me to get out of his life. Instead he was telling me that he was willing to get to know me as a *gay* person. I could feel something being lifted from me. I was able to play football; I was able to be an openly gay person; I was able to be myself.

By the end of my senior year I decided I wanted to go into teaching, at least for a couple of years until I got a "real job," as my mother put it. I wanted to go back to an environment like Exeter and be a black role model. I wanted to go back to a school like Exeter because I felt I understood what these students were going through in a way most of the other teachers didn't.

I went right into my first job that fall at Brewster Academy in Wolfeboro, New Hampshire. I was the only black teacher and, eventually, the only openly gay one as well. Coming in as a 22-year-old, I didn't realize what effect that would have on me. As a gay black man, I was never allowed the experience of being a young teacher. I found myself playing the role of spokesperson for two communities, while simultaneously trying to learn and understand what was still a new profession for me. Often, I would seek out a senior faculty member for advice on a basic educational issue and end up debating, explaining, or defending an unrelated topic dealing with racism or homophobia. Although the work was meaningful and rewarding, the stress that came with it was more than any beginning teacher should have to face.

The recurring thing I heard around the dorm, around the school, around the playing fields, was people constantly demeaning others with words like "faggot" or "dyke" or "cocksucker" or "lesbian." Initially I would ask those students why they used those words, and they would say it was just teen slang. I would ask how they thought someone who was gay or lesbian would feel if they overheard, and they would reply that no one at our school *was* like that. I started answering their homophobic remarks by saying, "What if I were gay? That might offend me." They would say, "You can't be gay. You were a big football player at Yale and all the girls want

you." I would then say, "Well, what if I was offended by that, even though I was straight?" I was walking the line between admitting I was gay and just being pro-gay.

I asked faculty members why they didn't stop such homophobic language. They said that if they stopped it every time they heard it, they'd never have time to teach their classes. Another new faculty member at the school was attracted to me and I decided that I had to tell her I was gay. She was taken aback but then said she respected that I could share that with her. She warned me that I'd better not tell anyone else, though, because I might get harassed or fired. I told more and more faculty after that, and always got that same response.

One situation that helped me to come out was when I noticed a student named Jean wearing a pink triangle. I asked if he knew what it stood for and he said, "Of course. It stands for gay rights." He was in one of my classes and, after this conversation, it sort of sparked him. He started paying attention and his grades started improving. He had been one of the problem students in the school, but the more he realized I supported his wearing the pink triangle, the more he began to turn around. Eventually we got into a conversation where we both personalized it – he was gay and I was gay. From then on, Jean blossomed academically. He started to shine in all his classes and began to try on some new activities.

While neither of us came out to the entire community, we did establish a relationship where we could talk about what was going on for us as gay people at the school. Not having any formal support system, we coordinated meetings with an administrator to whom we felt it would be safe to talk. Eventually, Jean felt comfortable enough to talk to his mother about his sexuality. Although I'd never advised him to do so (I would never advise a student to do that, as one never knows how a parent might react, and thus the student must make the final decision), he felt our conversations had given him enough confidence that he could deal with however his mother reacted. He felt she would be supportive since there was already another openly gay relative in the family. He told me afterwards that she had been mildly shocked but had then told him that of course she still cared for him and loved him as her son. I was surprised, then, when she

proceeded to call me and started screaming accusations: "You convinced my son to be gay" and "You
had a relationship with my son that made him gay."
After hanging up, I immediately headed over to the
home of the administrator who had been helping us
through this situation. She convinced me that I had
nothing to worry about and that Jean's mother was
simply taking out her frustration and shock on me.
Just as importantly, she let me know that I had the
school's support should this woman try to place any
professional blame on me. Although still a little
shaky, I was convinced I had handled the situation
appropriately, and felt I would be all right, thanks to
this administrator's support and the clear turn-
around in Jean's academic and personal performance since we had begun our work together.

I continued to let more students know that I was
gay. Initially some of them stopped talking to me.
They didn't know how to deal with the situation
since they had never known an openly gay person
before. Although I was initially hurt by this reaction, I held to my convictions.

One of the most painful initial rejections ended
up being one of the most rewarding. In my first
year, a student named Sim was also beginning at
the school. We instantly formed a strong student-
teacher relationship. Although I was not his official
advisor, he often came to me for personal and academic counseling. His parents wrote to me about
the wonderful effect I was having on their son's life.
They said he referred to me as the older brother he
had always wanted but never had. They even extended an open invitation for me to visit them at
their home.

Needless to say, when the time came for me to
tell Sim I was gay, I was extremely anxious about
what his reaction would be. At first, he seemed to
have no problem with my gayness. He then proceeded to avoid me in every possible way for the
next three weeks. I then got a message from his
parents. Already saddened by Sim's reaction, I expected an even worse one from his parents. Instead,
they were calling to convince me not to give up on
their son, explaining that they thought he was just
trying to adjust to a situation that was completely
new to him and needed space and time to work it
out. My biggest fear had always been the possible
reaction of my students' parents; here, in one of my
first encounters, they were encouraging me to hang
in there and affirming my decision to come out!

They closed by thanking me for being one of the
best teachers and role models their son had ever
had.

The headmaster was the last to know. The first
time we ever had a conversation about it was when,
as part of a "viewbook" featuring write-ups on
teachers that the school was publishing, I told him I
wanted to include the fact that I was a member of
GLSTN, the Gay, Lesbian, and Straight Teachers
Network. After all, other teachers were mentioning
that they were part of women's teachers groups
or people-of-color teachers groups. He told me I
couldn't because this was a school publication, and
I told him he was denying a part of me. Basically he
said he was sorry, but he didn't want to leave a "bad
mark" on the school. Even when I pointed out that,
at one time, it would have been considered to be a
"bad mark" to have a black teacher or a black students' support group at his school, he still refused to
allow me to mention my affiliation with GLSTN. I
felt enraged hearing my employer say he was willing to accept one part of me while so blatantly
refusing to acknowledge another. Even though he
admitted that he had been pleasantly surprised by
the community's reaction to my coming out, he said
he did not want to test how the general public
might respond. He added that he had been so elated
when he read my application folder: imagine, a
black teaching candidate who went to Phillips Exeter Academy and Yale University who wanted to
work at his school! Without even being asked, he
then volunteered that if he had known then that I
was gay, my folder would have been "darkened." I
will always remember that phrase because of his
unintentional pun.

I worked for two years at Brewster trying to
show people why it was important for people to be
able to be openly gay. We had workshops on why
we needed to change our policies and curriculum,
but the school steadfastly refused to do any of this.
I decided I had to leave. I was saddened because all
of my relationships with students had turned out to
be positive. Jean's mother had cornered me at his
graduation, asking me to forgive her for the accusations she had made and insisting that I had probably
saved her son's academic career as well as possibly his relationship with her; Sim and I had re-
established our friendship in the last year, with him
eventually calling me two years later to tell me of
his own homosexuality. Nevertheless, I felt that if I

were to survive emotionally and professionally, I had to change workplaces.

When I came to my second school, Nobles, I planned to continue to speak out. While interviewing, I decided that I needed to find out if my identity and work would be supported by the school. I had set up my interview for the day following the GLSTN conference, which was held at a school only twenty minutes from Nobles, thinking I could save myself a four-hour round trip from New Hampshire by doing so. The interview went quite well. The headmaster, Mr. Baker, was impressed by my resume as well as my teaching experiences and philosophy. At one point, he casually asked how I had been able to come down in the middle of the week on a school day. I realized that I could come out to him by telling about my participation in the GLSTN conference, or would have to make up some excuse while praying that he didn't find out I was gay before offering me a position. Since I was leaving Brewster because of the lack of professional and personal support for gay people there, I decided that now was the time to find out if Nobles was going to be different. I told him about the GLSTN conference and came out to him. Although it seemed that we were at the interview's end, we then proceeded to talk for another twenty minutes about my work as an openly gay teacher and what I would like to see happen on gay issues at Nobles. When we finished I asked him what he thought of my candidacy now. He replied that it seemed that what we had discussed could only make me a better candidate and teacher. A few days later, I was offered a position as a Spanish teacher, dorm parent, and football coach. Having already felt pretty good about myself for having the courage to come out in the interview, I was elated to actually win a job after doing so.

At Nobles I coached football for the first time. Even though I had a great time at Yale as an openly gay football player, I was still afraid of all the stereotypes the sport carried toward homosexuals. I wasn't sure how to deal with being an openly gay coach. Within the first few weeks, though, I felt the students had come to respect me as a coach and a player, and we had developed a very good relationship. I decided to first tell the captains that I was gay. When I approached them to tell them, they said they already knew from students who'd known me when I taught at the school the summer before. I asked how they felt. They said that initially they didn't know what to expect, but as the season went on, they had come to understand that I was a football coach who just happened to be gay and they had learned to respect that.

I then always wore a pink triangle, either on my whistle or on my cap, at practice. One day, the largest player on the team, who epitomized everything you could be afraid of, approached me and asked me what it stood for. I held my breath and said that it was a pin that stood for gay rights and that I wore it because, not only did I think that everyone should be treated equally, but also because I was gay. He said, "Oh, I thought so. I have a couple of pink triangles myself. My mother's a lesbian." That completely blew me away again, and taught me again the lesson that you have to trust people.

Recently I went to a people-of-color teachers conference. We had several workshops on how to deal with race in the school setting. But this was my third year there and I still didn't feel like I was a part of it. I had originally come just to be around other black teachers, but now I was wondering why I still didn't feel fulfilled by this conference. It really struck home with me at a breakfast for men of color that I attended. The men leading the workshop were telling us that we had to teach our boys to be strong black men, that we had to teach them to be aggressive, that we had to teach them "how to treat their women." It was these words that had helped me see why I had not felt at home in this conference, why I had not felt at home coming up all my life in the black community. I went up to the mike in the closing session and decided to address the entire group there. I didn't know what I was going to say but I knew what I wanted to get across. I was nervous, having never spoken up before at the conference because I had never wanted to risk being rejected by the crowd, my crowd, a crowd of people of color. I said that until we learn to deal with the fact that not all men are going to be aggressive and that not all men are going to have relationships with women, we were not addressing the entire black community. I then told them that I was a black gay man, that I was a *proud* black gay man. I told them that, if this conference was to represent all people of color, it had to address the issue of sexuality within race because it plays a huge part, especially within the black race. By the time I sat down I was so nervous that I was shaking and sweating.

But the audience stood up and gave me a standing ovation. I left feeling I could come back to the conference with my head held up, seeing that we had taken the first step toward addressing the issue of sexuality within the black community.

It was only a summer ago that I told my father that I was gay. The previous fall he had been really sick, and while he made it through the winter, I realized that I didn't want him to die without really knowing his youngest son. When I was home that summer I sat him down and told him I was gay. He asked me why I had chosen to do that and I told him it wasn't a choice; it's the way I am. After my lecturing him for fifteen or twenty minutes, I asked what he thought as a Baptist minister, as a "man of God," about my being homosexual. He said, "As a minister, I can only follow what the Bible says, and it says homosexuality is a sin. If you don't change, you're going to hell because you will be judged. But as a man on this earth, I am a father first, and you're my son, and I love you no matter what. I will always pray that you will not be hurt in any way, just as I pray for all your brothers and sisters. Only God Himself can judge us – we as humans can only love one another. I want you to know that I will always love you."

My father taught me the ultimate lesson. You just have to trust people who care for you. They will try to understand you, and make you a part of their lives, if only you give them the chance.

KENT KOPPELMAN

The Perversion of Homophobia

The word "perversion" has historically been used to describe homosexuality, but the au-thor argues that it is the homophobic response to gay men and lesbians – from hostile words to violent actions – that ought to be described as a perversion because of the effect of homophobia on how people think about their friends, family, and faith.

The young woman was awakened at 3:00 in the morning by the sound of the phone ringing. Struggling to wake up, she fumbled for the phone. She couldn't comprehend at first the torrent of words spewing at her, but it was a woman's agitated voice. Eventually she understood that the caller had cancer and that: "I have this cancer because of you!" After a few minutes the caller hung up, leaving the young woman to wonder who the caller was.

At 3:00 the next morning, the phone rang again. The same caller made the same hostile accusation. The young woman interrupted to ask, "Who is this?" but to no avail. The caller ranted for several minutes about the young woman causing her cancer and then hung up. The calls continued to come, night after night, at exactly 3:00. Such calls would upset anyone, but this young woman was a lesbian and she was worried that the caller might become violent, might use this allegation about her being the cause of the cancer as an excuse to stalk her and harm her. She became increasingly distraught.

The young woman and her partner discussed the bizarre situation, but they didn't know what to do. She didn't want to call the police. What was espe-cially frustrating was that the voice sounded vaguely familiar, but she could not identify it, nor could she think of anyone who would make up such a story to harass her. She couldn't call her fam-ily. They were fundamentalist Christians who had ostracized her years ago when she came out of the closet. Her mother refused to see her or talk to her. She was no longer welcome in her parent's home.

After receiving the calls for several weeks, the young woman began to recognize the voice. Listen-ing intently, she said nothing for several more nights until she felt certain she knew the identity of her tormentor. She did not want to believe her sus-picions, but she was determined to have a con-frontation. When the next call came she only listened for a minute, then interrupted, "Mother, why are you doing this? Why are you saying this to me?" Her mother responded, "God is punishing me because you're a lesbian! I have cancer because of you!"[1]

This story comes not from a soap opera script but from a reality scripted by homophobia. Because of her religious beliefs, the mother had denounced her daughter's homosexuality as a perversion and an abomination. Her child was living in sin and bound for eternal condemnation. When she learned she had cancer she was convinced it was divine punish-ment for having given birth to such a sinful daugh-ter. In her anger, the mother lashed out at the willful child who had "chosen" such a perverse lifestyle and rejected all that was good in the world,

From *Values in the key of life: Making harmony in the human community.* (Amityville, NY: Baywood Publishing Company, 2001).

including her mother. And the mother's fury was boundless.

There is a perversion here, but it is not the one perceived by the mother. Human existence, both past and present, is filled with stories of *motherlove*. Daughters may be selfish, sons may be abusive but mothers continue to love their children. *Fatherlove* is often perceived and portrayed as having a price attached. Working hard and being successful may earn *fatherlove*, but *motherlove* has been the model of unconditional love. Murderers, even serial killers, have been executed in the sight of a mother weeping for her little child lost. Yet here is a mother denouncing her daughter, a daughter who had not abused or murdered anyone, a daughter who was hard working and successful in her career, a daughter faithful to her partner, but her partner was someone of the same sex. Does this act define the limits of *motherlove?*

Parental rejection is the reason many argue that homophobia is the worst kind of prejudice because it can even turn family members against each other. Those who suffer from the actions of prejudiced people know they can always go home, that they can count on their family to welcome them and to love them and to help heal the hurt caused by others. Only gay men and lesbians may find that even their own families can harbor such homophobia that they will not be a harbor against the storm. The family may refuse to offer any comfort or compassion. It should surprise no one that drug and alcohol abuse have been major problems for many gay men and lesbians. Many people use drugs and alcohol to escape from pain.

One of the major components in viewing homosexuality as a perversion is that heterosexuals tend to focus on the sexual behavior of gay men and lesbians. Heterosexuality is usually viewed through the lens of love and intimacy and procreation whereas homosexuality is usually viewed through the lens of lust and immorality and perversion. Human beings share common concerns and needs, and one need is to be loved and to express love in an intimate relationship. Another need is to respond to the sex drive, but sexual activity represents just one part of a person's life. During the day we eat and bathe and dress and undress and work and play and gossip and watch television and listen to music and read and write and think and cele-brate. . . . Why should sexual behavior alone be the basis for rejecting another human being?

Rejection . . . another story.

A lesbian couple worked in a medium sized city but wanted to live in a small town because both had been born and raised in small towns. They looked at houses in nearby communities and purchased an attractive home in a town close enough to the city to permit a comfortable commute to their jobs. Because both women had also been raised in evangelical families and retained their Christian faith, they hoped to find a church that would accept them. After attending several different services, they heard one minister who seemed broad minded and thoughtful so they went to see him. They explained that they would like to come to his church but they wanted him to be aware of their relationship. If lesbians were not welcome in his church, they would not intrude. He accepted them warmly and encouraged them to consider attending the church he served.

After the two women had attended services for several months, the rumors began. The two women were living together; they bought their house together; they never seemed to go on dates nor did they bring men into their home. People wondered if they were lesbians, and in the time tested tradition of gossip, the question became rhetorical. Everyone knew. One couple in the church was so convinced by the rumor that they came to see their minister. They told him it was well known in the community that these two women were lesbians and they demanded that he tell these women they were no longer welcome in the church.

The minister listened respectfully and when they finished he asked, "Are you saying that I should be involved in the private sexual activities of my parishioners?" They nodded, that was exactly what they were saying. "All right," said the minister as he reached for his paper and pen, "Let's start with you. Tell me everything you enjoy doing sexually." Neither the husband nor his wife wanted to talk about that. "But you just told me I am supposed to be involved in the sexual activities of my parishioners, so I am just doing what you say you want me to do." The couple still refused to discuss their sexual activities. "All right, so I guess you do not want me to poke my nose into what people do in their bedrooms." He put his pen and paper down. "And that's what I prefer as well." When the couple left his office that day they also left the church. No doubt they found another church that permitted them to persist in their prejudice.

The Christian church has played a major role in fanning the flames of homophobia for a long time. Literally. The medieval Christian church condoned burning men and women to death who were guilty of being attracted to people of the same sex. Sometimes they were accused of being heretics or witches, but such wickedness often included betraying their nature, heterosexuality being considered the only sexual orientation that was natural. When men were burned they were often bound tightly with ropes that gave them the appearance of tightly tied bundles of kindling called fagots. According to some scholars, the pejorative term "faggot" was crafted in these flames of faith and hatred,[2] creating another chapter in a history of atrocities committed by a religion whose fundamental principles are love and mercy and forgiveness, but whose leaders and followers have promoted and engaged in anti-Semitism, misogyny, and slavery.

In 1997, the Southern Baptist Church confessed that it had defended and legitimized slavery before the Civil War. The Church issued a formal proclamation apologizing for their mistake, but these same Southern Baptists were also denouncing the Disney Corporation and sponsoring a boycott of Disney for having gay friendly policies such as providing benefits for people in domestic partnerships. How long will it be before we can expect the next apology?

Why do people calling themselves Christians feel justified in maintaining this prejudice? There is very little mention of homosexuality in the Bible, and even where it seems to be condemned one must cautiously consider the context. The concept of homosexuality – having a persistent erotic attraction for someone of the same sex — is of relatively recent origin. The term was first coined in the middle of the 19th century and did not gain popular usage until the 20th century. Previously most western societies had simply assumed that men and women were heterosexual by nature. When Biblical writers denounced men sleeping with men, they were chastising heterosexual men for going against their nature and for wasting their procreative potential by "spilling their seed" on infertile ground. They

were exhorting men to reject this perversion of their nature and to behave the way a heterosexual man should behave. This is not a condemnation of homosexuality but of heterosexuals engaging in inappropriate sexual activity. With this in mind, one can argue that the Bible says nothing about homosexuality given what we now understand about sexual orientation.[3]

Scientists still have much work to do to determine the genetic basis of sexual orientation and how it is influenced during fetal development and early childhood, but there is little support for the claim that being sexually attracted exclusively to members of the opposite sex is the natural orientation. Animal studies, as well as human history, clearly reveal the persistence of sexual activity among same sex participants as a naturally occurring phenomenon. Many homosexuals report having strong feelings of sexual attraction for people of the same sex early in their lives. Lesbians had "crushes" on favorite female teachers while their girl friends were having the same feelings for favorite male teachers. Gay men heard their teenage peers fantasizing about the latest cinema sex symbol while they were dreaming about handsome male actors.

Such self-reports, along with other evidence, support Alfred Kinsey's bell shaped curve of human sexuality suggesting that some people are born with a strong inclination toward being exclusively attracted to members of the same sex, just as others on the opposite end of the continuum are exclusively attracted to members of the opposite sex. Kinsey argues that the majority of people have a mixture of feelings but in a society that emphasizes heterosexuality, people feel pressured to reject any feelings of attraction toward members of the same sex.[4]

If it's true that a certain percentage of people are born with a sexuality oriented exclusively toward homosexuality, then it makes no sense to persecute homosexuals on the basis of having made bad moral choices. There are gay men and lesbians who insist that they didn't choose to be homosexual, that they were born this way. Many people reject this idea because to accept it means they must recognize homophobia for what it is: a prejudice. Some Christian churches staunchly resist the claim of many gay men and lesbians that "God made me this way" because it compels them to question conventional beliefs about the Creator and the nature of the Creation.

Some Christians accept the idea that homosexuality is innate and not a choice, but still insist that homosexual behavior is a sin. They exhort gay men and lesbians to resist temptations to engage in homosexual activity, to be celibate or try to find satisfaction in heterosexual activity. They say the homosexual orientation is a test from God. Why God should concoct such a test and assign it only to a certain percentage of people is not clear, nor is it clear why the sin of homosexuality is so abominable. A thief deprives a person of rewards earned; a murderer deprives a person of life; a homosexual loves and cares for another person who happens to be of the same sex. And the sin is . . .?

If Americans accepted the idea that some people are born with a sexual attraction exclusively for same sex partners, would that eliminate homophobia in our society? Probably not. People could use Kinsey's studies to argue that most people have a bisexual orientation which means they have the capacity for engaging in homosexual activities, but they can make a choice. The arguments in support of encouraging people to reject homosexual activities and be exclusively heterosexual would range from religious to pragmatic, but they would be grounded in the idea that there is a choice to be made and the choice affects the entire society.

What is this choice? It is a choice about a person to love and making love with that person. What moral or ethical principles should be upheld? Someone who wants to maintain traditional values could advocate for the principles historically used for heterosexual relationships by exhorting all couples whether in marriages or domestic partnerships to be loving and kind and generous and faithful. Since society's mores now recognize that people make mistakes and allow heterosexual couples to divorce and marry someone else, the same allowance should be given to same sex couples in domestic partnerships. Since our society now takes a more permissive attitude toward premarital sexual activity among heterosexuals, it should take the same kind of attitude toward such activity among gay men and lesbians.

If someone chooses to be involved in a same-sex relationship that is no excuse for hatred or prejudice. People make many personal choices in life, but should any choices be considered a legitimate basis for perpetuating prejudice and animosity? Consider the following:

Is it acceptable for North Dakotans to be suspicious of a New Yorker who chooses to move to Bismark?

Is it acceptable for Protestants to condemn a Lutheran who chooses to convert to Catholicism?

Is it acceptable for Caucasians to denounce a white woman who chooses to marry a black man?

Is it acceptable for Christians to hate the Jews for choosing not to acknowledge Jesus Christ as the Messiah?

The problem is not the choice but our response to choices. Our response to homosexuality is to hate and fear it. Our response to homosexuality is homophobia.

Homosexuality is not the perversion, homophobia is. It perverts the family by sowing seeds of rejection and hostility that tear families apart. It perverts Christianity by turning the Christians who are supposed to love everyone, even their enemies, into people who hate. It perverts our humanity by diminishing our compassion for other human beings. For proof of this, consider the issue of gay bashing. Most attacks are unprovoked. The gay basher assaults his victim simply because he believes the victim is homosexual. In the vast majority of cases the gay basher is a teenage male, apparently so insecure about his own sexuality that he needs to attack a gay man to prove his masculinity to himself and to others. Reports from schools document that students are verbally harassed and even physically attacked if they are perceived to be homosexual. Where is the source of the problem? By any standard of justice and decency, whose behavior is perverse?

Once I discussed this issue for over two hours with a young man who was a fundamentalist Christian. He did not to want to condemn homosexuals but he believed the Bible left him no choice. We discussed Old Testament rejections of abominations and New Testament admonitions to love and forgive. How to reconcile the two? Near the end of our conversation we agreed that it didn't matter whether or not we had the same interpretation of what the Bible said about homosexuality, but we could agree on other passages, "Why do you see the speck that is in your brother's eye, but do not notice the log that is in your own eye?" (Matthew 7:3). "Judge not lest ye be judged" (Luke 6:37). In these passages and many more, Christians are encouraged to behave toward others in ways that reflect God's love and mercy and compassion. For human beings to judge others is a usurpation of God's role. Most religions agree that human beings should not judge others but should look for ways to improve themselves. When one human being judges another that implies that this individual can make judgments as well as God. It is an act of arrogance. Such judgments ignore Paul's unequivocal assertion that human beings can only see "through the glass darkly" (Corinthians 13:12).

Homophobia will continue to affect all of us until some of us stand up and name it for what it is – a perversion of the human spirit. Homophobia will continue to produce prejudice and hatred in our society until institutions and corporations and government agencies declare it unacceptable and refuse to sanction it. Homophobia will receive a mortal blow when religious leaders of all faiths discard their sermons on the evils of homosexuality and persuade their followers that the universal call for compassion should be answered every day and that no human being should be excluded from that compassion.

Is this mortal blow forthcoming? Instead of promoting understanding and empathy, many religious leaders are silenced by the power of ancient prejudices still strong among the masses of people. As this society struggles to overcome homophobia, that struggle should be viewed as a litmus test for measuring our compassion. The extent to which each of us is prepared to resist and reject the forces that demonize those who are different, the extent to which we do not allow differences to divide us, is the extent to which we extend our vision of humanity to include all of those who are here and who belong here . . . among us . . . and beside us.

Notes

[1]Karen Harbeck, *A matter of justice and compassion*, presented at the Statewide Equity and Multicultural Education Conference, Nov. 3, 1995, Milwaukee, WI.

[2]Martin Kantor, *Homophobia: Description, development and dynamics of gay bashing.* (West Point, CT: Praeger, 1998), p. 138.

[3]Gary Doupe, True to our Tradition (pp. 187–204). In W. Blumenfeld (Ed.) *Homophobia: How we all pay the price,* (Boston: Beacon Press, 1992).

[4]June Reinisch (Ed.), *The Kinsey Institute New Report on Sex: What you must know to be sexually literate.* (New York: St. Martin's Press, 1990), p. 140.

Appearances

Martin Luther King, Jr., said, "Injustice anywhere is a threat to justice everywhere . . . Whatever affects one directly affects all indirectly." The author provides examples of homophobic behavior that had negative consequences for people who were not gay. To create better communities, the author suggests specific ways to challenge homophobia.

North of Market Street and east of Twin Peaks, where you can see the white fog mushroom above San Francisco's hills, is a place called the Castro. Gay men, lesbians, and bisexuals stroll leisurely up and down the bustling street. They jaywalk with abandon. Night and day they fill the cafes and bars, and on weekends they line up for a double feature of vintage classics at their ornate and beloved Castro theater. . . .

Brian boarded the 24 Divisadero bus and handed his transfer to the driver one late June night. Epithets were fired at him the moment he turned for a seat. He slid his slight frame into an empty seat next to an old woman with silver blue hair who clutched her handbag and stared straight ahead. Brian stuffed his hands into the pockets of his worn brown bomber jacket and stared with her. He heard the flip of a skateboard in the back. The taunting shouts grew louder. "Faggot!" From the corner of his eye, he saw a beer bottle hurtling past the window and crash on the street. A man in his forties, wearing a Giants baseball cap and warmup jacket, yelled at the driver to stop the bus and get the hoodlums off. The bus driver ignored him and pulled out.

Brian dug his hands deeper into his pockets and clenched his jaw. It was just five stops to the top of the hill. When he got up to move toward the exit, the skateboard slammed into his gut and one kick followed another until every boy had got his kick in. Despite the pleas of the passengers, the driver never called the police. Brian spent a week in a hospital bed, afraid that he would never walk again. . . .

On the south side of Market Street, night brings a chill wind and rough trade. On a brisk November night, men with sculptured torsos and thighs wrapped in leather walked with precision. The clamor of steel on the heels of their boots echoed in the darkness. Young men and women walked by the men in leather, who smiled in silence. They admired the studded bracelets on Mickey's wrists, the shine of his flowing hair, and the rise of his laughter. They were, each of them, eager to be among the safety of like company where they could dance with abandon to the pulse of hard rock, the hypnotism of disco, or the measured steps of country soul. They looked forward to a few drinks, flirting with strangers, finding Mr. or Ms. Right or, maybe, someone to spend the night with.

At the end of the street, a lone black street lamp shone through the mist. The men in leather walked under the light and disappeared into the next street. As they reached the corner, Mickey and his friends could hear the raucous sounds of the Garden spill

From Warren J. Blumenfeld (Ed.) *Homophobia: How we all pay the price.* Copyright © 1992 by Warren J. Blumenfeld. Reprinted by permission of Beacon Press, Boston.

onto the street. They shimmied and rocked down the block and through the doors.

The Garden was packed with men and women in sweat-stained shirts. Blue smoke stung the eyes. The sour and sweet smell of beer hung in the air. Strobe lights pulsed over the dancers. Mickey pulled off his wash-faded black denim jacket and wrapped it around his waist. An iridescent blue tank top hung easy on his shoulders. Impatient with the wait for a drink, Mickey steered his girlfriend onto the crowded dance floor.

Reeling to the music and immersed in the pleasure of his rhythms, Mickey never saw the ice pick plunge into his neck. It was just a bump with a drunk yelling, "Lame-assed faggot . . . Punk faggot." Mickey thought it was a punch to the neck. He ran after the roaring drunk man for seven steps, then lurched and fell on the dance floor, blood gushing everywhere. His girlfriend screamed. The dance floor spun black.

Mickey was rushed to San Francisco General Hospital, where thirty-six stitches were used by trauma staff to close the wound on his neck. Doctors said the pick used in the attack was millimeters away from his spinal cord. His assailant, charged with attempted murder, pleaded innocent.

Mickey and Brian were unfortunate stand-ins for any gay man. Mickey was thin and wiry, a great dancer clad in black denim, earrings dangling from his ear. Brian was slight, wore a leather jacket, and boarded a bus in the Castro. Dress like a homo, dance like a homo, must be a homo. The homophobic fury directed at lesbians, gay men, and bisexuals in America most often finds its target. Ironclad evidence of sexual orientation, however, is not necessary for someone to qualify as a potential victim of deadly fury. Appearances will do.

The incidents described above are based on actual events reported to the San Francisco Police and Community United Against Violence (CUAV), an agency serving victims of antilesbian and antigay violence where I worked for four years. The names of the victims have been changed. Both men assaulted were straight. Incidents of antilesbian and antigay violence are not uncommon or limited to San Francisco. . . .

Why does it happen? I have no definitive answer to that question. Understanding homophobic violence is no less complex than understanding racial violence. The institutional and ideological reinforcements of homophobia are myriad and deeply woven into our culture. I offer one perspective that I hope will contribute to a better understanding of how homophobia works and why it threatens all that we value as humane.

At the simplest level, looking or behaving like the stereotypical gay man or lesbian is reason enough to provoke a homophobic assault. Beneath the veneer of the effeminate gay male or the butch dyke, however, is a more basic trigger for homophobic violence. I call it *gender betrayal*.

The clearest expression I have heard of this sense of gender betrayal comes from Doug Barr, who was acquitted of murder in an incident of gay bashing in San Francisco that resulted in the death of John O'Connell, a gay man. Barr is currently serving a prison sentence for related assaults on the same night that O'Connell was killed. . . . When asked what he and his friends thought of gay men, he said, "We hate homosexuals. They degrade our manhood. We was brought up in a high school where guys are football players, mean and macho. Homosexuals are sissies who wear dresses. I'd rather be seen as a football player."

Doug Barr's perspective is one shared by many young men. I have made about three hundred presentations to high school students in San Francisco, to boards of directors and staff of nonprofit organizations, and at conferences and workshops on the topic of homophobia or "being lesbian or gay." Over and over again, I have asked, "Why do gay men and lesbians bother you?" The most popular response to the question is, "Because they act like girls," or, "Because they think they're men." I have even been told, quite explicitly, "I don't care what they do in bed, but they shouldn't act like that."

They shouldn't act like that. Women who are not identified by their relationship to a man, who value their female friendships, who like and are knowledgeable about sports, or work as blue-collar laborers and wear what they wish are very likely to be "lesbian baited" at some point in their lives. Men who are not pursuing sexual conquests of women at every available opportunity, who disdain sports, who choose to stay at home and be a househusband, who are employed as hairdressers, designers, or housecleaners, or who dress in any way remotely resembling traditional female attire (an earring will do) are very likely to experience the taunts and sometimes the brutality of "fag bashing." . . .

It is a frightening reality. Dorothy Ehrlich, executive director of the Northern California American Civil Liberties Union (ACLU), was the victim of a verbal assault in the Castro several years ago. Dorothy lives with her husband, Gary, and her two children, Jill and Paul, in one of those worn and comfortable Victorian homes that grace so many San Francisco neighborhoods. Their home is several blocks from the Castro, but Dorothy recalls the many times she and Gary could hear, from the safety of their bedroom, shouts of "faggot" and men running in the streets.

When Jill was an infant, Gay and Dorothy had occasion to experience for themselves how frightening even the threat of homophobic violence can be. One foggy, chilly night they decided to go for a walk in the Castro. Dorothy is a small woman whom some might call petite; she wore her hair short at the time and delights in the comfort of jeans and oversized wool jackets. Gary is very tall and lean, a bespectacled and bearded cross between a professor and a basketball player who wears jean jackets and tweed jackets with the exact same slouch. On this night they were crossing Castro Street, huddled close together with Jill in Dorothy's arms. As they reached the corner, their backs to the street, they heard a truck rev its engine and roar up Castro, the dreaded "faggot" spewing from young men they could not see in the fog. They looked around them for the intended victims, but there was no one else on the corner with them. They were the target that night. They were walking on "gay turf," and it was reason enough to make them a target. "It was so frightening," Dorothy said. "So frightening and unreal."

But it is real. . . . Tom and Jan Matarrase, who are married and have a child, lived in Brooklyn, New York, at the time of their encounter with homophobic violence. Tom and Jan were walking down a street in Brooklyn lined with brown townhouses and black wrought-iron gates. It is snowing, and, with hands entwined, they walk slowly down the street where they were assaulted. Tom was wearing a khaki trenchcoat, slacks, and loafers. Jan is almost the same height as Tom, and she was wearing a black leather jacket, a red scarf, and burnt orange cords. The broadness of her hips and

softness of her face belie the tomboy flavor of her carriage and clothes, and it was hard for her to believe that she would be mistaken for a gay man. But she was.

They were walking home, holding hands and engrossed in each other. On the other side of the street, Jan saw a group of boys moving toward them. As they approached, Jan heard a distinct taunt meant for her and Tom: "Aw, look at the cute gay couple." Tom and Jan quickened their step, but it was too late. Before they could say anything, Tom was being punched in the face and slammed against a car. Jan ran toward Tom screaming desperately that Tom was her husband. Fists pummeled her face as well. Outnumbered and in fear for their lives, Tom yelled at Jan to open her jacket and show their assailants that she was a woman. The beating subsided when Jan was able to show her breasts. . . .

Enforced heterosexism and the pressure to conform to aggressive masculine and passive feminine roles place fag bashers and lesbian baiters in the same psychic prison with their victims, gay or straight. Until all children are free to realize their full potential, until all women and men are free from the stigma, threats, alienation, or violence that come from stepping outside their roles, we are all at risk.

The economic and ideological underpinnings of enforced heterosexism and sexism or any other form of systematic oppression are formidable foes and far too complex for the scope of this essay. It is important to remember, however, that bigots are natural allies and that poverty or the fear of it has the power to seduce us all into conformity. In Castro graffiti, *faggot* appears right next to *nigger* and *kike*. Race betrayal or any threat to the sanctimony of light-skinned privilege engenders no less a rage than gender betrayal, most especially when we have a great stake in the elusive privilege of proper gender roles or the right skin color. *Queer lover* and *fag hag* are cut from the same mold that gave us *nigger lover*, a mold forged by fears of change and loss of privilege

Unfortunately, our sacrifices to conformity rarely guarantee the privilege or protection we were promised. Lesbians, gay men, and bisexuals who have tried to pass know that. Heterosexuals who have been perceived to be gay know that. Those of us with a vision of tomorrow that goes beyond tolerance to a genuine celebration of humanity's diversity have innumerable fronts to fight on. Homophobia is one of them.

But how will this front be won? With a lot of help, and not easily. Challenges to homophobia and the rigidity of gender roles must go beyond the visible lesbian and gay movement. Lesbians, gay men, and bisexuals alone cannot defuse the power of stigmatization and the license it gives to frighten, wound, or kill. Literally millions of us are needed on this front, straight and gay alike. We invite any heterosexual unwilling to live with the damage that "real men" or "real women" messages wreak on them, on their children, and on lesbians, gay men, and bisexuals to join us.

We ask that you not let queer jokes go unchallenged at work, at home, in the media, or anywhere. We ask that you foster in your children a genuine respect for themselves and their right to be who and what they wish to be, regardless of their gender. We ask that you embrace your daughter's desire to swing a bat or be a carpenter, that you nurture your son's efforts to express affection and sentiment. We ask that you teach your children how painful and destructive words like *faggot* or *bulldyke* are. We ask that you invite your lesbian, gay, and bisexual friends and relatives into the routine of your lives without demanding silence or discretion from them. We invite you to study our history, read the literature written by our people, patronize our businesses, come into our homes and neighborhoods. We ask that you give us your vote when we need it to protect our privacy or to elect open lesbians, gay men, and bisexuals to office. We ask that you stand with us in public demonstrations to demand our right to live as free people, without fear. We ask that you respect our dignity by acting to end the poison of homophobia.

Until individuals are free to choose their roles and be bound only by the limits of their own imagination, *faggot, dyke,* and *pervert* will continue to be the playground words and adult weapons that hurt and limit far many more people than their intended victims. Whether we like it or not, the romance of virile men and dainty women, of Mother, Father, Dick, Jane, Sally, and Spot is doomed to extinction. . . . There is much to be won and so little to lose in the realization of a world where the dignity of each person is worthy of celebration and protection. The struggle to end homophobia can and must be won, for all our sakes.

Convention (A Play in One Scene)

In this play, the author satirizes homophobic attitudes by describing and making fun of common stereotypes, and also by showing how homophobia can generate "logical" thinking that ultimately leads to an absurd conclusion.

A room in a medium priced New York hotel. Two twin beds. Two luggage racks. A night table with a lamp, an ashtray, and a telephone on top of it. A door in the middle of the back wall.

It is evening. There is a knock at the door. After a moment, it opens and Riley enters, carrying a suitcase. He is a conservatively dressed man in his late thirties, and wears a gray business suit with a conventioneer's badge on his lapel.

Riley puts his suitcase down on one of the luggage racks and opens it. He takes off his jacket, puts it on the bed, looks briefly at the other bed, and unloosens his tie.

There is another knock at the door and before Riley can get there it opens, revealing Walters. Walters is also in his late thirties, also wears a business suit with a conventioneer's badge on his lapel, but he is broader and bigger than Riley.

Walters: Hi. (*Enters room, looks around, puts down his suitcase, and sticks out his hand toward Riley*) Name's Walters, Marshal City.

Riley: (*Shakes hands*) Riley, Terre Haute.

Walters: Glad to meet ya, Riley. You in town for the same confab I am?

Riley: Reckon so.

Walters: Looks like we're gonna be bunkmates for a couple days then, Riley, if that's OK with you.

Riley: Suits me Walters. Guess they're really packin' them in here this time.

Walters: Yep. (*Swings his suitcase onto his luggage rack and snaps it open*) Two in every room. Three in some, I hear. (*Takes off his jacket and throws it on the bed. Loosens his tie.*)

Riley: I don't mind sharing a room at all. Less lonely that way.

Walters: (*Looks at him quickly. Pause*) I usually try and get a room to myself if I can. Less like a barracks that way, if you know what I mean.

Riley: (*Quick look at Walters. Pause*) I asked them for a private room. They said they were doubling up to accommodate the convention.

Walters: Don't get me wrong. I don't *mind* sharing a room. With *you*, I mean. (*Pause*) I mean, I don't know you from Adam but you look like a good guy to me. (*Pause. Laughs uncomfortably*) I mean, you don't look like no queer anyway. (*They both laugh uncomfortably. Pause*) Lots of queers in the service. You been in the service, Riley?

Riley: Uh, yeah.

Walters: What service?

Riley: Navy.

Walters: The Navy, eh? I was in the Marine Corps myself. The Navy ain't too bad, I guess. (*Pause*)

Originally appeared in *Avant Garde* magazine, November, 1969. Reprinted by permission of the author, Dan Greenburg, 645 Broadway, #16, Hastings-On-Hudson, NY 10706, or dan@dangreenburg.com.

At least it's not as loaded with them as the Air Force, eh? (*Both laugh*) I hear they do have quite a few queers in the Navy, though. (*Pause*)

Riley: (*Suddenly flops down on floor, does ten fast push-ups, flips over on his back and does ten sit-ups, then stands up and slaps the dust off. Slightly out of breath*) I do that about six times a day. It's the only way to keep in shape. Been doing that every day since I was a kid, as a matter of fact, Chin-ups and sit-ups during the day, burpees and running-in-place every night before I go to bed. Little tennis and swimming on the weekends, squash at the Y if I get home early enough on week nights. (*Pause*) You work out at all?

Walters: Naw, not much. Little golf on the weekends. Little sandlot ball in the summer with the company team. That's about all. You can overdo that physical stuff, too, you know?

Riley: What do you mean?

Walters: Oh, you know. Those guys who are always running over to the gym to lift weights and stuff like that. Always pumping up their biceps. Rubbing grease on their bodies and looking at themselves in the mirror. If ya ask me, those physical-culture guys are bigger queers than the ones who wear ladies' underpants under their suits.

Riley: (*Pause*) I've never lifted weights, myself.

Walters: Neither have I.

Riley: You couldn't pay me to lift one of those barbells.

Walters: Me either.

Riley: (*Pause*) Not that I couldn't if I wanted to. (*Pause*) The only exercise *I* do is the kind that *lengthens* the muscles. Athletics. Your team sports. Baseball . . . (*Checks Walters to see if he approves*) . . . basketball . . . volleyball . . .

Walters: Volleyball? That's a girls' game.

Riley: (*Quickly*) I meant boys' rules – but there are others I like better. Soccer . . .

Walters: Isn't that what those British queers play?

Riley: (*Quickly*) . . . and, of course, football, which is probably my favorite sport of all. Yes sir. There's nothing quite like slipping into the old football gear on a brisk October afternoon with the leaves all red and gold or crunchy brown

under your spikes, hearing the ball being snapped from center, taking the hand-off, spinning and running wide around your own right end and down the far sidelines for ten, fifteen, *twenty* yards before you're stopped and brought down hard by a solid wall of human flesh.

Walters: (*Pause*) I don't know. All that body contact. All that reaching down behind a man between his legs to get the ball. All those men lying on top of other men after a tackle. If you ask me, those football guys are bigger queers than the physical culture queers.

Riley: (*Pause*) I don't, uh, actually play anything but *touch* football. (*Pause*) You sure seem to know a lot about queers.

Walters: I hate the bastards.

Riley: So do I. I hate 'em like poison.

Walters: Any time I see one, I beat the hell out of him.

Riley: Me too. The bastards.

Walters: I can spot 'em a mile off, too.

Riley: Me too. (*Pause*) How do *you* spot 'em?

Walters: Well, outside of the *obvious* things – like being a dancer, an actor, a painter, a writer, a musician, or owning a cat or a poodle, or having long hair, or knowing how to cook, or being skinny or fat or built too good, or being a Communist or a member of some fruity protest group – you can tell by the way they move. By the fruity way they do things.

Riley: I know just what you mean. (*Pause*) Like what kind of things, for example?

Walters: Oh, you know. Like the way they sit.

Riley: Yeah. How do they sit?

Walters: You know. The way they cross their legs. (*Pause*) Sit down.

Riley: What?

Walters: Sit down.

Riley: (*Pause*) Sit down?

Walters: Yeah, sit down.

Riley: (*Pause*) Why?

Walters: Because I said to. (*Pause. Riley sits down very cautiously on the bed*) Cross your legs.

Riley: (*Pause*) Cross my legs?

Walters: Right. (*Pause. Riley very cautiously crosses his legs by resting his right ankle on his left knee*) There. You did it right. If you was a queer, you would of done it like this. (*Sits down on bed and crosses his legs by resting his right knee on his left knee*)

Riley: Oh. (*Relieved smile. Stands up*)

Walters: (*Suddenly*) Look at your fingernails! (*Riley, startled, raises his hand – palm up and closed – and looks at his fingernails*) You did that right, too. A queer would of done it like this. (*Raises hand – palm down and open – and looks at his fingernails*)

Riley: Right.

Walters: (*Reaches for a pack of cigarettes and offers one to Riley*) Smoke?

Riley: Oh, thanks. (*Takes one out of pack and sticks it in extreme right side of mouth*)

Walters: Match?

Riley: Thanks. (*Pause*) Oh, I'm sorry. (*Goes to bed, fumbles in his jacket pockets, finds a book of matches, starts to light one, reconsiders and does it over again with cupped hands and an exaggerated masculine manner, as Walters watches him carefully. Riley waves the flame of the match out*)

Walters: Good. A queer would of *blown* it out.

Riley: Right. (*Puffs on cigarette. walks across room, gets ashtray, and returns. Takes cigarette out of mouth in an exaggerated Marlboro-ad fashion, holding it with the thumb and tips of all four fingers. He holds it over the ashtray and taps the ash off by flicking the opposite end of the cigarette with his finger*)

Walters: A queer would of done it like this. (*Holds cigarette between tips of thumb and second finger, taps cigarette just behind ash with first finger*)

Riley: Right.

Walters: Do you drink?

Riley: Drink? Hell, yes. Every chance I get. Usually I have a drink the minute I get up in the morning and just keep going that way all day long. I'm sort of a chain-drinker. I also hold my liquor damned well. Never had a hangover or thrown up a single day in my life. Not only that –

Walters: There's nothing wrong with hangovers.

Riley: Oh.

Walters: What do you drink? None of them fruity *mixed* drinks, I hope?

Riley: Hell, no. Although, in all fairness I must admit that somebody once gave me a martini by mistake. Didn't like it much, however. Spit it out on the floor, as a matter of fact.

Walters: What do ya drink when you're not drinking martinis?

Riley: Whiskey. Good old *bourbon* whiskey.

Walters: (*Pause*) With what?

Riley: With nothing. Straight. No sissy soda, no faggy water, nothing.

Walters: (*Looks cagily away from Riley*) Ever mix it with ginger ale?

Riley: (*Outraged*) With what?

Walters: Ginger ale.

Riley: Hell no!

Walters: With ice?

Riley: Up your ass!

Walters: (*Pause*) What brand do you drink?

Riley: (*Pause. A note of panic creeps into his voice*) What brand do I drink?

Walters: Yeah. What brand do you drink?

Riley: (*Pause. Bravely*) What brand do you drink?

Walters: I don't drink bourbon. I drink beer.

Riley: (*Pause. Miserably*) Beer, eh?

Walters: Yeah, beer.

Riley: (*Pause*) I see. (*Pause*) Listen, do you have the time?

Walters: The time?

Riley: Yeah.

Walters: (*Looks at his watch*) It's just about midnight. Why?

Riley: Midnight! (*Slams his fist into his open palm*) Shit!

Walters: What's the matter?

Riley: (*Slams his fist into his palm again*) Piss!

Walters: What's wrong?

Riley: (*Slams his fist into his palm again*) Turd!

Walters: What is it?

Riley: (*Slams his fist into the wall*) Crap!

Walters: Riley?

Riley: (*Slams his fist into his suitcase*) Fart!

Walters: What's the matter?

Riley: (*Kicks a chair*) Tit!

Walters: Hey Riley?

Riley: (*Kicks the bed*) Yeah?

Walters: What the hell is wrong with you?

Riley: I just realized I haven't had a woman in over two hours.

Walters: (*Impressed*) Two hours?

Riley: Yeah. Christ, I'm nearly going out of my mind! (*Begins feverishly pacing around the room*)

Walters: Who did you have two hours ago?

Riley: The girl at the desk. (*Punches the wall*) God, I can hardly stand it!

Walters: What do you wanna do? You wanna send for one?

Riley: (*Pause*) Right now, you mean?

Walters: Yeah, now.

Riley: Sure, how?

Walters: This is New York, isn't it? This is a convention isn't it? (*Walks over and picks up phone*) Hello, room service? Yeah, this is Room 346. We'd like a woman up here. (*Pause*) Yeah, a woman. (*Pause*) Just a minute, I'll ask. (*To Riley*) Blonde, brunette, or redhead?

Riley: Blonde.

Walters: (*Into phone*) Blonde. (*Pause*) Yeah. (*Pause*) Just a minute, I'll ask. (*To Riley*) Platinum, honey, or strawberry?

Riley: Strawberry.

Walters: (*Into phone*) Strawberry. (*Pause*) Right. (*Pause*) Just a minute, I'll ask. (*To Riley*) Ecto-morph, endomorph, or mesomorph?

Riley: Endomorph.

Walters: (*Into the phone*) Endomorph. (*Pause*) Right. (*Pause*) Just a minute, I'll ask. (*To Riley*) Catholic, Presbyterian, or Jewish?

Riley: Ask them if they've got Ethical Culturist. If not, I'll take Seventh-Day Adventist.

Walters: (*Into phone*) Listen, ya got any Ethical Culturists down there? (*Pause*) Good. We'll take one of those.

Riley: And tell them as fast as possible.

Walters: (*Into phone*) Right. And as fast as possible. (*Pause*) Right. OK, thanks. (*Hangs up phone*) She'll be right up.

Riley: Good. They really have a nice selection here in New York, don't they?

Walters: Yeah.

Riley: I'm glad I suggested this. I was really getting horny.

Walters: Yeah. You know something? You're OK, Riley, I mean it.

Riley: Thanks.

Walters: When I first came in here tonight I thought you might be a queer or something, but I was wrong. You're a regular guy.

Riley: Thanks, Walters.

Walters: With some guys you never can tell, not even with guys you've known for years. They may *look* OK. They may *act* OK. But then some time when you least expect it – usually when you're in some place alone somewhere with them – suddenly they'll up and do something fruity.

Riley: I know.

Walters: I had this friend once. Knew him for years. *Years.* I never suspected a thing. And then one day when we were off hunting together he ups and touches my God damned *arm*, for Christ's sake!

Riley: You're kidding me.

Walters: He just ups and touches my God damned arm. A guy I've known for years. Can you beat that?

Riley: It's frightening, that's what it is. The bastards.

Walters: Who can ya trust, for God's sake, if a guy you've known for *years* would put that kind of shit on you?

Riley: You're right. (*Pause*) What did you say to this guy?

Walters: What did I *say* to him? I laid him out cold, that's what I said to him. I've never seen the bastard since.

Riley: Boy, I don't blame you. (*Pause*) I sure wish that little blonde would hustle her ass up here already.

Walters: Me too. I can hardly wait.

Riley: Me either. (*Begins pacing off to the left*) What time is it now?

Walters: (*Looks at his watch*) Almost 12:20.

Riley: Almost 12:20! Boy, I wish she'd hurry! (*Continues pacing*)

Walters: Me too. (*Begins pacing feverishly off to the right. Suddenly there is a knock at the door. They both jump*)

Riley: It's her!

Walters: Come in! (*The door opens and a blonde Call Girl walks breathlessly into the room and closes the door behind her*)

Riley: Well, hello.

Call Girl: I got here as fast as I could. (*Walters suddenly frowns and begins to stare fixedly at Girl, in obviously deep concentration*)

Riley: I'm Riley, and this here is Walters.

Call Girl: Pleased to meet ya. (*Pulls dress over head and hangs it up in closet, smoothes out her short chemise*) I'm Brenda. Who's first?

Riley: Well, I don't know. (*Turns to Walters*) Who goes first, Walters, me or you?

Walters: (*Still frowning*) Listen, Riley, you go ahead and do whatever you want. I'm not going in on this after all. (*Both Girl and Riley turn and stare at him*)

Riley: Your aren't? Why the hell not?

Walters: Because I've been thinking and I just realized something in the nick of time.

Riley: Oh yeah? What did you realize?

Walters: That going to bed with a woman is just another way some guys try to prove they're real men. You show me any man who goes to bed with women and I'll show you a queer every time.

(*Curtain*)

Multicultural Education in American Schools

> "If you are thinking one year ahead, plant a seed. If you are thinking ten years ahead, plant a tree. If you are thinking one hundred years ahead, educate the people."
>
> **Chinese Proverb**

How should a nation educate its people if the population is heterogeneous? For several decades educators and scholars have promoted the concept of pluralism for schools and society; yet a nation can contain diverse groups of people and still not be a pluralistic nation. Diversity simply refers to the diverse groups existing in a society; pluralism refers to a perspective whereby members of a diverse society value that diversity. Political and financial leaders of a diverse society could believe that one particular group within that society was the superior group, and require all people to conform to the attitudes and behaviors of that "superior" group. They could implement policies and practices to reward the "superior" group even if these policies and practices disadvantage the groups viewed as inferior. Because of the existence of numerous groups in such a society, it would have to be identified as diverse, but it could not be described as pluralistic. A pluralistic society would be a nation whose values, policies, and practices assumed the value of diversity and mandated equal opportunity for all members of diverse groups within that society.

Historically many immigrants coming to the United States increased the nation's diversity while they were subjected to a deliberate practice known as "Americanization," especially in schools. Being Americanized meant immigrants were forced to abandon their native language and heritage and adopt the white, middle class norms established in the American society. As in the hypothetical example given in the previous paragraph, prejudices held by the dominant white group in the United States against racial and ethnic groups, women, poor people, gay men and lesbians, and people with disabilities were translated into policies and practices that disadvantaged these groups and benefited white males. White male supremacy was open and blatant in schools and society until after World War II, but in the aftermath of that war, the nation began to change.

There were many reasons for the changes. Because the Nazis captured the horror of the Holocaust on film, Americans saw outrageous scenes that shocked them. Despite the denials of the German people, these films documented the capacity of ordinary people to engage in evil if prejudice and bigotry were allowed to flourish. In addition, African Americans, Japanese Americans, and individuals from other oppressed groups had joined the military and made enormous sacrifices during the war. Returning veterans had seen many individuals from their group lose their lives, and the survivors would no longer tolerate being treated as second-class citizens. The civil rights movement began by addressing racial segregation in schools and in transportation, and later discrimination in voting rights, services for the poor, and job opportunities, especially in southern states where the racism was usually more blatant than elsewhere.

While the marches and demonstrations and sit-ins were occurring, some scholars revived a concept first described in the 1920s called "cultural pluralism."[1] They argued that if Americans would commit to this concept, it was possible to resolve problems caused by prejudice and discrimination and that Americans could have a more just and equitable society. As affirmative action requirements helped open doors of opportunity to people of color and women, some businesses began to implement "diversity training,"[2]

which would eventually become common at corporate and government workplaces and in the military services. Teachers and administrators were exposed to ideas from "multicultural education," an educational reform based on curricular and instructional strategies that reflected a pluralistic vision. Preparing students and workers and soldiers and leaders to function effectively in a diverse society is becoming largely perceived as a pragmatic response to a society as diverse as the United States.

As revealed in the writings of some critics of multicultural education, its purposes and strategies are often misunderstood; therefore, this reform effort has encountered much resistance. Because of misconceptions about who benefits from it and what it is trying to accomplish, James A. Banks addresses these issues in "Misconceptions of Multicultural Education" and provides an accurate description of what multicultural education is, what it has achieved and what challenges it is likely to confront in the future. Similarly, the strategy of ability grouping or "tracking" students also has its share of misconceptions as scores from standardized tests have been used to justify "tracking" certain students into remedial classes and others into accelerated classes. In this way, schools continue their historic practice of sorting students into categories that affect the education they receive and what they do after graduation. In "Tackling

66 America is a heterogeneous nation of many different people of different races, religions, and creeds. Should this experiment prosper, we will have offered humans a new way to look at life; should it fail, we will simply go the way of all failed civilizations. 99

Nikki Giovanni (1943–)

> ❝I refuse to believe that the American public intends to have its children sorted before their teens into clerks, watchmakers, lithographers . . . and treated differently in their schools according to such prophecies. Who are we to make these prophecies?❞
>
> **Charles Eliot Norton (1827–1908)**

Tracking," Ian McFeat's students research the topic of tracking and discover the problems that have been reported in various studies. The students request and take responsibility for planning a "learn-in" at school to present their findings and make recommendations to students, teachers, and invited guests. These students presented data and represented a perspective that echoed sentiments of earlier critics of schools engaging in sorting practices.

The next two essays focus on instructional strategies designed to promote pluralistic perspectives in schools. Jane Bolgatz conducted her research at an urban high school with diverse students and she documents how two teachers addressed issues of race and racism in their classroom. Despite the sensitivity of the topic, these teachers created a safe place for students to discuss controversial issues. The essay provides an example of how teachers can engage in anti-racist pedagogy, which is a major commitment for many multicultural educators, including Christine Sleeter. Sleeter's essay describes anti-racist activities in classrooms where students are

not diverse, but it is important that courses preparing primarily white teacher education candidates challenge them to become more critical thinkers about racial issues and diversity issues in general. In "Reflections on My Use of Multicultural and Critical Pedagogy When Students Are White," Sleeter discusses several successful strategies for her predominantly white students, such as having them research and write papers from the perspective of people in an oppressed group, reading and discussing ethnographies, and writing their own text on issues pertaining to diversity and social justice. Because historically teachers have consisted primarily of white people and predictions are that this trend will continue into the foreseeable future, it is important that teacher education programs prepare them to be effective as they work with diverse students.

One of the major goals of multicultural education is to teach about social justice issues in a way that empowers students to believe that change is possible and that we can improve our communities and create a more just society. Jonathan

> ❝The role of the teacher remains the highest calling of a free people. To the teacher, America entrusts her most precious resource, her children; and asks that they be prepared, in all their glorious diversity, to face the rigors of individual participation in a democratic society.❞
>
> **Shirley Hufstedler (1925–)**

> ❝When I despair, I remember that all through history, the way of truth and love has always won. There have been murderers and tyrants, and for a time they can seem invincible. But in the end they always fall. Think of it, always.❞
>
> **Mohandis K. Gandhi (1869–1948)**

Kozol believes that one way to do this is to share the stories of social reformers. Years ago I read an account of Gandhi as a young lawyer living in South Africa. One day he was running to board a train as it pulled out from the station, but as he clambered aboard the last car, one of his shoes slipped off his foot and landed on the railroad track. Gandhi immediately pulled off his other shoe and threw it in the direction of the lost shoe. Now Gandhi was well dressed befitting his profession, so another passenger asked why he did that. Gandhi said some poor man might now find a pair of shoes rather than only one that would do him no good.

From this story, it is easy to perceive the moral vision shaping Gandhi's social commitments and lifelong achievements. Kozol wants teachers to share such stories with students, but in his essay on "Great Men and Women," he is critical of the way school curricula tend to ignore moral reformers or distort their beliefs and achievements. He challenges teachers to provide accurate information about the values, beliefs, and actions of such individuals so that their lives can inspire children and youth to become passionate about addressing social injustices and to believe (as Gandhi believed) that people and societies can change for the better.

Notes

[1]Louis Menand, *The metaphysical club*. (New York: Farrar, Strauss, & Giroux, 2001).

[2]Sonia Nieto, *Affirming diversity: The sociopolitical context of multicultural education*, 5th ed. (Boston: Pearson, 2004).

Misconceptions of Multicultural Education

Because of confusion about what multicultural education means and how it would manifest itself in classrooms, the author describes some common misconceptions of multicultural education and discusses its future.

The bitter debate over the literary and historical canon that has been carried on in the popular press and in several widely reviewed books has overshadowed the progress that has been made in multicultural education during the last two decades. The debate has also perpetuated harmful misconceptions about theory and practice in multicultural education. Consequently, it has heightened racial and ethnic tensions and trivialized the field's remarkable accomplishments in theory, research, and curriculum development. The truth about the development and attainments of multicultural education needs to be told for the sake of balance, scholarly integrity, and accuracy. But if I am to reveal the truth about multicultural education, I must first identify and debunk some of the widespread myths and misconceptions about it.

Adapted with permission of Phi Delta Kappa and the author from James A. Banks, "Multicultural education: Development, dimensions, and challenges." *Phi Delta Kappan,* September, 1993, Volume 75, Number 1, pages 22–28.

Multicultural Education Is for the Others

One misconception about multicultural education is that it is an entitlement program and curriculum movement for African Americans, Latinos, the poor, women, and other marginalized groups.[1] The major theorists and researchers in multicultural education agree that the movement is designed to restructure educational institutions so that all students, including middle-class white males, will acquire the knowledge, skills, and attitudes needed to function effectively in a culturally and ethnically diverse nation and world.[2] Multicultural education, as its major architects have conceived it during the last decade, is not an ethnic- or gender-specific movement, but is a movement designed to empower all students to become knowledgeable, caring, and active citizens in a deeply troubled and ethnically polarized nation and world.

The claim that multicultural education is only for people of color and the disenfranchised is one of the most pernicious and damaging misconceptions with which the movement has to cope. It has caused intractable problems and has haunted the multicultural education movement since its inception. Despite all that has been written and spoken about multicultural education being for all students, the image of multicultural education as an entitlement program for the "others" remains strong and vivid in the public imagination as well as in the hearts and minds of many teachers and administrators. Teachers who teach in predominantly white schools and districts often state that they don't have a program or plan for multicultural education because they have few African American, Latino, or Asian American students.

When multicultural education is viewed by educators as the study of "the other," it is marginalized and prevented from becoming a part of mainstream educational reform. Several critics of multicultural education, such as Arthur Schlesinger, John Leo, and Paul Gray, have perpetuated the idea that multicultural education is the study of the "other" by defining it as synonymous with Afrocentric education.[3] The history of intergroup education teaches us that only when educational reform related to diversity is viewed as essential for all students – and as promoting the broad public interest – will it have a reasonable chance of becoming institutionalized in the nation's schools, colleges, and universities.[4] The intergroup education movement of the 1940s and the 1950s failed in large part because intergroup educators were never able to persuade mainstream educators to believe that the approach was needed by and designed for all students. To its bitter but quiet end, mainstream educators viewed intergroup education as something for schools with racial problems and as something for "them" and not for "us."

Multicultural Education Is Opposed to the Western Tradition

Another harmful misconception of multicultural education has been repeated so often by its critics that many people take it as self-evident. This is the claim that multicultural education is a movement that is opposed to the West and to Western civilization. Multicultural education is not anti-West

because most writers of color, such as Rudolfo A. Anaya, Paula Gunn Allen, Maxine Hong Kingston, Maya Angelou, and Toni Morrison, are Western writers. Multicultural education itself is a thoroughly Western movement. It grew out of a civil rights movement grounded in such Western democratic ideals as freedom, justice, and equality. Multicultural education seeks to extend to all people the ideals that were meant for an elite few at the nation's birth.

Although multicultural education is not opposed to the West, its advocates do demand that the truth about the West be told, that its debt to people of color and women be recognized and included in the curriculum, and that the discrepancies between ideals of freedom and equality and the realities of racism and sexism be taught to students. Reflective action by citizens is also an integral part of multicultural theory. Multicultural education views citizen action to improve society as an integral part of education in a democracy; it links knowledge, values, empowerment, and action. Multicultural education is also postmodern in its assumption about knowledge and knowledge construction; it challenges positivist assumption about the relationships between human values, knowledge, and action.

Positivists, who are the intellectual heirs of the Enlightenment, believe that it is possible to structure knowledge that is objective and beyond the influence of human values and interests. Multicultural theorists maintain that knowledge is positional, that it relates to the knower's values and experiences, and that knowledge implies action. Consequently, different concepts, theories, and paradigms imply different kinds of actions. Multiculturalists believe that in order to have valid knowledge, information about the social condition and experiences of the knower are essential.

Multicultural Education Will Divide the Nation

Many of its critics claim that multicultural education will divide the nation and undercut its unity. Schlesinger underscores this view in the title of his book *The Disuniting of America: Reflections on a Multicultural Society.* This misconception is based partly on questionable assumptions about the nature of U.S.

society and partly on a mistaken understanding of multicultural education. The claim that multicultural education will divide the nation assumes that the nation is already united. While we are one nation politically, sociologically our nation is deeply divided along racial, gender, and class lines. The debate that occurred about admitting gays into the military underscored the deep divisions in U.S. society.

Multicultural education is designed to help unify a deeply divided nation rather than to divide a highly cohesive one. Multicultural education supports the notion of *e pluribus unum* – out of many, one. The multiculturalists and the Western traditionalists, however, often differ about how the *unum* can best be attained. Traditionally, the larger U.S. society and the schools tried to create unity by assimilating students from diverse racial and ethnic groups into a mythical Anglo American culture that required them to experience a process of self-alienation. However, even when students of color became culturally assimilated, they were often structurally excluded from mainstream institutions.

The multiculturalists view *e pluribus unum* as an appropriate national goal, but they believe that the *unum* must be negotiated, discussed, and restructured to reflect the nation's ethnic and cultural diversity. The reformulation of what it means to be united must be a process that involves the participation by diverse groups within the nation, such as people of color, women, straights, gay, the powerful, the powerless, the young, and the old. The reformulation must also involve power sharing and participation by people from many different cultures who must reach beyond their cultural and ethnic borders in order to create a common civic culture that reflects and contributes to the well being of all. This common civic culture will extend beyond the cultural borders of each group and constitute a civic "borderland" culture.

In *Borderlands*, Gloria Anzaldua contrasts cultural borders and borderlands and calls for a weakening of the former in order to create a shared borderland culture in which people from many different cultures can interact, relate, and engage in civic talk and action. Anzaldua states that "borders are set up to define the places that are safe and unsafe, to distinguish *us* from *them*. A border is a dividing line, a narrow strip along a steep edge. A borderland is a vague and undetermined place created by the

residue of an unnatural boundary. It is in a constant state of transition."[5]

Multicultural Education Has Made Progress

While it is still on the margins rather than in the center of the curriculum in most schools and colleges, multicultural content has made significant inroads into both the school and the college curriculum within the last two decades. The truth lies somewhere between the claim that no progress has been made in infusing the school and college curriculum with multi-ethnic content and the claim that such content has replaced the European and American classics.

In the elementary and high schools, much more ethnic content appears in social studies and language arts textbooks today than was the case twenty years ago. In addition, some teachers assign works written by authors of color along with the more standard American classics. In his study of book-length works used in high schools, Applebee concluded that his most striking finding was how similar present reading lists are to past ones and how little change has occurred. However, he did note that many teachers use anthologies as a mainstay of their literature programs and that 21 percent of the anthology selections were written by women and 14 percent by authors of color.[6]

More classroom teachers today have studied concepts of multicultural education than at any previous point in our nation's history. A significant percentage of today's classroom teachers took a required teacher education course in multicultural education when they were in college. The multicultural education standard adopted by the National Council for the Accreditation of Teacher Education (NCATE) in 1977, which became effective January 1, 1979, was a major factor that stimulated the growth of multicultural education in teacher education programs. The standard stated: "The institution gives evidence of planning for multicultural education in its teacher education curricula including both the general and professional studies components."[7]

The market for teacher education textbooks dealing with multicultural education is now a substantial one. Most major publishers now have at least one text in the field. Textbooks in other required courses, such as educational psychology and the foundations of education, frequently have separate chapters or a significant number of pages devoted to examining concepts and developments in multicultural education.

Some of the nation's leading colleges and universities have either revised their general core curriculum to include ethnic content or have established an ethnic studies course requirement. The list of universities with similar kinds of requirements grows longer each year. However, the transformation of the traditional canon on college and university campuses has often been bitter and divisive. All changes in curriculum come slowly and painfully to university campuses, but curriculum changes that are linked with issues related to race evoke primordial feelings and reflect the racial crisis in American society. For example, at the University of Washington a bitter struggle ended with the defeat of the ethnic studies requirement.

Changes are also coming to elementary and high school textbooks. I believe that the demographic imperative is the major factor driving the changes in school textbooks. The color of the nation's student body is changing rapidly. Nearly half (about 45.5 percent) of the nation's school-age youths will be young people of color by 2020.[8] Black parents and brown parents are demanding that their leaders, their images, their pain, and their dreams be mirrored in the textbooks that their children study in school.

Textbooks have always reflected the myths, hopes, and dreams of people with money and power. As African Americans, Hispanics, Asians, and women become more influential, textbooks will increasingly reflect their hopes, dreams, and disappointments. Textbooks will have to survive in the marketplace of a browner America. Because textbooks still carry the curriculum in the nation's public schools, they will remain an important focus for multicultural curriculum reformers.

Multicultural Education and the Future

The achievements of multicultural education since the late Sixties and early Seventies are noteworthy and should be acknowledged. Those who have shaped the movement during the intervening decades have been able to obtain wide agreement on the goals and approaches to multicultural education. Most multiculturalists agree that the major goal of multicultural education is to restructure schools so that all students will acquire the knowledge, attitudes, and skills needed to function in an ethnically and racially diverse nation and world. As is the case with other interdisciplinary areas of study, debates within the field continue. These debates are consistent with the philosophy of a field that values democracy and diversity. They are a source of strength.

Multicultural education is being implemented widely in the nation's schools, colleges, and universities. The large number of national conferences, school district workshops, and teacher education courses in multicultural education are evidence of its success and perceived importance. Although the process of integration of content is slow and often contentious, multicultural content is increasingly becoming a part of core courses in schools and colleges. Textbook publishers are also integrating ethnic and cultural content into their books, and the pace of such integration is increasing.

Despite its impressive successes, however, multicultural education faces serious challenges. One of the most serious of these challenges is the highly organized, well-financed attacks by the Western traditionalists who fear that multicultural education will transform America in ways that will result in their own disempowerment. Ironically, the successes that multicultural education has experienced during the last decade have played a major role in provoking the attacks.

The debate over the canon and the well-orchestrated attack on multicultural education reflect an identity crisis in U.S. society. The American identity is being reshaped as groups on the margins of society begin to participate in the mainstream and to demand that their visions be reflected in a transformed America. In the future, the sharing of power and the transformation of identity required to achieve lasting racial peace in America may be valued rather than feared, for only in this way will we achieve national salvation.

As the ethnic texture of nations such as the United States, Canada, and the United Kingdom continues to deepen, educational programs related to ethnic and cultural diversity will continue to emerge and will take various shapes and forms. New challenges will continue to evolve in pluralistic democratic societies. The extent to which these challenges will be transformed into opportunities will be largely dependent on the vision, knowledge, and commitment of each nation's educators.

Notes

[1]Nathan Glazer, In Defense of Multiculturalism, *New Republic*, 2, (1991, September), pp. 18–22; and Dinesh D'Souza, Illiberal education, *Atlantic* (1991, March), pp. 51–79.

[2]James A. Banks. *Multiethnic education: Theory and practice* (3rd ed.). Boston: Allyn and Bacon (1994); James A. Banks and Cherry A. McGee-Banks, *Multicultural education: issues and perspectives* (2nd ed.) Boston: Allyn and Bacon (1993); and Christine E. Sleeter and Carl A. Grant, *Making choices for multicultural education: Five approaches to race, class and gender* (Columbus, OH: Merrill, 1988).

[3]Arthur M. Schelsinger, Jr., *The disuniting of America: Reflections on a multicultural society,* Knoxville, TN: Whittle Direct Books (1991); John Leo, A fringe history of the world, *U.S. News & World Report,* 12, (1990, November), pp. 25–26; and Paul Gray, "Whose America?," *Time* (1991, July 8), pp. 13–17.

[4]Hilda Taba et al., *Intergroup education in public schools,* Washington, D.C.: American Council on Education (1952).

[5]Gloria Anzaldua, *Borderlands: The new Mestiza.* (San Francisco: Spinsters/Aunt Lute, 1987), p. 3.

[6]Arthur N. Applebee, Stability and change in the high school canon, *English Journal,* (1992, September) pp. 27–32.

[7]*Standards for the Accreditation of Teacher Education.* (1977). Washington, D.C.: National Council for Accreditation of Teacher Education, p. 4.

[8]Pallas, A. M., Natriello, G. and McDill, E. I. (1989, June/July). The changing nature of the disadvantaged population: Current dimensions and future trends. *Educational Researcher,* p. 16-22.

Tackling Tracking

Studies have shown that "tracking" – grouping students by ability – is not an effective pedagogical approach; students in middle to low groups tend to perform much worse than when they are with students with diverse academic abilities. Even so, many schools continue to track students. The students of this author/teacher looked at the research on tracking and decided to do something about tracking in their school.

"I don't want *my* son with *those* kids!" one of the parents shouted.

"Yeah. How are you going to challenge my daughter when these kids can't even read?" another said. "You can't make all kids learn at the same rate. That's unfair."

The classroom where we held the community meeting on small school reform erupted into finger pointing and shouting as some faculty explained plans to de-track courses for the incoming ninth graders. We were one year into the process of converting to small schools and the parents of the "academically motivated" were turning up the heat.

Our school, Henry Foss High School in Tacoma, Washington, had received a small schools grant from the Bill and Melinda Gates Foundation. The foundation granted $950,000 for professional development and other activities to help us begin converting our comprehensive high school into smaller learning communities.

While other high schools in my district are physically located within their school communities, Henry Foss draws its nearly 2,000 students from both the wealthy Fircrest community that borders it and neighborhoods not well off enough to have formal names other than those on the apartment building billboards. Students are drawn to Henry Foss primarily for the International Baccalaureate program (I.B.) that offers a leg up for college credit and a prestigious certificate of merit for those who complete the diploma requirements.

Yet more than half of the students at Henry Foss receive free or reduced-price lunches, and some staff members believe this number should be much higher because many of the students don't take the free lunches to avoid being stigmatized or labeled as "poor." Our school is culturally diverse, with enrollment of African Americans near 30 percent, Asian Americans and Pacific Islanders around 28 percent, and recent immigrants from Eastern Europe and other minority groups hovering around 10 percent. Nearly half the students who enter Foss as freshmen do not graduate as seniors. This number parallels national trends, but dropouts are overwhelmingly the non-Fircrest students.

When we undertook small school reform, one tough issue was the integration of students from separate tracks. The grant itself vaguely required that "all" students be provided with a "rigorous"

From *Rethinking Schools*, 2005, Vol. 19, #4. Reprinted with permission of Rethinking Schools, www.rethinkingschools.org.

education. Rigor was a requirement; de-tracking our institution was not. The plan for integration came from a few teacher-leaders of the academies. These leaders, in agreement with the administration, saw the need to refocus our schools for equity.

Some parents wanted to ensure that no one would infringe upon their I.B. turf. They didn't want their "highly capable" students mixed with the "regular" kids. Fircrest parents organized to preserve the prestigious I.B. program. These parents got involved in the reform effort. They went to community meetings where we discussed the focus of the small schools; they helped plan booster meetings in the faculty lunchroom; they went to school board meetings to voice their desires that the I.B. courses remain untracked.

In sharp contrast to Fircrest, the other communities whose children attended Foss were fractured: divided by a freeway on one side, a minor league baseball park on the other, a business district choked with fast food restaurants, and the parks and recreation softball fields. These communities, although close in proximity to the affluent one, lacked the organizing power of the economically endowed Fircrest neighborhood, and had not been involved in the school reform activities. A few teachers saw this small school grant as an opportunity to organize our school around equity, de-track our high school, and provide quality education for all of our students. The parents of the academically "gifted" had advocates. We thought this reorganization would give us a chance to stand up for "regular" kids.

As part of the grant our school district gave teachers eight late-start days. Students would arrive at school late so we could meet as faculty in our academies to discuss the school's future. By the time students rolled into class in the late morning, I was drained, and my freshman "regular" civics students could tell. I taught two freshman civics courses. The first was full of "high achieving" students, and my second was loaded with so-called "regular" students.

Deshawn, a student in the latter class, was a curious student who lived in a house that bordered the mall and a Pizza Hut. "What are you guys talking about in those meetings anyway?" he asked. I told him that we were studying how to break our school into smaller learning communities. "So, who shows up?" he asked.

"Well, it's faculty now."

"So, you're gonna decide for us, aren't you?" he asked. I thought about it. There wasn't a single student at the meetings. The usual suspects drove the reform: teachers, administrators, and parents of the academically talented. Students were shut out of the process, relegated to the sidelines. We had never asked them about the education they'd like to create or included their dreams and aspirations alongside our own.

Deshawn's comment made me think twice about what I wanted to teach next. I realized I wanted to include my students in the conversation that was going on around them about their schooling.

I talked to Deshawn the next day: "I'll show you what we talked about on Monday. We'll study it."

With the help of a small schools collaborative coach who was hired with the Gates Foundation money, I organized a civics unit around the study of school. I wanted my freshmen to uncover the hidden curriculum at Foss, to begin to put clothes on the institution that remained invisible. I wanted students to critique the institution in order to create greater equity at our school.

We began the unit on schooling with a role-play activity that examined the issue of tracking, as well as the historical and cultural aspects of power and privilege in public schooling. The role-play emphasized that schools were created to instill patriotism at the expense of questioning, that the tracking of public high schools was used to segregate laborers from leaders, and that biased standardized tests were utilized to justify this stratification. I hoped that my students might begin to imagine how similar stratification continued to exist in some form today in our tracked school. And I wanted them to consider how they might ultimately change these structures to ensure more democratic participation in their own school lives.

After the role-play, I provided the students with data from Henry Foss High School about the failure rate and information about the International Baccalaureate program. My presentation included statistics on student success in the I.B. program broken out by race and gender. More than half of the 200 students who entered the I.B. program freshman year quit during their senior year, approximately the same as the rate for our "regular" classes. But the I.B. dropout rate for African-American students was nearly three times the rate of our white students. And, while Asian-American students tended to complete the program, they tended not to receive diplomas, which award college credit. Eleven of 35 males who began pre-I.B. were people of color and 37 females of color began the program that same year, but only 15 total students received I.B. diplomas by their senior year. Fourteen of these students were white and one was Latina.

Joey, a non-Fircrest student, appeared to be surprised at the end of the presentation. "Wow," he said, "I never knew this stuff was happening at our school."

Next we read the chapter "Sorting" in Ted and Nancy Sizer's book *The Students Are Watching*. The chapter helps unearth a reality behind tracking: Students in the "high-ability" tracks are offered more rigorous course work and greater access to rich and creative schooling experiences than other students.

I wrote the phrase "Sorting Is . . ." in the center of about 10 feet of butcher paper with enough space for plenty of comments and taped it on the wall. I told the students that this activity was called a Chalk Talk. I explained that a Chalk Talk is a silent activity: No one may talk during it, yet anyone may add to the Chalk Talk as they please. I had used this activity with students previously and knew that it provided opportunities for expression for those who might be reluctant to make comments out loud. In my experience, Chalk Talk also democratized discussion by allowing many voices to share simultaneously in a conversation. I didn't set limits on how many students could "talk" at the same time, but I told them that there might be periods of long "silence" or times when we'd all be up at the front, "talking" and responding to each other's comments. Students were already familiar with the activity, so I handed out different colored markers and told them to write as they felt for 15 to 30 minutes. They were to use the article to apply their thinking about sorting to our school.

Marissa, who lived near the apartments next to Highway 16, wrote on the paper first, "Sorting is systematic racism, and it's a cheap way to determine the intelligence of us." Her comment got three students out of their seats ready to respond.

"This happens because of powerful parents," one wrote.

"This becomes like a group of kids that stay together through most of their high school courses," wrote another. "It separates us from each other and puts us into categories."

Jeremy, a quiet student, wrote:

[Sorting is] extremely stupid and affects people's lives in the long run, whether you realize it or not. When a young child is accustomed to sorting and grows up they will think it is the proper way to live and grow up believing that the world should be sorted. It shouldn't. A child that believes that sorting is right will have a very hard life ahead.

Some students also caught on to the larger implications of sorting. One student wrote, "[sorting is] a class system." To which another replied, "It is wealth segregated."

When we debriefed, I asked how two of the comments in particular related to our study. I pointed to one student comment, "Oh well, what all can kids do?" Then I pointed out a student question, "So do we have to deal with it?" Jacob explained that we had a responsibility to do something about this stuff. Marisa added, "Yeah, if I had never studied tracking then I would never have known about it. We have to let others know."

Marissa hit on an important point. The system of segregation at Henry Foss was so embedded that the majority of students had no idea it was even going on. And more to the point, the institution had convinced students in most of the tracks in the school that they deserved their slots. Silence on the issues of tracking and segregation had been the norm until now. I wanted students to reflect, speak out, and take action.

Some students wanted to protest at the main office, carrying signs that labeled themselves as they had experienced in the testing and tracking role-play. Students advocating this action believed it would forever expose the silent quality of tracking – the ways students from disadvantaged neighborhoods were slipped and slotted into lower tracks without their knowledge. My students believed this action might spread awareness to the student body and force the administration to open more classes in the I.B. track or make I.B. accessible to all students. With only 200 out of 2000 students enrolled in the I.B. program, there were serious inequities. Others wanted to march on over to the next school board meeting to demand that students be included in the reform efforts and have votes on major policy issues that involved our conversion to smaller schools. Still others wanted vaguely to "fight the power."

After deliberating, we decided to host a "learn-in" on democracy and education. We decided to bring in professors from around the area and use students in the class to teach lessons. As a class we created a general list of topics that might explain tracking and our work on equity. Students chose topics on unpacking white privilege, looking at school through the eyes of students, raising the issue of *Brown vs. Board of Education* at our school, and looking closely at the social construction of intelligence.

Students wanted to build interest from their peers to analyze the I.B. program and its disproportionate benefits to white male students; to provide an alternative forum to the student government which had some power in student activities but a nonexistent role in shaping our school; to include a student voice on schooling personalization and the new structure of our small schools; to influence teachers to see students as active participants in the small schools work; and to critically examine the failure rate at Henry Foss and gather support for a student-led organization that would hold our school accountable to all of its students. . . .

On the day of the learn-in my students looked nervous. Near the front of the cafeteria, before an anxious audience of professors, community members, and teachers, the opening act wasn't taking place. The microphone wasn't working. Finally the microphone came on and from that point on, the day quickly slid by. . . .

At the end of the day we had accomplished a lot. More than 18 professors, seven students, and four faculty members led discussions on equity issues with titles such as: "The Education of Racism," "Ebonics and the Skin We Speak," and "The Deficit of Deficit Thinking Widens the Gap," and included discussion emphasizing some practical approaches to equity: "Reaching Toward Equity in College Readiness and Access" and "Student Profiles and Student Needs." Using 23 classrooms, we could not

accommodate the demand as more than half of Foss's students (at least a thousand) participated in at least one of the lessons, and 600 students had been in three or more sessions.

Reflecting on the experience Jessie said, "I never knew learning could be so real. This was learning and doing together. We can't let this die down." Immediately following the learn-in, some students talked of building a coalition or alternative group that would have an impact on school policies. A few students from some of the presentations got together and drew up plans for an interest group called STAT (Students and Teachers Against Tracking). . . .

Perhaps the most tangible effect of our efforts came when our English courses in Academy 1 agreed to mix "honors" students with the "regular" ones for the next academic year. This has led to more inclusive classrooms now, where students are mixed heterogeneously in at least one subject area in one-fourth of the school. . . .

But the learn-in also had its problems. I had failed to enlist the support of students in the I.B. program, and one of them who wasn't so thrilled with the day's events said, "All we see is the good and the bad. Nothing else" Also, although it was appropriate to have faculty from state universities teach lessons, student evaluations showed the student-run lessons had the highest ratings. . . .

During the debriefing with the professors, someone said he thought the learn-in failed to connect to what students would return to at school. Although he believed it was important to study school and these issues, he thought the learn-in built animosity without giving hope to students.

Despite these shortcomings, my students and I learned important lessons about civics and educational democracy. Students like Deshawn wanted to be included in the conversation about their future, about the future of our conversion to small schools at Henry Foss. Without listening to their voices, we would have missed out on the insights they had to offer; insights that the adults needed to hear.

Teachers Initiating Conversations About Race and Racism in a High School Class

Many teachers are too intimidated to address diversity issues in the classroom, and yet there is nothing more important for our students today than to find a safe place to explore the complexity of diversity issues. The author shows us two teachers who have made their classroom a safe place to talk about racial issues.

Race and racism are complicated historical and current phenomena that students need to understand if they are going to grapple effectively with the ongoing racial tensions in our society. Unfortunately, teachers often do not know how to broach these subjects with students. The topics are often considered too taboo or controversial for discussion in schools, and teachers have few tools to overcome the difficulties associated with initiating conversations about these subjects. For research purposes, I observed the techniques, materials and processes of a White teacher and a Black teacher who introduced issues of race and racism in their team-taught high school class. The teachers explicitly put the issues of race and racism on the table, asked questions that challenged students to think about these topics, and used race-related curricular materials and assignments. The teachers' initiative encouraged the students in the class to speak out about the language and meaning of race and racism.

For decades many teacher educators have advocated that teachers help students understand cultural differences among groups and reduce students' racial prejudice. In recent years, school districts and public policy makers have espoused rhetoric about recognizing diversity and preparing students to function in a multicultural society. Critical multicultural theorists have suggested that teachers should bring up the subjects of race and power . . . and discuss differences without normalizing Whiteness or any other position, while at the same time examining the historical and social creation and continuation of conditions of oppression in society.

Yet, despite this encouragement, talking about race and racism in classrooms remains a challenge. Research has shown that some, especially White, teachers feel they lack understanding of or reject information about the nature and causes of social inequities.[1] In my teacher education classes, preservice and in-service teachers, usually White, wonder how they will be able to "fit" multicultural education into their already over-stuffed curricula. They

From *Multicultural Perspectives*, 2005, 7(3). Reprinted by permission of Taylor and Francis Group who may be contacted at www.informaworld.com.

also fear that examining race explicitly will some-how create or reinforce racism. Research has shown that White teachers often do not like to talk about whiteness,[2] leave race out of the teaching of U.S. History,[3] and do not even take up the topic of race when they are using books with explicitly racial content.[4] Many teachers wonder how or if they should address "sensitive" topics like slavery, partic-ularly with younger students. . . .

Because I was interested in studying this gap be-tween the theory and practice of multicultural edu-cation, I decided to look at how two teachers, Ann and Lewis, introduced race and racism in their team-taught, U.S. History and Language Arts class. Their interdisciplinary class covered United States history from 1950 to the present. I chose this class for two reasons. First, it was a required course, and I wanted to observe a cross-section of students in the context of a general course, rather than stu-dents specifically interested in race or racism or a class devoted to those topics. Second, the teachers focused on issues of power in society, and I sus-pected that the topics of race and racism would come up in discussion.

I was a participant-observer in the class for one term (12 weeks). I chose to be a participant-ob-server because the teachers told me that students might trust me more if I participated in the class to some degree rather than simply watching and tak-ing notes. Because I wanted to influence the course of the class as little as possible, I only occasionally offered ideas and questions; for most of the time I was observing. . . .

The class took place at a public alternative school in a Midwestern city. The alternative school admit-ted students who had either dropped out of or been dismissed from one of the city's three large conven-tional schools, and its student population was 82% White. The class met four times a week for 80 min-utes. Out of 24 students in the class – mostly juniors and seniors, and mostly boys – 18 identified as White, three as Black, and one each as Chicano, Asian and mixed Black and White. Most students came from low-income families.

The teachers were Ann, a 65-year-old White Language Arts teacher, and Lewis, a 49-year-old Black Social Studies teacher. Ann had taught at the school for 22 years, and Lewis for 8. . . . Ann ex-plained that she and Lewis were able to reach a

wider audience in a general history class than they might have by teaching a course specifically about difference, intolerance, or oppression. But she added, "I think the emphasis ended up being quite a bit on racism because that was our particular in-terest."

The teachers fostered conversations in the class by cultivating an environment that encouraged stu-dents' participation and ownership. Ann and Lewis worked to make sure that all students had a voice in the conversation. They often went "around the cir-cle," asking each student to share an answer to the question that they had responded to in writing when the class started. Although this took time, it allowed all students a specific time to talk in class. The teachers also worked hard to ensure that stu-dents were respectful of each other. For example, when several students fired questions at one girl at one time, Ann reprimanded them: "You can ask that in different ways so that people don't feel like they are being attacked."

The teachers explicitly taught students how to listen, back up their opinions with evidence, and make use of their own experiences in discussions. Moreover, because they had worked to build a trusting tone in the class, they were able to encour-age a great deal of student-to-student interaction. Such a class structure freed students to interact on a subject as potentially difficult as racism without being led every step of the way by a teacher. . . .

Ann and Lewis talked easily about race and racism. Such ease normalized the idea of talking about these topics. By talking personally about their racial positions in society, the teachers investigated the construction of race and modeled the process for students. Lewis especially shared his personal experiences with students, moving beyond the rhetoric of the social studies curriculum to bring the issue of equity alive. Introducing the civil rights unit, for instance, he related a story about the seg-regation in his hometown:

> We had one Black pool in this small town, one
> public swimming pool. They closed that. We had to
> go back to swimming in the creek. Because they
> said, "The races will not mix." . . .

Although she did not raise the issue as much as Lewis did, Ann was also comfortable with discussions of race. In one class she talked about how it was often difficult for her to figure out what language to use when referring to groups of people. "Do you say 'Black,' or do you say 'African-American'?" she asked rhetorically, and then explained that the night before she had seen a man on television say that most Indians preferred the term "Indian" to the term "Native American." Throughout the explanation, she was open and at ease with what might have been seen as a delicate issue. . . .

Another way the teachers brought race into the conversation was through questioning. In one discussion, students argued about the existence of institutionalized racism as a result of Lewis asking them to think about racial profiling. Lewis explicitly called attention to the racial make-up of prisons: "Who is the biggest majority of people in the state's prisons?" Lewis asked the students to look carefully at the factors that might have caused more Blacks to be imprisoned. He gave a specific example from his own experience and asked if a White teacher would have faced the same treatment:

> Would it be the fact that I'm more likely to get stopped? I drove to school up here. Police followed me. I'm coming to school. Would George Doyle [a White teacher] be stopped? I don't know.

In response to this challenging question, there was a heated argument about institutionalized racism (the race of the student is identified in parentheses).

> *Tim (W) (crying out):* I get followed, too! I get followed, too! . . . Wouldn't that be there's more Black people in jail in [our city] so wouldn't that mean there's more Black criminals [here]? Or do you think that you guys just get messed with more?
>
> *Edmund (B):* The majority of the people in prison in [this state] for violent crimes are White people. The majority of the Black people in prison in [this state] are in there for crimes like –
>
> *Tim:* Drugs.
>
> *Edmund:* Drugs.
>
> *Tim:* Well, do you think more Black people are doing drugs?
>
> *Edmund:* No. It's impossible! Because . . . the majority of the people here –

> *Malik (B):* There's not as many Black folks here in [this state] as there is White folks here.
>
> *Edmund:* Exactly.
>
> *Ann (teacher):* I think it does have to do with being caught. I think that there (are) some studies, Tim, that are really kind of interesting. It really does have to do with being picked up and caught.
>
> *Tim:* But I get pulled over, too, man. Like I get followed and I get messed with too!

Although the pace was quick and not everyone participated, this discussion resulted in at least some students examining and articulating their views and acknowledging at least the possibility of institutionalized racism. For example, Hank and Chris, both White students, talked about the bias of the legal system:

> *Hank:* Yeah we [Whites] are followed, too. But, you know, even though you may not realize it, but Black people are, like, followed by cops. They do get stopped more.
>
> *Chris:* Yes, I admit it! I get off because I'm White.

Another powerful example of questioning the racist institutions in society occurred when the class discussed the U.S. military involvement in Kosovo. Both teachers asked questions that allowed students to see the war through the lens of race. Ann pointed out the discrepancy between military policy in Europe, which has a predominantly White population, and Africa, which is predominantly Black. She asked students why the U.S. was fighting in Kosovo but not Africa. Her question was not detached or academic; rather her tone suggested her genuine concern and curiosity:

> There are a lot of wars and killing going on . . . in Africa. Are we bombing them? Are we worried? I was told by the people who got us into this war [in Kosovo] that the purpose was to stop the killing.

Students responded with objections that the reason that the United States did not go to war in Africa was because Africa was not as financially important. Lewis, in an even bolder question, pointed to the racial element of the response by the United States: "Could it be that if you're White you're right?"

In discussing the topic in a small group afterwards, Tricia, a White student, said that she had been surprised by the idea that military policy would have to do with race. "I remember than when [Lewis] brought the color into it . . . That totally threw me off, cuz I wasn't thinkin' it had anything to do with that." Realizing that the military might perpetuate institutionalized racism was a new awareness for Tricia. Lewis and Ann's questions had opened the question of racism for several students:

Jake (W): I still don't think [the war in Kosovo] had anything to do with [race].

Edmund (B): Hey, you know, it was a good point, because it does – And Ann was trying to get at the same thing. It made sense to me.

Antoine (B): You're trying to say that Black folks aren't as important?

Tricia (W): But I think that the countries in Africa would be as important if they had, like, the military stuff, like the bombs.

Antoine: The reason why they don't have that . . .

Edmund: . . . is because nobody's helping them.

Antoine: Yes, exactly.

Edmund: Because they're not important enough. That's [the point Lewis] was trying to make, and I agree with it. I'm not trying to be like – I agree with that point. That's what he was trying to get at and I know it was.

Tricia: Well, I see that now. Like no one's helping them get the education to go out and do it.

The students conflated being important because a country has a predominantly White population with being important because "they had, like, the military stuff, like the bombs" or because a population is sufficiently educated. The students did not question these ethnocentric assumptions. Nevertheless, they wrestled with the idea of racism.

Questions also served to prompt students to think about subtle forms of racism, such as the ways that people of color are discredited in society. When the students saw a picture of Elvis Presley shown as one of the famous people of the 1950s, Ann asked a question that served to call into question the Eurocentric bias of the picture: "Where did Elvis get his music?" Two students responded to the question:

Vic (A): African music.

Antoine (B): Rhythm and blues.

Their answers widened the scope of history that was unacknowledged in the image. Although there was no extended discussion about the African or African-American influences on Presley's music, Ann's question did serve to expand the conversation. She helped students examine how race frames our view of the world. The teachers often explicitly pointed out the element of race in historical and current events. . . .

During one discussion, Ann asked if the way the class was talking about racism was intellectualizing, and she countered that approach by describing a photograph that evoked students' emotional responses: "There's a picture of a little kid – whose grandfather is in the Ku Klux Klan. It's a little White kid. And the grandfather is helping the child sort of adjust his robe. He's got a little tiny Ku Klux Klan robe on. And that, I mean that picture hits you right – " [she pressed a fist against her chest].

"That's child abuse," a student exclaimed and several students debated whether or not it is child abuse to teach your child to be racist. Ann's representation of a family's perpetuation of racism was a powerful catalyst for discussion.

The teachers did not only ask students to think about race and racism in relation to isolated texts. The final project in the class was for the students to research the progress of a particular group in society since the 1960s, and present their findings to the class. These presentations engendered provocative conversation. One student's presentation about Native Americans, for example, led to a heated discussion about the use of racial names for sports teams. Vic, an Asian American student, asked why Native Americans objected to the Cleveland Indians. Another student wondered, "How come they get mad about the Cleveland Indians but not the Jeep Cherokee?" In the ensuing discussion, students argued about the offensiveness of various images. . . . The prevailing sentiment in the class was that logos such as the Cleveland Indians and other cartoon depictions were not insulting. One student, however, held that turning the Fat Albert character into a logo would be offensive.

Finally, the teachers were willing to examine their own positions, modeling reflection for students and opening the door to conversations about race and racism. . . . In a discussion, Ann used the pronoun "we" to describe the Europeans who had taken or purchased land in the Midwest in the 1800s. She laughed after she spoke and then explained that she was surprised to find herself unconsciously identifying with White Europeans. In response, three students referred to their own ancestry, which was different from that of White Europeans. They agreed with Ann's self-correction, calling into question the accuracy of an inclusive "we." . . .

In their responses to Ann's comment, students connected themselves to racial groups from the past. Vic, for instance, who had been born in Korea and adopted by White parents, identified with Asian immigrant railroad workers of the previous century. In doing so the students opened the question of racial identity – who am I? At the same time, they questioned the way that race is often constructed – indicating that being White is not a universal experience. With Ann as the model, they challenged the norm of Whiteness. It was striking that these students voiced their beliefs and challenges out loud.

Teachers' willingness to talk about race is the funnel through which any curriculum that addresses issues of race or racism either flows or is thwarted. When race is ignored, the hidden curriculum teaches a powerful message that race and racism are not worthy of students' attention. In their class, however, Ann and Lewis made racism part of the explicit curriculum. . . . By broaching the subject, they normalized the discussion and pushed students to talk more critically and broadly about race and racism. . . .

Putting the issue of race on the table is not a matter of charisma. Rather it is about taking risks, being open to hearing what students think, and maintaining an atmosphere of respect. The teachers I observed incorporated interrelated strategies to initiate race talk – open, nonjudgmental dialogue; frequent references to and reflections on race and racism in conversations; and explicit reference to race and racism through materials, questions, and assignments. These strategies represent possible avenues for engaging students in vital conversations about their lives and futures.

Notes

[1]Gloria Ladson-Billings, Toward a theory of culturally relevant pedagogy, *American Educational Research Journal*, 1995, *32*(3), pp. 465–491.

[2]Alice McIntyre, *Making whiteness a topic of inquiry in teaching and research,* Paper presented at the NCTE Assembly for Research Midwinter Conference: Teaching and researching across color lines, February, 2003, Minneapolis, MN.

[3]D. Almarza, and B. R. Fehn, The construction of whiteness in an American history classroom: A case study of eighth grade Mexican American students, *Transformations*, 1998, *9*(2), pp. 196–211.

[4]Gloria Ladson-Billing, *Still playing in the dark: Whiteness in the literary imagination of children's and young adult literature teaching,* Paper presented at the NCTE Assembly for Research Midwinter Conference: Teaching and researching across color lines, 2003, Minneapolis, MN.

Reflections on My Use of Multicultural and Critical Pedagogy When Students Are White

According to current data and demographic predictions, over 80 percent of teachers are white, and will continue to be for many years; yet these teachers will encounter an increasingly diverse student population. The author addresses the issue of preparing aspiring white educators to engage in teaching that has value for all students.

Multicultural education and critical pedagogy are conceptually linked, although such links are not always articulated. Advocates of critical pedagogy seek to reinvigorate democracy as a public process and to grapple with ethical issues of domination and control. Critical pedagogy "would stress student participation in the learning process with the intention of enabling students to challenge the social order."[1] . . .

But what if one's students occupy social positions of privilege? How might one prompt students to challenge the social order who largely stand to benefit from it as it exists? Or is that even possible? For example, Jonathan Kozol summed up a huge challenge:

> No matter what devices are contrived to bring about equality, it is clear that they require money-transfer, and the largest source of money is the portion of the population that possesses the most money.[2]

And the most power and authority. Now, imagine what multicultural critical pedagogy might mean if one is teaching those with the most, rather than the least. Banks (1988) recognized that curriculum for powerful groups needs to differ from that for oppressed groups. He explained that the "Enlightening Powerful Groups" model of curriculum should attempt "to modify the attitudes and perceptions of dominant ethnic groups so that they would be willing, as adults, to share power . . . and willing to take action to change the social system so it would treat powerless ethnic groups more justly."[3] However, he expressed pessimism that one could achieve significant change by trying to educate powerful groups and saw more hope in strategies to empower oppressed groups.

While I agree with his emphasis on empowering oppressed groups, I believe there is value in attempting to educate others who (like me) are white and relatively secure economically. This is a challenge I have struggled with for several years . . . Early on, I recognized an unsatisfactory but common dichotomy in pedagogical orientations that Elshtain described as the "coercive" classroom versus the "non-authoritarian" classroom.[4] Teachers who wish to critique structural oppression want their students to learn to engage in the same form of critique. The greater the likelihood their students will find social critique threatening and foreign, the greater the tendency of the teacher to control the selection and flow of ideas, which many students experience as coercive rather than liberating. This coercive pedagogy contradicts the participatory mode of critical teaching. So, many teachers instead construct a non-authoritarian classroom in which students are invited to create knowledge by sharing their own perspectives and feelings – which often are not critical at all. Liberatory classrooms are neither non-authoritarian nor coercive, but, as Elshtain says, involve shifting relations of power as students engage with ideas they may find threatening; the long-range goal is construction of "a theory of human liberation" that includes all of us.[5]

So again, how does one do that? How, for example, does one involve a class of male and female white students from mainly middle class backgrounds in a critique of various forms of oppression grounded in emancipation of other people?

(One) fall semester . . . I assigned a class of twenty-two undergraduate pre-service students a paper in which they were to ask a "Why?" question involving some aspect of race, social class, and/or gender that they genuinely did not understand. They were to attempt to answer the question from a perspective of the oppressed group(s) the question was about, with relatively little direct help from me. All of the students were white; sixteen were women and six were men. They ranged in age from about twenty-one to thirty-five and in social class from working to middle class.

Their papers surpassed what I would have expected several years ago. In most pre-service teacher education classes, if one poses a question such as, "Why do children of poor families disproportionately not complete school?" one is likely to receive answers that focus on inadequacies of their families and communities, changes in the moral climate among students over the past three decades, or the problem of gangs. My students learned to proceed quite differently. . . .

(Consider) two perspectives about the nature of society and the nature of "have not" groups which derive from different positions in an unequal social order. The dominant perspective holds that society is free and open to anyone who tries to advance, although one may encounter barriers one must work to overcome. To explain inequality, "deficiencies " of "have not" groups are highlighted: deficiencies of language, effort, education, culture, family, and so forth. "Minority position" perspectives hold that society is unfair and rigged to favor groups with power. "Have not" groups are more accurately understood as oppressed; they may lack access to society's resources, but culturally have generated a considerable reservoir of strengths.

Teachers enter teaching with some ideas about diverse American groups and about why groups occupy different social positions, based on their lived experience and the ideology they have learned to use to interpret those experiences. It is very possible to study the "Other" and retain one's own ideas about justice and the existing social system. When multicultural education is reduced to teaching about "other" people, educators are usually allowed to retain their perspective and theories about the workings of society.

The pedagogical approach I will describe aims to help students learn that there is more than one perspective and learn to use a "minority position" perspective to examine school issues. When attempting to teach "minority position" perspectives, teachers often bombard students with them, leaving intact the assumption that there is one correct interpretation of society: the teacher's interpretation. This creates what Elshtain termed the "coercive" classroom, which many students resist. Partly what students resist is the implication that the sense they have made of their lives is wrong. I have found them far more likely to entertain another perspective, as long as it is not presented as the only "correct" one.

Embedded within the project of attempting to reposition perspectives, however, is the recognition that students' perspectives are not singular. Each student can learn to engage in a "minority position" perspective regarding some issues and in some circumstances, but retain a dominant perspective in other situations. Further, to the extent that my pedagogical process is "liberating," it is not necessarily liberating my students. Rather, my work attempts to connect students with discourses that others find liberating, so that when they enter the classroom as teachers, they will recognize and hear (and, one hopes, begin to act with) the words and visions of disenfranchised people.

During their second semester with me, twenty-two pre-service students posed "why" questions about a variety of issues. They formulated their questions on the basis of personal experiences or observations; most opened their "Why?" papers with very specific examples of the questions they addressed. Most of their questions had to do with race and culture; some involved gender issues. Their sources of information were mainly interviews with people who are members of the group(s) their questions involved; papers also drew on scholarly articles written by members of such groups. I will share examples of their work, then discuss the teaching they had experienced.

Four young white women wondered why African American males experience difficulties in schools. Their papers explored a variety of factors; their conclusions differed but fit within the context of observations made:

> The "black male crisis" becomes reified in isolation and addressed outside the full cultural, historical, political, and economic contexts of African Americans' lives. Eurocentric formation of the issue defines it as a "black" issue, thus making it both the product and the responsibility of black people.

One of the papers focused on African American community self-help strategies, noting that white society, though creating problems that impact on the African American community, cannot be relied on to help. Another examined African American males' cultural coping mechanisms for racial oppression. Yet another white woman concluded that the greatest problem African American male students face in school is white female teachers who, afraid of them, refer them to remedial and special education programs in order to rid themselves of a "problem" they fear.

> So I feel the first main objective to help make a change for the young African American male is to work with the white female teacher and work to change their perceptions about the African American male.

Several papers examined facets of institutional racism. One of these concluded that social services for low-income Hispanic children in the local community are appallingly inadequate largely because of indifference of the dominant community. Another asked why low-income Hispanic children do not attend school regularly even though their parents regard school as important; she concluded that schools are structured such that they force a choice between school versus family, requiring those who place family responsibility first to make "a choice they shouldn't have to make." A young woman who previously had not believed that institutional racism exists asked why many educational institutions that serve mainly people of color do not employ pedagogical strategies that would benefit the students. She concluded (with many specific examples she had observed) that schools were structured initially to reproduce society as it is; those who control schools are mainly white males, and many teachers in schools are prejudiced. As a result, she asked:

> How many times have we heard teachers and administrators blame the failure of the students on their environment? Hardly ever do we hear of a teacher saying that his/her methods of teaching are not beneficial to students. Instead we are given explanations of students' deficiencies as being the source of failure.

A young woman asked why the omission of minorities from training videos in industry matters. She argued that, although it would make good business sense to produce material that reflects the diversity of the public, corporations are run mainly by white men who often don't do that. Her paper then raised the questions of whether capitalism can reduce racism or supports it, noting W. E. B. DuBois' argument that capitalism is part of the problem of racism.

Two young men wondered why males exhibit more interest and success in math than females in secondary schools and higher education. One focused on adolescence and the dilemma young women face trying to please the peer group, especially boys who do not like girls who seem "smarter than the average guy." He reflected personally on how the male peer culture suppresses displays of female academic achievement without placing similar restrictions on boys, realizing that boys learn early to blunt girls' aspirations. The other young man (a prospective math teacher) focused on the university level, uncovering more blatant sexism in math and engineering departments than he had previously recognized.

The remainder of the papers addressed similarly interesting questions, such as why Spanish-speaking students use Spanish instead of English to communicate, even in an ESL class; why complexion variation makes a difference within the African American community; why students of color drop out of school disproportionately more than white students; and why African American and Hispanic community groups experience difficulty coalescing to effect political change. Although their papers focused mainly on why patterns exist, most also recommended strategies for change – strategies that oppressed groups advance.

Readers may critique some of these examples for limits of their political analysis. However, I regarded the great majority of the students as successful in beginning to use a minority position perspective; they framed concrete observations of inequality in terms of institutional discrimination and uncovered strategies oppressed groups use to cope with or attempt to advance from a minority position. The students sought answers from members of oppressed groups themselves and recognized social change strategies that oppressed groups advocate.

I will discuss the strategies used in (my) two sequential, required preservice courses. . . . Initially, I used my power as teacher to make assignments, organize activities and discussions, present material, evaluate work, and so forth. However, over the two courses, spaces for student authority enlarged. . . . I explicitly teach a framework I expect students to practice. It is predicated on an ideal that Americans share: that people should be able to achieve what they work for. . . .

The framework delineates three levels for analysis: the individual, institutional, and symbolic levels.[6] At the individual level, one examines an individual's ability, effort, desire, and so forth. In dominant discourse, most explanations for inequality are drawn from this level (for example, in the assertion that few women are school administrators because women do not desire that career). At the institutional level, one examines the availability of rewards people work for (such as housing, jobs, good grades, entry to college) and the social rules for distributing rewards. Social rules include both written and unwritten rules and procedures and organized patterns of behavior. At the symbolic level,

one examines social expression of beliefs, particularly through various media. One also examines the impact of media on individual behaviors, and connections between media, institutional structures, and control. . . .

In the first course we practice using the framework, focusing on the institutional and symbolic levels of analysis. I tell students that my goal is to help them learn to pose questions and examine factors within the context of the framework. I explain that doing this will challenge much of their thinking, but it will also help them understand where other groups are coming from. Ultimately, their personal beliefs are their own business; as a teacher, my responsibility is to help them see a different perspective. . . .

For critical pedagogy to be empowering, it must involve "a process of knowledge production" in which students work together to generate their own text.[7] . . . I divide (the class) into three groups to conduct mini-investigations on racism, poverty, and sexism. Beginning with the racism group, I . . . ask the class as a whole to generate as many questions as they can about possible current examples of racism at the institutional and cultural levels. As they ask questions, I write them on the board, asking for ideas as to how questions might be investigated. Then each of the students who selected racism volunteers to take a question; I give them a week or two to conduct their investigations. One of the most effective investigation processes is for students to replicate testing procedures used to investigate housing and job discrimination: to pair with a student of another race and find out whether they receive the same treatment in a particular context such as a bank, real estate agency, retail store, and so forth.

About ten students at a time share what they found out, and usually considerable discussion follows. For example, with respect to poverty, one student acquired published information about available child care for low-income people, then pretended to be a single mother looking for child care and actually made the telephone calls specified; she found out that print descriptions can differ widely from the treatment low-income single women may actually receive. Another student assembled paperwork a woman must fill out to receive welfare. Another looked into local homeless shelters and was shocked to discover how many homeless people the city had. (While shopping), a white student was shocked to realize that while salespeople helped her, they often followed her African American peer around the store to make sure she did not shoplift. . . .

A second form of collective knowledge production occurs in the context of (reading) ethnographies. This is a rather complex assignment, using jigsaw cooperative learning. Each student reads one ethnography of schooling; about ten or twelve different books are available from which to choose. For discussion I first group together students who have read the same or similar books, to make sure they understand the main ideas in their books. Then I mix students so that four or five books are represented by one student each, per group. I give the groups four to five questions to answer collectively that require them to synthesize the information and ideas in the books; I also encourage students to use their own experience. . . . Sometimes the groups put on a skit illustrating what they learned; other times they collectively write a short paper.

The culminating experience for these two courses is the production and use of a text about issues related to multicultural education. Students are to complete their "why" papers about halfway through the semester. I read them, give students feedback, and give them about two weeks to complete any revisions they wish to make. Then I collect their papers, organize them around common topics or themes, and have them duplicated and bound to form a text that the class uses for the remainder of the semester. At this point, students take control of the production and discussion of knowledge. I participate in discussions with the students, but am no longer "in charge."

I have turned students' "why" papers into a class text three times, after having found that the papers are consistently strong enough to do this effectively. Of all the reading assignments I have ever given, students seemed to take this the most seriously. They told me that they wanted to find out what their peers learned and found important, and that this had more meaning to them than any other reading assignment, no matter how interesting other reading assignments may be.

Multicultural teaching is not simply a list of teaching strategies. Rather, it is an orientation to listening to oppressed people, including scholars, with the aims of learning to hear and understand what is being said, of building dialog, and of learning to share decision-making power with oppressed communities. The process of listening, engaging in dialog, and power-sharing is very difficult to learn. Educated whites are very accustomed to believing that we can construct good solutions to other people's needs ourselves. I want students to leave my class having begun a process of listening and dialog; I deliberately reduce my own position as "the" source of information about multicultural teaching. While I do not know the extent to which students continue to seek minority position perspectives for themselves from their students, students' parents or professionals of color, at least they will have begun this process.

Notes

[1] W. B. Stanley, *Curriculum for utopia.* (Albany: SUNY Press, 1992), p. 102.

[2] Jonathan Kozol, *Savage inequalities.* (New York: Crown Publishers, 1991), p. 233.

[3] James, A. Banks, *Multiethnic education,* 2nd ed. (Boston: Allyn & Bacon, 1988), p. 182.

[4] J. B. Elshtain, The social relations of the classroom: A moral and political perspective (pp. 97–110), *Telos,* 1976.

[5] Ibid., p. 110.

[6] P. H. Collins, Toward a new vision: Race, class, and gender as categories of analysis and connection (pp. 25-46), *Race, Sex & Class,* 1993, *1*(1).

[7] J. Gore, What we can do for you! What can "we" do for "you"? Struggle over empowerment in critical and feminist pedagogy, pp. 54–73. In C. Luke and J. Gore (Eds.), *Feminisms and critical pedagogy.* (New York: Routledge, 1992), p. 68.

Great Men and Women

Famous people in our history should be used as role models for our children and youth, but some of the staunchest advocates for social justice are not portrayed accurately in the curriculum. The author argues that we need to be honest about the values, beliefs, and actions of great men and women so that students can appreciate what they stood for.

"I don't give a damn about semi-radicals."

Helen Keller, 1916[1]

Teachers face a difficult job when they sit down to work out lesson plans on U.S. history. How do these [representatives] of the leading counter-revolutionary nation on the face of earth cope with a history that has been studded with so many bold, and revolutionary, and subversive, and exhilarating men and women?

Schools know well the dangers that can be provoked by ethical upheaval in the consciousness of those within a social order that depends on managed views, on manufactured tastes and falsified perceptions of our own experience. Private ethics and public management are not compatible. Schools cannot leave it to the idle chance of later years to see how open minds respond to burning mandates. Instead, the mandates are themselves examined, outlined, categorized, congealed, within the basic framework of our school experience. Each radical name, each dangerous idea is given its ordered place within the course of study. Each name, each statement, each quotation, snaps and fits into its own pre-designated slot. If each item can be locked into its proper place, there is no risk of confrontation or surprise in later years when we are on our own and do not have, between ourselves and justice, a curricular protection.

There is, by now, a sequence by which historic figures of strong radical intent are handled in the context of the public school. First, we drain the person of nine tenths of his real passion, guts and fervor. Then we glaze him over with implausible laudations. Next we place him on a lofty pedestal that fends off any notion of direct communion. Finally, we tell incredibly dull stories to portray his school-delineated but, by this time, utterly unpersuasive greatness.

Dr. Martin Luther King, Jr., by classic process of detoxification, comes to be a kindly, boring and respectful "Negro preacher" with very light skin and rather banal views, who went to college to "improve himself," believed in God, believed in "fellow man" and won, as a reward for his respectable beliefs and his non-violent views, the reverence of most U.S. citizens, "both white and black" – and, then, the Nobel Prize for Peace. Left out of focus is the whole intensity, the tactical genius and the ardent fervor that awoke within his soul . . . which inspires and establishes his greatness. Teachers do not tell their pupils, if they are not forced, that Dr. King urged his disciples to defy the law, to interrupt

From *The Night Is Dark and I Am Far from Home.* (New York: Touchstone, 1990). Reprinted by permission of the author.

its normal processes and openly obstruct its execution, so long as both appear to stand in conflict with good conscience.

Thoreau comes to mind in much the same regard: a man to whom, today, the nation pays considerable – but nervous – tribute. For more than fifty years after his death he was ignored. In his own day he was no more well-received than younger rebels of his stamp and character are loved today. He spoke of freedom, conscience and dissent and offended nearly everyone then living in the State of Massachusetts. Moreover, he did not restrict himself to words alone, but took explicit action on his views: "How does it become a man to behave toward this American government today? I answer, that he cannot without disgrace be associated with it."[2]

In evidence of this conviction, and in clear enactment of the sense of disaffiliation, Thoreau refused to pay his tax and was, for one brief night, put into Concord jail. His willingness to stand out from his neighbors and to differentiate his own views from those of his time was seldom blurred in the accepted manner that is now taken for agreeable dissent. Thoreau sought none of the palliations that are used by those who cloud their statements with the satisfying ambiguities that pass for truth within the press and public schools today. "The greater part of what my neighbors call good I believe in my soul to be bad, and if I repent of any thing, it is very likely to be my good behavior. What demon possessed me that I behaved so well?" He also wrote: "You may say the wisest thing you can old man, – you who have lived seventy years, not without honor of a kind, – I hear an irresistible voice which invites me away from all that. One generation abandons the enterprises of another like stranded vessels."

In 1844, Thoreau made up his mind to leave behind his neighbors altogether and went to live alone outside of Concord. There was, throughout this time, a sense of living absolutely at the center of his soul, at that decisive place within himself at which he knew that it was he alone who lived his life and that it could not be lived for him by any other: "When a sixth of the population of a nation which has undertaken to be the refuge of liberty are slaves, and a whole country is unjustly overrun and conquered by a foreign army, and subjected to military law, I think that it is not too soon for honest men to rebel and revolutionize... As for adopting the ways which the state has provided for remedying the evil, I know not of such ways. They take too much time, and a man's life will be gone."

Thoreau had words of scathing hatred for the cautious philanthropic people of his day. He also made clear what it was within their brand of philanthropic action he despised. They knew very well that what they did could not transform the social order, nor undermine their own unshakable position at the top. Thoreau, himself, did not abstain, of course, from straightforward ethics – nor from compassion of a strong and active form. Nor did he hesitate to claim a moral basis for his work or to take recourse, in a time of indecision, to the voice of his own conscience. It was the guarded character of philanthropic action and the pompous tone of philanthropic self-promotion, which he hated and attacked. They boast, he said, of spending "a tenth part" of their income in charity; perhaps they ought to spend "the nine-tenths so" and then be done with it. His own rebellion, at once more bold and less confined, took him in a more exhilarating and more dangerous direction: "We should be men first and subjects afterward..."

Today Thoreau is well-entombed in high school literature courses, wherein he is given limitless admiration as a nature writer. Those who wish to probe a little deeper into the political and moral implications of his views are urged by their intimidated and uneasy teachers to wait, if they can, until they are "a little older."

None of this should come to us as an immense surprise. The government is not in business to give voice to its disloyal opposition. Thoreau is dangerous. He disobeyed the law, in keeping with the dictates of his own intense and uninhibited intellectual and personal integrity that lends so much of leverage, strength and of sustained veracity to his best work. Public school is not in the business to produce Thoreau and, even less, young citizens who may aspire to lead their lives within the pattern of his courage and conviction. School is in business to produce reliable people, manageable people, unprovocative people: people who can be relied upon to make correct decisions or else to nominate and to elect those who will make correct decisions *for* them.

It should no longer be perceived by us as either unreflective, unintended or erroneous that public schools will view with reservation and contain with care the words and voices of those men and women who call forth in us the best things we are made of. To pretend that public schools cannot perceive, and will not logically suppress, the danger constituted by the burning eyes of Malcolm X or the irreverent brilliance of Thoreau is to assign to those schools a generous ineptitude which they do not in fact possess. To undermine a man like Martin Luther King, or to speak of Thoreau as a naive, brilliant but eccentric country-farmer, is not, as liberal critics like to say, a mindless error of the U.S. public schools. It is an ideal instance of their true intent.

The manner in which the schools contrive to decontaminate exhilarating women is, in part, a separate issue. In this situation, it is not so much a problem of the ethical debilitation of specific women. It is, instead, a matter of their virtual exclusion. In practical terms, great women don't exist in public schools. Those who do are, with few notable exceptions, sterile relics of devitalized respectability: Martha Washington, Betsey Ross, Mary Todd Lincoln and the like. Harriet Tubman comes out of the wash with more than the average portion of her spirit still intact; yet even she ends up with much of the same bloodless character as Dr. King. Emma Goldman, Elizabeth Flynn and Rosa Luxembourg, having spoken in specific revolutionary terms, will not likely win a place in public schools for decades yet to come. If, and when, in fifty years, one or another of these women wins her paragraph, or her "subsection" in a text, it is not easy to believe she will escape that special exercise of decontamination that is reserved for those who voice not only earnestness, but pain: not only righteous protestation, but authentic rage.

Helen Keller's decontamination in the public school offers by far the clearest parallel to that of Thoreau. Most of us know well the standard version of the deaf-blind-mute, glazed, dead and boring Helen Keller of the Fourth Grade bookshelf. She emerges earnest, brave, heroic and undangerous. Harriet Tubman with white pigmentation, Eleanor Roosevelt with a few less faculties, but with the same high-pitched, pathetic voice.

"Helen Keller is a famous deaf-blind lady who can read, write and speak. She fought against great, even formidable odds, a battle that many people felt could not be won – and never would, perhaps, if it had not been for her trusted friend and teacher. Together, the two achieved things that seem all but past belief. Among the many important people whom they knew were Andrew Carnegie, King George, Queen Mary, Samuel Clemens, Lady Astor, and Alexander Bell. In every respect, Helen Keller represented courage, perseverance and the highest moral values of her day . . . "[3]

This is the standard Helen Keller whom two million children read about each year in public school, about whom they write tedious book reports, almost unreadable because over the years they have remained identical, unchanging, banal and, in factual terms, dead wrong. Here, for one moment, is the voice of Helen Keller as in fact she lived and spoke, fighting with passion to expose the unfair labor practices of the first decades of the Nineteen Hundreds and to do battle with the U.S. social order as it still exists today:

"Why is it that so many workers live in unspeakable misery? With their hands they have built great cities, and they cannot be sure of a roof over their heads. With their hands they have opened mines and dragged forth with the strength of their bodies the buried sunshine of dead forests, and they are cold. They have gone down into the bowels of the earth for diamonds and gold, and they haggle for a loaf of bread. With their hands they erect temple and palace, and their habitation is a crowded room . . . They plow and sow and fill our hands with flowers . . . Their own hands are full of husks . . ."[4]

In another passage, Helen Keller speaks of factory visits she has made: "I have visited sweatshops, factories [and] crowded slums. If I could not see it, I could smell it . . . With my own hands I could feel . . . dwarfed children tending their younger brothers and sisters, while their mothers tended machines in nearby factories." She then says this: "People do not like to think. If one thinks," she writes, in one of those remarks which, taken at face value, would transform from top to bottom every school in the United States: "If one thinks, one must reach conclusions . . . Conclusions are not always pleasant." She makes clear her own conclusions after visits in the factories and slums: "The foundation of society is laid upon a basis of . . . conquest and exploitation." A social order "built upon such wrong and basic principles is bound to retard the development of all . . ."

The result, she says, in words prophetic of Marcuse, "is . . . false standard." Trade and material reward are viewed as the chief purposes of human life: "The lowest instincts in human nature – love of gain, cunning and selfishness – are fostered . . . The output of a cotton mill or a coal mine is considered of greater importance than the production of healthy, happy hearted [and] free human beings . . . "

Of war, she says this: "The few who profit from the labor of the masses want to organize the workers into an army which will protect [their] interests . . . "

Of voting, she says this: "We the people are not free. Our democracy is but a name. We vote? What does that mean? We choose between Tweedledum and Tweedledee."

Of education, she has these choice words to speak: "We can't have education without revolution. We have tried peace education for one thousand nine hundred years . . . Let us try revolution and see what it will do now."

Of revolution, she says this: "The time of blind struggle is drawing to a close . . . This is not a time of gentleness." It is not a time either of lukewarm beginnings: "It is a time for . . . open speech and fearless thinking . . . a time of all that is robust and vehement and bold."

Is she afraid? Is she intimidated by her chosen stand? Far from intimidation, she is inflamed with passion: "I love it . . . It thrills me . . . I shall face great and terrible things. I am a child of my generation. I rejoice that I live in such a splendidly disturbing time."

There is the temptation to go on: to quote page after page of this undaunted and subversive prose. Less clever than Thoreau, less skilled as craftsman in the use of words, she is more capable of soaring indignation.

The point at stake can be subsumed in these words: The special humiliation women undergo within the twelve-year interlock of public school (and, to a degree, still worse, within the Schools of Education) is evil enough to call for anger on its own. In the particular case of Helen Keller, I believe, she is not decontaminated in the public school by special reason of her being "woman," but rather in the same way as Thoreau – and for much the same cause. She comes out: laundered, low-key, admirable, heroic and yet, somehow,

non-infectious. Schools speak often of the dangers of infection among children. They offer tetanus shots to ward off tetanus, Salk vaccine to ward off paralytic illness. The way they fend off ethical epidemic has a genius all its own. It is difficult to think that Communist teachers, for all supervision and political control, ever could fashion a more gross, more ruthless or more wholesale labor of historical revision.

There are certain men and women who break all the rules and cannot be defused with the same deceit and glib abandon as Thoreau or Keller. These are, for the most part, rebels of a saintly, somewhat self-abasing character, often with religious implications: people, for example, like Saint Francis, Gandhi or Saint Joan. The radical provocations of these kinds of "heroes" are such that schools cannot . . . label men and women of this sort as evil or insane. Whatever public schools may wish, therefore, a certain number of prophetic figures of this kind must, in some fashion, be respected or revered.

There is, however, a vast gulf between respect and imitation. It is at this point that the schools have carried out a solemn act of disaffiliation. The knife-blade falls between respect and imitation: between a "conscientious interest in a decent, and, indeed, an interesting and important person" and unclothed dialogue with the mandate which, in his utterance, resounds and resonates.

There is a quick and bitter instant of semantic surgery. Some people, we say, command our love and adoration. These, we say, are fine and admirable people. In certain ways, we say, they are the best and bravest, most remarkable, most admirable of human beings – but therefore (as we seem to say) just for that reason, not in any sense, by no miscalculation . . . are they anything like ordinary folk: i.e., like you or me. To be a brave, heroic and risk-taking man or woman, to be a person who is not afraid to be entirely different, whether saint or soldier, martyr or eccentric or incorrigible rebel: *to be someone like this is not to be someone like you or me.*

It is affirmed to start with, it is comprehended, it is unconditionally agreed, that we can afford to pay lip service to these dangerous and intoxicating human beings only because we do not have the obligation to be *like* them. Some people we honor, others we emulate, reward and ask for cocktails. This is an ugly but, I think, realistic designation of the range of proper options open to a person who intends to grow into serene and uncomplex adulthood.

"The social purpose of education," Friedenberg has said, "is not to create a nation of actively insatiable truth seekers . . . It is to create a nation which can see clearly, and agree on what it sees, when it looks in certain directions."[5] What it is expected to see, when it looks in the direction of Saint Francis, Thoreau, Helen Keller, Dr. King, is a possible object for arm's-length admiration and respect, but in no case an appropriate model for acceptable or even sane behavior.

There is, of course, a cold and brutal desecration in this process of dichotomy and insulation. It is, however, more at our expense than at that of those men and women whom we so insultingly, and so inadequately, revere. In the long run, as we seem to say, we are not sufficiently important – not enough "central to our own lives" – to believe ourselves good people but just "ordinary" folks. We live out some place on the flatlands where the stakes are low and where the issues do not count. Unlike Dr. King, we have not been to the mountain and we do not plan to go there. If we did, we might come back to our old friends and "fellow man" with a sense at the very least of disconcerting irony. What then would we experience? How then would we be able to respond? What would we say?

The man who has been to the mountain does not come back to pick up in the conversation where he left off. If he comes back at all, it is to interrupt the conversation. It is to say he is no longer what he was before and that he cannot answer to the same ideas with the same mixture of delight and acquiescence. It is, most certainly, not the business of a school that serves the interests of a social order such as ours to send its pupils out on pilgrimage, or even on a two-day round-trip expedition of this kind. I believe it is at least in part for just this reason that we have been trained to feel respect for people of this sort only in their distant power or past excellence. We honor decent people after they are dead: cowards, cynics and amusing people while they are still living. There is no danger that a dead man will arise to tell us that we are degrading his best work, or that we have been invalidating all its deepest worth.

It is still more than this. A man, once dead, cannot come back to say to us that we might someday be strong and courageous too. He cannot look to us with trust, or with a sense of love or invocation. He cannot tell us to leave what we have been, and who we are, and go with him. This point goes beyond the realm of politics alone. It is not a mere decision as to which of certain men or women we may find most suitable to our ideas. Rather, it is a matter of belief that any person who, in any sense, has lived deeply, and felt strongly, and struggled bravely and spoken boldly, with a voice of real conviction, is a person with whom we might converse as child and teacher, follower and leader, friend and friend. Everything in our education, and much in our social order, takes away from us the sense of power to look to the people that we most revere as fitting correspondents for our inept dialogue. They are too lofty: We are too banal. The distance from the flatlands to the mountains is too far.

"In this life," Robert Coles has written, "we prepare for things, for moments and events and situations . . . We worry about wrongs, think about injustices, read what Tolstoi or Ruskin . . . has to say . . . Then, all of a sudden, the issue is not whether we agree with what we have heard and read and studied . . . The issue is *us*, and what we have become."[6]

It is clear, by now, that "what we have become" is, to a considerable degree, what we have first been told it is within our right or "logical range of yearning" to imagine that it is appropriate to wish to be. The writer who tells us: the teacher who instructs us: the schooling –apparatus that persuades us that our logical, sane and proper place is on the flatlands of relaxed intent and genial undertaking, has exercised thereby a fearful power. It is the power either to endow our dreams with richness and vocation or to reduce our aspirations to the size of an inept concern and the dimensions of an uninspired concept of inert compassion.

Low expectation . . . is a self-fulfilling prophecy. Children become, to a considerable degree, what they are told it is "appropriate" to wish to be. In this respect, I think it can be said that most of us need a sense of sanction or authentication – an empowering voice – in order to believe it is our right or our vocation to become just, passionate and risk-taking human beings. Conversely, there is limitless power of expropriation, for most children, in the voice that tells them it does not belong to them to yearn to be such men or women. We build perimeters around the ethical aspirations of our students by the very terms we teach them how to bring to their own act of self-description.

The schools instruct our children to believe in their own marginal position in relation to the kinds of people they are trained to look upon with reverence, adulation, love. The schools instruct our children to regard these women and these men as dwelling apart, within another realm, beyond our small peripheral existence. These people, as school seems to say, command our love but live beyond our dreams. Dr. King goes to the mountain, Thoreau to Walden, Christ to Gethsemane, and Gandhi to the sea. As for us, we stay in class and write term-papers on the "question" of vocation or about the "symbolism" in a young man's or young woman's quest for truth and justice. Moreover, school goes further and makes certain that we get full credit for the time that we put in, whether in terms of grades, degrees and recommendations, prizes, publication or material reward. In such a way, school does not only stand between the child and the person he reveres, but also cheapens the relationship between them by showing the child how to turn his sense of admiration into coin that can be bartered on the common market. In a nation in which all forms of produce, intellection and vocation can be sold, consumed, exploited or traded-in, the ultimate triumph of the values of the state and social order in the face of those real dangers which subversive people such as King, Thoreau, or Keller represent is to be able to turn them into a term-paper.

Nothing is sacred: least of all a man or woman whose whole being constitutes an invocation to the sense of risk, of ethics, of rebellion. It is bizarre that we should look for something different. What do we really think these schools are for?

Notes

[1]Helen Keller is quoted here from *The Little Red White and Blue Book,* by Johnny (Appleseed) Rossen, (New York: Grove Press, 1969), p. 84. This book is a collection of quotations from a number of distinguished men and women who are canonized in U.S. history. The irreverent tone of the quotations chosen from our "Founding Fathers" makes this book a small but useful instrument for change.

[2]Henry David Thoreau is quoted from *Walden and Civil Disobedience* (New York: Washington Square Press, 1968), p. 7, 55, 344, 346, and 351.

[3]The passage on Helen Keller quoted here is a pastiche of standard biographical works on Keller (found) in the public schools.

[4]Helen Keller is quoted from P. Foner (Ed.), *Helen Keller: Her socialist years.* (New York: International Publishers, 1967), p. 31, 43, 55, 56, 75, and 84.

[5]Edgar Friedenberg, *The vanishing adolescent.* (New York: Dell Publishing, 1972), p. 76.

[6]Robert Coles, *Erik Erikson: The growth of his work.* (Boston: Little, Brown and Company, 1970), p. 339.

Pluralistic Responses to the Diversity of American Society

> We must acknowledge that as a people – E Pluribus Unum – we are on a slippery slope toward economic strife, social turmoil, and cultural chaos. If we go down, we go down together.
>
> Cornel West (1953–)

ornel West's words may seem prophetic, as people in the United States have had to struggle to regain their sense of stability in the wake of the recession that began in 2008 and continued into 2009. Social scientists have expressed numerous concerns over the past three decades about the growing disparity between rich and poor, the shrinking of the middle class, and the fact that the current generation is the first one that cannot expect to be better off financially than their parents. These warnings crossed racial and ethnic lines and social class boundaries. Although there is evidence that families of color have suffered more from the mortgage crisis, layoffs, and other aspects of the economic downturn, most white middle class families have also been affected. In response, Americans placed their hopes in Barack Obama, the first African American to be elected President of the United States. Many hope that his election symbolizes a shift among Americans away from the divisiveness of

racism and other forms of oppression and toward a greater acceptance of others that will be reflected in the growth of pluralistic attitudes and actions.

Although the history of American institutions does not reveal many people who advocated for diversity or for providing opportunity to women, people of color, or other groups, there have been individuals in every era who advocated for a more just, more equitable society. For example, Edward Everett was the President of Harvard University from 1846–1849, and he rejected the racial prejudices inherent in the debates about slavery. When he issued an announcement that Harvard was considering the admission of a black student, white students were indignant and threatened to leave the school. In response to their threat, Everett said, "If (the black applicant) passes the examination, he will be admitted; and if the white students choose to withdraw, all the income of the college will be devoted to his education." After passing the exam, the black applicant was admitted, and the white students remained.[1]

Combining such examples from our history with recent achievements, Americans can reject the pessimism stemming from our economic decline and imagine an America different from what it has been, and better. From Studs Terkel's interview with "C. P. Ellis," we can learn how an individual benefits from rejecting prejudice and bigotry and embracing pluralistic values. Despite being the leader of a local Ku Klux Klan chapter, Ellis began to understand that poor whites and poor blacks had the same problems, and that both were being manipulated by white people who held positions of power. His transformation from a racist to a human rights activist was affirmed during a labor union election when many black workers voted for Ellis to be their union representative.

"Dancing with Bigotry" proves that you don't have to live in the south like C. P. Ellis to be subjected to racist messages in our society, while emphasizing the need to identify and respond to these messages. In their essay, Donaldo Macedo and Lilia Bartolomé analyze racism in words and phrases found in tirades of talk-show hosts, in uncritical reporting of mainstream journalists, in political speeches, and even in some calls for "tolerance." The authors call for a pluralistic commitment by being attentive to racist language and confronting those who use it. They encourage educators to look to the future and teach children and youth to be pluralistic by implementing what they call a "pedagogy of hope" that encompasses not only our nation but also our global diversity. It is a similar hope that was expressed much earlier by the American woman who was awarded the Nobel Prize in Literature in 1938 – Pearl Buck:

> I am grateful . . . that the people of our country are of more races than one. It gives us a matchless opportunity of working out upon our own soil the world problems of equality and of cooperation between different peoples.

In "My Class Didn't Trump My Race: Using Oppression to Face Privilege," Robin DiAngelo analyzes her own experience growing up in poverty while still enjoying some degree of white privilege. As a professor who has observed white students minimizing the problems of race because of their own experiences with poverty, she describes how poverty should be used to gain insights into the oppression experienced by people of color. In working with white people, she has observed patterns of "internalized dominance." She describes the patterns and explains how white people who fall into these patterns become oblivious to the impact of racism on people of color.

Tim Wise contributes to DiAngelo's analysis by discussing male privilege and white privilege in "Membership Has Its Privileges: Thoughts on Acknowledging and Challenging Whiteness." Wise describes how racism creates disadvantages for people of color, and he also discusses how it creates advantages for white people. Wise argues that ultimately everyone pays a price for allowing the perpetuation of racial discrimination in our society, and he provides a list of specific actions for white people to confront racism and promote social justice. If our future is to be better than our past, white people need to be engaged in the kinds of activities that Wise proposes to demonstrate that they want to be part of the evolving, diverse American "family" described by journalist Leonard Pitts:

> (America is) a vast and quarrelsome family, a family rent by racial, social, political and class divisions, but a family nonetheless.

In "Yellow Woman and the Beauty of the Spirit," Leslie Marmon Silko focuses on a past that provides lessons for the future, as she describes her life as a child on a Navajo reservation and discusses what she learned, especially from her great-grandmother. These lessons are often in conflict with the norms of mainstream society, but they make sense in the context of a diverse society. This is why they speak to America's future. In the stories we learn that Yellow Woman's beauty is not like Snow White's, but stems from her passionate, risk-taking behaviors. Silko describes her as a role model for people in a diverse society who are trying to develop pluralistic attitudes. As the world continues to evolve into a global village, pluralistic attitudes will become increasingly necessary for understanding and interacting with diverse people in nations around the world. African novelist Cheikh Hamidou Kane spoke of this future many years ago, but his words are as pertinent today as they were when he first wrote them:

> Every hour that passes brings a supplement of ignition to the crucible in which the world is being fused. We have not had the same past . . . but we shall have the same future. The era of separate destinies has run its course

Notes

[1]David Wallechinsky and Irving Wallace. *The People's Almanac.* (New York: Doubleday, 1975).

C. P. Ellis

It's hard to imagine that someone could be a leader of a local Ku Klux Klan and then become a supporter of civil rights and a spokesman for a union where most of the workers were black, but that's what C. P. Ellis did. He overcame his bigotry and began to understand that all people have the same needs and desires. His story is one of hope.

We're in his office in Durham, North Carolina. He is the business manager of the International Union of Operating Engineers. On the wall is a plaque: "Certificate of Service, in recognition to C. P. Ellis, for your faithful service to the city in having served as a member of the Durham Human Relations Council. February 1977."

At one time, he had been president (exalted Cyclops) of the Durham chapter of the Ku Klux Klan . . .

He is fifty-three years old.

My father worked in a textile mill in Durham. He died at forty-eight years old. It was probably from cotton dust. Back then, we never heard of brown lung. I was about seventeen years old and had a mother and sister depending on somebody to make a livin'. It was just barely enough insurance to cover his burial. I had to quit school and go to work. I was about eighth grade when I quit.

My father worked hard but never had enough money to buy decent clothes. When I went to school, I never seemed to have adequate clothes to wear. I always left school late afternoon with a sense of inferiority. The other kids had nice clothes, and I just had what Daddy could buy. I still got

some of those inferiority feelin's now that I have to overcome once in a while.

I loved my father. He would go with me to ball games. We'd go fishin' together. I was really ashamed of the way he'd dress. He would take this money and give it to me instead of putting it on himself. I always had the feeling about somebody looking at him and makin' fun of him and makin' fun of me. I think it had to do somethin' with my life.

My father and I were very close, but we didn't talk about too many intimate things. He did have a drinking problem. During the week, he would work every day, but weekend he was ready to get plastered. I can understand when a guy looks at his paycheck and looks at his bills, and he's worried hard all the week, and his bills are larger than his paycheck. He'd done the best he could the entire week, and there seemed to be no hope. It's an illness thing. Finally you just say: "The heck with it. I'll just get drunk and forget it."

My father was out of work during the depression, and I remember going with him to the finance company uptown, and he was turned down. That's something that's always stuck.

My father never seemed to be happy. It was a constant struggle with him just like it was for me. It's very seldom I'd see him laugh. He was just tryin' to figure out what he could do from one day to the next.

From *American Dreams: Lost and Found,* (New York: Ballantine Books, 1980). Reprinted by permission of Donadio & Olson, Inc. Copyright © 1980 by Studs Terkel.

After several years pumping gas at a service station, I got married. We had to have children. Four. One child was born blind and retarded, which was a real additional expense to us. He's never spoken a word. He doesn't know me when I go to see him. But I see him; I hug his neck. I talk to him, tell him I love him. I don't know whether he knows me or not, but I know he's well taken care of. All my life, I had work, never a day without work, worked all the overtime I could get and still could not survive financially. I began to say there's somethin' wrong with this country. I worked my butt off and just never seemed to break even.

I had some real great ideas about this great nation. (Laughs.) They say to abide by the law, go to church, do right and live for the Lord, and everything'll work out. But it didn't work out. It just kept getting' worse and worse.

I was workin' a bread route. The highest I made one week was seventy-five dollars. The rent on our house was about twelve dollars a week. I will never forget: outside of this house was a 265-gallon oil drum, and I never did get enough money to fill up that oil drum. What I would do every night, I would run up to the store and buy five gallons of oil and climb up the ladder and pour it in that 265-gallon drum. I could hear that five gallons when it hits the bottom of that oil drum, spatters, and it sounds like it's nothin' in there. But it would keep the house warm for the night. Next day you'd have to do the same thing.

I left the bread route with fifty dollars in my pocket. I went to the bank and I borrowed four thousand dollars to buy the service station. I worked seven days a week, open and close, and finally had a heart attack. Just about two months before the last payments of that loan. My wife had done the best she could to keep it runnin'. Tryin' to come out of that hole, I just couldn't do it.

I really began to get bitter. I didn't know who to blame. I tried to find somebody. I began to blame it on black people. I had to hate somebody. Hatin' America is hard to do because you can't see it to hate it. You gotta have somethin' to look at to hate. (Laughs.) The natural person for me to hate would be black people, because my father before me was a member of the Klan. As far as he was concerned, it was the savior of the white people. It was the only organization in the world that would take care of the white people. So I began to admire the Klan.

I got active in the Klan while I was at the service station. Every Monday night, a group of men would come by and buy a Coca-Cola, go back to the car, take a few drinks, and come back and stand around talkin'. I couldn't help but wonder: Why are these dudes comin' out every Monday? They said they were with the Klan and have meetings close-by. Would I be interested? Boy, that was an opportunity I really looked forward to! To be part of somethin'. I joined the Klan, went from member to chaplain, from chaplain to vice-president, from vice-president to president. The title is exalted Cyclops.

The first night I went with the fellas, they knocked on the door and gave the signal. They sent some robed Klansmen to talk to me and give me some instructions. I was led into a large meeting room, and this was the time of my life! It was thrilling. Here's a guy who's worked all his life and struggled all his life to be something, and here's the moment to be something. I will never forget it. Four robed Klansmen led me into the hall. The lights were dim, and the only thing you could see was an illuminated cross. I knelt before the cross. I had to make certain vows and promises. We promised to uphold the purity of the white race, fight communism, and protect white womanhood.

After I had taken my oath, there was loud applause goin' throughout the buildin', musta been at least four hundred people. For this one little ol' person. It was a thrilling moment for C. P. Ellis.

It disturbs me when people who do not really know what it's all about are so very critical of individual Klansmen. The majority of 'em are low-income whites, people who really don't have a part in something. They have been shut out as well as the blacks. Some are not very well educated either. Just like myself. We had a lot of support from doctors and lawyers and police officers.

Maybe they've had bitter experience in this life and they had to hate somebody. So the natural person to hate would be the black person. He's beginnin' to come up, he's beginnin' to learn to read and start votin' and run for political office. Here are white people who are supposed to be superior to them, and we're shut out.

I can understand why people join extreme right-wing or left-wing groups. They're in the same boat I was. Shut out. Deep down inside, we want to be part of this great society. Nobody listens, so we join these groups.

At one time, I was state organizer of the National Rights party. I organized a youth group for the Klan. I felt we were getting old and our generation's gonna die. So I contacted certain kids in schools. They were havin' racial problems. On the first night, we had a hundred high school students. When they came in the door, we had "Dixie" playin'. These kids were just thrilled to death. I begin to hold weekly meetin's with 'em, teachin' the principles of the Klan. At that time, I believed Martin Luther King had Communist connections. I began to teach that Andy Young was affiliated with the Communist party.

I had a call one night from one of our kids. He was about twelve. He said: "I just been robbed downtown by two niggers." I'd had a couple of drinks and that really teed me off. I go downtown and couldn't find the kid. I got worried. I saw two young black people. I had the .32 revolver with me. I said: "Nigger, you seen a little young white boy up here? I just got a call from him and was told that some niggers robbed him of fifteen cents." I pulled my pistol out and put it right at his head. I said: "I've always wanted to kill a nigger and I think I'll make you the first one." I nearly scared the kid to death, and he struck off.

This was the time when the civil rights movement was really beginnin' to peak. The blacks were beginnin' to demonstrate and picket downtown stores. I never will forget some black lady I hated with a purple passion, Ann Atwater. Every time I'd go downtown, she'd be leadin' a boycott. How I hated – pardon the expression, I don't use it much now – how I just hated that black nigger. (Laughs.) Big, fat, heavy woman. She'd pull about eight demonstrations, and first thing you know they had two, three blacks at the checkout counter. Her and I have had some pretty close confrontations.

I felt very big, yeah. (Laughs.) We're more or less a secret organization. We didn't want anybody to know who we were, and I began to do some thinkin'. What am I hidin' for? I've never been convicted of anything in my life. I don't have a court record. What am I, C. P. Ellis, as a citizen and a member of the United Klansmen of America? Why can't I go to the city council meeting and say: "This is the way we feel about the matter? We don't want you to purchase mobile units to set in our schoolyards. We don't want niggers in our schools."

We began to come out in the open. We would go to the meetings, and the blacks would be there and we'd be there. It was a confrontation every time. I didn't hold back anything. We began to make some inroads with the city councilmen and county commissioners. They began to call us friend. Call us at night on the telephone: "C. P., glad you came to that meeting last night." They didn't want integration either, but they did it secretively, in order to get elected. They couldn't stand up openly and say it, but they were glad somebody was sayin' it. We visited some of the city leaders in their home and talk to 'em privately. It wasn't long before councilmen would call me up: "The blacks are comin' up tonight and makin' outrageous demands. How about some of you people showin' up and have a little balance?" I'd get on the telephone: "The niggers is comin' to the council meeting tonight. Persons in the city's called me and asked us to be there."

We'd load up our cars and we'd fill up half the council chambers, and the blacks the other half. During these times, I carried weapons to the meetings, outside my belt. We'd go there armed. We would wind up just hollerin' and fussin' at each other. What happened? As a result of our fightin' one another, the city council still had their way. They didn't want to give up control to the blacks nor the Klan. They were usin' us.

I began to realize this later down the road. One day I was walkin' downtown and a certain city council member saw me comin'. I expected him to shake my hand because he was talkin' to me at night on the telephone. I had been in his home and visited with him. He crossed the street. Oh shit, I began to think, somethin's wrong here. Most of 'em are merchants or maybe an attorney, an insurance agent, people like that. As long as they kept low-income whites and low-income blacks fightin', they're gonna maintain control.

I began to get that feeling after I was ignored in public. I thought: Bullshit, you're not gonna use me any more. That's when I began to do some real serious thinkin'.

The same thing is happening in this country today. People are being used by those in control, those who have all the wealth. I'm not espousing communism. We got the greatest system of government in the world. But those who have it simply don't want those who don't have it to have any part of it. Black and white. When it comes to money, the green, the other colors make no difference. (Laughs.)

I spent a lot of sleepless nights. I still didn't like blacks. I didn't want to associate with 'em. Blacks, Jews, or Catholics. My father said: "Don't have anything to do with 'em." I didn't until I met a black person and talked with him, eyeball to eyeball, and met a Jewish person and talked to him, eyeball to eyeball. I found out they're people just like me. They cried, they cussed, they prayed, they had desires. Just like myself. Thank God, I got to the point where I can look past labels. But at that time, my mind was closed.

I remember one Monday night Klan meeting. I said something was wrong. Our city fathers were using us. And I didn't like to be used. The reactions of the others was not too pleasant: "Let's just keep fightin' them niggers."

I'd go home at night and I'd have to wrestle with myself. I'd look at a black person walkin' down the street, and the guy'd have ragged shoes or his clothes would be worn. That began to do somethin' to me inside. I went through this for about six months. I felt I just had to get out of the Klan. But I wouldn't get out.

Then something happened. The state AFL-CIO received a grant from the Department of HEW, a $78,000 grant: how to solve racial problems in the school system. I got a telephone call from the president of the state AFL-CIO. "We'd like to get some people together from all walks of life." I said: "All walks of life? Who you talkin' about?" He said: "Blacks, whites, liberals, conservatives, Klansmen, NAACP people."

I said: "No way am I comin' with all those niggers. I'm not gonna be associated with those type of people." A White Citizens Council guy said: "Let's go up there and see what's going' on. It's tax money bein' spent." I walk in the door, and there was a large number of blacks and white liberals. I knew most of 'em by fact 'cause I seen 'em demonstratin' around town. Ann Atwater was there. (Laughs.) I just forced myself to go in and sit down.

The meeting was moderated by a great big black guy who was bushy-headed. (Laughs.) That turned me off. He acted very nice. He said: "I want you all to feel free to say anything you want to say." Some of the blacks stand up and say it's white racism. I took all I could take. I asked for the floor and I cut

loose. I said: "No, sir, it's black racism. If we didn't have niggers in the schools, we wouldn't have the problems we got today."

I will never forget, Howard Clements, a black guy, stood up. He said: "I'm certainly glad C. P. Ellis come because he's the most honest man here tonight." I said: "What's that nigger tryin' to do?" (Laughs.) At the end of that meeting, some blacks tried to come up and shake my hand, but I wouldn't do it. I walked off.

Second night, same group was there. I felt a little more easy because I got some things off my chest. The third night, after they elected all the committees, they want to elect a chairman. Howard Clements stood up and said: "I suggest we elect two co-chairpersons." Joe Beckton, executive director of the Human Relations Commission, just as black as he can be, he nominated me. There was a reaction from some blacks. Nooo. And, of all things, they nominated Ann Atwater, that big old fat black gal that I had just hated with a purple passion, as co-chairman. I thought to myself: Hey, aint' no way I can work with that gal. Finally, I agreed to accept it, 'cause at this point I was tired of fightin', either for survival or against black people or against Jews or against Catholics.

A Klansman and a militant black woman, co-chairmen of the school committee. It was impossible. How could I work with her? But after about two or three days, it was in our hands. We had to make it a success. This give me another sense of belongin', a sense of pride. This helped this inferiority feelin' I had. A man who has stood up publicly and said he despised black people, all of a sudden he was willin' to work with 'em. Here's a chance for a low-income white man to be somethin'. In spite of all my hatred for blacks and Jews and liberals, I accepted the job. Her and I began reluctantly work together. (Laughs.) She had as many problems workin' with me as I had workin' with her.

One night, I called her: "Ann, you and I should have a lot of differences and we got 'em now. But there's somethin' laid out here before us, and if it's gonna be a success, you and I are gonna have to make it one. Can we lay aside some of these feelin's?" She said: "I'm willing if you are." I said: "Let's do it.'

My old friends would call me at night: "C. P., what the hell is wrong with you? You're sellin' out the white race." This begin to make me have guilt feelin's. Am I doin' right? Am I doin' wrong? Here I am all of a sudden makin' an about-face and tryin' to deal with my feelin's, my heart. My mind was beginnin' to open up. I was beginnin' to see what was right and what was wrong. I don't want the kids to fight forever.

We were gonna go ten nights. By this time, I had went to work at Duke University, in maintenance. Makin' very little money. Terry Sanford give me this ten days off with pay. He was president of Duke at the time. He knew I was a Klansman and realized the importance of blacks and whites getting along.

I said: "If we're gonna make this thing a success, I've got to get to my kind of people." The low-income whites. We walked the streets of Durham, and we knocked on doors and invited people. Ann was going' into the black community. They just wasn't respondin' to us when we made these house calls. Some of 'em were cussin' us out. "You're sellin' us out, Ellis, get out of my door. I don't want to talk to you." Ann was getting' the same response from blacks: "What are you doin' messin' with that Klansman?"

One day, Ann and I went back to the school and we sat down. We began to talk and just reflect. Ann said: "My daughter came home cryin' every day. She said her teacher was makin' fun of me in front of the other kids." I said: "Boy, the same thing happened to my kid. White liberal teacher was makin' fun of Tim Ellis's father, the Klansman. In front of other peoples. He came home cryin'." At this point – (he pauses, swallows hard, stifles a sob) – I begin to see, here we are, two people from the far ends of the fence, havin' identical problem, except hers bein' black and me bein' white. From that moment on, I tell ya, that gal and I worked together good. I begin to love the girl, really. (He weeps.)

The amazing thing about it, her and I, up to that point, had cussed each other, bawled each other, we hated each other. Up to that point, we didn't know each other. We didn't know we had things in common.

We worked at it, with the people who came to these meetings. They talked about racism, sex education, about teachers not bein' qualified. After seven, eight nights of real intense discussion, these people, who'd never talked to each other before, all of a sudden came up with resolutions. It was really somethin'; you had to be there to get the tone and feelin' of it.

At that point, I didn't like integration, but the law says you do this and I've got to do what the law says, okay? We said: "Let's take these resolutions to the school board." The most disheartening thing I've ever faced was the school system refused to implement any one of these resolutions. There were recommendations from the people who pay taxes and pay their salaries. (Laughs.)

I thought they were good answers. Some of 'em I didn't agree with, but I been in this thing from the beginning, and whatever comes of it, I'm gonna support it. Okay, since the school board refused, I decided I'd just run for the school board.

I spent eighty-five dollars on the campaign. The guy runnin' against me spent several thousand. I really had nobody on my side. The Klan turned against me. The low-income whites turned against me. The liberals didn't particularly like me. The blacks were suspicious of me. The blacks wanted to support me, but they couldn't muster up enough to support a Klansman on the school board. (Laughs.) But I made up my mind that what I was doin' was right, and I was gonna do it regardless what anybody said.

It bothered me when people would call and worry my wife. She's always supported me in anything I wanted to do. She was changing, and my boys were too. I got some of my youth corps kids involved. They still followed me.

I was invited to the Democratic women's social hour as a candidate. Didn't have but one suit to my name. Had it six, seven, eight years. I had it cleaned, put on the best shirt I had and a tie. Here were all this high-class wealthy candidates shakin' hands. I walked up to the mayor and stuck out my hand. He give me that handshake with that rag type of hand. He said: "C. P., I'm glad to see you." But I could tell by his handshake he was lyin' to me. This was botherin' me. I know I'm a low-income person. I know I'm not wealthy. I know they were sayin': "What's this little ol' dude runnin' for school board?" Yet they had to smile and make like they were glad to see me. I begin to spot some black people in that room. I automatically went to 'em and that was a firm handshake. They said: "I'm glad to see you, C. P." I knew they meant it – you can tell about a handshake.

Every place I appeared, I said I will listen to the voice of the people. I will not make a major decision until I first contacted all the organizations in the city. I got 4,640 votes. The guy beat me by two thousand. Not bad for eighty-five bucks and no constituency.

The whole world was openin' up, and I was learnin' new truths that I had never learned before. I was beginnin' to look at a black person, shake hands with him, and see him as a human bein'. I hadn't got rid of all this stuff. I've still got a little bit of it. But somethin' was happenin' to me.

It was almost like bein' born again. It was a new life. I didn't have these sleepless nights I used to have when I was active in the Klan and slippin' around at night. I could sleep at night and feel good about it. I'd rather live now than at any other time in history. It's a challenge.

Back at Duke, doin' maintenance, I'd pick up my tools, fix the commode, unstop the drains. But this got in my blood. Things weren't right in this country, and what we done in Durham needs to be told. I was so miserable at Duke, I could hardly stand it. I'd go to work every mornin' just hatin' to go.

My whole life had changed. I got an eighth-grade education, and I wanted to complete high school. Went to high school in the afternoons on a program called PEP – Past Employment Progress. I was about the only white in class, and the oldest. I begin to read about biology. I'd take my books home at night, 'cause I was determined to get through. Sure enough, I graduated. I got the diploma at home.

I come to work one mornin' and some guy says: "We need a union." At this time I wasn't pro-union. My daddy was anti-labor, too. We're not getting' paid much, we're having to work seven days in a row. We're all starvin' to death. The next day, I meet the international representative of the Operating Engineers. He give me authorization cards. "Get these cards out and we'll have an election." There was eighty-eight for the union and seventeen no's. I was elected chief steward for the union.

Shortly after, a union man come down from Charlotte and says we need a full-time rep. We've got only two hundred people at the two plants here. It's just barely enough money comin' in to pay your salary. You'll have to get out and organize more people. I didn't know nothin' about organizin' unions, but I knew how to organize people, stir

people up. (Laughs.) That's how I got to be business agent for the union.

When I began to organize, I began to see far deeper. I began to see people again bein' used. Blacks against white. I say this without any hesitancy: management is vicious. There's two things they want to keep: all the money and all the say-so. They don't want these poor workin' folks to have none of that. I begin to see management fightin' me with everything they had. Hire anti-union law firms, badmouth unions. The people were makin' a dollar ninety-five an hour, barely able to get through weekends. I worked as a business rep for five years and was seein' all this.

Last year, I ran for business manager of the union. He's elected by the workers. The guy that ran against me was black, and our membership is seventy-five percent black. I thought: Claiborne, there's no way you can beat that black guy. People know your background. Even though you've made tremendous strides, those black people are not gonna vote for you. You know how much I beat him? Four to one. (Laughs.)

The company used my past against me. They put out letters with a picture of a robe and a cap: Would you vote for a Klansman? They wouldn't deal with the issues. I immediately called for a mass meeting. I met with the ladies at an electric component plant. I said: "Okay, this is Claiborne Ellis. This is where I come from. I want you to know right now, you black ladies here, I was one time a member of the Klan. I want you to know, because they'll tell you about it."

I invited some of my old black friends. I said: "Brother Joe, Brother Howard, be honest now and tell these people how you feel about me." They done it. (Laughs.) Howard Clements kidded me a little bit. He said: "I don't know what I'm doin' here, supportin' an ex-Klansman." (Laughs.) He said: "I know what C. P. Ellis come from. I knew him when he was. I knew him as he grew, and growed with him. I'm telling' you now: follow, follow this Klansman." (He pauses, swallows hard.) "Any questions?" "No," the black ladies said. "Let's get on with the meeting, we need Ellis." (He laughs and weeps.) Boy, black people sayin' that about me. I won one thirty-four to forty-one. Four to one.

It makes you feel good to go into a plant and butt heads with professional union busters. You see black people and white people join hands to defeat the racist issues they use against people. They're tryin' the same things with the Klan. It's still happenin' today. Can you imagine a guy who's got an adult high school diploma runnin' into professional college graduates who are union busters? I gotta compete with 'em. I worked seven days a week, nights and on Saturday and Sunday. The salary's not that great, and if I didn't care, I'd quit. But I care and I can't quit. I got a taste of it. (Laughs.)

I tell people there's a tremendous possibility in this country to stop wars, the battles, the struggles, the fights between people. People say: "That's an impossible dream. You sound like Martin Luther King." An ex-Klansman who sounds like Martin Luther King. (Laughs.) I don't think it's an impossible dream. It's happened in my life. It's happened in other people's lives in America.

I don't know what's ahead of me. I have no desire to be a big union official. I want to be right out here in the field with the workers. I want to walk through their factory and shake hands with that man whose hands are dirty. I'm gonna do all that

one little ol' man can do. I'm fifty-two years old, and I ain't got many years left, but I want to make the best of 'em.

When the news came over the radio that Martin Luther King was assassinated, I got on the telephone and began to call other Klansmen. We just had a real party at the service station. Really rejoicin' 'cause that son of a bitch was dead. Our troubles are over with. They say the older you get, the harder it is for you to change. That's not necessarily true. Since I changed, I've set down and listened to tapes of Martin Luther King. I listen to it and tears come to my eyes 'cause I know what he's sayin' now. I know what's happenin'.

POSTSCRIPT: *The phone rings. A conversation.*

"This was a black guy who's director of Operation Breakthrough in Durham. I had called his office. I'm interested in employin' some young black person who's interested in learnin' the labor movement. I want somebody who's never had an opportunity, just like myself. Just so he can read and write, that's all."

Dancing with Bigotry

Because of the rapidly increasing diversity in the United States, some people have responded with anger, fear, and alarm. The authors analyze the role of language and some negative responses in the media and from political leaders. They challenge all of us not to demonize those who are different, but to recognize our common humanity.

One of the most pressing problems facing educators in the United States is the specter of an "ethnic and cultural war," which constitutes, in our view, a code phrase that engenders our society's licentiousness toward racism. . . . The popular press and the mass media educate more people about issues regarding ethnicity and race than all other sources of education available to U.S. citizens. By ignoring the mass media, educators are missing the obvious: that more public education is done by the media than by teachers, professors, and anyone else. . . .

Central to the idea of an ethnic and cultural war is the creation of an ideologically coded language that serves at least two fundamental functions: on the one hand, this language veils the racism that characterizes U.S. society, and on the other hand, it insidiously perpetuates both ethnic and racial stereotypes that devalue identities of resistance and struggle. Although the present assault on Latinos is mostly characterized by a form of racism at the level of language, it is important to differentiate between

language as racism and the experience of racism. For example, former presidential candidate Patrick Buchanan's call for the end of illegal immigration "even if it means putting the National Guard all along the Southern frontier" constitutes a form of racism at the level of language.[1] This language-based racism has had the effect of licensing institutional discrimination whereby both documented and undocumented immigrants materially experience the loss of their dignity, the denial of their humanity, and, in many cases, outright violence by the border patrol. . . . Terms like "border rats," "wetbacks," "aliens," "illegals," "welfare queens," and "nonwhite hordes" used by the popular press not only dehumanize other cultural beings but also serve to justify the violence perpetuated against subordinate groups. . . .

We need to understand fully the interrelationship between symbolic violence produced through language and the essence of the experience of racism. . . . By deconstructing the cultural conditions that give rise to the present violent assault on undocumented immigrants, affirmative action, African-Americans, and other racial and ethnic groups, we can single out those ideological factors that enable even highly educated individuals to embrace blindly, for example, conservative radio talk-show host Rush Limbaugh's racist tirades designed to demonize and dehumanize ethnic and

From Dancing with bigotry: The poisoning of racial and ethnic identities in *Dancing with bigotry: Beyond the politics of tolerance.* (New York: Palgrave, 1999). Reproduced with permission of Palgrave Macmillan.

cultural identities other than his own. Here are two examples:

- There are more American Indians alive today than there were when Columbus arrived or at any other time in history. Does that sound like a record of genocide?
- Taxpaying citizens are not being given access to these welfare and health services that they deserve and desire. But if you're an illegal immigrant and cross the border, you get everything you want.[2]

The racism and high levels of xenophobia we are witnessing in our society today are not caused by isolated acts by individuals such as Limbaugh or the onetime Louisiana gubernatorial candidate David Duke. Rather, these individuals are representatives of an orchestrated effort by segments of the dominant society to wage a war on the poor and on people who, by virtue of their race, ethnicity, language, and class, are reduced at best to half-citizens, and at worst to a national enemy responsible for all the ills afflicting our society. We need to understand the cultural and historical context that gives rise to over 20 million Limbaugh "ditto heads" who tune in to his weekly radio program.

We also need to understand those ideological elements that inform our policymakers and those individuals who shape public opinion by supporting or rewarding Limbaugh's unapologetic demonizing of other cultural subjects. For example, television commentator Ted Koppel considers Limbaugh "very smart. He does his homework. He is well informed." George Will considers him the "fourth branch of government."[3] What remains incomprehensible is why such highly educated individuals cannot see through Limbaugh's obvious distortions of history and falsification of reality. We posit that the inability to perceive distinctions and falsifications of reality is partly the result of an educational process that is acritical due to the fragmentation of bodies of knowledge. Such a process makes it very difficult for students (and the general population) to make connections among historical events so as to gain a more critical understanding of reality.

The promotion of an acritical education was evident when David Spritzler, a twelve-year-old student in Boston refused to recite the Pledge of Al-

legiance, which he considered "a hypocritical exhortation to patriotism" in that there is not "liberty and justice for all." According to Spritzler, the pledge is an attempt to unite:

> (the) oppressed and the oppressors. You have people who drive nice cars, live in nice houses, and don't have to worry about money. Then you have the poor people, living in bad neighborhoods and going to bad schools. Somehow the Pledge makes it seem that everybody's equal when that's not happening. There is no justice for everybody.[4]

The inability of teachers and administrators at Spritzler's school to see the obvious hypocrisy contained in the Pledge of Allegiance represents what Noam Chomsky calls "a real sign of deep indoctrination [in] that you can't understand elementary thoughts that any ten-year-old can understand. That's real indoctrination."[5] . . . Meanwhile the forces employed by Immigration and Customs Enforcement (ICE) have been increased with few safeguards in place to ensure that the new hires will not continue to increase the human rights abuses perpetrated along the U.S. Mexican border. . . .

Liberals appear to progressively idealize liberty and equality . . . On the other hand some liberals accept the notion of difference and call for ways in which difference is tolerated. For example, there is a rapid growth of textbooks ostensibly designed to teach racial and multicultural tolerance. But what these texts in fact do is hide the asymmetrical distribution of power and cultural capital through a form of paternalism that promises to the "other" a dose of tolerance. In other words, since we coexist and must find ways to get along, I will tolerate you. Missing from this posture is the ethical proposition that calls for mutual respect and even racial and cultural solidarity. . . .

Tolerance for different racial and ethnic groups not only constitutes a veil behind which liberals hide their racism, it also puts them in a compromising racial position. While calling for racial tolerance, a paternalistic term, they often maintain the privilege that is complicit with the dominant ideology. Thus many white liberals willingly call and work for cultural tolerance but are reluctant to confront issues of inequality, power, ethics, race, and ethnicity in a way that could actually lead to social transformation that would make society more democratic and humane and less racist and discriminatory. . . .

The separation of the individual from the collective consciousness is part of the dominant white ideology's mechanism to fragment reality, which makes it easier for individuals to accept living within the lie that we exist in a raceless and colorblind society. The real issue behind the present assault on multiculturalism and affirmative action is that we must never fall prey to a pedagogy of big lies.[6] . . .

The real issue is not Western civilization versus multiculturalism or affirmative action versus individual effort and merit. Cultural dominance and racism are the hidden issues that inform the pernicious debate on cultural diversity and its ramifications such as affirmative action. We cannot speak of our American "common culture" and democracy in view of the quasi-apartheid conditions that have relegated American Indians to reservations, created ghettoes, and supported the affirmative action of redlining and Robin Hood policies in reverse. How can we honestly accept the mythical reality of our common culture when its major proponents are simultaneously engaged in a permanent process of putting other cultural identities on trial? . . .

Culture is intertwined with language and represents a sizable dimension of its reality, but language is rarely studied as part of our multicultural understanding; we rarely question the role of the dominant language in the devaluation of the cultural and ethnic groups under study. Put simply, we understand little how the English language can subordinate and alienate members of the cultures we study through English.

"Welfare reform for the poor" represents a positive phrase to the majority of white middle-class individuals who feel put upon by paying high taxes to, in their view, support lazy individuals who are poor because they do not want to work. When one points out that a higher percentage of their taxes goes to support welfare for the rich, the cry is uniform, immediate, and aggressive: there is no room in the United States for incitement of class warfare. When the call is to reform welfare for the rich, the reaction is as swift as it is disingenuous. By changing the context of welfare reform from the poor to the rich, the impact of the language changes accordingly, from a positive to a negative effect.

Many working-class white people are misled by the positive illusion of "welfare reform" without realizing that they themselves are, perhaps, one paycheck away from benefiting from the very social safety net they want reformed or destroyed. In an age of institutional downsizing (which is a euphemism for corporate greed and maximization of profit), the economic stability of both the white middle and working classes is fast disappearing. This creates an urgent need for the white middle and working classes to be given a scapegoat in order to blame the "other" for their present economic insecurities.

The dominant discourse uses the presence of taboo words such as "class" and "oppression" to dismiss a counter-discourse that challenges the falsification of reality. Thus, to call for welfare reform for the rich is immediately dismissed as "class warfare," a taboo concept not in keeping with the myths that the United States is a classless society. If in fact we live in a classless society, why do we constantly refer to the existence of the working class versus the middle class? What is omitted from the dominant discourse is the existence of the term "upper class.". . . To suppress the term "upper class" is to deny its existence.

Another example, consider the negative effect of the word "migrant." Why do we designate Latinos who migrate to other geographical areas to seek better economic opportunities as "migrants" and, in contrast, use the term "settlers" for the English migrants who came to Plymouth, Massachusetts? And why do we continue to call the Hispanic community of migrant workers that has been here for centuries "migrant" yet fail to use the same term to categorize the Massachusetts workers who migrated to Florida and elsewhere during the last recession? Clearly, the term is not used to describe the migration of groups of people moving from place to place but to label and typecast certain Hispanics ethnically and racially, while using this typecast to denigrate and devalue the Hispanic culture. "Migrant" not only relegates the Hispanics labeled as such to a lower status in our society, but it also robs them of their citizenship as human beings who participate in and contribute immensely to our society.

The following poem was distributed to Republican legislators in California by State Assemblyman William Knight:

Ode to the New California

I come for visit, get treated regal.
So I stay, who care illegal.
Cross the border poor and broke,
Take the bus, see customs bloke.
Welfare say come down no more,
We send cash right to your door.
Welfare checks they make you wealthy,
Medi-Cal it keep you healthy.
By and by, I got plenty money,
Thanks, American working dummy.
Write to friends in mother land,
Tell them come as fast as can.
They come in rags and Chebby trucks,
I buy big house with welfare bucks.
Fourteen families all move in,
Neighbor's patience growing thin.
Finally, white guy moves away,
I buy his house and then I say,
Send for family, they just trash,
But they draw more welfare cash.
Everything is much good,
Soon we own the neighborhood.
We have hobby, it's called "breeding,"
Welfare pay for baby feeding.
Kids need dentist? Wife need pills?
We get free, we got no bills.
We think American damn good place,
Too damn good for white man's race.
If they no like us, they can go,
Got lots of room in Mexico.[7]

When the legislator's Latino caucus complained that the poem was racist, Knight explained without apologizing that he thought the poem was "clever" and "funny,"[8] adding that it was not intended to offend anyone. In the United States, how can we honestly speak of human freedom in a society that generates and yet ignores ghettos, reservations, human misery, and savage inequalities, and then have the audacity to joke about it? . . .

We challenge everyone, especially educators, to reject the social construction of images that dehumanize the "other." . . . The creation of otherness not only fosters more ignorance on the part of those in power, but also fails to provide the dominant group with the necessary tools to empathize with this demonized other. The dominant group loses its humanity in its inability to feel bad for discriminating against other human beings. The dominant group's ability to demonize and its inability to empathize with "the other" points to the inherent demon in those who dehumanize.

We conclude by proposing a pedagogy of hope that is informed by tolerance, respect, and solidarity. . . . A pedagogy that points out that in our construction of the other we become intimately tied with that other; a pedagogy that teaches us that by dehumanizing the other we become dehumanized ourselves. In short, a pedagogy of hope should guide us toward the critical road of truth, rather than myths and lies, toward reclaiming our dignity and our humanity. A pedagogy of hope will point us toward a world that is more harmonious and more humane, less discriminatory, less dehumanizing, and more just.

Notes

[1] Michael Rezendes, Declaring 'Cultural War': Buchanan Open '96 Run, *Boston Globe,* March 21, 1995, p. 1.

[2] Steven Randall, Jim Naureckus, and Jeff Cohen, *The Way Things Ought to Be: Rush Limbaugh's Reign of Error* (New York: New Press, 1995), p. 47–54.

[3] Ibid. Comments from Ted Koppel and George Will were quoted on p. 10.

[4] Donaldo Macedo, *Literacies of Power: What Americans Are Not Allowed to Know* (Boulder, CO: Westview Press, 1994), p. 10.

[5] C. P. Otero, Ed., *Language and Politics* (New York: Black Rose Books, 1988), p. 681.

[6] Donaldo P. Macedo, Literacy for stupidification: The pedagogy of big lies, *Harvard Educational Review* 63 (1993), pp. 183–206.

[7] From "I Love America!" a poem distributed in May 1995 to California Legislators by State Assemblyman William J. Knight, quoted in Dan Morain and Hank Gladstone, "Racist Verse Stirs Up Anger in Assembly," *Los Angeles Times,* May 19, 1993.

[8] Morain and Gladstone, Racist Verse Stirs Up Anger in Assembly" *Los Angeles Times,* May 19, 1993, p. 3.

ROBIN J. DIANGELO

My Class Didn't Trump My Race: Using Oppression to Face Privilege

Individuals are often shaped by having membership in multiple groups; for example, one individual could be a gay person of color with a disability. The author explains how you can use your experiences as a member of an oppressed group to understand oppression of a group in which you are part of the dominant, not the oppressed group.

I grew up poor and White. Although my class oppression has been relatively visible to me, my race privilege has not. In my efforts to uncover how race has shaped my life, I have gained deeper insight by placing race in the center of my analysis and asking how each of my other group locations have socialized me to collude with racism. In so doing, I have been able to address in greater depth my multiple locations and how they function together to hold racism in place. Thus my exploration of what it means to be White starts with what it means to be poor, for my understanding of race is inextricably entwined with my class background. I now make the distinction that I grew up poor *and* White, for my experience of poverty would have been different had I not been White. For Whites, the experience of oppression in other areas of our lives (such as class, gender, religion, or sexual orientation) can make it difficult to center a location through which we experience privilege.

When leading discussions in multicultural education courses, I find that White students often resist centering racism in their analysis, feeling that to do so invalidates their oppressions. These students also feel that their oppressions make them "less" racially privileged. As I work to unravel my internalized racial dominance, I have found two key questions useful:

1. How does internalized dominance function collectively for Whites, regardless of our other social locations?
2. How did I learn racism *specifically through my class (or other) oppression*?

I was born to working class parents; my father was a construction worker and my mother was a switchboard operator. When I was 2, my parents divorced and my mother began to raise us on her own; at that point we entered into poverty. I have never understood people who say, "we were poor but we didn't know it because we had lots of love." Poverty hurts. It isn't romantic, or some form of "living simply." Poor people are not innocent and child-like. The lack of medical and dental care, the hunger, and the ostracization are concrete. The stress of poverty made my household much more chaotic than loving.

We were evicted frequently, moving four to five times a year. There were periods when oatmeal was the only food in our house. I had no health or den-

From *Multicultural Perspectives*, 2003, 8(1). Reprinted by permission of the Taylor and Francis Group who may be contacted at www.informaworld.com.

tal care during my childhood, and today all of my front teeth are filled because by the time I was 10 they were rotten. If we got sick, my mother would beat us, screaming that we could not get sick because she could not afford to take us to the doctor. We occasionally had to live in our car, and I was left with relatives for eight months while my mother tried to secure housing for us. My teacher once held my hands up to my fourth-grade class as an example of poor hygiene. With the class as her audience, told me to go home and tell my mother to wash me.

I used to stare at the girls in my class and ache to be like them; to have a father, to wear pretty clothes, to go to camp, to be clean and get to sit with them. I knew we didn't have enough money and that meant that I couldn't join them in school or go to their houses or have the same things they had. But the moment the real meaning of poverty crystallized for me came when we were visiting another family. As we were leaving I heard one of their daughters ask her mother, "What is wrong with them?" I stopped, riveted. I, too, wanted to know. Her mother held her finger to her lips and whispered, "Shhh, they're *poor.*" This was a revelatory moment for me. The shock came not just in the knowledge that we were poor, but that it was exposed. There was something wrong with us, indeed, and it was something that was obvious to others and that we couldn't hide, something shameful that could be seen but should not be named. It took me many years to gain a structural analysis of class that would help shift this sense of shame.

I begin this narrative with my class background because it so deeply informs my understanding of race. From an early age I had the sense of being an outsider; I was acutely aware that I was poor, that I was dirty, that I was not normal, and that there was something "wrong" with me. But I also knew that I was *not* Black. We were at the lower rungs of society, but there was always someone just below us. I knew that "colored" people existed and that they should be avoided. I can remember many occasions when I reached for candy or uneaten food laying on the street and was admonished by my grandmother not to touch it because a "colored person" may have touched it. The message was clear to me; if a colored person touched something it became dirty. The irony here is that the marks of poverty were clearly visible on me: poor hygiene, torn clothes, home-

lessness, and hunger. Yet through comments such as my grandmother's, a racial Other was formed in my consciousness, an Other through whom I became clean. Race was the one identity that aligned me with the other girls in my school.

I left home as a teenager and struggled to survive. As I looked at what lay ahead, I could see no path out of poverty other than education. The decision to take that path was frightening for me; I had never gotten the message that I was smart and academia was a completely foreign social context. But once I was in academia, I understood that a college degree is not conferred upon those who are smarter or who try harder than others, it comes through a complex web of intersecting systems of privileges that include internal expectations as well as external resources. In academia, racism, a key system that I benefit from, helped to mediate my class-based disadvantages.

Upon graduation, with my degree in sociology and a background in adult education, I answered a call for diversity trainers from a state department that had lost a civil rights lawsuit and been mandated to provide 16 hours of diversity training to all employees. They needed 40 diversity trainers to train 3,000 people. Looking back from where I am now, I see how naive I was when I started that contract. I thought that being "liberal" qualified me because after all, racists were people who didn't have an open mind. I had an open mind and was thus not a racist; these employees just needed help opening their minds. As often happens, those in the position to hire me (primarily other White people) did not have the ability to assess the qualifications of someone leading discussions on race, and I was hired, along with 39 other people from a range of backgrounds.

I was completely unprepared for the depth of hostility and the disconnection from racial realities that I encountered from White people in these trainings. It was unnerving to be in a room composed exclusively of White employees and hear them bitterly complain that because of Affirmative Action, White people could no longer get jobs. That White employees would feel free to express this hostility to my co-leader of color (who was racially isolated in the room) was another piece of the puzzle that I was yet to put together. Even more significantly, the training teams were always interracial, and the very dynamics that I sought to enlighten my participants on were actively manifesting between my co-trainers and myself.

Over time, I began to see racial dynamics more clearly, and after many years in the field, along with much personal work and some very patient mentors. I became more grounded in the dynamics of racialized knowledge construction. These trainings provided an extraordinary opportunity to observe first hand the processes by which a White racial identity is socially constructed and privileged, and the mechanisms by which White people receive and protect that privilege. I also reflected on my own responses to the ways in which I was being racially challenged, for unlike the middle class culture of academia that I found foreign, the culture of Whiteness was so normalized for me that it was barely visible. I had my experience of marginalization to draw from in understanding racism, which helped tremendously, but as I became more conversant to the workings of racism, I came to understand that the oppression I experienced growing up poor didn't protect me from learning my place in the racial hierarchy. . . .

As I reflect back on the early messages I received about being poor and being White, I now realize that my grandmother and I needed people of color to cleanse and realign us with the dominant White culture that our poverty had separated us from. I now ask myself how the classist messages I internalized growing up lead me to collude in racism. For example, as a child who grew up in poverty, I received constant reminders that I was stupid, lazy, dirty, and a drain on the resources of hard-working people. I internalized these messages and they still work to silence me. Unless I try to uproot them, I am less likely to trust my own perceptions or feel like I have a "right" to speak up. I may not attempt to interrupt racism because the social context in which it is occurring intimidates me.

My fear on these occasions may be coming from a place of internalized class inferiority, but in practice my silence colludes with racism and ultimately benefits me by protecting my White privilege and maintaining racial solidarity with other White people. This solidarity connects and realigns me with White people across other lines of difference, such as the very class locations that have silenced me in the first place. I am also prone to use others to elevate me, as in the example with my grandmother. So although my specific class background mediated the way I learned racism and how I enact it, in the end it still socialized me to collude with the overall structure.

It is my observation that class dictates proximity between Whites and people of color. Poor Whites are most often in closest proximity to people of color because they tend to share poverty. I hear the term "White trash" frequently. It is not without significance that this is one of the few expressions in which race is named for Whites. I think the proximity of the people labeled as White trash to people of color is why; race becomes marked or "exposed" by virtue of a closeness to people of color. In a racist society, this closeness both highlights and pollutes Whiteness. Owning class people also have people of color near them because people of color are often their domestics and gardeners – their servants. But they do not interact socially with people of color in the same way that poor Whites do. Middle class Whites are generally the furthest away from people of color. They are the most likely to say that, "there were no people of color in my neighborhood or school. I didn't meet a Black person until I went to college" (often adding, "so I was lucky because I didn't learn anything about racism"). Looking specifically at how class shaped my racial identity has been very helpful to me in attempting to unravel the specific way I manifest my internalized racial superiority.

I am no longer poor. Although I still carry the marks of poverty, those marks are now only internal. But these marks limit me in more than what I believe I deserve or where I think I belong; they also interfere with my ability to stand up against injustice, for as long as I believe that I am not as smart or as valuable as other White people, I won't challenge racism. I believe that in order for Whites to unravel our internalized racial dominance, we have two interwoven tasks. One is to work on our own internalized oppression – the ways in which we impose limitations on ourselves based on the societal messages we receive about the inferiority of the lower status groups we belong to. The other task is to face the internalized dominance that results from being socialized in a racist society – the ways in which we consciously or unconsciously believe that we are more important, more valuable, more intelligent, and more deserving than people of color. . . .

After years of facilitating dialogues on race with thousands of White people from a range of class positions (as well as varied gender, sexual orientation, religious, and ability positions), and bearing witness to countless stories and challenges from people of color about my own racism and that of other Whites, I have come to see some very common patterns of internalized dominance. These patterns are shared across other social positions. Regardless of one's other locations, White people know on some level that being White in this society is "better" than being a person of color, and this, along with the very real doors Whiteness opens, serves to mediate the oppression experienced in these other social locations. I have identified ten patterns of internalized dominance that are generally shared among Whites.

1. **We live segregated lives.**   Growing up in segregated environments (schools, workplaces, neighborhoods, media images, historical perspectives, etc.), we are given the message that our experiences and perspectives are the only ones that matter. We receive this message day in and day out, and it is not limited to a single moment, it is a relentless experience. Virtually all of our teachers, history books, role models, movie and book characters, are White like us. We are taught not to feel any loss about the absence of people of color in our lives; in fact, their absence is what defines our schools and neighborhoods as "good." And we get this message regardless of where we are oppressed in other areas of our lives. Because we live primarily segregated lives in a White-dominated society, we receive little or no authentic information about racism and are thus unprepared to think critically about it. . . . Upward mobility is the great class goal in the United States, and the social environment gets tangibly Whiter the higher up one goes, whether it be in academia or management.

2. **We are taught in our culture to see our experience as objective and representative of reality.**   The belief in objectivity coupled with setting White people up as outside of culture and thus the norm for humanity, allow us to see ourselves as universal humans who can represent all of human experience. People of color can only represent their own racialized experience; . . . we keep White ex-

perience and people centered and people of color in the margins.

3. **We are raised to value the individual and to see ourselves as individuals rather than as part of a socialized group.**   Individuality allows us to present ourselves as having "just arrived on the scene," unique and original, outside of socialization and unaffected by the relentless racial messages we receive. This also allows us to distance ourselves from the actions of our group and demand that we be granted the benefit of the doubt (because we are individuals) in all cases. We get very irate when we are "accused" of racism because as individuals we are "different" from other White people and expect to be seen as such. . . . Seeing ourselves as individuals erases our history and hides the way in which wealth has accumulated over generations and benefits us, *as a group*, today. . . .

If we use the line of reasoning that we are all individuals and social categories such as race, class, and gender don't matter and are just "labels" that stereotype us, then it follows that we all end up in our own "natural" places. Those at the top are merely a collection of individuals who rose under their own individual merits, and those at the bottom are there due to individual lack. Group membership is thereby rendered inoperative and racial disparities are seen as essential rather than structural. . . .

4. **In our dominant positions we are almost always racially comfortable and expect to remain so.**   We can often choose if and when we will put ourselves into racially uncomfortable situations. . . . Thus racial comfort becomes not only an expectation, but something to which we feel entitled. If racism is brought up and we become uncomfortable, then something is "wrong" and we blame the person who triggered our discomfort (usually a person of color). Because racism is necessarily uncomfortable, insisting that we remain comfortable guarantees that we will never really face it or engage in authentic dialogue with others about it. . . .

5. **We feel that we should be judged by our intentions rather than the effects of our behavior.**   A common form of White reasoning is that as long as we didn't intend to perpetuate

racism, then our actions don't count as racism. . . . We spend great energy explaining to people of color why our behavior is not racist at all. This invalidates their perspective while enabling us to deny responsibility. . . .

6. **We believe that if we can't feel our social power, then we don't have any.** White social power is so normalized that it is outside of our conscious awareness. Yet we often expect that power is something that one can feel rather than something one takes for granted. . . . In discussing race, I often hear White working class men protest that they don't have any social power. They work long and grueling hours, often in jobs in which they have no long-term security, and come home feeling beaten and quite disempowered. . . . These men are indeed struggling against social and economic barriers, but race is simply not one of them; in fact, race is a major social current running in their direction and not only moving them along, but helping them navigate their other social struggles. Not feeling power is not necessarily aligned with how others perceive or respond to us, or our relationship to social and institutional networks.

7. **We think it is important not to notice race.** The underlying assumption of a colorblind discourse is that race is a defect and it is best to pretend that we don't notice it. But if we pretend we don't notice race, we cannot notice racism. If we don't notice racism, we can't understand it or interrupt it in ourselves or others. . . . White people and people of color do not have the same racial experience; this has tangible consequences that need to be understood if we want to stop colluding with racism.

8. **We confuse not understanding with not agreeing.** Because of the factors discussed previously, there is much about racism that Whites don't understand. Yet in our racial arrogance, we have no compunction about debating the knowledge of people who have lived, breathed, and studied these issues for many years. We feel free to dismiss these informed perspectives rather than have the humility to acknowledge that they are unfamiliar to us, reflect further on them, or seek more knowledge. . . .

9. **We will be the judge of whether or not racism has occurred.** . . . White people tend to regard racism as specific acts that individuals either do or don't do, and think we can simply look at a specific incident and decide if "it" happened. But racism is infused in every part of our society, our beings, and our perspectives. It is reinforced everyday in countless and often subliminal ways. . . .

10. **Racism has been constructed as belonging to extremists and being very bad.** Racism is a deeply embedded, multidimensional, and internalized system that all members of this society are shaped by. Yet the dominant culture constructs racism as primarily in the past and currently occurring only as isolated acts relegated to individual bad people (usually living in the South or "old"). Although many White people today sincerely believe that racism is a bad thing, our abhorrence of racism coupled with a superficial conceptualization of it causes us to be highly defensive about any suggestions that we perpetuate it. Many Whites (liberal Whites in particular) think that we can deal with racism in our heads (and without ever interacting with people of color) by deciding that we have not been affected because we don't want to have been affected. . . .

I have found that a key to interrupting my internalized racial dominance is to defer to the knowledge of people whom I have been taught, in countless ways, are less knowledgeable and less valuable than I am. I have had to reach for humility and be willing to *not know*. I may never fully understand the workings of racism because I have been trained my entire life to perpetuate racism while denying its reality. Having an expectation that I could ever fully understand racism is part of my internalized dominance, but I do not have to understand racism for it to be real. . . .

My class position is only one social location from which I learned to collude with racism. For example, I have also asked myself how I learned to collude with racism as a Catholic, or as a woman. . . . Some argue that making racism the center of my analysis denies my other oppressions, but by asking myself these questions, I have been able to gain a much deeper and more useful analysis of racism. I have found that making racism the center of my analysis of oppression has been a profound way to address the complexity of all my social locations.

Membership Has Its Privileges: Thoughts on Acknowledging and Challenging Whiteness

Just because a white male benefits from both white privilege and male privilege does not mean that a white male should not fight against oppression. Indeed, a white male is in a unique position to do just that. The author explains why white males should challenge the oppression of others, and describes some actions they could take.

Being white means never having to think about it. James Baldwin said that many years ago, and it's perhaps the truest thing ever said about race in America. That's why I get looks of bewilderment whenever I ask, as I do when lecturing to a mostly white audience: "what do you like about being white?" Never having contemplated the question, folks take a while to come up with anything.

We're used to talking about race as a Black issue, or Latino, Asian, or Indian problem. We're used to books written about "them," but few that analyze what it means to be white in this culture. Statistics tell of the disadvantages of "blackness" or "brownness" but few examine the flipside: namely, the advantages whites receive as a result.

When we hear about things like racial profiling, we think of it in terms of what people of color go through, never contemplating what it means for whites and what we don't have to put up with. We

might know that a book like *The Bell Curve* denigrates the intellect of blacks, but we ignore the fact that in so doing, it elevates the same in whites, much to our advantage in the job market and schools, where those in authority will likely view us as more competent than persons of color.

That which keeps people of color off-balance in a racist society is that which keeps whites in control: a truism that must be discussed if whites are to understand our responsibility to work for change. Each thing with which "they" have to contend as they navigate the waters of American life, is one less thing whites have to sweat: and that makes everything easier, from finding jobs, to getting loans, to attending college.

On a personal level, it has been made clear to me repeatedly. Like the time I attended a party in a white suburb and one of the few black men there announced he had to leave before midnight, fearing his trip home—which required that he travel through all-white neighborhoods—would likely result in being pulled over by police, who would wonder what he was doing out so late in the "wrong" part of town.

Used by permission of the author, Tim Wise, author of *White Like Me: Reflections on Race from a Privileged Son.*

He would have to be cognizant – in a way I would not – of every lane change, every blinker he did or didn't remember to use, whether his lights were too bright, or too dim, and whether he was going even 5 miles an hour over the limit: as any of those could serve as pretexts for pulling one over, and those pretexts are used regularly for certain folks, and not others.

The virtual invisibility that whiteness affords those of us who have it is like psychological money in the bank, the proceeds of which we cash in every day while others are in a state of perpetual over-draft.

Yet, it isn't enough to see these things, or think about them, or come to appreciate what whiteness means: though important, this enlightenment is no end in itself. Rather, it is what we do with the knowledge and understanding that matters.

If we recognize our privileges yet fail to chal-lenge them, what good is our insight? If we intuit discrimination yet fail to speak against it, what have we done to rectify the injustice? And that's the hard part: because privilege tastes good and we're loath to relinquish it. Or even if willing, we often wonder how to resist: how to attack unfairness and make a difference.

As to why we should want to end racial privilege – aside from the moral argument – the answer is straightforward: The price we pay to stay one step ahead of others is enormous. In the labor market, we benefit from racial discrimination in the relative sense, but in absolute terms this discrimination holds down most of our wages and living standards by keeping working people divided and creating a surplus labor pool of "others" to whom employers can turn when the labor market gets tight or work-ers demand too much in wages or benefits.

We benefit in relative terms from discrimination against people of color in education, by receiving, on average, better resources and class offerings. But in absolute terms, can anyone deny that the cre-ation and perpetuation of miseducated persons of color harms us all?

And even disparate treatment in the justice sys-tem has its blowback on the white community. We may think little of the racist growth of the prison-industrial complex, as it snares far fewer of our chil-dren. But considering that the prisons warehousing black and brown bodies compete for the same dol-lars needed to build colleges for everyone, the im-pact is far from negligible.

In California, since 1980, nearly 30 new prisons have opened, compared to two four-year colleges, with the effect that the space available for people of color and whites to receive a good education has been curtailed. So folks fight over the pieces of a diminishing pie—as with Proposition 209 to end af-firmative action – instead of uniting against their common problem: the mostly white lawmakers who prioritize jails and slashing taxes on the wealthy, over meeting the needs of most people.

As for how whites can challenge the system – other than by joining the occasional demonstration or voting for candidates with a decent record on race issues – this is where we'll need creativity.

Imagine, for example, that groups of whites and people of color started going to local department stores as discrimination "tester" teams. And imagine the whites spent a few hours, in shifts, observing how they were treated relative to the black and brown folks who came with them. And imagine what would happen if every white person on the team approached a different white clerk and re-turned just-purchased merchandise, if and when they observed disparate treatment, explaining they weren't going to shop in a store that profiled or oth-erwise racially discriminated. Imagine the faces of the clerks, confronted by other whites demanding equal treatment for persons of color.

Far from insignificant, if this happened often enough, it could have a serious effect on behavior, and the institutional mistreatment of people of color in at least this one setting: after all, white clerks could no longer be sure if the white shopper in lady's lingerie was an ally who would wink at unequal treatment, or whether they might be one of "those" whites: the kind that would call them out for doing what they always assumed was accept-able.

Or what about setting up "cop watch" programs like those already in place in a few cities? White folks, following police, filming officers' interactions with people of color, and making their presence known, when and if they observe officers engaged in abusive behavior.

Or contingents of white parents, speaking out in a school board meeting against racial tracking in class assignments: a process through which kids of color are much more likely to be placed in basic classes, while whites are elevated to honors and advanced placement, irrespective of ability. Protesting this kind of privilege – especially when it might be working to the advantage of one's own children – is the sort of thing we'll need to do if we hope to alter the system we swear we're against.

We'll have to stop moving from neighborhoods when "too many" people of color move in.

We'll have to stop running to private schools, or suburban public ones, and instead fight to make the schools serving all children in our community better.

We'll need to consider taking advantage of the push for publicly funded charter schools by joining with parents of color to start institutions of our own, similar to the "Freedom Schools" established in Mississippi by the Student Non-Violent Coordinating Committee in 1964. These schools would teach not only traditional subject matter, but also the importance of critical thinking, and social and economic justice. If these are things we say we care about, yet we haven't at present the outlets to demonstrate our commitment, we'll have to create those institutions ourselves.

And we must protest the privileging of elite, white male perspectives in school textbooks. We have to demand that the stories of all who have struggled to radically transform society be told: and if the existing texts don't do that, we must dip into our own pockets and pay for supplemental materials that teachers could use to make the classes they teach meaningful. And if we're in a position to make a hiring decision, we should go out of our way to recruit, identify and hire a person of color.

What these suggestions have in common – and they're hardly an exhaustive list – is that they require whites to leave the comfort zone to which we have grown accustomed. They require time, perhaps money, and above all else, courage; and they ask us to focus a little less on the relatively easy, though important, goal of "fixing" racism's victims (with a bit more money for this or that, or a little more affirmative action), and instead to pay attention to the need to challenge and change the perpetrators of and collaborators with the system of racial privilege. And those are the people we work with, live with, and wake up to every day. It's time to revoke the privileges of whiteness.

Yellow Woman and the Beauty of the Spirit

In this essay about the Laguna Pueblo culture, the lessons of the past demonstrate a plu-
ralistic attitude that is appropriate for the increasingly diverse society of the present and
future. In describing the practices and stories of the old-time people, the author provides
parables for becoming new people, prepared to enter into a new age.

From the time I was a small child, I was aware that I was different. I looked different from my playmates. My two sisters looked different too. We didn't look quite like the other Laguna Pueblo children, but we didn't look quite white either. In the 1880s, my great-grandfather had followed his older brother west from Ohio to the New Mexico Territory to survey the land for the U.S. government. The two Marmon brothers came to the Laguna Pueblo reservation because they had an Ohio cousin who already lived there. The Ohio cousin was involved in sending Indian children thousands of miles away from their families to the War Department's big Indian boarding school in Carlisle, Pennsylvania. Both brothers married full-blood Laguna Pueblo women. My great-grandfather had first married my great-grandmother's older sister, but she died in childbirth and left two small children. My great-grandmother was fifteen or twenty years younger than my great-grandfather. She had attended Carlisle Indian School and spoke and wrote English beautifully.

I called her Grandma A'mooh because that's what I heard her say whenever she saw me, *A'mooh* means "granddaughter" in the Laguna language. I remember this word because her love and her acceptance of me as a small child were so important. I had sensed immediately that something about my appearance was not acceptable to some people, white and Indian. But I did not see any signs of that strain or anxiety in the face of my beloved Grandma A'mooh.

Younger people, people my parents' age, seemed to look at the world in a more modern way. The modern way included racism. My physical appearance seemed not to matter to the old-time people. They looked at the world very differently; a person's appearance and possessions did not matter nearly as much as a person's behavior. For them, a person's value lies in how that person interacts with other people, how that person behaves toward the animals and the earth. That is what matters most to the old-time people. The Pueblo people believed this long before the Puritans arrived with their notions of sin and damnation, and racism. The old-time beliefs persist today; thus I will refer to the old-time people in the present tense as well as the past. Many worlds may co-exist here.

I spent a great deal of time with my great-grandmother. Her house was next to our house, and I used to wake up at dawn, hours before my parents or younger sisters, and I'd go wait on the porch swing or on the back steps by her kitchen door. She got up at dawn, but she was more than eighty years old, so she needed a little while to get dressed and to get the fire going in the cookstove. I had been carefully instructed by my parents not to bother her and to behave, and to try to help her any way I could. I always loved the early mornings when the air was so cool with a hint of rain smell in the breeze. In the dry New Mexico air, the least hint of dampness smells sweet.

My great-grandmother's yard was planted with lilac bushes and iris; there were four o'clocks, cosmos, morning glories, and hollyhocks, and old-fashioned rosebushes that I helped her water. If the garden hose got stuck on one of the big rocks that lined the path in the yard, I ran and pulled it free. That's what I came to do early every morning: to help Grandma water the plants before the heat of the day arrived.

Grandma A'mooh would tell about the old days, family stories about relatives who had been killed by Apache raiders who stole the sheep our relatives had been herding near Swahnee. Sometimes she read Bible stories that we kids liked because of the illustrations of Jonah in the mouth of a whale and Daniel surrounded by lions. Grandma A'mooh would send me home when she took her nap, but when the sun got low and the afternoon began to cool off, I would be back on the porch swing, waiting for her to come out to water the plants and to haul in firewood for the evening. When Grandma was eighty-five, she still chopped her own kindling. She used to let me carry in the coal bucket for her, but she would not allow me to use the ax. I carried armloads of kindling too, and I learned to be proud of my strength.

I was allowed to listen quietly when Aunt Susie or Aunt Alice came to visit Grandma. When I got old enough to cross the road alone, I visited them almost daily. They were vigorous women who valued books and writing. They were usually busy chopping wood or cooking but never hesitated to take time to answer my questions. Best of all they told me the *hummah-hah* stories, about an earlier time when animals and humans shared a common language. In the old days, the Pueblo people had educated their children in this manner; adults took

time out to talk to and teach young people. Everyone was a teacher, and every activity had the potential to teach the child.

But as soon as I started kindergarten at the Bureau of Indian Affairs day school, I began to learn more about the differences between the Laguna Pueblo world and the outside world. It was at school that I learned just how different I looked from my classmates. Sometimes tourists driving past on Route 66 would stop by Laguna Day School at recess time to take photographs of us kids. One day, when I was in the first grade, we all crowded around the smiling white tourists, who peered at our faces. We all wanted to be in the picture because afterward the tourists sometimes gave us each a penny. Just as we were all posed and ready to have our picture taken, the tourist man looked at me. "Not you," he said and motioned for me to step away from my classmates. I felt so embarrassed that I wanted to disappear. My classmates were puzzled by the tourists' behavior, but I knew the tourists didn't want me in their snapshot because I looked different, because I was part white.

In the view of the old-time people, we are all sisters and brothers because the Mother Creator made all of us – all colors and all sizes. We are sisters and brothers, clanspeople of all the living beings around us. The plants, the birds, fish, clouds, water, even the clay – they all are related to us. The old-time people believe that all things, even rocks and water, have spirit and being. They understood that all things want only to continue being as they are; they need only to be left as they are. Thus the old folks used to tell us kids not to disturb the earth unnecessarily. All things as they were created exist already in harmony with one another as long as we do not disturb them.

As the old story tells us, Tse'itsi'nako, Thought Woman, the Spider, thought of her three sisters, and as she thought of them, they came into being. Together with Thought Woman, they thought of the sun and the stars and the moon. The Mother Creators imagined the earth and the oceans, the animals and the people, and the *ka'tsina* spirits that reside in the mountains. The Mother Creators imagined all the plants that flower and the trees that bear fruit. As Thought Woman and her sisters thought of it, the whole universe came into being. In this universe, there is no absolute good or absolute bad;

there are only balances and harmonies that ebb and flow. Some years the desert receives abundant rain, other years there is too little rain, and sometimes there is so much rain that floods cause destruction. But rain itself is neither innocent nor guilty. The rain is simply itself.

My great-grandmother was dark and handsome. Her expression in photographs is one of confidence and strength. I do not know if white people then or now would consider her beautiful. I do not know if the old-time Laguna Pueblo people considered her beautiful or if the old-time people even thought in those terms. To the Pueblo way of thinking, the act of comparing one living being with another was silly, because each being or thing is unique and therefore incomparably valuable because it is the only one of its kinds. The old-time people thought it was crazy to attach such importance to a person's appearance. I understood very early that there were two distinct ways of interpreting the world. There was the white people's way and there was the Laguna way. In the Laguna way, it was bad manners to make comparisons that might hurt another person's feelings.

In everyday Pueblo life, not much attention was paid to one's physical appearance or clothing. Ceremonial clothing was quite elaborate but was used only for the sacred dances. The traditional Pueblo societies were communal and strictly egalitarian, which means that no matter how well or how poorly one might have dressed, there was no social ladder to fall from. All food and other resources were strictly shared so that no one person or group had more than another. I mention social status because it seems to me that most of the definitions of beauty in contemporary Western culture are really codes for determining social status. People no longer hide their face-lifts and they discuss their liposuctions because the point of the procedures isn't just cosmetic, it is social. It says to the world, "I have enough spare cash that I can afford surgery for cosmetic purposes."

In the old-time Pueblo world, beauty was manifested in behavior and in one's relationships with other living beings. Beauty was as much a feeling of harmony as it was a visual, aural, or sensual effect. The whole person had to be beautiful, not just the face or the body; faces and bodies could not be separated from hearts and souls. Health was foremost in achieving this sense of well-being and harmony;

in the old-time Pueblo world, a person who did not look healthy inspired feelings of worry and anxiety, not feelings of well-being. A healthy person, of course, is in harmony with the world around her; she is at peace with herself too. Thus an unhappy person or spiteful person would not be considered beautiful.

In the old days, strong sturdy women were most admired. One of my most vivid preschool memories is of the crew of Laguna women, in their forties and fifties, who came to cover our house with adobe plaster. They handled the ladders with great ease, and while two women ground the adobe mud on stones and added straw, another woman loaded the hod with mud and passed it up to the two women on ladders who were smoothing the plaster on the wall with their hands. Since women owned the houses, they did the plastering. At Laguna, men did the basket making and the weaving of fine textiles; men helped a great deal with the child care too. Because the Creator is female, there is no stigma on being female; gender is not used to control behavior. No job was a man's job or a woman's job; the most able person did the work.

My Grandma Lily had been a Ford Model A mechanic when she was a teenager. I remember when I was young, she was always fixing broken lamps and appliances. She was small and wiry, but she could lift her weight in rolled roofing or boxes of nails. When she was seventy-five, she was still repairing washing machines in my uncle's coin-operated laundry.

The old-time people paid no attention to birthdays. When a person was ready to do something, she did it. When she no longer was able, she stopped. Thus the traditional Pueblo people did not worry about aging or about looking old because there were no social boundaries drawn by the passage of years. It was not remarkable for young men to marry women as old as their mothers. I never heard anyone talk about "women's work" until after I left Laguna for college. Work was there to be done by any able-bodied person who wanted to do it. At the same time, in the old-time Pueblo world, identity was acknowledged to be always in a flux; in the old stories, one minute Spider Woman is a little spider under a yucca plant, and the next instant she is a sprightly grandmother walking down the road.

When I was growing up, there was a young man from a nearby village who wore nail polish and women's blouses and permed his hair. People paid little attention to his appearance; he was always part of a group of other young men from his village. No one ever made fun of him. Pueblo communities were and still are very interdependent, but they also have to be tolerant of individual eccentricities because survival of the group means everyone has to cooperate.

In the old Pueblo world, differences were celebrated as signs of the Mother Creator's grace. Persons born with exceptional physical or sexual differences were highly respected and honored because their physical differences gave them special positions as mediators between this world and the spirit world. The great Navajo medicine man of the 1920s, the Crawler, had a hunchback and could not walk upright, but he was able to heal even the most difficult cases.

Before the arrival of Christian missionaries, a man could dress as a woman and work with the women and even marry a man without any fanfare. Likewise, a woman was free to dress like a man, to hunt and go to war with the men, and to marry a woman. In the old Pueblo worldview, we are all a mixture of male and female, and this sexual identity is changing constantly. Sexual inhibition did not begin until the Christian missionaries arrived. For the old-time people, marriage was about teamwork and social relationships, not about sexual excitement. In the days before the Puritans came, marriage did not mean an end to sex with people other than your spouse. Women were just as likely as men to have a si'ash, or lover.

New life was so precious that pregnancy was always appropriate, and pregnancy before marriage was celebrated as a good sign. Since the children belonged to the mother and her clan, and women owned and bequeathed the houses and farmland, the exact determination of paternity wasn't critical. Although fertility was prized, infertility was no problem because mothers with unplanned pregnancies gave their babies to childless couples within the clan in open adoption arrangements. Children called their mother's sisters "mother" as well, and a child became attached to a number of parent figures.

In the sacred kiva ceremonies, men mask and dress as women to pay homage and to be possessed by the female energies of the spirit beings. Because differences in physical appearance were so highly valued, surgery to change one's face and body to resemble a model's face and body would be unimaginable. To be different, to be unique was blessed and was best of all.

The traditional clothing of Pueblo women emphasized a woman's sturdiness. Buckskin leggings wrapped around the legs protected her from scratches and injuries while she worked. The more layers of buckskin, the better. All those layers gave her legs the appearance of strength, like sturdy tree trunks. To demonstrate sisterhood and brotherhood with the plants and animals, the old-time people make masks and costumes that transform the human figures of the dancers into the animal beings they portray. Dancers paint their exposed skin; their postures and motions are adapted from their observations. But the motions are stylized. The observer sees not an actual eagle or actual deer dancing, but witnesses a human being, a dancer, gradually changing into a woman/buffalo or a man/deer. Every impulse is to reaffirm the urgent relationships that human beings have with the plant and animal world. In the high desert plateau country, all vegetation, even weeds and thorns, becomes special, and all life is precious and beautiful because without the plants, the insects, and the animals, human beings living here cannot survive. Perhaps human beings long ago noticed the devastating impact human activity can have on the plants and animals; maybe this is why tribal cultures devised the stories about humans and animals intermarrying, and the clans that bind humans to animals and plants through a whole complex of duties.

We children were always warned not to harm frogs or toads, the beloved children of the rain clouds, because terrible floods would occur. I remember in the summer the old folks used to stick big bolls of cotton on the outside of their screen doors as bait to keep the flies from going in the house when the door was opened. The old folks staunchly resisted the killing of flies because once, long, long ago, when human beings were in a great deal of trouble, a Green Bottle Fly carried the desperate messages of human beings to the Mother Creator in the Fourth World, below this one. Human beings had outraged the Mother Creator by neglecting the Mother Corn altar while they dabbled with sorcery and magic. The Mother Creator disappeared, and with her disappeared the rain clouds, and the plants and the animals too. The people began to starve, and they had no way of reaching the Mother Creator down below. Green Bottle Fly took the message to the Mother Creator, and the people were saved. To show their gratitude, the old folks refused to kill any flies

The old stories demonstrate the interrelationships that the Pueblo people have maintained with their plant and animal clanspeople. Kochininako, Yellow Woman, represents all women in the old stories. Her deeds span the spectrum of human behavior and are mostly heroic acts, though in at least one story, she chooses to join the secret Destroyer Clan, which worships destruction and death. Because Laguna Pueblo cosmology features a female Creator, the status of women is equal with the status of men, and women appear as often as men in the old stories as hero figures. Yellow Woman is my favorite because she dares to cross traditional boundaries of ordinary behavior during times of crisis in order to save the Pueblo; her power lies in her courage and in her uninhibited sexuality, which the old-time Pueblo stories celebrate again and again because fertility was so highly valued.

The old stories always say that Yellow Woman was beautiful, but remember that the old-time people were not so much thinking about physical appearances. In each story, the beauty that Yellow Woman possesses is the beauty of her passion, her daring, and her sheer strength to act when catastrophe is imminent.

In one story, the people are suffering during a great drought and accompanying famine. Each day, Kochininako has to walk farther and farther from the village to find fresh water for her husband and children. One day she travels far, far to the east, to the plains, and she finally locates a fresh-water spring. But when she reaches the pool, the water is churning violently as if something large had just gotten out of the pool. Kochininako does not want to see what huge creature had been at the pool, but just as she fills her water jar and turns to hurry away, a strong sexy man in buffalo-skin leggings appears by the pool. Little drops of water glisten on his chest. She cannot help but look at him because he is so strong and so good to look at. Able to transform himself from human to buffalo in the wink of an eye, Buffalo Man gallops away with her on his back. Kochininako falls in love with Buffalo Man, and because of this liaison, the Buffalo People agree to give their bodies to the hunters to feed the starving Pueblo. Thus Kochininako's fearless sensuality results in the salvation of the people of her village, who are saved by the meat the Buffalo People "give" to them.

In another story, Kochininako has a fling with Whirlwind Man and returns to her husband ten months later with twin baby boys. The twin boys grow up to be great heroes of the people. Once again, Kochininako's vibrant sexuality benefits her people.

The stories about Kochininako made me aware that sometimes an individual must act despite disapproval, or concern for appearances or what others may say. From Yellow Woman's adventures, I learned to be comfortable with my differences. I even imagined that Yellow Woman had yellow skin, brown hair, and green eyes like mine, although her name does not refer to her color, but rather to the ritual color of the east.

There have been many other moments like the one with the camera-toting tourist in the schoolyard. But the old-time people always say, remember the stories, the stories will help you be strong. So all these years I have depended on Kochininako and the stories of her adventures.

Kochininako is beautiful because she has the courage to act in times of great peril, and her triumph is achieved by her sensuality, not through violence and destruction. For these qualities of the spirit, Yellow Woman and all women are beautiful.

Index

Note: Italicized page numbers indicate references to or in fictional work.

Evangelical Christians, 124,
125–129
Everett, Edward, 326

F

Fairly, Juliet, 171
Faludi, Susan, 237, 240
Falwell, Jerry, 124, 128
Family Cap policy, 183
Farrell, Walter, 170–171
Fay, Robert, 244
Fear
of bilingualism, 93
Jewish experience, 144–145
of others, 9–13
Feminism, 255–259, 260–263
Fiedler, Craig, 207, 221
Fine, Michelle, 122, 130
Flynn, Elizabeth, 322
Folake (Nigerian student),
115–120
Founding Fathers, 21–22,
124–129
Fowles, Jib, 244–245
Fox, Vincente, 74, 75
Frank, Anne, 144
Frank, Debbie, 183–184
Franklin, Benjamin, 21, 87, 88,
125–126
Freaks, 213–215
Freud, Sigmund, 46
Friedenberg, Edgar, 324
Fuller, R. Buckminster, 268
Funderburg, Lise, 168

G

Gaither, Billy Jack, 143–144
Gandhi, Mahatma, 141
Gandhi, Mohandis K., 300
Gardner, John, 181
Gay people. *See* LGBT (lesbian, gay,
bisexual and transgendered)
people
Gender
culture and, 236–237
male social behavior, 250–254
relative size and, 246–249
Zuni culture and, 215
Gender betrayal, 289
Genetic variation, 14–19, 285
George, Dan (Native American),
150
German Americans, 87–88
German language, 87–88, 143
Gilchrist, Jim, 77, 79

Gill, Carol, 220
Giovanni, Nikki, 298
Glickman, C. D., 224
Goldman, Emma, 322
Gould, Stephen Jay, 169, 237–238,
246
Government
disabled people and, 205, 206,
216–220, 223
European *vs.* native models for,
20–23
illegal immigration and, 74–79
language issues and, 88, 89, 90,
91, 93
multiracial category and, 169
poverty and, 179, 183–184,
185–186, 187
Graham, Sandy, 77
Great Awakening, 125–126
Greenburg, Dan, 268, 292
Greene, Bob, 261
Griffin, John Howard, 151
Group membership. *See also*
Minority groups
identity formation and, 32–35
racism and, 340–347
within-group violence, 11
Guerrero, Rosa, 84

H

Haddon, Mark, 207, 232
Hage, Rawi, 30, 50
Haitian immigrants, 80–82
Haizlip, Shirlee Taylor, 170
Hall, Ronald, 170
Hamer, Fannie Lou, 48
Happiness, 133–135
Harding, William, 88
Harrington, Michael, 188
Harris, Emmylou, 267
Harris, Sidney, 3
Hart, Elva Treviño, 55, 58
Hatch, Nathan, 128
Hate crimes, 136, 138, 143–144
Heath, Shirley Brice, 85, 103
Heinlein, Robert, 121
Hemings, Sally, 14–15
Henry, Patrick, 126–127, 128
Hernandez, Miguel, 222
Heroes. *See* History
Herr, S., 223
Hershey, Laura, 205
Heterosexual violence, 11,
288–291
Hiawatha, 21

Higher education. *See* Colleges
and universities
Highwater, Jamake, 206, 213
Hindu community, 138, 139
Hispanics. *See* Latinos/Latinas
History
accuracy in teaching, 320–325
inclusiveness in teaching, 111,
165–166
Native-American, 21–23
Hite, Shere, 240–241, 242
Hitler, Adolph, 121
Hoang Vinh, 56, 63–68
Hobson, Thayer, 121
Homophobia
Christians and, 284–287
language of, 279, 290
parental rejection and, 284
as perversion, 283–285, 286,
287
satire on, *292–296*
violence and, 143–144, 288–291
Homosexuality. *See* LGBT (lesbian,
gay, bisexual and
transgendered) people
hooks, bell, 238–239, 260
Hufstedler, Shirley, 299
Hunger, 183–186
Hunt, J. M., 227
Hyppolite, Joanne, 57, 80

I

"I" *vs.* "we" classroom perspectives,
112–113
IDEA (Individuals with Disabilities
Education Act), 205, 223
Identity
American, 1, 2, 5–8, 14–19
biracial, 39–42, 168
complexity of, 31
group membership and, 32–35
multiracial concept, 168–171
Muslim American, 131–132
privilege and, 43–49
relationships and, 1, *50–53*
sexual, *264–265*
Illegal immigration, 74–79
Immersion method, 92, 97
Immigrants. *See also specific group*
acculturation, 66–68, 72–73
Americanization, 297
arrival stories, 69–72
diversity, 55
illegal, 74–79
immigration trends, 54